The National Security Enterprise

The National Security Enterprise
Navigating the Labyrinth

Roger Z. George and Harvey Rishikof, Editors
Foreword by Lt. Gen. Brent Scowcroft, USAF (Ret.)

In cooperation with the Center for Peace and Security Studies

Edmund A. Walsh School of Foreign Service

Georgetown University

Georgetown University Press
Washington, DC

Library of Congress Cataloging-in-Publication Data

The national security enterprise : navigating the labyrinth / Roger George and Harvey Rishikof, editors.
   p. cm.
"In cooperation with the Center for Peace and Security Studies, Edmund A. Walsh School of Foreign Service, Georgetown University."
Includes bibliographical references and index.
ISBN 978-1-58901-698-9 (pbk. : alk. paper)
1. National security—United States. 2. Interagency coordination—United States. 3. Administrative agencies—United States. 4. Executive departments—United States. 5. Research institutes—United States. I. George, Roger Z., 1949- II. Rishikof, Harvey. III. Georgetown University. Center for Peace and Security Studies
UA23.N2487 2011
355'.033073—dc22

2010022402

15 14 13 12 11 10   9 8 7 6 5 4 3 2
First printing

Printed in the United States of America

Acknowledgments

To our teachers and mentors
    Judge Leonard I. Garth
    Peter A. Gourevitch
    Stanley Hoffman
    Sam Beer
    Larry T. Caldwell
    John E. McLaughlin
    Joseph S. Nye
    William E. Nelson

We would like to acknowledge the support of our parents—Lowell Edwin and Elizabeth Zane George and Issie and Marjorie Cryer Rishikof—for their encouragement, love, and understanding over a lifetime.

Contents

List of Illustrations

Foreword

National security decision making is particularly difficult in this new era of emerging challenges. To develop a comprehensive U.S. national security strategy requires the integration of all elements of American power, many of which reside in an increasingly complex governmental enterprise. What this book describes is a virtual labyrinth of agencies and actors who participate in shaping American national security policy. At the end of the day, however, it is the president and his national security team who must make and implement the critical decisions that will keep the nation secure, prosperous, and at peace.

In my experience, each president seeks to shape his national security decision-making process to suit his own personal style and policy priorities. Every president faces the challenge of organizing the executive branch, working with the Congress, and managing the national debate over national security policy, which involves numerous other players. A president also faces the realities that the organizations and institutions through which he must work have their own customs, operational styles, and capabilities. Understanding those strengths and weaknesses is imperative for a president and his advisers if they are to craft successful policies and implement them.

Today, the problem is much harder than it was during the Cold War. Then, we faced a single overriding challenger, a reality that shaped the world and our policies. The world was tense but had defined lanes of authority. That world is gone. Today's world is anything but tidy. In some respects it is the exact opposite of the Cold War. There is no place on earth that cannot become tomorrow's crisis. Globalization is eroding borders and individual states' abilities to manage transnational challenges such as financial crises, environmental damage, networked terrorists, and international crime, to name a few. Shaping policies to deal with these transnational threats is daunting, as they—even more than the traditional threats emanating from states—blur the distinctions between foreign and domestic; moreover, they demand the use of more than simply military force or traditional diplomacy. In many cases, problems will require the use of all forms of U.S. power and influence, be it hard military or economic power, persuasive diplomacy, development aid for nation building, or soft power to attract nations and peoples toward seeing the world more like we do. This requires an extraordinary degree of coordination of these instruments across the entire U.S. government.

Today's national security decision makers face four principal challenges. First, they must determine where the lines of authority lie among the national security agencies for dealing with complex contingencies, like Iraq or Afghanistan. No single agency can manage such challenges, and departments must combine their strengths as well as minimize their weaknesses. Understanding the cultures as well as the capabilities of these agencies is important in crafting effective policies.

Second, today's decision makers are burdened by institutions and organizational habits of mind that were built for the Cold War, not the twenty-first century. These institutional mindsets, often manifested as resistance to new ways of doing business or new missions for which they were not originally established, need to be brought into line with the globalized security agenda we face. Organizational changes are and will be necessary, but so too are flexible organizational cultures that inhabit those organizations.

Third, the composition and concept of the national security team needs to be broadened. The Cold War notion that the National Security Council (NSC) team composed only of the secretaries of State and Defense, along with the Joint Chiefs of Staff and the director of CIA, is seriously outdated. Periodic adjustments to the composition of the NSC have occurred but may still be insufficient. Perhaps we have reached the point where every cabinet officer should be considered a member of the NSC; accordingly, they should attend meetings whenever their agencies' policies and capabilities are involved. Similarly, there may be a need to develop small NSC cells within each department to ensure close cooperation with the NSC staff and other agencies. This could be a useful alternative to constantly expanding the size of the NSC staff, with the danger of it becoming so large as to challenge effective integration of all elements of power.

Fourth, and perhaps most important, national security strategies will succeed or fail depending on whether they are implemented effectively. Too often a brilliant strategy can flounder for lack of resources or agencies' commitment to implementing the president's decisions. There should be a closer link between the NSC staff and the Office of Management and Budget (OMB) to ensure that the resources are available to implement the policy and that agencies have committed their resources to achieve the president's policy objectives. To its credit, this volume is one of the first I have seen that acknowledges the centrality of the resource question and treats the OMB as a key player in the national security enterprise.

These challenges should not be considered overwhelming for the U.S. system. Indeed, no country has been as successful in marshaling its ideas, people, and resources to confront the world's problems as the United States. By recognizing some of our own shortfalls, Americans can correct and improve on what overall has been a successful national security enterprise. I would expect no less from our twenty-first century's leaders than from those whom I have served in the past.

Lt. Gen. Brent Scowcroft, USAF (Ret.)

Preface

Crafting a book on the national security enterprise has been both a challenge and a pleasure. As educators we found it an essential contribution to our efforts to teach national security policies at the graduate level. In our teaching at the National War College, we were struck by the paucity of literature on the cultures of the national security agencies. Having been practitioners earlier in our careers, we were familiar with the hidden incentive systems of our agencies and how the other tribes of the national security enterprise navigated the policymaking labyrinth. However, we failed to find a text for our students that presented the cultures of the organizations in a systematic manner. We agreed that it would be extremely beneficial to gather together a group of professionals who are familiar with their respective cultures and allow them to reflect on their particular institutions and the interagency processes.

Writing about organizational cultures is extremely difficult. Readers will find that the chapters approach this topic in different ways, as there was no possibility of asking authors to use a cookie-cutter approach. Given the diversity of the agencies and institutions this book covers, each author had to approach it in his or her own idiosyncratic fashion. However, we believe that the whole is greater than the sum of its parts. To provide some anchors or pilot stars—and to allow readers to see just how different the organizations truly are—we invited authors to target some of their insights regarding their organization's culture on recent events in Iraq and the fight against terrorism.

Time and space required that we focus on core organizations. Clearly, many more agencies and institutions might have been added to this volume. If we have an opportunity to revisit this topic in a few years, we might easily add another set of agencies. In an era of nation building—should this persist—we suspect we need to add a chapter on the United States Agency for International Development (USAID), which has become so central to the efforts in Iraq and Afghanistan. Similar arguments could be made for including other economic agencies where aspects of the national security enterprise are increasingly found. For now, we are content to focus our energies on getting a first-cut look at the key organizational cultures that coexist within the national security enterprise. We hope that we have succeeded.

No book that involves this many contributors can truly be the result only of its editors. The chapter authors deserve many thanks for committing to this enterprise and producing some unique and insightful contributions. In addition, the volume would not have been possible without the generous support of Georgetown University's Center for Peace and Security Studies (CPASS) and its impressive teaching arm, the Security Studies Program. Its recent director, Daniel Byman, and deputy director, Ellen McHugh, have provided not only critical research resources, but also advice, patience, and other intangible forms of encouragement throughout the project. Don Jacobs of Georgetown University Press has been characteristically understanding of some slipped deadlines when so many busy and overcommitted authors are involved. Likewise, the Georgetown University Press staff has helped us expedite the completion of this volume and given it a very professional look. In preparing this manuscript we also are extremely grateful to our two outside reviewers, Jennifer E. Sims and Colton Campbell, for their thoughtful comments and suggestions that improved it immensely. And, for a book about bureaucracies, there were indeed a few organizational hurdles, and we appreciate the CIA Publication Review Board and the National Defense University for their speedy reviews of our manuscript.

Both of us owe a huge debt of gratitude to the National War College, which is part of the National Defense University. We have benefited greatly from discussions with our colleagues and have continually been challenged by our students, whose dedication and integrity we admire immensely. It is our hope that institutions such as the National War College and senior government training schools will continue to question and debate the ideas we have put forward.

We dedicate our book to our wives, Trudi and Cindy, for their unwavering support and a lifetime of understanding. They both have a high tolerance for the lost weekends and interminable phone conversations the editors conducted at all hours of the day and night. Harvey is forever indebted to Trudi, as she is usually his first critic in all that he writes and inevitably after her red pen there is always improvement both in clarity and style. Roger wishes to thank Cindy for her patience with a disorganized academic as a husband and her encouragement to take on this challenge when we were making so many other changes in our lives.

We would be remiss if we did not single out for special thanks our Georgetown University research assistant extraordinaire, Kirsten McNeil, whose careful manuscript preparations, fact checking, graphic creation, and mastery of the style guide have made the text not only more presentable but understandable. Kirsten went beyond the call of duty in toiling over the manuscript. It is our hope that one reason the book may appeal to the next generation is due to her thoughtful input.

Finally, our collaboration has been extremely enjoyable and rewarding. Through this adventure we learned to appreciate each other's intellectual eccentricities—whether one was prone to more legal Cartesian logic or the other's penchant for detail and flow—there never was a harsh word or awkward moment. Our respect and friendship has only grown and deepened as a result of the months of working on the project. The book is now done but the friendship continues to grow.

List of Abbreviations

CIA	Central Intelligence Agency
COCOM	Combatant Commander
CPA	Coalition Provisional Authority
DCI	Director of Central Intelligence
DHS	Department of Homeland Security
DNI	Director of National Intelligence
DOD	Department of Defense
DOJ	Department of Justice
DOS	Department of State
EOP	Executive Office of the President
FBI	Federal Bureau of Investigation
FEMA	Federal Emergency Management Agency
FSO	Foreign Service Officer
IC	Intelligence Community
IMF	International Monetary Fund
JCS	Joint Chiefs of Staff
NASA	National Aeronautics and Space Administration
NATO	North Atlantic Treaty Organization
NCTC	National Counterterrorism Center
NGO	Nongovernmental Organization
NSA	National Security Advisor
NSC	National Security Council
NSCS	National Security Council Staff
NSE	National Security Enterprise
NSPD	National Security Presidential Directive
NSPG	National Security Planning Group
ODNI	Office of the Director of National Intelligence
OMB	Office of Management and Budget
OSD	Office of the Secretary of Defense
PDD	Presidential Decision Directive
PNSR	Project on National Security Reform
PPBS	Planning, Programming, Budgeting System
USAID	United States Agency for International Development
WH	White House
WTO	World Trade Organization

Introduction   # The National Security Enterprise: Institutions, Cultures, and Politics

ROGER Z. GEORGE AND HARVEY RISHIKOF

> In enacting this legislation, it is the intent of Congress to provide the comprehensive program for the future security of the United States; to provide for the establishment of integrated policies and procedures for the departments, agencies, and functions of the Government relating to the national security. . . .
>
> *Public Law 80-253, sec. 2 (1947)*

> Every organization has a culture; that is, a persistent, patterned way of thinking about the central tasks of and human relationships within an organization.
>
> *James Q. Wilson, Bureaucracy*

Organizing the national security process has been a constant feature of the American government. More than sixty years ago, the United States embarked on a fundamentally new way of formulating its foreign and defense policies. It no longer had the luxury of mobilizing the country and its political, military, and economic power to counter threats once war had occurred. Rather, it needed a permanent national security policy framework to identify, deter, and if necessary defend against international threats to the nation. The National Security Act of 1947, subsequent legislation, and innumerable executive actions of a dozen presidents have built up an elaborate national security process to safeguard Americans. That system, as remarkably flexible as it has been, is no longer satisfactory for the twenty-first century and the many transnational and complex challenges it confronts. Studies (more than two dozen major ones since the designing of the national security system of the 1940s) continue to identify conceptual as well as structural flaws that inhibit effective planning, formulation, and implementation of national security policies. The latest is a bipartisan U.S. Institute of Peace report on the 2010 Quadrennial Defense Review that concludes, yet again, that there is an urgent need to replace the existing national security planning process with one that is more comprehensive, up-to-date, and effective given the new challenges of the twenty-first century.[1]

This book is not another study of those structural flaws found in past and current national security systems. Instead, this book examines the specific organizations and cultures of the institutions and agencies that make up the national security enterprise. The book takes a consciously Washington perspective, focusing on the headquarters' mentalities, as most strategic decisions are made inside the Beltway rather than in embassies, commands, or stations; one often hears of the "Washington clock" versus "Baghdad or Kabul clock." No doubt the people in the field have their own perspectives, but they most often react to Washington and are seldom defining or driving their organizations in the same way that the Washington bureaucrats and politicians can. The central premise, then, is that the dysfunction often described in the current national security enterprise gives little rigorous attention to the internal organizational cultures that comprise it; moreover, no conceptual or structural fix to the current system is likely to succeed unless it understands the organizations and people that make up that system. In this sense, our book is a gap filler, as there is scarcely any literature on the individual organizations that make up the growing set of agencies that comprise our national security enterprise. Two recent textbooks on the foreign policy process written by Steven Hook and Howard Wiarda devote only a short chapter to the dozen or more executive branch agencies that formulate the nation's foreign policies.[2] Likewise, some of the early groundbreaking work done on the role of organizational behavior on foreign policy outcomes by Graham Allison and Morton Halperin is also surprisingly brief in their description of those cultures.[3] The most complete discussion of the role of organizational behavior in recent policies is to be found in Amy Zegart's study of the organizational behavior of the Central Intelligence Agency (CIA) and Federal Bureau of Investigation (FBI) in the 9/11 attack; however, this excellent study is far from complete in describing the many other organizations that make up this enterprise.[4]

The absence of more attention to the institutional organizational cultures is surprising given that many of the government and nongovernment studies of the national security enterprise regularly complain about the parochial nature of the organizations and institutions that make up the system. The massive 2008 Project on National Security Reform (PNSR) report, to take one example, squarely identifies the problems as being organizational in nature: "[T]he basic deficiency of the current national security system is that parochial departmental and agency interests, reinforced by Congress, paralyze the interagency cooperation even as the variety, speed, and complexity of emerging security issues prevent the White House from effectively controlling the system."[5]

The PNSR notes that in the midst of huge international changes, the National Security Council (NSC) system is still essentially a hierarchically organized structure, which relies on the traditional agencies and their disciplines. Such a structure reflects an assumption, perhaps a conviction, that the government is a unitary actor that develops foreign affairs strategies according to a logical process of matching means with ends and developing courses of action that maximize those ends with the use of all elements of power. Such means–ways–ends models may work well to explain how an ideal national security strategy should be developed, but they have little relevance to how governments actually operate. Although traditional academic study of the foreign policy process gives lip service to the role of bureaucracy and organizational culture, it never is the focus of the models. Yet, these cultures shape the process of policy deliberation, as well as its execution within the national security enterprise. Out of frustration and distrust of such behaviors, however, some presidents have ignored or worked outside this system, sometimes to their political detriment.

WHAT IS THE NATIONAL SECURITY ENTERPRISE?

We have adopted the term "national security enterprise" to capture the notion that the enterprise is more than simply the formal government institutions found in the executive branch and the Congress. Typically, when reformers speak of the national security system they mean executive branch departments and separate agencies and the office of the president with its NSC staff. Many of the reform studies recommend changes in the way the various national security agencies operate, interact with each other, or respond to the president. In a few cases, most recently the 9/11 Commission, reformers have suggested that both executive *and* congressional branch reforms are needed if the system is to function more effectively.

However, as this book argues, the enterprise is much broader than those two institutions. Imagining that the enterprise is a series of concentric circles, the core functions of government—executive branch departments—make up the nucleus of the national security system. However, outside that nucleus lies another layer of the enterprise: the other branches of government. Most significantly is the Congress, which has sizable foreign affairs and security policy responsibilities, but also the courts, which increasingly have an impact on the formulation and conduct of foreign and national security policies.

Beyond these two levels, however, lies a more informal set of players in the national security enterprise. Those players include the media, which is instrumental in setting the agenda, evaluating the formal players' performance, and publicizing alternative views. This outer ring also includes the think tank world, where former government officials and nongovernment experts likewise formulate new initiatives alongside their critiques of government as well as act as informal partners with parts of the formal executive branch and congressional players. Similarly, that outside layer contains important lobby groups that provide expertise and represent domestic interest groups with foreign policy objectives as well as foreign groups who hope to influence the legislative process and executive branch policy priorities.

THE ORGANIZATIONAL DIMENSION

The nature of government generally and national security policies in particular have become so complicated that specialized organizations are necessary to fulfill the nation's will. Public policy has become bureaucratized to ensure a rational and orderly administration of the government's responsibilities. Positively seen, a bureaucracy, in the Max Weber sense,[6] is a group of individuals who operate by a set of rules and standards to achieve certain agreed-upon goals; they are expected to be professionals, sometimes technocrats, who hold their positions by virtue of their expertise, education or training, and other unique characteristics of those professions. Be they government lawyers or economists, military officers, diplomats, legislators or lobbyists, or intelligence officers, they were all selected for certain skills. National security professionals bring expertise to the interagency table but they often carry other organizational, cultural, and professional baggage as well. These professionals are schooled in the correct procedures used to accomplish their specific tasks, and rewarded and promoted according to the organizational interests they represent. This is more than "where you sit" determining "where you stand;" it is "how you tick." So, the military officer spends years in training to develop war-fighting methods and understanding what a proper civil-military relationship is; or the diplomat masters foreign languages and hones the art of negotiation and report writing; or the intelligence officer develops the skill of clandestine operations, handling of foreign spies, and the evaluation of raw intelligence reports. Each such organization, then, develops special processes and practices that can improve its efficiency and, most importantly, its reliability. On a permanent basis we expect our diplomats to represent our government according to certain principles; likewise, we expect our military services to follow the code of military conduct and for intelligence officers to conduct espionage overseas under appropriate executive orders.

Box I.1   An Organizational Culture Defined

An organization, namely a group of people organized and managed often hierarchically to accomplish a specific set of tasks, quickly institutionalizes a way of doing business to get the job done. This institutionalization of the specialized functions it performs begins to form what becomes known as the organizational culture. The founders of any organization have an especially powerful impact on socializing the work force and developing the norms, values, and practices of such organizational cultures. They pass down these values but also become some of the legends and models to which newer members aspire.

An organizational culture is widely seen as a system of shared meaning or values that the organization's membership holds and that distinguish it from other groups. The essence of an organization is often characterized by the extent to which the organization defines and values its mission, rewards results and risk taking, pays attention to details or facts, and the way it develops and retains its people.

A dominant culture is one that expresses the core values held and shared by most members of the organization. Subcultures are possible, especially in large organizations containing divisions separated by their different missions, location, or selection process. A strong culture is one where the members accept and enforce the values. Such a culture can build cohesion and loyalty but also is more resistant to change than weaker ones. The organization's process of selecting, training, evaluating, and promoting people tends to keep and reward those who fit the culture and encourage nonconformists to find other work.

Such behaviors become routinized and second nature to the professionals within these bureaucracies. They are unquestioned, for the most part, as they seem to have worked in the past to both accomplish the organization's goals and to ensure that the individual is promoted within the system. So, it should come as no surprise that change is not something that organizations always willingly embrace.[7] Bureaucracies are designed to accomplish certain specific organizational tasks using procedures, doctrines, and regulations to achieve certain goals so there is no question as to how they should operate. Although our intent is not to review the extensive literature on organizational behavior, we do accept the principles embedded in those studies that suggest that there are certain behaviors that many organizations, be they private or public, often exhibit:

- Organizations promote outcomes and decisions that advance their own interests and minimize costs to their operations.
- Agencies try to avoid taking on tasks that are not central to their understanding of their core mission.
- When an agency has more than a single internal culture, conflicts over priorities often occur.
- Senior officials' positions tend to be defined by the combination of their personal views and the culture they represent.
- Successful changes in a culture have to be seen as central to the perceived mission of the agency.

Social scientists have observed such organizational behaviors in virtually all kinds of private and public sector organizations. Whether it is the firm, the foundation, or the foreign service, certain organizational norms flourish. This is the phenomenon that this book will explore. It is important to remember that organizations are made up of both people and processes. As the chapters will document, the different agencies and institutions self-select people who will perform certain operations successfully; but more importantly, agencies train those people to conduct themselves in certain ways so that these practices become second nature and frame any approach to a problem. To understand the organization, one has to look at the type of people as well as the special skills and processes that they employ to achieve their objectives.

At the outset, we acknowledge that the national security enterprise and its many constituent organizations have changed over time. No organization is totally impervious to new missions, tasks, and structural adaptations. However, sometimes the change is not in the right direction or effective; at other times organizations resist or defeat the intent of those new missions or tasks. It is not fair to criticize our institutions as totally dysfunctional, nor is it correct to say that all the change we see has been positive. These chapters will try to describe both the good and the bad of our bureaucracies.

COMMON CHALLENGES

A number of themes are addressed in the book that represent challenges to the national security enterprise. Each chapter touches on these, and the cumulative effect of our volume is to address them from a variety of perspectives.

First, the 2010 world reflects a set of institutional players that has vastly increased since the 1947 National Security Act. What once was a function largely focused on the president, his secretaries of state and defense, and his military and intelligence advisors is now spread across virtually every department. So, when senior meetings are held on international topics, the range of agencies will span the foreign and security field but also law enforcement agencies and the Department of Homeland Security (DHS); the economic departments of Treasury, Commerce, and Agriculture; or the technical fields of the Centers for Disease Control and Prevention, NASA, or the Office of the Science Advisor. The blending of such different cultures and priorities makes for an unruly interagency process, brings more congressional voices into the discussion as well, and means that even more outside interest groups and experts are interested in what American policies will emerge from the government deliberations.

Second, and related to this first reality, is the very uneven nature of the different agencies' capabilities and interests. Some critics have argued that U.S. foreign policy has become overly militarized, partly as a result of the massive resources and skills of the Pentagon and relatively underdeveloped resources and capabilities of the State Department and other civilian agencies. Even within the military, the adage that "you fight the war with the army you have" makes it clear that developing resources and capabilities requires time and planning, something that far too few agencies have when an emergency develops and the interagency calls for them to step forward with new programs. The uneven strengths and weaknesses of the players definitely affect policy outcomes, both in how they are decided but also in how they are implemented.

Third, information sharing remains a major challenge for effective decision making and policy implementation. As agencies control information, they can use it to maximize their influence over decisions or undercut those agencies that are its bureaucratic opponents. Yet, most reform recommendations are adamant that better information sharing is essential to a smoother operation of government. This info-sharing admonition runs counter to the natural stovepiping of organizations. Their hierarchical nature and their desire to control information discourage them from sharing. In some cases, it is the need-to-know principle, but in others it is driven more by information is power or a professional resistance to share based on bureaucratic principles.

In addition, information can be used for bureaucratic purposes to impact policy. As is often the case, "leaks" and unauthorized disclosures based on open source material by the media often seizes the headlines and may at times put at risk individuals and national security programs. Balancing First Amendment rights and security needs has always been a tricky task and has grown even more difficult in this world of cyber and electronic data storage.

Fourth, priorities are constantly changing. Every four years there is either a new president or a new term that calls for new directions and ideas. Each new administration has approximately 3,000 appointments to harness and direct the executive branch. Congressional elections and changing majorities in the legislative process can also influence the types of initiatives that will be welcomed or opposed. Moreover, the world itself is an unpredictable place. President George W. Bush started his presidency thinking he would focus on building relationships with the key powers of Russia, China, and India but quickly found his presidency marked by what he felt justified to call the global war on terror. Eight years later, a new president has dispensed with this term, preferring such euphemisms like "ongoing contingency operations," and has instructed that there be a new look into how we conduct the battle against terrorism, and has significantly altered U.S. plans for Iraq and Afghanistan. Even these plans might be subject to major changes, as 2009–10 saw the worst economic and budget conditions since the Great Depression; this, too, might again force an alteration of presidential priorities, to which agencies and institutions will be obliged to adjust.

ORGANIZATION OF THE BOOK

The book is organized to highlight the different domains of the national security enterprise. In the first section we introduce this notion of an enterprise with some history of how the system itself arose and evolved. We then discuss how the NSC and OMB have developed an ethos of their own, reflecting the presidents they have served. In the second section we examine the executive agencies and departments that make up the bulk of the formal interagency process: the Departments of State and Defense, the military services, the CIA and the director of national intelligence, and the FBI and DHS. There could have been more written about other agencies but space does not permit us to include every agency. Subsequent studies might easily expand on the list of critical economic agencies, including USAID and Treasury, or include greater discussion of the role of field operations in shaping organizational cultures.

A second set of chapters focuses on the Congress and the courts. The Congress has long vied for more control over the foreign and national security policies of the executive branch; it can be both ally and enemy, sometimes different parts of it aligned with separate agencies. The courts too play a role, albeit less obvious but no less fundamental to the national security process. The controversies swirling around detention and interrogation policies make clear how important the rule of law is to American foreign policy.

The final section contains the outer, informal set of players in the enterprise. The media, the think tanks, and the lobbyists play major roles in shaping, supporting, and critiquing U.S. security policies. They too can be partners or protagonists to the interagency process, depending on the clash or convergence of ideology as well as the opportunity to advance their own interests.

The argument of the book is that the effectiveness and coherence of the national security enterprise is challenged by both our constitutional structure and the nature of our professional bureaucracies. No one group or entity is charged with a grand strategy; each organization is in a way preoccupied with its own professionalism and therefore coordination is difficult. With every new administration a new layer of political actors arrives, somewhat divorced from power and not well versed in how to use the ways and means of institutional power but understanding their goals. During the Cold War there was continuity across administrations—containment, the Marshall Plan, the WTO, full spectrum domination by our military—because the problem set was relatively constant. The new problem set of the twenty-first century—nuclear proliferation, terrorism, failing states, cyber threats, global warming, and the international economic reshuffle—has revealed the weaknesses of the current national security enterprise. These issues do not fit neatly into the repertoires of individual agencies but will necessitate collaboration among many different agencies and organizational cultures.

In the concluding chapter we lay out some modest suggestions for creating more collaboration across these very different agencies and cultures. Redesigning the national security enterprise is clearly not a one-time event; rather, it is an ongoing task that must not rely simply on changing the structures, authorities, and procedures for reaching and implementing decisions. Improving the effectiveness of the national security enterprise means understanding what motivates and drives different organizations so that the right incentives can be developed to build collaboration. Hence, greater understanding of those cultures—their strengths and weaknesses as well as their roles and missions—will be an important step in the right direction.

NOTES

1. See the United States Institute of Peace review of the quadrennial defense report, a bipartisan panel led by Stephen J. Hadley and William J. Perry. The report, *The QDR in Perspective: Meeting America's National Security Needs in the 21st Century; The Final Report of the Quadrennial Defense Review Independent Panel* (July 2010) warns of an impending all-volunteer force "train wreck," and advocates for new approaches and institutions for national security at www.usip.org/files/qdr/qdrreport.pdf.

2. See Steven W. Hook, *U.S. Foreign Policy: The Paradox of Power*, 2nd ed. (Washington, DC: CQ Press, 2008), chapter 6, "The Foreign Policy Bureaucracy," 162–97; and Howard J. Wiarda, *Divided America on the World Stage: Broken Government and Foreign Policy* (Washington, DC: Potomac Books, 2009), chapter 11, "Bureaucratic Politics: Turf Battles among Agencies," 257–81.

3. See Morton H. Halperin and Priscilla A. Clapp, *Bureaucratic Politics and Foreign Policy*, 2d ed. (Washington, DC: Brookings Institution, 2006); and Graham Allison and Philip Zelikow, *The Essence of Decision: Explaining the Cuban Missile Crisis*, 2d ed. (Boston: Little Brown, 1999).

4. Amy Zegart, *Spying Blind: The CIA, the FBI, and the Origins of 9/11* (Princeton, NJ: Princeton University Press, 2007).

5. Project on National Security Reform, *Forging a New Shield*, November 2008 (Washington, DC: PNSR), Executive Summary, 7.

6. For Weber a bureaucracy constituted a professional corps of career officials with formal qualifications organized in a hierarchical pyramid of authority with specific divisions of labor, governed by impersonal, uniform rational rules and procedures so that promotion could be based on the principles of both seniority and performance. Bureaucratic administration is rational since the exercise of control is based on knowledge. See "Bureaucracy," *Encyclopedia Britannica*, at: http://lilt. ilstu.edu/rrpope/rrpopepwd/articles/bureacracy2.html.

7. Zegart, Chapter 3, p. 45 explains how the organizational cultures resisted change. As Zegart notes, "the internal barriers to organizational change are powerful and deeply entrenched. . . . [E]mployees inside organizations become wedded to habits, thinking, routines, values, norms, ideas, and identities, and these attachments make change difficult."

Part I   The Interagency Process

Chapter 1 History of the Interagency Process for Foreign Relations in the United States: Murphy's Law?

Jon J. Rosenwasser and Michael Warner

> "Will you please tell me what in hell the State Department has to do in an active theater of war?"
> *Question posed to diplomat Robert Murphy in North Africa, 1942*

The processes for making and executing foreign policy in the United States have grown more centralized, more rationalized, and more inclusive of multiple institutional viewpoints since World War II. Nevertheless, they still remain remarkably dispersed and their coordination ad hoc. This situation results in large part from the constitutional fragmentation of power between and among the executive and legislative branches of government, reinforced by customs and precedents forged during a time when the geography of two oceans alone provided the Republic significant security and masked institutional deficiencies. The demands of global engagement in World War II and the Cold War, however, prompted presidents and Congress to experiment with new legal and institutional forms for coordinating policymaking, diplomacy, and military efforts. Chief among these forms have been the National Security Act of 1947 and the National Security Council that it created. Reorganizations and reforms within the nation's military, diplomatic, economic, and intelligence arms have also had significant impacts. Since the Cold War the challenges of state disintegration and transnational threats, punctuated by the September 11, 2001 terrorist attacks, have prompted further innovation in the interagency system, from presidential directives on complex emergencies to the creation of a Department of Homeland Security and sweeping intelligence reform. Although these have resulted in greater exchange of views and information (and increased cooperation in the field), the basic difficulties of coordinating the plans and actions of highly independent cabinet departments endure.

ORIGINS OF THE INTERAGENCY PROCESS IN THE UNITED STATES

Veteran diplomat Robert Murphy had a good answer to the question above, posed to him by an American major general not long after the Anglo-American invasion of North Africa in 1942. In his memoir, he explained that the State Department "had direct responsibility in the preparatory stage leading to the invasion. It was directly concerned in the political decisions inevitably made during the military operations, and will have to deal with the postwar political effects of this campaign. . . . And that is why I am here."[1] Murphy's experience encapsulates a history of interagency relations in American foreign and security policy. He compensated for the irregularity of his formal authorities ("Don't bother going through State Department channels," President Roosevelt had told him), and his scant preparation ("I became aware of my appalling ignorance of military matters"), by dint of tireless work, personal grit, and indomitable common sense. By and large his colleagues in the army, navy, State Department, and Office of Strategic Services did likewise, fashioning ways to work together in the common cause with their British (and ultimately French) allies. Their effort saw its share of missteps and even comic opera episodes, but it worked, if sometimes only by the narrowest of margins. Many other American ventures overseas have shared this ad hoc manner.

Before considering the history of the interagency process to understand the persistence, but also the gradual diminution, of the "Murphy spirit" in U.S. foreign policy, it is important to consider a framework that can guide analysis of its form, because its form shapes its operation and, ultimately, the policy outcomes. A useful framework to consider is that the interagency system comprises two dimensions: dynamics and levels. The dynamics of the interagency system—in the United States or any other nation—are the function of six underlying structural factors: the nature of the threat environment; a state's geostrategic position; constitutional frameworks; leadership proclivities; technology (particularly its military character); and prevailing public management paradigms. As these factors evolve, so does the interagency process. In addition, the interagency process operates at three levels, corresponding to the place (both physical and institutional) at which the interaction occurs. At the strategic level, policy planning and coordination happens, dominated by the dynamics of the national capital. At the intermediate or operational level, initiatives that comprise larger policy are conceived and managed. At the tactical level, military commanders and other personnel deployed in the field execute plans (for war, diplomacy, development, trade, etc.) that contribute to those initiatives. (At all three levels, other actors such as foreign partners, inter- and nongovernmental partners, and industry are increasingly involved.)

The historical circumstances of the United States' first 150 years decisively shaped its interagency process. Born from revolutionary separation from Great Britain, America has mistrusted central authority at home while recognizing the need for unified leadership abroad. With good reason, the Founding Fathers feared both tyranny by kings and tyranny by the masses. Article I of the Constitution gave Congress explicit powers to "provide for the common Defence," "declare War," "raise and support Armies," "provide and maintain a Navy," and "make Rules for the Government and Regulation of the land and naval Forces," backed by its power of the purse. Though the Senate held the right to advise the president in appointing certain officers and to approve treaties (with the high bar of a two-thirds majority), these formal powers were essentially passive; the chief executive held the initiative to act or not act in the myriad cases and ways of his office.

As a practical matter, therefore, the executive branch naturally assumed primacy in national security affairs. For the first 150 years of the nation's history, the national security establishment comprised the State Department and the two military departments (a War Department for the army and a Navy Department for the navy and marine corps). All reported directly to the president. The president's authorities were few but clear in this domain: the power to negotiate treaties, to appoint the heads of the several government departments, and to exercise command in war. Once Congress appropriated the necessary funds, the president did not have to share these powers with anyone or seek approval or advice before ordering diplomats abroad or the nation's forces into harm's way. Presidents could keep their own counsel or ask one or more aides to help them reach decisions; no formal coordinating or decision-making machinery existed under them. The lack of technological or analytical means to amass, analyze, or disseminate information reinforced presidential autonomy. Matters of national importance might well be discussed by the department secretaries comprising the cabinet: a body that could be counted on to bring a broad range of experience and exquisitely sensitive political instincts to bear, but rarely much in the way of expertise on foreign topics.

The congressional committee structure, organized around oversight of a defined set of departments, reinforced this separation of institutions. It let committees exert more influence over the executive branch, and it also let members do more for their constituents; Congress's desire to influence the location of installations and the purchase of material is not a modern phenomenon. When it first created committees in 1816, Congress then fashioned ones explicitly for each of these three departments: Foreign Relations for the State Department, Military Affairs for the War Department, and Naval Affairs for the Navy Department. Under this model, the departments submitted appropriations requests directly to their committee of jurisdiction, with little input from the president or his staff. With this division of labor suiting the strategic landscape of the Republic's early decades and hewing to congressional interests to keep the executive branch fragmented, each tool of national power developed its own institutional narrative, organizational ethos, and operational coda.

U.S. foreign policy long focused on guarding the nation's westward expansion, winning the Civil War, and protecting trade. The early secretaries of state held an enviable position as *primus inter pares* with regard to their fellow cabinet secretaries, discharging a range of diverse but important domestic duties (for a time these included supervising the census and the U.S. Mint) as well as the conduct of foreign relations. With notable exceptions like Thomas Jefferson and John Quincy Adams, secretaries typically had little direct diplomatic experience, but instead were selected on the basis of their achievements in business or law—and their support for the president's ticket and party. Several of them made up in ability what they lacked in experience.

Secretaries of state oversaw a bifurcated department. The diplomatic service helped represent the president in advancing the United States' world interests, while the consular service promoted opportunities for American business overseas and protected U.S. citizens abroad. Secretaries of state since Jefferson lodged bureaucratic power with the diplomatic service. Ambassadors and diplomats typically won their appointments through political connections, with the result that the United States sent some very able men and some appalling embarrassments to represent its interests abroad.[2] Continuity and competence instead was provided through career staff in Washington. William Hunter and Alvey A. Adee, to name two members of that cadre, between them served from 1829 to 1924 and were described by one historian as "walking encyclopedias of precedent, international law, and diplomatic procedure."[3] By 1940, remembered Dean Acheson, the real bureaucratic power in the department "had come to rest in the [geographic] division chiefs and the advisers, political, legal, and economic." The result of this "nineteenth-century" arrangement, argued Acheson, was that "most matters that concerned the Department arose from specific incidents or problems and then evolved into policies, rather than beginning as matters of broad decision and ending in specific action. In this way the departmental division having jurisdiction to deal with the incident became the basic instrument for the formulation and execution of policy."[4]

With relatively little urgency to have a robust overseas presence as the early American Republic grew, Congress only reluctantly spent money on overseas missions and activities. As a result, the foreign service was "traditionally ill-chosen, ill-treated, ill-paid, ill-housed, ill-coordinated, and under-manned."[5] It became a home away from home for the nation's elite, who perforce paid most of their overseas expenses but who—at least in the age before the telegraph—also had unambiguous authority to represent the United States in foreign capitals. As a result, diplomacy served as the principal tool of statecraft, unless and until armed conflict erupted, in which cases armies and navies were raised and the military departments oversaw the conduct of combat. In short, the president and the Department of State were preeminent in peacetime, and the president and the military departments and armed services took preeminence in wartime.

The military developed its own organizational ethos based on four structural features. First, the armed services were small, only surging in wartime. Second, they fought different forms of war; the army fought one kind of war on land, and the navy another at sea, which reinforced their unique cultures and independent approaches.[6] Third, the army and navy, at least in peacetime, were decentralized structures dominated not by their line commanders but by their several service and support bureaus. Appointed civilians set strategy, policy, and doctrine, such as they were. The domination of the armed services by officials and staff officers who did not actually fight was an arrangement that allowed Congress to exert strong influence over the services' bureaus, which only strengthened their institutional clout. This arrangement of the American military not infrequently resulted in inefficiency, unclear command relationships, and friction between the War and Navy departments.[7] The military's fourth structural feature was technology. Although military technology remained relatively static through the nineteenth century, two inventions provided new opportunities for coordination by shrinking the distance between national capitals (including Washington) and the field. The introduction of the railroad allowed the transport of supplies to far-flung territories to protect the borders or encroach upon neighbors. The telegraph, moreover, enabled short communication bursts to distant outposts, including ambassadors and military field commanders. The age of the proconsul was ending.

The three departments did exchange information and cooperate; they just did so in their own time, on their own terms. Presidents interfered minimally with the departments' autonomy, and did not demand that they adopt common strategies or programs. The interagency coordination that occurred was largely at the strategic level in Washington. Presidents created no formal governing or coordinating body apart from whatever aides were hired to handle the chief executive's paperwork and schedule. When coordination was necessary, the proximity of the departments' headquarters to one another and to the president doubtless helped. All three departments occupied buildings on the same (rather large) city block as the White House until after the Civil War, and then were colocated until just before World War II in a grand Second Empire structure (naturally dubbed the "State-War-Navy Building") beside the executive mansion.

This system could work well, and it could work poorly. It did both in America's "splendid little war" with Spain in 1898, when the United States suddenly emerged as one of the great powers. Having been goaded to war by congressmen and journalists appalled by the frightful Spanish counterinsurgency campaign in Cuba, President William McKinley and his cabinet ran the affair with a marked amateurism. Their proximity and familiarity meant that the president and his lieutenants received advice from many quarters, and also that decisions could be made and implemented swiftly. On the other hand, their decisions were not always well considered. An assistant secretary of the navy named Theodore Roosevelt, on his own authority, concentrated the U.S. Asiatic fleet near the Philippines to strike the first blow against the Spanish. It did, and then waited impotently for weeks in Manila's harbor for troops to arrive and seize the city. The U.S. army had been wholly unprepared for the conflict and its commanders coordinated haphazardly with the navy in Cuba. Having found his country in possession of Manila, President McKinley and his advisors also found themselves with seemingly no alternative to acquiring the entire Philippine archipelago from Spain and also found themselves saddled with a grueling counterinsurgency campaign featuring scenes as grim as those from Cuba under Spanish rule.[8]

The early decades of the twentieth century—the Progressive Era—introduced new ideas about public management and organizational planning that began a long process of updating this segmented interagency system. President Theodore Roosevelt's commitment to rooting out the spoils system by professionalizing the civil service promoted a transformation over the next two decades in State Department entrance standards, pay, and training. The Rogers Act (1924) merged the diplomatic and consular services to unify America's overseas presence, as well as institutionalized the selection of career foreign service officers through competitive examinations. Shortly thereafter, the Porter Foreign Service Buildings Act (1926) provided major upgrades in American missions abroad to reflect the nation's growing international prestige.[9]

Innovations also came to the military, albeit slowly. In the wake of the mishaps in the Spanish-American War, and with the obvious modernization of European militaries proceeding apace, President Theodore Roosevelt's secretary of war Elihu Root centralized the army's technical services under his direction and proposed a joint Army-Navy board to adjudicate interservice matters.[10] The navy, meanwhile, remained highly decentralized, reflecting the deeper tradition of autonomy given to ships at sea and the strength of the naval bureaus.[11] Thus, whereas World War I spurred great technological advances in the weapons that the armed services employed, it made little effect on their degree of cooperation.

A more subtle but equally important change to the interagency system came with the new thinking in resource management. Up to this period, predominant attention was paid to internal controls to monitor "inputs," that is, money and people, which were exclusively handled between each federal department and its relevant congressional oversight committee. The 1921 Budget Act, which created a new bureau of the budget in the White House (the precursor to the Office of the Management and Budget), did not change the focus on inputs or allow for analysis of overlaps, gaps, and synergies between and among departments, but it did provide the president with greater insight into individual departments' spending so that the administration could explain to Congress how appropriations were actually obligated.

The last significant change ushered in with the Progressive Era was the creation of public policy centers that straddled the line between academia and government. The Carnegie Endowment for International Peace (1910), the Brookings Institution (1916), and the

Council on Foreign Relations (1921) paved the way in providing independent research to the foreign policy debate. Over the next few decades such institutions—whether for research or straight advocacy—would proliferate and serve as a foil for spawning, testing, and refining foreign policy ideas. In fact, over time, such public policy institutions became proving grounds and holding pens for those who would serve at the most senior levels of government.

Coincidental with these progressive reforms were several technological innovations that provided new means of communication and amplified the destructive capacity of military force. The radio and early incarnations of the telephone provided leaders with new instruments to reach and control their diplomatic and military representatives in the field while also creating new opportunities for societal mobilization (for causes both ill and good). Mechanization, longer-range artillery, and the airplane all gave the military important new means to bring greater firepower to bear over greater distances. Chemical weapons (the first weapons of mass destruction) threatened terrifying effects on civilian populations. Together, these technologies compelled further coordination among the instruments of national power to prevent conflict (or manage its dramatically greater consequences if prevention failed).

It took World War II to finally force the departments to cooperate in unprecedented ways. The ancient premise that land and naval warfare were unique propositions eroded with the development of air power and made congressmen and officials reconsider the division of labor between the army and navy. With each service developing aviation capabilities that performed overlapping roles and missions, interservice rivalry increased—as did the need for a more unified war effort to stave off defeat at the hands of Nazi Germany and Imperial Japan.[12] The nation's far-flung forces could not win without tight coordination of supplies, shipping, and operations and the imperative to gain and keep allies (while keeping neutrals out of the fray on the Axis powers' side) made it essential for generals, admirals, and diplomats like Robert Murphy to work together closely and constantly. Such exertions called forth prodigious applications of expertise of all kinds, mobilized in the State, War, and Navy departments as well as in an array of emergency entities like the Joint Chiefs of Staff and war agencies such as the Office of Strategic Services, the Office of War Information, and the Coordinator for Latin American Affairs. Furthermore, the introduction of the atomic bomb as the ultimate weapon, as Bernard Brodie termed it, gave the world pause to contemplate the devastation that war could impose in the modern age if events spiraled out of control. The lessons learned in World War II, the reshaping of international politics thereafter, and this technological Rubicon had a decisive imprint on the interagency process in the United States.

Problems with the nation's diplomatic and military performance, ironically enough, were glaringly obvious to knowledgeable observers as America celebrated victory in 1945. Dean Acheson, at the time an assistant secretary of state, later complained that "the Department had no ideas, plans, or methods for collecting the information or dealing with the problems" created by the need to mobilize resources and wage war on a global scale.[13] Scant weeks after the Japanese surrender, General of the Army George C. Marshall told Congress in public session that it was only the looming threat of defeat in 1942 that had persuaded the army and navy to stop fighting each other and fight the Axis powers instead.[14] A study prepared contemporaneously for navy secretary James Forrestal echoed this lament.

Its authors applauded the unified command structure adopted by the military after Pearl Harbor, in which all forces in-theater answered to a single regional commander regardless of home service (that officer would later be titled a combatant commander, or COCOM). The study noted, however, that this innovation broke down as Allied forces neared Japan. No one in Washington selected a supreme commander for the impending assault on the Home Islands and, thus, the army and navy in the western Pacific began to revert to their old, separate ways as the invasion of Japan loomed closer. American diplomacy was hardly better coordinated with its military power: "Many times, when there has been disagreement about a matter of policy, instead of meeting together for common discussion and decision, there have been independent appeals to the President." These examples and others convinced the authors of the report to recommend unification of the armed services and a series of measures and bodies, such as a national security council, to coordinate policies.[15]

A NEW CHARTER

The change in America's global position after World War II had made the need to coordinate the national security institutions of the U.S. government increasingly obvious. The Soviet menace after 1945 led to a series of policy choices that endured through the ensuing Cold War: maintaining a large standing military deployed around the world; the creation of a nuclear arsenal to deter general war; security guarantees to allies in Europe and the Pacific; and participation in new institutions to oversee global affairs and trade (e.g., United Nations, the International Monetary Fund [IMF], the World Bank, and the General Agreement on Tariffs and Trade).

These choices had practical implications for interagency relations over the next generation. First, the United States needed an integrated approach to all possible intensities of armed conflict across the land, sea, and air domains. Second, the civilian and diplomatic instruments of power needed to be managed more carefully to properly signal intent and capability to adversaries so as to avoid the catastrophe of nuclear war. Finally, Washington needed more precise and capable intelligence support to win and keep allies, halt Soviet expansionism, and ensure that Moscow did not gain (or believe it had gained) a clear lead in military power. The rapid adoption of real-time communication over long distances, moreover, gave both the impetus and means for long-needed reforms.

President Harry Truman recognized the need for an overhaul of the United States' "antiquated defense set-up."[16] The 80th Congress agreed, convinced in part by the sudden and chaotic demobilization of the enormous fighting force the nation had mobilized for World War II. The National Security Act of 1947 thus preserved the traditional diplomatic and military departments but changed the ways in which they related to one another, centralizing power in certain cases, while clarifying roles and responsibilities in others. In large measure, the Act's core features endure to this day: a National Security Council (NSC) in the White House; a secretary of defense to oversee the armed services with a statutory Joint Chiefs of Staff (JCS) to provide advice and a small number of regional combatant commanders to execute orders under the "Unified Command Plan"; and a loosely configured intelligence system to support the whole. For the next four decades, presidents and Congresses sought to enhance the effectiveness of the components of this system while ironically making relatively little effort to improve their collective operation.

National Security Council

The 1947 National Security Act created a NSC (comprising the president and vice president, along with the secretaries of state and defense), to operate as a standing venue to coordinate the foreign and defense policies of the departments and of the government as a whole. This innovation provided the president his own institution to coordinate foreign policy, as well as a mechanism for crisis management. The NSC's size, role, and influence ebbed and flowed depending on each president's proclivity for maintaining a policy-coordinating mechanism separate from his cabinet and his bilateral relationships with top advisors. That proclivity varied according to each national security advisor's relationship with the president he or she served, and with the interplay among the national security advisor and the cabinet secretaries (especially the secretaries of state and defense). The NSC staff proper remained relatively small, usually less than one hundred people. Outside of a brief period of overseeing operations under President Eisenhower, the staff mostly focused on high-level policy formulation and coordination.

The NSC reflects its president's governing style. Dwight Eisenhower's NSC functioned like an Army staff. John Kennedy's operated less formally, with much of its work influenced by his brother, Attorney General Robert Kennedy. National security advisors did not really come into their own as institutional players until Kennedy's choice for the post, Harvard dean McGeorge Bundy. Henry Kissinger raised the role to its zenith of power and influence for Presidents Richard Nixon and Gerald Ford; he made and directed policy and, for a time, served concurrently as secretary of state. President Jimmy Carter had criticized the Kissinger model and thus allowed the NSC's power to recede to the departments while maintaining a strong directive voice from his national security advisor, Zbigniew Brzezinski. President Ronald Reagan vacillated among these models before establishing one that would endure under his successors George H. W. Bush, William Clinton, George W. Bush, and Barack Obama: a staff balanced between politically appointed officials close to White House staff (and even the president himself) and career civil servants rotated from the departments. In this model, several staff directorates organized around core regions and cross-cutting challenges were complemented by a nested set of committees of increasing seniority to handle topics of presidential and interagency import.[17]

The Department of Defense

The National Security Act did not exactly unify the armed services, but it did create a secretary of defense to oversee the army, the navy, and the (now independent) air force. Amendments to the National Security Act in 1949, 1953, and 1958 created the Department of Defense, clarified the originally amorphous roles of the secretary of defense and the JCS, and provided them with greater authority and staff to manage the armed services and the department itself. The sheer size, expense, political salience, and global footprint of the nation's military lent the Department of Defense influence over most aspects of foreign policymaking and the interagency process during the Cold War (and thus competed with the State Department's long dominance of foreign policy).

Without unifying concepts, analytic tools, or bureaucratic discipline, however, neither the secretary of defense nor the joint chiefs could manage the defense establishment as an integrated whole. In 1961 Secretary Robert McNamara began to change this situation. McNamara, who had revolutionized management at Ford Motor Company, adopted a three-pronged strategy to enhance civilian control and focus the defense effort around national security goals. Organizationally, he expanded the Office of the Secretary of Defense (OSD), centralizing decisions on weapons development, forming an Office of Systems Analysis, and elevating the department's comptroller to outrank the military services. Substantively, he infused defense decision making with new analytic techniques (many developed at RAND) whose chief metrics were economy and efficiency rather than military judgment and intuition. Procedurally, and perhaps most importantly, he initiated a planning-programming-budgeting system (PPBS), managed by civilians in OSD, to link their strategic guidance, the services' programs, and fiscal constraints. Although these reforms did not penetrate the operational side of the armed services (which fought distinct and largely separate wars in Vietnam), the goal of integrating the management of the nation's military was no longer in question.

Department of State

The State Department adjusted with difficulty to the changed world and interagency environment of the Cold War. Secretaries of state, of course, can execute only the authorities delegated to them by the presidents they serve, and not all presidents viewed them as did President Truman, who "looked principally to the Department of State in determining foreign policy and—except where force was necessary—exclusively in executing it," in words of Dean Acheson.[18] Acheson himself may have been the last secretary who could say such a thing about the department. Several of his successors perhaps matched his personal influence in policy circles, but none of them—not even Henry Kissinger or George Shultz—could argue that the department was the unrivaled leader in making and executing foreign policy.

This is not to say that the department did not grow in stature and ability in the postwar era. State was indeed "woefully unprepared to handle the staggering amount of work imposed on it" at the end of World War II, remembered Robert Murphy in his memoir. Its "failure to make preparations for responsibilities in Germany, Japan and elsewhere caused unbelievable administrative confusion," and forced the armed services to step into the vacuum as occupiers and nation-builders.[19] Secretary of State Dean Acheson credited his predecessor, George Marshall, with essential modernization of the department's governance. Marshall (with Acheson, for a time, as his undersecretary) brought a more military-style efficiency to its procedures and decision making, and also created a policy planning staff to keep deliberations from fixating on the *crise du jour*.[20] Acheson's successor John Foster Dulles continued the reforms of the department's organization, personnel system, and culture in the 1950s, better integrating the Foreign Service and the departmental staffs and seeking to ensure that State's officials had the training to function alongside the military and other agencies of government whose work took them overseas. State's regional bureaus remained the locus of power in the Department, but increasingly important work was being done by functional bureaus covering economic, environmental, and scientific issues. By the 1960s, moreover, new independent organizations that reported directly to the president with a "dotted reporting line" to the secretary of state, most notably the Agency for International Development, the U.S. Information Agency, and the Arms Control and Disarmament Agency, also played an ever-larger role in making policy in Washington and implementing it abroad. This arrangement elevated important areas of U.S.

foreign policy (development, public diplomacy, and nuclear arms control), but created bureaucratic sprawl that complicated the coordination of State Department activities and broader foreign policy objectives.

Intelligence Community

The National Security Act created a new Central Intelligence Agency (CIA) under a director of central intelligence (DCI) that would inform the NSC's deliberations and implement its decisions by covert means. As with the JCS, however, congressional concerns in 1947 about possible overreaching and threats to civil liberties proscribed the DCI's influence over the intelligence activities in the armed services and the other departments. Directors of central intelligence held marginal influence over intelligence activities and policymaking before the tenures of Gen. Walter B. Smith and Allen Dulles (the younger brother of the secretary of state) under Presidents Truman and Eisenhower. Despite their efforts to coordinate clandestine activities and analyses, however, the nation thus grew what was essentially a three-part intelligence system (dubbed the "intelligence community" in the 1950s). Most of the money and personnel stayed with the armed services, which dominated the increasingly sophisticated national technical means of surveilling the Soviet Union and other adversaries. Internal security intelligence remained the purview of the FBI, a national law enforcement agency based in the Justice Department that was hindered as much as helped by the tenure of its long-serving director, J. Edgar Hoover. National-level analytical work and clandestine activities overseas fell almost by default to the DCI and the CIA, which also performed useful coordination functions and services of common concern for the community.

Congress

Capitol Hill largely deferred to the executive branch during the height of the Cold War in the 1950s and 1960s. But the trauma of Vietnam and President Richard M. Nixon's downfall revolutionized Congress's membership, committee structure, and approach to oversight. Motivated by an unpopular war, a younger generation unseated older members and forced several changes in chamber and party caucus rules that devolved power from older committee chairmen to more youthful subcommittee chairmen. To enable this agenda, the Legislative Reorganization Act of 1970 expanded the staffs of congressional committees and its auxiliary arms, the General Accounting Office and the Congressional Research Service, while the Congressional Budget and Impoundment Control Act of 1974 gave the Congress greater power in reviewing the president's federal budget request and its execution. Particular to national security, the War Powers Resolution of 1974 placed a brake on presidential prerogative regarding the unilateral deployment of military power and epitomized the new leadership's assertiveness. The Church and Pike committees' investigations of intelligence community excesses in Latin America and at home led to the creation of new select committees on intelligence in each chamber, reporting requirements for covert action, and establishment of the Foreign Intelligence Surveillance Court regime to review proposed collection on U.S. persons. By the end of the 1970s, Congress had turned into an activist arm of government in foreign policy to counterbalance the imperial presidency. But although oversight of each tool of national power was much more robust, overseeing the entire apparatus from an integrated perspective remained wanting.

Nonfederal Actors

The Cold War also saw a proliferation of several important actors outside the U.S. government that shaped and thus contributed to the interagency dialogue. National laboratories and federally funded research and development centers provided the government with independent analyses in niche areas, most notably nuclear weaponry. The government funded substantial university-based education and research in areas including nuclear physics, development economics, and languages. Think tanks and advocacy groups, backed by increasingly well-endowed foundations like Ford and MacArthur, sprang up on increasingly specialized topics, from human rights and refugees to international trade and labor rights. In addition, international institutions—the constellation of United Nations organizations, NATO, and the IMF and the World Bank—played an important role in providing the international collective goods of global diplomacy, security, and financial liquidity. The media, building on Edward R. Murrow's pioneering reporting during World War II, also became increasingly sophisticated on foreign policy matters. The net result was an environment in which U.S. departments and agencies benefited from but also were constrained by the knowledge and clout of institutions beyond their power.

DEFENSE REFORMS

By the 1970s, the seemingly static security environment dominated by the superpower competition was itself becoming more complex. A blue-ribbon panel chartered by Congress (and chaired by now-retired diplomat Robert Murphy in one of his last public acts) noted in 1975 that "the nature of foreign policy problems facing this country has changed dramatically since 1947. So has the nature of international power. Increasingly, economic forces define the strength or weakness of nations, and economic issues dominate the agenda of international negotiation."

Because of this sea change, "[n]o important foreign policy problem now falls within the jurisdiction of a single department."[21] Although the Murphy Commission's recommendations did not prompt an overhaul of the interagency process, they added volume and insight to the growing recognition in Washington that economic dilemmas and the new issues crowding the headlines, like uncertain energy supplies, human rights, international terrorism, and narcotics trafficking, were demanding ever-greater expertise and collaboration among the offices of the U.S. government.

The interagency process needed new mechanisms to enable such collaboration. At the policy and coordination level in Washington, the process confronted the fundamental dilemma of balancing expertise with authority. Cabinet secretaries are by nature too busy running and representing their departments to spend the requisite time with each other coordinating government-wide policies. Their employees may have the time and expertise to do so, but they lack the authority to make binding joint decisions for their departments. Someone possessing authority, time, and expertise therefore must be delegated to attend numerous meetings at the NSC as well as bilateral sessions with counterparts at other agencies—while remaining fully briefed on developments in his or her own departments. Without a copious supply of such officers who have tended in practice to serve at the deputy or assistant secretary levels, the process bogged down or failed.

Military mishaps in the early 1980s prompted new thinking about interagency coordination, particularly at the operational level. The abortive Iran hostage rescue mission (1980); the terrorist bombing of a marine barracks and the United States withdrawal from Lebanon (1983–84); and the chaotic Grenada invasion (1983) highlighted systemic problems. In particular, the JCS, with its committee-like structure, its institutionally weak chairman, and mediocre staff cadre, gave inadequate and untimely joint advice and direction to the services, the secretary of defense, and the president. Second, at the operational level, the regional combatant commanders lacked clear authority over the forces they led, which had of course been raised, trained, and equipped by their home services and still lacked a joint ethos.

The Department of Defense Reorganization Act of 1986 (commonly known as the Goldwater-Nichols Act after its twin sponsors, Sen. Barry Goldwater and Rep. Bill Nichols) made three broad reforms to meet these challenges. The chairman of the JCS received greater statutory authority (including becoming a member of the NSC) so he could operate independently of the other service chiefs; he was also given a larger staff to handle the range of interservice issues and a more robust analytical capacity to render independent advice. The chain of command was streamlined to give the combatant commanders explicit control over the forces assigned to them, including joint training, logistics, organization, and doctrine. Finally, the joint personnel system was imbued with greater professionalism.

The Act had barely begun to be implemented when the reforms it mandated faced a real test. In the 1991 Persian Gulf War to liberate Kuwait from Iraqi occupation, the Pentagon deployed roughly 500,000 military personnel under the unified command of Gen. H. Norman Schwarzkopf. Their swift success in battle, while not flawless, seemed to vindicate the Goldwater-Nichols reforms and the entire project of compelling the armed services to plan, train, and fight jointly. And yet, victory also exposed lingering problems. General Schwarzkopf proved to be a capable field marshal, but he had no plan to deal with the political and humanitarian turmoil in southern Iraq once combat abruptly ceased. Fighting the actual war and holding together the international coalition that had mounted it had consumed the attentions of the NSC and Defense and State Departments for months, and thus no one in Washington had better ideas for handling the dilemmas that Schwarzkopf suddenly (and not unpredictably) faced. In the resulting policy and security vacuum, Iraqi dictator Saddam Hussein and his ruling Ba'athists mercilessly suppressed a Shi'a uprising almost in sight of coalition forces, and sowed seeds of fear and distrust of the United States that would be reaped by a later coalition foray into the country. The American military had been greatly improved, but the interagency process in which it operated still did not seem to afford the larger integration of national power that was needed.

AFTER THE COLD WAR

The Persian Gulf War occurred in the midst a larger restructuring of international politics that would profoundly affect the interagency process in the United States. The collapse of Soviet communism and the Warsaw Pact left a sudden security vacuum in Central Europe while creating strong centrifugal forces in countries (including Yugoslavia, Czechoslovakia, and the Soviet Union itself) comprising multiple ethnic and/or religious populations once united by oppressive central authority. Some leaders may have expected America's role in world affairs to shrink with the resolution of the Cold War, but the opposite ensued. As the sole superpower, the United States saw itself as perforce the final provider and guarantor of international order. The United Nations Security Council, no longer divided by the threat of a Soviet veto, now invited the United States to play a leading role in peacekeeping and humanitarian missions in places like Somalia, Bosnia, Haiti, and Kosovo. The explosion in telecommunications technology (which fueled the growth of real-time, global media), and increasingly organized advocacy groups provided new public pressure for politicians to "do something—now."

The shifting terminology used to describe these missions indicated the fuzzy conceptual understanding of their requirements. Were they peacekeeping operations, peace enforcement, postconflict operations, or military operations-other-than-war? Regardless of the confusion, the missions typically shared several elements: a humanitarian cause and rationale; a set of actors who could be tough to categorize as friend or foe, or even as state or nonstate; a desire on the part of an international coalition to impose, or create the conditions for, a peace accord; the involvement of multilateral institutions (often the UN) and nongovernmental organizations (mostly providing aid); and dramatic coverage by the international news media (the "CNN effect").

Such missions required new institutional postures by American departments and agencies that had long adapted themselves to the imperatives of the Cold War. Diplomacy needed to operate much more proactively to forestall state disintegration that could create destabilizing refugee flows and violence. The U.S. military needed stronger capabilities for missions such as policing and riot control. The intelligence community needed to watch events in many regions simultaneously and assess the political implications of moves by a wider range of international actors. The Treasury and Commerce departments, the Agency for International Development, and the U.S. trade representative needed to support long-term reconstruction efforts and promote the modernization of infrastructures to provide postconflict stability. And they all increasingly recognized the contributions and technical assistance that globally active nonprofit organizations could offer in austere regions. Although each institution could meet these challenges in individual crises, the underlying interagency process often complicated the integration of their responses, particularly at the strategic and operational levels (in the field, as always, the deployed units from across the government often found ways to work together out of necessity).

The Clinton administration established new policies for these peace missions, and thereby portended important changes for the interagency process. Presidential decision directive (PDD)-25 ("Reforming Multilateral Peace Operations"), issued in 1994, demonstrated the opportunities and limits of reform. The PDD provided a framework for evaluating which missions to undertake, sharing costs among departments, compensating for inadequate UN capabilities, maintaining command and control of American forces operating in multilateral operations, supporting congressional oversight, and improving interagency decision-making capacity. But PDD-25 was limited in its impact on the interagency process. It addressed bureaucratic elements (e.g., requiring the Defense Department to take management and financial responsibility for operations undertaken under Chapter VII of the UN Charter) without explaining how the departments would plan or work together. PDD-25 also embodied the traditional American assumption that crises proceeded in phases, including a combat phase that would be dominated by military imperatives and then a separate postconflict phase in which the State Department and other civilian agencies could take primary responsibility.

Experiences in Haiti and the Balkans led the Clinton administration to update PDD-25 with PDD-56 (on complex contingency operations) in 1996. While the new PDD offered a checklist of requirements for undertaking any such operation, it still assumed that interagency planning was relevant mostly for the postconflict phase of a crisis, and not for the combat phase or the even-earlier shaping activities to avoid conflict in the first place. In addition, PDD-56 paid little attention to economic and development aspects of national power, and it did not address how the interagency process should operate for missions other than these complex contingencies. In short, interagency coordination remained relatively tangential to the operation of the national security establishment.

SINCE 9/11

The massively destructive terrorist attacks against New York and Washington on September 11, 2001, marked a watershed in the development of the interagency system. The global war on terror declared by President George W. Bush required an interdisciplinary approach in some ways akin to that undertaken by earlier administrations. Because terrorism was a transnational plague that often was steeped in remote and ungoverned spaces in the developing world, many of the diplomatic, military, economic, and intelligence capabilities developed for contingency operations in the 1990s were equally if not more relevant. The new situation differed, however, in other respects. The terrorists' ability to target Western cities and to exploit American missteps and debates over strategy for public relations gains gave new salience to public diplomacy efforts and made officials concerned with hitherto domestic issues like internal security and infrastructure protection into full foreign policy partners.

Congress and the Bush administration created new institutions in response to the terrorism challenge. Each of them, however, assumed a different model of interagency coordination. The president founded a Homeland Security Council to complement the National Security Council, with a focus on internal security and protection for the nation's critical infrastructure, including the transportation, financial, and energy sectors. (In 2009, this council was folded back into the National Security Council.) In 2002, Congress and the president also established a Department of Homeland Security (DHS), which gathered in some 22 federal agencies and 170,000 workers. This step brought together a range of functions and specialties, although forging a unity of purpose and a shared culture at DHS has proved to be as difficult as it initially was at the Department of Defense. The intelligence community underwent changes as well, many of them inspired by the Goldwater-Nichols reforms in the Defense Department. A series of amendments to the National Security Act in 2004 replaced the DCI with a somewhat more powerful director of national intelligence (DNI) to coordinate the programs and findings of the IC's 16 agencies and lead a set of "mission managers" working to integrate intelligence efforts against selected issues and targets (most notable among them being the National Counterterrorism Center). The DNI has wielded new authorities over budgets and personnel but still shares authority in many areas with the six cabinet department heads who host IC elements. To complement these new institutions, the Bush White House also issued several national strategies and accompanying implementation plans to integrate the government's efforts in the fields of terrorism, maritime and aviation security, weapons proliferation, cyber security, pandemic illnesses, emergency response, and others. These generally served as vehicles for departments and agencies to state their unique roles rather than for articulating new cross-cutting approaches or capabilities.

The planning and conduct of the wars in Afghanistan and Iraq highlighted the need for more effective interagency coordination. Both campaigns (launched in 2001 and 2003, respectively) achieved quick success on the battlefield, demonstrating how the U.S. military had adopted the Goldwater-Nichols Act's emphases on joint operations and clear chains of command, as well as how national-level intelligence support to battlefield commanders had been dramatically improved. Once again, however, the transitions between the combat and postcombat phases showed that Washington's ability to conceptualize and integrate military and political planning was still incomplete. In both Afghanistan and Iraq, the military found itself the only institution on the ground in significant strength, and thus by default responsible for fighting insurgents while providing day-to-day security, building new political structures, and overseeing large-scale economic repair and development projects.

In the wake of the flawed Iraq postwar effort, a number of reforms built on the efforts of the 1990s, and also employed the assumption that the crux of the interagency problem resided in an alleged postconflict phase. The Senate Foreign Relations Committee in 2004 instigated the creation of a State Department-led office of a coordinator for reconstruction and stabilization (known by its acronym S/CRS). The new office, comprising less than a hundred predominantly non-State Department personnel, aimed to strike a new balance in the interagency relationship between the State and Defense departments. Still, the office's mission, "to lead, coordinate and institutionalize U.S. Government civilian capacity to prevent or prepare for post-conflict situations, and to help stabilize and reconstruct societies in transition from conflict," had a narrow scope.[22] For its part, the White House issued National Security Presidential Directive (NSPD)-44 in December 2005 to replace the Clinton-era PDD-56 and buttress the State Department's lead role in postconflict affairs and recovery efforts.[23] It provided S/CRS with greater authority to set reconstruction and stabilization strategy, to develop policy and manage program execution, and to coordinate with foreign and nongovernmental organization (NGO) partners. State nonetheless remained outmanned and outplanned by the Defense Department during the Bush administration, a problem lamented even by Secretary of Defense Robert Gates.[24]

Toward the end of George W. Bush's administration, the White House began tilting toward more expressly corporate models for interagency management. In a way, the Bush administration had extended Clinton administration efforts to institutionalize interagency coordination to their logical conclusion and now was trying the new approach of making such coordination not mandatory but instinctive. The surge in the penetration of the internet across the globe, the rapid rise in computing power, and the use of collaborative and social networking tools together gave additional evidence that interagency reform was not only necessary to breed integration but inevitable.

In May 2007, the White House issued an executive order on national security professional development to promote the education, training, and experience of current and future professionals in national security positions across the U.S. government.[25] Modeled on the military's requirement (under the Goldwater-Nichols Act) to train officers for joint duty who could thus rise above the parochialism of their separate services, this NSPD resonated with midlevel national security officials throughout the government who increasingly work across departmental lines as a matter of course. The challenge remained, however, to evolve personnel incentives to ensure that taking advantage of such interagency training, education, and rotations in fact advances, not hampers, careers. Finally, in August 2008, the White House issued NSPD 60 to foster strategic planning through the creation of a policy-coordinating committee comprised of senior officials across the national security establishment to focus on longer-term policy and plans. The Obama administration has embraced this directive and is continuing its implementation. The findings of the Project for National Security Reform, a nonprofit effort focused exclusively on interagency reform—with many board members accepting senior posts in the Obama administration—is fueling such efforts.[26]

THE PAST AND FUTURE OF THE INTERAGENCY PROCESS

The blue-ribbon commission that Robert Murphy chaired in 1975 began its final report by noting "good organization does not ensure successful policy, nor does poor organization preclude it. But steadily and powerfully, organizational patterns influence the effectiveness of government."[27] The comment and the report together marked an implicit retort to the question posed to Murphy in North Africa three decades earlier: "Will you please tell me what in hell the State Department has to do in an active theater of war?" Four decades later, it is possible to see how much and how little the U.S. government has learned in terms of fixing its interagency process. If Murphy's gifted amateurism, which exemplified the careers of so many other senior officials, commanders, and diplomats, is no longer the rule, coordination and integration of departmental plans, processes, and capabilities is still by no means automatic or even routine.

Modern states need their own interagency processes because international challenges rarely confine themselves to a single dimension of state power. Although the U.S. government is predominantly organized along departmental lines that align to core functions of the state, for example, the military, diplomacy, and the treasury, the interagency process tries to stitch the seams between those institutions and capabilities. The long and tortuous path of interagency reform illustrates the complexity and difficulty of this task. At the tactical level among elements deployed in the field, coordination and collaboration have steadily increased. At the operational and strategic levels, however, the system has been only modestly adjusted to reflect modern challenges that by their nature require interagency collaboration in policy formulation and operational planning, not just for a presumed postconflict phase, but as an integral element of U.S. foreign and national security policy.

History suggests that several obstacles will remain in the path of significant changes in the interagency process, which itself will be required to work better and faster in the years ahead. Current organizational models geared around departments and agencies will need to be increasingly flexible to integrate the various tools of national power, particularly at the strategic and operational levels, to cope with the transnational challenges, from protecting the cyber domain to managing the impact of climate change, that are facing the United States and every nation. The interagency system must be prepared to affect the entire range of national security missions (not just complex emergencies or stabilization and reconstruction) in all phases of overseas engagement from shaping activities to develop partners and forestall threats, to combat, to postconflict reconciliation and development. And yet, the benefits of significant interagency reform are sufficiently general and distributed across the national security establishment that no one department or leader (even the president) is likely to decide that a significant investment of political capital in this endeavor will yield dividends to him or his institution commensurate with the cost (the "tragedy of the commons" problem).

At a time when the interagency system increasingly includes partners beyond the federal government, to include industry, nongovernmental organizations, foreign powers, and state/local/tribal governments, departmental bureaucracies are likely to continue praising the virtue of interagency collaboration in principle but resist ceding their autonomy in practice. The U.S. government rarely goes it alone anymore; a host of actors are increasingly entwined in all American engagements overseas. Departments, however, can and have resisted collaboration with other agencies and actors because it creates interdependencies that seem to threaten successful execution of their own core missions. The departments and agencies of the national security establishment have developed elaborate standard operating procedures, technical standards, and organizational structures to perform missions assigned to them in law and in presidential directives, and are leery of reforms that cause uncertainty in meeting these basic requirements. Civil servants, furthermore, see few professional benefits from involvement in interagency activities, which take them out of sight of their day-to-day management, and may force them to articulate career-jeopardizing positions that advance the broader national interest but undermine their own department's autonomy.

Reform of the interagency system at the strategic and operational levels has always required White House attention. Organizing and managing by mission, rather than by department, will likely be the main dimension along which the interagency system will adapt, while departments and agencies continue to foster capabilities that have broad utility across multiple operational environments. The NSC staff might need to lead this effort, but unless it grows in size or undergoes a significant change in organization and emphasis of its own, it could lack the capacity to do so. In any event, devising an effective NSC staff model that survives the administration of the president who fashions it will remain problematic. Presidential leadership, moreover, will be needed to foster government-wide changes like a new human capital model that breeds senior leaders versed in multiple government disciplines; a technological infrastructure that enables safe, secure, and reliable communication and interaction across departmental lines; integrated programming, budgeting, and tasking processes; and mechanisms to ensure that plans are implemented and meet performance expectations.

Finally, interagency process reform has always required a sustained partner in Congress. Legislative oversight of the executive branch principally by department enables effective work by committees but complicates development of interagency approaches that spill across committee jurisdictions. Congressional committees since the nineteenth century have preferred to exercise exclusive jurisdiction to maximize their power and influence over the executive branch. Establishing new committees for national security that look across traditional jurisdictions could work, but unless existing committees were disbanded (as the Military and Naval Affairs Committees gave way to the Armed Services Committees in both houses in 1947), such new bodies might only confuse matters. Effective congressional oversight could potentially be achieved by informal comity among the chief oversight committees, by creating another oversight body, or through the leadership empowering a few select members who can work across committee lines and with senior executive branch officials. It may take a crisis, or a series of crises, to inspire a model of congressional oversight befitting the challenges of interagency collaboration.

NOTES

1. Robert D. Murphy, *Diplomat among Warriors* (Garden City, NY: Doubleday, 1964), 155.

2. Thomas A. Bailey, *A Diplomatic History of the American People* (New York: Appleton-Century-Crofts, 1958 [1940]), 13.

3. Ibid., 9.

4. Dean Acheson, *Present at the Creation: My Years in the State Department* (New York: W. W. Norton & Co., 1969), 15.

5. Bailey, *A Diplomatic History of the American People*, 11.

6. Of course, there were examples of joint army–navy operations. For example, they jointly defended Washington, DC, Baltimore, Plattsburgh, and New Orleans in the War of 1812 and fought together at Forts Henry and Donelson, Vicksburg, Richmond, and Albemarle and Pamlico Sounds in the Civil War. See Allan R. Millett, "The Organizational Impact of Military Success and Failure: An Historical Perspective," in *The Reorganization of the Joint Chiefs of Staff: A Critical Analysis*, ed. Allen R. Millett et al. (Washington, DC: Pergamon-Brassey's, 1986).

7. John Norton Moore and Robert F. Turner, *The Legal Structure of Defense Organization: Memorandum Prepared for the President's Blue Ribbon Commission on Defense Management* (Washington, DC: U.S. Government Printing Office, 1986), 36.

8. Details of all of these points can be found in Michael Blow's *A Ship to Remember: The Maine and the Spanish-American War* (New York: William Morrow, 1992); see also Ernest R. May, *Imperial Democracy: The Emergence of America as a Great Power* (New York: Harper & Row, 1977 [1961]).

9. Bailey, *A Diplomatic History of the American People*, 9–10, 14.

10. For a summary of the origins of the Root reforms, see Paul Y. Hammond, *Organizing for Defense: The American Military Establishment in the Twentieth Century* (Princeton, NJ: Princeton University Press, 1961), 12–24.

11. On a more philosophical level, the army's centralization reflected the neo-Hamiltonian view of administration where control was exerted through clear lines of accountability, whereas the navy's continued decentralization demonstrated its commitment to the neo-Jeffersonians' principle of devolved power.

12. Gordon N. Lederman, *Reorganizing the Joint Chiefs of Staff* (Westport, CT: Greenwood Press, 1999), 7–10.

13. Acheson, *Present at the Creation*, 16.

14. Frederick R. Barkley, "Marshall Urges Unified War Arm," *New York Times*, October 19, 1945.

15. The panel that drafted the study was led by Ferdinand Eberstadt; its report was reprinted by the Senate Committee on Naval Affairs in October 1945 as *Unification of the War and Navy Departments and Postwar Organization for National Security* (Washington, DC: Government Printing Office, 1945), 53, 55, 79. For a good summary of the genesis and assumptions of the Eberstadt Report, see Douglas Stuart, "Constructing the Iron Cage: The 1947 National Security Act," in *Affairs of State: The Interagency and National Security*, ed. Gabriel Marcella (Carlisle, PA: Strategic Studies Institute [U.S. Army], 2008), 67–71.

16. Harry S. Truman, *Memoirs, Volume 2, Years of Trial and Hope* (Garden City, NY: Double-day, 1956), 46.

17. A useful summary of the changes in the NSC's structure and procedures is contained in part II, "Description and Historical Background of the System," of the final report of the Project on National Security Reform, *Forging a New Shield*, November 2008; www.connectusfund .org/resources/project-national-security-reform-report-forging-new-shield.

18. Acheson, *Present at the Creation*, 734.

19. Murphy, *Diplomat among Warriors*, 451.

20. Acheson, *Present at the Creation*, 213–14.

21. Commission on the Organization of the Government for the Conduct of Foreign Policy [the Murphy Commission], *Final Report* (Washington, DC: Government Printing Office, 1975), 32, 34. The Commission was charged by Congress to suggest "a more effective system for the formulation and implementation of the nation's foreign policy"; see Murphy's transmittal letter, dated June 27, 1975 and reprinted as the report's foreword.

22. Office of the Coordinator for Reconstruction and Stabilization, Frequently Asked Questions. Available at www.state.gov/s/crs/66427.htm.

23. NSPD-44's stated purpose was "improved coordination, planning, and implementation for reconstruction and stabilization assistance for foreign states and regions at risk of, in, or in transition from conflict or civil strife." National Security Presidential Directive/NSPD-44, "Management of Interagency Efforts Concerning Reconstruction and Stabilization," President George W. Bush, December 7, 2005. Available at www.fas.org/irp/offdocs/nspd/nspd-44.html.

24. Secretary Gates complained in a speech at National Defense University on September 29, 2008, that the State Department and AID "have been gutted over the last 15 years."

25. Executive Order 13434: National Security Professional Development, President George W. Bush, May 17, 2007, available at http://edocket.access.gpo.gov/2007/pdf/07-2570.pdf.

26. Project on National Security Reform, *Forging a New Shield* and *Turning Ideas into Action*, available at www.pnsr.org/data/files/pnsr_turning_ideas_into_action.pdf. Officials on PNSR's governing coalition that joined the Obama administration included Dennis C. Blair as director of national intelligence, James L. Jones as national security advisor, James B. Steinberg as deputy secretary of state, and Ashton B. Carter and Michèle Flournoy as undersecretaries of defense.

27. Murphy Commission, *Final Report*, 1.

Chapter 2   The Evolution of the NSC Process

DAVID AUERSWALD

A principal danger at the top level of government is that discussion may be based on a presentation that is one-sided (however earnestly proposed) or that lacks a critical analysis in which all agencies freely participate at the formative stage.

Robert Cutler, special assistant to the president for national security affairs,
Eisenhower administration

The National Security Council (NSC) and the NSC staff as led by the national security advisor (NSA), serve critical functions at the heart of the interagency, national security process. Formal NSC members, and frequently the NSC staff, coordinate security policy across federal agencies. The NSC staff manages the flow of information and policy recommendations between the president and the various departments. At times the staff engages in long-range, strategic thinking. At other times they engage in short-term crisis policy. On occasion the NSC staff has run particularly sensitive security operations. A competent staff, working within a well-functioning NSC system, greatly facilitates the coordination of U.S. government efforts to achieve security goals. A dysfunctional staff and system can bring about disastrous results.[1]

This chapter explores how and why the NSC's structure and process have changed over time. A number of factors combine to explain the evolution of the NSC system. The institutional needs of the president appear to be a consistent reason why the NSC staff generally—and the national security advisor in particular—has played a central role in national security policy since the Eisenhower administration. The NSC staff belongs to the president, without loyalties or reporting requirements to federal agencies or the legislative branch—a particularly valuable commodity in an international environment characterized by massive and increasingly complex U.S. commitments and a domestic environment characterized by increasingly fragmented political and media conditions. Yet different presidents have used the NSC system, the NSC staff, and the national security advisor (NSA) in particular ways. Variations across and within administrations appear to depend on the operating styles of individual presidents and NSAs, and important external events that shock the national security or domestic political systems and create the need for organizational change.

The first section reviews the root causes of the NSC system's importance, focusing attention on the institutional needs of the presidency. I then explore the proximate reasons why presidents change the NSC system. In so doing, I document the main structural and procedural changes that have occurred since the creation of the NSC and its associated staff. I link those changes to the management styles and events that confront each administration to include each administration's reaction to its predecessor's NSC system.

Finally, I conclude with an initial assessment of the Obama administration's NSC structure and operating style.

ROOT CAUSES OF THE NSC SYSTEM'S IMPORTANCE

The NSC was established by the National Security Act of 1947 and was placed within the executive office of the president in 1949.[2] There are two components to the NSC that are important for our purposes. First, there are the statutory members of the NSC. These individuals have varied over time, but since 1949 have included the president, vice president, secretaries of state and defense, and advisors from the military and intelligence communities (currently the director of national intelligence and the chairman of the Joint Chiefs of Staff). Other senior officials attend NSC meetings in an advisory capacity at the president's discretion but are not statutory members of the NSC. The second component is the NSC staff, which has grown from a handful of people in the late 1940s and 1950s to upward of 150 people in recent times, depending on the administration and the counting rules. The NSC staff advises the NSC and the president, but individual staff assistants are not members of the NSC. Any president must decide on how the NSC and the NSC staff will be structured and make decisions. Structural choices include the size of the NSC staff, how they are organized into policy directorates, and what entities will consider policy decisions and who will serve on them. Procedural choices include who will chair and attend NSC and staff meetings, what role the NSC will play in executive branch decision making, the frequency of meetings, etc. Since 1953 the special assistant to the president for national security affairs, now known as the national security advisor, has directed the NSC staff.

The NSC system contains an intriguing mix of continuity and change over time. It embodies continuity in the sense that the basic role of the NSC staff and key structural elements of the NSC system have remained relatively constant across time, at least from the beginning of the Kennedy administration to the present.[3] Amy Zegart characterizes the post-Eisenhower NSC system as having strong national security advisors, powerful and capable NSC staffs, and relatively underutilized formal NSC meetings.[4] Considering each post-Kennedy president, Zegart concludes that "none has successfully altered the system's three essential features."[5]

To explain the continuity identified by Zegart, we would normally begin by examining an agency's culture and norms. Although organizational culture and bureaucratic norms influence a typical federal agency's behavior, this does not appear to be true with the NSC staff. The staff is different for three reasons. First, almost without exception, tenure at the NSC staff lasts no longer than a president's term in office. The NSC staff is in large part recreated out of whole cloth with the transition to a new administration. Often, NSC staff members burn out significantly faster than a four- or eight-year presidential term.[6] Second, the staff represents an ever-changing mix of officials detailed from federal departments, transplanted legislative branch staff, academicians, and think tank personnel. Third, staff detailed from federal agencies are chosen carefully and asked to set aside their bureaucratic loyalties for the duration of their NSC tenure. As a result, few if any traditions or behavioral norms pass from administration to administration or staff to staff, which prevents the NSC staff from developing the long-term culture prevalent in so many other government agencies and which helps distinguish foreign service officers from civil service employees at the State Department, fighter pilots from transport pilots, intelligence community analysts from operators, cavalry soldiers from infantry, or submariners from surface warfare officers. In short, other than sharing a penchant for ambition and hard work, the NSC staff would be hard pressed to develop a corporate identity or culture that is distinct from that of the president they serve or the NSA that leads them.

A better explanation for consistent behavior comes from the study of American political and institutional behavior. That literature focuses attention on the incentives confronting presidents when they choose what strategies and tools to use to achieve policy and political objectives.[7] The argument here is that presidents turn to the personnel in the executive office of the president (EOP) in general, and their White House (WH) staff in particular, for their most important and sensitive policy initiatives. Presidents cannot rely on anyone else. Federal agencies have preferences and interests that may not align with those of the president, the Congress has institutional incentives to counterbalance executive power, and the growth of the federal government's responsibilities has raised public expectations to the point that presidential inaction is tantamount to political suicide. In short, presidents need an entity that will respond to them and only to them if they are to survive politically while advancing U.S. interests. The EOP and WH fit the bill.

It should be no surprise then that the same logic applies to presidential reliance on national security advisors and their NSC staffs.[8] Presidents routinely depend on both to develop the country's most important security initiatives because the NSC has advantages for the president that other bureaucratic entities do not. The NSC staff serves at the pleasure of the president and has been part of the EOP since 1949. With one exception, the national security advisor has had a West Wing office, which puts him or her in close proximity to the president, with the access to match.[9] NSC staff members are not subject to Senate confirmation and cannot be subpoenaed to testify regarding their advice to the president. At the same time, the NSC staff is not beholden to a federal agency for money or influence, preventing the staff from developing institutional loyalties beyond the White House. From a political perspective then, the NSC staff is an attractive tool of presidential power and influence.

The same is true from a policy perspective. The NSC system was created at the beginning of the Cold War, which was a time of dramatically expanded U.S. international commitments. Creating an NSC staff provided the president with a means of coordinating the complex policies and demands associated with those commitments (to say nothing of managing the dramatically expanded federal work force devoted to defense and security affairs), just as the need for a government response to the Great Depression led to the creation of the EOP in the late 1930s.[10] Indeed, the NSC system was created in 1947 as part of the broader national security reorganization that also created the Defense Department, the Air Force as a separate military service, and the Central Intelligence Agency. The reason for such dramatic reforms, noted one influential 1945 report, was because, "the necessity of integrating all these elements into an alert, smoothly working and efficient machine is more important now than ever before. Such integration is compelled by our present world commitments and risks."[11] The NSC system gave presidents tools to meet Cold War challenges and the even more complex trials of the modern, post-Cold War era. From a policy perspective then, it is easy to see why the NSC staff and the national security advisor continue to play a central role in the national security processes of most administrations.

The empirical record supports these intuitions. Consider the size of the NSC staff. From a relatively small number of influential policy advisors in 1960, the NSC staff had grown in size to over one hundred people by the end of the George W. Bush administration.[12] Growth has not been uniform across time, however. Presidents Ford, Carter, Reagan, and both Bush administrations cut the size of the NSC staff at the beginning of their terms, only to add those positions back as time went on, in most cases to surpass the numbers employed by their predecessors. The trend line shows that presidents have increasingly relied on their NSC staffs for national security advice and coordination.

Or consider the choice of national security advisors. Most presidents since Eisenhower have picked powerful national security advisors to lead the NSC staff. The exceptions were Ronald Reagan, whose first four NSAs were considered insufficiently senior, expert, or both; and George W. Bush, whose first NSA was considered too junior relative to the administration's other senior foreign policy players.[13] Those exceptions notwithstanding, presidents have by and large chosen influential experts as their NSAs, consistent with the importance of the NSC staff for vital policy initiatives. Table 2.1 lists national security advisors by presidential administration.

Finally, there is evidence to support the idea that few presidents since Eisenhower have utilized the formal NSC process on a regular basis. Instead, presidents tend to use informal gatherings to reach agreement or coordinate among their core foreign policy team, or have tasked/allowed their national security advisors to do so on the president's behalf. They do so for two main reasons. First, informal meetings have tended to be relatively small compared to formal NSC meetings, which is attractive for administrations that have allowed a broad range of agencies to participate in NSC meetings. Second, small group meetings in theory allow the president or the NSA to have better control over debate and any decisions made.[14] For example, Lyndon Johnson preferred informal Tuesday lunches over NSC meetings because the intimate lunch format allowed him to persuade, test, or bluntly intimidate his advisors, just as he had done in one-on-one and small groups meetings with his Senate colleagues when he was majority leader.[15] Some

Table 2.1   National Security Advisors, 1961–Present

President	National Security Advisor	Dates
John F. Kennedy	McGeorge Bundy	1961–63
Lyndon Johnson	McGeorge Bundy	1963–66
	Walt Rostow	1966–69
Richard Nixon	Henry Kissinger	1969–74
Gerald Ford	Henry Kissinger	1974–75
	Brent Scowcroft	1975–77
Jimmy Carter	Zbigniew Brzezinski	1977–81
Ronald Reagan	Richard Allen	1981–82
	William Clark	1982–83
	Robert McFarlane	1983–85
	John Poindexter	1985–86
	Frank Carlucci	1986–87
	Colin Powell	1987–89
George H. W. Bush	Brent Scowcroft	1989–93
Bill Clinton	Anthony Lake	1993–97
	Samuel Berger	1997–2001
George W. Bush	Condoleezza Rice	2001–5
	Stephen Hadley	2005–9
Barack Obama	James Jones	2009–10
	Thomas Donilon	2010

Table 2.2   Informal, Alternative Security Forums, 1961–Present

President	Alternative Security Forums and Participants
John F. Kennedy	Executive Committee ("ExComm")
Lyndon Johnson	"Tuesday Lunches": POTUS, DOS, DOD, NSA plus the DCI, CJCS, and White House aides at times
Richard Nixon	Kissinger meetings: POTUS and NSA
Jimmy Carter	"Friday Breakfasts": POTUS, NSA, DOS plus DOD and White House aides at times
Ronald Reagan	National Security Planning Group: POTUS, VP, DOS, DOD, DCI, NSA, WH aides. "Family Group" lunches: DOS, DOD, DCI, NSA
George H. W. Bush	"Big Eight" meetings: POTUS, VP, NSA, Dep NSA, WH COS, DOS, DOD, CJCS "Inner Circle" meetings: POTUS, NSA, and either DOS or DOD
Bill Clinton	Foreign policy team meetings: POTUS and various advisors Albright-Berger-Cohen (ABC) lunches: DOS, NSA, DOD plus DCI, CJCS, UN ambassador, and VP NSA at times Special envoys (Russia, Balkans, Middle East, etc.): POTUS and various advisors
George W. Bush	Parallel vice presidential NSC process: 15-person VP national security staff Vulcan meetings in White House: POTUS, VP, DOD, NSA, and their deputies Lead agency: DOD in Iraq

POTUS, president of the United States; VP, vice president; DOS, State Department; DOD, Defense Department; NSA, national security advisor; DCI, director of central intelligence; WH, White House; CJCS, chairman of the Joint Chiefs of Staff.

presidents have even chosen to use presidential envoys (i.e., Clinton) or designate a lead agency (i.e., George W. Bush) to make policy for particular regions or crises rather than requiring coordination across cabinet agencies. The various informal mechanisms used by presidents to improve their control over security policy are listed in table 2.2.

PROXIMATE CAUSES OF CHANGE

Despite continuity in the growth of the NSC staff and informal advisory systems, the empirical record shows significant variation across and within administrations in terms of the NSC system's structure and processes.[16] This is particularly true with regard to the role played by the national security advisor.[17]

The most common explanation for changes to the NSC system is that each system reflects the incumbent president's personality to include such things as the president's operating style, comfort level with divergent views and disagreement, knowledge of foreign policy, and his reactions to previous administrations' policies and procedures.[18] Adherents to this perspective are not limited to academicians. Robert Cutler, President Eisenhower's special assistant for national security affairs, noted, "fundamentally, the Council is a vehicle for a President to use in accordance with its suitability to his plan for conducting his great office."[19] Colin Powell, President Reagan's final national security advisor, argued that, "at the end of the day, the duty of the National Security Council staff and the assistant is to mold themselves to the personality of the president."[20] Variants of personality-based explanations focus on the operating style of the national security advisor, or how the NSA meshes with the president and various cabinet members. All are said to help determine the roles and procedures of each NSC staff and the overall structure of the NSC system.

A second proximate cause of change at the NSC is the international and domestic context within which each administration operates. Here the argument is that important external and internal events provide exogenous shocks to the national security system, which creates the need for institutional innovation and organizational change. In this view, the NSC remains a relatively static organization until it is confronted with significant international or domestic policy crises, at which time the institution rapidly adjusts. The parallel in biology would be the punctuated evolution of species in response to regional, environmental, or global cataclysms. International failure can be one generator of change, as can be a desire to advance a dramatically new policy agenda. A desire to separate a new administration's tone or policies from those of its predecessor can be another. To see the degree to which personality and/or context explains change to the NSC system's structure and process, we must review the main developments associated with the NSC and its staff.[21]

Dwight Eisenhower

President Dwight Eisenhower took office at a time of international crisis for the United States. By January 1953, the United States had suffered a series of setbacks in the increasingly frigid Cold War, to include crises in Greece and Turkey; communist control of Bulgaria, Romania, Poland, Hungary, Czechoslovakia; the Berlin blockade; and the fall of China, to say nothing of the two-year-old and then-stalemated Korean War. The United States appeared to be playing defense in a losing game. At the same time, the United States was at a crossroad when it came to defense spending. The United States could try to match the Soviets and Chinese in terms of conventional forces, at great expense, or it could focus on deterring communist aggression via nuclear weapons, which would save money but be domestically and internationally risky. The new administration chose the latter option but would need discipline and unity to implement it.

President Eisenhower came to the presidency from a long and distinguished military career. He brought a sense of military organization and hierarchical structure to the NSC system. Eisenhower saw the staff as providing systematic support for his cabinet, and the statutory NSC participants as working for him.[22] In the words of his national security assistant, "President Eisenhower has made it clear that he regards the Council as a 'corporate' body, consisting of officials who are advising the President in their own right and not simply as the heads of their respective departments."[23] With regard to the NSC staff, Eisenhower wanted them to thoroughly prepare for each NSC meeting. "Eisenhower transformed the Council into a forum for vigorous discussion against a background of painstakingly prepared and carefully studied papers."[24]

These preferences and events translated into a formal, regularized, predictable NSC system structure and practice. The administration set up a four-stage NSC system.[25] Agencies would come up with policy proposals. The NSC planning board, staffed with assistant secretary-level personnel, would review those proposals twice per week and highlight disagreements between agencies. The NSC, usually chaired by the president, would hold a weekly meeting to consider those proposals. Monitoring the implementation of NSC decisions fell to the operations coordinating board, staffed at the undersecretary level. The NSC staff prepared the background and options papers associated with this process but had no substantive policy role.[26] In sum, the Eisenhower NSC was the epitome of a structured, systematic NSC process, something that the administration thought was needed given both the circumstances confronting it and the personality of the president.

John F. Kennedy

John F. Kennedy came to office wanting a less formal, more diverse NSC system than Eisenhower had. A priority for Kennedy was to have access to multiple sources of information. In the words of Walt Rostow, an NSC staffer under Kennedy and eventual NSA for Lyndon Johnson, President Kennedy "was determined not to be imprisoned by the options the bureaucracies might generate and lay before him."[27] He did not like formal meetings, preferring instead to have private, informal conversations with a variety of experts on his staff, even to the point of calling in relatively junior staffers for consultations on issues within their portfolios.

Kennedy's NSA, McGeorge Bundy, fit well with this style. He was widely regarded as a brilliant strategist, an academician, and moderate Republican who had known Kennedy for years.[28] He loved the informal give-and-take of academia and the think tank world, and brought that style to the White House.[29] The president and Bundy agreed to a large extent on Bundy's role: provide the president with information and act as an honest broker that would accurately represent cabinet members' views. They thought alike and "liked each other immensely."[30]

Kennedy and Bundy structured the NSC staff system in reaction to two external events. Domestically, they were responding to a Senate report that argued the Eisenhower NSC structure was too bureaucratic and slow to respond to international events.[31] Internationally, the Kennedy NSC system was to some extent a reaction to the failed Bay of Pigs invasion at the beginning of the administration's tenure. The administration attributed that failure to the relatively limited information and biased sources available to the president at the time.[32]

Combined with Kennedy's and Bundy's preferences and operating styles, these two events led to a very different NSC system than had existed under President Eisenhower. Kennedy's thirst for information translated into the creation of the White House Situation Room, and a relatively flat NSC staff organization in which any staffer was able to go directly to the president if necessary. According to Carl Keysen, a Kennedy NSC staff member, "Kennedy made very clear we were his men, we operated for him, we had direct contact with him."[33] Kennedy's aversion to formal meetings translated into the NSC system essentially being ignored, with only monthly meetings for most of the administration's tenure.[34] During the Cuban Missile Crisis the NSC was essentially replaced by the less formal executive committee. And even the executive committee was too large a body for the most sensitive discussions regarding trading Soviet missiles in Cuba for U.S. missiles in Turkey. Indeed, many in the administration, including members of the NSC, did not know about those discussions until after the crisis.

Lyndon B. Johnson

President Lyndon Johnson entered office with a domestically oriented agenda focused on enacting the Great Society program and civil rights legislation. Both were politically charged issues that had the potential to divide the Democratic Party. By themselves, they would dominate the full agenda of any president. Unfortunately for Johnson, he also had a deteriorating situation in Vietnam with which to contend. Focusing on Vietnam, however, would take attention away from the domestic agenda. Moreover, Johnson simply had little interest in foreign affairs. The result was that Johnson tried to keep Vietnam off the national radar for as long as possible. Johnson's desire to control the policy agenda, both domestically and internationally, would help shape his administration's NSC system.

Johnson had a very different operating style compared to his predecessor. He was a retail politician who preferred to build coalitions one person at a time rather than engage in long debates in large groups. That translated into a preference for working through his cabinet secretaries individually rather than with the NSC staff or in large meetings. Johnson had a difficult relationship with the NSC staff for another reason: He came from relatively humble roots and distrusted the intellectuals with whom Kennedy had surrounded himself, including NSA Bundy. Johnson did not want the large volume of information Bundy had provided to Kennedy. Nor did he want his NSA to maintain a neutral broker position. He much preferred his NSA to advocate on behalf of the president's preferred policies instead of trying to forge a compromise among the national security agencies. After all, compromise positions could shift attention away from, and derail progress on, his domestic agenda. In that sort of world, the NSC staff increasingly moved from preparing analytical options papers to monitoring the implementation of presidential decisions.

All this translated into a distrust of the formal NSC process greater even than had existed under the Kennedy administration. From the president's perspective, the forum was too big to meet his needs, it provided too few opportunities for individual persuasion, and was staffed by individuals that the president did not respect or trust.[35] Yet there were limits to how much Johnson could change the NSC system, at least initially, in that he came to office via the national tragedy of Kennedy's assassination. Keeping the appearance of the Kennedy structure made sense from a political perspective, so Bundy was initially kept on as NSA. That relationship deteriorated, however, to the point where Walt Rostow replaced Bundy. Rostow was much more of a policy advocate than Bundy, which served him well with the president but at times put him at odds with the other NSC members.[36]

At the same time the NSC staff's influence was downgraded when Rostow was denied the title of national security advisor. The two main NSC committees, the NSC senior interdepartmental group and the interdepartmental regional group, were both chaired by State Department officials rather than the NSC staff. Finally, even these NSC committees were largely ignored in favor of the much smaller Tuesday lunch discussions listed in table 2.2.[37] The problem, of course, was that the Tuesday lunch meetings did not include NSC staff, so no official records were kept of their discussions or decisions, and the staff had no way to ensure that decisions were implemented across the federal bureaucracy. In short, NSC meetings appeared to be pro forma ratifications of decisions already made by Johnson, particularly when it came to Vietnam.[38]

Richard M. Nixon

The Nixon administration's initial intent was to bring some order back into the informal NSC system of the Kennedy/Johnson years. Henry Kissinger, Nixon's national security advisor, created nine formal NSC committees, including the senior review group that previewed policy proposals before NSC meetings, the Washington special action group on crisis policy, the verification panel on arms control negotiations, the 40 committees for covert operations, the Vietnam special studies group, the intelligence committee and the intelligence resources advisory committee, the international energy review group, and the defense program review committee.[39] The staff initially was tasked to produce two types of documents: national security study memoranda to explore long-range strategy and decision memoranda that presented the president with a series of options. The NSC staff grew tremendously under the Nixon administration, from a dozen members to almost 55 by the middle of the first term.

This elaborate system was quickly ignored, however, for reasons related to personalities and the administration's ambitious foreign policy agenda. President Richard Nixon's personal style has been well documented elsewhere.[40] To some extent he was a walking contradiction. He has been called secretive, solitary, controlling, and even paranoid but also politically astute and strategically brilliant. He is said to have wanted a structured, formal NSC process but then systematically ignored that process because he was unable to personally confront those he disagreed with.[41] Kissinger was and continues to be one of the most influential NSAs ever to have held the office.[42] He and Nixon had a very close working relationship, shared a similar realist worldview, and were both concerned about media leaks (to the point of having some of the NSC staff wiretapped). That said, there was allegedly a significant element of distrust between the two, which bordered on jealousy.

The other reason the formal system was ignored relates to the sensitive nature of the administration's foreign policy agenda. Three issues dominated that agenda: a greatly expanded commitment in Vietnam that had been the undoing of the Johnson administration; the creation of a new, pragmatic relationship with the Soviets, which had implications for many issues, for example, U.S.–Soviet détente allowed the Nixon administration to create a linkage between missile defense and U.S.-Soviet arms control negotiations, which eventually led to the SALT I agreement; and establishing relations with China, which was a hugely controversial initiative at the time.

That ambitious agenda, combined with Nixon's and Kissinger's suspicion of leaks and their need for control, led them to regularly cut out all other statutory NSC members from important policy deliberations. Kissinger certainly was not the honest broker that Bundy had initially been eight years earlier. Rather, Kissinger was a policy advocate of the first degree. He wound up running several important foreign policy initiatives for the president, including negotiations with the North Vietnamese, arms control with the Soviets, and most famously the opening to China.[43] Despite early intentions of a highly structured process, the NSC system effectively boiled down to Kissinger and Nixon.

Jimmy Carter

President Carter came to office with the country still recovering from the abuses of the Nixon administration, including Watergate and the secret bombings in southeast Asia. The national counterreaction to Nixon extended to Nixon's national security policy process in general and the role played by Kissinger in particular. In June 1975, the "Commission on the Organization of the Government for the Conduct of Foreign Policy" recommended that the NSC staff's role be greatly curtailed.[44] The Carter administration took those recommendations to heart in the design of its NSC system.

There were other reasons to change the Nixon system. President Carter wanted a more inclusive system with balanced input from his cabinet secretaries and himself at the center. This is explained in part by Carter's micromanager personality, and in part to conflicts within the cabinet. Carter's NSA, Zbigniew Brzezinski, was an aggressive, opinionated policy advocate, "one of the most controversial national security advisors."[45] He and Secretary of State Cyrus Vance regularly disagreed on foreign policy toward China, Iran, and arms control negotiations, with these disagreements often spilling out into public view. As such, Brzezinski was not considered an honest broker, but was instead seen as someone trying to dominate the foreign policy decision-making process.

For all these reasons, Carter and Brzezinski greatly simplified the NSC system that they inherited from the Nixon administration. The NSC staff was cut in numbers from the mid-fifties down to the thirties. They dropped the junior-senior staff designations that had existed in Nixon's NSC staff.[46] The plethora of NSC committees were replaced by a policy review committee that reviewed security issues affecting individual agencies, and a special coordination committee that reviewed issues that cut across several agencies.[47] This minimal structure was matched by a minimal use of formal NSC meetings, of which there were only ten during the entire administration.[48] Instead, the president preferred using so-called Friday Breakfasts to discuss national security issues, supplemented by a huge number of informal meetings in 1979 on arms control, the Middle East, and eventually the Iranian hostage crisis.[49] Policymaking was not as concentrated in the Carter White House as it had been in the Nixon administration, but decision authority had by no means devolved out to the cabinet secretaries.

Ronald Reagan

A huge volume of research discusses the personality and operating style of President Ronald Reagan.[50] President Reagan has been characterized as principled, a visionary, and an unparalleled communicator, but also as distant, detached, and incurious about policy details. He is said to have wanted a collegial policy process with robust debate among his staff.[51] The administration certainly did not want a repeat of the Brzezinski-Vance feud from the Carter years and the widespread perceptions of disunity within the national security apparatus created by that feud. After all, that disunity and the policy vacillations it created was seen by the Reagan administration as a large reason for the Soviet invasion of Afghanistan and the taking of U.S. hostages in Iran. That said, Reagan was not willing to side with one advisor over another in his own administration; he liked to split the difference when given conflicting recommendations.[52] He also rarely made the effort to become well versed on the details of an issue. He was famous for taking long vacations in California and for working short days when in Washington. The details of governing were left to a troika of White House advisors: Ed Meese, the counselor to the president; James Baker, the chief of staff; and Michael Deaver, deputy chief of staff. For foreign and security policy recommendations, President Reagan relied on the secretaries of state and defense and the director of central intelligence rather than on his national security advisor.

Reagan vested almost all foreign policy authority in the State Department, which greatly curtailed the power of the NSC staff and the NSA.[53] The administration cycled through six national security advisors over two presidential terms. The choice of the first four was consistent with the expressed organizational priorities of the administration; each NSA lacked the experience or knowledge to be an equal to the secretaries of state or defense. In terms of process, the first NSA, Richard Allen, was put under the authority of Ed Meese, and was given no direct access to the president.[54] The NSC staff was tasked with providing staff assistance to the cabinet rather than giving direct advice to the president.

The NSC structure reflected the decreased role of the NSC staff. The administration created four NSC committees: defense policy, intelligence, foreign policy, and crisis management. Agency or department secretaries chaired each committee, with the vice president leading the crisis management committee. There was no leadership role for the NSA or his designee. Sitting above these committees was the national security planning group (NSPG), which contained the statutory and advisory members of the NSC as well as the aforementioned White House troika.[55] The difference between the NSPG and the NSC was that the NSC staff was not allowed to participate in or provide staff support for the NSPG, on the orders of Ed Meese. As a result, there were no minutes taken during meetings and no process existed to disseminate NSPG decisions out to relevant agencies.[56]

The Reagan NSC staff is perhaps best remembered for its genesis of the Iran-Contra scandal. A detailed treatment of the scandal is beyond the scope of this chapter, but a brief review of the policymaking environment between 1983–86 helps explain why the NSC staff was able to run an illegal covert operation.[57] Reagan's second NSA, William Clark, succeeded in regaining some of the authority enjoyed by other NSAs over the protests of Secretary of State Al Haig.[58] Yet he would soon be confronted with an emerging feud in the latter half of 1982 between newly appointed Secretary of State George Schultz (who replaced Al Haig in July 1982) and Secretary of Defense Caspar Weinberger, a feud that Clark was powerless to prevent and that threatened to deadlock most major foreign policy and security initiatives. Clark's successor, Colonel Robert "Bud" McFarlane, was too junior to break that deadlock, despite attempts to do so via informal "Family Group" lunches.[59] "The result was a virtual free-for-all, in which Shultz, Weinberger, [CIA Director William] Casey, and ultimately, the NSC sought to get to Reagan and sell him on their latest ideas. Getting the president's approval, and then quickly acting on it before opponents of the proposed policy could stop you, was how foreign policy was increasingly made in the mid-1980s."[60] The result was that relatively junior NSC staff members under the direction of McFarlane, and then Vice Admiral John Poindexter, Reagan's fourth national security advisor, could run a rogue operation seemingly unbeknown to senior officials across the national security bureaucracy.

The Iran-Contra scandal led to a wholesale change in the Reagan administration's NSC structure and processes, a change that would be amplified during the George H. W. Bush administration. When Frank Carlucci replaced Poindexter as NSA, he reorganized the NSC structure to emphasize reporting requirements in a hierarchical chain of command.[61] He divided the NSC staff into eleven directorates, each led by a senior director. Each directorate had a staff, and each reported to Carlucci, who ran formal NSC meetings. The bitterness between Schultz and Weinberger did not end, but at least Carlucci forced each side to air their differences in a formal setting (and in informal meetings as well).[62] By all accounts the new system was a huge improvement.

George H. W. Bush

George H. W. Bush assumed the presidency under what was arguably the most hostile friendly takeover of any transition in history, despite Bush having served as Reagan's vice president. Bush was a foreign policy realist where Reagan had been an idealist. Bush was a pragmatic, traditional conservative where Reagan had been more ideologically extreme. Bush was engaged where Reagan had been somewhat detached.

Bush had witnessed firsthand the dysfunction of Reagan's NSC and the late attempts by Carlucci and Powell to bring order to that system. And a regularized, orderly process had advantages during a time that included the end of the Cold War, the reunification of Germany, the invasion of Panama, and the first Gulf War, to name just a few of the events during Bush's tenure. The president's experience certainly helped. When it came to foreign and security policy, President Bush was among the most experienced, prepared presidents ever to have served. He had been vice president for eight years and, before that CIA director, ambassador to the UN, ambassador to China, and a two-term member of Congress. He was very hands-on when it came to foreign policy. He is quoted as having said, "I wanted the foreign policy players to know that I was going to involve myself in many of the details of defense, international trade, and foreign affairs policies."[63] He also wanted an extremely collegial team working for him, perhaps in part as a reaction to the bitter divisions on the Reagan NSC. That translated into a White House-centered foreign policy apparatus, with cabinet members chosen who would not challenge the White House, or each other, for primacy.

Bush's national security advisor, Brent Scowcroft, shared many of the president's foreign policy views and the belief in a White House-centered NSC system. Scowcroft was a true expert when it came to the NSC, having risen to the rank of lieutenant general in the Air Force, served as a military assistant in the Nixon White House, and then as Gerald Ford's national security advisor. He had been a principal author on the Tower Commission investigation of Iran-Contra. He saw the NSA role as that of a broker (i.e., similar to Bundy) rather than an advocate (à la Brzezinski or Kissinger) or an operator (à la Poindexter). He succeeded in a broker role by gaining the trust of his colleagues, establishing a cooperative NSC process, and maintaining a very close relationship to the president.[64] On the last point, "no other Bush adviser has had more influence on the agenda of American national security policy."[65]

Scowcroft added structure to the NSC system. He created a four-level NSC process. At the top was the formal NSC chaired by the president. Next was the principals' committee (PC), comprised of the NSC members minus the president. Scowcroft chaired PC meetings. Under the PC was the deputies' committee (DC), with participants drawn from the deputy secretary level. The deputy national security advisor chaired the DC. Further down the hierarchy were a series of eight issue-specific policy coordinating committees (PCCs). Most policy decisions were made at the deputies' committee level after being drafted by the various PCCs. Only debates for which consensus could not be reached at the DC level made it to the principals' committee. It was a rare issue that required a formal NSC meeting involving the president.

As elegant as this NSC structure was, the Bush administration developed two alternative, informal venues with which to develop policy: the "Big Eight" (see table 2.2) and the "Inner Circle." They existed probably as a result of the shared worldviews and close interpersonal relationships among the main players in the Bush administration, and the fast pace of events that confronted the administration in quick succession, including the invasion of Panama, the end of the Cold War, the reunification of Germany, and the Gulf

War. In essence, there was no need for a large, formal NSC meeting when the president could gather his closest advisors, who also happened to be close friends, and devise a policy initiative.

Bill Clinton

President Bill Clinton came to office having run on a platform of fixing the domestic economy; "It's the economy, stupid," was a campaign mantra. Clinton had virtually no foreign policy experience and an uncomfortable relationship with the uniform military. During the 1992 campaign he had been pilloried for his opposition to the Vietnam War and his first weeks in office were marred by the controversy over his policy regarding gays in the military. On other issues he was an insatiable consumer of information and a true policy wonk, frequently holding debates late into the night or calling aides and colleagues in the wee hours of the morning to discuss ideas. His political instincts were legendary as were his character flaws. Finally, he was a politician at heart who believed that his personal charisma and persuasive abilities, combined with carefully calculated compromises, could always win the day. He saw political implications in any policy choice.[66]

Upon assuming office Clinton was confronted with a novel set of international challenges. The Cold War was over, peacefully, thanks in part to the Bush administration, but nothing had yet replaced it as a guiding principle to international affairs. Internal conflicts and humanitarian crises were cropping up worldwide. States were breaking apart. The United States was engaged in a humanitarian intervention in Somalia, even while the presidential transition was occurring, but had no overarching rationale for future interventions.

Clinton chose Anthony Lake as his first national security advisor. Lake was a surprising choice from some perspectives because he did not know Clinton well and believed that politics should be kept out of national security policy, which was the antithesis of the president's view.[67] But, that said, Lake and Clinton believed the NSA should be a broker, not a policy advocate, similar to the role Scowcroft had played in the Bush administration. Lake also was well respected and without obvious ideological axes to grind. That fit with Clinton's desire for a collegial staff that would provide him with a diverse set of views.

The Clinton NSC kept the same basic structure of PCs and DCs that was used by the previous administration with changes at the margins. The Clinton team renamed and recast the PCCs as interagency working groups, and created new transnational directorates at the NSC staff level on nonproliferation, environmental affairs, global issues, democracy and human rights, transnational threats, and international health, to supplement a series of traditional regional and functional directorates.[68] The NSC staff was expanded to almost double its previous size. Senior NSC staff members were treated as equals to their cabinet-level counterparts.

The administration made three more fundamental changes from the Bush model, two of which can be attributed to the increasingly fuzzy distinction between the domestic and international realms, and the ever-closer relationship between security and economic issues. First, Clinton created the National Economic Council, a coordinating entity similar to the NSC but focused on economic issues. Second, the administration expanded the NSC membership to include the treasury secretary, the president's economic advisor, the White House chief of staff, the UN ambassador, the national security advisor and his deputy, and the vice president's national security advisor. Third and finally, the vice president and his staff were given a much more active role in NSC deliberations during the Clinton administration than had existed in the past.[69] These changes meant that the Clinton NSC was larger and more diverse than was the case under Bush and it was complemented by (or competing with) a parallel economic forum.

The question was how one could find consensus with the large number of participants in policy debates, the president's brainstorming style, and his desire for collegiality. The answer during the first term was that the NSC process was largely ignored in favor of smaller, ad hoc forums. The principals' committee met infrequently. Unstructured foreign policy team meetings often replaced NSC meetings, where no one really drove the discussion and decisions were rarely reached.[70] The administration created several special envoys to deal with specific problems, from Russia to Northern Ireland to the Middle East and the Balkans, which left it unclear who was really making policy for the administration. On many issues, particularly with regard to Somalia, Haiti, and the Balkans, the administration appeared unable to settle on a course of action.

Lake's attitude slowly changed during the latter part of the first term as debate within the administration failed to produce cohesive policies. His role evolved from neutral broker to policy advocate, particularly on NATO enlargement and intervention in Bosnia.[71] A more activist NSA role would continue on selective issues during the second term, when Sandy Berger would take over as national security advisor.

Samuel Berger was Clinton's first choice as national security advisor in 1992. At the time, Berger was Clinton's closest foreign policy aide (the two had known each other since 1972), a distinction he would retain throughout the eight years of the administration. Berger deferred to Lake in the first term, however, believing that the more experienced Lake should lead the NSC. Once Berger assumed the NSA duties in 1997, some believed he was "perhaps the most influential national security advisor since Henry A. Kissinger."[72] Berger had many of the same qualities attributed to Scowcroft: an excellent relationship with the secretaries of state (Albright) and defense (Cohen) based on trust, Berger's ability to get the job done, and Berger's belief that the policy process should be fair and transparent to those involved.[73]

Berger took a leadership role in the second term, particularly when President Clinton became consumed with impeachment proceedings. Berger developed the "ABC lunches," involving Berger and Secretaries Albright and Cohen, as an informal means of coordinating with state and defense. He was well known for frequently reaching out to both secretaries multiple times a day. He also used the principals' committee more frequently than was done in the first term, and his combination of credibility, trustworthiness, and his relationship with the president seemed to succeed, in that the PC was able to make decisions on Kosovo, arms control, the Middle East, and counterterrorism policy, the last of which would become the driving force for the subsequent administration.

George W. Bush

President George W. Bush, like Clinton before him, came to the presidency from a governor's mansion and had little experience with or knowledge of foreign and security policy. President Bush's style was similar to Reagan's. Both presidents believed in setting an agenda, making decisions, and leaving the implementation to his cabinet officials. Bush showed little inclination toward mastering the details of policy or revisiting decisions once made. Before the attacks of 9/11, Bush appeared to be searching for an overarching theme for his administration's foreign policies. Balancing against China and deploying missile defenses were topics frequently raised by administration officials. More generally, the Bush administration separated itself from the Clinton era by abolishing many Clinton administration policies, a pattern that was colloquially known as ABC, standing for "Anyway But Clinton." The ABC mantra was applied to everything from counterterrorism to North Korea, the Middle East peace process, and stability operations.[74] The 9/11 attacks gave the administration its missing theme. Preventing future terrorist attacks on the U.S. homeland became the guiding principle for the administration.[75]

Condoleezza Rice became the NSA in Bush's first term. Bush had turned to her to guide him on international politics during the presidential campaign.[76] She grew to be closer to the president than perhaps any other advisor in the history of the NSC and was frequently referred to as an adopted member of the Bush family. She had total access to the president and was consulted on virtually every aspect of the administration's foreign policy and security agenda.[77] Given that close relationship, it is no surprise that Rice saw the NSA's primary role as staff for the president and ensuring that his priorities were disseminated across the government, with managing the national security process as a secondary function. In her words, "I consider it my first responsibility to be staff and counsel to the president, because he doesn't have anywhere else to go for that. The second most important responsibility is to make sure that when he wants to move an agenda in a particular direction that you can get this huge ship of state turned around and moved in the direction he wants to go. . . . The third most important function is to coordinate the rest of the government."[78]

The NSC's *structure* did not change fundamentally under Rice's leadership from what had existed during the Clinton administration. The Bush administration kept the same basic PC and DC structure originated by Scowcroft in the first Bush administration and used by Clinton. As with many other administrations, the Bush team initially cut the size of the NSC staff, only to increase staff levels over time. They did away with a number of Clinton-era policy directorates, mainly dealing with Europe, international health, the environment, and legislative and media affairs.[79] But all told, the NSC structure remained relatively unchanged from what had existed in the previous two administrations.

A more fundamental structural change was the creation of the Homeland Security Council (HSC) in late October 2001. *Homeland Security Presidential Directive 1* (HSPD-1) established a council that "shall ensure coordination of all homeland security-related activities among executive departments and agencies and promote the effective development and implementation of all homeland security purposes."[80] The HSC was structured like the NSC, with principals, deputies, and policy coordinating committees. The membership was quite different, however, emphasizing domestically focused agencies, such as Treasury, Health and Human Services, Transportation, the FBI, FEMA, etc. HSPD-1 empowered the assistant to the president for homeland security (colloquially known as the homeland security advisor, or HSA) to call HSC PC meetings, to craft meeting agendas, and to prepare background papers for those meetings. In an effort to ensure coordination on counterterrorism issues between the HSC and NSC, the national security advisor and the homeland security advisor would share the above tasks.

Two changes in NSC's *processes* during Bush's first term represented more fundamental differences from the Clinton administration. The first was the central and unprecedented role played by the vice president. Vice President Cheney was specifically empowered to attend any and all meetings of the NSC or HSC principals, deputies, or policy coordinating committees.[81] The vice president had his own fifteen-person NSC staff, parallel to the president's NSC staff, which dwarfed the three-person staff of Vice President Al Gore. Numerous Bush administration officials noted that Cheney's staff had real power. According to NSA Rice, "The vice president's staff actually sits in on the deputies meetings . . . his groups of deputies sit in with Steve [Hadley]'s deputies, so they're very well integrated into our process."[82] Richard Haass, director of the State Department's policy planning staff during the first term, noted that "The vice president's office has become the equivalent of a separate institution or bureaucracy. . . . The vice president has his own mini-NSC staff."[83] Some critics argued that agencies even reported directly to the vice president's staff, often without informing the regular NSC staff.[84] If true, this would seem to undermine the central role played by the NSC staff under most previous administrations.

The second procedural change in the Bush administration's NSC system related to the Defense Department. According to observers both within and outside the administration, Defense Department officials, up to and including Secretary of Defense Donald Rumsfeld, repeatedly undermined the formal NSC process. Defense officials would refuse to provide advance copies of decision papers or status reports ahead of scheduled meetings or leave copies of reports for further examination. No one except Secretary Rumsfeld was empowered to speak for or commit the Defense Department at PC, DC, or PCC meetings. And, finally, defense officials repeatedly failed to attend scheduled meetings. For whatever reason, Secretary Rumsfeld ignored demands from the NSC staff in general and Rice in particular.[85] According to one senior administration official, "I have never seen more high-level insubordination in the U.S. government in almost thirty years than I have seen in this administration."[86] Indeed, Rice was not perceived or treated as an equal by the secretary of defense, to say nothing of Vice President Dick Cheney, despite her bond with President Bush.[87]

A representative example comes from the early stages of the Iraq conflict. L. Paul "Jerry" Bremer was chosen by the Pentagon to head the coalition provisional authority (CPA) in Iraq. He reported directly to Secretary Rumsfeld and the president. Though Defense Department civilians apparently approved Bremer's decision to disband the Iraqi army and de-Ba'athification of the Iraqi government in the summer of 2003, neither the president nor the NSC staff was provided with advance notice or the chance to review these decisions.[88] Certainly the intelligence community, which had warned of the adverse consequences of such actions in a prewar estimate, was not consulted by Bremer on the aforementioned decisions.[89] More generally, Bremer believed that Rumsfeld and his aides repeatedly withheld CPA reports from the NSC staff.[90]

Critics argued that the Bush NSC process during the first term suffered as a result of these factors.[91] Formal NSC meetings became meaningless exercises on many issues, with cabinet officials reading talking points but not engaging each other in any real sense.[92] According to published reports, real decisions were made during informal gatherings in the White House, at Camp David, or at Bush's ranch in Crawford, Texas. The problem was that these informal meetings often excluded Secretary of State Powell and CIA Director George Tenet, which meant that there was inadequate coordination across agencies when it came to Afghanistan and Iraq policies.[93] Moreover, Rice did not ensure that the NSC staff produced the background materials or ask the tough questions (i.e., questioning assumptions, examining consequences, assessing risks, and comparing policy options) during either these informal gatherings or formal NSC meetings.[94] In short, Rice and the NSC staff did not appear to be managing the interagency process in any real sense.[95]

The NSC process appeared to work more smoothly during the Bush administration's second term. Part of this can be attributed to personnel changes. Rice replaced Powell as secretary of state in 2005 and Robert Gates replaced Rumsfeld as secretary of defense in late 2006. Rice and Gates brought in their own senior staff and the combination of new cabinet members and senior staff improved the dynamic across all levels of the NSC structure. But as important, Hadley took on a more traditional broker role common to many previous NSAs. The two best examples of that came when the NSC coordinated the surge in Iraq in the winter and spring of 2007, and the administration's broad review of Afghanistan policy at the end of the administration's tenure. But by then many of the administration's major decisions already had been taken, such as whether to invade Iraq, the extent and means by which to conduct postconflict operations in Iraq, and how to treat detainees captured in Afghanistan, Iraq, and elsewhere.

THE NSC IN THE OBAMA ADMINISTRATION

This chapter began by noting patterns of continuity across NSC systems, particularly a White House-centered system with relatively strong national security advisors, robust NSC staffs, and the use of advisory groups outside the NSC system. Although there are limits as to what we can deduce about the Obama NSC system because of the brief time he has been in office, the administration has signaled certain key clues about its intent. The early evidence suggests that the Obama administration is acting consistently with expectations regarding continuity and change in the NSC system.

Presidential Policy Directive 1 (PPD-1) makes clear that President Obama, his national security advisor, and, by extension, the NSC staff are at the heart of the administration's national security system.[96] PPD-1 sets out a broad NSC membership on par with that of the Clinton administration and far broader than the membership of the recent Bush NSC. Yet it firmly situates authority at lower levels in the NSC system, with each level run by the NSC staff. Specifically, the NSC is organized around the PC/DC/subordinate committee structure used by every administration since the first Bush presidency. In the Obama NSC, however, the NSA chairs PC meetings, calls those meetings, sets their agenda, and ensures that the appropriate supporting materials are prepared in advance and that decisions are communicated in a timely manner. In theory, this gives the NSA a tremendous amount of power and influence. The DC is focused on policy implementation, periodic reviews of major initiatives, crisis management, and preparation of complete options papers for the PC to consider. The deputy NSA chairs DC meetings. Below these are interagency policy committees (IPCs), charged with ensuring daily interagency coordination. The appropriate NSC staff member chairs or cochairs each IPC. In sum, PPD-1 structures the NSC in such a way that the NSC staff should have firm control over the timing, agenda, preparation for, and dissemination of NSC products. And that, by extension, should give the White House control over the security policy process.[97]

In addition, the administration has demonstrated a preference for using special envoys that cut across traditional agency and departmental divisions. Remember, special envoys answer directly to the president in most cases, which to some extent weakens the power of cabinet secretaries and bolsters White House control over major policy initiatives. Vice President Biden has played that role in Pakistan, Latin America, the Balkans, and in Iraq. Obama named Richard Holbrooke as his envoy for Pakistan and Afghanistan. George Mitchell is the special envoy for the Middle East. Dennis Ross was the special envoy for Southwest Asia before moving to the NSC staff. Retired Air Force General Scott Gration is the special envoy for Sudan. Carol Browner is the special envoy for global warming. According to one press report on these moves, "Obama's moves formalize what White House veterans have always known—the Cabinet is close to a president, [but] his White House team [is] closer and more influential."[98]

In terms of process, we would expect the NSC process to reflect both the personalities of the president and the NSA, as well as their reaction to past events. There is ample evidence that suggests that President Obama's temperament and operating style will play an important role in NSC procedures. Consider the president's operating style.[99] Obama's response to the financial crisis has been pragmatic rather than ideological. He is methodical, as witnessed by his Senate career and his presidential campaign strategy. He is an excellent communicator, as witnessed by his many speeches during the campaign, the inauguration, and in response to the financial crisis. Most important, he wants to hear all sides of an issue before making a decision, as he made clear in a December 2008 news conference:

"I think that's how the best decisions are made. One of the dangers in a White House, based on my reading of history, is that you get wrapped up in groupthink and everybody agrees with everything and there's no discussion and there are no dissenting views. So I'm going to be welcoming a vigorous debate inside the White House. But understand, I will be setting policy as president. I will be responsible for the vision that this team carries out, and I expect them to implement that vision once decisions are made."[100] Retired Marine General James Jones, Obama's national security advisor, believes in taking a low-profile approach to his job, similar to Scowcroft or Lake's early behavior.[101] He is said to have a pragmatic, collegial style, well suited for the broker role he sees as his job.[102] In his words, "I want to make sure the right people are at the table and that they're able to say what they want—so that nobody walks away angry that their views weren't heard. So far at the principals' level it has been very collegial. Collegiality allows me not to have to be so much in the forefront. . . . This is what suits the president's comfort level, so he can go around the table and speak to every member of the NSC."[103]

In a March 18, 2009, memo to national security agencies titled "The 21st Century Interagency Process," Jones detailed specific ideas as to how the NSC process would work. The memo's content seemed aimed at reversing many of the perceived shortcomings of the George W. Bush administration's NSC process. In an implicit criticism of Bush-era decisions on Iraq, Jones noted that he will ensure that a variety of opinions are heard during NSC meetings to "avoid the emergence of a premature policy consensus." In an implied criticism of Cheney, Jones noted that the NSC process will be transparent: "agencies have a right to be aware and participate," with the NSC staff "communicating information appropriately and comprehensively." In what could be a reaction to the rift between Powell and Rumsfeld regarding Phase IV in Iraq, Jones instructed NSC cabinet members to leave their bureaucratic interests behind and focus on advancing the administration's overall goals. Finally, in what seemed a critique of Rumsfeld's disdain for the NSC process,

Jones noted that "The process—and the President—are not well served by interagency meetings that are held on short notice and defined by inadequate preparations . . . [including] when papers are circulated for approval at the last minute, when agencies fail to send appropriate level representatives to meetings, and when those who attend meetings are routinely unable to advocate on behalf of their 'Principals' when a decision is needed." To ensure that these mistakes do not occur, Jones then set out a series of requirements, including regular meeting schedules, an agreed-upon agenda, discussion papers circulated at least 48 hours before meetings, clear agreement on what was decided at each meeting, and mandatory attendance by two representatives from each agency who can speak for their agency. To make this work, of course, requires the cooperation of the other NSC members, the top cover of the White House, and a larger NSC staff. So far, Jones seems to have the first two and he is said to have asked for the third, if only to create a new strategic planning group within the staff.[104] How all this will work in practice, however, and where decision-making authority will ultimately reside, remains to be seen.

As this book goes to press, we are witnessing the transition from General Jim Jones to Tom Donilon as national security advisor. Jones reinstituted a structured process to NSC deliberations centered around the NSC staff, consistent with the historic pattern of centralizing national security decisions in the White House. The selection of Donilon, reportedly a long-standing confidant of President Obama and a savvy bureaucratic and political operative, supports the idea that individual NSAs ultimately rise or fall based on their relationship with the president they serve.

CONCLUSIONS

The previous discussion intentionally begs the question as to which NSC system worked best, in large part because there are so many definitions of "best" as applied to the NSC. Some have argued that a good NSC system is one in which the NSA plays the role of the honest broker within a well-articulated process, as exemplified by the tenure of Brent Scowcroft. Others, including some presidents (Johnson comes to mind), believe the NSC staff should act as the president's advocate in policy debates. A variant of that logic is that a good NSC system is one in which the president gets the policies that he wants, regardless of whether or not policy was made via the formal NSC process. Still others think that international outcomes, and whether those outcomes advance U.S. interests, best reflect the success or failure of an NSC system. In the end then, it may be impossible to know which NSC system works best because such an assessment relies on an inherently subjective judgment.

What is certain is that the NSC system has exhibited both continuity and change over time. Since the 1947 National Security Act created the NSC system, presidents have operated in an era of expanded U.S. international commitments, a huge national security bureaucracy, and tremendous public expectations. Presidents have responded by turning to a combination of NSC staff support and special envoys. Both are under direct presidential control and are not beholden to federal agencies or the legislative branch. The formal NSC system has suffered as a result. NSC meetings have been replaced by alternate forums that often do not have adequate staff support or exclude key foreign policy players.

Continuity, however, does not extend to the particular structures or organizational precepts of the NSC system itself. Nor does it hold for the role of specific national security advisors. Change on these fronts seems to depend on the personalities and desires of each president and NSA, and to the international and domestic contexts in which they find themselves. Consider the role of the NSA. For whatever reason, that role has fluctuated in a predictable manner across administrations. Eisenhower did not empower his advisors. Kennedy gave McGeorge Bundy significant authority. Johnson consciously took power away from his two advisors. Nixon empowered Kissinger. Ford had a caretaker in Scowcroft. Carter gave Brzezinski significant authority and influence. Reagan and his White House advisors demoted the NSA position significantly for most of the administration. George H. W. Bush empowered Scowcroft. Clinton did not cede as much power to Lake, though Berger appeared to wield more power and influence in the second term. George W. Bush certainly valued Rice's counsel but did not empower her vis-à-vis his cabinet secretaries or the vice president. Obama put Jones at the center of the national security debates. Obama's selection of Tom Donilon as the next NSA suggests that the president wants a confidant more than a practitioner, and that the NSA will maintain a central role in policy. It seems likely, however, that future NSC systems will exhibit a combination of continuity and change that their predecessors would easily recognize.

NOTES

1. For a summary of the evidence linking various NSC decision processes and foreign policy behavior, see John Burke, "The Neutral/Honest Broker Role in Foreign Policy Decision Making: A Reassessment," *Presidential Studies Quarterly* 35, no. 2 (June 2005): 229–59.

2. See PL 80-235 and PL 81-216, respectively.

3. The main differences between the Eisenhower and Kennedy NSC structures included a change from an administrative to a policy formulation role, from a core of nonpartisan, professional staff to a set of political appointees, and from a NSA with subcabinet status to the equivalent of cabinet rank. See Andrew Preston, "The Little State Department: McGeorge Bundy and the National Security Council Staff, 1961–65," *Presidential Studies Quarterly* 31, no. 4 (December 2001): 635–60.

4. Amy Zegart, *Flawed by Design: The Evolution of the CIA, JCS, and NSC* (Stanford, CA: Stanford University Press, 1999), 85–87.

5. Ibid., 89.

6. One well-known exception is Richard Clarke, who served as a counterterrorism expert on the NSC staff throughout the Clinton administration and into the George W. Bush presidency.

7. Terry Moe, "The Politicized Presidency," in *The New Direction in American Politics*, ed. John Chubb and Paul Peterson (Washington, DC: The Brookings Institution, 1985), 235–46.

8. Bert Rockman, "America's 'Departments' of State: Irregular and Regular Syndromes of Policy Making," *American Political Science Review* 75, no. 4 (December 1981): 911–27.

9. The exception was Richard Allen, Ronald Reagan's first national security advisor.

10. Stephen Hess, "Franklin Roosevelt: 1933–1945," in *Organizing the Presidency, 2nd Edition*, ed. Stephen Hess (Washington, DC: The Brookings Institution, 1988), 23–39.

11. Ferdinand Eberstadt, "Postwar Organization for National Security," in *Fateful Decisions: Inside the National Security Council*, ed. Karl Inderfurth and Loch Johnson (New York: Oxford University Press, 2004), 17–20.

12. For staff totals and trends, see Ivo Daalder and I. M. Destler, "Policy Brief No. 68: A NSC for a New Administration" (Washington, DC: The Brookings Institution, November 2000).

13. See Ivo Daalder and I. M. Destler, *In the Shadow of the Oval Office* (New York: Simon & Schuster, 2009).

14. The exception was Kennedy's ExComm, which had as many as nine cabinet members in attendance, plus roughly a dozen other advisors as necessary. See Graham Allison and Phillip Zelikow, *Essence of Decision, 2nd Ed.* (Reading, MA: Prentice Hall, 1999).

15. For a discussion of the Tuesday lunches, see John Prados, *Keeper of the Keys* (New York: William Morrow and Co., 1991), 149–51. For Lyndon Johnson's operating style, see Chris Matthews, *Hardball* (New York: Free Press, 1999), 19, 25–34.

16. Burke, "The Neutral/Honest Broker Role in Foreign Policy Decision Making," 239.

17. Cecil Crabb and Kevin Mulcahy, "The Lessons of the Iran-Contra Affair for National Security Policy Making," in *Fateful Decisions: Inside the National Security Council,* ed. Inderfurth and Johnson, 162–72.

18. Daalder and Destler, *In the Shadow of the Oval Office*; Matthew Shabat, *PNSR Chronology of National Security Structures, working draft #10* (Washington, DC: Project on National Security Reform, July 23, 2007); Inderfurth and Johnson, *Fateful Decisions*; David Rothkopf, *Running the World* (New York: Public Affairs, 2004); Richard Best, *National Security Council: An Organizational Assessment* (New York: Novinka Press, 2001); Christopher Shoemaker, *The NSC Staff: Counseling the Council* (Boulder, CO: Westview Press, 1991); and Prados, *Keeper of the Keys*.

19. Cutler, "The Development of the National Security Council," 442.

20. Quoted in Ivo Daalder and I. M. Destler, "The Role of the National Security Advisor," (Washington, DC: The Brookings Institution, October 25, 1999), 52. For similar thoughts, see Colin Powell, "The NSC Advisor," *The Bureaucrat* (Summer 1989), reprinted in Inderfurth and Johnson, *Fateful Decisions,* 158–61.

21. This review does not include the relatively brief and largely caretaker Ford administration. President Ford essentially continued many of the Nixon administration's structures and procedures in place. For instance, Ford kept Henry Kissinger as national security advisor for the administration's first year, replacing him with Brent Scowcroft during the administration's final year. In addition to the specific citations below, this review draws extensively from Rothkopf, *Running the World*.

22. Rothkopf, *Running the World,* 65–72.

23. Cutler, "The Development of the National Security Council," 442.

24. Ibid., 443.

25. Best, *The National Security Council,* 55–57. For a discussion of this process, with particular emphasis on the role of the NSC Planning Board, see Andrew Krepinevich and Barry Watts, "Lost at the NSC," *The National Interest*, January 6, 2009, www.nationalinterest.org/Article.aspx?id520498, accessed on January 7, 2009.

26. Best, *The National Security Council,* 57. For an organizational chart of the Eisenhower NSC staff structure, see Inderfurth and Johnson, *Fateful Decisions,* 30.

27. Preston, "The Little State Department: McGeorge Bundy and the National Security Council Staff, 1961–65."

28. Henry Kissinger, "What Vietnam Teaches Us," *Newsweek* (November 3, 2008), 44.

29. Kai Bird, "McGeorge Bundy," in *Fateful Decisions,* 185.

30. Ibid., 186.

31. See Shabat, *PNSR Chronology of National Security Structures, working draft #10,* 15.

32. Preston, "The Little State Department: McGeorge Bundy and the National Security Council Staff, 1961–65."

33. Quoted in Daalder and Destler, *In the Shadow of the Oval Office,* 33.

34. Best, *The National Security Council,* 60–61.

35. Kevin Mulcahy, "Walt Rostow as National Security Advisor, 1966–1969," *Presidential Studies Quarterly,* 25, no. 2 (Spring 1995): 223–36.

36. Mulcahy, "Walt Rostow as National Security Advisor, 1966–1969."

37. Best, *The National Security Council,* 64.

38. Larry Berman, *Planning a Tragedy: The Americanization of the War in Vietnam* (New York: W. W. Norton and Company, 1983).

39. For an organizational chart of the Nixon NSC staff structure, see Inderfurth and Johnson, *Fateful Decisions,* 69. See also Best, *The National Security Council,* 19.

40. For a selection, see Robert Dallek, *Nixon and Kissinger: Partners in Power* (New York: Harper, 2007); Gary Wills, *Nixon Agonistes* (Boston: Houghton Mifflin, 2002); Stephen Ambrose, *Nixon, volume 2: The Triumph of a Politician* (New York: Simon and Schuster, 1989).

41. Daalder and Destler, *In the Shadow of the Oval Office*, 61, 69.

42. For a profile, see Marvin Kalb and Bernard Kalb, *Kissinger* (Boston: Little, Brown, 1974).

43. Daalder and Destler, *In the Shadow of the Oval Office*, 63, 92.

44. Shabat, *PNSR Chronology of National Security Structures, working draft #10*, 18.

45. Daalder and Destler, *In the Shadow of the Oval Office*, 94.

46. Dom Bonafede, "Zbigniew Brzezinski," in Inderfurth and Johnson, *Fateful Decisions*, 197.

47. For an organizational chart of the Carter NSC staff structure, see Inderfurth and Johnson, *Fateful Decisions*, 72. See also Best, *The National Security Council*, 23–24. For a discussion of the NSC staff's daily operations, see Bonafede, "Zbigniew Brzezinski," 200–202.

48. Best, *The National Security Council*, 70.

49. Daalder and Destler, *In the Shadow of the Oval Office*, 119.

50. Some of the more well-known Reagan biographies include: James Mann, *The Rebellion of Ronald Reagan: A History of the End of the Cold War* (New York: Viking, 2009); Haynes Johnson, *Sleepwalking through History: America in the Reagan Years* (New York: W.W. Norton and Co, 2003); Peggy Noonan, *When Character Was King: A Story of Ronald Reagan* (New York: Penguin, 2002); Lou Cannon, *President Reagan: The Role of a Lifetime* (New York: Public Affairs, 2000).

51. Daalder and Destler, *In the Shadow of the Oval Office*, 129, 137.

52. Ibid., 152.

53. Shabat, *PNSR Chronology of National Security Structures, working draft #10*, 21.

54. Daalder and Destler, *In the Shadow of the Oval Office*, 133, 146, 161; Best, *The National Security Council*, 73.

55. Best, *The National Security Council*, 73–74.

56. Daalder and Destler, *In the Shadow of the Oval Office*, 140.

57. The Tower Commission is the authoritative source on the scandal. See *Report of the President's Special Review Board* (Washington, DC: Government Printing Office, February 27, 1987).

58. Prados, *Keeper of the Keys*, 469 quotes Clark as having said to Haig in mid-June 1982, "You've won a lot of battles in this administration, Al, but you'd better understand that from now on it's going to be the *President's* foreign policy."

59. Prados, *Keeper of the Keys*, 482, 491.

60. Daalder and Destler, *In the Shadow of the Oval Office*, 154. See also Prados, *Keeper of the Keys*, 481.

61. For background on Carlucci, see Prados, *Keeper of the Keys*, 538–40.

62. See Frank Carlucci's comments at the "Forum on the Role of National Security Advisor, April 21, 2001," reprinted in Inderfurth and Johnson, *Fateful Decisions*, 145. Colin Powell did not have to deal with that rivalry when he became Reagan's sixth and last NSA, as Carlucci had replaced Weinberger at the Department of Defense.

63. Daalder and Destler, *In the Shadow of the Oval Office*, 172.

64. Ibid., 180. See also David Lauter, "The Man behind the President," *Los Angeles Times*, October 14, 1990, reprinted in Inderfurth and Johnson, *Fateful Decisions*, 203–7.

65. Lauter, in Inderfurth and Johnson, *Fateful Decisions*, 203.

66. Joe Klein, *The Natural: The Misunderstood Presidency of Bill Clinton* (New York: Doubleday, 2003); also Sidney Blumenthal, *The Clinton Wars* (New York: Farrar, Straus and Giroux, 2003); and David Gergen, *Eyewitness to Power* (New York: Simon and Schuster, 2000), 249–342.

67. Daalder and Destler, *In the Shadow of the Oval Office*, 235.

68. For an organizational chart of the Clinton NSC staff structure, see Inderfurth and Johnson, *Fateful Decisions*, 103.

69. Best, *The National Security Council*, 78.

70. Daalder and Destler, *In the Shadow of the Oval Office*, 216, 227–29.

71. On NATO enlargement, see James M. Goldgeier, *Not Whether but When: The U.S. Decision to Enlarge NATO* (Washington, DC: The Brookings Institution, 1999). On Lake's role in the

Balkans, see David Auerswald, *Disarmed Democracies* (Ann Arbor, MI: University of Michigan Press, 2000).

72. R. W. Apple, "A Domestic Sort with Global Worries," *The New York Times*, August 25, 1999, reprinted in Inderfurth and Johnson, *Fateful Decisions*, 208–12.

73. Ibid. Berger's perceptions of the role of the NSA are reprinted in "Forum on the Role of National Security Advisor, April 21, 2001," reprinted in Inderfurth and Johnson, *Fateful Decisions*, 141–57.

74. Rothkopf, *Running the World*, 403–4.

75. For reviews of the administration's mindsets immediately after the 9/11 attacks, see Bob Woodward, *Bush at War* (New York: Simon and Schuster, 2002); and Ron Suskind, *The One Percent Doctrine* (New York: Simon and Schuster, 2006).

76. For a profile, see Elaine Sciolino, "Compulsion to Achieve—Condoleezza Rice," *The New York Times*, December 18, 2000, reprinted in Inderfurth and Johnson, *Fateful Decisions*, 213–15; also Rothkopf, *Running the World*, 394–95.

77. Rothkopf, *Running the World*, 393.

78. Quoted in Rothkopf, *Running the World*, 405. See also Daalder and Destler, *In the Shadow of the Oval Office*, 257, 260. Critics argued that she accomplished the first task but not the others, for reasons discussed below.

79. Rothkopf, *Running the World*, 405; Daalder and Destler, *In the Shadow of the Oval Office*, 260.

80. For the text of HSPD-1, see www.fas.org/irp/offdocs/nspd/hspd-1.htm.

81. HSPD-1, for instance, ends with an assertion of vice presidential power: "The Vice President may attend any and all meetings of any entity established by or under this directive."

82. Quoted in Rothkopf, *Running the World*, 421.

83. Ibid., 407.

84. Daalder and Destler, *In the Shadow of the Oval Office*, 275.

85. See Rothkopf, *Running the World*, 418–19, for numerous examples.

86. Quoted in Rothkopf, *Running the World*, 414. See also Daalder and Destler, *In the Shadow of the Oval Office*, 273.

87. Daalder and Destler, *In the Shadow of the Oval Office*, 257, 273, 275, 281. Rothkopf, *Running the World*, 407, quotes a member of the deputies committee making these exact arguments.

88. Bob Woodward, *State of Denial* (New York: Simon and Schuster, 2006), 197.

89. See Senate Select Committee on Intelligence, *S. Report 110-76: Report on Prewar Intelligence Assessments about Postwar Iraq* (Washington, DC: Government Printing Office, May 31, 2007).

90. Woodward, *State of Denial*, 236.

91. Numerous examples can be found in Rothkopf, *Running the World*, 406.

92. Woodward, *State of Denial*, 241.

93. Ibid., 230; Rothkopf, *Running the World*, 408; Daalder and Destler, *In the Shadow of the Oval Office*, 277.

94. John Burke, "The Contemporary Presidency: Condoleezza Rice as NSC Advisor," *Presidential Studies Quarterly*, 35, issue 3 (September 2005): 554–74; also Woodward, *State of Denial*, 241.

95. Glenn Kessler and Thomas Ricks, "Rice's Tenure Complicates New Post: Failure to Manage Agency Infighting Cited," *Washington Post*, November 16, 2004.

96. PPD-1 was signed on February 13, 2009.

97. Laura Rozen, "Obama's NSC Takes Power," *The Cable*, March 3, 2009, http://thecable.foreignpolicy.com/posts/2009/03/03/jones_s_nsc_moves_to_assert_greater_control_over_interagency_process.

98. Jonathan Martin, "West Wing on Steroids in Obama W.H.," *Politico*, January 25, 2009.

99. This section draws heavily on Fred Greenstein, "The Leadership Style of Barack Obama: An Early Assessment," *The Forum*, 7, issue 1, article 6 (2009).

100. Quoted in Greenstein, "The Leadership Style of Barack Obama: An Early Assessment," 8.

101. That approach has generated some early debate as to Jones's effectiveness. See Karen DeYoung, "In Frenetic White House, A Low Key 'Outsider'," *Washington Post*, May 7, 2009; Helene Cooper, "National Security Adviser Tries Quieter Approach," *New York Times*, May 7, 2009.

102. Secretary of Defense Robert Gates called Jones an "honest broker," noting that "I can trust Jim to represent my views on an issue to the president . . . He is a facilitator, not an obstacle, and that hasn't always been true in that job." See David Ignatius, "Jim Jones's Team," *Washington Post*, June 7, 2009, p. A17.

103. David Ignatius, "National Security Facilitator," *The Washington Post*, April 30, 2009.

104. Ibid. Support exists in the Defense Department's senior ranks for such an NSC directorate. See Michele Flournoy and Shawn Brimley, "In Search of Harmony: Orchestrating 'the Interagency' for the Long War," *Armed Forces Journal* (July 2006), available at www.armedforcesjournal.com/2006/07/1857934/.

Chapter 3 The Office of Management and Budget: The President's Policy Tool

Gordon Adams

> OMB is unexplainable to everyone who lives outside the Beltway and misunderstood by nearly everyone who lives inside the Beltway.
>
> *Paul O'Neill, former Treasury secretary*

> The OMB is staffed by the "abominable no-men."
>
> *Unnamed agency budget official*

INTRODUCTION

In national security, as with the federal budget as a whole, it is the president's budget.[1] Although presidents have had different appetites for being involved in budget planning, the preparation of the annual budget request is a responsibility they cannot ignore. Their budget requests provide the key opportunity to leave a mark on policy and implement the policy objectives they brought to office. This is especially true in the national security arena, where the executive must not only plan budgets for policy initiatives and priorities, but also react to events the government does not fully control: international conferences, new tensions, the outbreak of war, military interventions, humanitarian crises, or terrorist attacks, among others, all of which have resource implications. The emerging agenda of national security, which includes a complex and growing set of issues, demands both more of the federal agencies and greater coordination at the White House level. As a result, the policy, program, and budget activities of the executive office of the president (EOP) are a year-round responsibility, with both routine and unforeseen elements.

The Office of Management and Budget (OMB) is at the heart of the White House budgeting and resource planning process.[2] The OMB is the key White House player in executive branch budgeting and management decisions, White House approval of agency plans and programs, and the relationship between the executive branch and the Congress with respect to budgets and management.[3] It plays a key role in setting and implementing any administration's budgetary, legislative, and policy agenda. It serves as a technical and programmatic memory bank and implementer for the White House and as a funnel for executive branch operations and proposals as they move toward the Congress.[4]

The OMB manages the executive branch budget process, integrates agency budgets, develops the budget dimensions of White House policy actions, adjudicates resource disputes and coordinates resource planning among the agencies, carries out oversight of agency budgeting and management, approves all legislative proposals from the executive branch to the Congress, and draws up the administration's views on pending congressional legislation. It is the president's right hand on budget, management, regulatory, and

---

Box 3.1   The National Security Budget Process

The OMB process for planning national security budgets begins roughly eighteen months in advance of the start of the fiscal year for which the White House is requesting funds.

In the spring of any given year, OMB is dealing with three budgets simultaneously: the budget being implemented in that current fiscal year; the budget the president has already submitted to Congress for the next fiscal year; and the budget being planned for the following fiscal year. As a result, the planning of the third budget takes place in a context of uncertainty; how funds will be spent in the current fiscal year and how much funding and for what programs will Congress provide in the coming fiscal year.

The OMB resolves this uncertainty as best it can and provides guidance based on the out-year projections contained in previous budgets, new presidential priorities, deals cut with the Congress, electoral considerations, and emerging economic and fiscal realities (growth of the economy, inflation, deficits, etc.).

The guidance given national security agencies, as a result, can be affected by broader fiscal, budgetary, policy, and political priorities that may have little to do with national security requirements, per se. For example, President Bush's decision in 2001 to focus on tax reductions led to lower than expected defense budgets, as revenue projections declined. This externally imposed budget discipline ended, however, with the terrorist attacks of 2001, which led to major increases in defense and homeland security spending, and the reappearance of large spending deficits, as a result.

The OMB staff maintains a dialogue with agencies over the spring and summer, as the agencies carry out their own budget planning, in order to identify major budget issues and disagreements that could appear in OMB's fall budget process. By the middle of the summer, OMB delivers more formal budget planning instructions to agencies, which describes in detail the types of data and information agencies must provide in their budget submissions (called Circular A-11).[1]

A-11 provides OMB's expectations about the types of budget information each agency should provide, with detailed schedules (formats) for reporting that data. It describes the materials agencies should provide to justify their budgets (justification requirements). Moreover, A-11 also lays out expectations for agencies preparing emergency supplementary budget requests outside the normal budget process. These have been particularly important in the national security arena, as emergency supplemental requests for spending on operations in Iraq, Afghanistan, and against terrorists grew in size and frequency after the 9/11 terrorist attacks. The submission of agency budgets occurs in late September except for defense, which continues its dialogue with OMB until a final set of agreed data is supplied in December before the release of the budget.

---

1. Circulars are the OMB mechanism for providing guidance and instructions to executive branch agencies. A-11 is titled Preparation, Submission, and Execution of the Budget. Each year's version differs, following White House priorities and policies, and is generally available at the OMB website.

---

legislative issues. With a staff of roughly 450, OMB is the only large, permanent civil service staff for the EOP. The staff has detailed knowledge of executive branch operations, budgeting, and management that a president needs to shape and implement policy, ensure that resources support that policy, and control, to the extent possible, executive branch operations.

Created in the Budget and Accounting Act of 1921 as the Bureau of the Budget (BOB) in the Treasury Department, OMB's role has grown steadily as the budgeting process has become more complicated and as the federal budget itself has become a much larger element of the U.S. economy. The OMB's capabilities gradually grew, especially during the Roosevelt administration. Expanding budgets and the growing importance of federal spending in the depression led to a decision to bring BOB directly under the president in 1939.[5] After World War II, BOB's responsibilities both for budget and management processes expanded further. Recognizing the central importance of this presidential tool, BOB was reorganized in 1970 as the Office of Management and Budget and was given responsibility for administering the budget process, enforcing presidential priorities in that process, providing budgetary and management advice to the president and the agencies, and advocating for the budget after it was sent to the Congress.

The OMB's knowledge of the executive branch and congressional processes and its analytical capability are critical to a president. Each chief executive develops policies and initiatives he or she wants to implement. The OMB plays a key role in shaping these initiatives, ensuring they are included in agency budgets, and overseeing their implementation once the funds have been provided. The strength of the organization lies in its permanence and its reputation as an impartial advisor, evaluating programs based on data and previous experience. This role is generally valued as neutral.

The OMB is known for giving the best advice it can, regardless of the political stripe of the administration. The staff is renowned for its expertise on agency programs and operations and its willingness to provide unvarnished advice to the president.[6] Over time, however, as OMB's functions have expanded to include shaping program and congressional and public advocacy, these more politicized roles have conflicted with the agency's neutral and more technical image.[7] In the budget deficit reduction era of 1985–2002, doubt was cast on OMB's economic and budgetary projections, which were described as a "rosy scenario," or "cooking the books."[8] In general, however, OMB is seen by outside analysts and by the Congress as the most neutral and credible source of information and views on administration policies and budgets.

OMB's budget and planning role has become even more complex in the post-Cold War era, as U.S. national security policies, programs, and commitments have expanded to cover a widening agenda of global and regional issues. This expansion of the scope of national security is accompanied by an increasing amount of interagency activity at the White House level, activity that requires OMB involvement in the processes of other White House offices, particularly the National Security Council (NSC). Both OMB and NSC are playing growing roles in coordinating the interagency process for dealing with these cross-cutting issues, leading to proposals for reforming and strengthening the White House and particularly the OMB role in strategic planning, cross-agency guidance, and in interagency coordination.

OMB CULTURE: THE BUCK STOPS HERE

The OMB is one of the least understood, most influential, and sometimes most disliked institutions in the executive branch of the U.S. government. The standard mantra, certain to produce an uncomfortable and mistrusting chuckle in a non-OMB audience, is for an OMB political or career official to begin a presentation with the remark: "I'm from OMB; I'm here to help you." Most agencies would rather OMB did not exist and find that they tolerate, rather than appreciate, OMB's role in their institutional lives and processes. Most outsiders do not understand what OMB is responsible for and wonder why it has a reputation for having such power.

And yet, as one former associate director of OMB put it, when senior OMB policy officials reflect on their work, they find: "You sit at the pure epicenter of policy. You're in a position to make a difference. And eventually, everything will come across your desk."[9] The centrality of OMB to executive branch decision making and the speed with which it must work for the White House, combined with a very private institutional ethos, shapes the organizational culture of what is known as the president's budget office. Bluntly put, OMB is unique. It is the only large, career-staffed institution in the EOP. Its organizational culture can be summed up as flat, swift, hard-working, loyal, trustworthy, professional, skeptical, and insular.

First, the organization has a very flat culture. With its wide array of responsibilities and only 450 career employees, capped by a thin layer of policy officials, the OMB culture cannot afford to stand on ceremony or spend lengthy amounts of time waiting for decisions to be processed through a hierarchy. When information, a briefing table, an options paper, or the pricing of a presidential initiative is needed, there are only a few formal processes for working down into the organization for a response. The director and associate directors at the top can reach quickly to the examiner level for the answers. Typically, deputy associate directors (DADs), the senior level for career staff, will call branch chiefs and examiners together in a conference room for a quick review of papers, requests, or options, reaching a conclusion on the spot. Associate directors will frequently participate in these meetings, speeding the decision process. When the director needs a brief on a particular topic, all layers of the organization may appear in his or her office with the necessary information, examiners (the lowest layer) frequently providing the briefing.

Second, the organization prides itself on its speed. The responses it gives to senior policymakers' requests can arrive the same day as the request. A table on budget options for the defense top line will be produced in 24 hours. Analytical papers on options for defense procurement reform will be done in a matter of a few days at most. A detailed review, described in OMB terms as a "scrub," of a State Department emergency supplemental budget submission may take a day or two. An entire two-hundred-page briefing book for an incoming policy official may even be ready ahead of time or produced virtually overnight. When OMB officials and staff are responding to the need to price out policy options developed by the NSC, the NSC cannot wait for days; the options are priced in hours or days. There is possibly no other organization in the executive branch of government that can produce information and analysis with the speed of the OMB.

Third, because OMB is small and expected to respond swiftly, the organizational culture is one of hard work. Although officials throughout the government are generally prepared to work hard, OMB responsibilities rarely respect weekends or vacations. Because the White House is a 24/7 operation, OMB works the same hours and days. The standard joke at OMB is, "Thank God, it's Friday; only two more working days until Monday!"

As this discussion suggests, the OMB staff members also are extremely loyal, in the most professional sense of the term: they are committed to support the office of the presidency. In the OMB case, this loyalty has particular features. They are loyal to the organization

Box 3.2   Other White House Office Budget Players

The president and his personal office play a central role in the White House budget process. Some presidents are highly involved in the details of budgeting. President Carter was well known for his detailed review of budget proposals, particularly the budget requests of the Defense Department. President George H. W. Bush was also involved in final decisions, especially on national security issues and on overall budget policy. President Clinton chaired virtually every final appeal and decision-making meeting in the December before his budgets were sent to the Congress. Other presidents have been less directly involved, including Ronald Reagan and George W. Bush.

The presidential office can also play an important role in the budget process by acting on the president's behalf. Leon Panetta, who had been OMB director, continued to play a direct role in budget decisions as presidential chief of staff by holding regular budget decision meetings on key issues in his office and negotiating on budget bills with members of Congress.[1] Other staff members also intervene in the process on specific issues. In the Clinton administration, for example, the president was strongly committed to a new technology reinvestment program (TRP) at the Department of Defense (DOD), which provided funds for companies to use defense technologies for civilian and commercial applications. The White House staff of the National Economic Council (NEC) would regularly arrange three-way meetings between NEC, DOD, and OMB at which they would advocate higher levels of funding for the TRP program than DOD wanted to request.[2]

Historically, vice presidents have had a reputation for being at the margin of policymaking. However, the office of the vice president (OVP) has played a growing role in the budget process in recent years, starting with Walter Mondale and George H. W. Bush, and increasingly with Al Gore and particularly with Dick Cheney. As OVP staffs have expanded with this activist role, their participation in the budget process has also grown. Vice presidents also develop personal commitments to certain national security issues—global climate change and Russia programs in the case of Al Gore or national defense and counterterrorism in the case of Dick Cheney. Vice President Gore participated actively in virtually every appeals meeting held with the president. Vice President Dick Cheney played an even broader role in the White House budget process. He actively supported higher budgets for programs he was involved in, particularly Iraq and Afghanistan. In addition, Cheney played a central role in the overall budget process, particularly for national security, chairing the agency budget appeals process that followed OMB pass back.[3]

Other EOP offices also intervene in the OMB process. The U.S. Trade Representative, the trade agreement negotiating office in the White House, not only lobbies for its own operating budget but plays a key role in helping Treasury and OMB identify revenue options needed as offsets to compensate for the impact of trade agreements on projected federal receipts.[4] The White House Office of Science and Technology Policy frequently advocates higher levels of funding for research and development, including national security-related investments, than those requested by DOD, NASA, NSF, the Energy Department, or other agencies with research and development investment programs.

---

1. Author's experience.
2. Ibid.
3. Interviews with White House staff.
4. These offsets were required between 1990 and 2002, as a result of the Budget Enforcement Act of 1990, which set out a number of deficit-reduction requirements, including the need to pay in budgetary terms for budget decisions on the mandatory side of the budget that would cause a loss of projected federal revenues (so-called PAYGO). See Allen Schick, *The Federal Budget: Politics, Policy, Process*, 3rd ed. (Washington, DC: Brookings Institution Press, 2007), 162–90.

and know they share in a high-intensity, high-demand work experience that is unusual in government. In addition, they are loyal to each president. This has particular meaning, for presidencies come and go, but OMB stays permanently in place. Frequently, a new administration will come into office skeptical about OMB because it is a bureaucracy that served the previous administration well. There is always some initial doubt that the organization will be loyal to the policy priorities of the incoming team and flexible enough to help carry them out.

It sometimes takes a year or more for those doubts to recede. Regardless of individual party registration of any given OMB staff member, the staff is willing to work with the policy priorities of any administration. The staff prides itself on this sense of loyalty and it soon comes to be valued by a new White House. For example, when Vice President Al Gore came into office, he created an entirely separate vice presidential office, the National Performance Review (NPR), to carry out his responsibilities for reforming government management (the reinvention in government initiative). Initially, the vice president and the NPR staff were skeptical of the OMB commitment to such reform and saw the budget office as needing its own reform. After a year in office, however, the NPR office realized that, through its budget and management responsibilities, OMB had the leverage to execute NPR policies and goals that the NPR office lacked. The OMB and NPR swiftly became partners in the enterprise, overcoming the initial skepticism.

Overall, administration after administration has discovered the value of OMB as the most effective, flexible, and loyal instrument the president has to shape his policies, massage the budget to carry them out, and monitor the outcomes in the federal agencies. As one former associate director put it: "They are the only people I've ever met who work equally diligently on behalf of Democrats and Republicans."

Working effectively and loyally to execute the president's priorities, the OMB culture puts a priority on trustworthiness. There is, perhaps, no more discreet institution in the White House or in the entire executive branch. Although various National Security Councils have been known to leak or be tight with information, there is no such variation with OMB. There is virtually no history of a porous OMB. Staff is known for their ability to hold information close. Reporters repeatedly express frustration at their inability to obtain access to key policy and budget details being developed at OMB. When budget details are dispensed ahead of official release times, it is generally the result of a policy decision at the most senior level in the White House to obtain early or favorable coverage of their policies, not the result of an intentional disclosure at lower levels in the organization.

In general, OMB staffers, particularly in the National Security Programs division, are party to a wide range of information that would produce headlines, were it to become public. It simply does not happen; that is a key element in the organizational culture. The reason for this organizational discretion is relatively straightforward. If the organization came to be known as one that leaked information, it could not be trusted. That trust is the most critical commodity at OMB. If the president cannot trust OMB, he cannot rely on it to produce budgets and policy analysis he can use as part of his program. And, if the agencies with whom OMB works cannot trust OMB to safeguard the decision process and its contents, they will not trust it with the information OMB needs to do its job. Trustworthiness is built into the organizational responsibilities.

Many of these features of organizational culture can be grouped together in the word "professional." One of the distinguishing features of OMB professional culture is that the organizational positions are uniquely named: examiner, branch chief, deputy associate director. Even the policy positions have unusual names: program associate director (PAD), deputy director, director. While these titles have rough equivalents in standard executive branch agencies, their uniqueness sets OMB apart.

Coming into the organization, OMB staff is highly trained (frequently from public policy schools, political science or economics departments, or from the private sector). The OMB culture does not include significant training in the form of time off for training programs. Rather, they are substantially trained on the job at OMB. Many of them hit the ground running, handed responsibility for agency budgets and programs with little prior knowledge. Examiners pride themselves on getting up to speed quickly and eventually knowing nearly as much about agency programs and processes as the agencies themselves. As the examiners move up the institutional hierarchy, they acquire broader experience of agencies and programs. Branch chiefs and deputy associate directors are frequently promoted to these senior executive service positions from the career staff.

Because much of the OMB staff moves across subject matter and agency issues and because many of them remain with the organization throughout their professional careers, they are highly experienced, which is another part of the professional ethos of the OMB culture. An incoming policy official finds that he or she can rely on the staff to produce top-quality work swiftly and reliably. Moreover, because of their professional knowledge and experience, OMB staffers are precisely the kind of official executive branch agencies like to recruit. Lateral movement of the OMB staff to the budget and planning offices of agencies occurs frequently, with two great advantages for the hiring agency: they are certain to be obtaining a skilled, experienced staffer and, as a bonus, they have a staffer who knows its unique culture and has access to OMB. As one former associate director put it: "Your single biggest asset is the OMB career staff . . . [the DADs are] smart, experienced, accustomed to transition and ready to help you. Use them. You can trust them completely. The OMB staff is the most effective, analytic, pragmatic, and discreet group in government."[10]

The OMB organizational culture is also skeptical. At times, the most respected examiners are described as "junkyard dogs" in terms of their attitude toward agencies. Skepticism is a key value; no agency proposal or budget is taken on faith. No proposal is automatically accepted and approved. The staff is prepared to dig in hard, raise tough questions, and demand more information. In general, OMB staff suspect that agencies do not conduct adequately detailed analysis of their program and budget proposals, that they seek more funding than they need, and do not execute policy effectively or efficiently, until proven otherwise.

As a result, throughout the government, the OMB organizational default position is seen as "No." This characteristic can be of enormous value to a White House, as agency willingness to follow an administration's agenda is not always a given. It can also have a downside for the White House, by stimulating excess friction with agencies and resistance to White House priorities. The best OMB staffers learn how to manage this duality both to restrain agency independence and resistance and to encourage agency responsiveness to the White House agenda.

The OMB organizational culture is also characterized by pride. The staff is in a unique position for civil servants. They work for the president, not a federal department. They have unusual access across a range of policies and processes not available to other agency staff, sometimes including policy staff. The OMB examiners, branch chiefs, and deputy associate directors participate in senior-level meetings in the Cabinet Room, the Situation Room, and interagency deliberations covering virtually every aspect of government operations. They become part of crisis management teams for situations in Iraq, Afghanistan, and Pakistan. They plan emergency budgets for major U.S. national security operations. They have immense authority over agency planning and budgeting, with White House access and cachet. And, at the same time, they are civil servants, career officials across administrations. Few agency officials have this level of experience and access on a regular basis, which can lead to a certain amount of pride in the OMB staff.

Finally, like any organization, these characteristics of OMB culture can also make the organization insular, or turned in on itself at times. The organization is structured in a way that parallels executive branch agencies. As a result, the internal culture does not always promote cross-agency perspectives and knowledge. Although this is not unique to OMB, it can be an organizational handicap when major policy issues like terrorism, proliferation, postconflict reconstruction, or homeland security cut across agency boundaries. The OMB has found it difficult to carry out true cross-agency resource planning on a systematic basis because of this stovepiping.

In addition, much of the OMB staff see issues from a budgetary perspective rather than a policy perspective. This can lead to a focus and concern with the budgetary tradeoffs and efficiency issues, but does not always include a focus on policy priorities. That focus is more the concern of senior policy officials, both inside and outside OMB. Moreover, the budget process and focus of OMB, combined with the speed with which it must operate, comes at the cost of being able to plan strategically and think long term. There is often not time at the organization to focus on the future and carry out long-term planning.

OMB AND NATIONAL SECURITY

In the area of foreign policy and national security, OMB's National Security Programs office has responsibility for diplomacy, foreign assistance, defense, intelligence, and veterans affairs budgets, and legislation. It is organized into two units: the International Affairs Division and the National Security Division. International Affairs (150), in turn, has two branches, one for state and one for economic affairs. The National Security Division has four branches: Command, control, communications, computers, and intelligence; operations and support; force structure and investment; and veterans affairs and defense health. Each of these branches distributes to staff the responsibility for different agency budgets or program areas. The OMB's involvement with the national security agency budget processes takes different forms, depending on the agency in question.

Homeland security programs and agencies, however, are not concentrated in one resource management organization (RMO). Instead, like homeland security programs themselves, they are scattered among the existing RMOs, with central responsibility for the Department of Homeland Security located in the RMO for "general government." A deputy associate director is responsible for coordinating homeland security budgets.

International Affairs (150 Account)

International affairs agency budgets are handled like most other federal agency budgets, though this process has evolved over time. Typically, the budget for the State Department operations is prepared internally by the agency and transmitted to OMB sometime in September. Similarly, the USAID budget, covering development assistance, USAID operating expenses, and other USAID programs is transmitted separately from the State Department by September.

The uneven integration of international affairs agencies and budgeting, however, led to changes in the internal State Department/USAID budget process during the 1990s, which, in turn, slowed part of the international affairs budget submission to OMB. The secretary of state was directly responsible for a significant part of non-USAID foreign assistance program funds (such as Foreign Military Financing [FMF], International Military Education and Training [IMET], Economic Support Funds [ESF], counterterrorism, nonproliferation, counternarcotics, non-UN international organizations, and peacekeeping activities). In addition, several other foreign policy agencies do not report to the secretary of state and present their budgets separately to OMB.

In the early 1990s, the new State Department Office of Resources, Plans, and Policies (S/RPP), which reported to the secretary, began to coordinate budget planning for USAID and State and to hold budget hearings for other international affairs agencies to present their budget proposals to senior State Department officials. These internal reviews and hearings led to the secretary's recommendations to OMB on funding levels for all international affairs budgets, which generally arrived later in the fall, sometimes as late as November. This late transmittal made it difficult for OMB to move to the next stage of its budget review.[11] Moreover, the secretary's views were not authoritative for all international affairs agencies. As a result, OMB continued to deal separately with the budget submissions from international affairs agencies that did not report to the secretary of state, including USAID, acting as the de facto integrator of the international affairs budget function.

Early in the second Bush administration, the State Department created a Bureau of Resource Management, led by an assistant secretary, which tightened coordination between State and USAID's budget planning. The OMB remained involved in these more integrated internal hearings. The coordination grew even closer with the creation of the Office of the Director of Foreign Assistance (F) at State, which virtually integrated State and USAID budget planning. The OMB continued, however, to deal directly with the other, non-State/USAID international affairs agencies. The appointment of a second deputy secretary of state for management and resources in 2009 further tightened the integration of budget planning, at least between State and USAID.[12]

As the elements of the international affairs budget are received, they are distributed to ten to fifteen budget examiners in the OMB international affairs division, each of whom "scrubs" a particular account or agency budget. The "scrub" includes hearings or meetings of an hour to a full day with State, USAID, and other international affairs program and budget personnel.

The hearings force agencies to explain budget requests for which there may not be adequate justification. The hearings also can provide an opportunity to make sure White House policy preferences are reflected in agency budgets. Without this, budget requests may reflect only the agency preferences and not White House priorities. The OMB hearings can begin a process of bargaining with agencies to ensure that White House policy goals are adequately funded.[13]

A director's review, based on the earlier hearings, is conducted in November and early December to examine a budget options book prepared by the OMB staff. It is a closed meeting between the career OMB staff and senior OMB policy officials that generally does not include other White House or agency officials.[14] From this review, an OMB director's letter, known as the pass back, is sent to the international affairs agencies around Thanksgiving. State, USAID, and the other Function 150 agencies review the pass back and decide which decisions they will accept and which they wish to appeal.

Senior-level appeals meetings do occur and often must be resolved by the OMB director, the president, or the latter's designee.[15] Many of these meetings involve only the president, the vice president, the White House senior staff, the OMB director, PAD, and staff. Some cabinet-level secretaries, however, seek a presidential meeting to clarify agency budget priorities directly, appeal for a higher level of spending, or simply to have face time with the president. In the Bush administration, Secretaries of State Colin Powell and Condoleezza Rice won significant budget increases through such meetings.[16] Not surprisingly, the budgetary endgame in the White House is an intense moment in the process.[17]

National Defense (050 Account)

OMB's relationship with the Department of Defense (DOD) differs significantly from the process used with international affairs agencies. Beginning in the 1970s, with some interruptions, OMB staff has been integrated earlier and more deeply into the internal budget process at DOD, more so than with virtually any other federal agency. The central budget planning system for DOD, the Planning, Programming, Budgeting System (PPBS), is lengthy and elaborate. This OMB/DOD interaction is sometimes referred to as the joint review of the DOD budget. This interaction generally takes place in the summer, as issue groups begin to discuss major budget questions for the services and across the services and start to lay out decision priorities for the secretary of defense. The OMB examiners actively participate in these cross-service/office of the secretary groups, providing the White House's analytical and programmatic views.

There has been much discussion over the years about the advisability of this joint review. For OMB, it has some distinct advantages. The defense budget is the largest and most complex on the discretionary side of federal spending. Waiting until final decisions are made inside DOD and come to OMB in September would put OMB under intense pressure, given the need to close a final budget by the end of the year and the difficulties reversing internal DOD decisions. The OMB's defense staff is small, at roughly forty-five people, making it difficult to scrutinize every part of DOD's budget request. Early identification of the key issues, and early participation by OMB staff in the DOD process, allows the White House to focus on priority programs and policies. It makes it possible for the White House at an early stage to insert key programs, views, and policies that DOD might not rank highly into the DOD budget process. And it gives the White House early access to the DOD process before internal negotiations have locked down decisions that are hard to reverse.

The disadvantage is that DOD can co-opt OMB, gaining approval of DOD programs and policies ahead of the other agencies and before OMB has conducted its own hearings and director's review process. This is likely to limit OMB's options at later stages in the budget process.

There are advantages and disadvantages for DOD, as well. The advantage is to expose OMB to DOD preferences early in the process and obtain White House agreement, rather than wait until late in the process when negative OMB reactions could lead to chaos in internal DOD planning. The disadvantage is that OMB gets an early view of DOD decisions and options before DOD has finalized its own views. Later in the process, once DOD decisions have been set, OMB can continue to raise alternative budget options in the director's review, which can lead to pass-back decisions that are based on OMB's knowledge of options that DOD might have rejected in its internal process.

Because of the joint review, DOD does not submit a formal budget proposal to OMB by the September deadline. The OMB/DOD interaction at this stage does, however, allow the White House to bring its priorities to bear in DOD defense budget decisions. The OMB holds fall hearings with DOD and military service staff on key budget issues, analyzes the key budget and policy issues that emerge, and conducts a director's review. That review generally concerns issues OMB does not feel were resolved through OMB's involvement in the DOD process, or issues the White House wants to inject into that process. The director sends a pass-back letter on these issues, which usually leads to a DOD appeal. As with the secretary of state, the secretary of defense generally meets with the OMB director and with the president on these final issues.[18]

Homeland Security

The OMB's involvement with homeland security budgets is different, again, from the other two processes. Homeland security is not a budget function. The Department of Homeland Security (DHS) does not have responsibility for all homeland security-related funding. Other agencies such as DOD and Health and Human Services carry out a number of homeland security programs and activities. In addition, nearly half of the DHS budget is committed to programs that are not pure homeland security activities, such as Coast Guard rescue-at-sea responsibilities.[19] As a result, the White House involvement with homeland security budgets is complicated.

The complexities have made OMB a key player in integrating the homeland security budgets because it is the only institution in the executive branch that has the cross-agency responsibilities that can pull all the elements together. The OMB played a key role in the creation of DHS in 2004, helping the small White House planning team identify which parts of federal spending might be considered part of the homeland security budget. The OMB staff continues to analyze homeland security spending across agencies and prepares an annual analysis of that spending for the annual *Analytical Perspectives* volume of the president's budget request.

DHS prepares its agency budget request, which it submits to OMB in September; OMB and the Homeland Security Council staff in the White House coordinate the related budget requests from other agencies in preparing the annual analysis.[20] As a result, the OMB involvement in homeland security budgeting is neither as structured as its participation in the DOD process, nor as traditional as its role in international affairs budgets.

The traditional OMB process does prevail with respect to DHS itself. Budget preparation is done inside the agency, with a budget delivered in September, followed by hearings with the department. Because of the breadth of homeland security programs across departments, however, the OMB hearings cover other departmental budgets, including DOD, Justice/FBI, Health and Human Services, the Centers for Disease Control and Prevention, Agriculture, Labor, Interior, and the Environmental Protection Agency, among others. The new OMB Division for Homeland Security coordinates those hearings with the OMB divisions responsible for the other agencies. Pass back is given to several agencies with respect to their parts of the homeland security budget.

Intelligence

The OMB's involvement with intelligence budgeting is the responsibility of the command, control, communications, computers, and intelligence branch of the National Security Programs division. This branch has a small, highly cleared staff who are knowledgeable in the various intelligence disciplines and generally have a professional background in the intelligence community (IC). For many years, OMB's involvement in the IC's budget processes was minimal. Because 80 percent of intelligence funding is the responsibility of the DOD, the IC/DOD relationship is critical to budget planning for intelligence. The IC and DOD intelligence agencies generally resisted OMB involvement in this relationship.

The coordination of intelligence budgets at the White House level has been challenging. All intelligence budget submissions do pass through the OMB. However, historically, each agency's budget request was submitted in a different format from the others, with different categories and definitions of spending, which made it difficult to establish a crosswalk for the IC request as a whole. Nevertheless, OMB dealt with a growing number of intelligence budget issues during the 1990s. Senior OMB officials were regularly in discussion with the director of central intelligence (dual-hatted as the director of the CIA) on the overall level of intelligence funding in the post-Cold War era. Discussions at the working level with the DCI's community staff (which was responsible for IC management and cross-agency program and budgeting) covered such issues as the balance among intelligence disciplines and skills, and intelligence personnel requirements for the post-Cold War era. The OMB is a regular participant in White House discussions and decision making on covert action findings and operations.

From the public point of view, most of this involvement is beneath the radar screen because intelligence budgets are largely buried in other agency budgets, mostly at the Department of Defense, and are highly classified. In the 1990s, however, spending and budget issues at the National Reconnaissance Organization (NRO) brought greater visibility to intelligence budget issues in general. They became more visible with the 1994 Senate Select Committee on Intelligence staff investigation into the costs of the new NRO headquarters. This investigation revealed that the $350 million budget for the new headquarters building had not been reported in full to the Congress or even inside the executive branch.

The headquarters issue was followed by disclosures in 1995 involving NRO satellite program funding practices. In general, NRO funded future satellite programs in advance, known as forward funding. Essentially, NRO appropriations were requested and received for future spending on satellites. In 1995, Congress found that the size of this forward funding was so large and so slowly obligated that it rescinded these funds from satellite programs, used them to fund other defense programs, and demanded a Pentagon/CIA review of NRO's financial management.[21]

The growing number of intelligence budget issues in the 1990s led to closer OMB scrutiny of IC planning and budgeting in general. The intelligence budget system changed again with the creation of the Office of the Director of National Intelligence (ODNI) in 2004, which assumed and significantly expanded on the coordination and budgeting responsibilities formerly held by the DCI. The ODNI was given specific responsibility for providing budgetary guidance to the sixteen agencies participating in the national intelligence program (NIP). Based on their budget submissions, he is then to "develop and determine an annual consolidated National Intelligence Program budget."[22] The ODNI was also given the authority to direct the apportionment of appropriated funds to these agencies.

Both of these roles have brought OMB more directly into intelligence budget planning than had previously been the case. The OMB has helped ODNI develop an integrated budget planning system to examine the intelligence agencies' budget submissions, and has participated in a joint intelligence budget review with ODNI. Because OMB is the office responsible for providing apportionment of funds to agencies, the ODNI direction of apportionment is worked with the OMB intelligence staff. The OMB has been more deeply involved with this process since that time.[23]

Agency Cross-Cut Reviews

In addition to its focus on national security agency budgets, OMB also carries out budget reviews that cut across agency budgets, known as agency cross-cuts. The OMB agency cross-cuts include reviews of such policy areas as counternarcotics, counterterrorism, and counterproliferation programs. The purpose of a cross-cut is to gather data and program information on a policy area in which several agencies are involved. The goal is usually to identify the level of agency effort, gaps in program coverage, and duplications of activity.

The cross-cut process can ask agencies to identify spending and programs in the policy area in question. Agencies sometimes resist such a data call, arguing that it is too difficult to separate out programs dedicated to the specific policy area from broader agency activities. The Defense Department, for example, has argued that much of the force structure could be considered an investment in counterproliferation, as preventing proliferation is one mission of the forces.

The OMB staff will then analyze the agency programs, identify gaps and duplications in coverage, and prepare a review document similar to those prepared for director's review meetings. That document may simply review agency spending and identify overlaps and gaps. It might also serve as a budget planning document, leading to a cross-agency request for funding, commonly through a supplemental budget request. Such an options paper might also be part of a director's review of agency budgets, leading to funding and program decisions to be included in the pass-back letters to agencies.

BUDGETARY ROLE OF THE NATIONAL SECURITY COUNCIL

The National Security Council (NSC) is the principal White House institution that is responsible for coordinating national security strategy, advising the president on national security issues, overseeing policy implementation through the interagency process, and responding to national security crises.[24] The NSC does not have a formal role in the OMB budget process, nor do NSC staff members typically have expertise in resource planning. Nevertheless, virtually every decision made in the NSC framework has resource implications. Because of this, OMB and NSC interact constantly on resource issues.

Although the missions of NSC and OMB differ, NSC views and interagency discussions in the NSC framework can have important implications for the contents of the president's budget. In return, budget decisions made in the OMB process can facilitate or limit NSC and interagency policy options.[25] NSC views on program priorities can sometimes differ from the programs and funding levels requested by national security agencies and departments. These views reflect presidential program and funding priorities, or those of senior NSC officials, which are often expressed as if they were presidential priorities.

The NSC process for articulating and communicating these views to OMB can differ from administration to administration and from year to year within an administration.[26] Sometimes there is no internal coordination at NSC, and budget views are simply expressed by the different NSC offices, if they choose to do so. At other times, an NSC senior director may be tasked to gather budget recommendations from the other NSC offices, and will set priorities in consultation with the deputy national security advisor, and communicate those views to OMB. These views are usually communicated to the RMO for national security programs at OMB. The OMB might also invite affected NSC directors and senior directors to attend director's review meetings to express their views.

Given the irregularity of this process, OMB can often receive multiple, even conflicting budgetary recommendations from the NSC. This is especially true for international affairs budgets (Function 150). NSC responsibilities in foreign policy are distributed widely. Regional desks will have views about priority programs and spending levels within their region. Functional offices may have differing priorities with respect to such cross-agency programs as counternarcotics funding, democracy promotion, or postconflict reconstruction and stabilization. During the Clinton administration, for example, the senior director for global affairs would recommend a very high level of funding for counternarcotics programs but more restricted support for democracy promotion. At the same time, the senior director for democracy might recommend a reverse priority.

The NSC/OMB relationship is not restricted to the preparation of the president's budget. NSC is the critical agency for crisis response and planning, and for preparing the agenda for presidential travel and visitors. Both of these activities take place outside the budget cycle, but can clearly have significant budget implications. As a result, the NSC/OMB relationship is constant throughout the year. Lacking a resource planning culture, however, the NSC can frequently fail to make the connection between these responsibilities and the budgetary requirements. At times the NSC staff may take actions that involve budgetary obligations without realizing the budgetary implications. In 1994, for example, the NSC Near East desk coordinated commitments to a visiting Middle East head of state that included the forgiveness of that country's bilateral debt to the United States, not knowing that debt forgiveness required a budgetary action that had not been included in the budget that had just been submitted to Congress. Several months later, preceding a state visit by that leader, NSC staff became aware of that budgetary requirement, which lead to a rapid revision to the president's budget request that was already pending before the Congress.[27]

Occasionally, an NSC office might seek to coordinate program and budget planning separately from the normal OMB process, which can lead to conflicts. For example, in 1996 the NSC senior director for global affairs sought to coordinate a supplemental budget request for counterterrorism programs, outside normal OMB budget planning channels. Conversations at a senior level between OMB and NSC reversed this course, making OMB the coordinator of the budget supplemental planning effort.[28]

The NSC/OMB relationship is critical to successfully planning the president's policy priorities. When the two organizations work in tandem, the White House can exercise considerable influence over national security agency planning. When they do not, budget decisions may not reflect presidential priorities, or they may actually frustrate their achievement.[29] Moreover, the NSC historically has focused on short-term crises and the requirements generated by international events and the president's schedule. It has little commitment to or expertise on long-term planning, linked to resource decisions. As a result, there is not a consistent, institutionalized relationship between the two organizations.[30]

OMB, NSC, AND THE INTERAGENCY PROCESS

In the twenty-first century, the agenda for U.S. national security policy has both expanded and diversified. Terrorist threats, the proliferation of nuclear weapons, global economic instability, clashes of religion and identity, failures and weaknesses of governance in a number of countries, as well as climate change, migration, global trafficking in drugs, people, and weapons, and the risks of infectious disease are all now central concerns of U.S. national security strategy. The common characteristic of these issues is that the responsibility for dealing with them cuts across U.S. government agencies.

The processes and structures of the U.S. government are not yet well suited to these interagency tasks.[31] In particular, strategic planning capabilities at OMB and the NSC are weak or nonexistent. There is no systematic cross-agency process in the White House for giving agencies guidance for applying resource planning to strategic priorities. And the OMB and NSC coordination processes for planning, implementation, and resourcing of cross-agency operations are weak, at best. Recent experience suggests that OMB together with NSC can and should play a more central role in providing such planning, guidance, and operational oversight.

Both NSC and OMB operate in a short-term time frame. Moreover, while the NSC writes a national security strategy and has written other strategic documents that focus on such policy priorities as homeland security, proliferation, and terrorism, these documents have been disconnected from White House or agency budget planning, providing little resource guidance.[32]

At the level of overall national security strategic planning, there have been proposals to strengthen this process.[33] Reforms could include a statutory requirement for a quadrennial review of national security, similar to the quadrennial defense review carried out at the Defense Department. They could also include a biennial, classified White House guidance to agencies that would detail specific tasks by agency and the budget resources that they should request to perform those tasks, particularly with respect to national security priorities such as terrorism, proliferation, development, or fragile state support. And the reforms could include a statutory requirement for every OMB to transmit to Congress an annual budget volume covering the gamut of national security programs: diplomacy, foreign assistance, defense, intelligence, and homeland security. This volume could discuss the links among agency budgets that have focused the interagency process on the administration's strategic priorities.

Institutionalizing a more systematic and structured national security planning and guidance process, especially through statute, would not be easy. However, if recent experience is any indication, ad hoc White House efforts to integrate agency planning and resourcing with respect to terrorism and homeland security, and contingency operations/postconflict stabilization and reconstruction have fallen short of what is needed for effective central steering of the interagency process. Moreover, broader ad hoc efforts to integrate OMB and NSC deliberations on policy and budgets may be effective for a single administration or White House team, but they do not have continuity across administrations. Each new White House has to recreate the internal White House and interagency relationships from scratch.

Counterterrorism and Homeland Security Policy

The Intelligence Reform and Terrorism Prevention Act of 2004 legislated a requirement for interagency planning with respect to U.S. counterterrorism policy and operations. The act created the ODNI and gave the DNI the authority to approve and coordinate the budgets of the intelligence community agencies. The act also created the National Counterterrorism Center (NCTC), which reported to the DNI on counterterrorism intelligence but reported to the president with respect to the requirement that it "conduct strategic operational planning for counterterrorism activities, integrating all instruments of national power, including diplomatic, financial, military, intelligence, homeland security, and law enforcement activities within and among agencies."[34]

The follow-on NSC directive on counterterrorism programs (NSPD46/HSPD 15) tasked NCTC to prepare a strategic plan and agency guidance for the counterterror effort through a National Implementation Plan (NIP) for counterterrorism. The plan was to focus on denying terrorists resources, preventing the proliferation of weapons of mass destruction, defeating terrorist organizations, countering state and nonstate support for terrorists, and countering ideologic support for terrorists. This tasking led to an interagency planning process and guidance to agencies on counterterrorism priorities and tasks, which was agreed to by two hundred department and agency representatives. The classified guidance was drawn up in 2005–6, providing more than five hundred detailed taskings to agencies engaged in counterterror operations.

The NIP for counterterrorism is the most ambitious effort to date to provide cross-agency direction for a key area of national security policy. While NCTC had the formal responsibility for the plan, the NSC was directly involved in the planning effort at the level of the deputy national security advisor level. The structure did not explicitly provide a role for OMB. It was, however, deliberately included in the planning process in order to ensure that agency budget planning incorporated the priorities and tasks set out in the guidance and to allow OMB to track these commitments through the budget process.

The evaluation of the NIP process was mixed. There were too many priorities in the guidance and agencies resisted the process, fearing that the interagency priorities would require reductions in funding for other agency programs. The NSC and OMB staffs committed to the process were small, making follow-up difficult. In the end, it was not clear that many agency priorities changed as a result of the process or the guidance. Nevertheless, the NIP process showed that such an interagency planning process is possible.[35]

The Homeland Security Council (HSC) in the White House is a related precedent for interagency planning and budgeting. The HSC was created a year before DHS. Its task was to integrate planning and programs of the many federal agencies involved in homeland security. Even after the creation of the department, a significant number of homeland security programs continue to be implemented by other government departments, notably DOD and HHS.[36] The HSC played a coordinating role for overall policy and resource planning, working directly with OMB on the resource side. Over time, however, this coordinating role shrank, as the department has become the central agency for the majority of homeland security policy and programs. The OMB continues to have a key role in coordinating interagency budgets, however, through its division for homeland security.[37] However, even inside OMB, other divisions are responsible for agency budgets that are not part of DHS.[38] Moreover, in the Obama administration, the HSC has now been absorbed into the NSC structure, leaving its coordinating role on policy, priority setting, and resource planning unclear.[39]

There are important lessons from the NIP and homeland security cases. Even with a statutory requirement for planning, unless the tasking explicitly includes the NSC and OMB, the risk is that agencies will not be responsive to central tasking and guidance on a key interagency policy priority. Moreover, staffing at both OMB and NSC needs to be sufficient to oversee a planning process and provide the detailed follow-through. In addition, there needs to be some kind of formal reporting requirement to the Congress to ensure accountability for the results of the planning and agency guidance.

Contingency Operations and Postconflict Reconstruction Policy

Overseas contingency operations and postconflict reconstruction and stabilization provide a second important case study in the role of OMB and NSC in coordinating the interagency process.[40] Although much attention has focused on U.S. experience in Iraq and Afghanistan, these were not the first instances of a need for interagency coordination of contingency operations and postconflict planning for stability and economic recovery. During the Clinton administration, the experiences of U.S. involvement in Haiti, Somalia, Northern Iraq, and Bosnia stimulated an effort to define how the interagency process might function more systematically in responding to what was called complex contingency operations, involving both the military and civilian agencies. Presidential Decision Directive (PDD)-56 gave the NSC the lead in overseeing a planning process for such operations. PDD-56 dealt explicitly with the need for interagency coordination of budgets and authorities and created an interagency coordination process with responsibility for advance contingency planning, operational oversight, and resource coordination. PDD-56 was honored in the breach, however, in subsequent Clinton administration contingency operations, which continued to be planned and overseen in an ad hoc manner. As the RAND Corporation noted, "successive administrations have treated each new mission as if it were the first and, more importantly, as it if were the last."[41]

PDD-56 was rejected by the Bush administration. As a consequence, the invasions of Afghanistan and Iraq continued the ad hoc precedent. Both operations faltered because of insufficient planning for the civilian/military interface and for postcombat stability, governance, and economic recovery. In the Afghan case, after an initial focus on post-Taliban governance and an initial infusion of international funding, responsibility for planning, military operations, and longer-term funding were handed over to the DOD, with little or no White House follow-up oversight.[42] Before the war in Iraq began, the Department of Defense, not NSC, was given responsibility for postwar planning (NSPD-24). The creation of the Coalition Provisional Authority (CPA) in April 2003 was a response to the realization that postconflict requirements in Iraq would be more demanding than anticipated. However, that office continued to report through the secretary of defense. There was scarcely any actual planning for the U.S. role in postconflict stabilization; an early study of governance, social, and economic issues prepared by the State Department was set aside by DOD officials.[43]

Military planners had assumed that a relatively rapid U.S. withdrawal would take place, with Iraqis assuming responsibility for security. No funding was in place to support a longer occupation. On the reconstruction side, the administration assumed that any postconflict crisis would be short-term and humanitarian in nature. Economic activity would resume quickly and reconstruction needs would be handled by the Iraqi government and bureaucracy, funded by sufficient oil revenues. No U.S. or international reconstruction funding was in place as the need for such assistance became clear. The U.S-run institutions created to administer postconflict stabilization and reconstruction operations were, as a result, ad hoc, from the initial Office of Reconstruction and Humanitarian Assistance (ORHA), to the CPA, to a new State Department office to support the new Iraqi government (the IRMO or Iraq Reconstruction Management Office) to the Iraq Transition Assistance Office (ITAO).

Given the initial leadership role of DOD, the relationship between State/USAID and Defense was contentious and noncommunicative for much of the first two years of the occupation. Lacking training and expertise for this task, DOD struggled to deliver both security and reconstruction assistance. Lacking authority, funding, and personnel, State and USAID were continually challenged in the field. The policies, programs, and projects for stability, reconstruction, governance, and military operations evolved constantly; personnel delivering those policies were often inexperienced and they rotated in and out of the country constantly.[44] Program implementation, especially for governance and reconstruction, was slow, chaotic, and largely ineffective.

The coordination and resourcing weaknesses were largely the responsibility of the White House, which did not have an integrated OMB/NSC capacity to develop policy, plan resources, conduct oversight over programs and projects, and authoritatively resolve disputes among agencies. The NSC did not create a working group responsible for oversight for more than a year and was constantly changing these structures thereafter. The OMB budgeting for stabilization and counterinsurgency operations was done on an incremental basis, with a constantly shifting definition of goals and objectives.[45]

The many problems in Afghanistan and Iraq led the Bush administration to develop a more systematic approach to interagency coordination and planning, though it still did not focus primary responsibility on NSC or OMB. At the end of 2005, DOD increased its focus on postconflict tasks, issuing a directive that put "stabilization and reconstruction operations" on a par with combat operations.[46] At the same time, the NSC issued a new

National Security Presidential Directive (NSPD-44) (Management of Interagency Efforts Concerning Reconstruction and Stabilization) that designated a new State Department Office of the Coordinator for Reconstruction and Stabilization (S/CRS) as the coordinator for interagency reconstruction and stability operations. S/CRS was to be the "(i) focal point . . . to coordinate and strengthen efforts of the United States Government to prepare, plan for, and conduct reconstruction and stabilization assistance and related activities in a range of situations that require the response capabilities of multiple United States Government entities and (ii) to harmonize such efforts with U.S. military plans and operations. . . . The Secretary of State shall coordinate and lead integrated United States Government efforts, involving all U.S. Departments and Agencies with relevant capabilities, to prepare, plan for, and conduct stabilization and reconstruction activities."[47]

Although the S/CRS office was given some oversight responsibility with respect to resolving interagency funding disputes for such operations, its working relationship with the NSC and OMB in the interagency process, however, remained somewhat undefined. The directive clearly intended to limit the White House coordinating role of the White House. The S/CRS was "to recommend when to establish a limited-time PCC-level [NSC Policy Coordination Committee] group to focus on a country or region facing major reconstruction and stabilization challenges." A standing PCC for reconstruction and stabilization operations was also created, chaired by the S/CRS coordinator.

The NSPD-44 structure and process has clearly not succeeded. The S/CRS office was integrated into State's new Office of the Director of Foreign Assistance in 2007 but remained a lower-tier office at State with weak authority to coordinate interagency efforts. Even inside State, the S/CRS authorities conflict with the role and responsibilities of the powerful regional bureaus and country desks, as well as those of the USAID Offices of Transition Initiatives (OTI), and Foreign Disaster Assistance (OFDA). Outside State, it was far from clear that the other departments of government, notably DOD, were prepared to accept S/CRS leadership in any specific contingency.[48]

Repeated requests to Congress to create a contingency fund for S/CRS field operations were rejected, although the DOD was granted authority to transfer up to $200 million over two years to State for stability and reconstruction-related activities.[49] S/CRS budgets remained small as did its staff size, which depended heavily on its ability to obtain detailees from other agencies, until 2009.[50] In February 2008, the State Department sought $248 million in funding for a civilian stabilization initiative. This initiative would include a two-hundred-and-fifty-member active response corps, and a two-thousand-member standby response corps, created through S/CRS and drawn from a number of agencies: State, USAID, Justice, Commerce, Treasury, Agriculture, Health and Human Services, and Homeland Security. This civilian force would carry out actual reconstruction and stabilization operations.[51]

While the active and reserve forces may see the light of day, it is difficult to envisage S/CRS as the interagency coordinator described in NSPD-44. As an office in a single agency, its coordination and integration responsibilities are simply not at the right level to be effective. The lesson of Iraq and of S/CRS is that one federal department is simply not capable of coordinating the actions of another federal department, especially if, as in the case of DOD, one has significantly greater human and fiscal resources than the other. Should the leadership of these agencies be at loggerheads, a situation that clearly prevailed during the build-up to the Iraq invasion, there is little hope of a resolution without a significant White House role.[52] For postconflict operations, it makes more sense to create a new senior director position at NSC with responsibility for contingency planning and operational oversight, interagency coordination, and oversight of implementation. This office would develop presidential guidance for such operations and integrate interagency planning through the existing Policy Coordinating Committee for Reconstruction and Stabilization Operations. Operations would be conducted by the agencies, but NSC would retain a policy integration and oversight role, while interagency crisis planning teams could be created to develop campaign plans.[53] Both the State Department and DOD should plug into this architecture through their current postconflict stabilization and reconstruction offices (policy and JCS at Defense; S/CRS at State).

The problem of ensuring adequate and flexible funding for such operations, the coordination of agency budgets for this purpose, and the resolution of disputes over resources and authorities between agencies remains, however. It was evident in the Iraq case that the White House did not anticipate the fiscal requirements for postconflict reconstruction and stabilization or the need to coordinate resource planning and resolve disputes. Reconstruction funds were inadequate at the start and were only budgeted for eight months after the invasion. Beyond the initial $18.4 billion appropriated for reconstruction in 2003, Congress has only reluctantly provided small amounts of additional reconstruction funding.[54] As the Defense Science Board put it only eighteen months after the end of Iraq combat, "We have learned to provide adequate resources for 'as long as it takes' for combat, but we often don't provide adequate resources for a sufficient period for stabilization and reconstruction."[55] Moreover there were consistent conflicts between DOD, USAID, and State over the implementation of these funds on the ground.[56]

There is clearly a need for a more centrally coordinated White House resource planning process for stabilization and reconstruction operations, with OMB playing a central role. While specific operations cannot necessarily be anticipated, funds are needed to create the civilian capability that can plan and put in place a U.S. government response capability. More broadly, there is a need for some kind of contingency funding to enable a quick U.S. government response to the needs of a failing or postconflict state.[57] There is a precedent for such contingency funding in the emergency refugees and migration account (ERMA) at State, and the disaster assistance (OFDA) and transition initiatives (OTI) accounts at USAID, all of which are unearmarked, no-year funds available long term for response to emerging crises. The OMB should be linked closely to NSC in carrying out such contingency funding planning as well as in resolving disputes over funding among agencies.

THE OVERALL OMB/NSC ROLE

There remains the broader question of the role of OMB and NSC in overall strategic planning, as discussed above. The lessons of counterterror and postconflict planning and funding reinforce the need for a more central White House responsibility for strategic and resource planning across agencies. Neither NSC nor OMB currently possesses the personnel numbers and skills needed for this task. To carry out a national security strategy review and classified resource guidance, both agencies need to expand staff to include long-term planning capabilities.

In addition, both offices need a less ad hoc, more institutionalized process for working together, both on crisis response and on long-term planning. The OMB staff should be included in NSC structures and processes at all levels, from principals' and deputies' meetings, down through NSC working groups, to ensure a resource dimension is present in all policy discussions. Equally, NSC staff should be regular participants in the OMB process, for hearings, director's review, and cross-cut budget analyses. Because such cross-participation is not certain from administration to administration, consideration should be given to legislation that ensures that this process transfers across administrations. Ultimately, the best guarantee that the White House can plan strategically, provide adequate guidance to agencies, and respond efficiently and effectively to crisis is if OMB and the NSC are joined at the hip.

NOTES

This chapter draws on Gordon Adams and Cindy Williams, *Buying National Security: How America Plans and Pays for Its Global Role and Safety at Home* (New York: Routledge, 2010).

Note on the interviews: As part of research for the book on which this chapter is based, the author conducted a number of interviews with serving government officials who requested confidentiality. These are referenced as "confidential interviews" in the notes. In addition, some of the material was drawn directly from the author's own experience while serving as associate director for national security and international affairs at OMB, which are referenced as "author's experience" in the notes.

1. Allen Schick, *The Federal Budget: Politics, Policy, Process*, 3rd ed. (Washington, DC: Brookings Institution Press, 2007), 17. The estimates were bound together but not analyzed or changed by the Treasury Department.

2. For a detailed discussion of the history of OMB, see Shelley Lynne Tomkin, *Inside OMB: Politics and Process in the President's Budget Office* (Armonk, NY: M. E. Sharpe, 1998), esp. chapter 3.

3. The OMB's responsibilities for defining and approving federal regulations, through the Office of Information and Regulatory Affairs (OIRA), is also an important function but is one that touches national security programs less, as those agencies engage in much less regulatory activity than domestic agencies. On OIRA's role, see Tomkin, *Inside OMB*, 203–16.

4. Tomkin, 3, describes this function as an institutional memory. The memory bank function is critical for incoming administrations, especially if the new chief executive and his/her staff have little executive branch or Washington, DC, experience.

5. The OMB played an important role in World War II, assisting the White House with war mobilization programs and activities. See Tomkin, *Inside OMB*, 36–37, 191.

6. Paul O'Neill, once deputy director of OMB, described OMB's capabilities as "neutral brilliance." Quoted in Tomkin, *Inside OMB*, 3.

7. Schick, *The Federal Budget*, 98.

8. Tomkin, *Inside OMB*, 94, 163–64, suggests this was a problem in the initial Reagan/Stockman forecasts, and in the way a sequester under Gramm-Rudman-Hollings was avoided in the late 1980s.

9. Council for Excellence in Government, "Survey of Associate Directors," in *Prunes Online*, Washington, DC: CEG, December 7, 2008, available at www.excellenceintransition.org/prune/TOCPruneJobs.cfm?navItemNumber59745.

10. Ibid.

11. The delay of the secretary's recommendations also reflected an expectation that the foreign assistance budget might receive less intensive OMB scrutiny if it was received late in the OMB budget process. Author's personal experience, 1993–97.

12. For additional detail on State budgeting and organization, see chapter 4, this volume.

13. See discussion below on agency cross-cuts and the national implementation plan for counterterrorism.

14. Administrations differ in this regard. During the Clinton presidency, on occasion, NSC directors or senior directors would attend director's review sessions on national security agency budgets by invitation from OMB.

15. In the George W. Bush administration, vice president Dick Cheney was frequently the ultimate decision maker on agency appeals.

16. Interviews with senior State Department budget officials, 2007–8.

17. Schick, *The Federal Budget*, 96, notes that "dozens of decisions are made in the home stretch, when all the numbers have been tallied and the deadline nears for sending the budget to the printer."

18. Starting in the early 2000s, the national security division at OMB also took on responsibility for reviewing the budgets of the nuclear programs at the Department of Energy and the Department of Veterans Affairs, as well as DOD. These reviews tend to take the more typical form used for other departments, with the agencies preparing the budget submission, which is then reviewed by OMB in the fall process.

19. See Cindy Williams, *Strengthening Homeland Security: Reforming Planning and Resource Allocation* (Washington, DC: IBM Center for the Business of Government, 2008).

20. Ibid.

21. See Walter Pincus, "Spy Agency Hoards Secret $1 Billion," *Washington Post*, September 24, 1995; "White House Decries NRO's $1 Billion Hoard," *Washington Post*, September 25, 1995; Walter Pincus, "House, Senate Panels Make More Cuts in NRO Budget," *Washington Post*, September 26, 1995; Dan Morgan and Walter Pincus, "$1.6 Billion in NRO Kitty Helped Appropriators Fund Pet Projects," *Washington Post*, October 5, 1995.

22. *Intelligence Reform and Terrorism Prevention Act of 2004*, PL 108-458, Section 102A.a.2.c.1.A. and B; and Mark Lowenthal, *Intelligence: From Secrets to Policy*, 4th ed. (Washington, DC: Congressional Quarterly Press, 2009), 33.

23. For more detail on OMB's role in intelligence budgeting, see Adams and Williams, *Buying National Security*, 120–40.

24. On the structure, functioning, and evolution of the NSC, see Alan G. Whittaker, Frederick C. Smith, and Ambassador Elizabeth McKune, *The National Security Policy Process: The National Security Council and Interagency System* (Washington, DC: National Defense University, ICAF, April 2007); Loch K. Johnson and Karl F. Inderfurth, *Fateful Decisions: Inside the National Security Council* (New York: Oxford University Press, 2004); David Rothkopf, *Running the World: The Inside Story of the National Security Council and the Architects of America's Power* (New York: Public Affairs, 2005); and Amy B. Zegart, *Flawed by Design: The Evolution of the CIA, JSC, and NSC* (Stanford, CA: Stanford University Press, 2000).

25. According to the National Security Act of 1947, NSC "shall advise the President with respect to the integration of domestic, foreign, and military policies related to the national security . . . [and execute] other functions the President may direct for the purpose of more effectively coordinating the policies and functions of the departments and agencies of the government relating to the national security." The OMB, according to its Circular A-11 "evaluates the effectiveness of agency programs, policies, and procedures, assesses competing funding demands among agencies, and sets funding priorities."

26. At various times in the Clinton administration, NSC would transmit a single document aggregating the views of the different offices, but generally without setting out clear priorities.

27. Author's experience.

28. Ibid.

29. See, for example, a proposal made by President Bush in his State of the Union speech in January 2008 regarding a broadening of educational benefits for military families. The proposed policy was not funded in the president's budget request transmitted to Congress in February 2008. It was apparently inserted in the speech without budgetary analysis in the Defense Department or any coordination with the OMB budget process. Michael Abramowitz and Robin Wright, "No Funds in Bush Budget for Troop-Benefits Plan," *Washington Post*, February 9, 2008; and Adams and Williams, *Buying National Security*, 245–54.

30. For further discussion of NSC long-term planning capabilities, see chapter 2, this volume. For proposed reforms of OBM strategic planning capabilities, see below.

31. Cindy Williams and Gordon Adams, *Strengthening Statecraft and Security: Reforming U.S. Planning and Resource Allocation*, Occasional paper, Cambridge, MA: MIT Security Studies Program, June 2008. A CSIS study put this requirement quite broadly: "The U.S. government currently lacks both the incentives and the capacity necessary to support strategic thinking and long-range planning in the national security arena." Clark Murdock and Michele Flournoy, *Beyond Goldwater-Nichols: U.S. Government and Defense Reform for a New Strategic Era*, Phase 2 Report (Washington, DC: July 2005), 27.

32. For details on the strategy documents that an administration is required by statute to transmit to the Congress, see Catherine Dale, "National Security Strategy: Legislative Mandates, Execution to Date, and Considerations for Congress," Report RL34505 (Washington, DC: Congressional Research Service, May 28, 2008).

33. See Williams and Adams, *Strengthening Statecraft and Security,* and Project on National Security Reform, *Forging a New Shield*, Washington, DC: December 2008.

34. Intelligence Reform and Terrorism Prevention Act, Section 1020, PL 108-458, December 17, 2004.

35. Confidential interviews.

36. See Williams and Adams, *Strengthening Statecraft and Security.*

37. Ibid.

38. Interviews with HSC, OMB, and DHS officials.

39. White House statement by the president on the White House Organization for Homeland Security and Counterterrorism, Press Release, May 26, 2009.

40. See Gordon Adams, "Post-Combat Stabilization and Reconstruction: The Lessons for U.S. Government Organization and National Security Resource Planning," in Ellen Laipson and Maureen S. Steinbruner, eds., *Iraq and America: Choices and Consequences* (Washington, DC: Henry L. Stimson Center, 2006); and Gordon Adams, "Stabilization and Reconstruction in Iraq," in Williams and Adams, *Strengthening Statecraft and Security.*

41. James Dobbins et al., *America's Role in Nation-Building: From Germany to Iraq* (Santa Monica, CA: RAND, 2003), xxv.

42. Interviews with White House and DOD staff.

43. See Bob Woodward, *Plan of Attack* (New York: Simon and Schuster, 2004); and Tom Ricks, *Fiasco: The American Military Adventure in Iraq* (New York: Penguin, 2006).

44. See Rajiv Chandrasekaran, *Imperial Life in the Emerald City: Inside Iraq's Green Zone* (New York: Vintage, 2007).

45. Interviews with administration officials.

46. Department of Defense Directive 3000.05, "Military Support for Stability, Security, Transition, and Reconstruction (SSTR) Operations," released November 28, 2005, at www.dtic.mil/whs/directives/corres/pdf/d300005_112805/d300005p.pdf.

47. NSPD-44, dated December 7, 2005, is available at www.fas.org/irp/offdocs/nspd/nspd-44.html.

48. Interviews with executive branch officials.

49. This is known as "Section 1207" authority, for the section of the National Defense Authorization Act that created this transfer authority. The S/CRS is the State Department gatekeeper for proposals for using these funds, which are generally submitted by embassies and regional bureaus at State. The funding is not used for S/CRS field operations.

50. S/CRS has personnel and administrative budget of roughly $17 million and no contingency funding to start planning operations or conducting early missions. Only in 2007 did it look possible that Congress might appropriate funding for the proposed civilian reserve corps, which is still being defined. Former coordinator Ambassador Carlos Pascual estimates that S/CRS should be funded at $60 million for personnel and operations, another $50 million for a civilian reserve corps, and $200 million for a contingency response fund. "An Interview with Carlos Pascual," *Joint Force Quarterly*, 42, (2006): 80–85.

51. In addition, the funds would support the creation of a 2,000-person civilian reserve corps based in the private sector. See Department of State, "The Budget in Brief: Fiscal Year 2009," 63–65, at www.state.gov/documents/organization/100033.pdf.

52. An Army War College paper describes this as follows: "The principle problem of interagency decision-making is lack of *decisive authority*: there is no one in charge." See Gabriel Marcel,

"National Security and the Interagency Process," in *U.S. Army War College Guide to National Security Policy and Strategy*, ed. J. Boone Bartholomees (Carlisle, PA: U.S. Army War College, July 2004), 253. Stewart Patrick and Kaysie Brown arrive at a similar conclusion in Kaysie Brown, *Greater Than the Sum of Its Parts: Assessing "Whole of Government" Approaches to Fragile States* (New York: International Peace Academy, 2007).

53. The Center for Strategic and International Studies has proposed such a model. See Murdock and Flournoy, *Beyond Goldwater-Nichols*, 26–65. A bill sponsored by Senators Richard Lugar and Joseph Biden proposed a directorate at NSC to oversee interagency contingency planning. "Reconstruction and Stabilization Civilian Management Act of 2006." Bill S.3322 of the 109th Congress. Marcel, 253, calls for an "NSC-centric national security system, consolidating the State Policy Planning Staff and DOD's strategic planning, to deal with the need for authoritative decisions." For a summary of various reform proposals for the interagency process, see Neyla Arnas, Charles Barry, and Robert B. Oakley, "Harnessing the Interagency for Complex Operations" (Washington, DC: Center for Technology and National Security Policy, National Defense University, August 2005), available at www.ndu.edu/ctnsp/Def_Tech/DTP%2016%20Harnessing%20the%20Interagency.pdf.

54. See Joel Brinkley, "Give Rebuilding Lower Priority in Future Wars," *New York Times*, April 8, 2006.

55. Tomkin, *Inside OMB*, 8.

56. See the multiple reports of the Office of the Special Inspector General for Iraq Reconstruction at www.sigir.mil for documentation of the difficulties coordinating and implementing the reconstruction funds.

57. See Gordon Adams, William I. Bacchus, and David Glaudemans, "Civilian Surge: Providing Authorities and Resources," in Hans J. Binnendijk and Patrick Cronin, eds., *Civilian Surge: Key to Complex Operations, A Preliminary Report* (Washington, DC: National Defense University, 2008), 147–60. The cross-national study by Patrick and Brown, above, supports the call for contingency funding.

Chapter 4   The State Department: Culture as Interagency Destiny?

Marc Grossman

> Without a doubt, the State Department has the most unique bureaucratic culture I've ever encountered.
>
> *James Baker, former secretary of state*

INTRODUCTION

There is no simple way to describe a culture as kaleidoscopic as the one at the State Department. This chapter provides a perspective that argues that it is important first to understand the international culture of diplomacy and how American diplomats both place themselves inside and outside of this umbrella culture. Recognizing the pros and cons of generalization, this chapter proposes some observations about the prevailing State Department culture, a culture on display, both positively and negatively, after 9/11 and as the United States pursued military action and postconflict challenges in Afghanistan and Iraq.

The State Department has changed a great deal in the last fifteen years. The challenge for the future will be to have a transformed department ready to provide twenty-first century leadership in areas such as whole government responses to crises, the continuing need to defeat extremism, nonproliferation, and living sustainably on the planet. Will the State Department keep changing? The nation will look to today's State Department leadership and employees, foreign service and civil service, for answers to that question.

Diplomats and the institutions that instruct and support them are as old as the earliest contact between groups of people who sought ways to interact other than fighting.[1] Sophisticated systems of formal communication existed in the ancient Middle East and Anatolia, Persia, India, China, Greece, Rome, and Byzantium.[2] Scholars like Leguey-Feilleux, Kissinger, Lauren, Craig, and George use diplomacy's past both to illuminate contemporary challenges and to make observations about the behavior of diplomats over the centuries and their institutions and subcultures.[3]

Modern diplomacy began in Renaissance Italy.[4] Garrett Mattingly and others who write about this "revolution in diplomacy" showcase Bernard Du Rosier's "Short Treatise about Ambassadors," written in 1436, as a foundation for international diplomatic culture. Du Rosier wrote, "diplomats must be as clear as possible in exposition, but one need not say everything one has in mind at once before feeling out the opposite point of view. One must listen attentively and look especially for points of possible agreement; these it is usually desirable to settle first. One must adjust one's methods to circumstances, and be prepared to make all concessions consistent with the dignity and real interests of one's principle and the clear tenor of one's instructions. One must press steadily and persistently but patiently toward an agreement. . . . One must remember that the diplomat's hope is in man's reason and good will."[5]

AMERICANS AS DIPLOMATS: A STATE DEPARTMENT CULTURE

American diplomats are part of the international diplomatic culture that has built up over the centuries, but they also consciously put themselves outside of traditional diplomatic society because they represent the United States, a nation of optimism, idealism, universal values, and a belief that sustained effort can lead to progress. As Robert Kagan argues, "The Declaration of Independence is America's first foreign policy document."[6]

There is a unique State Department culture that influences the way its diplomats formulate and carry out U.S. foreign policy. No one has described the cultural anthropology of the State Department and the foreign service more incisively than Henry Kissinger. Secretary Kissinger wrote in *Years of Upheaval* in 1982 that he came to the State Department skeptical of the foreign service and left "a convert." He describes foreign service officers (FSOs) as "competent, proud, clannish and dedicated." Kissinger recalls America's historic distrust of diplomacy by noting that, "The conventional criticism, that they (diplomats) were a group of 'cookie pushers' contributed to a sense of beleaguered solidarity. . . long service abroad created greater sensitivity to the intangibles of foreign societies than to those of our own." Kissinger also makes this crucial point: "The Foreign Service emphasizes negotiability—which is another way of saying consciousness of what the other side will accept. . . . Institutionally, the Foreign Service generates caution rather than risk taking; it is more comfortable with the mechanics of diplomacy than with its design, the tactics of a particular negotiation rather than an overall direction, the near-term problem rather than the longer term consequences."[7]

Secretary Baker made a similar observation in his 1995 memoirs: "Most FSOs are talented and loyal public servants, and any Secretary would be foolish not to harness their strength. I did so, and was served very ably by many of them. But as with any large group, some of them tend to avoid risk taking or creative thinking."[8] Richard Haass brings these observations up to date as he describes the administration of President George W. Bush: "On almost every issue . . . the State Department was isolated and outnumbered. To some extent this was a matter of foreign policy outlook. The State Department and those who worked there are by temperament and training inclined toward diplomacy and working with others. In this Administration, those elsewhere were not."[9]

Of course Kissinger and Baker (and the many others who have commented on the State Department as an institution) do not define the outlook of every State Department employee and some of the challenges they identified have ameliorated over time. But the attitudes they portray are still held by enough people to create an institutional culture that influences the way recommendations are shaped for the secretary of state (and for the president) and defines the way people at the State Department promote and defend their proposals and policies in the interagency arena, in foreign countries, and at international organizations. And while Kissinger and others focus on the foreign service, these traits define a larger State Department culture, including the vital members of the civil service, and affect the attitudes of the thousands of locally engaged staff at embassies around the world.

The institutional power of the State Department and a secretary of state's relationship to the foreign service and the civil service are separate questions. The State Department's influence can increase even if a secretary of state uses the institution episodically. Conversely, the foreign service and civil service may occupy the commanding heights of the department, but without a strong connection to the White House the department's influence over policy will recede. For example, Baker's strong relationship with the president and his compelling ideas for foreign policy enhanced the clout of the institution even as Baker preferred to work closely with a small group of trusted advisors and assistants who were not FSOs.[10] Kissinger and Secretary George Shultz had close relationships with the White House, important ideas about foreign policy, and made substantial use of the department. Shultz in particular invested time and effort into building the institution and the department's influence rose in these years. Secretary Colin Powell made many positive changes to the institution and was deeply admired by State's employees, but his belief in engagement and alliances was met with disdain at the White House and the Pentagon, and the department's influence waned.

Eight observations about the State Department culture and the system in which today's American diplomats work are relevant to this examination of the American national security enterprise.

First, the State Department (like other agencies) has a culture defined by patriotism and a commitment to service to the nation in a dangerous world. The definition of patriotism and service is largely self-defined and encompasses what may seem contradictions to outsiders; the commitment of State Department employees to their country allows the institution to function even when faced with internal tensions over policy, procedure, or external criticism. This is the deeper lesson of the controversy over whether Secretary Rice would need to force people to take assignments in Iraq and Afghanistan in 2007. At a town hall meeting, one or two officers made headlines by saying they would not serve.[11] The reaction of the majority at State, however, was to volunteer for vacancies in both war zones and in the end, no one had to be forcibly assigned. The diplomatic service prides itself on serving the president, regardless of party or individual policy preferences, and the number of resignations over policy differences is few in any administration.

Second, State has consistently suffered from a crushing lack of human and financial resources, highlighted by the disparity between defense spending and spending on America's civilian capacity in foreign affairs. As a result, employees at the State Department have grown resigned (or accustomed) to getting by with much less than their military counterparts. As Secretary of Defense Gates noted in a speech at the Center for Strategic and International Studies (CSIS) in January 2008, the total foreign affairs request for FY2008 was $36 billion, which is about what the Pentagon spends on military health care. (President Bush's last budget and supplemental request and President Obama's first supplemental and budget requests have produced substantial increases to this number.) The Obama administration asked for $58.49 billion for international affairs in its FY2011 budget request. In March 2009, there were 6,761 FSOs; 5,011 foreign service specialist support staff; and 9,334 civil service personnel in the State Department. By contrast, in mid-2008, there were 1.6 million active-duty military personnel, nearly 1.6 million members of the Reserves and the National Guard, and 673,000 civilian employees in the Defense Department.[12] The U.S. Agency for International Development (USAID) currently has only

2,200 personnel following cumulative staff reductions of nearly forty percent during the past two decades. This disparity distorts policymaking because "money is policy." Lean budgets also increase the State Department and USAID reliance on contractors and make supervision of their work a serious challenge.[13]

In his CSIS speech, Gates noted that the army planned to add seven thousand more soldiers in 2008, the equivalent of adding the entire U.S. FSO corps to the Army in one year.[14] There are more lawyers at the Defense Department than in the entire U.S. diplomatic corps. Unlike U.S. military forces, over sixty percent of the foreign service is always deployed overseas.[15]

Gates made the additional crucial point that "A certain percentage of (military) officers, even in time of war and when the force is stretched, is always enrolled in some kind of advance training and education in leadership, strategy or planning at the Staff or War Colleges and at graduate school. No such float of personnel exists for the Foreign Service."[16] It is important to note that both Secretary Rice and Secretary Clinton succeeded in obtaining substantial new hiring for the State Department and for USAID.

Third, while the department has greatly benefited from changes in the way it recruits new foreign and civil service officers to enhance diversity, language skills, and technological capacity, more needs to be done. As Harry Kopp and Charles Gillespie note in their 2008 study of American diplomacy, "The Foreign Service in the first half of the 20th century was very much a white man's organization. As late as 1970, the core of Foreign Service officers was 95% male and only 1% African American. All female Foreign Service officers were single and, until 1971, required to resign if they wed." As a result of internal and external pressures, Kopp and Gillespie continue, "by 2005, 49% of Foreign Service entrants were women and 22% were racial or ethnic minorities . . .(although) minorities are still under represented in the Foreign Service."[17]

The average age of today's incoming officers is lower than in the 1990s, which has resulted in recruiting people more interested in action on the front lines in hard places with excellent technological (especially IT) skills, less patience for hierarchy, and ready to demand more professional education and a better balance between work and family.

Fourth, the State Department simultaneously embraces and rebels against institutional hierarchy. Most State Department employees say they want clear direction from the top. But Kissinger described a well-known tactic: An assistant secretary who, "because he opposed the decision he feared I would make," used "the splendid machinery so methodically to 'clear' a memorandum I had requested it took weeks to reach me; when it arrived it was diluted of all sharpness and my own staff bounced it back again and again for greater precision—thereby serving the bureau chief's purposes better than my own. Alternatively, the machinery may permit a strategically placed official's hobby horse to gallop through, eliciting an innocent nod from a Secretary unfamiliar with all the code words and implications."[18]

An additional complication in managing hierarchy is the presence of noncareer (political) appointees in the department. While the State Department benefits from first-rate outsiders who bring new energy, perspectives, and modern ways of doing business, and many outstanding noncareer appointees have served at home and abroad (and there have been poor career appointees as well), presidents have appointed noncareer leaders at the State Department or to embassies to pay off political debts. Since the Kennedy administration, the percentage of career to noncareer appointees at embassies abroad has generally been two-thirds career and one-third political. The *Washington Times* reported in July 2009 that the Obama White House, apparently unaware of this historic percentage, had been on track to give more than the usual thirty percent of ambassadorial jobs to political appointees until objections from career diplomats forced it to reconsider.[19] Given the global opportunities and threats that America faces, the American Academy of Diplomacy in June 2008 called on the presidential candidates to reduce the number of noncareer appointees overseas to ten percent and to pay extra attention to the qualifications of noncareer people to be appointed.[20]

Fifth, the State Department, like other agencies in the government, has a mix of norms and organizational structures and behaviors, some still relevant, others legacies well beyond their shelf life. As former ambassador Craig Johnstone has described one legacy habit, hundreds of people at State write talking points that move up the system as if the senior leadership of the department can solve foreign policy problems by reciting these lines in public to foreign leaders or in interagency meetings. This might have been the right structure when the only conversation that mattered was between the secretary of state and the Soviet foreign minister. However, in today's world, the major challenges cannot be solved by talking points. Fighting extremism, defeating narcoterrorism, preventing genocide, promoting sustainable development, stopping the trafficking in human beings, for example, require front-line action by the State Department and other U.S. government agencies.

Baker described it this way: "The State Department has the most unique bureaucratic culture I've ever encountered . . . at State, the inanimate came alive. While to most people the State Department is just a rather ugly, monolithic post-World War II eight-story monstrosity overlooking the Mall in Foggy Bottom, to its inhabitants it's 'the building'—a living breathing being that has opinions and policies of its own."[21] The "building" can also produce action and information channels that promote the interests of some bureaus within the department over others. The result is often conflict instead of collaboration. For example, State's unresolved tension between regional bureaus—which historically have the upper hand, as they have a major say in follow-on personnel assignments, especially to posts abroad—and functional bureaus is a significant impediment to collaboration. While regional bureaus can most quickly bring the art of what is possible to the table and galvanize embassy action, they also suffer the most "clientitis," the tendency to be overly concerned with another country's sensitivities. Regional bureaus have also historically resisted incorporating the new parts of the diplomatic agenda, such as human rights or environmental protection, into their work. This has resulted in a proliferation of functional bureaus, some demanded or established by Congress. To compound this challenge, functional bureaus have often struggled to recruit FSOs to serve in them and the fact that functional bureaus have more civil servants reinforces (wrongly) their second-class status in the institution.

One structure that has stood the test of time is the country team, the organizing principle in American embassies abroad, which brings together under the ambassador's leadership the representatives of all of the federal agencies with personnel in that country. The CSIS study, *Embassy of the Future*, describes the interagency character of embassies: "The scope and scale of representation from other Federal agencies at Embassies have been growing steadily, with 27 agencies (and numerous sub-agencies) represented overseas. In some large Embassies, the proportion of State Department representation relative to other Federal agencies can be less than one-third of full-time U.S. personnel."[22]

An ambassador's ability to inspire all country team elements to pursue common objectives is enhanced by a letter from the president describing the ambassador's roles and mission, including responsibility (with some important exceptions) for all executive branch personnel assigned to his or her country. The *Embassy of the Future* report notes that twenty-first century challenges will require strengthening this presidential letter to increase ambassadorial authorities; as U.S. diplomats become more dispersed geographically and technologically, and even more interactions abroad involve law enforcement, the need for an in-country authority to ensure that U.S. interests are being pursued increases.[23]

Sixth, despite recent efforts—promoted especially by former Deputy Secretaries of State Richard Armitage and Jack Lew—there is still an aversion at State to strategic planning and to making the crucial operational link between policy and resources. This is not just to increase the resources available to the department, but also to draw institutional interests together simultaneously through joint planning and reviews. And this is not a new observation. Writing in 1969, Andrew Scott noted that among the beliefs held by FSOs is that the "skilled conduct of foreign affairs involved more of art than of science . . . one of the reasons that the conduct of foreign policy is art rather than of science is that each problem that confronts the Foreign Service Officer is unique. He must take up each problem as it presents itself . . . and deal with it as best he can. He must then pass on to the next problem, knowing that its solution will owe very little to the solutions found in earlier problems. Since this is the case . . . efforts at 'planning' can be of little use."[24] Secretary of State Clinton announced in July 2009 a renewed effort to draw together policy and resources through the quadrennial diplomacy and development review (QDDR).

Seventh, the culture oscillates between the classified information system's restrictive need-to-know principle and the need for ever-larger numbers of people to know so that they can collaborate. In the 1980s, a state department executive secretary decreed that only he could have a fax machine at the State Department because he believed it his job to control all of the information all of the time. Even with new means and methods for significantly more efficient sharing of information widely available, the State Department has not yet leveraged these tools across the institution. In 2001, Powell had to order that internet access be made available on every state department employee's desk, and it was not until the middle of Powell's tenure that the State Department retired the last Wang word processor from the department.

State has begun to focus intently on outward-facing communication, crucial in today's environment. To more effectively recruit new FSOs, the State Department uses Facebook sites; over sixty percent of the people who log on to a State Department Facebook site to seek information subsequently sign up to take the foreign service exam. Richard Holbrooke, the U.S. envoy to Afghanistan and Pakistan, designed a media plan for Pakistan based on disseminating information via cell phone. State recognized the opportunities for U.S. engagement as opposition to the results of the 2009 Iranian election was organized on Facebook and documented by Twitter and cell phone cameras.[25]

Eighth, there is a lack of clarity, even though lengthy promotion precepts are published each year, about what actually constitute criteria for advancement. State has an internal caste system based on functional cones, and an informal guild system based on regional expertise; language training (creating further subcultures of Arabists, Chinese language officers, Japanese language officers, the German Club, etc.); and other skill-based subcultures such as staff and special assistants. As Kopp and Gillespie note, "Assignments in today's Foreign Service are made through a formal process that is largely transparent, and a parallel informal process that is largely opaque."[26] The assignment and promotion system still favors political officers who remain at the top of the caste system at State and who, especially before 1989 and certainly before 2001, tended in most embassies toward traditional reporting and not program development and direction.

NEGOTIATING IN THE INTERAGENCY: LOOKING BACK

The international culture of diplomacy, American diplomacy's adaptation of that culture, and the lessons drawn from observations and analyses of how the State Department behaves as an institution, all influence the way State defines and then plays its role in the interagency process. The State Department's history and its contemporary culture and challenges directly influenced the way America's diplomats reacted to the murderous attacks of September 11, 2001, and then participated in the interagency debate about both pre- and post-conflict U.S., allied, and partner actions in Afghanistan and Iraq.

Post-September 11, 2001: Afghanistan

The State Department's immediate response to 9/11, diplomatically and in the interagency process, drew on the positive aspects of the diplomatic culture, seeking to create the widest coalition against terrorism. NATO declared the attacks of 9/11 an attack on all NATO members, invoking Article V of the NATO treaty for the first time in history. Even if for their own reasons, Russia and China supported an international effort against terrorism that translated (with the strong backing and creative diplomacy from our traditional allies, especially the United Kingdom) into international obligations to fight terrorism, including cutting off terrorist financing.

Post-9/11 interagency groups confronted new fears and drew in participants not previously considered part of the national security establishment before 9/11, especially after the domestic anthrax attacks in the fall of 2001, such as the Department of Health and Human Services and the Department of Transportation. September 11, 2001, highlighted another factor as well. Richard Haass notes that, "In principle and design, the NSC ought to be neutral on policy or at least determined to make sure that its honest broker role enjoys pride of place before it assumes the stance of counselor." But it was "at least two and a half to one against State on almost every issue just by the time we sat down with our interagency peers."[27]

Based on work begun in the Clinton administration, State Department leaders had been focused since the Bush 43 inauguration on the overseas threat to U.S. interests from the Taliban and al-Qaeda. Department managers were convinced that al-Qaeda would attack American interests outside of the United States. Alert levels at diplomatic installations around the world in the spring and summer of 2001 were increased and Washington directly warned the Taliban that if al-Qaeda attacked American interests anywhere in the world they would be held responsible.

State actively supported the president's decision to invade Afghanistan and, working closely with central command, performed the diplomatic work required to gain the support of nations surrounding Afghanistan so that U.S. forces could base and stage from these countries in the effort to destroy al-Qaeda and the Taliban.

During this period, conflict in the interagency system, especially between the Department of Defense (DOD) and State, was often based on personality clashes at all levels, but at root the struggle had cultural and ideological foundations. There was profound disagreement, for example, about whether the United States should engage in nation building, a policy President Bush had campaigned against in 2000. State Department professionals were generally proud of the effort the United States had made in nation building and in peacekeeping: supporting the deployment of U.S. military forces to participate in the multinational force and observers (MFO) in the Sinai, which the DOD was determined to end; and peacekeeping and nation-building activities in East Timor, Haiti, and the Balkans, including strong continuing support for the Dayton accords; and for the restoration of civil society after NATO military action in Serbia and Kosovo. Most department officials believed nation building, properly funded and done right, could be an effective long-term foreign policy tool of the United States.

Another source of conflict over nation-building activities was the State Department's inclination to promote and define military missions for the Pentagon and the armed services in an increasing number of situations important, but not vital, to U.S. national interests, such as peacekeeping in Liberia. The department's readiness to volunteer U.S. military forces was often a direct result of the lack of U.S. civilian capacity to do the jobs required.

There were other examples of institutional cultural traits highlighted by the war in Afghanistan. By joining the U.S. government consensus to reject NATO's offer of alliance military assistance in Afghanistan, the State Department jettisoned too much of its cultural desire for allies and engagement in the aftermath of 9/11.[28] While department leaders were grateful for NATO's declaration of Article V immediately after 9/11, the department too quickly accepted the notion that a formal NATO role in support of U.S. forces would provoke a clash of civilizations. The DOD opposed NATO's involvement as an alliance because they felt it would constrain U.S. military operations. The interagency was thus united in opposition to NATO participation for different (and both wrong) reasons. Individual allied forces (NATO and non-NATO) operated in Afghanistan with great valor and effect, but an approach that had initially embraced a NATO role would have better served the larger cause.

The State Department argued from the beginning of the military operation in Afghanistan that targeting and destroying Taliban storehouses of opium should be a U.S. objective. In a world of simultaneous challenges, State argued, the destruction of this narcotics stash, and a commitment to use military forces in a counternarcotics role, would take existing drugs off the market and set the right example for a future Afghan government. Defense maintained that counternarcotics was not a U.S. military mission in Afghanistan.

One of the main fears during and after U.S. military intervention in Afghanistan was starvation among the Afghan population. The State Department and the Agency for International Development argued that the United States should not only air-drop food (to which DOD initially objected) but also get wheat into Afghanistan through Iran; the United States would have to talk to Iran to arrange the shipments. The DOD opposed Iran as a geographic conduit, and the interagency process stalled before the president reminded agencies that his policy was that the United States would not use food as a weapon.

In 2002, Powell and the department argued for an expansion of the International Security and Assistance Force (ISAF) in Afghanistan, including deployment of U.S. forces to

ISAF, arguing that the inclusion of U.S. troops would open the door to thousands more international troop contributions. The DOD opposed this recommendation.

Collaboration, competition, or misunderstanding between agencies is not, of course, limited to interactions between the DOD and the State Department, nor do these attributes apply only to the most senior levels of the interagency process. Thirty years ago the State Department's relationship with operational elements of the intelligence community was often contentious. These relationships have over time become more routine and collaborative. As law enforcement took an increasingly important role in American foreign policy after the mid-1980s, the State Department (and especially ambassadors abroad) struggled to establish an understanding with the Department of Justice and with those of its elements, such as the FBI, deployed overseas. As counterterrorism became a priority for the U.S. government, agencies fought over turf, information and credit, frighteningly well described by Lawrence Wright in *The Looming Tower*.[29] The creation of the Department of Homeland Security (DHS) after the attacks of September 11, 2001, also required adjustment on the part of the State Department and other players in the interagency arena, especially as DHS deployed officers abroad and began to adjudicate visa questions.

The relationship between the State Department and the national security advisor and her or his staff has also had its moments of collaboration and tension; foreign service and civil service employees of the State Department who have the opportunity to work at the National Security Council staff (or, indeed, in any of the other government agencies and in Congress) come back with a clearer-eyed view of their home institution. This opportunity to see both the positives and the negatives is a forceful argument for more rotation of personnel among the national security agencies in the future and for more joint training, starting with entry-level employees across the national security structure and should be required at intervals throughout a career in government.

Iraq

State Department leadership generally saw Iraq as a diversion from Afghanistan and in 2001–3 not central to the war on terror. Saddam Hussein was a dictator and a menace, but in a box, posing no immediate direct threat to the United States; focus should be kept on defeating al-Qaeda in Afghanistan and supporting the new Afghan government.[30] Iraq had been a source of tension and disagreement inside the State Department (reflecting the debate in the country) since the beginning of the administration. Some at State sought to move department policy first and then U.S. policy away from support for revised—or smart—UN sanctions and toward an aggressive posture regarding Saddam. Conversely, and especially once planning for action against Iraq began in earnest in 2002, many within State warned their leadership that department participation in planning for conflict signaled acquiescence in a decision that had perhaps already been made to proceed.

The department's culture of negotiability did not serve as a good guide to institutional behavior for most of the senior State people who participated in the interagency debate leading to the invasion of Iraq. Senior department officers participated in planning for the conflict and its aftermath assuming—or, perhaps better put, hoping—that events either at home or abroad would turn preparations for conflict into successful coercive diplomacy rather than the military action that took place in the spring of 2003. Then State Department Director of Policy Planning Richard Haass observed that while he was "60-40 against going to war" (he was assuming that Iraq had weapons of mass destruction [WMDs]; if he had known they did not he would have been 90-10 against the war), "no organization could function if people left every time they lost out on a 60-40 decision."[31] Haass's recollection is a reflection on the challenges of making policy at the most senior levels of government, especially when the information on which people base their judgments turns out to be wrong.

While State Department leaders were reluctant to invade Iraq in spring 2003, many did not rule out the use of force against Saddam forever; the department sought instead to use the year to try to recreate the successful Gulf War coalition of President George H. W. Bush, an outcome more consistent with State Department culture. The department argued that the United States and its allies might compel Saddam to submit through a show of force in early 2003, or, if this failed, there should be a sustained diplomatic effort to create a broad coalition to move militarily in the fall of 2003. The White House and the DOD were on a different timetable; this possibility lost all relevance on January 20, 2003, when the French government announced Paris would never support a second UN Security Council resolution to authorize the use of force in Iraq.

While one intensive diplomatic effort ended, another began in earnest. From January 20, 2003 on, the State Department supported CENTCOM Commander General Franks in order to make the war as short and successful as possible to limit American, allied, and Iraqi civilian casualties. Just as in the run-up to the invasion of Afghanistan, the department worked with military commanders to seek access to facilities for U.S. forces and to participate in the public diplomacy effort to gain as much support as possible for the armed liberation of Iraq from Saddam Hussein. Ironically, one of the areas in which there was substantial State–DOD collaboration, the effort to convince Turkey to allow the Fourth Infantry Division to transit that country to create a northern front in the battle against Saddam forces, was unsuccessful. Although the department had serious reservations about the size of DOD's request to Ankara, State worked closely with both civilian and military authorities at the Pentagon to try to meet the need that had been identified by the chairman of the Joint Chiefs of Staff, but joint DOD–State diplomacy could not overcome a negative vote in the Turkish Parliament.

Afghanistan and Iraq: Postconflict

The State Department's response to the challenges of postconflict Afghanistan and Iraq displayed both the pluses and minuses of the department's culture and the influence of resource restraints under which U.S. foreign policy operates.

The political effort to create a new Afghan government, which drew on the diplomatic strengths of the department, is described in Ambassador James Dobbins' book *After the Taliban*.[32] At Powell's direction, Dobbins supported the regional negotiation hosted by the Germans in Bonn, including promoting a key role for the United Nations, which put Hamid Kharzai in a position to lead Afghanistan; the culture of negotiability and U.S. engagement and leadership were here excellent guides to process and objectives. Much less successful was the U.S. attempt to get sufficient amounts of U.S. or international assistance to Afghanistan and U.S. acceptance of the diffusion of responsibility in Afghanistan where the British took charge of counternarcotics, the Italians the justice sector, the Germans training police. Postconflict resources focused by the United States on Afghanistan were small compared to other postconflict situations, including Kosovo.[33] The desire to have other nations take on specific responsibilities in Afghanistan was consistent with Washington's wish to share the load. As America shifted its focus to Iraq, burden sharing often seemed a way for the United States to ignore Afghanistan rather than making the commitments required to ensure that Afghanistan never again became a launching pad for terror attacks on America, its friends, and allies.

Although the State Department participated in planning for postconflict Iraq, the department did not have the capacity to take responsibility for the immediate postconflict administration.[34] Although it might have made more sense to have State in charge, the department leadership, understanding the lack of State resources, agreed to the executive order creating the postconflict Iraq structure that reported to the secretary of defense. On July 1, 2004, the State Department did officially open (on time and on budget) an embassy in Baghdad that allowed an expansion of diplomacy in Iraq and more effective senior civilian cooperation with U.S. military forces.

Interagency disagreement during the immediate postconflict period often focused on how and on what American money should be spent, which again exposed fundamental disagreements about whether nation building was good or bad for the United States. The State Department supported a $1 billion investment to provide clean water to Iraqis. The DOD opposed this expense, arguing that Iraq was a third world country and needed only a third world water system. The State Department also sought in 2003 to find some way to allow Iraqis to create a system of rudimentary representation by using the rolls developed for the United Nations' Oil for Food distribution program as electoral rolls. The DOD responded that Iraqis had a different conception of legitimacy and that early elections of any kind would not promote stability in the country.

A CULTURE TRANSFORMING?

The State Department can further close the gap Kissinger identified as existing in an institution that can be more interested in the mechanics of diplomacy and negotiation than the creation of policy. Indeed, the simultaneity of today's global challenges requires that the State Department close this gap. President Obama discussed these global challenges at the National Defense University on March 12, 2009: "Terrorism and extremism make up just one part of the many challenges that confront our nation . . . an historic economic downturn has put at stake the prosperity that underpins our strength, while putting at risk the stability of governments and the survival of people around the world. We are threatened by the spread of the world's deadliest weapons, by emerging cyber threats, and by a dependence on foreign oil that endangers our security and our planet. Poverty, disease, the persistence of conflict and genocide in the 21st century challenge our international alliances, partnerships and institutions."[35]

American diplomacy had of course been adjusting to these challenges for some years. With American leadership and support, NATO was expanded and transformed before and after 9/11 to better meet the demands of the twenty-first century, including participating in active combat in Kosovo. Plan Colombia, begun under President Clinton and continued by President Bush, promoted broad human security, focusing simultaneously on defeating narcoterrorism, promoting economic development, and enhancing human rights in

Colombia. No one at State (or within the interagency process) involved in Plan Colombia could be successful pursuing objectives in their own silo, and the program created new ways of interaction both inside the U.S. embassy in Bogotá and across executive and legislative branches in Washington. The Millennium Challenge Corporation (MCC) was created in 2004 as a new way to address development assistance, supporting sustainable economic growth by investing in poor countries that rule justly, invest in their people, and promote economic freedom. State Department employees supporting the MCC confront—simultaneously—a wider range of considerations than the legacy stovepiped assistance bureaucracies. The Proliferation Security Initiative, a partnership of more than ninety countries using their own laws and resources to stop shipments of WMD, delivery systems and related material on the sea, in the air, or on land, is a new way to address nuclear proliferation while avoiding the traditional diplomatic structures of communiqués and international conferences. State defined the structure of the international response to the tsunami that struck Southeast Asia in December 2004 by creating an informal coalition of countries and international organizations that focused on building capacity to provide immediate assistance to the victims (delivered by U.S. and other military forces) without seeking to create even a semipermanent multilateral institution.[36]

The wars in Afghanistan and Iraq have produced new structures and experiences for State Department employees, especially the provisional reconstruction teams (PRTs), which require close interaction with U.S. military forces at a more junior level than has been the norm since Vietnam, also producing wider experience in program direction and execution for State Department officers and employees. Service in these war zones is also influencing promotions and assignment; service in Iraq or Afghanistan will be a key ticket for future advancement.

Reform of America's diplomatic infrastructure had also accelerated in the late 1990s.[37] Secretary of State Madeline Albright supported major changes in the way the department recruits and retains its personnel. Secretary Powell launched the Diplomatic Readiness Initiative, hiring almost 1,200 new State Department employees during his tenure and emphasizing leadership and accountability by senior managers. Secretary Rice continued to highlight the need for diplomatic transformation and put more resources (especially personnel) in President Bush's FY2009 budget.[38] Gates has been an especially forceful spokesman for this strengthening of the civilian capacities of the U.S. government,[39] and a report by the American Academy of Diplomacy and the Stimson Center (funded by the Una Chapman Cox Foundation), recommended an increase in State Department and USAID staffing of 4,735 officers at a cost of $3.3 billion between 2009 and 2014.[40] Secretary of State Hillary Clinton has taken advantage of the tipping point that has been reached in favor of increasing civilian capacity: her objective is to expand the State Department by 25% over four years.

A TWENTY-FIRST CENTURY STATE DEPARTMENT

The tension between an American diplomacy that draws both on the international diplomatic culture and on America's unique history, objectives, and style will never be completely reconciled, but there is cause for optimism for more successful management of it. A State Department pursuing a definition of America's national interests that recognizes that security—international, national and human—will follow what Walter Russell Meade calls the need to focus on "economics, the problems of international order building or globalization, and the relationship of democracy and foreign policy."[41] This will be a stronger institution, better connected to the American public, and able to lead the international diplomatic culture in a uniquely American manner.

There will be no successful American diplomacy efforts without the support of a president who sees diplomacy as a key tool of American strength. President Obama told students at the National Defense University in March 2009 that: "My administration is committed to renewing diplomacy as a tool of American power and to developing our civilian national security capabilities."[42]

The recognition that diplomacy is a key element of national security cannot be seen by the State Department as the victorious end to a campaign for attention. But the international culture of diplomacy is attractive, bureaucratic interests strong, and some will argue that it is not State's job to try to close the gap Kissinger identified; reactions at State to Rice's 2006 and 2008 speeches at Georgetown on diplomatic transformation were mixed. And as the CSIS report *Embassy of the Future* made clear, more people and more money are only part of the answer: better training, better technology, and a continued evolution in the department's attitude from strict force protection to risk management (so that, for example, ambassadors can make risk-based judgments about security in the service of the mission and not have the perception that any security incident at their posts would question their judgment about carrying out the mission) are necessary to create a State Department fully ready to take its place as a twenty-first century instrument of American national power.[43]

There are additional factors added to the challenge of transforming American diplomacy. Americans are impatient, but successful diplomacy is based on long-term campaigns to promote America's interests. Although there is a broad consensus that State and USAID need more resources, the economic crisis and large budget deficits may move rebuilding America's civilian capacity down on the national agenda. In June 2009, eight former secretaries of state drafted and signed an op-ed piece calling for more resources for the State Department. It was published on June 25, 2009, in Politico.com after the *Washington Post*, the *New York Times*, and the *Wall Street Journal* all apparently decided it was "not newsworthy."[44] There will always be a strain in American thinking that equates diplomacy with weakness.[45] Events and the divergent interests of others can complicate rather than simplify even the most earnest commitment to diplomacy and engagement. Emerging or re-emerging global power structures may also constrain the possibilities for diplomacy.[46] It is also crucial to recognize that diplomacy alone is not the answer to every question. Maintaining a strong defense and demonstrating the willingness to use force (preferably with others in coalitions, but alone if necessary) are essential to successful diplomacy.

President Obama and Secretary Clinton have posed another test of the department's culture: the appointment of a large number of special envoys to carry out the president's foreign policy in areas such as the Middle East, Afghanistan/Pakistan, climate change, and Eurasian energy. Reaction to the envoys in the department has been mixed, reflecting cultural ambivalence to those outside the institutional structure taking roles that appear to diminish the primacy of the traditional leadership in the regional bureaus. Some regional bureaus have embraced the special envoy and have tried to use the special envoy's presence as a way to enhance the department's role in diplomacy. Other parts of the bureaucracy hope that the permanent institutions of the department will overwhelm the newcomers. Can the department's culture accommodate a president committed to diplomacy as a tool of national security, a secretary of state committed to additional resources for the institution (with a talent for diplomacy and a close relationship with the president), with the new structures of special envoys? While there is a number of special envoys that is too high, can the foreign service and the civil service recognize that it is possible for the department's institutional influence to grow (and by extension the influence of the permanent bureaucracy) through the special envoys if they are focused and properly supported? An increasingly flexible department culture would shape these opportunities to inspire a renaissance of American diplomatic skill and capacity. There are possibilities for a State Department that has closed Kissinger's gap by adapting its culture, producing policy recommendations for the president, and then carrying out the president's decisions on the front lines, that show the potential of twenty-first century diplomacy.

Although there is still work to be done to defeat extremism that will require the use of force, America can leverage the simultaneity of the challenges to create opportunities rather than constraints and pursue what Phillip Bobbitt calls a strategy of "preclusion."[47] Drawing on a department culture that seeks allies, friends, and coalitions, there is a range of policies and institutions that can be harnessed to manage the global instability which leads to extremism and threatens America's well being and security.[48] One key aspect the new culture must embrace is a focus on reversing what Ambassador Ed Djerejian called in a 2003 report, "a process of unilateral disarmament in the weapons of advocacy."[49] Parag Khanna calls for what amounts to a "rebranding" of America and for the deployment of more FSOs, more Peace Corps volunteers, and more efforts by our private sector to influence the future around the world.[50]

A State Department empowered to lead an interagency effort and drawing on its historic culture can keep focused on building a twenty-first century nonproliferation diplomacy. Policies in this area would include both new forms of multilateral cooperation, such as the Proliferation Security Initiative, focusing on the new START Treaty, following up the Non-Proliferation Treaty Review Conference that took place in spring 2010, and seeking broader participation in missile defenses. Crucial also will be meeting the tests set by Graham Allison to make sure that WMDs never come into the hands of terrorists.[51]

The State Department can help galvanize the global conversation about how better to live sustainably on earth. Jared Diamond argues that there is a strong correlation between environmental degradation and regional instability.[52] It will take diplomatic creativity to address climate change beyond Copenhagen, perhaps basing effort not on formal treaties but on transparent national obligations that can be judged systematically by others in the international system. Integrated environmental diplomacy, backed by an interagency effort to include the Department of Energy and other agencies, could also promote a "Manhattan Project" for the joint pursuit of clean coal technologies with the United States, China, India, Australia, and Japan; an effort to increase the diversity of global energy supplies through rejuvenated pipeline diplomacy in Eurasia; and collaboration on energy security with NATO and the European Union.[53] Pursuing environmental diplomacy will require further changes in the State Department culture, with additional focus on science, technology, and long-term planning.

The department should continue to lead a "whole of government" approach to managing postconflict situations. As Philip Bobbitt has described it, "The problem is the picture (of warfare) to which we cling. The picture unfolds in this way: peacemaking by diplomats; war making by the Armed Forces, peace building by USAID and reconstruction personnel. The reality of the 21st century, however, is that all of these tasks must be performed simultaneously."[54] Powell, in an initiative continued and strengthened by Rice and Clinton, created in July 2004 the Office of the Coordinator for Reconstruction and Stabilization. President Bush empowered this State Department office through NSPD-44 in December 2005, requiring the secretary of state to lead and coordinate the U.S. government response to postconflict situations across all agencies. The department has also created the civilian stabilization initiative to strengthen its capacity to manage and implement reconstruction and stabilization activities including ready-to-deploy active, stand-by, and reserve staffed and trained specialists from inside and outside the federal government.[55]

One area in which the president and the secretary will need to pay special attention (and their backgrounds as senators will be a big advantage) is in improving the department's image and effectiveness on Capitol Hill. Some State Department officers forget that the Congress is not just another branch of government but is an equal branch of government; some members of Congress think everyone at the State Department is an incurable victim of "clientitis." When State Department officers testify in the House or the Senate sitting next to a military officer in uniform, it is apparent that a military uniform is a more persuasive statement of service to the nation than a dark suit. It was not until Powell's tenure that the State Department opened offices on Capitol Hill, offices that the DOD had used for years to increase contacts and understanding of DOD's institutional priorities. But even with a substantial effort, and, despite the relatively modest amounts of money involved, as Gates has said, "Getting the additional resources and authorities for soft power is not an easy sell politically. It simply does not have the built-in domestic constituency of defense programs."[56] The key question is whether this structure will survive the first real crisis. Despite the State Department's major effort (supported by Senator Richard Lugar) to take on this responsibility, State still may not have the people or resources to successfully lead a "whole of government" stability or reconstruction task.

This is not an argument for preemptive capitulation. It should instead be a challenge taken on by all department officers: a key job for a transformed State Department is to create a positive relationship with the Congress. One area in which the department has a particular advantage is the opportunity to convey the importance of diplomacy as a national security tool when members of Congress travel abroad. Here too there has traditionally been a cultural struggle. The announcement of a congressional delegation (CODEL) is still taken at too many embassies as a distraction from the real work of State Department officers, and thus the opportunity to interact with members that could produce future collaborative relationships is often missed. A few congressional delegations may not have work as their sole priority, but failing to take advantage of these visits is a missed opportunity for the department.

Harry Kopp and the late Charles Gillespie start their book *Career Diplomacy* by describing a talk between a businessperson and a former FSO. The businessperson wanted to know why we needed diplomats in the twenty-first century. It seemed to him we could get all the information we needed from the news. Kopp and Gillespie write: "We need to make sense of the world, and we need to make sure the world makes sense of us. We need to understand, protect, and promote our own interests. Whenever and wherever we can, we need to shape events to our advantage."[57] These objectives are principles worth recalling as President Obama and his secretary of state work to further change the culture of American diplomacy and deploy enough well-trained diplomats as America's first line of defense around the world.

NOTES

The author wishes to express his appreciation to The Cohen Group, The Woodrow Wilson International Center for Scholars, and The Harvard Kennedy School Project on the Future of Diplomacy for their support in thinking systematically about these issues. The author also wishes to thank Ms. Toni Getze for her invaluable assistance in preparing this chapter. The author thanks Ambassador Beth Jones, Ambassador Tom Pickering, and Mark Steinberg for reading an early draft. The author also thanks Mildred Patterson and Anne Witkowsky for their careful reading of the chapter and for their wise counsel. All errors of fact and judgment are, of course, solely the responsibility of the author. The author also expresses his appreciation to Chuck Daris of the State Department for his review of the chapter and wishes to be clear that the opinions and characterizations in this book are those of the author alone and do not necessarily represent official positions of the U.S. government.

1. Paul Gordon Lauren, Gordon A. Craig, and Alexander L. George, *Force and Statecraft: Diplomatic Challenges of Our Time*, 4th ed. (London: Oxford University Press, 2007).

2. Jean-Robert Leguey-Feilleux, *The Dynamics of Diplomacy* (Boulder, CO: Lynne Rienner Publishers, 2009), 23–36.

3. Lauren, Craig, and George, *Force and Statecraft*; Leguey-Feilleux, *The Dynamics of Diplomacy;* and Henry Kissinger, *Diplomacy* (New York: Simon and Schuster, 1994).

4. Garrett Mattingly, *Renaissance Diplomacy* (New York: Courier Dove Publications, 1988).

5. Mattingly, *Renaissance Diplomacy,* 35.

6. Robert Kagan, *Dangerous Nation* (New York: Knopf, 2006), 41.

7. Henry Kissinger, *Years of Upheaval* (London: Little, Brown, 1982), 442–45.

8. James A. Baker, III, *The Politics of Diplomacy* (New York: GP Putnam's Sons, 1995), 31.

9. Richard Haass, *War of Necessity, War of Choice* (New York: Simon and Schuster, 2009), 182.

10. Baker, *The Politics of Diplomacy,* 31.

11. Helene Cooper, "Foreign Service Officers Resist Mandatory Iraq Postings," *New York Times,* November 1, 2003.

12. J. Anthony Holmes, "Where Are the Civilians? How to Rebuild the U.S. Foreign Service," *Foreign Affairs* 88, no. 1 (January/February 2009): 151.

13. Gordon Adams and Cindy Williams, *Buying National Security* (New York: Routledge, 2010), 1; and Allison Stanger, *One Nation under Contract* (New Haven, CT: Yale University Press, 2009), 34–83.

14. Secretary of Defense Robert Gates's speech at the CSIS, Washington DC, January 26, 2008, available at www.defenselink.mil/speeches/speech.aspx?speechid=1211.

15. Holmes, "Where Are the Civilians?" 150.

16. Gates's speech at CSIS, January 26, 2008.

17. Harry Kopp and Charles A. Gillespie, *Career Diplomacy: Life and Work in the U.S. Foreign Service* (Washington, DC: Georgetown University Press, 2008), 20–21.

18. Kissinger, *Years of Upheaval,* 440.

19. Nicholas Kralev, "Career Diplomats Protest Obama Appointments," *Washington Times,* July 10, 2009.

20. American Academy of Diplomacy letter to Senator Obama dated June 24, 2008, available at www.academyofdiplomacy.org/media/Ambassadorial_Qualifications_Sen_Obama_6_2008.pdf.

21. Baker, *The Politics of Diplomacy,* 28.

22. George L. Argyros, Marc Grossman, and Felix G. Rohatyn, *Embassy of the Future* (Washington, DC: Center for Strategic and International Studies, 2007), 47.

23. Argyros, Grossman, and Rohatyn, *Embassy of the Future,* 48.

24. Andrew M. Scott, "The Department of State: Formal Organization and Informal Culture," *International Studies Quarterly* 13, no. 1 (March 1969), 3.

25. *Time Magazine*, June 1, 2009, 56; *International Herald Tribune*, May 27, 2009, 4; *New York Times*, June 17, 2009, A–10.

26. Kopp and Gillespie, *Career Diplomacy*, 168.

27. Haass, *War of Necessity, War of Choice*, 184.

28. State Department employees were affected by the 9/11 attacks not just as professionals (State Department officers had been the victims of terrorism for 30 years), but as citizens; they too were surprised and shocked. Many offices in the State Department building look out across the Potomac to the Pentagon and so hundreds, if not thousands, of State Department employees watched the smoke rise as DOD colleagues, friends, and family perished, were injured, or fought the flames. The *Washington Post* columnist David Ignatius has said that the surprise and violence of the 9/11 attacks knocked America's individual and national gyroscopes off center. State Department employees (I certainly include myself) suffered from this gyroscopic imbalance. One example of this loss of balance is that our post-9/11 foreign policy became militarized. This seemed required at the time. It was not. The imbalance between civilian and military capacities in our government is a continuing national challenge.

29. Lawrence Wright, *The Looming Tower: Al-Qaeda and the Road to 9/11* (New York: Vintage Books, 2007).

30. Haass, *War of Necessity, War of Choice*, 211–12.

31. Haass, *War of Necessity, War of Choice*, 247. Haass's book contains other examples of the cultural clash between the State and Defense Departments over Iraq.

32. James Dobbins, *After the Taliban* (Washington, DC: Potomac Books, 2008).

33. James Dobbins, John G. McGinn, Keith Crane, Seth G. Jones, Rollie Lal, Andrew Rathmell, Rachel M. Swanger, and Anga R. Timilsina, *America's Role in Nation-Building: From Germany to Iraq* (Santa Monica, CA: RAND, 2003).

34. Much of the NSC-led postwar planning was detailed, but focused on lessons learned from the first Gulf War. There were elaborate plans to forestall another Kurdish refugee crisis and plans that would no doubt have successfully stopped starvation. The department's *Future of Iraq Project*, while important, would not have solved Iraq's postwar problems.

35. President Obama's remarks at Lincoln Hall Dedication, March 12, 2009.

36. Marc Grossman, "The Tsunami Core Group: A Step Toward Transformed Diplomacy in Asia and Beyond," *Security Challenges (Australia)*, 1, no. 1 (2005): 11–14.

37. Marc Grossman, "An American Diplomacy for the 21st Century," speech given at Foreign Affairs Day, Washington, DC, September 10, 2001, available at http://164.109.48.103/p/us/rm/6581.htm.

38. Dr. Condoleezza Rice's speeches at Georgetown University, January 18, 2006, and February 12, 2008.

39. Gates's speech at CSIS, January 26, 2008.

40. American Academy of Diplomacy, *Foreign Affairs Budget for the Future: Fixing the Crisis in Diplomatic Readiness,* October 2008, available at www.academyofdiplomacy.org/programs/fab_project.html.

41. Walter Russell Mead, *Special Providence: American Foreign Policy and How It Changed the World* (New York: Routledge, 2002), 78.

42. President Obama's remarks at Lincoln Hall Dedication, March 12, 2009.

43. Argyros, Grossman, and Rohatyn, *Embassy of the Future.*

44. Former secretaries of state Henry Kissinger, George Shultz, James Baker, Lawrence Eagleburger, Warren Christopher, Madeleine Albright, Colin Powell, and Condoleezza Rice, "U.S. must deploy more foreign diplomacy personnel," Politico.com, June 25, 2009.

45. Angelo M. Codevilla, *Advice to War Presidents* (New York: Basic Books, 2009), 75–109.

46. A key observation in Robert Kagan, *The Return of History and the End of Dreams* (New York: Vintage Books, 2009).

47. Philip Bobbitt, *Terror and Consent: The Wars for the Twenty-First Century* (New York: Penguin, 2008), 137.

48. *Managing Global Insecurity*, Brookings Institution, (Washington, DC: March 21, 2007), available at www.brookings.edu/events/2007/0321terrorism.aspx; and Richard L. Armitage and Joseph S. Nye Jr., cochairs, *CSIS Commission on Smart Power: A Smarter, More Secure America* (Washington, DC: Center for Strategic and International Studies, 2007) available at www.csis.org/media/csis/pubs/071106_csissmartpowerreport.pdf.

49. U.S. Department of State Advisory Group on Public Diplomacy for the Arab and Muslim World, Edward P. Djerejian, Chairman, *Changing Minds, Winning Peace: A New Strategic Direction for U.S. Public Diplomacy in the Arab & Muslim World,* October 1, 2003, 13. Available at www.state.gov/documents/organization/24882.pdf.

50. Parag Khanna, "Waving Goodbye to Hegemony," *New York Times Magazine,* January 27, 2008.

51. Graham T. Allison, *Nuclear Terrorism: The Ultimate Preventable Catastrophe* (New York: Macmillan, 2005).

52. Jared Diamond, *Collapse: How Societies Choose to Fail or Succeed* (New York: Penguin, 2005), 497.

53. Senator Richard Lugar's speech at NATO Summit, Latvia, November 27, 2006, available at www.rigasummit.lv/en/id/speechin/nid/36/. See also Marc Grossman and Simon Henderson "Foreign pipeline plan matters," *Dallas Morning News,* July 21, 2009.

54. Philip Bobbitt, *Terror and Consent,* 155.

55. An excellent discussion of this requirement can be found in *Improving Capacity for Stabilization and Reconstruction Operations,* by Nora Bensahel, Olga Oliker, and Heather Peterson, RAND Corporation, 2009. Interested readers will also want to consult *Civilian Surge,* edited by Hans Binnendijk and Patrick M. Cronin, National Defense University Press, Washington, DC, 2009, especially chapter 5 by James A. Schear and Lesley B. Curtin, "Complex Operations: Recalibrating the State Department's Role," 93–114.

56. Gates's speech at CSIS, January 26, 2008.

57. Kopp and Gillespie, *Career Diplomacy,* 3.

Chapter 5 The Office of the Secretary of Defense: Civilian Masters?

FREDERICK C. SMITH AND FRANKLIN C. MILLER

> This office will probably be the biggest cemetery for dead cats in history.
> *James V. Forrestal, 1947*

> I have no patience with the myth that the Defense Department could not be managed.
> *Robert S. McNamara, 1995*

INTRODUCTION

A familiar aphorism says that mighty oaks from little acorns grow. Nothing could be a more apt description of the role of the office of the secretary of defense (OSD) in influencing the direction of national security policy over the past several decades. Few legislators or presidential advisors who helped create the department would recognize their work. More importantly, they would scarcely recognize the interagency process that the National Security Act has morphed into, or the power that the Pentagon and the secretary of defense would wield. Moreover, neither would they have envisioned that the secretary would not only become the key player both in the internal bureaucratic process of managing the largest department in the government and the military services, but also a key player in formulating and implementing national security policies, requiring skills in dealing with other executive branch officials as well as the Congress.

When the National Security Act of 1947 created the post of secretary of defense, the holder of the post was virtually powerless. The act gave the secretaries of the services substantial authority by acknowledging that their departments "shall be administered as individual executive departments by their respective Secretaries and all powers and duties relating to such departments not specifically conferred upon the Secretary of Defense by this Act shall be retained by each of their respective Secretaries."[1]

In 1947, the secretary was authorized to have only three special assistants—political, budgetary, and international—and three other civilian and military assistants to run the three statutory agencies (the Joint Chiefs of Staff [JCS], Munitions Board, and Research and Developments Board) under what was then called the national military establishment. The first secretary of defense, James V. Forrestal, initially brought forty-five employees from the Navy Department, mostly low-level support staff, to run the new cabinet position. Forrestal believed that large staffs "begin to gather the attribute of God to themselves very fast."[2]

Forrestal, however, soon realized he had no authority over the services and that the department lacked a central decision maker. As the official history of the OSD notes, he

Box 5.1 Secretary of Defense Challenges

"The Secretary was surrounded by antagonists. In front were the State Department and the NSC, presumably pointing out the path of national policy; behind him, the Treasury and the Budget Bureau, always acting as a drag; on either side, the Joint Chiefs and the Comptroller, pushing him off the road in one direction or another. The Secretary, however, was institutionally naked and defenseless. It was not surprising that his functions were encroached upon by other agencies or that he himself found it necessary to identify his interests and role with that of some other agency. He had no support with which to maintain an independent stand."[1]

1. Samuel P. Huntington, *The Soldier and the State: The Theory and Politics of Civil-Military Relations* (Cambridge: Belknap, 2000), p. 449. Writing in 1957, Huntington noted that in the United Kingdom, the minister of defense was aided by fifty military officers and high-level civil servants headed by a chief staff officer and permanent secretary. But the secretary of defense was weak in comparison as he had no such staffs to assist him.

had hoped to exercise authority by coordinating the activities of the military departments rather than by command authority, but he soon realized he had misjudged the scope of his problems.[3] Other scholars have also concluded that the greatest deficiency of the department was "the absence of the proper staff" for the secretary.[4] Thus, he and successive secretaries of defense worked to increase the power and authority of their role to keep pace with the expanding scope and influence that the DOD would have in the post-WWII era. Early on, Forrestal established three assistant secretaries of defense, including one for foreign military affairs and military assistance, in recognition that the secretary of defense needed to have one central official who could deal with the Department of State on foreign affairs issues. While the State Department initially objected because it might limit contact with other Pentagon officials, it proved to be one of the necessary centralization tasks to help manage the interagency process as it became more complex.[5]

From that small staff has sprung a large, multifunctional staff of nearly four thousand professionals. Today, it commands over a half-trillion dollars a year in federal funds, with U.S. forces spread across the globe at hundreds of installations and with military commanders conducting wars and military operations, as well as diplomacy, in numerous places; the Department of Defense (DOD) has become the so-called eight-hundred pound gorilla in the interagency discussion of national security issues. That image, both of its size and presumed uncontrollability, is a tool but also a burden for those in the OSD who are trying to be effective players in the interagency process.

EVOLUTION OF OSD

Since Forrestal first established the OSD, it has grown tremendously and become a major player in the interagency process. As the Cold War deepened and U.S. defenses and alliances grew, so too did the complexity of DOD operations, necessitating a growing role for a staff that could help the secretary of defense manage this large military–civilian complex. Changes in the National Security Act in 1949, 1953, and 1958 substantially increased the secretary of defense's authorities. According to the new legislation in 1949, "no function . . . should be performed independent of the direction, authority and control of the secretary of defense."[6] His three assistant secretaries became nine. These were the first of many steps taken to broaden the secretary's control and direction of the defense effort.

When Robert McNamara assumed the job in 1961, he introduced a host of organizational changes to give him leverage over the services and rationalize the defense procurement, budgeting, and evaluation process. Among the most important were the creation of an independent program and evaluation office and a separate defense intelligence agency, two innovations that gave the secretary access to independent assessments of weapons systems programs as well as foreign military threats. In so doing, McNamara made himself and future secretaries less dependent on the threat assessments and military judgments of the uniformed military; a secretary of defense could therefore challenge, if not overrule, service weapons decisions. These innovations were not welcomed by the uniformed military, who viewed the so-called defense intellectuals, or whiz kids, as self-impressed amateurs who often had never seen military combat and were far more junior to the flag officers they were often questioning.[7]

Outside the Pentagon, McNamara was also one of the most powerful interagency figures in the Kennedy administration. He convinced President Kennedy to allow him to select his own deputies, a luxury not afforded all the other cabinet secretaries, and, as Vietnam increasingly became the key foreign policy issue during Kennedy's term, McNamara attempted to coordinate—and in so doing control—the far-reaching interagency process to mount the counterinsurgency operations in Southeast Asia. This involved not only usual national security agencies like Defense, State, and CIA, but also USAID, USIA, Treasury, and others.[8] The publishing of annual defense posture reports to Congress also began during these years, which laid out the plans and programs and budgetary figures as a way to get the Pentagon the resources it needed to accomplish the defense mission.[9]

In the intervening years, the OSD staff has become a powerful bureaucratic player, both within the department itself and with the other national security agencies. In both cases, power and influence remains shared. Within the Pentagon, OSD must work in a mutually trusting and cooperative manner with the JCS and Joint Staff, the combatant commanders, and the military service chiefs who run the day-to-day operations of the army, navy, marines, and air force. The internal bargaining process among OSD, the Joint Staff, and the services is often focused on the development of long-term defense guidance and national military strategy documents. These planning documents must reflect the combined views of civilian and military leaderships, accord with the secretary's own preferences, and be consistent with the president's overall national security strategy. Equally challenging for a secretary of defense is to develop a common Pentagon view on a myriad of weapons development and procurement decisions, driven primarily by the budget process. Not infrequently, the civilian OSD leadership and the services disagree on procurement decisions. This leaves the secretary to make controversial decisions; these regularly produce appeals to the White House, the Office of Management and Budget (OMB), or the Congress, as well as media stories that reveal divisions within the Pentagon bureaucracies over the nation's defense priorities and fuel legislative-executive branch battles over where to spend defense dollars.[10]

The government-wide national security decision-making process also thrusts OSD into the center of a complex interagency process. The OSD's role is to reflect the secretary's priorities and equities in the shaping of not only a national military strategy, but also the development of a broader national security strategy (NSS).[11] Mandated by Congress, this national security strategy document is intended to guide all national security agencies and so must reflect the DOD interests and equities as much as any other national security agency's. As the largest national security agency, the Pentagon has been very much involved in the interagency preparation of these public strategy documents. Similarly, when the national security council (NSC) calls upon the interagency to re-examine current security policies, be they on a regional crisis, new foreign policy initiative, or merely a general policy review, OSD represents the secretary's interests and works to craft an OSD policy that accords as well with those held by the JCS chairman's and Joint Staff's perspective.

Today, the OSD has a work force of nearly four thousand civilians and military personnel, organized into five major sections headed by undersecretaries who report to the secretary through a deputy secretary:

- Policy
- Acquisition, Technology, and Logistics
- Intelligence
- Personnel and Readiness, and
- Comptroller

The five undersecretaries exercise enormous influence in their respective areas. Their staffs, organized into units headed by assistant secretaries, develop policies, budget recommendations, and supporting analyses and generally run the day-to-day operations of their respective areas of responsibilities. These functions are performed both independently and in coordination with the staffs of the chairman of the JCS, combatant commanders, and military services. Depending on the topic, these undersecretaries also have to work closely with other parts of the interagency. For example, the undersecretary of defense for intelligence (USD/I) is the secretary's representative to the U.S. intelligence community (IC); as such, major DOD intelligence agencies like the National Security Agency, National Geospatial-Intelligence Agency, and Defense Intelligence Agency must report through him to the secretary. The USD/I also serves as the secretary's key person to deal with the director of national intelligence (DNI). Because the DNI and secretary of defense now jointly make decisions regarding the budgets and operations of these defense intelligence agencies, the OSD staff has a key role in representing the secretary within the IC's own interagency process. Another example would be the key role the comptroller has in working with the OMB when it conducts joint reviews of DOD budget proposals. As recent Obama administration decisions on defense cuts indicate, the secretary and OMB director worked closely to ensure that dissent within the department did not derail cuts by leaking these ideas early to congressional supporters of those programs.[12]

It is important to note that, in contrast to the British model of an integrated central staff (wherein the functions of the staffs reporting to the civilian defense secretary and the four-star chief of defense staff are interwoven functionally into a single reporting chain), the OSD is an independent body that interacts with but does not direct the Joint Staff, combatant commander's staffs, and individual service staffs. The difference in the two systems lies in the fact that the British defense secretary receives one recommendation from the integrated civilian-military staff, whereas the U.S. secretary of defense may receive opposing or differing recommendations from the OSD staff and the chairman of the JCS.

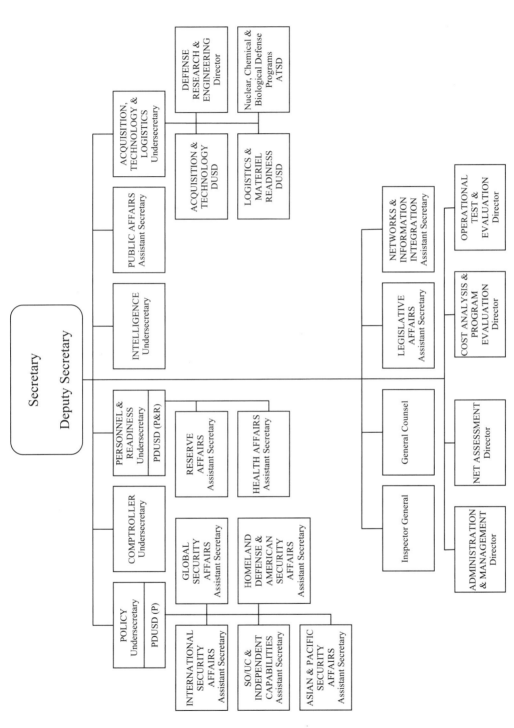

Figure 5.1   The Office of the Secretary of Defense, 2009.

SECRETARIES OF DEFENSE: SHAPERS OF THE INTERAGENCY PROCESS

The OSD's role and influence in the interagency process has been shaped in large measure by the personality and style of the secretary of defense. Hence, the nearly two dozen occupants have brought their personality, management skills, and experience in national security and with the military into play. Ideally, the skill set that the secretary should bring to the position includes (1) able leadership and management skills with a strategic vision; (2) political skills and an ability to deal with Congress; (3) both national and international credibility; and (4) the ability to influence the president and his cabinet in the interagency arena.

Some secretaries have viewed interagency cooperation as useful and necessary to the effective operation of the U.S. government. Others have perceived their cabinet colleagues and their staffs as meddlesome interlopers in the DOD's business and have been inclined to disdain interagency cooperation. Some have been outspoken opponents of working with the interagency, whereas others have embraced participation as a necessary evil, if not always a good thing.

The Opponents

The opponents tended to be the strong-willed individuals who saw the department as having a major and essentially self-contained role in developing and implementing U.S. defense strategies, which should not be meddled with by other agencies or outsiders, including the Congress. These secretaries relied on their closeness to their president, their perceived decisiveness, and self-confidence to weather the interagency process and battles with the Congress.

Robert S. McNamara (1961–68)

McNamara had dominant control over the interagency process on Vietnam. He fought strenuously, and for a long time successfully, to block the State Department and others from providing independent assessments of the U.S. efforts to carry out what is now called "nation-building" in South Vietnam. For better or worse, Vietnam became known as "McNamara's War" in light of his single-handed management of both the strategy and the public defense of it. The Pentagon's tight control over Vietnam policy included pressuring intelligence agencies to alter their bleak assessments or self-censor themselves to "keep with the policy." Unfortunately for McNamara, he was ill-served by his generals in the field and their overly optimistic reports and by civilian micromanagement of the war throughout the U.S. government. McNamara's legacy, however, was not limited solely to Vietnam. Apart from his key role in crisis management as mentioned earlier, he also helped to develop U.S. nuclear strategy, rationalize the development of weapons and budgets, and increase intelligence resources available to the department and the U.S. government.

McNamara remains probably the most controversial secretary of defense, either revered or reviled by his subordinates and colleagues. He applied an active management philosophy by providing "aggressive leadership, questioning, suggesting alternatives, proposing objectives, and stimulating progress."[13] He instituted systems analysis as the basis for making key decisions on force requirements and weapon systems, as well as policy decisions. By turning the OSD into a powerful civilian bureaucracy, he made it possible for later secretaries to play either powerful or destructive roles in the interagency process.

Caspar W. Weinberger (1981–87)

Caspar Weinberger primarily saw his role as restoring American military capabilities.[14] To that end, he saw strengthening the services to be more important than building up his own role as secretary, as McNamara had done. However, on policy issues he found himself frequently at odds with secretaries of state on arms control and Soviet policies. His close relationship to President Reagan helped him enormously in those interagency battles. Moreover, President Reagan's decision to demote the importance of his national security advisors (of which he went through six in eight years), made the NSC staff largely irrelevant and gave freer rein to cabinet secretaries like Weinberger. One symptom and cause of this NSC dysfunction was the Iran-Contra affair, which not only tarnished Weinberger's reputation but also caused him ultimately to step down.

Despite early deference to the military, Weinberger became a believer in the OSD staff and pioneered the plea of giving the staff increased responsibilities in the direction and implementation of the war-planning process. For example, he allowed the career civilian staff to lead the work that overhauled strategic war planning (nuclear forces) and to write the contingency planning guidance for conventional war planning. These are two seminal planning areas that he felt comfortable assigning to the long-term careerists rather than to political appointees or the military. Weinberger also asserted himself in articulating for the Reagan administration the terms on which U.S. military forces should be employed. Termed the Weinberger principles and later adopted by JCS Chairman Colin Powell, he argued that U.S. forces should only be employed when vital interests and clear objectives were identified and there was both public and congressional support.[15]

Donald H. Rumsfeld (2001–6)

Donald Rumsfeld exhibited total disdain for the interagency process and encouraged his staff to obstruct and hamper interagency cooperation to the maximum extent possible. As the only secretary to have held this position twice (previously under President Ford in 1976–77), Rumsfeld was confident of the changes he wanted to make in the department, including gaining more control over the military, introducing new transformational concepts, and keeping more control over any foreign policy initiative that involved DOD resources. He constantly reminded his military commanders that he was "in the chain of command" and expected to be the one to issue orders. As one senior aide recounts, Rumsfeld told U.S. central command (CENTCOM) commander General Tommy Franks in preparation for the Iraq War that, "It's clear to you and everyone that DOD is in charge of the war. You're in charge and I'm in charge and other departments put in ideas, but we make the decisions, right?"[16] Likewise, some recently published memoirs of senior OSD advisors to Secretary Rumsfeld acknowledge that they believed the interagency system was broken and that no senior official in the DOD felt it necessary to fix it or work with it.[17] Indeed, Secretary Rumsfeld admitted to Bob Woodward in a 2006 interview that he felt the interagency process was ill-suited to twenty-first century warfare and, by inference, not reparable.[18]

The Participants

Conversely, a number of secretaries of defense were much more inclined to work coopera-
tively with their cabinet colleagues, as they had confidence in the national security advisors
who ran the process or they saw the virtue of gaining interagency views and cooperation
in order to run an effective DOD.

Harold Brown (1977–81)

Harold Brown brought hard work, discipline, strong technical skills, and a wealth of experience in national security to the office as President Jimmy Carter's secretary of defense.
The interagency process was disciplined by Zbigniew Brzezinski and worked reasonably
well. Brown and Brzezinski, both intense in their work habits and approaches to national
security, were more hawkish in their views than others in the Carter administration. It was
only after the Soviet invasion of Afghanistan in late 1979 that their true (hard-line) tendencies were allowed to dictate over the interagency process, including a fairly substantial
increase in the FY1981 defense budget.

Dick Cheney (1989–93)

Dick Cheney was an extremely effective secretary of defense for several discernible reasons.
His time in office was defined primarily by the first Gulf War (1990–91), which caused the
department to stay focused on a major international event and was viewed as highly successful. Second, an outstanding chairman of the JCS, General Colin Powell, assisted Cheney,
which, in turn, led to excellent civil–military relations. Third, Secretary Cheney served at
a time of a well-functioning NSC that was characterized by good working relationships
among the principals (Scowcroft, Baker, and Cheney), which reinforced collaborative relationships among second-tier political appointees within their departments. Fourth, Cheney
had developed a deep understanding of defense policies and programs while in Congress
and he put this to good use. Last, he was prepared to reach out to and trust his civilian staff.

William J. Perry (1994–97)

William Perry was also an extremely effective secretary of defense. Armed with a technical
background, he was a strong manager who kept the OSD staff as well as the military involved
at all levels of DOD's activities. By doing this, he engendered staff loyalty and their sense of
ownership of the issues. Perry was an active secretary of defense who constantly worked issues
before they became problems. Given the smooth OSD–military working relationship within the
Pentagon, the DOD under Perry's leadership was an influential player in the interagency arena.
Perry himself was highly respected in the interagency arena by his peers (namely, Secretary of
State Warren Christopher and National Security Advisor Tony Lake). Because of his highly
intelligent and informed positions on national security, coupled with his calm demeanor and
strong work ethic (he was particularly recognized for his personal engagement with many foreign officials), he was one of the most effective cabinet members in President Clinton's first term.

Robert M. Gates (2006–Present)

When Robert Gates was nominated to be the 22nd secretary of defense in November
2006, he was given a clear mandate: (1) manage the Iraq strategy to ensure a successful outcome; (2) get the DOD budget under control, especially in light of the wars in

Iraq and Afghanistan; and (3) repair the civil–military relations in the DOD that had suffered greatly under Donald Rumsfeld. Given that he was expected to hold the office for only two years until the end of the George W. Bush administration, these were monumental tasks. Fortunately, Bob Gates was a seasoned government civil servant and possessed the requisite management skills and personality to accomplish even the most difficult tasks.

Prior to coming to the DOD, Bob Gates served for twenty-six years in the government as a career analyst at the Central Intelligence Agency and on the National Security Council staff. In 1991, he was nominated and confirmed as the DCI and director of the CIA under President George H. W. Bush. From 1989–91, Gates served as deputy national security advisor under Brent Scowcroft and George H. W. Bush. Brent Scowcroft is considered the quintessential national security advisor and Gates learned his lessons well. He had the reputation, especially during the first Gulf War, of running very efficient meetings and clearly laying out the interagency process that was expected. It was not surprising, therefore, that he has been supportive of a functioning interagency process now that he was sitting in the Pentagon.

As secretary of defense, Gates has also proven to be a tough yet fair manager. In 2007, he relieved the secretary of the Army when the incumbent seemed incapable of improving conditions that had been exposed in the press at the Walter Reed Hospital. That same year he took the unprecedented action of not renominating the sitting chairman of the JCS for reasons that were not entirely clear to the public, but believed to be tied to the Iraq strategy. In 2008, he fired the secretary of the Air Force and Air Force chief of staff over mishaps in handling nuclear weapons and their components. These actions, all of which were viewed necessary by the public, the administration, and within the Pentagon, established Gates as a manager who holds his people accountable. His decision-making process within DOD has also improved immensely the civil–military relations since he took office.

Given Bob Gates's success and the credibility he established with the Congress and public in his first two years as secretary and also given the sensitivity of the two ongoing wars and other issues within DOD, President-elect Obama made the decision in November 2008 to retain him in his cabinet. This decision was widely applauded and has proven to be a good one. Bob Gates works well within the national security structure of the Obama administration—he gets along well with Vice President Biden, Secretary of State Clinton, National Security Advisor Jones, and others. He proved himself the ultimate team player during testimony for Congress in April 2009 when, as secretary of defense, he advocated more resources for the Department of State.

GOLDWATER-NICHOLS ACT

Personalities aside, nothing transformed the dynamics of the Pentagon and how OSD operated in the interagency as much as the Goldwater-Nichols Department of Defense Reorganization Act of 1986. Much has been written about this major legislative change to how the military services, combatant commanders, and JCS were to relate to each other, but less has been said about how that would impact the military's relationship to the civilian side of the Pentagon. In an effort to create jointness, the act put in place measures that ensure that a unified commander's authorities transcends military service biases. Accordingly, it accomplished several significant changes in the military command structure:

- Made a stronger, more active chairman, JCS as the principal advisor to the president and secretary of defense
- Increased the chairman's power in relation to the service chiefs; gave the JCS chairman full authority over the Joint Staff
- Created a vice chairman, JCS
- Strengthened the role of the combatant commanders; in many respects, combatant commanders became dominant over the service chiefs, including with regard to budgetary issues
- Mandated personnel requirements for joint service.

Goldwater-Nichols had consequences, both positive and negative, within the combatant commands and the Joint Staff. But for our purposes, we should underscore how it altered the military's relationship to OSD and thereby also changed the DOD's approach to the interagency process. From a positive perspective, Goldwater-Nichols improved significantly the quality of personnel assigned to joint tours. Previously, the services filled positions on the unified commands, the Joint Staff, and in OSD strictly out of necessity, while their best people were retained on their respective staffs to fight interservice battles. Generally, joint tour assignments, including assignments to OSD, were not seen by military officers as career enhancing. Time spent away from the mother service was not considered relevant when promotion boards convened. After the passage of Goldwater-Nichols, joint tours were a prerequisite for promotion to the senior ranks. The OSD benefited substantially from the number and quality of officers (generally at the lieutenant colonel and colonel level) seeking assignments in policy and the other OSD directorates.

An unintended consequence of Goldwater-Nichols, however, affected DOD's position in the interagency process. Before 1986, OSD and the JCS and Joint Staff would collaborate on a given position, submit a single DOD paper to the NSC staff, and OSD would take the lead in the interagency meetings. This strengthened the DOD's position and often gave it the upper hand with the other agencies, especially the Department of State, which frequently came to the meetings still trying to sort out policy differences among its regional and functional bureaus.

After enactment of Goldwater-Nichols, the JCS and Joint Staff interpreted the act to mean that they enjoyed an autonomous position. The Joint Staff, for example, insisted on sending separate papers. At the meetings, although the separate Pentagon positions did not differ widely, Defense's arguments did not have the strength as when presented as a single view.

INTERAGENCY PROCESS AND USD(P)

While the work of each of the five undersecretaries and their teams variously affect the development and implementation of U.S. national security policy, and while their staffs interact to a lesser or greater degree with the interagency community, the office of the undersecretary of defense for policy (USD[P]) is the arm of OSD that works most frequently with the other elements of the U.S. government's national security team. This includes most notably the State Department, IC, NSC staff, office of the vice president, Joint Staff, and combatant commanders' staffs. The policy organization is rather large, with between four hundred and five hundred personnel.

It was not always this big. In 1949, one of the three special assistant positions allocated to the secretary of defense was upgraded by statute to be the post of assistant secretary of defense for international security affairs (ASD ISA). For the first thirty years of OSD's existence, ISA was *the* policy organization. Often known as the Pentagon's Little State Department, ISA was a relatively small organization with vast responsibilities. It was staffed by a mix of career civilian officials (many of whom were retired military officers or people who had served in the military) and active duty officers. Four deputy assistant secretaries of defense (DASDs) had regional responsibilities (Europe-NATO, Near East-South Asia, Asia-Pacific, and Latin America; Africa was not assigned a DASD until the 1980s) and an additional DASD was in charge of policy planning. The DASDs reported to the ASD ISA, who was the secretary's principal advisor on all defense policy and international security related issues. The regional DASDs had responsibilities for geographical areas that aligned with those of assistant secretaries of state. This alignment of responsibilities, in effect, gave the DASDs as much authority and span of responsibility as State Department assistant secretaries who ran large bureaus.

In 1977, Congress created the post of USD(P). While the first undersecretary simply sat atop the ISA organization with a small personal staff (and was frequently the victim of bureaucratic end-runs by the ASD/ISA), in 1979 parts of ISA were stripped out to become direct reports to the undersecretary. In 1981, a new ASD for international security policy was created, taking responsibility for NATO/Europe, nuclear forces, arms control, and export control policy. The assistant secretary for ISA was left with responsibility for Asia, Latin America, Near-East South Asia, and Africa, and conventional forces policy.[19] The undersecretary oversaw both ASDs. After numerous changes in the Bush, Clinton, and Bush administrations, policy took on its current form under its ninth undersecretary, Michele Flournoy, who took office in February 2009.

UNDERSTANDING THE ORGANIZATION: WHAT IS OUSD(P)?

The office of the undersecretary of defense for policy (OUSD[P]) is in every respect a much more diverse organization than it was in 1977. While its staff is still comprised of a mix of career civilian officials and military officers, the civilian side of the house is very different than that which Policy inherited from ISA in the late 1970s. Unlike the early decades of the organization, Policy careerists tend to have broadly based skills and experience. In the late 1970s (when the authors joined Policy) many of the career civilians, particularly those who were military retirees, sought to remain in one job for their entire career (i.e., colloquially known as the German desk officer for life syndrome). Ironically, people in other agencies thought this staff longevity and institutional memory gave DOD an advantage in the interagency process. The State Department, for example, thought it was plagued by ever-changing personnel as foreign service officers (FSOs) were constantly rotated.

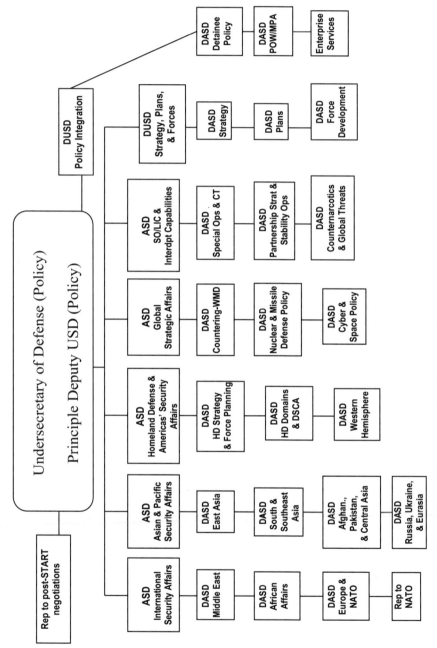

Figure 5.2   The Office of the Undersecretary of Defense for Policy, 2009.

The ISA/OUSD(P) leadership found this static personnel situation acceptable; or stated differently, the senior-level political appointees did not have interest in changing the situation during their relatively short tenure at the DOD. It was not, however, acceptable for the health of the Policy organization and its career personnel. It was a by-product of the fact that no career development program existed for the civilian staff in Policy and none of the senior political appointees ever felt the need to create one. As more young people joined the organization with ambitions beyond being a narrow subject matter expert and faced limited promotion potential, a mechanism needed to be created to produce a broad-based and flexible professional staff. To that end, in the mid-1990s, the authors with then Undersecretary Walter Slocombe's blessing and active encouragement, created the policy career development program, which both regularized promotion opportunities throughout the organization and instituted a mechanism for career officials to rotate jobs within the overall OUSD(P) organization.[20] Its net result was to increase significantly the professionalism of the career officials, to create a more homogenous USD(P) culture (rather than one confined to a particular ASD's or DASD's organization), and to provide management opportunities to allow careerists to develop the leadership and management skills that would permit them to perform in senior-level posts.

Many of the career personnel entered OSD through the presidential management fellows (PMF) program, which brings the best graduate students in the nation into federal service. At times, the PMF has been the only source of new blood in the organization, aside from political appointees. In fact, a high percentage of the senior career officials now in Policy were once PMFs. More than any other organization in the national security arena, OSD's leadership—and OUSD(P)'s—is made up of political appointees.

Political Appointees versus Careerists

One major difference in OSD compared to other interagency players is the extent to which it is driven by political appointees and not by DOD career civil servants. Few other interagency players are so dominated by outsiders. The entire IC has less than a handful of political appointees, typically the top two or three officials of the DNI and CIA. The office of the JCS has no political appointees (occasionally, a civilian may serve as an advisor or consultant to the chairman, JCS, but this person rarely interacts with the interagency process). At the State Department, careerists (i.e., FSOs) dominate the senior policy ranks below the secretary and deputy secretary. Typically, eighty-five percent of the deputy assistant secretaries and approximately fifty percent of the assistant secretaries (and at least one undersecretary) are career FSOs. In sharp contrast, until 2009 no OSD careerist has ever been nominated for a post within the department requiring Senate confirmation (assistant or undersecretary), although career FSOs have twice served as USD(P) and twice as assistant secretaries in Policy.[21]

Similarly, until the late 1980s, only one of the many deputy assistant secretary positions in OSD Policy was filled by a careerist. Despite a major change brought about by Undersecretary Walter Slocombe in the mid-to-late 1990s, which saw better than fifty percent of those posts filled by career staff, the George W. Bush administration reverted to the practice of staffing policy's senior leadership almost exclusively with political appointees (and indeed filled several office director positions with appointees as well). The Obama administration, and in particular Undersecretary of Defense for Policy Flournoy, appears to be allowing careerists once again to assume senior leadership roles in Policy.

From an organizational management standpoint, the net effect of such a high number of political appointees is that the top five to six levels (undersecretary down to office director) of OUSD(P) are replaced every four to eight years. Not only does this turnover tend to decapitate the organization in the early months of an administration (thereby reducing its ability to contribute to the early formulation of policy by a new team), it also undercuts continuity, institutional memory, and, most importantly, long-term morale of the career staff. Moreover, in the absence of new political appointees in the upper ranks of OSD, a new secretary or deputy secretary may be reluctant to give their proxies to careerists who might still represent a previous administration's priorities and philosophy. Having more careerists in the undersecretary and assistant secretary positions might reduce this tendency, if not eliminate it entirely.

The influx of numerous political appointees in Policy also creates a dysfunctional human dynamic early in a new administration. The appointees tend to regard the careerists they inherit as holdovers from the previous administration and, accordingly, tend to distrust them and the advice they provide. This in turn creates uncertainty and doubt on the part of the careerists. The distrust this breeds undercuts Policy's ability to act effectively both within the DOD and more broadly in the interagency arena. Ultimately, over time, the appointees come to recognize the value, and indeed loyalty, of the career staff and the "we-they" dynamic becomes an "us," but the loss of effectiveness, particularly early in an administration, is a cause for concern. Moreover, Secretary Rumsfeld's Policy team removed all but one of the career deputy assistant secretaries it inherited and relegated them to low-level positions well outside the Policy mainstream simply because they were careerists. This sent a chilling message through the ranks that officials who rose to leadership positions were imperiling their careers.

The long-term effect of an abundance of political appointees on the morale of career civil servants is significant. If nearly all the DASD positions, and many of the office director jobs, are filled with political appointees (or FSOs), there is little opportunity to achieve a senior-level position in the department for those who deserve it. FSOs are trained and aspire to be ambassadors. In the military services, career officers compete for major commands. There is nothing comparable for a DOD career civil servant. Careerists covet being selected for the senior executive service (SES), but obtaining the SES rank does not necessarily relate to being given senior-level responsibilities.

Generational Changes

Other generational changes have also occurred in the Policy area which both benefit and disadvantage the organization's effectiveness. Previously (in the late 1970s and 1980s), most of the career civilians had some military experience, which not only gave the civilian staff valuable knowledge and background experience, but also engendered a feeling of trust with their military counterparts. Today, very few of the civilians are military retirees; in fact, most of the civilians have not served in the military.

Another factor affecting the OSD Policy staff is the number of active duty military personnel assigned to it. In the early 1980s, approximately one-half of the staff was military officers. This high percentage contributed significantly to Policy's technical expertise, which in turn gave OSD Policy credibility with the Joint Staff and services. Over time, however, as military positions were converted to civilian slots, the percentage of active duty military officers assigned to Policy has been reduced to less than twenty percent. The organization is perceived as made up of exclusively of suits, which is not healthy for the overall civilian-military relationship.

Another change has been the gender of the personnel. Where ISA was almost exclusively a male organization, women now fill a large number of positions at every level of the Policy organization.

IS THERE AN OSD/POLICY CULTURE?

It would be something of a stretch to suggest that, given the diversity of the organization, that a Policy culture exists that colors the way OSD approaches either interagency discussions or specific interagency policy issues. That said, OSD career officials tend to be more innately conservative in their approach to issues and, therefore, more skeptical of foreign governments' intentions or promises than other elements of the interagency. It was long a maxim in OSD "to focus on adversary capabilities rather than adversary intentions." This view, heightened by daily interaction with colleagues in the Joint Staff and combatant commanders staffs (which have to worry about the risks and ramifications of military action should diplomacy fail), tends to be reflected in a risk-averse approach to policymaking. Where possible, the OSD staff seeks to have a common position with its Joint Staff colleagues in interagency deliberations; this magnifies OSD's tendency to view situations as being risks rather than opportunities. (Paradoxically, when dealing with force structure or budgetary issues internal to the DOD, OSD over the decades has evolved to be more questioning—even to the point of being confrontational—when dealing with military colleagues who are perceived to be less than forthcoming regarding information or details.)

Inevitably, the career staff's approach to dealing with the interagency is also influenced by the attitude of Policy's senior political appointees. Although historically there have always been specific issues that sparked bureaucratic warfare across the Potomac, generally speaking comity prevailed among the people in the interagency arena, if only for the reason that policymaking is a marathon event and one always has to keep dealing with the players from the other agencies. Twice in recent memory, once for a short period of time in the Reagan years and more pronouncedly during the tenure of Donald Rumsfeld, OSD treated the interagency process with an abiding animosity. This is relevant here only to the degree that it makes clear that if senior political appointees are adverse to working issues through the interagency process, the career staffs will in no small measure be pressured into adopting the attitudes of their bosses, which inevitably causes a stalemate or breakdown in the process. When this happens, senior administration officials are forced to adopt more informal and, most likely, less inclusive policymaking mechanisms.

THE 2003 IRAQ WAR: "THEY NEVER SUITED UP"

The foregoing discussion suggests that OSD is likely to have a major impact on the interagency process regardless of whether its senior officials embrace or reject that process. In most cases, the secretary of defense and his senior advisors recognize the necessity to engage in the process, if only to ensure that other agencies do not complicate defense and military strategies. However, the case of the 2003 Iraq War was unique and in some ways anomalous. Both in the development and planning for Operation Iraqi Freedom (OIF) and in the subsequent postwar reconstruction phase—the so-called Phase IV—OSD/Policy took little active interest in interagency work needed to prepare for potential combat operations in Iraq and took even less interest in postwar reconstruction activity in 2002–4. As active participants in the both OSD and NSC actions during this time, the authors are in a position to provide some direct observation of the interagency dysfunction. Capturing the sense of disarray was the common perception that the Pentagon "never suited up" for the game.

Except for weekly high-level strategy sessions of the deputies committee (DC) that began in early 2002, no interagency planning for possible combat operations in Iraq was permitted during the first half of 2002; at its most senior levels, the administration did not want any interagency work occurring on this. Echoing what has been said in other chapters regarding the lack of senior level decision making, there seemed to have been an assumption there would be war and hence no actual decision was formally taken.

In a curious twist, a Joint Staff effort, begun as an internal exercise to identify tasks that the interagency needed to accomplish before possible combat operations could begin—if the president so directed—quietly evolved into a tightly circumscribed NSC staff-led effort to plan a war that was not yet announced. Meetings were held three times a week to identify, review, and most importantly resolve the various tasks. This effort was given the innocuous title "executive steering group (ESG)" to deflect attention from its purpose and taskings; similarly, almost all ESG meetings were held in the Joint Staff area of the Pentagon to avoid the rest of the bureaucracy from noticing them, as would be the case if assistant-secretary level civilian and military officials arrived at the State Department or NSC offices next to the White House. The ESG's role was *not* to tee up fundamental decisions for potential debate among cabinet officials, but rather it was to focus on the implementation of tasks necessary to prepare for and to support possible combat operations.

From the very beginning, OSD/Policy showed lukewarm interest in the ESG and its work. In the words of one ESG participant, "It's not just that OSD wasn't 'in the game,' they didn't even come to the stadium and suit up." The ESG's first tasks were to obtain approval from various allied and friendly governments for several dozen construction projects in the CENTCOM and European command (EUCOM) areas of responsibility. CENTCOM Commander Tommy Franks had declared that completion of the projects was essential prior to the beginning of combat operations. At the ESG's first meeting, however, no one from either OSD or the Joint Staff could produce a list of projects. At the second meeting a list was produced but the ESG was then informed that an unknown issue was preventing the projects from being funded. Again, no one from OSD/Policy knew why, nor had these representatives consulted with their counterparts in the DOD comptroller's office to find out what was obstructing these projects. At the ESG chair's insistence, the comptroller became a member of the ESG thereafter. This passive-aggressive pattern continued throughout the ESG's operation until the onset of the March 2003 invasion. Of the over one hundred separate issues the ESG considered (including such critical tasks as building an OIF allied coalition, obtaining required overseas over-flight access, and getting basing rights for CENTCOM forces), OSD/Policy took an interest in only one rather tangential issue: namely, creating a training facility in Europe at which a "Free Iraqi Brigade" could be organized and made battle ready. OSD/Policy was forecasting the availability of thousands of recruits; however, at the end of the day, fewer than one hundred signed up.

Nevertheless, the ESG saw to it that a NATO ally provided an extensive training facility and a full training establishment that was headed by a U.S. major general.

At the direction of President Bush, through National Security Advisor Rice, the ESG did begin to examine the postinvasion issues. The ESG representatives provided input into and first-level clearance of major strategy briefs, which went through the deputies and principals committees and to formal NSC meetings. In January 2003, however, President Bush accepted Secretary Rumsfeld's recommendation to approve the national security policy directive 24 (NSPD-24), which assigned primary responsibility for postwar Iraq—and tactical planning as well—to the DOD. OSD/Policy made clear thereafter that the ESG's assistance in this area was neither necessary nor desired. It effectively stopped by March 2003. Ironically, deteriorating security, political, and socioeconomic conditions in Iraq caused growing Washington concern shortly thereafter in April and May. Yet, consistent with NSPD-24, OSD/Policy did not seek any interagency support, even though many of the problems occurring on the ground fell well outside the DOD's expertise and competence.

Finally, in early July 2003, Dr. Rice reestablished the ESG with the mission of coordinating interagency activity to help stabilize and improve conditions on the ground. The Justice Department, USAID, Treasury, and the Coalition Provisional Authority (CPA) were added to the ESG's membership. In its second life, the ESG met three to four times a week by secure video conference. While other agencies were almost always represented at the assistant secretary or deputy assistant secretary level, OSD invariably sent lower-ranked office directors who had less authority to speak for the department. Moreover, these officials seldom attended regularly, severely limiting the group's ability to develop any continuity needed to deal with critical issues like electricity supplies, security for humanitarian aid missions, translators for U.S. troops, and the detailing of skilled specialists to the CPA from other agencies. Simply put, OSD Policy never brought an issue to the table to be solved, nor sought to assist in resolving those that were on the table. The obvious policy disarray was partly due to OSD/Policy's uncharacteristic unwillingness to play in what amounted to the most important interagency agenda of the Bush administration. U.S. policy and strategy for Iraq were in disarray, reconstruction and security efforts were floundering, and American soldiers were dying.

The OSD's disdain for the postwar effort was apparent in how it dealt with creating the office in Washington to support the CPA, led by Ambassador Paul Bremer. By the summer of 2003, it became evident that the CPA required better support from Washington, especially from the DOD.[21] A decision was made to establish a "CPA Rear" to mirror in Washington all the staff functions being performed by the CPA in Baghdad to relieve it from many daily Washington-driven taskings (e.g., congressional and media inquiries, contract negotiations, personnel recruitment, etc.). But OSD support for CPA Rear was marginal, at best. None of the tasks, personnel assignments, office space, authorizations to participate in interagency meetings, etc., were ever given a high enough priority to succeed. Most importantly, CPA Rear was never able to get other agencies to approve the assignment of their personnel to Baghdad to serve the CPA. OSD/Policy was itself unwilling to assign its own staff to the CPA, which further undercut the effectiveness of the postwar reconstruction effort. In sum, as the organization so eager to take on the Iraq problem, the DOD failed to live up to its own responsibility and to take advantage of the necessary interagency skills needed to avert the chaos that ensued in 2003–4.

CONCLUDING THOUGHTS

The evolution of the OSD has led it to become in many respects the most powerful player in the interagency process. The command over more than a million military and civilian employees, a half-trillion dollar budget, and a powerful array of transportation, communication, and weapons systems makes it the 911 for many urgent problems facing the U.S. national security enterprise. Recent statements from Defense Secretary Gates and other officials suggest that there is a desire to shift the heavy burden of nation-building back onto other civilian national security agencies rather than assume the Pentagon is the appropriate and most capable agency for such functions. That debate may lead to some rebalancing, but is unlikely to alter dramatically the DOD's major role in all aspects of national security planning.

As the foregoing discussion suggests, the power of the DOD and the secretary's policy shop is such that it can dominate or destroy the interagency process. As the 2003–4 period demonstrates, no single agency was prepared to handle the military, social, political, economic, and cultural complexities that this nation-building exercise required. Secretary Rumsfeld may have believed that twenty-first-century challenges, such as transnational terrorism and proliferation, have made the interagency process irrelevant; however, pursuing a go-it-alone strategy or obstructivism is no solution. Rather, success may demand a re-examination of how the interagency process needs to be organized and where the locus of control—probably at the White House-NSC level—needs to be established early to ensure effective collaboration and information sharing on any given crisis or complex contingency operation.

A second observation that can be made is that the personality and style of the secretary can shape how the policy process works within the department and how OSD will play in the interagency process. Strong secretaries, having either regard or disdain for other agencies, shape the attitude of their close advisors and all the many political appointees brought into the department. Unlike other agencies, OSD policy is remade every time there is a new administration or even a new secretary, meaning the behavior of the department can shift quite dramatically. A key question is whether so many critical positions within the OSD should be offered to political appointees, guaranteeing that there is less continuity of operation from administration to administration. Establishing the principle that DASDs should, on balance, remain careerist positions and then developing a career cadre of policy officers could improve OSD's ability to operate during political transitions. Moreover, breaking the well-known pattern of excessive political turnover might depoliticize OSD processes. Future secretaries could then be assured that the careerists are clearly apolitical and not holdovers from a previous administration's own effort to stuff political favorites into mid-level positions within the department. This might get ideology out of the department and bring expertise and experience back into the process.

A third observation would be that a policy culture as such is still very much lacking. In light of the dominance of political appointees and the demoralization of the OSD careerists, what organizational culture does exist is still very weak and not very highly self-regarding. When the interagency becomes stalemated on some issue, OSD culture is probably not to blame, rather it is under orders from a political appointee. Before the Goldwater-Nichols reforms, it was easier to speak of a common DOD culture that reflected the native conservatism that the Pentagon brought to the table; in that pre-1986 period, OSD Policy and the Joint Staff would hammer out their differences—sometimes minor, sometimes great—and then present a more united front to the interagency process. Now, with the Joint Staff representing the chairman's and the military's views separately, OSD Policy has to fend for itself. Given its weak self-image, what amounts to OSD Policy's approach is whatever the senior political officials say it is. Ironically, development of a stronger OSD culture, not a weaker one, might actually make the organization more effective in working the interagency process.

Finally, as we enter an era of constrained budgets and potentially increased involvement in failed states with special forces, the analysis provided by OSD for military force and stability operations will become even more critical. The OSD is one of the critical focal points for civilian-military relations, whereby the professional general officer corps provides advice and policy recommendations. As documented by different chapters in this volume, this relationship has undergone severe strain in the last few years. The modern problem set requires a coordinated civilian-military process inside the DOD, one that is open, analytical, and disciplined, and characterized by mutual respect. The failure to restore this relationship will hamper the efficacy of OSD and the broader national security enterprise in the process.

NOTES

1. Richard I. Wolf, *The United States Air Force: Basic Documents on Roles and Missions* (Washington, DC: United States Air Force, 1987).

2. Steve Vogel, *The Pentagon: A History: The Untold Story of the Wartime Race to Build the Pentagon—And to Restore It Sixty Years Later* (New York: Random House, 2007), 345.

3. Steve L. Rearden, *History of the Office of the Secretary of Defense, Volume 1: The Formative Years 1947–1950* (Washington, DC: U.S. Government Printing Office, 1984), 24. (Hereafter *History of OSD*).

4. Samuel P. Huntington, *The Soldier and the State: The Theory and Politics of Civil-Military Relations* (Cambridge: Belknap, 2000), 449.

5. *History of OSD*, vol. 1, 127–28.

6. Roger B. Trask and Alfred Goldberg, *The Department of Defense, Volume 4: Into the Missile Age 1956–60* (Washington, DC: Historical Office of the Secretary of Defense, 1997), 130.

7. "McNamara's Whiz Kids" were often drawn from the RAND Corporation or other university public policy and economic programs, which would apply strict quantitative methods to evaluating weapons systems' cost effectiveness. One so-called Whiz Kid, Les Aspin, would become a future chairman of the House Armed Services Committee and later secretary of defense under President Clinton.

8. *History of OSD*, vol. 5, 36–37. A high-level task force was established that met regularly and often included senior White House representatives like Robert Kennedy.

9. The Office of System Analysis produced these reports initially. For many years one of the McNamara whiz kids, William Kaufman, an MIT professor McNamara brought to Washington, was principally responsible for drafting these posture statements.

10. Christopher Drew, "Obama Wins Crucial Senate Vote on F-22," *New York Times,* July 21, 2009.

11. More than other agencies, the DOD operates according to plans. Thus, the secretary's staff prepares a quadrennial defense review, the defense program guidance, the national military strategy, and the annual defense posture statements. These documents, which involve the OSD, Joint Staff, and military services, help to shape the department's priorities and tell others in the government what the Pentagon is prepared to do.

12. August Cole and Yochi Dreazen, "Pentagon Pushes Weapon Cuts," *Wall Street Journal*, April 7, 2008. Gates's proposed 2010 DOD budget of $534 billion is still four percent larger than 2009, but it cut new orders for advanced F-22 fighter jets in favor of low-tech unmanned drones used in Afghanistan and Iraq; expected congressional opposition required a high degree of secrecy and signed secrecy agreements for those in the Pentagon who were knowledgeable about these proposals.

13. Roger B. Trask and Alfred Goldberg, *The Department of Defense, 1947–1997: Organization and Leaders* (Washington, DC: Historical Office of the Secretary of Defense, 1997), 78.

14. Charles F. Stevenson, *SECDEF: The Nearly Impossible Job of Secretary of Defense* (Washington, DC: Potomac Books, 2006).

15. Stevenson, *SECDEF*, 69.

16. Douglas Feith, *War and Decision: Inside the Pentagon at the Dawn of the War on Terrorism* (New York: HarperCollins, 2008), 106.

17. See Peter Rodman, *Presidential Command: Power and Leadership and the Making of Foreign Policy from Richard Nixon to George W. Bush* (New York: Alfred Knopf, 2009); and Feith, *War and Decision*.

18. Quoted in Bob Woodward, *State of Denial: Bush at War Part III* (New York: Simon & Schuster, 2006), 379.

19. This division of responsibility reflected the personal interests of the nominees for the ISA and ISP posts rather than any grand bureaucratic design.

20. Prior to the 1990s, promotions within the GS system and into the senior executive service (SES) were made by the individual assistant secretaries. Regular access to the assistant secretaries thus became a key consideration for career officials. In late 2008, the undersecretary of defense for personnel and readiness mandated that anyone applying for the DOD's two highest SES grades must have held positions in multiple agencies if they wanted to be promoted. A similar requirement is said to be in the offing for promotion into the SES. In 2008, a senior DOD careerist was nominated to be an assistant secretary of defense in OUSD(P), but was forced to resign from the civil service in order to accept the position. It is worth noting that the officials in OSD responsible for career personnel policy are all political appointees.

21. Because OSD Policy had asked for and been given responsibility for postwar Iraq, the authors found it surprising that OSD/Policy officials from the undersecretary down to office directors and action officers were supporting those efforts as a tertiary responsibility.

Chapter 6   The Military: Forging a Joint
            Warrior Culture

Michael J. Meese and Isaiah Wilson III

> Many feel that the Pentagon is like a giant log floating slowly down a turbulent river.
> The log has lots of ants running around on top who stick their legs into the water on occasion
> to try to steer the log in some direction or the other. Some of these ants have somewhat longer legs than others,
> some seem to avoid ever sticking their legs in the water, while some others fall or are pushed off the log.
> Most seem to be in a great hurry as they run from one side of the log to the other.
>
> *Perry Smith, Assignment Pentagon: How to Excel in a Bureaucracy*

INTRODUCTION

The U.S. Department of Defense (DOD) spends $693 billion annually and commands global forces that are unprecedented in their relative size compared with other forces throughout the world.[1] It is the ultimate expression of the military might of America as a superpower and undergirds much of U.S. influence in the world. Simultaneously, DOD has the greatest personnel system, budgetary process, bureaucracy, and government building in the world: the Pentagon. The "greatness" of the DOD gives it extraordinary resources that can achieve unequalled accomplishments, but also can have significant drawbacks. First, the sheer size and power of the military—occasionally referred to as the eight-hundred-pound gorilla—can have extraordinary power in both national and international policy environments.[2] Second, multiple competing organizational structures and bureaucratic cultures can make change within DOD problematic. Finally, DOD requires management structures to ensure that greatness does not mask inefficiency. Understanding both the positive and negative aspects of the greatness of DOD is essential to navigating the national security enterprise.

This chapter builds on the previous one by expanding the discussion beyond the office of the secretary of defense (OSD) to the overall structure of DOD to include the Joint Chiefs of Staff (JCS), military departments and services, the combatant commands, and the defense agencies. This chapter will first provide a general explanation of DOD itself, how it is organized, and the brief history of its evolution. Next, it will explain significant cultural and organizational influences on DOD, specifically the role of the military as a profession and the cultures of the several military services and the joint staff that affect DOD. Finally, it will illustrate the effect of organizational culture on policy by examining different case studies of DOD decision making and then draw conclusions concerning the future of the military establishment.

THE MILITARY ESTABLISHMENT AS AN INSTITUTION

The story of the establishment of DOD is one of independent services chafing at the loss of institutional identities amidst continued efforts toward unification to improve the coordination, efficiency, and effectiveness of U.S. military forces as a whole. Before 1947, the

War Department included the army and later the Army Air Corps; and the Department of the Navy included the navy, with its associated marine corps. Consequently, there was limited interservice rivalry because the services were in different cabinet departments and received legislative approvals from separate congressional committees.[3] During both world wars, the need for centralized coordination forced the development of ad hoc arrangements: President Wilson established the council on national defense during World War I and President Roosevelt established the State-War-Navy Coordinating Committee during World War II.[4] In the aftermath of World War II, the National Security Act of 1947 was the first attempt to unify formally the military services in peacetime.[5] Notably, the structure in Congress also changed, with the Military Affairs Committee and the Naval Affairs Committee being combined into a single Armed Services Committee to provide unified oversight over a newly unified national military establishment.

While the 1947 act was the most significant step toward unification, it was still a compromise document that required additional modifications. The first three amendments to the National Security Act, in 1949, 1953, and 1958, "were major landmarks . . . aimed primarily at strengthening the centralized entities on the civilian side of the Pentagon."[6] The Goldwater-Nichols Act of 1986 was the most recent piece of major legislation affecting the Pentagon organization. The Goldwater-Nichols Act generally defines the structure of DOD as it exists today with several major components: the management structure of DOD and the Joint Staff, the military departments and services, the combatant commands, and the defense agencies.[7]

DOD Management: OSD, JCS, and the Joint Staff

As described in chapter 5, the management of DOD is accomplished by the secretary of defense with the assistance of the deputy secretary, currently five undersecretaries, several assistant secretaries, and other staff members. Although there are some military assistants to these officials, all of the ultimate management decisions are made by civilian leaders appointed by the president and, in many cases, confirmed by the Senate. This reinforces the historical importance of civilian control of the military, which will be discussed in more detail below.

The Joint Chiefs of Staff (JCS) includes the chairman, vice chairman, and the chiefs of each of the military services: army, navy, air force, and marine corps. As specified in the 1986 Goldwater-Nichols Act, the chairman is the principal military advisor to the president, the National Security Council (NSC), and the secretary of defense and is the senior officer in the U.S. military. The vice chairman must be from a service other than that of the chairman and is the second-highest ranking military officer. The other four members of the JCS are also advisors to the president, NSC, and secretary of defense in addition to their roles as chiefs of their own services.[8]

The Joint Staff consists of approximately 1,500 military personnel, equally selected from all military services, who assist the chairman and other members of the JCS in the performance of their duties.[9] They interact with the OSD staff, the services, and the combatant commands, as well as the other agencies of government, to assist in providing strategic advice on planning, preparedness, requirements, programs, budgets, as well as joint doctrine, training, and education. Neither the chairman individually nor the JCS collectively are in the chain of command. Direction flows directly from the president to the secretary of defense to combatant commanders. The JCS and Joint Staff facilitate coordination and communication but "shall not operate or be organized as an overall Armed Forces General Staff and shall have no executive authority."[10] This prohibition of command by the Joint Staff reflects the concern for a powerful military staff that might undermine civilian control of the military or the role of individual military services.[11]

Taken together, OSD, the JCS, and the Joint Staff provide the strategic direction and management of the DOD. They engage with other agencies of government, Congress, the public, and other national and international actors on behalf of the national military establishment as a whole. However, they rely on the two other components of DOD—the services and the combatant commands—actually to execute any tasks.

The Military Services and Departments

The U.S. armed forces consist of the four military services: the army, the air force, the navy, and the marine corps. The U.S. Coast Guard is part of the Department of Homeland Security, but can have elements of it placed under operational control of the navy in time of war or when directed by the president.[12] The services are organized within military departments with their own civilian service secretaries, which are vestiges of the pre-World War II independent services; however, service secretaries no longer hold cabinet rank and are subordinate to the secretary of defense.

The primary purposes of the Department of the Army, the Department of the Air Force, and the Department of the Navy (which controls both the navy and the marine corps) are to recruit, organize, train, and equip their military forces so that they can be provided to combatant commands for employment. This includes all of the nonoperational and administrative functions that are necessary to prepare a soldier, airman, sailor, or marine as part of a unit before their engagement in a military mission:

- personnel functions (recruiting, education, leader development promotions, punishments, retirements, housing, finance, health care);
- material functions (research and development, procurement, fielding, sustainment, disposal);
- operations functions (doctrine, organization, training, evaluation, readiness); and
- support functions (budgeting, operating bases, communications, transportation, life support).

These tasks are detailed in Title 10 of the U.S. code and are often referred to as Title 10 functions. Because each service has the authority to execute them separately—not under the direction of the Joint Staff, for example—they can tailor their functions to their specific service, which can both account for and accentuate service-specific differences.

The chief of staff of the army, chief of staff of the air force, chief of naval operations (CNO), and commandant of the marine corps are the senior military officers in their services and both direct the functions of their service and participate as a member of the JCS. They do not employ any of their forces but prepare forces for operational employment in their service chief role and advise for (or against) employment of forces in their JCS role. Similar to the OSD staff, each military department has a staff of civilians, under- and assistant secretaries, that assist the service secretary in fulfilling his or her role. Each service chief has a military staff that works with the joint staff and the civilian leaders in their own service to develop and execute policy to accomplish their Title 10 functions. The vice chief of staff, vice CNO, or assistant commandant, in each service, normally runs the day-to-day operations of the staff.

The Combatant Commands

With OSD, the JCS, and Joint Staff providing management, and the services providing the forces, the ten combatant commands are the organizations that actually employ military forces on operational missions. Six of the combatant commands are geographically organized, as indicated in figure 6.1, with each part of the globe assigned to the responsibility of a four-star general or admiral. The U.S. Northern Command (NORTHCOM) is responsible for Canada, the United States, and Mexico. The U.S. Southern Command (SOUTHCOM) is responsible for Central and South America. The U.S. European Command (EUCOM) is responsible for Europe, to include Russia to the east and Israel to the south. The U.S. Africa Command (AFRICOM) is responsible for most of Africa, except Egypt. The U.S. Central Command (CENTCOM) is responsible for most nations in the Middle East and Central Asia from Egypt in the west to Pakistan in the east. Finally, the U.S. Pacific Command (PACOM) is responsible for India to the west and all nations bordering the eastern Pacific Ocean (except Russia).

Additionally, there are four functional commands that have global responsibility. The U.S. Strategic Command (STRATCOM) is responsible for strategic deterrence, which includes command and control of U.S. nuclear weapons and global missile defense, as well as military operations in space and cyberspace. The U.S. Special Operations Command (SOCOM) is responsible for the training, equipping, and employment of U.S. Special Operations units and has been given the additional mission of synchronizing global planning against terrorism. The U.S. Transportation Command (TRANSCOM) is responsible for global military deployment and distribution systems. Finally, U.S. Joint Forces Command (JFCOM) is responsible for providing joint-capable military forces. Because the services already provide service-trained military forces, JFCOM concentrates on joint exercises, experiments, doctrine, command structures, and training to integrate and provide military forces that can work together from all services. JFCOM is one of the major forces toward the unification of joint and increasingly interagency relationships, as reflected in figure 6.2.[13]

The Goldwater-Nichols Act substantially strengthened the power of the combatant commanders and today they operate with significant power, access, and authority in their regions. Some have described them as "the modern-day equivalent of the Roman Empire's proconsuls—well-funded, semi-autonomous, unconventional centers of U.S. foreign policy," with disproportionate power within their region that sometimes can dwarf the power and influence of ambassadors or other interagency players in the same region.[14] Not only do combatant commanders wield significant authority in their regions and in the interagency, but they have increasing influence within DOD itself. Combatant commanders have direct access to the president and the secretary of defense, and they represent the demand side for military forces. The services are the supply side of military forces and, in spite of the unprecedented size of the U.S. military, must apportion those forces among combatant commands that seemingly have an insatiable demand for military forces in their areas. This tension between combatant commanders and service chiefs has increased as

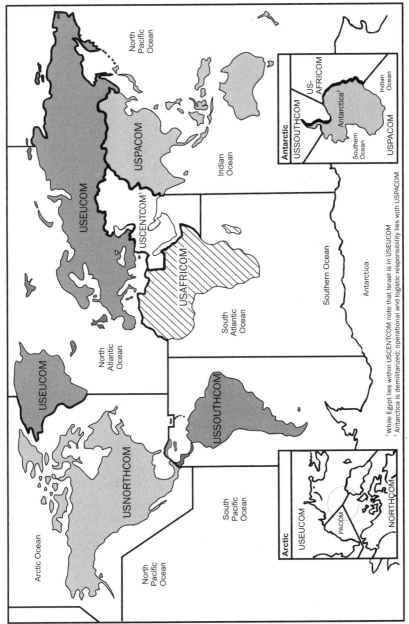

Figure 6.1   Geographical Combatant Commands (DOD, accessed at www.defenselink.mil/specials/unifiedcommand/ images/unified-command_world-map.jpg).

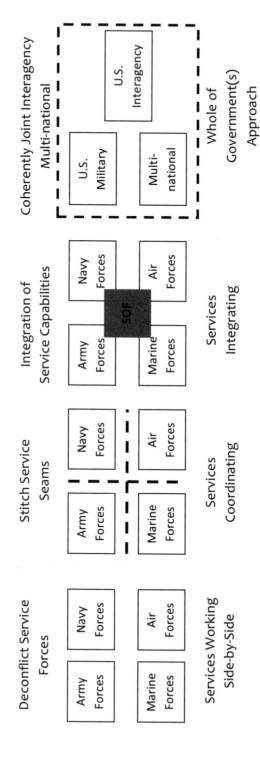

Figure 6.2   Increased Integration of Forces over Time.

some combatant commanders have become well known (e.g., Generals Petraeus, Abizaid, Franks, Jones, Clark, Zinni, and Schwarzkopf as well as Admirals Blair and Fallon) while most service chiefs are generally unknown outside of their service. While any four-star position is certainly important, as a significant cultural shift from decades ago when the pinnacle of any military career would have been to be the chief of one's own service, increasingly the more powerful and prestigious jobs are perceived to be that of combatant commanders, who are *executing* U.S. national security policy throughout the world.

The Defense Agencies

As an increased move toward unification and jointness, defense agencies have increased in numbers, size, and demands on the DOD budget. For example, many of the service logistics functions are integrated into the Defense Logistics Agency (DLA); many long-haul communications functions combined in the Defense Information Services Agency (DISA); schools for family members provided by the DOD Educational Activity (DODEA); and satellite reconnaissance and mapping functions combined into the National Geospatial-Intelligence Agency (NGA). Box 6.1 lists these agencies, which are normally commanded by three-star generals or admirals that reflect the breadth of the activities under DOD centralized control. In many cases, particularly those that are engaged with the intelligence community, these agencies can exert significant influence in national security decision making.

ORGANIZATIONAL CULTURE WITHIN DOD

Merely understanding the components of DOD provides a necessary but not sufficient knowledge of the way that DOD functions. While entire books have been written on DOD orga-

---

Box 6.1   Defense Agencies

American Forces Information Service (AFIS)
Armed Forces Radiobiology Research Institute (AFRRI)
Ballistic Missile Defense Organization (BMDO)
Defense Advanced Research Projects Agency (DARPA)
Defense Commissary Agency (DeCA)
Defense Contract Audit Agency (DCAA)
Defense Finance and Accounting Service (DFAS)
Defense Information Systems Agency (DISA)
Defense Intelligence Agency (DIA)
Defense Legal Services Agency
Defense Logistics Agency (DLA)
Defense Medical Programs Activity
Defense Prisoner of War/Missing Personnel Office

Defense Security Cooperation Agency (DSCA)
Defense Security Service (DSS)
Defense Technical Information Center (DTIC)
Defense Technology Security Administration
Defense Threat Reduction Agency (DTRA)
Department of Defense Education Activity (DODEA)
Department of Defense Human Resources Field Activity
National Geospatial-Intelligence Agency (NGA)
National Security Agency (NSA)
TRICARE Military Health System
Washington Headquarters Services

nizational culture, this section describes the most important features and sometimes least understood aspects of that organizational culture.[15] These include the military *as a profession*, the civilian control of the military, and the cultural perspectives of each of the services.

The Military as a Profession

On an organization chart, DOD appears to be analogous to, albeit bigger than, the other large bureaucratic cabinet departments that exist to carry out policies established by Congress and the president in accordance with appropriate laws, regulations, and policies. However, there are two critical distinctions in DOD, both of which significantly affect organizational culture.

First, while there are certainly many aspects of a bureaucracy involved in the day-to-day management of processes, in accomplishing the essential mission of DOD—defending the nation and fighting and winning the nation's wars—the military is entrusted with significant discretion. As a profession, military leaders must develop specialized expertise in the conduct of warfare so that they can effectively make judgments in the face of substantial uncertainty. No policymaker could ever imagine all of the circumstances in combat and specify bureaucratic responses to each, which is why the conduct of warfare is entrusted to the professional judgment of military leaders. As Don Snider observes with regard to the army in particular, "The Army must be a vocational profession—a calling—rather than just a big government bureaucracy, and it must be recognized as such by its client, the American people."[16] In a bureaucracy, the primary method of interacting with individuals is through rules and incentives that are developed to maximize the efficiency of the organization. In a profession, society delegates to the profession responsibilities to develop a specialized expertise and negotiate professional jurisdictions on behalf of the client—in this case, the nation. Part of the challenge, however, is that the military will always have some of the features of a bureaucracy. Don Snider further explains the tension and the resulting problem:

> Maintaining an appropriate balance between the Army's two natures is thus ever elusive; at any time, bureaucracy can come to predominate over profession. The result is an Army whose leaders, self-concepts, decisions, and organizational climate for soldiers reflect a high degree of bureaucracy and efficiency rather than military professionalism and effectiveness. In the bureaucratic mode, the self-concept of the Army's members is likely to become one of "employee," while in the mode of a calling their self-concept is one of professional. . . . Historically, militaries that do not resolve this tension in favor of their professional identity can experience the "death" of their professional character. As their bureaucratic nature comes to dominate, they cease to be a profession and become little more than an obedient military bureaucracy, treating their officers and soldiers as bureaucrats. One need only look to the current armies of western European nations, with one or two exceptions, for examples of this phenomenon.[17]

To address effectively the myriad uncertainties involved in the complexity of battle, military leaders must develop professional trust with their superiors and with the American people so that they can be given the appropriate discretion to employ the nation's violent force on behalf of the American people. Officers within each service are responsible for particular specialized expertise in their areas—land warfare, air warfare, or sea warfare—and they are expected to develop that expertise, convey that knowledge to civilian decision makers, and then execute the decisions of civilian leaders who represent the profession's client—the American people.

Second, in addition to being a profession, the military is generally a closed labor force that recruits individuals at roughly the time that they enter the work force and then develops, trains, educates, promotes, and selectively retains them.[18] There is very limited lateral entry into the military so that, for all intents and purposes, the workers that the military recruits this year will be the base from which it selects its middle-grade managers in twelve to eighteen years and its senior leaders in twenty-five to thirty-five years. While some have proposed increasing lateral entry into the military, most military officers and noncommissioned officers have spent their entire adult lives in their chosen service.[19] Consequently, they are collectively both benefactors and prisoners of their entire career worth of similar experiences. On a positive note, this provides a unique opportunity to use the military personnel system to educate, train, and develop officers in a particular way. For example, when Congress wanted to emphasize jointness in 1986, the Goldwater-Nichols Act provided incentives for officers to have education and assignments in joint specialties. Over the next twenty years nearly all officers increasingly developed joint backgrounds until joint operations became second nature. On a negative note, a lack of lateral entry can lead to generational groupthink. For example, when the Cold War ended and the generation of officers whose primary concept of war had been the defeat of the Soviet Army confronted situations such as Somalia, Haiti, Bosnia, Kosovo, and Afghanistan, the army's official term for those operations became "Operations Other Than War." The Cold War officers emphasized that these operations, while important, were distinctly subordinate to "real war," which many believed should be the primary, if not sole, focus of the army. It was only after challenges in Iraq that the army reexamined its preconceived notions of warfare expressed in doctrine and concluded that "stability operations . . . are now given the same weight as offensive operations and defensive combat operations and are considered a critical part of U.S. military operations."[20] Recognizing the implications of generational learning within the military's closed labor force is important to understanding the military's organizational culture and effectiveness.

The implication of the military as a profession with limited lateral entry is that, more than any other element of the U.S. government, education and training are significant and integral parts of DOD. By the time generals or admirals are advising policymakers in Washington, it is not uncommon for them to have spent up to ten years of their military career in various types of schools: from undergraduate education at service academies (four years); junior officer training (six months to two years); graduate education (two years); intermediate staff colleges (one year); senior service college (one year); and numerous other schools. In addition to educating officers, these schools develop and codify the specialized expertise of war fighting in military doctrine. What officers see, hear, and do at these schools really matters because the experience affects their self-concept and the way that they provide professional military advice.

Subordination to Civilian Control

If the military constituted only a power-seeking element within the DOD bureaucracy, then it might use its specialized expertise to dominate policy debates with a concurrent diminution of the authority of civilian leaders that are nominally superior to military officers. However, one of the integral components of the military, as a servant of society, is that it is both nonpartisan and subordinate to civilian control. That subordination to civilian control within the American military dates back to George Washington, who not only put down the Newburgh conspiracy in 1783 but also resigned his commission before becoming president and in so doing preserved the important separation between civilian and military leadership in the United States.[21] Today, that subordination of civilian control of the military is codified in law. Two examples are the prohibition from the Joint Staff acting as a general staff and the fact that no military officer can serve as secretary of defense or as a service secretary until he or she has been retired from the military for at least ten years or five years, respectively.[22]

More recently, some pointed to Army Chief of Staff Eric Shinseki's response to a congressional question in which he disagreed with the Bush administration's estimate of troops needed in Iraq as insubordination. General Shinseki addressed the importance of civilian control directly when he said: "So when some suggest that we, in the Army, don't understand the importance of civilian control of the military—well, that's just not helpful—and it isn't true. The Army has always understood the primacy of civilian control—we reinforce that principle to those with whom we train all around the world. So to muddy the waters when important issues are at stake, issues of life and death, is a disservice to all of those in and out of uniform who serve and lead so well."[23]

In the most recent issue of civil-military conflict, General Stanley McChrystal, commander of U.S. and NATO forces in Afghanistan, resigned after derogatory comments from him and his staff about civilian leaders involved in Afghanistan policy were published in a *Rolling Stone* magazine article.[24] In spite of the fact that General McChrystal fully supported the president's strategy, he offered his resignation and by doing so reinforced the importance of professional military conduct and subordination to civilian control. McChrystal said: "Throughout my career, I have lived by the principles of personal honor and professional integrity. What is reflected in this article falls far short of that standard."[25] Recognizing the standards of conduct is essential to the effectiveness of the military as a profession. This concept of civilian control of the military is of significant importance to military professionals and is reinforced through education and training throughout their careers.

An integral part of civilian control of the military is the fact that any advice is based only on the professional military judgment based on specialized expertise, education, and doctrine, and is not subject to the particular political party that happens to be in power. This historic nonpartisanship has even led some officers to the belief that they should abstain from voting in national elections.[26] While military officers have been steeped in the tradition of nonpartisan subordination to civilian leadership, some civilian leaders fail to recognize the importance of the proper civil-military relationship. For example, chief of staff of the army during World War II, General George Marshall, had to insist on his own nonpartisan independence from President Roosevelt: "Marshall did not visit Roosevelt's estate, Hyde Park. He made a point not to laugh at his jokes. When, on one occasion, Roosevelt called him George, Marshall said that he was George only to his wife. He insisted that the President call him General Marshall. Roosevelt was famed for his charm and powers of manipulation. Marshall felt it essential for the prosecution of the task ahead [World War II] that he maintain his full independence."[27]

Similarly, today American political leaders undermine this independence when they leverage close association with military leaders for political purposes. For example, President George W. Bush made a point of using General Petraeus's first name, David, when referring to military advice from Iraq several times in press conferences. Shortly after he did that, senior advisors explained the importance of an independent military and, after July 2007, President Bush virtually always referred to the Iraq commander as "General Petraeus" and never "David" again.[28] An independent, nonpartisan, subordinate, professional military that is believed by the American public to be independent, nonpartisan, and subordinate to civilian control is integral to DOD's organizational culture.

Service Cultures: Dominated by the Medium in Which They Fight

Aside from the concept of the profession and the subordination of the military to civilian control, which are common to all services, the significant service-specific education and closed labor force develops and perpetuates distinct organizational cultures that dominate each military service. These organizational cultures are a function of the services' individual histories, which are largely driven by the warfare in which they have been engaged. While any generalization is made with great trepidation because there are certainly many exceptions, the following is a broad attempt to depict the general culture of each military service.

The Army: Obedient Servant Emphasizing People

Carl Builder described the army as "first and foremost, the Nation's obedient and loyal military servant."[29] It focuses on the readiness and preparation of its personnel and emphasizes that the army's boots on the ground in an area is the ultimate expression of American national will and power. At the U.S. Military Academy at West Point, cadets spend four years walking past statues of Washington, MacArthur, Eisenhower, Patton, and other leaders, reinforcing the criticality of the human dimension of leadership. The army hallways of the Pentagon are adorned with division and regimental flags, pictures of battles, and tributes to individuals from the army's history. The army emphasizes cooperation and coordination both within and between services because success in battle requires the effective coordination of all arms and services. While officers from maneuver branches—infantry and armor—still tend to dominate leadership positions, no battle can be won without sea and air transport, fires from artillery, transport and fires from aviation, data from intelligence sources, communications from signal units, mobility from engineers, security from military police, sustainment from logisticians, and myriad other functions. This need for the complex coordination and independent synchronization of all units leads to a great emphasis on fairness, inclusiveness, and, to the extent possible, decentralization among all branches and units in the army.

Even as it is difficult to make generalizations about a service culture, it is even more difficult to generalize about intellectual progenitors of any organization's doctrine or thinking. And it is equally difficult to summarize a comprehensive body of thoughts about military power into a few sentences. However, making such generalizations is important because it provides a window through which the specialized expertise of a service can be understood. For the army, if one were to ask senior leaders to identify an intellectual godfather, many would name Carl von Clausewitz and his writings from the eighteenth century in *On War*.[30] Clausewitz's dictum that "war is an extension of politics by other means," resonates well with the army as the obedient and loyal military servant of political masters. His emphasis on the "fog and friction in war" reinforces the need for military judgment, indeed what Clausewitz calls "military genius." Army leaders are comfortable with his emphasis on the human dimension of warfare and the need for consistent linkages between political leadership and military decision making. They strive to develop the specialized expertise in land warfare that supports effectiveness in battle.

The Air Force: Victory through Technology

As the youngest service spun off from the army in 1947, the air force sees itself as the service that best embodies the modern American way of war—use of decisive technological superiority to overwhelm and defeat any potential foe while avoiding risk of American casualties. From General Billy Mitchell's use of airpower to sink battleships in 1921 and the World War II air raids over Europe, to the nuclear bombs dropped in Japan and the shock and awe at the opening of the Iraq War, the air force continues to emphasize the use of high technology to deliver decisive military victory. At the Air Force Academy, cadets hold formation in a quadrangle surrounded by airplanes on pedestals and gaze at the cold-metal roof of the academy chapel that sweeps up to the heavens. The air force halls in the Pentagon, like most air force headquarters and the newly dedicated air force monument, emphasize sleek, functional, modern designs, much as one would see in the corporate offices of a high-technology firm. In contrast to the army's general equanimity with regard to all branches, the air force prioritizes the pilot as the focus of their human capital strategy because it is the pilot who commands the sophisticated and expensive technology and renders the decisive power in combat.

Air force proponents will often point to several strategists who have recognized the decisive nature of air power in warfare, including Guiluo Dohet, Billy Mitchell, Hap Arnold, and Curtis LeMay. Recently, John Warden has been an influential strategist as he helped design and implement the use of air power in Desert Storm. Expanded information technology has enhanced centralization and prioritization of precision technology so that the air force can provide more effectively and efficiently decisive effects on targets anywhere in the world. This centralized control is embodied in two mainstays of air force operations—the Single Integrated Operational Plan (SIOP) for nuclear weapons and the Air Tasking Order (ATO) for conventional engagements. Both plans are developed by dynamically assimilating all possible intelligence and environmental information and then precisely allocating virtually every weapon of each plane or each warhead of each missile against an optimal target. With its penchant for precision application of technology, the air force has also pushed for leadership in the development of cyber warfare capabilities as well. With increasingly sophisticated intelligence and network connectivity, air power can become an even more decisive element of modern warfare.

The Navy: Independent Exercise of Sovereignty

The navy is "the supranational institution that has inherited the British navy's throne to naval supremacy . . . sea power [is] the most important and flexible kind of military power for America as a maritime Nation."[31] In spite of the 9/11 attacks on the U.S. homeland, the navy is quick to point out, "70 percent of the earth is covered by water, 80 percent of the world's population lives in close proximity to the coast, and 90 percent of the world's international commerce is transported via the sea."[32] The navy can exert American sovereignty throughout the globe and literally show the flag without the inconvenience of placing U.S. soldiers in harm's way on another nation's soil. Moreover, the navy is its own complete joint force with air power through navy aviation, land power through the marines, and navy SEAL teams providing special operations. At the Naval Academy, the midshipmen's lives are dominated by Bancroft Hall—a single imposing dormitory that houses all midshipmen. Like a large ship, it subordinates the accomplishments of any single individual to the overall success of the institution as a whole. In the Pentagon, the navy hallways exude tradition and imposing dignity with dark wooden walls, brass door hardware, and impressive model ships that reflect the extension of naval influence throughout the globe. In spite of modern communications that can impede the previously cherished independent sea operations, there is still great autonomy that is ascribed to a ship's captain or a navy admiral. Being accustomed to giving orders that cause a ship full of sailors and marines to change course, navy leaders are more deferential toward senior-ranking officers, who, in turn, are more likely to act autonomously and be somewhat less concerned with inclusiveness of all components in their decision making.

Most navy leaders would point to Alfred Thayer Mahan as the grand theoretician that underpins the navy's view toward global warfare. Mahan's belief that a state's power and sovereignty was inextricably linked to its sea power reinforces the navy's self-image and importance.[33] This view is consistent with the American founding fathers who specified in the Constitution that "Congress shall have the power . . . to provide and maintain a navy" but only to "raise and support armies," which reflects the nation's intended permanence of the naval service for the United States as a maritime power.[34] Currently, the navy, like the air force, has leveraged information technology to exploit network centric warfare and increased the effectiveness of its ships, while reducing the overall size of the navy.

The Marine Corps: The Nation's Force of Choice

The marine corps organizational culture is summed up in their recruiting motto: "The few. The proud. The Marines." Completely dependent on the navy for budgetary, administrative, and logistics support and competing with the army for many land power missions, the marines are the only military service that the nation could potentially choose to do without. Although that would never happen, marine leaders act as if it could happen any day if they fail to forcefully and publicly demonstrate their continuous relevance to U.S. national security. That is why marine documents advertise themselves as "the nation's 911 force," or "the expeditionary force of choice," and may explain why current marine leaders are rapidly transitioning all force from the "old" war in Iraq to the "new" U.S. national priority in Afghanistan.[35] And the marines make every individual believe that the fate of the marine corps (and the nation) is in their hands and they must make the corps proud. Every marine is first a rifleman and will endure any burden and suffer any sacrifice, being "prepared to 'live hard' in uncertain, chaotic, and austere environments" to accomplish any mission assigned without question.[36] The marines do not have their own academy, but derive many of their traditions from that of the navy and are always careful to never bite the navy hand that feeds, budgets, and equips them. In the Pentagon, the marines have a relatively smaller presence, preferring to have most of their headquarters in nearby Henderson Hall. But, any time there is a marine near any headquarters, just like the marine guards at every U.S. embassy, they are highly visible and exemplify spit-and-polish standards that are second to none.

The stereotype of a marine might imply that they have little or no intellectual godfather, but actually nearly all senior marine leaders are extremely well read and borrow extensively from both army and navy strategic thought to develop their own professional identity and specialized expertise. If pressed to name an individual that drives their thought, marines might identify the persona of heroic individuals such as Lieutenant General Lewis "Chesty" Puller, whose five Navy Crosses for heroism epitomizes the marine's can-do attitude.[37] It is more likely, however, that they might identify the current or a recent commandant of the marine corps as the source of their intellectual thought. In contrast to the other services, which frequently have from eight to eleven four-star generals or admirals each, the marine corps is much smaller and typically has only three or four four-star generals. Consequently, the commandant is truly king within the marine corps and when he issues directives, there is little pushback because, other than the assistant commandant, there is no other four-star general within the service proper.[38] The ability to carefully craft and then focus the marine corps on a single, compelling message is important to the marine corps' organizational culture.

The Joint Staff: A "Purple" Profession in the Making?

With over sixty years since the unification of the DOD and twenty-five years since the passage of the Goldwater-Nichols Act, one might ask whether a "joint profession" with a "purple" identity independent of the services is emerging.[39] There are several significant steps toward cooperation among the services that reflect integration. First, the planning and execution of wars in Iraq, Afghanistan, and elsewhere are fully developed by joint staffs with officers generally being strong advocates of their organizational perspectives much more than any particular service perspective. Correspondingly, the prevalence and prestige of joint assignments has increased, which coincides with the increased relevance and influence of combatant commanders. Second, several of the defense agencies and organizations have developed their own organizational cultures that supersede those of the services from which they draw their people. For example, personnel spending most assignments with the special operations command, defense logistics agency, or national security agency, soon develop their primary personal identity as members of the special operations, logistics, or intelligence communities, respectively, and only secondarily identify with the culture of their parent service. Third, as DOD increasingly engages with other agencies, the cooperation among military services in the joint staff is critical. This joint coordination facilitates the military providing a unified, powerful position as it engages with the Departments of State, Treasury, Justice, the Office of Management and Budget, and other elements of government. So while interservice rivalries still exist, especially with regard to roles, missions, and resource allocation, there is unquestionably a more unified approach among the military services.

On the other hand, the military is still a long way from developing a joint profession. Bureaucratic unification around issues is extremely slow to create long-term change in the overall DOD. Properly understanding the perspectives of individuals in the joint staff is vital to implementing any fundamental, lasting change in DOD. One of the reasons that Secretary of Defense Donald Rumsfeld's priority on defense transformation met with limited success, for example, is that he focused on technology and equipment and not people: "Rightly understood, military transformation is less about emerging technologies, hardware, and software and more about the mindset of military and civilian professionals, including the vision and commitment they carry into their future professional service in behalf of the American people . . . *Military institutions do not transform, people do; and in so doing they transform the institution.*"[40]

The Rumsfeld transformation planning guidance only briefly mentioned the human aspects of military transformation and never led to any long-term changes. To make fundamental changes within DOD, it is important to recognize and provide incentives for coordinated, joint approaches to defense challenges. Exercises by Joint Forces Command are a helpful step toward coordinated training and doctrine development, but the next logical step toward greater joint cooperation is the development of specialized professional expertise for the joint war fighter. While the joint staff has increasing influence in the national security enterprise, there is still a long way for it to develop so that the joint staff becomes as influential as any particular service.

CASES OF ORGANIZATIONAL CULTURE AFFECTING POLICYMAKING

Although some examples were provided above, the following three short case studies illustrate the impact of bureaucratic structure and organizational culture on security policy.

Prewar Planning for Postwar Iraq

The failure to effectively plan for the postwar occupation of Iraq has many explanations, including the impact of organizational culture and bureaucratic structures throughout the various levels of DOD. The CENTCOM staff was significantly underresourced for the coordination and execution of wars in two different theaters and had difficulty gaining additional support from the services (recall General Frank's comment that they were "Title 10 Mother F!@#$s."). JFCOM was actually asked to provide a planning headquarters for postwar planning but failed to do so because it did not want to degrade its overall mission of force experimentation and integration.[41] The army staff under General Shinseki had researched and identified the likely needs in postwar Iraq, but planning for postwar operations in Iraq was not within the army's Title 10 responsibilities, so the army's studies of the cost of occupation were viewed as interesting at best and a nuisance at worse.[42] The senior civilian leadership in the Pentagon (Secretary Donald Rumsfeld, Deputy Secretary Paul Wolfowitz, and Undersecretary [Policy] Douglas Feith) had articulated that there would be little need for postwar planning and as noted in chapter 5, they "never suited up." The chairman of the Joint Chiefs of Staff decided to provide his advice through the secretary of defense and deferred to his civilian supervisor.[43]

Ultimately, when a semipermanent postwar headquarters was established, first the Office of Humanitarian and Reconstruction Affairs (ORHA) under Lieutenant General (retired) Jay Garner and then the Coalition Provisional Authority (CPA) under Ambassador Paul Bremer, these offices reported directly to the OSD staff—not to the combatant command (CENTCOM). In contrast to combatant commands and services that are staffed for and used to executing policy, OSD, as discussed previously, is a management headquarters, which is not properly staffed to supervise operations in a combat theater. In spite of the best military judgment to the contrary, the historical subordination of military input to civilian control led to a combatant command that was overworked, a service that was ignored, and a management structure that leveraged its control over the military in a way that hampered any effective opposition to administration beliefs about the needs in postwar Iraq.

Had the civilian leadership recognized that they needed to be more receptive to military objections, which are historically, legally, and culturally muted; had CENTCOM been resourced either from the services or JFCOM with an adequate planning staff; had the army had a role to play other than merely being the loyal, obedient servant complying as a force provider, then the outcome of the immediate postwar crisis in Iraq might have been different.

The Role of Technology and Unmanned Aerial Vehicles (UAVs)

Changes in technology often illustrate the conflicts between the professional jurisdictions of the different services. In the 1950s, ballistic missile technology led to conflicts between the army and the air force known as the Thor-Jupiter controversy.[44] The relative degree of centralization, allocation, and control of aviation has frequently led to conflicts between the air force, navy, army, and marine aviation. In today's conflicts, the advent of highly capable and potentially armed unmanned aerial vehicles (UAVs) illustrates more than just disagreements over who will control a valuable asset and potentially increase service budgets and capability. It also highlights the difference between the different services approaches toward technology.[45] Although it is an oversimplification, the army's tendency is to decentralize new technology to enhance the mission effectiveness of units on the ground while the air force's tendency is to centralize new technology to improve decision making and thereby optimize all assets for overall mission accomplishment.

The army and marines strongly resisted allowing the air force to become the executive agent for UAVs because of concern that the tendency toward centralization of assets might preclude the decentralized allocation of UAVs as necessary to support ground units. As Richard Aboulafia explains, "What the Army suspects, rightly or wrongly, is 'thank you for filing your flight access request. We will get back to you within a 48–72 hour period and make certain that there are no air [requirements]. Thank you.'"[46] The army's cultural bias is that no amount of technology will be able to eliminate the fog and friction in war and so UAVs and other assets should be allocated to deployed Army units so that they can assist decentralized commanders with greater intelligence to support them in the completion of their missions. In contrast, the air force's bias is to centrally employ all UAV assets so that the intelligence could be continuously fed into an increasingly sophisticated information technology network to maximize the efficient allocation of intelligence and weapons platforms. DOD followed the request of the army (as well as that of the navy and marines) and did not grant the air force executive agency for UAVs, which forced the services to develop a compromise concept of operations.[47] As UAV and other technologies expand, however, the conflict among service professional jurisdictions and the degree of centralization or decentralization of resources will continue to recur.

Approaching Irregular Warfare

Another way of highlighting the differences among organizational cultures within DOD is to examine their responses when new challenges emerge. One such challenge was the situation confronted after the major combat operations in Afghanistan and Iraq where the greatest military in the world was confronted with bands of guerillas, insurgents, and terrorists. These groups challenged the strength of the U.S. military not in force-on-force battles but in what is termed irregular warfare, which the U.S. military conducts as part of "stability, security, transition, and reconstruction" operations. The DOD management (OSD and the JCS) responded by issuing a directive, DOD Directive 3000.05, which established the policy: "Stability operations are a core U.S. military mission that the DOD shall be prepared to conduct and support. They shall be given priority comparable to combat operations. . . . U.S. military forces shall be prepared to perform all tasks necessary to establish or maintain order when civilians cannot do so."[48] Simultaneously, the army had recognized the challenge and turned back to its home of doctrine and specialized expertise—Fort Leavenworth, Kansas—and developed an entirely new manual for counterinsurgency operations, FM 3-24, to confront irregular warfare. True to its organizational culture, the issuing of a manual did not necessarily resolve the issue and concentrate efforts on counterinsurgency for the army. The army did not emphasize counterinsurgency to the exclusion of any individual or branches whose engagement in other types of future warfare might prove critical. Consequently, a robust debate has ensued in the army among professionals who vehemently and publically disagree on the merits of counterinsurgency as a primary task for the U.S. Army.[49]

The marines, on the other hand, had no such debate. They fully participated with the army's counterinsurgency manual development (incorporating concepts from the marine corps' 1940 Small War Manual) and simultaneously issued the new manual as "marine corps Warfighting Publication No. 3-33.5."[50] The marines rapidly adapted their approach to focus on the pressing needs, stating: "Our unique role as the Nation's force in readiness. . .will ensure that we remain highly responsive to the needs of combatant commanders in an uncertain environment against irregular threats."[51] As soon as the nation identified the need to fight irregular warfare, the marines were ready to fight it—and would figure out how to do so as rapidly as they could.

The air force, on the other hand, while assisting the army in irregular warfare wherever it can, culturally views the messy, complex, and long-lasting irregular warfare as antithetical to the American public's preference for war that is quick, leverages American technology, and minimizes casualties. Air Force Major General Charles Dunlap decries the "boots-on-the-ground-zealots," explaining, "As television screens fill with heartbreaking stories of dead and wounded soldiers and their families, such images over time often create political limitations as to how long a democratic society will sustain an operation like that in Iraq." He explains that the solution is air power:

> Air power is America's asymmetric advantage. . . . For example, huge U.S. transports dropping relief supplies or landing on dirt strips in some area of humanitarian crisis get help to people on a timeline that can make a real difference. Air power . . . can apply combat power from afar and do so in a way that puts few of our forces at risk. If America maintains its aeronautical superiority, the enemy will not be able to kill 2,200 U.S. aviators and wound another 15,000, as the ragtag Iraqi terrorists have managed to do to our land forces . . . the nature of the air weapon is such that an Abu Ghraib or Hadithah simply cannot occur. The relative sterility of air power—which the boots-on-the-ground types oddly find distressing as somehow unmartial—nevertheless provides greater opportunity for the discreet application of force largely under the control of well-educated, commissioned officer combatants. . . . The precision revolution has made it possible for air power to put a bomb within feet of any point on earth. . . . Eventually any insurgency must reveal itself if it is to assume power, and this inevitably provides the opportunity for air power to pick off individuals or entire capabilities that threaten U.S. interests. The real advantage—for the moment anyway—is that air power can do it with impunity and at little risk to Americans. The advances in American air power technology in recent years make U.S. dominance in the air intimidating like no other aspect of combat power for any nation in history.[52]

From the perspective of the air force organizational culture, concentrating warfare into the identification of discrete targets that can be engaged with precision weapons will ensure that American military force is used most efficiently.

Interestingly, the navy's organizational culture steeped in tradition has not taken a strong position on irregular warfare, although the (re)emerging threat of piracy has provided an opportunity for the navy to engage irregular threats directly. While never forsaking the need for global maritime presence, without another blue water navy to compete with, the navy stresses the adaptation of navy units to support the fight on shore. The navy's posture statement, organizational documents, and professional writings emphasize the navy's contribution with many sailors being nominated by their service to serve as members of provincial reconstruction teams, explosive ordinance detachments, construction battalions, and other units that contribute to the current fight, even on shore.

CONCLUSION: NEW THREATS, OLD SERVICE "TRIBALISM," AND GETTING BEYOND BOTH

There is a long-standing truism in organizational politics that states "institutions matter because they persist."[53] It is through institutionalization that individuals, groups, and governments preserve practices, tactics, and techniques that work and replicate those best practices in the future. In the military, this process of institutionalizing best practices is called *doctrine,* simply defined as those concepts and practices agreed upon by the profession. Yet, just as the very "greatness" of the U.S. military establishment is a double-edged sword, so it is with institutional persistence. Sometimes institutions persist well beyond their optimal effectiveness and efficiency because of changes in objectives, strategy, threats, resources, or the environment. With military institutions, the challenge is compounded because the prospect of changing to something that places national security at risk is frequently raised and can cause military organizations to be even more inherently conservative than they otherwise would be. Additionally, generational learning in a closed labor system may make adaptation of military officers to circumstances that are different from their education and doctrine more difficult.

Therefore, it is particularly important for DOD to develop habits of a learning organization capable of adapting to changing circumstances so that their institutions can remain relevant. As the U.S. military establishment confronts changes, the 2008 national defense strategy identifies the future global threat environment and the necessary directions for future U.S. strategy and force development. It concludes that, although U.S. predominance in conventional warfare is not unchallenged, it is sustainable for the medium term given current trends. Secretary Gates wrote:

> The Pentagon has to do more than modernize its conventional forces; it must also focus on today's unconventional conflicts—and tomorrow's. . . . It is true that the United States would be hard-pressed to fight a major conventional ground war elsewhere on short notice, but as I have asked before, where on earth would we do that? U.S. air and sea forces have ample untapped striking power should the need arise to deter or punish aggression—whether on the Korean Peninsula, in the Persian Gulf, or across the Taiwan Strait. So although current strategy knowingly assumes some additional risk in this area, that risk is a prudent and manageable one.[54]

This changing set of global security challenges may demand more investments in "less-tech," manning, training, and equipping for counterinsurgency operations through trade-offs drawn from the high-tech of the conflict spectrum. The challenges that confront DOD, to include the headquarters, combatant commands, and services, is "how" and "with what" the nation's armed forces will prepare itself to maintain the peace and fight and win America's wars.

These challenges may be most stark as they reveal worrisome "tribalism" within the services. The nation, through DOD, must decide whether the army will require more machine-based, lethal/kinetic approaches or a newer, more indirect, hybridized, lower-tech/higher-ideational approach. The nation, through DOD, needs to address the navy's struggles with the new high-seas banditry of international piracy and the U.S. air force's struggles with the cultural implications of UAVs and their operational control, the future of cyber warfare, and the recent firings of both the secretary and chief of the air force for apparent failures to adapt to changing times, challenges, and missions.

An essential component of effectively implementing changes in DOD is to understand the organizational structure and culture of the agencies involved, recognizing that those cultures can significantly influence decision making. Recalling the two most substantial changes in DOD since the Vietnam War—the implementation of the All-Volunteer Force in 1973 and the Goldwater-Nichols Act of 1986—provides insights to the interplay of organizational culture and bureaucratic decision making. In both cases, most uniformed leaders in the services opposed the changes on the grounds that they would erode the effectiveness of their force or the quality of the people in their service. The president, secretary of defense, and Congress, in both cases, understood the organizational cultures involved, included professional military advice, made decisions that changed the incentive structures within the services, and then oversaw the implementation of those decisions. As a result, with the benefit of hindsight, most observers have praised both changes as essential to the current success of the U.S. military.

As the nation confronts the challenges of developing a military structure that is capable of both providing security in the near term and adapting to emerging threats, it must recognize the organizational dynamics that affect defense decision making. Organizational culture matters, because, like institutions, cultures persist and they can impede needed change. Organizational dynamics will influence both the type of change that is implemented and how long it will take to implement changes within DOD.

NOTES

The views expressed in this chapter reflect the opinions of the authors and are not the positions of the U.S. Military Academy or any other government agency.

1. The $693 billion budget is for Fiscal Year 2010. See DOD Fiscal Year 2011 Budget Request, (Washington DC: Office of the Undersecretary of Defense (Comptroller), February 2010), 1-1.

2. DOD is often called the 800-pound gorilla in reference to the joke: "Question: Where does an 800-pound gorilla sit? Answer: Anywhere it wants." See, for example, Lock K. Johnson, "The DCI vs. the Eight-Hundred-Pound Gorilla," *International Journal of Intelligence and Counterintelligence* 13 (January 2000), 35–48.

3. Allan R. Millett and Peter Maslowski, *For the Common Defense: A Military History of the United States of America* (New York: Free Press, 1984), 369.

4. Vincent Davis, "The Evolution of Central U.S. Defense Management," in Robert J. Art, Vincent Davis, and Samuel P. Huntington, *Reorganizing America's Defense: Leadership in War and Peace* (New York: Pergamon-Brassey's, 1985), 149–67.

5. Reference 1947 National Security Act. See Charles A. Stevenson, "Underlying Assumptions of the National Security Act of 1947," *Joint Forces Quarterly* 48 (1st Quarter, 2008) 129–33.

6. Davis, "The Evolution of Central U.S. Defense Management," 153.

7. *Goldwater-Nichols Department of Defense Reorganization Act of 1986*, Public Law 93-433, 99th Congress, 2nd session (1 October 1986).

8. The role of the JCS and joint staff are specified in Title 10, US Code, (hereafter Title 10), section 5, accessed at www.law.cornell.edu/uscode/10/usc_sup_01_10_10_A_20_I_30_5.html, June 1, 2009.

9. The size of the Joint Staff estimated at 1,500 is from Perry M. Smith, *Assignment Pentagon: How to Excel in a Bureaucracy* (Dulles, VA: Brassey's, 2002), 128.

10. Title 10, section 155(e).

11. In an interesting recent study, Chris Gibson proposes further increasing the unity of planning and execution by replacing the chairman of the JCS with a commanding general of the armed forces, who would command all combatant commanders with authority to provide direction to U.S. military forces. See Christopher P. Gibson, *Securing the State: Reforming the National Security Decisionmaking Process at the Civil-Military Nexus* (Stanford, CA: Hoover Institution, 2008).

12. Institute of Land Warfare, *Profile of the U.S. Army 2008* (Arlington, VA: Association of the U.S. Army, 2008), 3.

13. Secretary of Defense Robert Gates has recently proposed eliminating JFCOM, which may eliminate the headquarters but not the need for the integration of service and interagency capabilities. If JFCOM is eliminated, integration would then become the responsibility of other combatant commanders of the joint staff.

14. Dana Priest, "A Four-Star Foreign Policy," *Washington Post,* September 28, 2001, A1. See also Dana Priest, *The Mission: Waging War and Keeping the Peace with America's Military* (New York: Norton, 2003).

15. See among others, Perry M. Smith, *Assignment Pentagon*. Sam C. Sarkesian, John Allen Williams, and Stephen J. Cimbala, *U.S. National Security: Policymakers, Processes, and Politics* (Boulder, CO: Lynne Rienner, 2008); Carl H. Builder, *The Masks of War: American Military Styles in Strategy and Analysis* (Baltimore, MD: Johns Hopkins, 1989); and James M. Smith, "Service Cultures, Joint Cultures, and the US Military, *Airman-Scholar* (Winter 1998), 3–17.

16. Don M. Snider, "The U.S. Army as Profession," in *The Future of the Army Profession,* 2nd Ed., by Don M. Snider and Lloyd J. Matthews (New York: McGraw-Hill, 2005), 4.

17. Snider, "The U.S. Army as Profession," 15.

18. For a discussion of the evolution of the Army's management system since Vietnam and recommendations concerning potential modifications to OPMS 3, see Michael Meese and Samuel Calkins, "Back to the Future: Transforming the Army Officer Development System," *The Forum,* vol. 4, issue 1, article 3 (2006), available at www.bepress.com/forum/vol4/iss1/art3/.

19. One recent study concerning lateral entry (concerning enlisted soldiers rather than officers) concluded that "lateral entry for non-prior-service personnel is unlikely to be successful in reducing training costs on a meaningful scale without introducing serious force management risks." It recommended "a shift in focus to lateral entry of prior-service personnel, both active-duty and reserve component. A strategy emphasizing expansion of prior-service lateral entry would minimize cultural disruption, avoid training costs, and amortize costs already incurred over a longer career length. Dina Levy et al., *Expanded Enlisted Lateral Entry: Options and Feasibility* (Santa Monica, CA: RAND National Defense Research Institute, 2004), xvi.

20. Institute of Land Warfare, *The U.S. Army's Role in Stability Operations* (Arlington, VA: Association of the U.S. Army, October 2006), 3.

21. In March 1783, when the Continental Army was encamped at Newburgh, NY, some officers, believing that Congress had not supported the Army sufficiently, threatened to disband the Army and ignore the authority of Congress. Washington appealed to the nascent concept of the American military profession and put down the revolt: "how inconsistent with the rules of propriety!—how unmilitary!—and how subversive of all order and discipline." See David Ramsey, *The Life of George Washington* (New York, 1807), accessed at www.earlyamerica.com/earlyamerica/milestones/newburgh/text.html, 1 June 2009.

22. See Title 10, U.S. Code, sections 113(a); 3013(a)2; 5013(a)2; and 8013(a)2.

23. Eric K. Shinseki, "Retirement Ceremony Remarks," June 11, 2003, accessed at www.army.mil/features/ShinsekiFarewell/farewellremarks.htm, June 1, 2009.

24. Michael Hastings, "Runaway General," *Rolling Stone*, June 25, 2010.

25. General Stanley McChrystal as quoted in Peter Spiegel, "McChrystal Defensive for Remarks," *Wall Street Journal* Blogs, accessed at blogs.wsj.com/washwire/2010/06/21/mcchrystals-next-offensive/, July 3, 2010.

26. General David Petraeus has publicly said that he has refrained from voting since his promotion to the rank of major general. See Andrew Bacevich, "Petraeus Opts Out of Politics—or Does He?" *Huffington Post,* accessed at www.huffingtonpost.com/andrew-bacevich/petraeus-opts-out-of-poli_b_136891.html, June 1, 2009.

27. Greg Behrman, *The Most Nobel Adventure: The Marshall Plan and the Time When America Helped Save Europe* (New York: Free Press, 2007), 11.

28. Awkwardly, President Bush followed the appropriate independent respect for General Petraeus but often continued to refer to the U.S. ambassador by his first name without a title. See, for example, President Bush's remarks where he says, "General Petraeus and Ryan Crocker know the troops are necessary . . ." in "President Bush and Prime Minister Brown Remark on Iraq and Terrorism," *Washington Post,* April 17, 2008.

29. Builder, *The Masks of War*, 33.

30. Carl von Clausewitz, *On War,* ed. and trans. by Michael Howard and Peter Paret (Princeton, NJ: Princeton University Press, 1976).

31. Builder, *The Masks of War*, 32.

32. Donald C. Winter, "Posture Statement of the U.S. Navy, 2008" (Washington, DC: Department of the Navy, 2008), 3.

33. Philip A. Crowl, "Alfred Thayer Mahan: The Naval Historian," in *Makers of Modern Strategy: From Machiavelli to the Nuclear Age,* Peter Paret, ed. (Princeton, NJ: Princeton University Press, 1986), 444–77.

34. U.S. Constitution, article 1, section 8.

35. See Cami McCormick, "High Time to Move Marines to Afghanistan: U.S. Marine Commandant Tells CBS News 'Nation Building' in Iraq Not Best Use of Troops," *CBS News,* December 31, 2008, accessed at www.cbsnews.com/stories/2008/12/31/terror/main4694266.html, June 1, 2009.

36. The hardship that Marines must be prepared to endure is highlighted in James T. Conway, *Marine Corps Vision and Strategy, 2025* (Washington, DC: U.S. Marine Corps, 2008), 5. Hereafter *Marine Corps Vision.*

37. Jon T. Hoffman, *Chesty: The Story of Lieutenant General Lewis B. Puller, USMC* (New York: Random House, 2002).

38. Other Marine four-star generals may command combatant commands or serve as chairman or vice chairman of the CJCS.

39. The term "purple" is used in the Defense Department to describe joint issues and is reflected in the color of the joint publications. It started to be used in the 1960s when the main form of communication was from view graph slides. At that time, the backgrounds of many Army slides were usually green, Navy slides dark blue, Air Force slides lighter blue, and Marine slides red. When the slides were stacked on top of each other and shown on an overhead projector the color resembled purple (and, perhaps fittingly, none of the content was intelligible). Officers who reflected no particular services bias were known as a purple-suiter. One of the first public references to purple reflecting a joint approach is in "Defense News Policy Passes On Unmourned," *The Los Angeles Times,* July 16, 1967, F7.

40. Don M. Snider and Jeffrey Peterson, "Opportunities for the Army: Defense Transformation and a New Joint Military Profession," in *The Future of the Army Profession,* 2nd ed. (New York: McGraw-Hill, 2005), 238–39. Italics in the original.

41. After the Millennium Challenge exercise in fall 2002, a standing joint task force (JTF) was requested from JFCOM for postwar planning. Because the standing JTF was a secretary of defense priority, JFCOM did not want to commit the single standing JTF that was trained. Instead, a group of individual augmentees formed the nucleus of JTF-4 and they only received software and brief training from JFCOM. These would eventually combine with Jay Garner's Office of Reconstruction and Humanitarian Affairs (ORHA).

42. Conrad C. Crane and Dr. W. Andrew Terrill, *Reconstructing Iraq: Insights, Challenges, and Missions for Military Forces in a Post-Conflict Scenario* (Carlisle, PA: U.S. Army War College, February 1, 2003).

43. With regard to Gen. Myers' relationship with Secretary Rumsfeld, see, among other reports, John Hendren, "General Ranked on Rumsfeld Campaign," *Los Angeles Times*, May 9, 2005.

44. See Michael H. Armacost, *The Politics of Weapons Innovation: The Thor-Jupiter Controversy* (New York: Columbia University Press, 1969).

45. See Air Force Association, "Air Force vs. Army Concepts for UAV Employment," accessed at www.afa.org/grl/UAV_CONOPS.pdf, June 1, 2009.

46. Demetri Sevastopulo, "US Military in Dogfight over Drones," *Financial Times,* August 19, 2007.

47. Ann Roosevelt, "Army, Air Force Ready to Complete UAV Concept of Operations," *Defense Daily*, September 26, 2008.

48. Department of Defense, "Subject: Military Support for Stability, Security, Transition, and Reconstruction (SSTR)," Number 3000.05 (Washington, DC: Undersecretary of Defense [Policy], November 28, 2005), 2.

49. See among many other writings, the juxtaposed articles from two influential Army former battalion commanders each with PhDs in subjects of military strategy: John Nagl, "Let's Win the Wars We're In," and Gian Gentile, "Let's Build an Army to Win *All* Wars," *Joint Forces Quarterly* (1st Quarter 2009), 20–33.

50. U.S. Marine Corps, *Small Wars Manual* (Washington, DC: Government Printing Office, 1940).

51. *Marine Corps Vision*, 5.

52. Charles J. Dunlap, Jr., "America's Asymmetric Advantage," *Armed Forces Journal* (September 2006).

53. James G. March and Johan P. Olsen, *Rediscovering Institutions: The Organizational Basis of Politics* (New York: The Free Press), 1989.

54. Robert Gates, "A Balanced Strategy," *Foreign Affairs* (January/February 2009), 32.

Chapter 7   Office of the Director of National
Intelligence: Promising Start Despite
Ambiguity, Ambivalence, and Animosity

Thomas Fingar

> The new intelligence law makes the Director of National Intelligence (DNI) responsible for integrating the 15 independent members of the Intelligence Community. But it gives him powers that are only relatively broader than before. The DNI cannot make this work unless he takes his legal authorities over budget, programs, personnel, and priorities to the limit. It won't be easy to provide this leadership to the intelligence components of the Defense Department, or to the CIA. They are some of the government's most headstrong agencies. Sooner or later, they will try to run around—or over—the DNI.
> *Transmittal letter to the Report to the President of the United States.*

Proposals to create a director of national intelligence (DNI) whose primary responsibility would be to integrate and optimize the performance of intelligence community (IC) component agencies had been advanced, without effect, for decades.[1] The rationale for doing so was clear but not sufficiently compelling to overcome vested interests and the sense that IC performance was good enough to meet current and anticipated requirements. That changed dramatically on September 11, 2001. Although postmortems revealed that what happened was the result of inadequacies in many parts of the national security enterprise, publication of a badly flawed national intelligence estimate (NIE) on Iraq's weapons of mass destruction (WMDs) narrowed the search for scapegoats and the scope of reforms intended to fix the broader problem by fixing the IC.[2] The establishment of the Office of the Director of National Intelligence (ODNI) was the centerpiece of the reform legislation signed in December 2004, but it is still a work in progress that manifests many of the fissures and flaws of the agencies from which it was created. The ODNI is making a positive difference and has the potential to do more, but even if it persuades all components of the intelligence enterprise to pull in the same direction, that accomplishment will not cure most of the ills of the national security establishment.[3]

When President George W. Bush signed the Intelligence Reform and Terrorism Prevention Act (hereafter Intelligence Reform Act) on December 17, 2004, he described the legislation as "the most dramatic reform of our nation's intelligence capabilities since President Harry S. Truman signed the National Security Act of 1947."[4] That may prove to be the case, but at this point in the short history of the ODNI, its impact on the IC and the national security enterprise has been limited by ambiguity, ambivalence, and animosity. Inevitable start-up problems and the ODNI's limited impact to date have frustrated those with unrealistic expectations about how easily or quickly existing national security institutions could be transformed, but important strides have been made and the potential for greater coherence, efficiency, and effectiveness is real, at least within the intelligence components of the national security enterprise. Realizing that potential will take time, patience, and equally significant changes in the nonintelligence elements of the national security apparatus.[5]

GENESIS OF THE ODNI

As the chapters in this book make clear, the national security enterprise is less efficient and effective than it should be because of institutional rivalries, overlapping authorities, and a host of other deficiencies that are easier to describe than to correct. The performance of the enterprise as a whole is constrained by shortcomings in its constituent elements and shaped by structural and serendipitous imbalances in the relative clout of individual agencies and the leaders who head them. Rifts and rivalries within the IC have been—and remain—as problematic as they are in other parts of the national security establishment. This is widely recognized but Washington is a political town with strongly entrenched interests determined to limit the impact of any change to the status quo. Moreover, all attempts to improve the performance of the national security enterprise, including the creation of the ODNI, have been shaped and constrained by what appear to be iron laws of Washington politics.

One such law can be summarized as, "In Washington, there are only two possibilities: policy success and intelligence failure." In other words, if a policy proves ineffective—or misguided—the knee-jerk explanation is that the IC failed to provide accurate information, timely warning, or expertise-based insight. The second is the recurring pretense that even the most complex problem can be solved with an organizational solution, and that if the mandated organizational changes fail to achieve promised results, it is because those responsible for implementation have failed to overcome bureaucratic pathologies. Among other consequences, this gives individuals and institutions unhappy with some aspect of the mandated change an incentive to frustrate implementation in hope of rolling back or revising organizational changes they do not like. As predicted by the Commission on the Intelligence Capabilities of the United States Regarding Weapons of Mass Destruction (hereafter WMD Commission) in its letter of transmittal, the Department of Defense and the Central Intelligence Agency (CIA) have at times attempted to thwart or distort reform initiatives. The Federal Bureau of Investigation (FBI) has also been obstructionist at times, albeit on different issues.

Rivalries within the IC were and are a problem, but they were not the most important defect identified by those eager to correct deficiencies identified by the 9/11 Commission, the WMD Commission, and virtually every other examination of impediments to achieving better integration of and improved performance by the IC and other components of the national security establishment. Every postmortem assessment of what went wrong cited inadequate information sharing across institutional boundaries and impediments to cooperation between the realms of foreign intelligence and domestic law enforcement as reasons for the failure to discover and disrupt preparations for the attacks on September 11, 2001.[6]

The case for breaking down barriers and making the IC function as an integrated enterprise rather than a collection of special-purpose agencies was convincing, but it probably would not have been compelling without the shock caused by the 9/11 attacks and the political firestorm triggered by the war in Iraq and the badly flawed 2002 NIE on Iraq's WMDs.[7] The findings and recommendations of the 9/11 Commission were supplemented and reinforced by the preliminary conclusions of the WMD Commission.[8] The specific deficiencies identified by commission members surprised no one familiar with the workings of the intelligence and law enforcement communities, but their enumeration in yet another set of reports would not by itself have been sufficient to persuade Congress to create the ODNI. What made the situation different than when previous commission reports were issued was the combination of shock and chagrin caused by the 9/11 attacks, dismay and ire triggered by the flawed performance of the IC with respect to Iraq's WMDs, and politically charged assertions about the role of intelligence in the decision to overthrow Saddam Hussein's regime. Together, two high-profile events characterized as intelligence failures created a sense that it was necessary—or politically expedient—to fix the national security enterprise by correcting deficiencies in the IC.

Even the conjunction of obvious need for reform and imperatives to punish poor performance probably would not have overcome inertia, vested interests, and administration disinterest in undertaking another bureaucratic reorganization as big and complex as the creation of the Department of Homeland Security while waging wars in Afghanistan and Iraq, were it not for the political skill of 9/11 Commission members in making their proposals for intelligence reform the centerpiece of what became an unstoppable, and very rushed, congressional effort to fix intelligence.[9] The 9/11 Commission report was released on July 22, 2004, and both Houses had passed competing bills before the November election. When Congress and the executive branch refocused on these bills after the elections, it quickly became apparent that many senior administration and IC officials wanted to preserve as much of the status quo as possible, and that members of Congress had very different visions of what was desirable. What emerged from the legislative process proved to be ambiguous and left wide latitude for continuing the struggle during implementation.[10]

FORMAL ROLES AND RESPONSIBILITIES

Members of Congress, the IC, and the punditocracy disagree on precisely what the Intelligence Reform Act and the ODNI are supposed to accomplish. Differences in perception and prescription have fueled the continuing debate over authorities, expectations, and performance.[11] A more serious consequence was the need for and difficulty of achieving substantive revisions to the executive order that clarified DNI authorities on issues critical to his ability to lead and transform the IC.[12]

Ambiguities remain and the debate continues, but there is consensus with regard to most of the higher-order objectives of the Intelligence Reform Act and the recommendations that helped shape the legislation. Those objectives, and provisions incorporated into the reform legislation, define the formal roles and responsibilities of the ODNI. The principal responsibilities assigned to the DNI are:

1. Serve as head of the IC;
2. Act as the principal intelligence advisor to the president, to the National Security Council (NSC), and the Homeland Security Council (HSC) for intelligence matters related to the national security[13]; and
3. Consistent with section 1018 of the National Security Intelligence Reform Act of 2004, oversee and direct the implementation of the National Intelligence Program (NIP; i.e., the IC budget).[14]

Before examining how these and other enumerated responsibilities affect the national security enterprise, it will be useful to provide a brief summary of their genesis and additional detail on the problems the Intelligence Reform Act was intended to solve.

Although it sometimes muddied the water in doing so, the Intelligence Reform Act responded to oft-repeated arguments that the director of Central Intelligence (DCI)'s dual responsibilities as both head of the IC and head of the CIA effectively forced a choice between managing a very large agency and leading a collection of highly disparate organizations. History had proven that every DCI gave priority to managing the CIA. That was understandable, and perhaps inevitable, because the DCI had clear and extensive authorities with respect to the CIA but very little authority to "lead" other elements of the IC, all of which reported to the secretary of defense or other cabinet secretaries.[15] As a result, IC integration was more nominal than real, rivalries impeded cooperation, and opportunities for comparative advantage and synergy were lost. In essence, the Intelligence Reform Act divided the DCI's portfolio, assigning primary responsibility for oversight and integration of the IC as a whole to the DNI, and reducing the mandate of the position now designated as the director of the Central Intelligence Agency (DCIA).

Dividing the portfolio made it possible—and a priority—for the DNI to focus on integrating and improving the performance of the IC as a whole, but that step alone did not solve the problem of competing authorities or the DCI's (now DNI's) limited ability to influence or effect the work of IC components that reported to another cabinet-level official. As a result, DNI Mike McConnell frequently characterized his position as "Coordinator of National Intelligence" because of his limited ability to direct the activities of IC agencies other than the CIA.[16] Members of Congress recognized the need to give the DNI more power over IC component agencies than had been vested in the DCI, but Secretary of Defense Donald Rumsfeld waged a successful campaign within the executive branch and with key members of Congress to preserve his (and other cabinet members') authorities. As a result, the Intelligence Reform Act gave the DNI the ability to effect change through his/her authority for the NIP budget, but constrained his/her ability to act by specifying in Section 1018 that authorities granted to the DNI must respect and not abrogate the statutory responsibilities of the heads of departments.[17] The net effect was to give the DNI more power than had been accorded the DCI but less than was needed for uncontested leadership of the IC.

To address deficiencies identified by the studies that examined IC performance related to the 9/11 attacks and the decision to invade Iraq, the Intelligence Reform Act and a subsequent decision by the president to endorse most of the recommendations made by the WMD Commission assigned a number of specific tasks to the DNI.[18] The assigned tasks, individually and collectively, were designed to enhance the quality of intelligence support to the national security enterprise and to restore confidence in the accuracy, reliability, and objectivity of information and assessments prepared by the IC. Fixing the IC was an instrumental goal; the ultimate objective was to enhance the performance of the national security enterprise by improving the quality of intelligence support provided to senior members of the national security team, the agencies they lead, and to others requiring intelligence-derived information and insights to protect our nation and advance its interests. The ODNI-led efforts to accomplish the mandated tasks and to achieve other integration and quality-enhancing goals have been beneficial to the national security enterprise, but their impact is still nascent. Further improvement is possible and likely if new

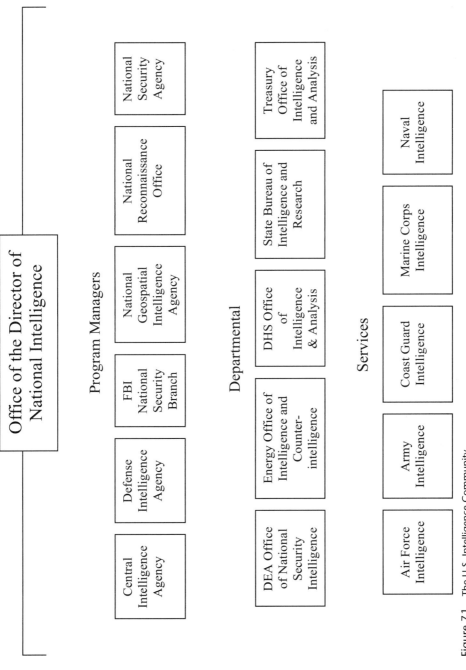

Figure 7.1   The U.S. Intelligence Community.

procedures are institutionalized and the IC is spared the turmoil of another near-term reorganization.

Space restrictions preclude a comprehensive review of mandated and self-initiated reforms designed to improve intelligence support to the national security enterprise but a few key examples will be sufficient to illustrate what is desired, what has been accomplished, and what remains to be achieved.[19] Perhaps the most important cluster of tasks, accomplishments, and impediments is that subsumed under the heading of information sharing. Reduced to its essence, one of the key conclusions of the 9/11 Commission report was that the failure to share information among agencies and across the once-sacrosanct barrier between intelligence and law enforcement had severely limited our ability to detect terrorist preparations to attack the United States.[20] The remedy was obvious and easy to assert: Reduce or eliminate impediments to information sharing. Actually doing so proved to be difficult and contentious.

The Intelligence Reform Act specified that, "The Director of National Intelligence shall have principal authority to ensure maximum availability of and access to intelligence information within the intelligence community consistent with national security requirements."[21] Although efforts focused initially on the sharing of terrorism-related information, it quickly became apparent that the need to share transcended terrorism. It also became apparent that Intelligence Reform Act ambiguities, previously concluded agreements with foreign governments restricting the sharing of their information even within the U.S. IC, proclaimed special sensitivities of many kinds, incompatible systems and software, and myriad other obstacles made the task far more difficult than most had anticipated. Resolution of some issues required revision of Executive Order 12333 governing intelligence activities and had to overcome protracted debate and bureaucratic maneuver. Others required changes to internal policies and operating directives, and still others required development of new software, risk management strategies, and metadata standards.[22]

The premise underlying all of these enabling measures was a simple one: The best way to ensure that nothing is missed, that collection resources are not squandered by seeking what we already know, that alternative explanations are examined, and that the expertise and experience of analysts across the IC can be brought to bear on any problem is to share information across bureaucratic boundaries within the IC. This will improve our understanding of difficult puzzles and enhance support to all IC customers. Nearly four years were required to put key prerequisites in place. Initial results are encouraging, but there is still a long way to go to realize fully DNI McConnell's mandate to change the paradigm from need to know to responsibility to provide.[23]

The second cluster of tasks and accomplishments is designed to enhance the accuracy, completeness, objectivity, and utility of analytic products. An equally important objective is to restore customer confidence in the quality of the assessments and judgments provided by IC analysts, and to build confidence in the quality of work done by colleagues across the IC in order to facilitate divisions of labor and reduce unnecessary duplication of effort. The ultimate objective, however, is to improve national security decisions by improving the quality and reliability of analytic support to the agencies and individuals that together constitute the national security establishment. Progress on all dimensions of this cluster has been quite good (e.g., mandatory analytic tradecraft standards for the entire IC were promulgated in June 2007, mandatory sourcing standards were issued in October 2007, and the Intelligence Reform Act–required ombudsman for analytic integrity was appointed in 2005).[24]

The net effect of these and other ODNI initiatives, such as the institution of a common course in basic analytic tradecraft (analysis 101) for analysts from across the IC, and the demonstration and pull effect of applying higher standards to the preparation of NIEs and articles for the *President's Daily Brief* (PDB), is improved analytic performance in every analytic component and across the IC as a whole.[25] Better analytic tradecraft and improved analytic products do not in and of themselves assure better national security decisions or more effective policy, but they do address key deficiencies identified by the WMD Commission. Over time, they should further enhance confidence in the analytic judgments of the IC, promote dialogue between policymakers and analysts with the potential to deepen and better focus analytic work in support of national security decision making, and facilitate trust-based divisions of labor and greater ability to engage experts from across the IC to address difficult issues.[26]

Improved information sharing, better analytic products, more effective use of experts from outside the IC, greater use of open-source (i.e., unclassified) information, strengthened capabilities to analyze scientific and technical issues, enhanced integration of and cooperation between law enforcement agencies and the foreign IC, and other objectives codified in the Intelligence Reform Act and the WMD Commission recommendations endorsed by President George W. Bush are still works in progress, but they are moving in the right direction. Senior officials in the IC have embraced the goals—some more enthusiastically than others—and further progress is likely, unless there is another failure-driven or politically motivated crusade to improve national security by fixing the IC.

The discussion thus far has focused on new requirements assigned to the DNI, but the ODNI also has important formal and informal roles in the national security enterprise resulting from the transfer of responsibilities from the DCI to the DNI. First and foremost is the DNI's role as "the principal intelligence advisor to the President, the National Security Council, and the Homeland Security Council for intelligence matters related to the national security." The transferred responsibilities include representing the IC in the NSC process.[27] In addition to these participatory duties, the DNI inherited the responsibility to inform—and ability to influence—national security decision making through other means, including the presentation of information and analysis through the PDB.

As inheritor of DCI responsibilities to support the NSC process, the DNI now attends NSC and principals committee (PC) meetings as the senior representative of the IC. However, he frequently has not been the only senior IC official at the meetings. The fact that the ODNI was created midway through the two-term Bush administration precluded a clean break with the past. Given the importance and complexity of the issues confronting the NSC, most of which antedated the appointment of the first DNI and were therefore far more familiar to the newly renamed DCIA, it was both natural and prudent that the DCIA continue to attend meetings during a period of transition. The same is true with respect to dual participation by ODNI and CIA senior officials in lower-level NSC meetings. This arrangement was appropriate for a transitional period but had become awkward and unnecessary long before the end of the Bush administration.

The DNI's formal role in the NSC process entailed four core responsibilities:

- Ensuring that he was up to speed on developments and intelligence information germane to the subjects to be discussed at each meeting, and that he or his "plus one" was prepared to provide an update briefing or answer questions about new developments or new intelligence.[28]
- Receiving and shaping intelligence-related requirements generated during the meeting and assigning tasks to appropriate collection or analytical components of the IC.
- Providing appropriate feedback on the discussion to elements of the IC working on the issues discussed and/or providing intelligence support to the other senior officials attending the meeting. The purpose of this feedback is to enable collectors and analysts to know what is already well understood, what officials said they needed, and what information and insights the senior intelligence professional thought would assist the deliberations even though no one else had requested it.
- Contributing to the decision-making process by commenting on proposed options and offering proposals of his own. This is the most ambiguous and trickiest of the DNI's responsibilities because he must maintain—and be seen to maintain—objectivity when presenting assessments and updates germane to the discussion while contributing his own insights and ideas as a responsible member of the group entrusted to make national security decisions. Other senior attendees could legitimately present the policy preferences of their agencies, but the IC as such is supposed to be objective and policy neutral.

When the DNI succeeded the DCI as the senior IC participant in the NSC process, John Negroponte decided to make a symbolic break with the past that had substantive consequences. Previously, analysts in the CIA's directorate of intelligence (CIA/DI) who had ready access to colleagues in the directorate of operations (now subsumed into the national clandestine service) routinely monitored developments and intelligence in order to prepare the DCI for participation in NSC meetings. DNI Negroponte reassigned this responsibility to the National Intelligence Council (NIC), which the Intelligence Reform Act had transferred from the DCI to the ODNI.[29]

The assignment of this new responsibility had profound consequences for the NIC and, subsequently, for efforts to integrate and improve the performance of IC analysts and analytic components. One consequence was that National Intelligence Officers (NIOs) had to assume greater responsibility for, and spend more time on, current policy issues. This eventually enhanced the utility and policy relevance of NIC products, including NIEs, but in the short term it both compelled and enabled the NIOs to engage analysts from across the IC. The CIA/DI had been able to handle this task internally. The NIC, which is roughly one-thirtieth the size of the DI, did not have that option.

As a practical matter, NIOs frequently turned to CIA analysts for help in preparing briefing materials for NSC, PC, and deputies committee (DC) meetings because they were located in the same building and had been doing this before the ODNI existed. But the NIOs were encouraged and empowered (by *Intelligence Community Directives 200* and *207*) to elicit written and verbal input from the most knowledgeable analysts in the IC, regardless of their bureaucratic home. The process was cumbersome and onerous at the beginning but quickly became routinized and proved to be an effective way to identify analytical differences and ensure that the DNI or other ODNI official attending a national security meeting understood why analysts with access to the same information had reached different conclusions. In addition, participation by analysts from multiple agencies in pre-meeting briefings of the DNI or other ODNI participants gave the analysts better understanding of the specific issues under discussion, the principal's thought process, and how their own work fit into the larger process. It also enabled them to provide better-informed support to other NSC officials (e.g., the secretary of state and the secretary of the treasury).

One additional formal DNI role in the NSC process warrants brief attention even though it is qualitatively different from those discussed above, namely, the role as chair of the Joint Intelligence Community Council (JICC). Membership of the JICC includes the statutory members of the NSC plus the secretary of energy, the secretary of homeland security, and the attorney general.[30] The function of the JICC is to assist the DNI to develop and implement a joint, unified national intelligence effort to protect national security. As a practical matter, this involves few meetings or JICC-specific interactions, largely because the DNI sees all of the members frequently in other venues. But it does provide a vehicle for periodic discussions to ensure that key national security policymakers understand DNI goals and priorities and that these priorities are consistent with and support the intelligence needs of the members and their agencies. The intelligence requirements and priorities of JICC principals are codified in the national intelligence priorities framework (NIPF), which is updated semiannually.[31] To date the JICC has not played a central role in linking the IC to other elements of the national security enterprise.

Since the inception of the ODNI, the DNI or his principal deputy has participated in the daily intelligence briefing of the president known as the PDB. The DCI participation in the daily briefing was episodic, and generally infrequent, before the administration of George W. Bush but became the norm after January 20, 2001. This gave the DCI, and subsequently the DNI, sustained time with the president, vice president, and national security advisor. Designated sessions also included other members of the NSC and the HSC, and they sometimes segued into formal meetings of the NSC. The subjects covered in these briefings were informed by the NSC agenda, but they also helped shape that agenda. The timing and focus of items prepared for the PDB often reflected IC knowledge of the issues being considered by NSC principals and were written to inform their deliberations. The converse was also true; decisions to add or defer discussion of specific subjects were sometimes influenced by developments reported in the PDB. Whether the resultant situation was an integral and beneficial part of the NSC process or a perversion of that process giving intelligence a larger role in the making of national security decisions than it should have can be argued both ways.

On the positive side of the ledger, this engagement provides information and analytic judgments that give the president an independent base for assessing the appropriateness and practicality of policy recommendations brought to him through the NSC process. The same is true, *mutatis mutandis*, of the briefings and written assessments provided by the IC to other NSC principals. When the system works properly, which it usually does, subordinate officials in each of the national security agencies receive essentially the same intelligence-based information as do their superiors. Subordinates also receive additional intelligence keyed to their specific responsibilities. Providing the information directly to superiors enables them to judge whether proposals developed by subordinates make sense in light of available intelligence and, if they seem inconsistent, to find out why. Intelligence should not automatically trump policymaker judgments, but it should be a visible part of the decision-making process at every stage.

Whether, or the extent to which, the DNI's (and therefore the IC's) potentially daily access to the president has a detrimental impact on the national security enterprise is probably more a function of personalities and interpersonal relationships than of structure. An attempt to preclude the possibility of adverse influence by eliminating the president's daily intelligence briefing or precluding, except in unusual circumstances, regular DNI participation in the briefing would be unwise, but it is appropriate for each DNI (and the presidents they serve) to consider carefully the opportunity costs of daily participation in the briefing session, especially the consequences of having less time for leadership of the IC.[32]

The PDB process also entailed other important elements of continuity and change. Perhaps the most notable continuity is the systematized effort to provide the same information to all NSC principals. Information provided through the PDB process certainly is not the only intelligence they receive (e.g., the secretary of state also receives intelligence-based analytic products from the State Department's Bureau of Intelligence and Research and the CIA), but it does ensure that all have access to the same core body of information. In addition, as a result of changes introduced by the ODNI, all are also made aware of the existence of, and reasons for, analytic disagreements.

ORGANIZATIONAL CULTURE OF THE ODNI

As a new organization, the ODNI has no hoary traditions, limited staff loyalty, and few routinized procedures. It exists because of dissatisfaction with the performance and procedures of the DCI-led structure and was intended to remedy a number of real and imputed maladies, but it did not emerge from the Congress like some latter-day Athena sprung from the head of Zeus. There were—and still are—almost as many different visions of what the ODNI is or should be as there are people with opinions on the subject. This is almost as true within the ODNI as without because, in many ways, the ODNI is a microcosm of the IC. With limited and partial exceptions, such as the requirement that the ODNI not be collocated with any component of the IC (a provision clearly intended to prevent the ODNI from becoming a captive of the CIA), both the legislation and the administration refrained from telling the DNI how to organize and run the new cabinet-level agency.[33]

For practical reasons, the ODNI took then-existing director of central intelligence directives (DCIDs) and CIA policies and procedures governing personnel, access to computer systems, etc., as its starting point. Disengaging from and replacing these legacy guidelines and requirements was difficult and time consuming, in part because of ambiguities in the legislation, disagreement over precisely what the ODNI should be and do, and the palpable desire of some to ensure that the new structure ended in failure. Moreover, as staff joined the ODNI from roughly two dozen organizations inside and outside the IC, they brought with them the cultures of their previous institutional homes. This bureaucratic baggage included both practices that were considered valuable and worth preserving, and behaviors and attitudes that were incompatible with the objectives of the

Intelligence Reform Act. Inevitably, people did not agree on what should be retained and what should be jettisoned. The challenge of forging a new organizational culture was further complicated by the fact that most of the new staff expected to return eventually to their home agencies.

The net result of the factors summarized above was that the ODNI lacked a distinct culture of its own, was populated by well-intentioned individuals who did what came naturally and/or resisted efforts to adopt new procedures or inculcate new values out of concern that following them might jeopardize return to their home agencies. In addition, most attached higher priority to mission (i.e., providing the best possible intelligence support to policymakers, military commanders, and those responsible for homeland security) than to institution building. The demands of two shooting wars, the war on terror, preparation of budgets, congressional requirements, and myriad other imperatives effectively precluded a sustained effort to create and inculcate a new organizational culture. This was further compounded by the decision, which the author believes to have been the right one, to limit the proportion of ODNI permanent cadre to roughly fifty percent of its staff. The inevitable result is the absence of a coherent organizational ethos with shared norms, values, and expectations.

The inability of persons inside and outside the ODNI to articulate a clear vision of what it is, what it does, and what it stands for impedes progress and contributes to the view of critics that it is little more than another layer of bureaucracy. That clearly is a problem, but the problem is bigger than the ODNI itself because it will be impossible to articulate and instill coherent norms and values for the ODNI without changing the cultures of IC component agencies. Simply stated, the ODNI exists in order to integrate the IC so that it can function as a single enterprise with specialized, mission-specific components, effective divisions of labor, and sufficient redundancy to avoid single points of failure or unchallenged analytic judgments. Key elements of the IC continue to resist that vision, view colleagues as competitors, and disparage the work of fellow professionals. Unless and until we can instill a shared view of the IC as a single body with many parts, it will be impossible to forge an organizational culture for the ODNI. Stated another way, the ODNI must instill and embody the new corporate culture of the IC because anything else would perpetuate the current disconnect between service in the ODNI and working in component agencies.

ILLUSTRATIVE CASES: IRAQ AND AFGHANISTAN

Intelligence—information, analytical insights, and operations—was critical to deliberations, decisions, and actions related to Iraq and Afghanistan (defined here to include terrorist safe havens along the Afghanistan-Pakistan border).[34] Such objective reasons for the close relationship between intelligence and decision making on Iraq and Afghanistan were reinforced—and complicated—by subjective and political factors affecting ODNI participation in the NSC process with respect to those theaters of operations.

The importance and impact of the political dimension derives from the perception and argument that U.S. involvement in both countries was the result of intelligence failures: 9/11 and the flawed 2002 NIE on Iraq's WMDs. As noted above, those factors more than any other led to the creation of the ODNI with a mandate to fix the IC. A third important element in the political stew was the increasingly poisonous and partisan political environment in Washington.

The IC was deeply wounded by its failure to detect and prevent 9/11 and by the poor tradecraft of the Iraq NIE. It was also stung by the intensity and perceived unfairness of the public excoriation of the entire community for the failings of a small percentage of the dedicated intelligence professionals working to keep our country safe. Collectors, analysts, and IC senior officials knew that everything they did, wrote, and said with respect to Iraq and Afghanistan would be closely scrutinized and greeted with skepticism by NSC principals, members of Congress, and the media. As a result, substantial resources were shifted to Iraq and Afghanistan—with inevitable consequences for the IC's ability to anticipate, monitor, and interpret developments germane to other national security issues. Even without other pressures to devote more resources to Iraq and Afghanistan (e.g., the imperative to support the troops), the IC would have made the decision to accept greater risk on other subjects in order to minimize the likelihood of failure on the highest-profile issues.

The creation of the ODNI added another element to the mix and additional incentives to restore confidence in the IC and its products by demonstrating that intelligence produced under the new organizational structure was better than it was before the ODNI was created. The challenge of doing so and steps taken to enhance performance far transcended Iraq and Afghanistan, but they had a number of specific manifestations with respect to those countries and associated issues. One of the first centered on the need to resolve authority and turf issues in the counterterrorism arena. After 9/11, every IC element took steps to improve coverage of terrorism-related issues. Everyone was eager to get into the fight and to demonstrate that countering the terrorist threat was a top priority. Even if nothing else had changed, there was both the opportunity and the need to rationalize the work of the many components working on counterterrorism. But now there was an additional player with a new mandate.

In addition to the ODNI, the Intelligence Reform Act gave statutory authority to the National Counterterrorism Center (NCTC). The act specified that it was to "serve as the primary organization in the United States Government for analyzing and integrating all intelligence possessed or acquired by the United States Government pertaining to terrorism and counterterrorism, excepting intelligence pertaining exclusively to domestic terrorists and domestic counterterrorism."[35] Reflecting larger problems of ambiguity and indecision, the NCTC director reports to the DNI on certain matters but reports directly to the president on others.[36] The story of multiple and conflicting mandates, turf issues, and the absolute requirement to avoid breaking anything while attempting to alleviate specific problems is important but beyond the scope of this chapter. Simply put, the DNI could not suspend the war on terror (or the military conflicts in Iraq and Afghanistan) while he reinvented the IC. Coping strategies and imperfect solutions were the best that could be achieved. In the case of work on counterterrorism, the imperfect workable solution was to establish clearer lanes in the road for each of the players.

A second and much easier structural adjustment was designed to improve NIC coverage of Iraq and Afghanistan by splitting the portfolio of the NIO for the Near East and South Asia and creating a separate NIO for South Asia. This change could have been made without creation of the ODNI but it was not. The purpose was primarily substantive: to bring more NIC and IC-wide expertise to bear on issues in each region, including Iraq and Afghanistan. But there was also a symbolic reason for giving greater prominence to IC coverage of South Asia, and that was to demonstrate understanding of how important it was that Afghanistan (not to mention Pakistan and India) not be disadvantaged by the increased focus on Iraq (and Iran).

As noted above, the period under discussion was intensely political and every decision was dissected with partisan scalpels and examined through hypercritical media lenses. In the highly charged political atmosphere, accusations that administration officials had misrepresented and misused intelligence gained currency through repetition. There were attempts, sometimes explicit, to use the IC as a stick with which to beat the administration and/or as a kind of truth squad providing an independent check on the veracity of what Congress was told by the executive branch. This was especially the case with respect to Iraq and Afghanistan. That this occurred is a testament of sorts to the success of efforts to restore confidence in the quality and objectivity of IC analysts, but it put the IC in a difficult position.

One reflection of this combination of increased confidence and politically motivated desire to challenge the administration was the advent of unprecedented congressional requests for (and, in some cases, legislatively mandated) NIEs (and other coordinated products) on Iraq, Afghanistan, and terrorism. Some of the requests called for unclassified reports or summaries; others requested unclassified statements for the record and open hearings. This created two types of tension relative to ODNI participation in the NSC process. One type involved the semi-zero sum character of analytic effort. Specific examples include the periods of intense policy review that preceded the so-called surge of troops into Iraq in 2007 and the review of Afghanistan strategy in late 2008. Given the obvious importance of both activities and determination to avoid errors that would again undermine confidence in IC competence or objectivity, the most experienced analysts in the IC were assigned to support the policy reviews. In both cases, there was a conscious decision to focus on the White House-led reviews because of their importance to the success of American efforts to restore stability and facilitate development and democracy. In both cases the preparation of rigorous estimative products on the core topics was relatively far along when the policy reviews began, making it easier than it otherwise would have been to make timely, informed, and important contributions to the policy reviews. Inevitably, this delayed the publication of the NIEs requested by members of Congress.

Confirming that it is sometimes impossible to win for trying, when the NIEs were published a few weeks after completion of the policy reviews, they were criticized by some as irrelevant to the policymaking process because they were not published until after policy changes had been announced. Such criticism misses the point; policymakers, in this case working under the auspices of the NSC, were well served by the dedicated support of experienced analysts with a mandate to reach into the IC to tap additional sources of expertise without regard to where in the IC the experts worked. As importantly, the published NIEs were made available to members of Congress in plenty of time to inform debate and decisions on whether/how to provide funding for the modified strategies.

CONCLUDING THOUGHTS

The ODNI is still very much a work in progress. Despite persistent problems, it has made substantial headway on most of the objectives enumerated in the Intelligence Reform Act, but it has yet to overcome the consequences of the ambiguity, ambivalence, and animosity that have plagued and constrained it from the start. The continuing impact of these constraints was illuminated and underscored when Dennis Blair, the third DNI, resigned after sixteen months on the job and one month after celebrating the fifth anniversary of the ODNI.[37] After five years, the DNI—and by extension the ODNI—continued to be hobbled by passive-aggressive behavior on the part of nominal subordinates, unrealistic expectations and political blame games, divided loyalties, and ambivalent support from the White House.[38]

If, or to the extent that, the experience of secretaries of defense and the Office of the Secretary of Defense is indicative of how long it takes to establish and institutionalize fundamental structural and procedural changes in the national security enterprise, it will be many more years before a DNI achieves effective control over the disparate agencies and missions of the intelligence community. Whether the process is accelerated or aborted will depend on politics, personalities, and political priorities.

Those who pretended that the ODNI would be a kind of magic bullet capable of instantly overcoming legal, policy, structural, cultural, and other impediments to the creation of a truly integrated IC decry its failure to correct all deficiencies in its first few years.

Those who predicted—or hoped—it would fail have been proven wrong. The reality is that it has achieved mixed results and been forced to spend inordinate amounts of time and effort on peripheral issues. But it has also scored a number of successes, particularly in the area of analytic tradecraft and information sharing. It also has enhanced the ability of the national security enterprise to understand the challenges it faces and to make better-informed decisions to address those challenges.

The IC needs time to refine what has been initiated, to take its game to a higher level, and to complete the transition from the dangerous but relatively simpler times of the Cold War to the myriad and multifaceted challenges of the twenty-first century. The ODNI has the potential to integrate the IC more effectively than it ever has been and thereby to enhance significantly the performance of the national security enterprise, but the goal of transforming the IC into a single enterprise with appropriate divisions of labor and constructive redundancies remains to be fully realized. Other dimensions of the national security enterprise must change in order to take full advantage of what the IC is able to do. As importantly, fundamental changes in other parts of the national security enterprise are needed in order to avoid failure on one or more of the issues already on the table.[39] If those changes are not made, and there is another failure, history suggests that the finger of blame will be directed at the IC.

NOTES

1. Michael Warner and J. Kenneth McDonald examine fourteen studies of the IC, the reasons they were undertaken, and the recommendations they proposed in *US Intelligence Community Reform Studies since 1947* (Washington, DC: Strategic Management Issues Office, Center for the Study of Intelligence, Central Intelligence Agency, April 2005).

2. The most detailed and influential postmortem was the National Commission on Terrorist Attacks upon the United States, *The 9/11 Commission Report* (Washington, DC: Government Printing Office, 2004) (hereafter 9/11 Commission report). See also Charles Perrow, "A Symposium on *The 9/11 Commission Report*," *Contemporary Sociology* 34(2) (March 2005), pp. 99–107; and Richard A. Falkenrath, "The 9/11 Commission Report," *International Security*, 29(3) (Winter 2004/05), pp. 170–90. The flawed estimate was *Iraq's Continuing Programs for Weapons of Mass Destruction* [hereafter *Iraq WMD*], October 2002. Declassified key judgments released on July 18, 2003, are available at www.fas.org/irp/cia/products/iraq-wmd.html. The legislative fix is the "Intelligence Reform and Terrorism Prevention Act of 2004," Public Law 108-458—December 17, 2004, Sec 102 (b) (hereafter Intelligence Reform Act) at www.dni.gov/history.htm.

3. Descriptions of the roles and missions of the institutional members of the IC can be found on the website of the ODNI. See in particular, "Members of the Intelligence Community" at www.dni.gov/members_IC.htm, and *An Overview of the United States Intelligence Community for the 111th Congress* at www.dni.gov/overview.pdf. These materials list sixteen constituent agencies, one more than the fifteen referenced in the quotation from the WMD Commission letter of transmittal cited in the chapter epigraph. The reason for the difference is the addition of the Drug Enforcement Administration's Office of National Security Intelligence in 2005.

4. White House Press Release, December 17, 2004 at http://georgewbush-whitehouse.archives.gov/news/releases/2004/12/20041217-1.html.

5. In certain respects the start-up of the ODNI and the challenges inherent in the attempt to reduce the independence of the sixteen constituent elements of the IC in order to achieve a more integrated and effective intelligence enterprise are similar to those attending the creation of the Office of the Secretary of Defense in 1949. It took more than a decade—and the strong-willed personality of Robert McNamara and strong backing of President Kennedy—for the secretary of defense to gain primacy over the military services. See, for example, Lawrence S. Kaplan, Ronald D. Landa, and Edward J. Drea, *History of the Office of the Secretary of Defense, V.5: The McNamara Ascendancy* (Washington, DC: Historical Office, Office of the Secretary of Defense, 2006).

6. *9/11 Commission Report*. See also Senate Select Committee on Intelligence and U.S. House Permanent Select Committee on Intelligence, *Joint Inquiry into Intelligence Community Activities Before and After the Terrorist Attacks of September 11, 2001*, 107th Congress, 2d Session, S. Rept. No. 107-351, H. Rept. No. 107-792, December 2002.

7. See Senate, *Report of the Select Committee on Intelligence on Postwar Findings about Iraq's WMD Programs and Links to Terrorism and How They Compare with Prewar Assessments together with Additional Views*, 109th Congress, 2d Session, September 8, 2006. See also Richard A. Best, Jr., *U.S. Intelligence and Policymaking: The Iraq Experience* (Congressional Research Service, December 2, 2005) at www.fas.org/spg/crs/intel/RS21696.pdf; and Senate Select Committee on Intelligence, *Report on Whether Public Statements Regarding Iraq by U.S. Government Officials Were Substantiated by Intelligence Information together with Additional and Minority Views*, 110th Congress, 2d Session, S. Report 110-345, June 5, 2008.

8. The final report was not published until March 2005 but many of its key findings were known when Congress and the administration were deliberating and debating what became the "Intelligence Reform and Terrorism Prevention Act of 2004." See Commission on the Intelligence Capabilities of the United States Regarding Weapons of Mass Destruction, *Report to the President of the United States* (Washington, DC: Government Printing Office, 2005).

9. Members of the 9/11 Commission aggressively and effectively lobbied the executive branch, the Congress, and the public to ensure that their report and recommendations did not suffer the fate of most such reports. In important respects, they drove the process that produced the Intelligence Reform and Terrorism Prevention Act of 2004. See, for example, Philip Shenon, "Sept. 11 Commission Plans a Lobbying Campaign to Push Its Recommendations," *New York Times*, July 19, 2004 at www.nytimes.com/2004/07/19/us/sept-11-commission-plans-a-lobbying-campaign-to-push-its-recommendations.html.

10. See Laurie West Van Hook, "Reforming Intelligence: The Passage of the Intelligence Reform and Terrorism Prevention Act," ODNI, National Intelligence University at www.dni.gov/content/IRTPA_Reforming-Intelligence.pdf.

11. See, for example, Peter Spiegel and Doyle McManus, "Spy Czar, Rumsfeld in a Turf War," *Los Angeles Times,* May 6, 2006; Greg Miller, "Intelligence Office Has Swollen, House Panel Says," *Los Angeles Times,* March 31, 2006; Richard A. Posner, *Uncertain Shield: The U.S. Intelligence System in the Throes of Reform* (Lanham, MD: Rowman & Littlefield, 2006); House Permanent Select Committee on Intelligence, Subcommittee on Oversight, *Initial Assessment on the Implementation of the Intelligence Reform and Terrorism Prevention Act of 2004,* July 27, 2006, at www.fas.org/irp/congress/2006_rpt/hpsci072706.pdf.

12. See Executive Order 12333, "United States Intelligence Activities" (as amended by Executive Orders 13284 [2003], 13355 [2004], and 13470 [2008]) at www.fas.org/irp/offdocs/eo/eo-12333-2008.pdf. For media commentary on the debate over how to revise the 1981 executive order signed by President Reagan, see, for example, Scott Shane, "Bush Issues Order Seeking to Unite the Efforts of U.S. Spy Agencies," *New York Times,* August 1, 2008; and Pamela Hess, Associated Press, "Agencies Fight for Spy Control," *USA Today,* May 28, 2008.

13. President Obama abolished the HSC and reassigned its responsibilities to the NSC on May 26, 2009. See Helene Cooper, "In Security Shuffle, White House Merges Staffs," *New York Times,* May 26, 2009, at www.nytimes.com/2009/05/27/us/27homeland.html?_r=1&ref=us.

14. Intelligence Reform Act.

15. IC agencies reporting to cabinet secretaries other than the secretary of defense are: Office of Intelligence and Counterintelligence (secretary of energy); Office of Intelligence and Analysis (secretary of homeland security); Bureau of Intelligence and Research (secretary of state); Office of Intelligence and Analysis (secretary of treasury); Office of National Security Intelligence [Drug Enforcement Administration] (attorney general); National Security Branch [FBI] (attorney general); and the Intelligence Component of the U.S. Coast Guard (secretary of homeland security). Agencies reporting to the secretary of defense are: Defense Intelligence Agency; National Geospatial Intelligence Agency; National Security Agency; National Reconnaissance Office; and the intelligence components of the Air Force, Army, Navy, and Marine Corps.

16. See, for example, J. Michael McConnell, "DNI Addresses the Richard W. Riley Institute of Furman University," March 28, 2008, at www.dni.gov/speeches/20080328_speech.pdf.

17. Intelligence Reform Act, Sec. 1018, "Presidential Guidelines on Implementation and Preservation of Authorities."

18. See "President Bush Administration Actions to Implement WMD Commission Recommendations," White House Press Release, June 29, 2005, at http://georgewbush-whitehouse.archives.gov/news/releases/2005/06/20050629-5.html.

19. This chapter focuses narrowly on analysis-related missions of the ODNI, in part because space limitations preclude even cursory discussion of ODNI responsibilities and innovations with respect to intelligence collection, personnel policy, acquisition, and other mission areas.

20. See, for example, Barbara A. Grewe, "Legal Barriers to Information Sharing: The Erection of a Wall between Intelligence and Law Enforcement," a declassified staff monograph prepared for the Commission on Terrorist Attacks upon the United States, August 20, 2004, at http://fas.org/irp/eprint/wall.pdf.

21. Intelligence Reform Act, Sec. 102 (g) "Intelligence Information Sharing."

22. For a partial list of steps taken to improve access to information and information sharing, see *ICD 501 Discovery and Dissemination or Retrieval of Information with the Intelligence Community* at www.dni.gov/electronic_reading_room/ICD_501.pdf; Tim Starks, "Intelligence Chief Says New Policy Will Dramatically Boost Information Sharing," *CQ Today Online News,* January 16, 2009; and Ben Bain, "A-Space Set to Launch This Month," *Federal Computer Week,* September 3, 2008.

23. See, for example, remarks by DNI Mike McConnell at the Project on National Security Reform Conference, Washington, DC, July 26, 2007, at www.dni.gov/speeches.html; and Intelligence Community Policy Memorandum 2007-20-2 Responsibility to Provide at www.dni.gov/electronic_reading_room.html.

24. Relevant IC policy documents can be found at www.dni.gov/electronic_reading_room.html. See particularly *Intelligence Community Directive (ICD) 203 Analytic Standards, ICD 206 Sourcing Requirements for Disseminated Analytic Products, ICD 208 Write for Maximum Utility,* and *Intelligence Community Policy Memorandum (ICPM) 2006-202-2 Role of the Office of the Director of National Intelligence Analytic Ombudsman.*

25. The ODNI is required to report to the Congress annually on the performance of the analytic community as measured against Intelligence Reform Act standards and the additional standards adopted in ICD 203. These reports are classified but they document the improvement noted in the text. The requirement to provide this report to the Congress can be found in Intelligence Reform Act, Sec. 1019.

26. Other ODNI initiatives to ensure that IC materials prepared for national security decision makers are informed by insights and information from experts who are not in the IC include *ICD 205 Analytic Outreach*, and consolidation and expansion of mechanisms to tap outside expertise through the IC affiliates program that the State Department's Bureau of Intelligence and Research manages for the IC.

27. The NSC process, as that term is used here, subsumes meetings and deliberations of the NSC chaired by the president as well as the cascade of principals committee, deputies committee, and other subordinate arenas. This chapter treats the HSC as part of the NSC process but it is important to note that the existence of two structures with overlapping missions further complicated the ability of the ODNI, and the IC more generally, to support the policymaking process.

28. "Plus one" is the NSC term for the person who accompanies the principal. A senior analyst, usually an NIO or deputy NIO, normally accompanied the DNI but when appropriate to the agenda, the "plus one" would come from the national clandestine service or another element of the collection community.

29. For additional information on the NIC, see the descriptive materials at www.dni.gov/nic/NIC_home.html.

30. Intelligence Reform Act, Sec. 1031.

31. For additional information on the national intelligence priorities framework process, see *ICD 204 Roles and Responsibilities for the National Intelligence Priorities Framework* at www.dni.gov/electronic_reading_room.html.

32. How much time the DNI devotes to directly supporting the president has been a recurring topic of debate. See, for example, Edward Maguire, ODNI, Office of the Inspector General, "Critical Intelligence Community Management Challenges," November 12, 2008, at www.fas.org/irp/news/2009/04/odni-ig-1108.pdf; and Mark Mazzetti, "Report Faults U.S. Spy Agencies," *New York Times*, April 2, 2009.

33. The proscription on collocation is in Intelligence Reform Act, Sec. 103 (e).

34. "Afghanistan" is used as a shorthand reference to the more inclusive category of Afghanistan, terrorist activities in the Afghanistan-Pakistan border region, and terrorism more broadly. This obscures important nuance but is sufficient to make the central arguments of this chapter.

35. Intelligence Reform Act, Sec. 1021. The National Counterterrorism Center had been established by executive order in August 2004. See Executive Order 13354 of August 27, 2004, at www.fas.org/irp/offdocs/eo/eo-13354.html.

36. Ibid.

37. See "Statement from Director of Dennis C. Blair to the ODNI and Intelligence Community Workforce," May 20, 2010, www.odni.gov/press_releases/DNI_Statement.pdf; and "ODNI Marks Five-Year Anniversary with Ceremony: DNI Blair Celebrates Achievements, Reflects on Challenges," at www.dni.gov/press_releases/20100421_release.pdf.

38. See, for example, Greg Miller and Walter Pincus, "Blair's Resignation May Reflect Inherent Conflicts in Job of Intelligence Chief," *The Washington Post*, May 22, 2010, www.washingtonpost.com/wp-dyn/content/article/2010/05/21/AR2010052104939.html; Mark Mazzetti, "Facing a Rift, U.S. Spy Chief to Step Down," *New York Times*, May 20, 2010, at www.nytimes.com/2010/05/21/us/politics/21intel.html?_r=1&hp; and Josh Gerstein, "Blair Exit Revives Concerns about DNI," Politico, May 21, 2010, at www.politico.com/news/stories/0510/37587.html.

39. See, for example, the 9/11 Commission report observation that the other reforms it had suggested could not work without reform of congressional oversight, *The 9/11 Commission Report*, (2004), 420–21.

Chapter 8

Central Intelligence Agency:
The President's Own

ROGER Z. GEORGE

> The sole element of the intelligence community independent from a cabinet agency is the CIA.
> As an independent agency it collects, analyzes, and disseminates intelligence from all sources.
> The CIA's number one customer is the president of the United States, who also has the
> authority to direct it to conduct covert operations.
>
> *The 9/11 Commission Report*

INTRODUCTION: HOW INTELLIGENCE BECAME CENTRAL

Intelligence has become a central feature of the national security enterprise but it was not always so. Indeed, until 1947, American intelligence was a marginal player in the formation of national security policy and was dominated by the military departments that focused on wartime needs. The drafting of the 1947 National Security Act challenged this bureaucratic tradition of departmentally focused wartime intelligence. The military services as well as the Federal Bureau of Investigation (FBI)—which had domestic as well as foreign counterintelligence authorities at the time—remained critical of the proposed new national security framework. The strong biases of the nation's diplomats, warriors, and law enforcement officials drove them to see no need for a new intelligence organization.[1]

Yet, the failings of intelligence at Pearl Harbor and the onset of the Cold War overrode those interests, propelling the president and the Congress to agree—reluctantly at first—that a more coherent intelligence function was important if future failures were to be averted. Between 1947 and 1951, the makings of the new Central Intelligence Agency (CIA) were evident. First, its director became the president's senior intelligence advisor. Second, the CIA was given the role of coordinating and bringing together the information available to various parts of the U.S. government for the National Security Council (NSC). Third, its intelligence collection function—carried over from the earlier Office of Strategic Services (OSS)—was reaffirmed by virtue of the growing need for information on the Soviet Union's political, economic, military, and scientific developments. And fourth, the CIA's covert action (CA) responsibilities (termed "special activities" in the 1947 NSC directives that laid the groundwork for such duties) also grew in response to the spreading Communist challenges faced in Europe, Asia, and other parts of the world.[2]

The 1947 National Security Act dictated a much more formal interagency process, which would require a more ambitious intelligence role than departmental intelligence units could provide. Scholars and the public are fixated on CIA's more colorful operational activities. Yet, the original and core mission of this new "central" intelligence agency was to inform the national security decision-making process and bring together all the available intelligence found throughout the U.S. government. Operations—either to collect secret information or to conduct CA in support of a president's policies—were not mentioned in the National Security Act of 1947. Some scholars believe their absence in the legislation was to avoid details and possibly congressional delays in approving the legislation's principal purpose: unifying the military and establishing a national security making process. In addition, playing down CIA operations would not highlight U.S. actions vis-à-vis its adversaries as well as its friends.

There would be lively debate over which function—analysis, collection, or CA—was now the core mission of CIA. Regardless, a unique feature of CIA—unlike other parts of the intelligence community (IC)—has been to provide *independent* and *non-departmental*, finished intelligence analysis that the president and his senior advisors need. That mission remains the one that dominates the CIA's role in the interagency process.

Although the CIA remains the only intelligence agency independent of a policy department, its direct reporting role to the president is now in flux. The 2004 Intelligence Reform and Terrorism Prevention Act (IRTPA) established the new director of national intelligence (DNI) as the president's principal intelligence advisor and made him responsible for coordinating the broader IC. This has meant that CIA's close relationship with the president may well be different in the future. Even so, the three core missions of all-source analysis, human intelligence (HUMINT) collection, and CA give CIA a special role in the interagency process.

As the core missions of the CIA—analysis, collection, and CA—grew, so too did the development of a new set of bureaucratic players: the analysts and the operators with their own unique cultures. Not surprisingly, then, the CIA began to emerge with interests and behaviors that were distinct from those of the other national security organizations. Two noticeable fault lines became evident—the internal one of analysts versus operators and an external one of intelligence versus policy. It is the interaction of these two sets of fault lines that characterizes much of CIA's operation in the interagency process.

THE INTERNAL FAULT LINE: CULTURES OF CIA

As former CIA Director Richard Helms remarked, "there is a CIA culture. Any circumscribed group of people engaged in a demanding, isolated and occasionally dangerous activity is likely in time to develop a culture."[3] Providing objective, accurate, and timely intelligence to every president since 1947 has shaped that culture for more than sixty years. Yet, the reality is more complex. The CIA contains subcultures reflecting its separate but intertwined analytic and operational missions. More importantly, they also reflect differing priorities, norms, and operational styles for CIA's role within the national security enterprise.

Analysts and the Culture of Objectivity

From its very early beginnings, CIA officials faced a challenge in providing objective intelligence to an inherently political policy process. By its very nature, policymaking is a battleground of ideas in which strong-willed players in the different departments would compete for the president's attention and support. In such a politically charged and personality-driven atmosphere, could independent and objective information and analysis actually make a difference? According to Sherman Kent, a Yale historian, OSS veteran, and early director of the CIA's Office of National Estimates, the proper role of intelligence was to raise the level of the policy debate, not take sides. Kent's 1949 book, *Strategic Intelligence for an American World Policy,* became the touchstone for how intelligence officers view their craft and its relationship to the policy process: "Intelligence is not the formulator of objectives . . . drafter of policy . . . maker of plans . . . carrier out of operations. Intelligence is ancillary to these: . . . it performs a service function. Its job is to see that the doers are generally well informed . . . to stand behind them with the book open at the right page, to call their attention to the stubborn fact they may be neglecting, and—at their request—to analyze alternative courses without indicating choice."[4] In Kent's view, intelligence must be close enough to policy to give guidance and support but not so close as to lose its objectivity and analytic integrity.[5]

Kent's larger-than-life impact—his professional career at CIA lasted from 1952 until 1967—shaped the thinking of generations of analysts and managers. Within the directorate of intelligence (DI) resided the largest number of all-source intelligence analysts serving the president, his key advisors, and increasingly the Congress. They came to see themselves as uniquely placed to provide objective and unbiased information from which policymakers could draw insight and wisdom. During Kent's tenure, CIA left the crowded spaces of its wartime offices in downtown Washington, DC, to take up permanent residence in the suburbs of Langley, Virginia. Situated on a sprawling campuslike compound more than a twenty-minute drive to the White House, this symbolized CIA's remaining apart from the world of departmental politics and White House intrigues.

The evolution of the DI over sixty years has seen numerous organizational changes to reflect the expanding list of intelligence priorities far beyond the Soviet threat. University-trained social scientists, economists, and military historians initially staffed the CIA, to be joined over time by scientists, engineers, and other technical disciplines.[6] The DI now represents a more diverse work force focused on the special political, economic, scientific, and military interests of U.S. government officials. Additionally, in-house training focuses on how to task secret collection systems, effectively write for and brief the busy policymaker, and apply analytic rigor to challenge one's own thinking process. Training and mentoring emphasize the analyst's responsibility for producing objective (free of any political agenda) analysis. This notion of objectivity and analytical integrity has become the sine qua non for a fully professional analyst.

An all-source analyst's performance is judged by his or her file of finished production, the ability to brief senior officials, and a willingness to accept critical assignments that require flexibility and a quick-study ability to cover suddenly emerging intelligence priorities. CIA analysts, by virtue of working inside the premier human intelligence (HUMINT) collection organization, also tend to profile clandestine reporting in their analysis; this inclination results in CIA analysts producing more highly classified—therefore, more restrictively controlled—analysis than is the case in other intelligence agencies. The 24/7 world of today has put an even higher premium on producing analysis that is both timely and concise. As one analyst admitted in a recent study of the analytical culture, he had not joined a university as much as a government-run newspaper business.[7] The rush to produce analysis carries with it the nagging analytic concern about correctly capturing "what we know and don't know." In a word, analysis is an error-prone business where uncertainty is as high as are the risks of being wrong. Intelligence failures come with the turf. No generation of CIA analysts escapes the searing experience of a spectacular failure or the damaging charge of producing biased or politicized intelligence.

Clandestine Service and the Operational World

The creators of the 1947 National Security Act probably did not anticipate how CIA's role would change so quickly to encompass other critical missions beyond those specified in the very vague legislation that established CIA. Although the CIA's collection of intelligence was not mentioned in the 1947 National Security Act, it was not long before espionage was added to the CIA's growing list of responsibilities. And it was the growth in CIA's collection operations and CA mission that gave rise to the agency's dominant culture found in the National Clandestine Service (NCS)—until 2005 known as the directorate of operations (DO). What now most distinguishes CIA from other intelligence agencies is its cadre of HUMINT collectors (often called case officers) who recruit agents, steal secrets, and mount CA operations at the direction of the president. This unique function has given the CIA a character and ethos all its own and strongly shapes the way the CIA operates in the policy process—even when it is primarily the DI that is engaged with Washington policymakers.[8]

By virtue of its authorities to operate overseas and to recruit foreign spies, the NCS values secrecy more than almost any other organization in the U.S. government. As the only career analyst to become a director of CIA, Robert Gates was uniquely situated to observe the operators' different culture: "Secrecy is not a convenience or a bureaucratic matter, but the essential tool of their craft—without it, sources are executed, operations fail, case officers' careers are cut short, and sometimes they and their agents die . . . [NCS] ran the Agency bureaucratically and dominated it psychologically. And few questioned the rightness of that."[9] To be accurate, however, outside critics have questioned this culture of secrecy, which they often complain is used by the agency to hide its failures and escape proper oversight.[10]

The selection and training of clandestine officers also tends to reinforce a feeling of uniqueness that binds clandestine officers together into a guildlike organization. Unlike the DI, which finds its work force largely in American universities, the NCS has recruited heavily from the military and the business world. It sees its origins in the wartime OSS, which had its own military traditions and operated (as one veteran described it) as an "extremely hierarchical organization."[11] The NCS cultivates the image of a can-do culture, not unlike the Marine Corps or an enterprising multinational corporation. Stationing many of its officers in overseas locations conveys a sense of independence from the Washington policy world as well as encourages a sense of self-reliance on each other. Specialized training, itself kept secret to protect the case officer's tradecraft from adversaries, builds this operator's code of behavior. Armed with countersurveillance and recruitment skills, these officers are rewarded for running agents, filing reports that gain the attention of senior policymakers, and handling difficult situations without causing publicity or blowback.

Clandestine operators' quest for secrecy extends even to other parts of the agency. Indeed, for the first several decades, physical barriers separated the NCS from the analysts; what contact existed was only at the very senior levels. Jack Smith, one of the early DI senior managers, admitted, "Most of us on the analytic side had little or no knowledge of the techniques of clandestine work and were prone to scoff at the excessively tight security about operations and to sneer at the bumbling of the 'spooks.'"[12] Conversely, Smith and others in the analytic ranks were well aware of the operational side's subtle disdain for their thinking profession. Analysts were sometimes viewed as security risks to highly sensitive operations, which were not shared with those not having a genuine need to know. Analysts routinely complained that they did not know enough about the clandestine sources—whose identities were well protected—to evaluate how credible they were.

This legacy of separation and secrecy remains important, even though it has diminished over time. Increasingly, more operators and analysts find themselves working together in fusion centers like the CIA's Counterterrorism Center and the DNI's National Counterterrorism Center. Some CIA analytical units have also been collocated with their clandestine service counterparts in the main headquarters building, just as analysts are now deployed overseas to work closely with case officers on many difficult intelligence topics. Analysts working closely with the NCS are also permitted more information regarding sources than they would have been only a few years ago. That said, differences remain at least on an interpersonal if not institutional basis. As recently as 2003 a senior operations officer in Afghanistan could openly dismiss the idea of having analysts in the field to lead operations.[13]

One reason for this sensitivity, of course, is the risky nature of the operations business. An enduring feature of the NCS culture is its long-standing history of doing a president's bidding and suffering the consequences of programs gone awry. Every president since Harry Truman has relied on the CIA to conduct clandestine operations. Many have also had reasons to distance themselves from those operations when they proved embarrassing or questionable, legally or ethically.[14] Since the 1970s Church Senate hearings (when a long list of illegal activities were revealed by then CIA Director William Colby to the congressional oversight committees), senior NCS officers have felt a sense of dread when asked to conduct risky activities to support a president. One recently retired officer put it this way: "[T]he Directorate of Operations, which is the heart and soul of the agency, has become a whipping boy. The truth is that without the clandestine service . . . the CIA would basically be a rather small think tank. Without it the analysts would have nothing out of the ordinary to analyze, the technical experts would have no one to invent for, and human resources would be twiddling their thumbs with no double agents to unearth and fewer eccentric individuals to manage."[15]

Other practitioners have echoed the sentiment that too often zealous policymakers place too much weight on CA. Former CA planners dispute the image of the rogue elephant and cowboys given to the clandestine service. In fact, "officers . . . who manage the covert action programs have always shied away from this side of the business as quickly as a pony shies from a rattlesnake." They tend not to be career enhancing and only a few officers warm to the thrill and risk of such operations.[16] The 9/11 Commission report similarly concludes that the NCS was largely unenthusiastic about CA as its leaders felt that it had gotten them in trouble in the past.[17] What critics call risk aversion, professionals call common sense or good political judgment. The fact remains that overseas operations are the stock-in-trade by which the NCS is measured, whereas the DI's mission as well as its hazards exist largely inside the Washington beltway.

Collaboration between these analytic and operational cultures has proven to be a challenge for running the agency effectively. Most famously, analysts and their substantive views

---

Box 8.1 Outsiders' View: A Risk-Averse NCS?

Richard Clarke argues that CIA could have done more in the pre-2001 war against terrorism but did not because of an institutional aversion to risk taking. CIA reversed itself after 9/11 to deflect accusations of being slow to act earlier. According to Clarke:

> CIA had not acted before because the career managers of its Directorate of Operations were risk-averse. The risks they sought to avoid were risks to them, to the reputation of the CIA, and more important, to the DO itself. Inserting CIA personnel into Afghanistan might have resulted in their becoming prisoners of al Qaeda, with all the attendant embarrassing publicity. Helping the Northern Alliance might have ended up with the managers of the DO hauled before congressional oversight committees having to answer whether

the money had been used for heroin traffic or for the abuse of Taliban prisoners.[1]

CIA had been subject to criticism before, when past White House staffs had gotten them involved in the civil war in Lebanon, in trading arms for hostages with Iran, in supporting Latin American militaries fighting communists, and trampling human rights. Secretary of State Madeline Albright, reflecting on the history of the CIA, said to me that it was easy to understand why it was risk averse: it acts in a passive-aggressive way, she said, as if "it has the battered child syndrome."[2]

---

1. Richard Clarke, *Against All Enemies: Inside America's War on Terror* (New York: Free Press, 2004), 277.
2. Ibid.

---

were excluded from the disastrous Bay of Pigs planning. Conflicts also raged between analysts and operators during the Vietnam conflict in the 1960s and the later Contra wars of the 1980s. Skeptics by nature, analysts were less sanguine about the outcomes for those conflicts than those in the field running operations and committed to the mission. CIA directors have found the collaboration between the analytic and operational cultures hard to manage. Speaking about the Vietnam era, Richard Helms lamented that he found the intelligence directorate very pessimistic on military prospects there, while the operations personnel in the field—working with South Vietnamese who were risking their lives—remained convinced the war could be won. In Washington, Helms said he "felt like a circus rider standing astride two horses, each for the best of reasons going its own way."[18]

A common perception was that CIA directors—either because they came from within the ranks of the clandestine service or because as outsiders they quickly appreciated the power and risks of the larger operational side—tended to favor operators over analysts. Many directors, including most recently retired General Michael Hayden, have made it a priority to develop a one-agency concept. Yet, many officers recognize that "despite all the 'bonding' and cross-fertilization that has taken place between the DI and the NCS over the past several years, with symbolic and real successes, the fact remains that the two cultures are very different."[19]

EXTERNAL FAULT LINE: INTELLIGENCE VERSUS POLICY

How the CIA's cultures and practices interact with the policy world has shifted over the years to reflect a changing view of what intelligence can bring to the national security-making process. In principle it was always there to serve the president. The NCS understood this by virtue of having to conduct CA at the president's behest. However, the DI for many years felt it had to remain more aloof from the policy arena. To be sure, even Sherman Kent appreciated that analysts needed to be cognizant of the policymakers' needs, but he and others cautioned not to get so close as to become advocates of the policy. Over time, a gulf developed that undermined the CIA's credibility. As a young analyst in the late 1970s, the author recalls senior analysts proudly saying, "It did not matter whether CIA papers were read downtown, this is what we believe." Yet the national intelligence estimates (NIEs), considered the most authoritative published intelligence, were often ignored or seen merely as CIA's biased views on what policy ought to be. Policymakers always wanted the facts, but seldom CIA's opinions.

A rising intelligence analyst who had the good fortune to work in several presidents' NSCs early in his career, Robert Gates observed this steady decline in intelligence's role. As Gates ascended the career ladder at CIA to become director of intelligence (the senior-most analytic position), deputy director of CIA, and ultimately director of CIA (DCIA), he steadily spread the message that relevance had to trump independence. Writing about his revelations in the White House, Gates noted, "CIA knew how foreign policy was made in every country in the world except one—our own. Analysts and their supervisors were oblivious to how information reached the president. They had no idea of the sequence of events preceding a visit by a foreign leader or a presidential trip abroad, or even the agenda of issues the president and his senior advisors would be working during a given week. In short, the distance from CIA's headquarters to the White House was vastly greater than the drive down the George Washington Parkway."[20]

Gates's insights and impact were both profound and far-reaching. As the Cold War wound down and the CIA's very existence was seen in doubt, the relevance factor became uppermost in the minds of intelligence professionals. Increasingly, it seemed the way to guarantee a significant role for CIA in the post-Cold War era.

The First Customer

By the 1980s, CIA was more focused than ever on providing tailored intelligence that focused explicitly on the president's agenda. The *President's Daily Brief* (PDB) became the coin of the realm, more so than the NIEs, which still seemed time-consuming to draft, ponderous to read, and prone to miss the mark for many policymakers. Primary attention was paid to what current intelligence was needed to inform the Oval Office and those closest to the president. Termed the *first-customer philosophy* by senior agency officials, they established an elaborate process for preparing, reviewing, and briefing the most highly prized—and usually highly classified—intelligence items in the daily meetings with the president and the few other senior cabinet officials designated to receive the PDB. Even after 2005, when the PDB became an IC product run under the auspices of the DNI, this attitude persisted. CIA proudly noted that as the largest all-source analysis organization it still provided most of the staffing of the PDB process and produced over eighty percent of the PDB items. One clear advantage of this first-customer approach was that it provided CIA much more impact and input to senior-level thinking. As the PDB was tightly controlled and therefore not widely read in the U.S. government, leaks also were seldom if ever a problem.[21]

Owing to the agency's unique mission of providing the president with the best intelligence, its relationship to the NSC has been especially close as well. CIA operators and analysts have served with the NSC regional directorates (e.g., Europe and Russia, the

Middle East, or Asia) and its functional directorates responsible for counterterrorism and defense; in a few cases, they have worked directly in the president's and vice president's personal offices. The NSC senior director for intelligence is typically a CIA officer who is the White House focal point for overseeing all intelligence programs and for preparing presidential findings for CA. Many future CIA leaders have spent time in this directorate to gain a presidential perspective on intelligence's role. Numerous junior CIA officers also have staffed the White House Situation Room, where raw intelligence and diplomatic reporting is received and disseminated throughout the NSC and White House.

Because of its small size, the NSC staff tends to use the CIA as a ready research service. It is not uncommon for NSC directors to commission analyses that can be used in developing internal working papers or briefing memos to the president and national security advisor. Nor is it unusual for NSC directors to arrange for regular weekly briefings or regular phone calls with their counterparts in the CIA and the National Intelligence Council. Such close cooperation between the CIA and the NSC has reinforced a feeling on the part of CIA that it works primarily for the president. This special relationship has reinforced the CIA officer's self-image of providing national, not departmental, intelligence.

This constant interaction, however, is not without its frictions. Historically, some presidents enter office distrusting the CIA bureaucracy either for its analytic views or for its operational methods. President Nixon is said to have blamed CIA and its analysis for undermining his campaign in 1960. Jimmy Carter—on the heels of the Church investigations and the Watergate scandals—wanted little to do with the agency; he allowed his national security advisor to screen intelligence provided to him, thereby preventing much direct contact with agency officers. On the latter point, CIA careerists have preferred to provide intelligence directly to a president. However, strong national security advisors—perhaps best typified by Henry Kissinger—have chosen to preview CIA analysis and select that which a president should see. Tony Lake as NSC advisor had galvanized the DI into re-engineering the PDB to be more relevant to the White House agenda; President George W. Bush took it a step further in admonishing CIA officials to bring him actionable intelligence. Regardless of the pattern selected, each White House and NSC has pressed CIA and now the DNI to adapt its intelligence support and priorities to match the president's style and interests.

One by-product of closeness to the policy arena was the ever-present danger of politicization. Like art, politicization is hard to define but people claim to know it when they see it. Efforts to slant intelligence to please policymakers—either by analysts themselves or through policy-driven pressures or preferences—challenged the analytic culture to its core. Hence, as CIA moved away from Kent's model of an arm's-length distance from the policy world and into the Gatesian world of policy relevance, the opportunities for politicization would seem to rise accordingly. Indeed, Robert Gates became the target of politicization charges during his 1991 confirmation hearings for CIA director. Senators invited CIA analysts to testify against him and on his behalf for his alleged altering of analytic judgments and pressure on analysts to develop an analytic line closer to the Reagan administration's view of the Soviet Union in the mid-1980s. This searing experience led to Gates's own admission that the agency had to fight harder against such pressures and avoid even the appearance of politicization. The establishment of an agency ombudsman for politicization, whose sole mission was to investigate such charges and recommend actions to rectify them, reaffirmed the analytic culture's core value of analytic integrity.[22]

Presidents and CIA Directors

Despite CIA's efforts to support the president, few officeholders have been entirely satisfied with the agency's performance. CIA directors have tried to forge close relationships with their principal customer to help educate and support the president. John F. Kennedy initially was impressed by Allen Dulles and CIA's abilities, but the Bay of Pigs incident caused him to find another director and to assign his brother Robert to watch over CIA and its CA plans thereafter. CIA Director Helms professed never to have developed a close relationship to Presidents Nixon or Johnson, nor was he accorded regular access to either. More recently, directors of central intelligence (DCIs) have found that their clout in the interagency process partly flowed from their closeness to the president and their ability to deliver actionable intelligence. One can contrast the short tenure of James Woolsey—who failed to develop a close relationship with President Clinton—with the nearly seven years that George Tenet served under Presidents Clinton and George W. Bush. Director Tenet's remarkably long tenure was partly the result of good chemistry between himself and the president, as well as his conscious effort to focus CIA's analytic skills and CA capabilities to satisfy President Bush's desire for actionable intelligence.

With the creation of the DNI in 2005, the CIA director's relationship with the president is changing. Now a key issue will be how the relationship between the DCIA and DNI develops. How easily the two senior advisors can coexist and collaborate within the IC as well as in the broader interagency process will be a major test of the IRTPA reforms. CIA's own image as the provider of national intelligence is also likely to evolve. Recent developments suggest this three-way relationship among the president, the DNI, and CIA director will remain highly unpredictable. In May 2006, CIA Director Portor Goss resigned under pressure after continual struggles with the newly appointed DNI John Negroponte; the CIA's morale was judged to be at a low point by well-informed outsiders, requiring a change at the top.[23] Then, under President Obama, DNI Dennis Blair was also summarily fired after repeated struggles with CIA Director Leon Panetta; Blair's failure to connect with Obama and his efforts to exert too much operational control over CIA proved to be his downfall.[24] Not surprisingly, the next DNI is likely to be one who is more sensitive to maintaining good relations with both the president and the CIA.

AFGHANISTAN AND IRAQ: FROM OPERATIONS TO ANALYSIS

No single case can capture the full range of CIA involvement in the policy process. However, a brief review of what is publicly known about CIA actions in Afghanistan and Iraq can at least illustrate some of the internal and external fault lines at work. From this brief narrative, one can draw some lessons regarding CIA's relationship to the interagency process.

Into Afghanistan: Are Operations Policy?

Following 9/11, the CIA was tapped to lead the United States into Afghanistan based on its knowledge of the country's tribes and its understanding of Osama bin Laden. More than any other agency, CIA had been following bin Laden and al-Qaeda and warning of its growing influence and intentions. President Bush gave CIA unprecedented authorities to fight and kill terrorists in not only Afghanistan but globally, which permitted CIA covert operators more freedom of action than the typical case officer would have. According to Bob Woodward's account, it authorized the CIA to disrupt the al-Qaeda network and other global terrorist networks on a worldwide scale, using lethal CA to keep the U.S. role hidden; it also instructed CIA to operate in Afghanistan with its own paramilitary teams, case officers, and the newly armed Predator drone.[25]

These presidential instructions thrust CIA into the middle of the War Cabinet and made it not just an observer of policy, but also a major operational partner and somewhat independent player alongside the Department of Defense (DOD), the State Department, and the NSC. Inevitably, when the CIA director or his deputy sat at the principals and deputies meetings, they now held both analytic and operational responsibilities.

In his own memoirs, CIA Director George Tenet acknowledges that CIA was built to gather intelligence, not conduct wars. However, now it had a leading role in defeating al-Qaeda, requiring that it devote far more resources and take more risks than anything the agency had been asked to do for some time. Within a week, the first CIA team had been inserted into Afghanistan to make contact with the Northern Alliance, a loosely organized set of tribes hostile to the Taliban. CIA clandestine officers led risky operations, making sure Northern Alliance forces got the necessary financial inducements, military equipment, medical supplies, and training to help defeat the Taliban. No fewer than one hundred sources and eight tribal networks already developed by CIA laid the groundwork for this new paramilitary operation and these networks were supplied with millions of dollars as well as tons of weaponry and equipment to keep them loyal.[26]

Despite the president's decision to send CIA in first, Tenet also claims "there was a lot of bureaucratic tension" with senior Pentagon officials on who would be in charge. In senior-level discussions, Tenet sensed that the White House's intervention to let CIA take the lead would be a continuing battle. U.S. Central Command (CENTCOM) Commander Tommy Franks's solution was, "you guys need to work for me," but CIA felt it needed more flexibility and tactical autonomy than would be permitted if CIA teams reported to CENTCOM. In the end, Tenet tried to solve this policy dispute by signing a memorandum of understanding with CENTCOM that would protect CIA prerogatives.[27]

Bureaucratic resistance to a growing operational voice for CIA was to follow. Echoing Tenet's own recollections, former undersecretary for policy in the Pentagon Douglas Feith recalls that CIA's Afghan experts disagreed with the Pentagon's support of a Northern Alliance-based Afghanistan strategy. Not appreciating the internal debates among CIA operators, Feith complained that CIA had good ties into the Northern Alliance but was arguing against using those to overthrow the Taliban. Instead, CIA was content to target only Taliban units containing foreign (Arab) forces as a way to play on the Afghans' well-known xenophobia.[28] That did not disturb him nearly as much as CIA taking too public a position against the views held by others in the interagency. Media leaks by former agency officials, he felt, were designed to undermine the Pentagon's view. Whether linked or not, he claimed, "CIA was not functioning properly in the interagency process."[29]

CIA's voice, however, was not as powerful as some of its critics seem to allege. In the end, the United States was unable to capture bin Laden despite having cornered him at Tora Bora in December 2001. Some CIA operatives blame CENTCOM leadership for not pursuing him with U.S. forces, instead allowing unreliable Afghan allies to attack the Tora Bora area.[30] Other critics of U.S. decision making, like Richard Clarke, echo the charges that the White House and CENTCOM ignored CIA advice and excluded such experts from key decisions regarding Afghan strategy.[31]

When all is said and done, however, the Afghan operations amounted to an unprecedented collaboration between CIA and the DOD. Under an agreement between Secretary Rumsfeld, CENTCOM Commanding General Tommy Franks, and CIA Director Tenet, CENTCOM would have operational control over CIA teams. From former CIA participants we learn that these teams often operated independently in practice but supplied CENTCOM with information on the military tactics, locations, and intentions of Northern Alliance fighters as well as the Taliban. They worked closely with Special Forces teams to designate targets. CIA also operated the armed unmanned aerial vehicle (UAV) called Predator in conjunction with the U.S. Air Force and CENTCOM to target key leaders. CIA operatives would identify targets but CENTCOM would ultimately give the go-ahead to strike the target. The lengthy process by which CIA and the military reached an accommodation on the Predator's use in Afghanistan is itself a study in bureaucratic politics (see box 8.2).

Iraq: The Intelligence-Policy Fault Line

Iraq is likely to take a special place in the CIA's history, but not simply to highlight failures in assessing Iraq's WMD program. Rather, CIA's support to policy beginning with the first Gulf War in 1990 until the end of the Saddam regime shows a mixed record of successes and failures—both in terms of its forecasts but also in its ability to support and influence the policymaking process. The tension between policy and intelligence was evident both in the 1990 Gulf War but also later in the 2002–3 run-up to the Iraq invasion. These episodes exposed the external fault line in a way that is likely to have a lasting impact on how CIA operates in the interagency in the future.

In August of 1990, when Saddam invaded Kuwait, CIA analysts were surprised, as were many in the first Bush administration. Most accounts have credited CIA for being on top of the steady buildup of forces on the Iraq-Kuwait border, but only a few CIA officials interpreted Saddam's military movements as actual preparation for war. An ominous warning of war memo was issued late on July 25, 1990. One week later, a full-scale invasion began, far exceeding what most CIA and other U.S. analysts believed Saddam was contemplating. Bush administration advisors, although surprised by this move and CIA's slowness in warning about it, took seriously subsequent intelligence reporting and assessments that CIA was making. These reports contributed to a U.S. decision to move forces to Saudi Arabia and prepare Operation Desert Storm to expel Saddam from Kuwait. More significantly, CIA analysis of the Iraqi military capabilities—describing its army as battle tested and the fourth largest in the world—proved wrong but influential in debates over a congressional resolution endorsing the plans. CIA briefings, along with many others provided by the Defense Intelligence Agency, to congressional intelligence committees, convinced some key Democratic leaders like Senators David Boren and Sam Nunn not to support the administration's request for a resolution backing the use of military force to oust Saddam from Kuwait.[32]

After the war, congressional hearings and after-action assessments dissected the role various analyses played in shaping policymakers' mindsets and decisions. For most intelligence professionals, it was an expected mixed record, not unusual for almost any important issue. However, according to journalist John Diamond, some key officials who would emerge later in the second Iraq war—perhaps especially then defense secretary Dick Cheney—seem to have drawn the lesson that an administration cannot ultimately rely on the CIA to fully

Box 8.2   Bureaucratic Politics: The Predator Program

After the USS Cole and African embassy attacks, the Clinton National Security Council (NSC) initiated measures aimed at taking down the bin Laden operation in Afghanistan. One was the decision to use an unmanned airborne vehicle (UAV) called the Predator to locate bin Laden. NSC participants viewed the CIA as reluctant to take on this role because operating a UAV was unproven and not considered a central CIA mission. One defense official claims the White House had to "cram it down the throat of the agency" presumably because those in the operations directorate thought it might complicate their relationships with the region's host governments. NSC Director Richard Clarke had to orchestrate presidential outrage to force the agency and the military to collaborate on this project.[1] Other NSC staff complained that the two were squabbling over the management and funding of the program. Neither the U.S. Air Force (USAF) nor CIA, according to them, wanted to pay for Predator UAVs.[2]

Even after 9/11, defense department officials questioned why the Joint Staff should take on this function, as it was not a military mission per se; likewise the CIA was not eager to pay for crashed UAVs. This argument intensified when the program shifted with the decision to arm the Predator with a Hellfire missile and thus give it not just an intelligence-gathering function but also a lethal counterterrorism measure. As NSC participants tell the story, "Whose finger would be on the trigger when the Predator went after bin Laden—the Air Force's or the CIA's?" Should the White House be involved? There were also likely to be policy consequences if it flew through neighboring countries' air space. CIA reportedly did not want the responsibility but neither did the USAF, which indicated that if given the job of killing bin Laden it would prefer to use B-52s, not Predators.[3] These bureaucratic tussles quickly became high-level policy issues in which CIA

was a major player, not a detached intelligence advisor.

Richard Clarke recounts that when the Clinton administration tried to get CIA to do more, George Tenet agreed to a series of things that CIA could do to be more aggressive, but the details had to be worked out on the new authorities, how much money would be spent, and where the money would come from. "CIA had said it could not find a single dollar in any other program to transfer to the anti-al-Qaeda effort. It demanded additional funds from the Congress."[4]

---

1. Daniel Benjamin and Steven Simon, *The Age of Sacred Terror* (New York: Random House, 2002), 321–22. The program reportedly had boosters as well as detractors in both the Pentagon, Joint Staff, and CIA. It was continued through summer 2000 with no clear resolution of who would run, fund, and shape the project.

2. In his testimony to the 9/11 Commission, Director George Tenet acknowledged that there had been interagency discussions of the management of the Predator program, noting that USAF and CIA ultimately agreed to split the cost of damaged or lost Predators; he claims the program was not delayed by such management issues, which Clarke seems to dispute, as he believed it could have been accelerated in 2000. As early as September 2001, the Predator was deployed to Afghanistan but remained "unarmed" until after the September 11, 2001, attacks. See George Tenet, *Written Statement for the Record of the Director of Central Intelligence Before the National Commission on Terrorist Attacks upon the United States,* March 24, 2004, 15.

3. Benjamin and Simon, *The Age of Sacred Terror,* 344. The former NSC directors claim that senior CIA officials worried if CIA had the responsibility for Predator it might endanger the lives of CIA operatives around the world, again reflecting what some would view as a parochial bureaucratic concern compared with the broader American objective of delivering justice to the perpetrator of the 9/11 attacks.

4. Clarke, *Against All Enemies,* 238.

understand a devious enemy.[33] Moreover, other skeptics of CIA like Donald Rumsfeld and Paul Wolfowitz—who had both served on commissions in the 1990s that were highly critical of the agency's military analysis—were also to become key players in the Second Gulf War.[34]

Iraq 2003: How Relevant Was Intelligence?

CIA involvement in the Iraq policy process during 2002–3 was dramatically different from what occurred in 1990. For much of this period, CIA stood on the sidelines of the policy process and only in the final phases played any role in the decision to invade. As participants to that policy process tell it, there was little formal discussion of the Iraq problem within the interagency until fall 2002.

From what senior participants have now said, the question of invading Iraq had appeared inevitable almost as soon as the dust had settled on the twin towers attacks. Yet there were no NSC meetings at which the question of war or peace was formally addressed.[35] Instead, within a few weeks of the Camp David meeting on the Afghanistan plan, Secretary of Defense Rumsfeld had asked CENTCOM commander Tommy Franks to review his war plan for dealing with Iraq. In early spring 2002, the Joint Staff and CENTCOM planners were revising these plans and getting major inputs from the secretary himself. The president is said to have asked General Franks to begin moving forces from Afghanistan to the Gulf. Other Pentagon officials have written that "the President's decision to go to war, made finally in January 2003, came after more than a year of deliberation within the administration." By one DOD account, dozens of meetings of the NSC, principals, and the deputies on all aspects of the war occurred; that view is confirmed by George Tenet's own recollection but they tended to operate on the assumption that war was coming and never engaged in whether a war was needed.

A formal working-level executive steering group was not set up until August 2002 to develop interagency plans, a fact confirmed in other chapters of this volume. It was at this point that the CIA began to see the need for assessments on all aspects of intelligence. In summer 2002 CIA Director Tenet established a mission manager for Iraq, whose role became organizing an internal agency taskforce; there was a need to ensure the NCS and analysts were exchanging information, particularly as CENTCOM began tasking the IC for information in preparing itself for possible action.

Until summer 2002, senior CIA officials felt in the dark about the extent to which serious war planning had begun. Paul Pillar, national intelligence officer (NIO) for the Near East at the time, recalls that until August 2002, when Vice President Cheney addressed the veterans of foreign wars and pronounced Iraq to be a serious threat, he was unaware of how actively the White House had been working to prepare for an Iraq operation. That speech caught George Tenet offguard as well. It was a speech touching on intelligence but was never shared with CIA officials for clearance; moreover, it went "well beyond what our [CIA] analysis could support."[36] In Tenet's view, the military had become convinced by early spring that war was inevitable, while most intelligence analysts came to this conclusion much later. He seems to conclude that by summer 2002 war became inevitable, although the rationale for it was still being fashioned and would ultimately involve the IC's own flawed assessments of Iraq's WMD capabilities.

After CIA Director Tenet and his analysts became convinced the United States was headed for war, serious analytical work on Iraq—including assessments regarding the regional and domestic consequences of removing Saddam—began. Even then, NIO Pillar felt he needed to justify such analysis by first getting a senior State Department official—in this case Richad Haass at policy planning—to request these assessments. As a nonpolicy agency, it would have been difficult to justify any self-initiated studies by the IC, given the sensitivity of the White House and the Pentagon to CIA questioning the correctness of the emerging Iraq policy. Tenet notes that a prescient CIA paper produced in late August for a national security team meeting in September 2002 was titled "The Perfect Storm: Planning for Negative Consequences of Invading Iraq." By then, the battle lines seemed well formed with Secretary Powell favoring more diplomacy through the UN and other advisors convinced that this was a road to nowhere. A subsequent deputies committee meeting the following week focused on developing the arguments for "Why Iraq?"

On the CIA's operations side, the unease with the sudden decision for war was also noticeable. During the Clinton administration, Iraq had taken a back seat to other higher priority collection concerns like Iran and North Korea. The U.S. reliance on UN inspections—aided by some tip-offs provided by U.S. intelligence—was deemed sufficient to monitor Iraq's disarmament. Containment, stated the U.S. policy, had effectively taken Saddam off the radar. Yet, when Saddam kicked out the UN inspectors in 1998, the CIA found itself without major sources. Now in late 2001 and early 2002, there was an urgent need to know as much about Iraq as possible. Many accounts of the later Iraq/WMD failure recount the absence of good HUMINT in reaching judgments on Saddam's WMD program. But CIA's Iraq Operations Group (IOG) suddenly ramped up to develop whatever sources it could on Saddam's WMD program.[37]

Perhaps the most important intelligence and policy dispute had nothing to do with WMD, but rather focused on the alleged links between al-Qaeda and Iraq. Ever since the 9/11 attacks there had been rumored reports of senior al-Qaeda connections to Iraq's security services. CIA analysts doubted such connections existed, and CIA Director Tenet himself says, "CIA found absolutely no linkage between Saddam and 9/11."[38] Over the course of 2002, CIA produced a series of papers trying to lay out the evidence and assess how close a connection there was or was not. One June 2002 paper, titled "Iraq and Al Qaeda: Interpreting a Murky Relationship" purposely took a devil's-advocate position in trying to find connections; it provoked such divisions among CIA's regional and terrorism analysts that some complained to the CIA's ombudsman for analytical integrity. Yet that same paper did not seem to satisfy some policymakers. Several subsequent visits to CIA headquarters by senior White House officials did not diminish policymakers' disagreements with CIA's judgments. Two later papers issued in September received similar testy reactions from policymakers, according to George Tenet.[39]

Civilian defense officials firmly believed that CIA had dismissed important information and had interpreted the data incorrectly. Then Undersecretary Feith led the charge in challenging the agency's judgments regarding the al-Qaeda–Iraq links. To bolster his case, he had intelligence professionals on his policy staff critique CIA analysis, which the Pentagon believed was filtering out data that did not support a benign view of Iraq. This dispute continued through much of 2002, culminating in an August 2002 briefing that Feith's staff provided to George Tenet and senior intelligence officials. In Feith's view, it had the effect of laying out an alternative way of viewing intelligence data and of subsequently qualifying CIA's earlier denials of any contacts between the two groups.

Tenet's version of this same meeting, however, was quite different; he termed the meeting "entirely inappropriate" and cautioned senior defense officials that this issue needed to be handled by professional analysts in intelligence channels rather than being driven by policy officials with agendas. At the end of the day, the absence of an interagency consensus on the role of al-Qaeda in Iraq prevented it from becoming a major public justification for the Iraq invasion. CIA's defense of its analytic integrity thus left the WMD threat as the strongest pillar of the administration's case against Saddam. Speaking to journalists later, Deputy Secretary Wolfowitz also acknowledged it was the lowest common denominator around which the interagency could agree. Even so, Secretary Powell's discomfort at leading the administration's case against Iraq using CIA evidence led him to insist that DCIA Tenet be present when he addressed the UN Security Council in February 2003.

LESSONS LEARNED: INTELLIGENCE MATTERS, BUT NOT ALWAYS

CIA's performance in the Afghan and Iraq cases provides a number of useful lessons about the relationship between intelligence and policy. Among the most important is the difficulty in drawing a line between what constitutes objective intelligence and policy advocacy. When vital issues of war and peace are at stake, strong-minded policymakers will view CIA analysis impacting the debate and either becoming a useful weapon or a major complication. CIA's involvement in the policy process, then, requires that intelligence officials acknowledge the inherently political nature of their work. To be naïve about how intelligence is likely to be used can allow CIA to become a victim of the contending forces on both sides of a disputed policy.

A second lesson learned is that CIA will periodically be at the interagency table not solely as an intelligence advisor but also as a policy player. Having its own programs—covert to be sure—to manage, fund, and implement gives it a voice along side the State and Defense Departments, which is not sufficiently appreciated. CIA, not surprisingly, is a bureaucracy with its own priorities, missions, and jurisdictions. So, when conflicts like the Predator program arise within the interagency process, it can be expected to defend its views no less firmly than the Pentagon, the services, or the State Department.

In an era where CA is seen as one of the important instruments for a president, CIA becomes the executive agent for parts of a presidential decision and will have to assume a policy-implementing role. Legitimately, it will at times question whether other policymakers are relying too much on this instrument—when other parts of the policy might not be working—and worry that it will be instructed to conduct operations that will eventually come back to haunt the agency. Other policymakers naturally may find CIA less eager to step forward to implement risky policies for which it is responsible, which is no different from the Pentagon's or the State Department's reactions to presidential initiatives for which they are going to be held responsible.[40]

Third, whenever CIA is actively supporting presidential policies with major operations as well as with analytic analysis, it will be a challenge to distinguish when senior CIA officials are speaking as policy advocates or as analysts. Particularly for other policy agencies, as seen in the case of Afghanistan, this becomes a murky area. Nonintelligence participants in the interagency process may resent this infringement on their turf and not see such fine distinctions being made by intelligence officials. They particularly resent former intelligence officials or their surrogates from using the media to argue their case.

Historically, CIA directors have found themselves becoming policy advocates. John McCone played a key role in Kennedy's executive committee deliberations over the Cuban missile crisis; likewise CIA Director William Casey, also a cabinet member, felt no qualms about expressing his own policy views on Central America and the Soviet Union even when they contradicted the intelligence analysis provided by the DI. The recent subordination of CIA director to the new DNI perhaps may help to remove the conflict between the CIA's analytic and operational roles. Hypothetically, CIA might be at the table as a policymaking agency when it conducts CA while the DNI might represent the entire IC and its analytic views regarding the issue at hand without feeling the same tug to be with the program that operators might feel.

Fourth, formal intelligence is not necessarily the most important information in forming a policy. Administrations and presidents rely on a range of opinions and information channels to reach important decisions. In many cases, CIA's analytic views will not count or be as instrumental as others' views in the policy community. Often policymakers come into government with strongly held opinions; they know what they think and they cannot be persuaded by CIA analysis. In the case of Iraq, there were competing sources of information to those provided by CIA, a situation that is not unique. Indeed, as other chapters in this book make clear, information was flowing from a variety of think tanks and advocacy groups that were just as influential as anything CIA might have been producing. Of course, policymakers have every right to accept or reject CIA analysis. CIA's job is to call it as it sees it, but there is no obligation on the part of policymakers to agree; moreover, policymakers also have a right to challenge CIA analysis. There is a fine line between a decision maker pressing analysts to explain and justify their conclusions and forcing changes in those judgments. At least in the case of Iraq, there has been no convincing evidence of blatant policy pressure that would cause a change in CIA judgments.

Fifth, in the real world intelligence is never perfect but seldom an entire failure. Intelligence can count on having both successes and failures on whatever issue the interagency is focused. Having provided strategic warning but no tactical warning of the 9/11 attacks, the CIA restored its reputation in the audacious and rapid implementation of a CA plan to bring down the Taliban and disrupt al-Qaeda's worldwide operations. Similarly, on Iraq the CIA's record is just as mixed. CIA's successes in the 1990 Gulf War tend to be forgotten in the wake of the Iraq WMD controversy; moreover, its analytic integrity on the al-Qaeda–Iraq connection as well as its sober warnings of what a post-Saddam Iraq and region might look like were similarly well done, if not well received at the time. Policy agencies, not to mention the Congress, the media, and the public, will tend to focus more on what the agency got wrong than on what it got right.

Finally, the CIA and the IC more generally cannot provide good intelligence support if the interagency process is not operating in a transparent and open fashion. Having regular interagency discussion of policy options, where issues are debated, allows CIA analysts to perform their role of producing analysis on those issues. When that interagency process is more informal, kept within a small circle, or entirely hidden, CIA is unable to understand what policy options are being considered and cannot produce timely and relevant intelligence. Analysts are not prone to guessing about whether policy options are under consideration and are reluctant to rely on media stories to explain where U.S. policy stands at any given moment. When operating in a vacuum they cannot, in Kent's words, raise the level of policy discourse. Hence, the CIA's unique role of serving the president rests on the national security system operating in a transparent fashion. As the national security enterprise evolves, efforts to ensure a healthy exchange of diverse opinions within the interagency process is one guarantee that the agency will play a positive role in formulating successful foreign policies.

NOTES

1. Amy Zegart, *Flawed by Design: The Evolution of CIA, JCS and NSC* (Stanford, CA: Stanford University Press, 1999).

2. NSC Directive 4/A (December 14, 1947) established CIA's covert action responsibilities, with political guidance from the State Department. Secretary Marshall did not wish State Department to be running these operations, nor did the military see it as their mission. Michael Warner's review of the origins of CIA's authorities discusses the changing focus and continuing ambiguity of the CIA director's responsibilities. See Michael Warner, "Central Intelligence: Origins and Reforms," in *Intelligence and the National Security Strategist*, ed. Roger Z. George and Robert D. Kline (Lanham, MD: Rowman & Littlefield, 2006), 47–56.

3. Richard Helms, *A Look over My Shoulder: A Life in the Central Intelligence Agency* (New York: Random House, 2003), vii.

4. Cited in Jack Davis, "The Kent-Kendall Debate of 1949," *Studies in Intelligence* 36, no. 5 (1992): 91–103.

5. The creation in 2000 of a Sherman Kent School for Intelligence Analysis was recognition of the need for a specialized set of training courses for analysts to improve their analytic methods. The school would also instill the sense of analytical integrity and transparency in the work force that would protect the reputation of CIA as providing independent and objective assessments to presidents and their advisors. The school was named after Sherman Kent, symbolizing the importance attached by the DI culture to Kent's legacy of objectivity and professionalism.

6. See John Hedley, "The Evolution of Intelligence Analysis," in *Analyzing Intelligence: Origins, Obstacles, and Innovations*, ed. Roger Z. George and James B. Bruce (Washington, DC: Georgetown University Press, 2008), 19–34.

7. Rob Johnston, *Analytic Culture in the U.S. Intelligence Community: An Ethnographic Study* (Washington, DC: Center for the Study of Intelligence, 2005), 27.

8. Discussion of the clandestine service's operations overseas would be a story in itself. Included would be mention of the chief of station's key role in advising the ambassador or chief of mission about the intelligence activities being conducted within that country. In this sense, the NCS has important, if more field-focused, relationships with policymakers. These experiences—the good, the bad, and the ugly—have done much to shape the trust to be found or lost between senior agency and state department officials.

9. Robert Gates, *From the Shadows: The Ultimate Insider's Story of Five Presidents and How They Won the Cold War* (New York: Simon & Schuster, 1996), 33. To underline the point, clandestine collection training often is conducted in separate locations and away from other agency training of analysts. It focuses on surveillance detection, escape (crash and bang) counterintelligence services, and tradecraft in recruiting, developing, extracting sources from hostile countries. All techniques are designed to conceal and protect. Compare this emphasis with state department attention to understanding foreign cultures, languages, consular duties, representational duties, cable writing, and one can quickly discern how the cultures of different agencies would be unique.

10. Tim Weiner's *Legacy of Ashes* argues that secrecy is used to hide agency failures and to avoid accountability.

11. Charles G. Cogan, "The In-Culture of the DO," in *Intelligence and the National Security Strategist*, 213. The NCS logo is a spear that the OSS had adopted as its logo from its military roots to reflect the martial nature of their work; its meaning was that intelligence must be the first line of defense and the leading edge of any military operation.

12. Russell Jack Smith, *The Unknown CIA: My Three Decades with the Agency* (Washington, DC: Pergamon-Brassey's, 1989), 140. Smith boasted that Dick Helms occasionally told outsiders that the clandestine service actually had a supporting, not primary, role, describing his DI as having the primary role of informing the president. Even so, the clandestine service maintained far larger budgets and personnel and considered itself the muscle of the CIA. Smith also recounts, "analysts characterizing the 'spooks' as reckless blunderers who were paranoid about secrecy, especially as it pertained to their reports, which, in the view of the analysts were often trivial and second- or third-rate compared to State Department reporting or intercepted communications of the National Security Agency" (p. 9).

13. Gary Berntsen, *Jawbreaker: The Attack on Bin Ladin and Al Qaeda* (New York: Crown Books, 2005), 9. The same complaint was made by long-time case officer Robert Baer, when a senior DI manager was selected to become the head of the DO (itself a deviation from the usual practice), that "he knew nothing about operations . . . never met or recruited an agent," and more importantly handed out overseas jobs to people (analysts) whose primary qualifications were being briefers, working at the NSC or being close to the DCI. See Robert Baer, *See No Evil* (New York: Crown, 2001), 233.

14. William Daugherty, a former CA operator, has written the definitive look at the presidential role in mounting covert operations. See William J. Daugherty, *Executive Secrets: Covert Action and the Presidency* (Lexington, KY: University of Kentucky Press, 2004). He asserts that even Presidents Carter and Clinton, who openly distrusted the CIA and the use of covert operations, ultimately relied on them when other overt methods proved insufficient.

15. Tyler Drumheller, *On the Brink: An Insider's Account of How the White House Compromised American Intelligence* (New York: Carroll & Graf Publishers, 2006), 138.

16. Daugherty, *Executive Secrets*, 4. Gary Schroen, in his own book on the Afghan War also describes himself as one of the few who thrived on these sorts of operations and which did not necessarily earn him promotions within the agency. See Gary Schroen, *First In: An Insider's Account of How the CIA Spearheaded the War on Terror in Afghanistan* (New York: Ballantine, 2005).

17. The 9/11 Commission, *Final Report of the National Commission on Terrorist Attacks upon the United States* (New York: W.W. Norton & Company, 2003), 351.

18. Helms, *Over My Shoulder*, 310.

19. Cogan, "The In-Culture of the DO," 214.

20. Gates, *From the Shadows*, 56.

21. As the PDB is for the president, it is regarded as having the protections of executive privilege. As of this writing only two PDBs—heavily sanitized—have been revealed as part of the 9/11 Commission investigations. Even commissioners had to fight to gain limited access to the PDBs written during the period under scrutiny.

22. Following his confirmation hearings, Gates addressed the work force and acknowledged the dangers of politicization, and set up a task force to investigate what could be done about the problem. He further created an independent ombudsman for politicization, a position held by a retired senior officer who would conduct annual surveys of politicization and be available to any officer who felt he or she was coming under management or policy pressure to alter an analytic line. This position is still operating and was active during and after the Iraq War controversies.

23. David Ignatius, "The CIA at Rock Bottom," *Washington Post*, May 7, 2006.

24. Max Fisher, "Why Director of National Intelligence Resigned," *The AtlanticWire*, May 21, 2010, at www.theatlanticwire.com/opinions/view/opinion/Why-Director-of-National-Intelligence-Blair-Resigned-3690.

25. Bob Woodward, *Bush at War* (New York: Simon & Schuster, 2002), 101.

26. George Tenet, *At the Center of the Storm: My Years at the CIA* (New York: Harper Collins, 2007), 213.

27. Ibid.

28. Douglas Feith, *War and Decision: Inside the Pentagon at the Dawn of the War on Terror* (New York: Harper, 2008), 78.

29. In this cited article by Milton Bearden, a retired senior NCS officer recites the same argument that a U.S. partnership with the Northern Alliance would unite the Pashtuns with the Taliban and ultimately backfire. See Milton Bearden, "Afghanistan, Graveyard of Empires," *Foreign Affairs* 80,

no. 6 (November/December 2001), 17–30. Feith later accuses other unnamed CIA and state officials of "leaking" to undermine efforts to revisit the containment policy toward Iraq (250). Another senior Pentagon official, Peter Rodman, also accuses CIA of repeated leaks and unprofessional behavior in the interagency process. See Peter Rodman, *Presidential Command: Power and Leadership and the Making of Foreign Policy from Richard Nixon to George W. Bush* (New York: Alfred Knopf, 2009), 365. Rodman accuses state and CIA of a breakdown in professionalism, which included allowing a senior officer to publish a book highly critical of policies "so long as the book was being used to bash the president." Rodman goes on to claim "politicization of intelligence professionals . . . [who] oppose the leadership of an administration, a trend in bureaucratic indiscipline that will haunt future presidencies."

30. Berntsen, *Jawbreaker,* 314–15.

31. Richard Clarke's interview with "PBS Frontline," January 23, 2006.

32. According to several eyewitnesses to this episode on both the congressional and executive branch sides, the most alarming briefings came from the Defense Intelligence Agency, which implied huge casualties would result. Nonetheless, when the invasion proved to be successful, congressional accounts recorded senior senators as most upset by CIA's analysis and few criticized DIA for its alarmist analysis of Iraq's conventional capabilities.

33. John Diamond, *CIA and the Culture of Failure* (Stanford, CA: Stanford University Press, 2008), 140.

34. The so-called Rumsfeld Commission (Commission to Assess the Ballistic Missile Threat to the United States) found CIA and IC analysis of the foreign ballistic missile threat to be deficient, and it warned that the United States would have little or no warning of missile threats coming from rogue states like North Korea and Iran. See *Report of the Commission to Assess the Ballistic Missile Threat to the United States,* July 15, 1998.

35. CIA Director Tenet claims there was never a single meeting at which the central questions were discussed. But Pentagon officials have since argued that the president already knew the minds of his key advisors and didn't need such a meeting. Undersecretary of Defense Douglas Feith also explains that disagreements between Defense on the one hand and CIA and State on the other led National Security Advisor Condoleezza Rice to avoid the debate rather than resolve it; hence, Feith concluded that this allowed the "bureaucracy's innate bias in favor of inaction."

36. Tenet, *At the Center of the Storm,* 316.

37. James Risen, *State of War: The Secret History of the CIA and the Bush Administration* (New York: Free Press, 2006), 76–83. Elsewhere, Risen recounts a senior-level meeting in November 2002, when CIA's Iraq Operations Group (IOG) representatives met with the agency's senior operators in Europe. There was clearly tension between those in the field and the headquarters where the sense of urgency was far higher. At this meeting IOG stressed that field officers needed to "drop their reluctance to engage on Iraq. War was just a few months away," 79.

38. Tenet, *At the Center of the Storm,* 341.

39. Other participants in those DOD–CIA meetings confirm that differences of view emerged but that it was contentious but cordial. They also highlight that CIA's terrorism analysts were more comfortable reaching forward-leaning judgments as they seldom get corroboration for some sensational reports; CIA's regional analysts typically take a skeptical view of single reports and demands more independent corroboration. Hence, these different analytical styles set up internal CIA tensions quite apart from the policy-intelligence frictions that existed at the time.

40. State and Defense have often resisted presidential initiatives to add new missions to their own responsibilities. The Pentagon did not embrace peacekeeping in the Balkans in the 1990s, nor had it wanted to take on nation-building in the Bush administration. Likewise, the State Department felt ill-prepared to do many of the postconflict reconstruction programs and found it hard to get sufficiently skilled foreign service officers to volunteer for assignments to Iraq. Many diplomats did not see this as a core mission or feared it was a distraction from other pressing issues. Ultimately, the State Department was able to fill its quotas without directing officers to these assignments; however, the pressure to volunteer hung over some younger officers who knew their future promotions might hinge on a willingness to serve in war zones despite their lack of relevant country or linguistic expertise.

Chapter 9   The Evolving FBI: Becoming a New
National Security Enterprise Asset

Harvey Rishikof

Meeting the strategic goals requires that the FBI supplement its reactive capability with bold and innovative proactive efforts designed to deter and prevent—to the maximum extent feasible—criminal activities that threaten vital American interests.

Draft FBI Strategic Plan (1998)

The Bureau is designed, and has always operated, as law enforcement and as an intelligence agency. It has the dual mission: (1) to investigate and arrest perpetrators of completed crimes (the law enforcement mission), and (2) to collect intelligence that will help prevent future crimes and assist policy makers in their decision making (the intelligence mission). History has shown that we are most effective in protecting the U.S. when we perform these two missions in tandem.

FBI Response to a Review of the FBI's Handling of Intelligence Information Prior to the September 11, 2001 Attacks Special Report (November 2004)

The FBI Mission is to protect and defend the United States against terrorism and foreign intelligence threats, to uphold and enforce the criminal laws of the United States, and to provide leadership and criminal justice services to federal, state, municipal, and international agencies and partners.

Department of Justice's Congressional Budget Justifications and Capital Asset Plan and Business (2009)

INTRODUCTION: THE EVOLVING FBI MISSIONS

The Federal Bureau of Investigation (FBI) plays a unique role in the national security enterprise. It is the domestic intelligence agency that has primary responsibility for counterintelligence, counterterrorism, and espionage. Created in the early twentieth century, it has been the envy of many law enforcement agencies due to its reputation and élan; however, to its critics it has at times stepped outside its boundaries and has been obstinate in how it shares information in the interagency process due to its criminal law enforcement mission. To others it is too constrained in the manner it carries out its missions due to its commitment to "American legal ethics."[1]

In this new era of threats, the FBI has been challenged to adapt its law enforcement organization and culture of the last fifty-plus years to address new transnational issues that are both domestic and foreign. This has not been an easy transformation for a number of reasons, among them historic legal restrictions, policy guidance, and organizational culture. To observers, the question of whether a domestic intelligence organization might be needed to replace the FBI turns on whether the FBI's culture proves to be too resistant to change.

New missions have created new challenges. For example, questions have been raised on how effectively the FBI has been combating economic or industrial espionage. At the time of the passage of the Economic Espionage Act in 1996 (EEA), twenty-three to twenty-six countries were identified as practicing suspicious collection and acquisition activities, and twelve in particular were targeting industrial trade secrets.[2] The FBI has seen the number of cases of suspected economic espionage under investigation leap from four hundred to eight hundred cases by 1996, but to many observers this may be only the tip of the iceberg. By 2005 the number of countries involved in collection efforts against sensitive and protected U.S. technologies had risen dramatically. As a result, in 2007 alone the FBI opened fifty-five new cases and pursued eighty-eight pending cases.[3] And the national security division (NSD) of the Department of Justice (DOJ), with the aid of the FBI and other agencies, has prosecuted over one hundred cases of export violations to stem the tide of information flowing out of the country.[4]

To understand the FBI's role in the national security enterprise, this chapter traces the historic origins and development of the pre-9/11 FBI culture and the challenges 9/11 presented. In the process, this chapter assesses how successful the reforms of its culture have been and provides recommendations for additional reforms. To some experts, the recent reforms still remain incomplete and insufficient and may prove to be unworkable, requiring even more institutional rearrangement. As the cliché goes, this is a work in progress—but a major attack on the United States would renew the debate on whether an independent, dedicated domestic intelligence agency is required.[5]

THE FBI CULTURE: SIZE, STRUCTURE, AND ETHOS

The history, organizational culture, and capabilities have left legacies of views and behaviors that make FBI agents stand out in the law enforcement community—professional, competent, and desirous of being in charge of investigations. Furthermore, the ability to arrest suspects or targets (unlike the Central Intelligence Agency [CIA]) and testify in court has reinforced a tough, court-oriented approach to evidence and prosecutions. This institutional characteristic has both enhanced and hindered an integrated approach to national security.

Origins: The Need for a Federal Law Enforcement Agency

In July 1908, when Attorney General Charles J. Bonaparte issued a memo describing a force of thirty-four special agents to investigate specific cases for the DOJ, it would have been impossible for him to imagine the complicated and varied missions the FBI would eventually be responsible for a century later.[6] As it grew and evolved, the FBI captured the imagination of the American public—whether as G-men in the 1930s or as Efrem Zimbalist Jr. on the 1970s television show *The F.B.I.* or as Agents Mulder and Scully in the 1990s *The X-Files* series.

In the beginning of the twentieth century there was no systematic way to enforce federal law across the nation.[7] Few federal criminal laws existed and the few federal law enforcement agencies, such as the Secret Service, were limited in resources. The advent of the Model-T automobile created cross-state gateways that handicapped local police who had no authority outside of their respective states. Meanwhile, the growth of a small anarchist movement that assassinated President McKinley finally pushed the government to create a federal law enforcement agency.

At its origin, the FBI would borrow agents from the Secret Service for investigations until the Congress banned this practice in 1908. Bonaparte's successor, George W. Wickersham, renamed the unit the Bureau of Investigation. The agents were special because the Congress, in its legislation, created special federal crimes. For the first fifteen years, the FBI focused on white-collar crime, civil rights, antitrust, and fraud cases. In 1910, with the passage of the Mann Act, a law to halt interstate prostitution and human trafficking, the FBI became the lead agency and gained resources. With World War I came the passage of the Espionage Act and the Sabotage Act and the FBI took primary jurisdiction for these federal crimes. Based on the new missions as a foundation, the FBI grew to 360 agents and support staff.

The continuing riddle for the FBI over the years has been how to balance its multiple missions while protecting and respecting the right of privacy and constitutional norms. This challenge arose following World War I, when domestic terrorism rocked the postwar celebrations and tranquility. Anarchists' bombs in front of Attorney General A. Mitchell Palmer's home and on Wall Street resulted in the infamous "Palmer Raids," whereby, over a few years, thousands were arrested without warrants in a preventive action.[8] Other bombs were planted that same day in eight other cities and over the next few months, bombs were intercepted in the U.S. mail.[9] Due to the massive arrests, both President Herbert Hoover and a young FBI agent named J. Edgar Hoover, who was in charge of the investigations, were widely criticized for civil rights violations based on who had been targeted. During the next few decades a wave of professional criminals courtesy of Prohibition and the emergence of the Ku Klux Klan (KKK) generated more work for the FBI.

During the Teapot Dome scandal in the 1920s, it was discovered that the FBI had spied on members of Congress, and calls for reform again were made. The attorney general was fired, and the new attorney general, Harlan Fiske Stone, promoted the then 29-year-old J. Edgar Hoover to lead the reform. With Hoover at the helm as the new director, a series of reforms were put into place to modernize the FBI. Agents were fired. A strict code of conduct was instituted with background checks for *new* hires. Prospective agents had to be between the ages of 25 to 35 and physically fit (lawyers and accountants were preferred). Regular inspection of headquarters and field offices (FOs) became the norm and, for the first time, a two-month course of formal training in Washington was mandatory. Finally, the nation's fingerprinting file collections were consolidated. During this period the total number of fingerprint cards grew from 100,000 in 1936 to 100 million by 1946.

Within five years Hoover had shrunk the agency from 650 agents to 441. But the legend of a tightly organized, professional, scientific, and special police force was forged. Fingerprint centralization, the collection and reporting of national crime statistics, and the creation of a scientific crime lab, which eventually grew to become the largest forensic laboratory in the world, all contributed to the FBI's image as the premier national federal law enforcement agency. Sensational cases before World War II such as those involving Machine Gun Kelly, Bonnie and Clyde, John Dillinger, and the Lindbergh kidnapping reinforced the image of a state-of-the-art agency.

With World War II, President Franklin D. Roosevelt expanded the primarily domestic intelligence-focused agency to handle overseas intelligence matters. Because there was no CIA and the Office of Strategic Services did not come into existence until 1942, the FBI created its special intelligence service. During the next few war years, over 340 undercover personnel were sent to Central and South America. By 1946, the FBI had assembled an impressive list of achievements: It had identified 887 Axis spies, 281 propaganda agents, 222 agents smuggling strategic war material, 30 saboteurs, and 24 secret Axis radio stations.[10] It had even participated in counterintelligence programs by passing false and misleading information back to the enemy.

In the immediate postwar period, the FBI continued its domestic focus in its anti-communism investigations in the 1950s such as the Rosenberg spy case and the KKK in the 1960s. Four assassinations—President John Kennedy, Senator Robert Kennedy, Dr. Martin Luther King Jr., and Malcolm X—set the stage for the turbulent 1960s. The advent of left-wing groups such as the civil rights movement, the Weathermen, the Black Panthers, women's liberation, and the anti-Vietnam War protests coalesced into a broad counterculture threat for the FBI. Without any guidelines for national security investigations, the FBI launched Cointelpro, or the counterintelligence program. The National Security Council had approved the Cointelpro in 1956 to oppose the Communist Party; the program was slowly expanded to include the Socialist Party, the KKK, the Black Panthers, and eventually leftist groups.[11] The use of infiltration techniques and discreditation against left-wing movements such as Dr. King's civil rights demonstrations, however, became a clear abuse of investigative power. Although these techniques were legitimate when used against communists and the KKK, these approaches (though warranted by the then attorney general) violated constitutional norms of the First Amendment when focused on protest groups. Congressional investigations in the 1970s of the FBI and CIA by Senator Frank Church and Representative Otis Pike produced a new attorney general, Edward Levi, who issued clear guidelines for domestic security investigations. Only protesting groups breaking the law or clearly engaging in violent activity were to be investigated. With the new guidelines, the number of domestic security investigations fell dramatically from 21,000 in 1973 to 626 in 1976.[12] In addition, in 1978 the Foreign Intelligence Surveillance Act (FISA) was passed, establishing a special court to hear requests for warrants and helping to establish the new rules for domestic foreign surveillance.

The history of FBI overreaction and congressional reprimand, particularly in the 1970s, made the FBI "more cautious and more willing to strictly delineate between national security and criminal investigations."[13] The experience of commingling investigative techniques used against both foreign threats and domestic protest movements had resulted in severe rebukes and a national loss of public reputation. In an ironic twist, this structure of controlling excessive domestic investigative aggressiveness pre-9/11 proved to be a political disaster post-9/11 because the FBI was subsequently attacked for not having integrated its foreign national security and criminal investigations.

FBI Culture: Becoming the Special Agent

To appreciate the culture of the FBI it is necessary to understand the incentive system of promotion and status for special agents. The goal of most agents is to become a special-agent-in-charge (SAC), head of an FO, or "captain of one's own ship." The journey begins at the FBI training academy as recruits at Quantico, Virginia. Wearing FBI blue polo shirts, khaki pants, and hiking boots, the candidates are given an eighteen-week course of instruction.[14] A significant number still come from military or law enforcement backgrounds but increasingly recruits come from other intellectual disciplines—the sciences, computer

Box 9.1   The Recent Record on Counterintelligence

The FBI's hard-working agents have occasionally strayed over the line in the name of protecting the public and have had "chalk on their cleats." The FBI has been rightly praised for prosecuting high-profile espionage cases: John Walker, Jonathan Jay Pollard, Larry Wu-tai Chin, Ronald William Pelton, Aldrich Ames, Harold Nicholson, and Ana Belen Montes. In the domestic terrorism arena, the capture of Eric Rudolph (the abortion clinic bomber), Theodore Kaczynski (the Unabomber), and Timothy McVeigh (the Oklahoma City bomber) demonstrated a commitment to marshal resources over a long period of time. The anthrax attack in early 2001 that killed five Americans resulted in an investigation over seven years ending with the suicide of the major suspect, Dr. Bruce Ivins, and the dropping of the investigation against all other subjects.

In contrast is the list of celebrated cases involving missteps: the laboratory investigation over whistle-blower Frederic Whitehurst's allegations of "cops in lab coats;" the shootings at Ruby Ridge; the Waco, Texas assault; the Centennial Olympic Park bombing and the false Richard Jewel accusation; the botched investigation of Wen Ho Lee as a spy stealing nuclear secrets; and, finally, the discovery of FBI agent Robert Hanssen as a double agent working for the Russians.[1] This medley of errors has conspired to create a negative image of the bureau as an effective counterintelligence agency.

Recent cases such as the 2009 conviction of State Department spies Walter Kendall Meyers and his wife, Gwendolyn, after having spent nearly thirty years passing classified information to Cuba's intelligence agency and the apprehending in Yonkers, Boston, and northern Virginia of the eleven-person U.S.-based Russian "Illegals" spy ring in 2010 and the subsequent Cold War-like "spy swap" have burnished the FBI's capabilities in the public's mind. Clearly, the next big challenge in counterintelligence will be cyber-related issues and the jury is still out on the FBI and IC capacity in general to respond to this particularly pernicious threat.

---

1. It is instructive to remember that many of these individuals operated undetected for years: Walker over seventeen years; Ames over seven years; Hanssen over twenty-one years; and Montes over fifteen years. See Michelle Van Cleave, "The NCIX and the National Counterintelligence Mission: What Has Worked, What Has Not, and Why," Project on National Security Reform at www.pnsr.org.

---

technology, accounting, or intelligence. The operational style, however, remains hierarchical and military-like. As one recruit recently noted about Quantico, "Until you get there, it's hard to explain. . . . It was the demands, the pressure, the lifestyle. It's much more of a military-type organization than I expected. A lot of the agents are police or military. I wasn't used to calling people 'sir' and 'ma'am.' I felt like it was going to be 18 weeks of boot camp."[15]

Following the initial training, agents usually spend two to three years in one office and then are moved to a new city. The intent is to prevent agents from becoming too close to local officials in order to retain their distance in public corruption cases. For many years, only agents had blue badges; the rest of the support staff had white so agents could pick each other out quickly in a meeting. Support staff, analysts, etc., felt like second-class citizens. Although this was changed in recent years, SACs still have a gold badge. The gold badge of an SAC is the equivalent of becoming a general officer in the army or admiral in the navy and reflects a senior position. To become a SAC, an agent has climbed up through the ranks. A typical career would include tours as agent, desk officer, unit chief, section chief, office of professional review (internal inspector general), and assistant division director with multiple tours at headquarters in Washington, DC, along with as many as five different FO assignments.

Toughness is part of the image and culture. At Quantico the recruits are given boxing gloves, headgear, and mouth guards and arranged in circles in the gym, according to weight, to fight each other. For many, this is the first time they have been in a physical fight. They must also pass a firearms qualification test and will carry a .40-caliber Glock 22, a 9mm Smith & Wesson, or a 9mm SIG Sauer. To pass the shooting test, each recruit has to fire a gun from four positions at four distances, 150 shots in all, and place at least 120 shots in the target. Agents are also polygraphed when joining the bureau and can expect to be polygraphed a number of times during their career, a requirement that separates the bureau from most agencies outside of the intelligence community (IC).

Trainees also receive seventy hours of instruction on a critical FBI skill: interviewing and interrogation. Over the course of their career they will probably conduct thousands of interviews and interrogations, honing their skills as questioners. The FBI inculcated the ethos of a law enforcement agency; the fact that it is an agency that makes arrests is enshrined as part of the early training. The objective of the interrogation is to preserve evidence and admissions for an eventual trial. For many years the key to success in the FBI was a criminal-focused career path in the criminal division, based on significant cases and successful trials. The counterintelligence or counterespionage jobs, although somewhat glamorous, did not have the status or resources of the criminal components. Agents made names for themselves by making cases, making arrests, and demonstrating an ability to get things done in the field leading to criminal convictions.

Capabilities: Small but Focused

The FBI is comprised of FBI headquarters and a network of FOs. The FBI headquarters located in Washington, DC, provides centralized operational, policy, and administrative support to FBI investigations conducted throughout the United States and in foreign countries.[16]

The FBI operates fifty-six FOs in major U.S. cities and over four hundred resident agencies (RAs) throughout the country. RAs are satellite offices that support the larger FOs and allow the FBI to maintain a presence in and serve communities that are distant from main FOs. FBI employees assigned to FOs and RAs perform the majority of the investigative and intelligence work of the FBI. The FBI also operates fifty-nine legal attaché (Legat) offices and fourteen suboffices in foreign countries around the world.

In comparison to the Department of Defense (DOD) or CIA, the FBI budget and agent power is quite modest. The 2009 FBI budget request proposed a total of $7.1 billion in direct budget authority, including 31,340 permanent positions—12,225 special agents, 2,647 intelligence analysts, and 16,468 professional support.[17] The 2009 FBI budget request represented an increase of 1,129 new positions, including 280 special agents, 271 intelligence analysts, and 578 professional support and approximately $185 million in associated personnel funding over 2008. That budget request of $7.1 billion as stipulated by the Senate Appropriations Committee is "for [the] detection, investigation, and prosecution of crimes against the United States," of which $2.7 billion "shall be for counterterrorism investigations, foreign counterintelligence, and other activities related to national security."[18]

Surprisingly, this relatively modest growth in the post-9/11 years, when compared to DOD, is evident when it is remembered that the FBI's total 2002 budget was $4.2 billion for 10,534 special agents, 1,156 intelligence analysts, and 13,641 professional support.[19] In fact, the New York City police department still has a larger police force than the FBI.[20] But the FBI has always been able to project a Wizard of Oz effect as being all-powerful and effective.

THE WALL: PRE-9/11 ATTEMPTS OF REFORM

Before the events of 9/11, the United States had established a legal regime that clearly distinguished between criminal law enforcement and national security.[21] This paradigm was established primarily to keep in check the broad investigative powers of the FBI separate from the roles and missions of the CIA. This framework was established in 1946 and, over the years, the two agencies have enjoyed periods of cooperation and intense competition. The two agencies have struggled for control over issues of domestic espionage, counterterrorism, counterintelligence, and national security.[22] Yet, by the end of the Cold War, the increase of transnational crimes (narcotics, terrorism, money laundering, economic espionage, and weapons of mass destruction trafficking) increasingly created challenges for the old paradigm. The 9/11 attacks finally shattered it.[23]

Two critical documents created a framework that shaped the FBI's mission and roles in the area of national security: the 1978 FISA and the 1981 Executive Order 12333. This framework, reinforced by court decisions, established a bright line between the domestic and international arenas. Under FISA, records could be sought only "for purposes of conducting foreign intelligence" when the target was "linked to foreign espionage" and an "agent of a foreign power."[24] Surveillance of "agents of a foreign power" was appropriate so long as the "primary purpose" was to obtain foreign intelligence information. Procedures were established to ensure that FISA warrants would not be issued as a way to overcome weak probable cause warrants on the criminal side of the FBI house.[25]

Over the past two decades, a regime of court rules and internal DOJ procedures developed surrounding the use of FISA warrants that barred FBI agents and other IC personnel working intelligence cases that employed the FISA tool from coordinating and swapping leads with agents working criminal cases. As a result of this legal wall, intelligence agents and criminal agents working on a terrorist target had to proceed without knowing what the other might be doing against that same target. The wall theory particularly gained prominence as an explanation of constrained performance during the 9/11 Commission hearings.[26] From this perspective, the FBI was fighting international terrorism with one arm tied behind its back. Ironically, as noted previously, FISA had been passed to stop previous perceived abuses of power by the executive branch and the FBI.

The classic view of the FBI argues that it was designed to be a law enforcement agency that investigates crimes and gathers evidence for criminal trial prosecutions. Prevention had never been a priority, nor had national security been the fast track for a career at the FBI. Although there have been some celebrated national security cases, this was not the focus of the organizational mission. Before 9/11, during the late 1980s and 1990s, a number of reforms and innovations took place to integrate the communities (FBI and CIA) and make intelligence and counterterrorism FBI priorities—the creation of the Counterterrorism

Center (1986); the National Drug Intelligence Center (1992); Intelligence-Law Enforcement Policy Board and Joint Intelligence-Law Enforcement Working Group (1994); National Counterintelligence Center (1994); and the Antiterrorism and Effective Death Penalty Act of 1996. Successes such as the investigation and arrest of double agent Aldrich Ames at the CIA and the arrest and prosecution of Katrina Leung, an FBI source and Chinese double agent, did not do enough to counter the general sense that the FBI was not up to the task.

The FBI continued to be viewed in the interagency process as an organization where the dominant culture was that of an elite national police force that did not share its information and expertise easily with local law enforcement or other agencies. Agents continued to be drawn primarily from police, military, and legal backgrounds, with little representation from other intellectual disciplines such anthropology, mathematics, logic, or philosophy. Senior FBI appointments of outsiders, or non-law enforcement experts, were usually restricted to the director or deputy director's staffs. (Only very recently have significant numbers of assistant directors been chosen from outside the ranks of the FBI.)

Before September 11, 2001, the bureau had no centralized structure for the national management of its counterterrorism program and terrorism cases were routinely managed out of individual FOs.[27] An al-Qaeda case, for example, might have been run out of the New York FO; the Washington FO might have managed a Hamas case. This arrangement functioned for years and, although it produced a number of impressive prosecutions, it did not reflect an integrated effort. Director Robert S. Muller III concluded that, as counterterrorism emerged, the FO focus had a number of failings in "that it (1) 'stove-piped' investigative intelligence information among field offices; (2) diffused responsibility and accountability between counterterrorism officials at FBI Headquarters and the lead Special Agents in Charge who had primary responsibility for the individual terrorism investigations; (3) allowed field offices to assign inconsistent priorities and resource levels to terrorist groups and threats; (4) impeded effective oversight by FBI leadership; and (5) complicated coordination with other federal agencies and entities involved in the war against terrorism. For all these reasons, it became apparent that the counterterrorism program needed centralized leadership."[28]

The first major systematic attempt to turn the FBI into a national security asset began with the *Strategic Plan of 1998*.[29] The plan was radical in a number of ways. First, it placed terrorism, espionage, and other national security threats in tier one, the top priority, whereas more traditional domestic crimes were given lower tiers of significance. Second, the plan called for more resources and improvements in the intelligence collection and analysis capabilities. Third, the plan identified the crucial need for improvements of the information and technology systems.

The strategic plan was to supplement and build on the Legat program, whereby the FBI stationed agents in embassies abroad to facilitate law enforcement to law enforcement cooperation and to create ties to an international network.[30] In the 1990s, recognizing that global crime and terror were on the rise, the FBI had made it a priority to open new Legat offices. In 1993, the bureau had twenty-one offices in U.S. embassies worldwide (mostly in Europe and Japan); within eight years that number had doubled. Offices were opened, for example, in such strategic locations as Pakistan, Egypt, Israel, Jordan, Turkey, South Korea, and Saudi Arabia.[31]

The stated goal of the strategic plan was to transform the bureau from being a reactive criminal prosecutorial law enforcement agency to a proactive intelligence processing national security asset that made counterintelligence and counterterrorism the focus. But the careerists resisted the strategic plan. The 9/11 Commission report recognized the attempt to reform but concluded that a number of forces undermined its success: The FBI had not shifted enough human resources to counterterrorism (twice as many agents remained devoted to drug enforcement); the new division of analysis faltered (not appropriate education and expertise); FBI intelligence collection was weak (not enough translators or appropriate tracking of source reporting); and finally, its notorious information technology system was woefully inadequate. In sum, the maximum capacity program, the attempt to bring the FBI FOs to maximum feasible capacity in counterterrorism was undermined by the fact that the FOs lacked analysts, linguists, or technically trained experts.[32]

A subsequent revealing document released in 2004 explains this culture of resistance to the new missions.[33] In a response to the DOJ Inspector General (IG), the bureau explained that historically it measured its performance to a large extent by the number of criminals it arrested. While useful for traditional law enforcement where the primary objective is arrest and prosecution, this standard was too restrictive when applied to counterterrorism or counterintelligence, where the primary objective is to neutralize and preempt terrorist intelligence threats. Such scorekeeping only captures that subset of terrorist intelligence threats that are neutralized by arresting terrorists and prosecuting them with charges of criminal terrorism. Significantly, it fails to count the terrorist intelligence threats that were neutralized through means other than formal prosecutions such as deportation, detention, arrest on nonterrorism charges, seizure of financial assets, and the sharing of information with foreign governments for their use in taking action against terrorists within their borders.

Furthermore, in 1998 plans to become involved in infrastructure defense such as the National Infrastructure Protections Center, or the National Office of Defense Preparedness, a program transferred from the DOD, simply did not engage most agents or analysts, as it seemed removed from the world of criminal arrests and performance evaluations. In fact, both programs would eventually be transferred to the new Department of Homeland Security (DHS). In the end the FBI leadership was unsuccessful in changing the cultural mindset of the institution and there was no similar change either at the DOJ or the U.S. Attorney's Office. The Congress in its oversight capacity lacked the fortitude to oversee the reform as it focused on one cause célèbre after another. The forces of reform retired or moved on, and a new director was appointed. The criminal culture mindset was reinforced with statutes and legal opinions that made resistance to change all the more effective. It would take 9/11 to usher in real cultural and structural reform.

POST-9/11 REFORM: THE FALL OF THE WALL

Robert S. Mueller III assumed the position of director of the FBI just a week before the terrorist attacks occurred on September 11, 2001. His immediate goal was to expand and develop the infrastructure of the information technology branch, to address records management issues, and strengthen the weaknesses in FBI foreign counterintelligence analysis and security that had been exposed in the 1999 Wen Ho Lee case.[34] Mueller's proposals were initiated partly to prevent future counterespionage and the damage that had been inflicted by former special agent Robert Hanssen, who was convicted on fifteen counts of espionage in July 2001. In the wake of 9/11, Mueller acted quickly to work with the new administration, law enforcement officials, other intelligence agencies, and foreign allies in the investigation process. Mueller's assessment of the FBI's counterterrorism performance was harsh. His analysis faulted the FBI for not developing the institutional structure and processes necessary for a fully functioning intelligence operation, notwithstanding the previous legal restrictions.[35]

The congressional enactment of the USA Patriot Act in 2001 fundamentally changed the "12333/FISA" paradigm that had shaped the FBI's culture for the past three decades.[36] Over the years, judicial rules and DOJ internal procedures had prohibited FBI counterterrorism agents working intelligence cases from coordinating and sharing information with criminal agents who often were working investigations against the same targets.[37] As then Democratic Senator Joe Biden explained during the Senate floor debate about the USA Patriot Act, "the FBI could get a wiretap to investigate the Mafia, but they could not get one to investigate terrorists. To put it bluntly, that was crazy! What's good for the mob should be good for terrorists."[38] The difference was that the Fourth Amendment applied to criminal investigations but after 1978 and the introduction of FISA, a different standard of review was required for a FISA investigation.

By definition, the FBI now understood that investigations of international terrorism were *both* intelligence and criminal investigations. They are intelligence investigations because their objective, pursuant to Executive Order 12333, is "the detection and countering of international terrorist activities." Therefore they may employ the authorities and investigative tools such as FISA warrants that are designed for the intelligence mission of protecting the United States against attack or other harm by foreign entities. On the other hand, they are criminal investigations because international terrorism against the United States constitutes a violation of the federal criminal code.

In essence, the USA Patriot Act eliminated the wall and the FBI subsequently believed it was now authorized to coordinate among agents working criminal matters and those working intelligence investigations. On March 6, 2002, the attorney general issued new intelligence-sharing procedures for foreign intelligence and foreign counterintelligence investigations conducted by the FBI to capitalize on this legislative change. These new procedures specifically authorized FBI agents working intelligence cases to disseminate to criminal prosecutors and investigators all relevant foreign intelligence information, including information obtained from FISA. Likewise, the new procedures authorized prosecutors and criminal law enforcement agents to advise FBI agents working intelligence cases on all aspects of foreign intelligence investigations, including the use of FISA.

In October 2002, Director Mueller went before the Senate Select Committee on Intelligence to describe the bureau's transformation process.[39] Mueller initiated programs to modify FBI structure and operations to focus on the prevention of potential attacks, to counter foreign intelligence operations against the United States, and to begin to assess the impact of cybercrime-based attacks and other high-technology crimes. In reorganizing the counterterrorism division, the bureau created a position for an assistant director to have oversight authority. The division recognized that counterterrorism had national and international dimensions that went beyond traditional local FO jurisdiction. Centralized coordination was required to ensure that individual pieces of an investigation could be compiled into a single and coherent picture. Before this new system, there was little accountability because responsibility had been diffused.[40] The assistant director for counterterrorism, however, was now accountable for taking all steps necessary to develop the bureau's counterterrorism capacity. Mueller also pledged to the committee that the FBI would continue to enhance its analytical, information-sharing, and technology departments to meet the demands of global counterterrorism efforts.

Nevertheless, the FBI still had primary responsibility for domestic law enforcement missions. According to the bureau's public website, it remained ". . . dedicated to protecting civil rights, combating public corruption, organized crime, white-collar crime, and major acts of violent crime."[41] While addressing issues of foreign intelligence and the war on terror, the bureau still placed the most emphasis on domestic security. The tension in performing both missions remained.

Mueller's new policies attempted to work with ideas of globalization to protect American citizens at home and abroad through an emphasis on counterterrorism. For Mueller, counterterrorism efforts had to address the threats posed by a multitude of international and domestic terrorists.[42] Through these policies, the Bureau believed that it had "strengthened its support to federal, county, municipal, and international law enforcement partners and (had) dedicated itself to upgrading its technological infrastructure to successfully meet each of its priorities."[43]

Internally the FBI contended that the FISA court opinions by the foreign intelligence surveillance court of review and its new reclassification systems had finally changed the culture and solved the wall problem. Reinterpretations of procedural guidelines by the FISA appellate court weakened the historic separation of criminal and intelligence matters. Now, under section 218 of the USA Patriot Act, the government had to show only a "significant purpose" for its request for foreign intelligence information, rather than a "primary purpose" as had been established by previous court opinions. The original, much higher standard had been there to ensure that prosecutors did not use FISA to avoid the even higher standards for warrants in criminal cases. Although there was some debate over whether the previous restrictive approaches had been necessary, the cultures of the FBI and the DOJ had conducted themselves with the view that the restrictions were necessary. To reflect this change internally, the FBI created a new classification for cases. This reclassification officially designated an international terrorism investigation as one that could employ intelligence tools as well as criminal processes and procedures. The FBI understood its new role:

> With the dismantling of the legal "wall" and the integration of criminal and intelligence personnel and operations, the FBI believed it would have the latitude to coordinate intelligence and criminal investigations and to use the full range of investigative tools against a suspected terrorist. On the intelligence side, the FBI could conduct surveillance on the suspected terrorist to learn about his movements and identify possible confederates; it could obtain FISA authority to monitor his conversations; and/or approach and attempt to cultivate him as a source or an operational asset. On the criminal side, it now had the option of incapacitating the target through arrest, detention, and prosecution. It could decide among these options by continuously balancing the opportunity to develop intelligence against the need to apprehend the suspect and prevent him from carrying out his terrorist plans. For the FBI this integrated approach has guided its operations and successfully foiled terrorist-related operations and disrupted cells from Seattle, Washington, to Detroit, Michigan, to Lackawanna, New York.[44]

In addition, the creation of the DHS and the Director of National Intelligence (DNI), the National Counterintelligence Executive (NCIX), the National Counterterrorism Center, and a newly amended Executive Order 12333, reinforced the ongoing process to integrate law enforcement and national security equities. The national security enterprise had created more institutions, more silos, and more integration mechanisms.

One measure of the FBI's new aggressiveness was the extent to which FISA coverage increased significantly post-9/11, reflecting an increased focus on counterterrorism and counterintelligence investigations. From 2001 to 2003, the number of FISA applications filed annually with the foreign intelligence surveillance court increased by eighty-five percent. There was a similar increase in the use of the emergency FISA process that permitted immediate coverage in emergency situations. In 2002, for example, the DOJ obtained a total of 170 emergency FISA authorizations, which is more than three times the number of emergency FISAs obtained in the twenty-three years between the 1978 enactment of FISA and September 11, 2001.

Although touted as a success by the administration, to the critics of the FBI it again was seen as failing to use the FISA tools properly by shortcutting the procedures. Soon the FBI was embroiled in a scandal on the improper use of national security letters (NSLs).[45] As critics noted in 2001, the Patriot Act significantly expanded this authority in several ways.[46] Under the Patriot Act, NSLs were no longer limited to foreign powers or agents of a foreign power but simply "relevant to" or "sought for" an investigation to protect against international terrorism or espionage. This included information on people who were not the subject of the investigation. Expanded as well was the number of people who could authorize the letters: headquarters officials, the heads of FOs or the SACs. In short these changes dramatically increased the number of NSLs being issued from 8,500 in 2000 to 39,000 in 2003; 56,000 in 2004; and 47,000 in 2005.[47]

Pursuant to the Patriot Reauthorization Act of 2005, the DOJ Office of the Inspector General (OIG) is required to review the use of NSLs issued by the DOJ. In 2007, the OIG released its first report and detailed significant violations of law and regulations by the FBI in its use of its "national security letter authority."[48] Although the FBI responded quickly to take corrective measures to make sure these abuses would not continue, to many outsiders it looked like the bureau had become lax, and had yet again let its detractors highlight a culture that was arrogant, sloppy, and not in control.[49] In fact, some believed the problem stemmed from the fact that issuing NSLs had become the new metric for the FBI to evaluate the aggressiveness of an FO and its SAC leadership.

Despite these attempts at reform, hard questions remained. Had these changes addressed the fundamental cultural sources of the FBI's weakness in the national security area? To its critics, the FBI continued to be primarily and organizationally focused on making cases for criminal investigations; moreover, its effort to maintain the integrity of the criminal prosecution, citing the evidentiary and chain of custody rationale, it still would not share bureau information. The reputation of the FBI was that it did not behave collegially in the interagency world. All incentives reinforced the view that agents were encouraged to be "reactive, case-driven, and conviction-oriented, working cases one by one and protecting information for use of trial."[50]

The second major criticism focused on the FBI's timidity to pursue investigations in the counterterrorism, counterintelligence, and national security arenas due to a reluctance to reignite the 1970s criticism by the Church Committee (United States Senate Select Committee to Study Governmental Operations with Respect to Intelligence Activities).

These investigations had documented how the FBI and the CIA, in the name of security and domestic intelligence in the 1960s and 1970s, had violated, among other things, certain First Amendment and Fourth Amendment rights in investigations of the alleged subversive movements when confronting domestic protest. The passing of the FISA flowed from the findings of the Church Committee and was the Congress's attempt to bring in the judiciary as a check into domestic surveillance issues.

The third criticism of the FBI was the lack of a talented, effectively trained, cyber-savvy special agent cadre as well as a modern, computerized record-keeping system to help analyze information in a coherent and timely manner. In short, the FBI continued to "not know what it knows" and even when it knew it, not perform effectively.

The fourth problem was too much poor and unverified information was still being collected in an uncoordinated manner, which added to the difficulty in transferring the information to the domestic and intelligence communities. The conclusion was the FBI remains a reactive institution that investigates crimes after the fact and does not prevent crimes or international incidents from happening.

To look more closely at one of the key areas of criticism—technology, information gathering, and information sharing—one theme stands out. Although in the area of technology the FBI has made great strides, "the FBI for a number of years has had an on-line computer database known as the Terrorist Information System (TIS) containing information on suspected terrorist groups and individuals. The system contains more than 200,000 individuals and over 3,000 organizations or enterprises. The individuals indexed include not only subjects of investigations but also known or suspected members of terrorist groups, associates, contacts, victims, and witnesses. The organizations or enterprises include not only terrorist groups but also affiliated organizations or enterprises. TIS was designed to allow the FBI to rapidly retrieve information and to make links between persons, groups or events."[51] But has the new computer system been functioning to its full capacity?

As technology advances, there is increasingly more access to more information, and historically the federal institution that organized and controlled information involving potential crime has been the FBI. Yet, as has been recognized by numerous commentators in this volume, crime, terrorism, and intelligence have many overlapping points. As recently as October 2009, yet again the IG for DOJ issued a report on the FBI's collection of wiretapped phone calls and intercepted e-mails and cited a continuing failure to review "significant amounts" of the backlog of recordings and data.[52] Significantly the report found that the FBI had failed to read 7.2 million electronic files collected by counterterrorism investigators.[53] Although it disagreed with some of the conclusions, the FBI pledged to hire or contract with more linguists; this has been a problem since 2001 and noted in many previous IG reports. However, the Congress may be losing its patience with the FBI on this continuing problem. So the question remains, should the FBI still be the agency to coordinate domestic information efforts or is some other framework required?

RENEWED FBI REFORMS AND RESTRUCTURING

As it continued to fight the war on terror, the FBI leadership also continued to restructure the organization. In 2004, Director Mueller came before Congress again to discuss new transitions in FBI culture, noting the need to adapt constantly because it was faced with diverse crimes such terrorism, corporate fraud, identity theft, human trafficking, illegal weapons trade, and money laundering.[54] Mueller believed that the bureau had to be "flexible, agile, and mobile in the face of these new threats."[55] As a result, the FBI under Mueller had:

- Refocused its mission and revised its priorities;
- Realigned its workforce to address these priorities;
- Shifted its management and operational environment to strengthen flexibility, agility, and accountability;
- Restructured FBI headquarters;
- Undertaken dozens of projects aimed at reengineering internal business practices and processes.[56]

In addition, Mueller discussed how the bureau would implement these new goals by building a more diverse and capable work force. It would do this through:

- Expanding the FBI's applicant base for critical skills and diversity;
- Updating new agent training to reflect revised priorities;
- Establishing new career tracks for counterterrorism, counterintelligence, cyber security, and for analysts;
- Improving management and leadership development.[57]

The bureau also was continuing to increase its efforts to expand communication between itself and other federal partners at the local, state, federal, and international level. By 2006, the FBI had finished most of its transitional development programs and presented its new look—the deputy director would focus on operational matters; a new associate deputy director (ADD) would focus on information management; and five new branches (including a National Security Branch [NSB]) would have three components: a counterterrorism division, a counterintelligence division, and directorate of weapons of mass destruction.[58]

Because of these new structural changes, the position of executive assistant director for law enforcement services became obsolete. The ADD now had a more streamlined oversight of the human resource branch, office of the chief information officer, inspection division, facilities and logistics services division, finance division, records management division, and security division.

The creation of the NSB at the FBI paralleled the creation of the NSD at the DOJ. The NSD at DOJ merges the primary national security elements: the counterterrorism and counterespionage sections, the office of intelligence, a new law and policy office, and the office of justice for victims of overseas terrorism. Working closely with DHS, FBI, Commerce, DOD, and other law enforcement agencies, the NSD has brought over one hundred cases since 2007.[59]

Ultimately, Mueller believed that the FBI has been revamped and transformed into a more vigorous, flexible, and pragmatic organization and "is now better equipped to confront the myriad of threats we face in a post-September 11th world. We will continue to evolve and make comprehensive changes in the overall structure, organization, and business practices of the FBI to ensure that we remain the very best law enforcement and intelligence agency in the world."[60]

Box 9.2   Reorganizational Reforms Post-9/11

The deputy director (DD) would continue oversight of the national security; the criminal, cyber, response and services branch; and the science and technology branch. Also reporting to the DD would be the assistant directors in charge/special agents in charge of FBI field offices, the office of public affairs, the office of congressional affairs, the office of the general counsel, the office of equal employment opportunity, the office of professional responsibility, and the office of the ombudsman.

Creation of the associate deputy director (ADD) with oversight functions of the management of the FBI's office of the human resources branch and the office of the chief information officer through the respective EADs, and exercises direct oversight of the inspection division, the facilities and logistics services division (FLSD), the finance division (FD), the records management division (RMD), the security division (SecD), and the resource planning office (RPO) or personnel, budget, administration, and infrastructure to ensure that these areas are aligned with the bureau's mission. This would allow the director and DD to focus on operations, intelligence, and liaison. Because of the growth of the bureau's work force and budget, new executive management policies and a larger focus on long-term strategic efforts were needed to adapt to the changes. The office of the ADD, therefore, would meet these new sorts of demands.

Five new branches: Each branch to be headed by an executive assistant director (EAD): the national security branch; the criminal cyber, response, and services branch investigations branch; the human resources branch; the science and technology branch; and the office of the chief information officer.

Reporting to the DD

National security branch (NSB): The branch would be composed of the counterterrorism division, counterintelligence division, and directorate of intelligence. In 2006 the NSB added a new weapons of mass destruction (WMD) directorate, which merged WMD and counterproliferation initiatives. This new directorate would study the consequences of a WMD attack, increase the bureau's level of preparedness, and coordinate the federal government's response in the event that the United States is attacked with a WMD.

Criminal cyber, response, and services branch (CIB): The branch encompasses the criminal investigative division, the cyber division, the critical incident response group, the office of international operations, and the office of law enforcement coordination. This directorate will be accountable for criminal and cyber investigations, coordination with law enforcement, international operations, and crisis response. By giving one individual complete responsibility over this directorate, it ensures that criminal programs receive strategic guidance and support, and that the FBI maintains its unparalleled level of excellence in criminal investigations.

The science and technology branch (S&T): The S&T branch would combine the criminal justice information services division, laboratory, the operational technology division, and the special technologies and applications section (formerly part of the cyber division). "The S&T branch will ensure that the FBI continues to provide exceptional service to the law enforcement community and stays on top of technical innovation and developments in the sciences to support investigative and intelligence-gathering activities."

Reporting to the ADD

Human resources branch (HR): This new branch combined the human resources division and the training and development division (TDD). The intent of this merger was for the bureau to restructure its human capital program and to focus on what the bureau sees as its most crucial assets, its people. The HR branch demonstrates that the bureau is committed to recruiting, training, developing, and retaining people who will further its reputation for excellence.

Office of the chief information officer (OCIO): The composition of this branch, when created, was not changed but was more aligned with the components handling strategic planning, finance, security, and facilities. Because information technology in the FBI's restructuring plan is important, this new alignment was critical.

Though much of the chapter has focused on the failings of the FBI and the question of its reform, its role in the war in Iraq and the professionalism it demonstrated in the context of the national security enterprise deserves mention and comment given the themes of the book and case studies.

THE GUANTANAMO INTERROGATION SCANDAL: IN DEFENSE OF CULTURE

FBI culture and its professionalism saved the bureau from the scandal over coercive interrogation techniques that have been the subject of much criticism and scrutiny. In the face of executive pressure, the bureau held fast to its criminal law procedures that limited interrogation of detainees to techniques that would be admissible in trial. When deployed to Guantanamo, a number of FBI agents reported abuses and "aggressive treatment of prisoners" in the interrogation process, which launched internal military investigations.[61] These complaints caused some friction in the interagency relationships as dueling views of military necessity came into conflict. For the FBI agents, from their culture, the detainees should have been *mirandized* or read their rights and be given attorneys; for the military, the detainees were prisoners of war and the military would decide which interrogation techniques would be used in military zones for prisoners of war.[62] The two cultures approached the issues of detention from two different institutional perspectives.

The conclusion of the DOJ IG was that "the vast majority of FBI agents in the military zones understood that existing FBI policies prohibiting coercive interrogation tactics continued to apply in the military zones and that they should not engage in conduct overseas that would not be permitted under FBI policy in the United States."[63] The IG praised the FBI for deciding in 2002 to continue to apply FBI interrogation policies to the detainees in military zones. The report found that "most FBI agents adhered to the FBI's traditional rapport-based interview strategies in the military zones."[64] The IG also "found no instances in which an FBI agent participated in clear detainee abuse of the kind that some military interrogators used at Abu Ghraib prison." The IG credited "the good judgment of the agents deployed to the military zones as well as guidance that some FBI supervisors provided."[65]

The FBI general counsel emphasized before a Senate hearing that the IG report noted after the Abu Ghraib disclosures, the FBI issued a written policy that reaffirmed existing FBI policy and reminded FBI agents that they were prohibited from using coercive or abusive techniques. The policy directed agents that they were not to participate in any treatment or interrogation technique that was in violation of FBI guidelines and that FBI agents were required to report any incident in which a detainee was either abused or mistreated. For the general counsel it was important to note in her testimony that the policy *relied on the education, training, and experience* of the FBI agents to have a sufficient understanding of the words "abuse" and "mistreatment" and to use the same *sound judgment required to make such determinations while executing their duties domestically* (emphasis added).[66] For the general counsel, it was the professionalism and culture of the interrogating agents that guided their actions.

CONCLUSION: HAS THE FBI CULTURE AND ORGANIZATION BEEN TRANSFORMED ENOUGH?

Will changing attorney general guidelines, new legal rules, and recent organizational restructuring solve the perceived problem of the FBI culture?[67] Was the FBI truly hamstrung in its efforts to combat domestic terrorism before 9/11? It is the general view within the bureau that before 9/11 there were restrictions to the FBI doing its job? One former FBI official was quoted as saying that "you have to wait until you have blood on the street before the bureau can act." Steven Emerson, a national security commentator, asserted that the FBI is severely restricted in infiltrating known extremist groups, that it has no terrorism database like the CIA's, and that it is powerless to stop extremist groups from masquerading as "religious" groups. Therefore, all of the changes will still not be effective.

There are different approaches a nation can pursue to balance national security and domestic criminal responsibilities. One of our closest allies, Great Britain, has divided domestic intelligence, international intelligence, and law enforcement among three agencies: MI5, MI6, and Scotland Yard. The FBI has always been a combination of MI5 and Scotland Yard, MI6 being the CIA. Resistance to creating a stand-alone domestic intelligence service in the United States has always been based on the fact that the FBI has the tradition, training, and discipline to perform the domestic mission within the boundaries of our constitutional framework of the First and Fourth Amendments. For example, as mentioned earlier in the post-9/11 world, the IG quickly reprimanded the FBI for its use of NSLs, an investigative tool that did not require judicial review, and the FBI quickly reformed its lax procedures.

Under the Clinton administration, the NCIX was created to act as a fusion center for terrorism and counterintelligence information; a mini MI5 with no arrest powers. The NCIX was to be a body of analytical thinkers with representation from all members of the IC tasked with coordinating the national counterintelligence agenda with ties to the relevant terrorist information. This group, as already envisioned by a presidential decision directive, answered to the director of the CIA, now the DNI, attorney general, the director of the FBI, and the secretary of defense.[68] The existing NCIX was to be responsible for coordinating and dealing with the relevant information from each component agency. Although the concept was sound, it faltered in its execution for a variety of reasons including early leadership, bureaucratic resistance, lack of resources, and an unclear mandate.[69] Currently NCIX has been moved to the DNI, and only time will tell if it can prove effective in coordinating the counterintelligence community and harnessing the FBI investigative power.

The DHS also has divisions for information analysis and infrastructure protection. The department was thus a fledgling federal institution defining itself in the more robust and institutionalized and turf-conscious IC. Its intelligence divisions have had a slow start due to lack of analysts, insufficient resources, and number of senior resignations, as documented in other chapters in this book. The decision to keep the FBI and CIA as separate institutions with DHS as a client for information guaranteed that the new organization would have to struggle to establish an intelligence role. As DHS continues to battle for identity and function, there will be a continuing bureaucratic tussle on whether the department's primary focus is on acting as a B team that reexamines all the intelligence assembled by the FBI and CIA, as point agency for tightening security on main street, or as primary liaison to the private sector in the critical infrastructure sectors outlined by the Marsh Commission on security.[70]

In early 2003, debate began to find an alternative solution to the FBI, an American version of British MI5. This would entail restructuring the FBI, DHS, and the Department of Treasury by hiving off the national security, counterterrorism, and counterintelligence analysis functions in order to combine all of the relevant analysts into one agency, as is currently the practice in Great Britain. MI5, like the CIA, has no arrest powers and specializes in analysis. The FBI would consequently function more like Scotland Yard and concentrate on traditional national crimes and organized crime violations. Presumably the new entity would also work closely with DOD assets to act as a clearinghouse for all the relevant information from the fifteen major intelligence-gathering agencies.[71] Needless to say, the resistance to the creation of an American MI5 comes not only from a philosophical aversion to the notion of a domestic spy agency but also from all the existing intelligence bureaucracies who oppose the concept of losing such assets. The creation of DHS without significant intelligence powers reflects this reservoir of resistance to an American MI5.

Given these constraints, a group of experienced former government officials suggested an interim MI5 approach that would prove to be more bureaucratically acceptable to the IC.[72] Arguing for more information domestically on terrorist cells and the need for the integration of counterintelligence with counterterrorism that goes beyond a case-file mentality, the group called for the creation of a new and accountable agency within the FBI. Using the National Security Agency and the National Reconnaissance Office as models, it envisioned the new agency embedded within the FBI with its director not from law enforcement but appointed by the president, responsible to the director of the DNI and CIA, governed by attorney general guidelines, having its own independent personnel system for hiring, and subject to direct oversight by the FISA court and Congress. The ultimate outcome was the creation of the NSB in the FBI: the bureau within the bureau. The FBI resisted the more radical aspects of the proposed reform by requiring the head of the branch to report to the director of the FBI.

As one can readily deduce from any proposed solution, one of the continuing questions is who is in charge of integrating domestic law enforcement intelligence from the approximately 650,000 police officers, domestic federal agencies, and foreign national intelligence? Although the new DNI is the titular head of the IC, the DNI has no control of approximately eighty percent of the intelligence budget, which is under the authority of the secretary of defense. As a matter of law, neither the DNI nor the CIA director can operate domestically without severe legal constraint.

All the proposals for reform agree that there is a problem with the FBI and for that matter with the IC in that the current institutional configuration was not established to counter the threat posed by domestic terrorism with international links that has both U.S. citizens and foreigners linked together in a conspiracy. Fighting terrorism requires the gathering of both domestic and international intelligence to prevent attacks and provide national security. The elaborate and enviable legal and bureaucratic structures that were created to protect and guarantee our privacy had become impediments to prosecuting and preventing terrorist acts. How to empower the agencies while maintaining privacy protection and avoiding abuse of power is the critical issue. Over the last nine years, new legislation has been passed to address the problems. The debate has rightly focused on how to reengineer this framework while sufficiently protecting our domestic liberties.

Three Recommendations for More Reform

What more can be done within the existing framework? Ideally, there is another set of reforms that would go to the heart of the FBI culture and would be short of creating an MI5: more senior executive service specialists from outside the FBI, a dedicated FBI IG, and a revamped training division.

A New Talent Base

The road to cultural change is through organizational structures and proper incentives. Director Mueller's proposed organizational changes have begun the painful process of structural change but they do not include several areas where culture is defined and reinforced. A series of new steps now should take place to further this process. Regardless of which organizational format is finally chosen, the director should appoint an advisory committee of seasoned experts from the private sector, academic, legal, and intelligence communities. This committee would include experienced senior managers who have transformed their industries, such as computer companies, complex financial institutions, and data mining firms, and foreign experts in domestic intelligence from among our allies. Currently, entry into the upper echelon of the FBI management, the senior executive service, requires at least one year of law enforcement experience; such a requirement discourages most non-law enforcement experts from joining the FBI. Although the original goal behind the restriction was to "de-politicize" the agency, the unintended consequence has been the elimination of outside expertise and diverse skill sets. Lower pay than that of other government executive service is another serious disincentive. The director needs outside assistance to evaluate both plans for change and new personnel. Relying solely on inside knowledge and FBI careerists makes a new director too captive to insider views.

An Inspector General for the FBI

Although the IG for the DOJ has traditionally done an excellent job, there should be an internal IG for the FBI. With expanded FBI powers there must be clear and transparent accountability. The director should create an IG for the FBI who reports to both the director and the attorney general. The IG would have broad powers to ensure that investigations followed constitutional limits and privacy restrictions. The historic turnaround of the FBI laboratory in the mid-1990s and the role played by an independent IG in the process is proof of how effectively it can work. But the OIG must be large enough to ensure its success. The current Office of Professional Responsibility, although staffed with agents of integrity and energy, is too small, with too limited powers. The reports of the DOJ IG have helped correct past abuses of the DOJ and FBI in the fight against terrorism in a number of cases. This type of transparency builds legitimacy in the long run. As the general counsel for the FBI noted when explaining the revised attorney general rules for investigation in 2009, "Those who say the FBI should not collect information on a person or group unless there is a specific reason to suspect that the target is up to no good seriously miss the mark. The FBI has been told to determine who poses a threat to the national security—not simply to investigate persons who have come onto our radar screens."[73] With expanded power must come expanded accountability—and an institutional office that guarantees impartial review.

A New, Revamped Training Division

Third, the director should revamp the training division at Quantico. Not only should the new agents come from a broader spectrum of graduate programs, policy institutes, accounting firms, and computer companies, but also a new curriculum must be created with an emphasis on terrorism analysis. Here the outside advisory committee mentioned previously would be of invaluable assistance. Analysis is the key to fighting terrorism. Analysis is the key to understanding what the new crown jewels of the modern state are. The problem is not gathering information; the problem is gathering the *right* information, analyzing it, and making sure decision makers have it in a timely fashion.

Moreover, all agencies continue to have a shortage of Arabic, Spanish, and Mandarin speakers. In the Cold War, when there was a shortage of Russian speakers, the government created government-sponsored language scholarships to create a critical mass of translators. Within four years of the introduction of such a program, the government was able to hire thousands of speakers with the appropriate security clearances. Such a program today would benefit both the students and meet the government's needs.

The Next Crossroads

But one should not believe that even if all of the suggestions were taken, even the creation of an American MI5, then we would not have any more acts of terrorism in the United States. Israel, a much smaller country and one with infinitely more experience in fighting terrorism without our evolved sense of private liberties, still has not been able to stop acts of suicide bombers on the West Bank and in Gaza. Moreover, given our vulnerabilities to cyber attacks, suicide lone gunmen, and the anthrax attacks, it has been demonstrated that we cannot be one hundred percent successful. The amount of the vulnerable structure controlled by the private sector makes government-private market cooperation vital but deeply complex. Many industries, such as the financial sector, have a structural disincentive to making known their computer vulnerabilities for fear of financial penalty. Our ports are so open that even the positioning of agents in foreign ports of origin will not secure the commercial traffic.

It is estimated by the International Institute for Strategic Studies, a London policy organization, that approximately 20,000 jihadist soldiers have graduated from the al-Qaeda training camps in Afghanistan and that U.S. operations have killed or captured around 2,000 of these militants.[74] In the film *Minority Report*, a top detective in an experimental "pre-crime" unit wires the brains of genetically altered "precogs" (short for "precognition") to computers that display their glimpses of the future. The super sleuth stands before the display as if he is conducting a symphony and directs the images so that he can find the perpetrators before they kill. There is no way to know if everyone who is arrested under this program would in fact have become a murderer, but, in the film, since the program has been in place, there has not been a single murder in the city.[75] Unlike in the film *Minority Report* we probably will never have a set of "precogs" at the FBI or CIA or DNI, who can predict when an act of violence will take place, days before it happens, so that corrective measures can be taken by the government to stymie the event? In reality we will have to infiltrate terror cells at home and abroad, use spy satellites to track movements, trace deposits with money-laundering specialists, increase eavesdropping, deploy code breakers, and then piece it all together.[76]

We seem ever at a crossroads on the issue of law enforcement and the national security enterprise. Law enforcement, properly integrated into the national security enterprise, is a critical asset. The national security enterprise at its worst is a process of overcoming turf battles, bureaucratic intransigency, incompetence, and limited budgets with misaligned priorities. In the end, terrorism is a political act. Although there may be a small number of self-destructive nihilists for whom violence itself is the goal, the U.S. response to reorganize the state is being made with political terrorism as the object. If in the desire to fight terrorism we create an intrusive state that erodes the right of privacy without effective checks and accountability on government officials to avoid abuses, the irony will be that in the attempt to fight terrorism we will have delegitimized the very institutions created to protect ourselves.

As we expand the FBI detention, questioning, and surveillance functions; as local police use new electronic identification profiling; as we increase Immigration and Naturalization Service magistrate powers without review; as we experiment with rules of evidence for military tribunals and federal courts; as we increase the use of the death penalty; as we use more special forces, targeted killing, and covert operations; as we institutionalize preemption doctrines; and as we continue to blur the line between domestic and international and citizen and noncitizen, it becomes even more imperative that we increase institutional accountability, regardless of the new reforms. For in the war of ideas, we will have defeated ourselves if accountability is not maintained and enforced.[77]

The emerging national security enterprise may not exhibit as much patience as the previous Cold War national security state, if it appears the FBI organization has failed to reform its culture and itself. The attack of Major Nidal Malik Hasan at Ft. Hood in 2009, killing U.S. soldiers preparing to deploy to war zones, has launched yet again investigations on the performance of the FBI. A new domestic intelligence institution may be no guarantor of success, but such repeated perceived institutional failures tend to lead to new organizations—it is the way of the national security enterprise and Washington political culture.

NOTES

I particularly would like to thank Trudi Rishikof and Roger George for their invaluable suggestions and assistance in writing this chapter.

1. Reuel Marc Gerecht, "Major Hasan and the Holy War," *The Wall Street Journal*, November 23, 2009, A21; and Harvey Rishikof, "Economic and Industrial Espionage," in *Vaults, Mirrors, and Masks: Rediscovering U.S. Counterintelligence*, edited by Jennifer E. Sims and Burton Gerber (Washington, DC: Georgetown University Press, 2009).

2. The technology categories, many of which are dual-use technologies, listed in the Military Critical Technology List published by the DOD were of great interest. The categories for 1997/1997 were: advanced material coatings; advanced transportation and engine technology; aeronautics systems; armaments and energetic materials; biotechnology; chemical and biological systems; directed and kinetic energy systems; electronics; ground systems; guidance, navigation, and vehicle control; information systems; information warfare; manufacturing and fabrication; marine systems; materi-

als; nuclear systems; power systems; semiconductors; sensors and lasers; signature control; space systems; weapons effects and countermeasures.

3. See DNI Reports for 2008 at www.ncix.gov/publications/reports/fecie_all/fecie_2008/2008_FECIE_Blue.pdf

4. See DOJ Release, *Fact Sheet: Major US Export Enforcement Prosecutions (2007 to the present)*, October 2009, at www.usdoj.gov.

5. Gregory F. Treverton, *Reorganizing U.S. Domestic Intelligence: Assessing the Options* (Santa Monica, CA: RAND, 2008).

6. See *The FBI: A Centennial History, 1908–2008*, U.S. Department of Justice (Washington, DC: U.S. Government Printing Office, 2008). The section on the origin of the FBI culture is drawn from this text.

7. See also for history Treverton, *Reorganizing U.S. Domestic Intelligence.*

8. See David Cole, *Enemy Aliens* (New York: The New Press, 2003), 116–28.

9. Ibid.

10. *The FBI: A Centennial History,* 1908–2008, 35.

11. Ibid., 57.

12. Ibid., 70.

13. Ibid.

14. See Sari Horwitz, "Over 18 Weeks, an Arduous Path to the Badge," *The Washington Post*, August 17, 2006. The next three paragraphs are drawn from the article.

15. Ibid.

16. Major FBI facilities include: the FBI Academy; the Engineering Research Facility; the FBI Laboratory at Quantico, VA; a large complex in Clarksburg, WV, for fingerprint identification and other services; information technology centers in Pocatello, ID; Fort Arsenal, AL, and Monmouth, NJ; operational support centers in Butte, MT, and Savannah, GA; and the Hazardous Devices (Bomb) School at Redstone Army Base at Huntsville, AL.

17. All of the numbers and description of the FBI are from DOJ justification for budget at www.usdoj.gov/jmd/2009justification/pdf/fy09-fbi.pdf. The total is further divided as $7,065,100, for salaries and expenses and $42,991,000 for construction.

18. See S.3182 of the 111th Congress: "Commerce, Justice, Science, and Related Agencies Appropriations Act," 2009.

19. See all of the numbers and description of the FBI from DOJ justification for budget, 1–13 at www.usdoj.gov/jmd/2009justification/pdf/fy09-fbi.pdf.

20. The NYPD employs more than 1,000 people in its counterterrorism division and spends about $173 million a year on counterterrorism. (Though both numbers are the highest of any American city, they still constitute a small fraction of the department's 36,000 uniformed and 15,000 civilian employees and $4.6 billion annual budget.) But according to the budget that Mayor Michael Bloomberg unveiled in early May 2009, the NYPD will lose about $225 million over the next two years, part of the $1.5 billion in budget cuts that the mayor has made for all city agencies. See Judith Miller, Counterterror and the Crunch, at www.city-journal.org/2009/nytom_counterterrorism.html. Though the department reached an all-time high of 40,311 officers in 2000, the department in mid-2009 was down to 35,758 and is expected to fall to 34,117 by 2010. Though the operating budget to run the department on a daily basis, covering salaries and equipment, is slated to be $4.3 billion in 2010, the department's actual cost to the city will be nearly $8 billion, due to the pension obligations entailed by each current officer. See Heather MacDonald, *New York's Indispensable Institution* at www.city-journal.org/2009/nytom_nypd.html.

21. The following text and the concluding paragraphs are drawn from a recent op-ed. See Harvey Rishikof Op-Ed in the Providence Journal Online at: www.projo.com/opinion/contributors/content/projo_20020727_ctrish27.721d2.htm.

22. See Mark Riebling, *Wedge: From Pearl Harbor to 9/11, How the Secret War between the FBI and CIA Has Endangered National Security* (New York: Simon & Schuster, 2002). For the lack of cooperation between the agencies during the early stages of the investigation of Aldrich Ames, see Michael R. Bromwich, "Review of the FBI's Performance in the Uncovering the Espionage Activities

of Aldrich Hazen Ames," in *Intelligence and the National Security Strategist*, ed. Roger Z. George and Robert D. Kline (New York: Rowman & Littlefield, 2004).

23. Richard A. Best, Jr., *Intelligence and Law Enforcement: Countering Transnational Threats to the U.S.*, CRS Report for Congress, updated December 3, 2001.

24. Dahlia Lithwick and Julia Turner, "A Guide to the Patriot Act, Part I: Should You Be Scared of the Patriot Act?" *Slate*, September 8, 2003.

25. See Michael J. Woods, *Foreign Intelligence Surveillance Act Procedures to Ensure Accuracy*, ("Woods Procedures"), April 5, 2001 at www.fas.org/irp/agency/doj/fisa/woods.pdf.

26. *The 9/11 Commission Report*, 78–80.

27. See the FBI Response to "A Review of the FBI's Handling of Intelligence Information Prior to the September 11 Attacks" Special Report, November 2004 (Released publicly June 2005), at www .usdoj.gov/oig/special/0506/app3.htm. The following paragraphs are drawn from the FBI response.

28. Ibid.

29. Description of the plan from Amy B. Zegart, *Spying Blind: The CIA, the FBI, and the Origins of 9/11* (Princeton, NJ: Princeton Press, 2007), 130–34.

30. The Legat program stemmed from World War II when agents had been dispatched to South and Latin America to combat Nazi spying operations, before the creation of the CIA. Following the end of the war the number of Legats operating from the 1950s through the 1980s fluctuated due to crime trends and budget allowances, with offices opening, closing, and reopening at various times.

31. The description of the Legat program is drawn from *The Legal Attaché: History* at www.fbi .gov/contact/legat/history.html. It is interesting to note that this program has continued today, and the bureau has more than two hundred special agents and support professionals in more than sixty overseas offices, pursuing terrorist, intelligence, and criminal threats with international dimensions in every part of the world. As part of the modern global outreach, the FBI also takes part in all manner of global and regional crime-fighting initiatives, including Interpol and Europol; the Budapest Project; and Resolution 6, which co-locates FBI agents in Drug Enforcement Agents offices worldwide to combat drugs.

32. *The 9/11 Commission Report*, 76–78.

33. See the FBI response to "A Review of the FBI's Handling of Intelligence Information Prior to the September 11 Attacks."

34. In the case, Dr. Wen Ho Lee, who worked at Los Alamos National Laboratory, was accused by federal investigators of giving nuclear secrets to China. Dr. Lee spent nine months in solitary confinement awaiting trial. Ultimately, he pleaded guilty to one felony count of illegally gathering and retaining national security data but received an apology on the record from the trial judge in the case for the way the government had handled the case. Dr. Lee then sued the government and five news organizations alleging the government had violated privacy laws by telling reporters about his employment history, finances, travels, and polygraph tests. The government eventually settled the case for $1,645,000. See Adam Liptak, "News Media Pay in Scientist Suit," *New York Times*, June 3, 2006, at www.nytimes.com/2006/06/03/washington/03settle.html?_r=1&pagewanted=print

35. Ibid. The following paragraphs are drawn from the response.

36. *Uniting and Strengthening America by Providing Appropriate Tools Required to Intercept and Obstruct Terror*, ("Patriot Act") H.R. 3162, 107th Congress, October 26, 2001, Pub. L. No. 107–56. For a quick summary of how the Patriot Act changed the legal framework, such as the introduction of the roving wiretap, see the DOJ web page at www.justice.gov/archive/ll/highlights.htm.

37. The following section is drawn from the FBI response to "A Review of the FBI's Handling of Intelligence Information Prior to the September 11 Attacks."

38. See Cong. Rec., October 25, 2001, quoted at www.justice.gov/archive/ll/highlights.html.

39. FBI, Testimony of Robert S. Mueller, III, Director, FBI, Before the Senate Select Committee on Intelligence and the House Permanent Select Committee on Intelligence, "Joint Intelligence Committee Inquiry," October 17, 2002, accessed through www.fbi.gov/congress/congress02/mueller101702 .html.

40. Ibid.

41. FBI, "History."

42. FBI, Robert Mueller Testimony, "Joint Intelligence Committee Inquiry."

43. FBI, "History."

44. FBI Response to "A Review of the FBI's Handling of Intelligence Information Prior to the September 11 Attacks."

45. An NSL is a letter request for information from a third party that is issued by the FBI or by other government agencies with authority to conduct national security investigations. NSL authority is provided by five provisions of law:

- The Right to Financial Privacy Act, 12 U.S.C.§ 3414(a)(5), for financial institution customer records;
- The Fair Credit Reporting Act, 15 U.S.C.§ 1681u(a) and (b), for a list of financial institution identities and consumer-identifying information from a credit reporting company;
- The Fair Credit Reporting Act, 15 U.S.C. § 1681v, for a full credit report in an international terrorism case. This provision was created by the 2001 USA Patriot Act;
- The Electronic Communications Privacy Act, 18 U.S.C. § 2709, for billing and transactional communication service provider records from telephone companies and internet service providers; and
- The National Security Act, 50 U.S.C. § 436, for financial, consumer, and travel records for certain government employees who have access to classified information.

NSLs are similar to federal executive branch administrative subpoenas in that a government agency issues the request for information without prior judicial approval. Like grand jury subpoenas and administrative subpoenas, NSLs can be used to acquire information relevant to an authorized preliminary or full FBI national security investigation. NSLs, however, are subject to two significant limitations. First, they are only available for authorized national security investigations (international terrorism or foreign intelligence/counterintelligence investigations), not general criminal investigations or domestic terrorism investigations. Second, unlike administrative subpoenas and grand jury subpoenas, NSLs can only be used to seek certain transactional information permitted under the five NSL provisions, and NSLs cannot be used to acquire the content. See FBI press release at www.fbi .gov/pressrel/pressrel07/nsl_faqs030907.htm.

46. See the Electronic Privacy Information Center (EPIC) description of NSLs at http://epic.org/ privacy/pdf/nsl_letter.pdf.

47. Ibid.

48. In particular, critics highlighted the following problems found by the OIG: The FBI is required to report to Congress on the number of NSLs issued; the OIG found that the FBI underreported this number. The OIG review looked at 77 case files containing 293 NSLs from four separate FBI FOs issued in the 2003–5 period. This review found that there were seventeen percent more NSLs in the sample of case files than in FBI reporting databases. Delays in data entry also caused about 4,600 NSLs not to be reported to Congress. The OIG concluded that the FBI database significantly understates the number of NSL requests issued, and that Congress has been misinformed about the scale of the usage of the NSL authority. The report further stated that violations are supposed to be self-reported by the FBI to the Intelligence Oversight Board. During the three-year period in question, the FBI self-reported 26 violations out of the 140,000 NSLs issued. The OIG, however, found 22 potential violations out of the sample of 293 NSLs it reviewed. The OIG has stated that there is no indication that the 293 NSLs it reviewed are not representative of all of the NSLs issued, thus indicating that the FBI is failing to self-report a very significant number of violations. The OIG also found over 700 exigent letters, which are not authorized by statute and some of which appear to have been issued when no exigency or emergency existed. These letters requested records from telephone companies and promised that proper subpoenas had been submitted or would follow. However, the OIG found no confirmation that subpoenas, NSLs, or other proper process did follow or had in fact been submitted. Report at www.usdoj.gov/oig/special/ s0703b/final.pdf.

49. See FBI IG report on NSLs at www.fbi.gov/pressrel/pressrel07/nsl_chart.htm.

50. Zegart, *Spying Blind*, 123; or Richard A. Posner, "Remaking Domestic Intelligence," Hoover Institution, Stanford University, June 16, 2005, at http://media.hoover.org/documents/oped_2821821.pdf.

51. This concludes the pages quoted from the Center for National Security Studies—The FBI Domestic Counterterrorism Program material at Gelman Library, April 26, 1995, at http://nsi.org/Library/Terrorism/terpolcy.html.

52. Charlie Savage, "F.B.I. Is Slow to Translate Intelligence, Report Says," *The New York Times*, October 27, 2009.

53. Ibid.

54. FBI, Testimony of Robert S. Mueller, III, director, FBI, before the Senate Appropriations Committee, Subcommittee on the Departments of Commerce, Justice, and State, the Judiciary, and Related Agencies, "Congressional Testimony," March 23, 2004, accessed through www.fbi.gov/congress/congress04/mueller032304.htm.

55. Ibid.

56. Ibid.

57. Ibid.

58. See Box 9.2.

59. See DOJ Release, *Fact Sheet: Major US Export Enforcement Prosecutions (2007 to the present)*, October 2009, at www.usdoj.gov.

60. FBI, "Congressional Testimony."

61. The executive summary of the Investigation into FBI Allegations of Detainee Abuse at Guantanamo Bay, Cuba Detention Facility ("Schmidt-Furlow Report") is available at www .defenselink.mil/news/Jul2005/d20050714report.pdf.

62. Police generally read *Miranda* rights to individuals about to be questioned in custody: "You have the right to remain silent. If you give up the right to remain silent, anything you say can and will be used against you in a court of law. You have the right to an attorney. If you desire an attorney and cannot afford one, an attorney will be obtained for you before police questioning." The *Miranda* rule was developed to protect the individual's Fifth Amendment right against self-incrimination. The *Miranda* warning ensures that people in custody realize they do not have to talk to the police and that they have the right to the presence of an attorney. If the *Miranda* warning is not given before questioning, or if police continue to question a suspect after he or she indicates in any manner a desire to consult with an attorney before speaking, statements by the suspect generally are inadmissible at trial—they cannot be used against the suspect. See American Bar Association Public Information at www.abanet.org/publiced/practical/criminal/miranda_rights.html.

63. All quotes from the IG report, "A Review of the FBI's Involvement in and Observations of Detainee Interrogations in Guantanamo Bay, Afghanistan, and Iraq," are from Valerie E. Caproni, General Counsel FBI, Statement before the Senate Committee on the Judiciary, June 10, 2008, available at www.fbi.gov/congress/congress08/caproni061008.htm. The IG report can be found at http://hosted.ap.org/specials/interactives/wdc/documents/oig_detainees052008.pdf.

64. Ibid.

65. Ibid.

66. Ibid.

67. Note the following paragraphs on Attorney General Guidelines and the FBI's pre-9/11 investigations are quoted from the Center for National Security Studies—The FBI Domestic Counterterrorism Program material at Gelman Library, April 26, 1995, at http://nsi.org/Library/Terrorism/terpolcy.html.

68. See Presidential Decision Directive (PDD) 75, "U.S. Counterintelligence Effectiveness—Counterintelligence for the Twenty-first Century," January 5, 2001 (President William J. Clinton).

69. See Michelle Van Cleave, "The NCIX and the National Counterintelligence Mission: What Has Worked, What Has Not, and Why," Project on National Security Reform at www.pnsr.org.

70. See John Mints, "At Homeland Security, Doubts Arise Over Intelligence," *The Washington Post*, July 22, 2003, A12; President's Commission on Critical Infrastructure Protection, 1997; ("General Marsh Commission"). Also see PDD-63.

71. Senator John Edwards, Homeland Security Address, Brookings Institute, Washington, DC, December 18, 2002.

72. Former Deputy FBI Director Robert Bryant; former Deputy Defense Secretary John Hamre; former Drug Enforcement Administration Administrator John Lawn; former Associate Deputy CIA Director for Operations John MacGaffin; former FBI General Counsel Howard Shapiro; and former CIA General Counsel Jeffrey Smith, "America Needs More Spies," *The Economist*, July 12–18, 2003.

73. Charlie Savage, "Wider Authority for FBI Agents Stirs Concern," *The New York Times*, October 29, 2009, A1.

74. Daniel Bergner, "Where the Enemy Is Everywhere and Nowhere," *New York Times Magazine*, July 20, 2003.

75. Plot summary from Movie Mom's Reviews at http://movies.yahoo.com/shop?d=hv&cf =parentsguide&id=1807592183.

76. Eric Lichtblau, "Connecting the Dots," *The New York Review of Books*, March 16, 2003.

77. See R. D. Howard and R. L. Sawyer, *Terrorism and Counterterrorism: Understanding the New Security Environment* (New York: McGraw-Hill, 2003); Harvey Rishikof, "Is It Time for a Federal Terrorist Court? Terrorists and Prosecutions: Problems, Paradigms, and Paradoxes," 8 *Suffolk J. Trial & App. Adv.* 1 (2003).

Chapter 10   The Department of Homeland Security: Chief of Coordination

GARY M. SHIFFMAN AND JONATHAN HOFFMAN

> The culture of DHS in 2009 is this: my job is not done until the entire mission is complete.
>
> *Secretary Michael Chertoff, July 2009*

INTRODUCTION

The many and varied institutions of U.S. homeland security do not accommodate an easy definition, and the evolving nature of the mission set suggests an evolutionary approach to the study of the Department of Homeland Security (DHS). U.S. political leaders created the department quickly, and it continued to change over its first seven years. This chapter will explain DHS by providing insights into the evolution of DHS. We propose a latitudinal and longitudinal framework for understanding the department. This chapter tells the chronology of major events in the history of the department, stopping where appropriate to emphasize the depths of relationships required in order for DHS to have any hope of successfully accomplishing the homeland security missions.

Most people recall with vivid clarity where they were on September 11, 2001. Once you learned the attacks were the work of al-Qaeda, a terrorist group, how did you feel? Vulnerable? Patriotic? Angry? Most of us asked ourselves, "What did we do or fail to do, and what can be done now?" U.S. political leadership had many of these same reactions to the attack on the American homeland and responded similarly, but also with a mandate and the authority to take action.[1]

Decision makers often face a tradeoff between expediency and effectiveness. Immediate actions, as satisfying as they might seem in the moment, may lack effectiveness. Complex actions may deliver effectiveness but require more time. Complex actions implemented too quickly might come out wrong. The pressing emotional desire for action tipped the scales toward expediency following 9/11; the challenge was to incorporate the right amount of complexity to deliver an effective response quickly. Those initial actions have evolved over the years since 9/11 and some have been validated. This chapter explores the primary institutional change to the national security community in the United States: the creation of DHS.

President George W. Bush chose to act quickly in creating the Office of Homeland Security (OHS) in the White House, and Pennsylvania's sitting governor, Tom Ridge, agreed to leave his job to be the first U.S. executive branch lead for the homeland security enterprise. Meanwhile, down Pennsylvania Avenue from the White House, Senator Joe Lieberman also acted swiftly, leading a strong and bipartisan group of members of Congress advocating for the creation of a department run by a Senate-confirmed secretary and a cadre of senior leadership with real budget authority—a significantly more complex endeavor. As Lieberman now states,

> Even before President Bush appointed Governor Ridge as his Homeland Security Advisor, I believed that an official needed to be in charge of homeland security and to have line authority over people and budgets. I recognized that creating a new department would take time and energy. However, it was clear to me that a White House-based homeland security advisor lacked authority over budgets, personnel and other resources necessary to marshal the U.S. Government's capabilities for ensuring homeland security. As a result, I believed that that landmark legislation creating a Department of Homeland Security, led by a Secretary, was essential for protecting our nation's security.[2]

With emotions running strong, and with 9/11-related stories still dominating news headlines, combined with a tremendous sense of urgency to do something, the president and Congress quickly negotiated the creation of this new department comprised of 180,000 people from twenty-two agencies across the federal government.[3] The compromise was to take action that would be seen as both expedient and effective.

From its inception, DHS was given one articulated mission: to manage the terrorist threat. The growth of DHS has been a multiyear process, and therefore the DHS culture, roles, and missions are not yet completely crystallized. March 1, 2003, the date DHS was "stood up," was a milestone in the process, but instead of establishing one new, powerful institution in the interagency with legitimacy derived from universal support and clean lines of authority, DHS remains a work in progress. Two issues may be seen as axes providing a framework for understanding the department's evolutionary culture. First, as the department has evolved over time it has become a product both of its premeditated design as well as of unrelated threats occurring since 9/11. As planned, the department deals with terrorism but it also deals with tornadoes, hurricanes, and even threats to public health. Second, in order to address such a wide array of threats to the homeland, the department constantly interacts with authorities not assigned directly to the department, and often not easily brought together.

Under the U.S. constitutional system that divides power between state and federal governments, military and civil authorities do not interact easily. For example, military authorities remain exclusively federal. However, state governors own and deploy the states' National Guard forces under state civil authorities, unless the guard becomes nationalized by the federal government. Law enforcement in the state remains under the purview of the governor, except when federal offenses allow federal law enforcement to exercise authority within the governor's state. Mayors maintain responsibility for public safety in cities where the mayor exercises chief law-enforcement authorities unless violations in state or federal law invite in other authorities. Because three chief executives, the president, the governor, and the mayor, each bear responsibility for the public safety of the population in a given city, for example, the lines of authority and communication can easily become conflicted and confused. Therefore, DHS must act as the coordinator yet not the operator for many efforts, and the lead operator for others.

In addition, national intelligence and law enforcement institutions have historically mixed only with great caution, even though a primary failing identified by the 9/11 Commission was their inability to share information.[4] Strict laws restrict U.S. federal intelligence agencies

undertaking domestic activities. Thick cultural precedents further inhibit information sharing between intelligence and law enforcement, even at the federal level. Systems facilitating
information sharing between intelligence communities and state or local law enforcement
pose legally and culturally significant challenges. DHS was designed to sit at the juncture of
these institutions. Realizing the vision, however, takes time and a lot of work.

If it were only as easy as addressing these constitutional and legal issues, then we might
have more definitive lines of authority today, but the bureaucratic politics of the interagency
exerted significant influence. The interagency problem arose when the Homeland Security
Act of 2002 took authorities, missions, and budgets from other federal departments to create
DHS. To this day, battles continue among DHS, the formerly independent Federal Emergency
Management Agency (FEMA), and the Departments of Defense, State, and Energy, to name
just a few. Outside of DHS headquarters, battles can also arise between agencies, such as
between FEMA and the Department of Health and Human Services (HHS).

What is the culture and organization of DHS? How has it evolved from its inception, in
reaction to real-world events? What operational authorities legitimately reside within the
department? How can DHS successfully accomplish the assigned mission sets while coordinating other legitimate and powerful institutions within the national security enterprise?
Is the secretary of homeland security an operator or a coordinator?

DHS EVOLUTION OVER TIME

To understand DHS today, we will use a chronological narrative while focusing on the
origin of the department, how external events influence that origin, and how authorities
across the federal, state, and local power centers further affect the evolution of its mission
within the broader global and U.S. homeland security mission set.

In retrospect, before 9/11, we had clues to concepts that today comprise many DHS
missions. The U.S. government knew of the changing threats and had even taken steps to
assess the threats and develop new strategies, yet there was a failure to act on these recommendations prior to 9/11. One of the most often-cited efforts to identify changing terrorist
and security threats was the U.S. Commission on National Security/21st Century (otherwise known as the Hart-Rudman Commission), which issued its final report in January
2001. Hart-Rudman addressed the shifting threat caused by the end of the Cold War and
the rise of globalization. Presciently, one of the core recommendations of Hart-Rudman
was the creation of a "new National Homeland Security Agency to consolidate and refine
the missions of the nearly two dozen disparate departments and agencies that have a role
in U.S. homeland security today."[5]

Another effective review of terrorism was the U.S. Congressional Advisory Panel to Assess
Domestic Response Capabilities for Terrorism Involving Weapons of Mass Destruction, a
review run by the RAND Corporation and commonly known as the Gilmore Commission.
Notably, 146 of the Gilmore Commission 164 recommendations issued between 1999 and
2003 have been adopted, though many of them only following the tragedy of 9/11.[6]

Other precursors included the 1997 Catastrophic Terrorism Study Group, cochaired by
Dr. Ashton Carter and former CIA Director John Deutch. Eerily, in the November–December 1998 issue of *Foreign Affairs*, Carter and Deutch were joined by future 9/11 Commission Executive Director Philip Zelikow in writing a "what if" article that considered the

implications if the 1993 bombing of the World Trade Center had succeeded in destroying the towers. Their foresight is interesting:

> The resulting horror and chaos would have exceeded our ability to describe it. Such an act of catastrophic terrorism would be a watershed event in American history. It could involve loss of life and property unprecedented in peacetime and undermine America's fundamental sense of security, as did the Soviet atomic bomb test in 1949. Like Pearl Harbor, the event would divide our past and future into a before and after. The United States might respond with draconian measures scaling back civil liberties, allowing wider surveillance of citizens, detention of suspects and use of deadly force. More violence could follow, either future terrorist attacks or U.S. counterattacks. Belatedly, Americans would judge their leaders negligent for not addressing terrorism more urgently.[7]

The fact that many of the major changes recommended by these three groups and others were not adopted until after 9/11 shows a failure not of imagination, but of will. The 9/11 terrorist attacks provided a focal point for historians and the impetus for public and political sentiment to take action. The ideas were not new on 9/11, only the imperative to act.

Whether or not one believes the nature of the threat changed before or on 9/11, these terrorist attacks on the U.S. homeland caused the creation of DHS and defined the initial mission. According to Jim Loy, the department's second deputy secretary, "Five hundred years from now, they will still be talking about the world before and after 9/11. Although we had won the Cold War twelve years earlier, we did not recognize the changes to the global security environment and adapt to them until the terrorist attacks forced that recognition and caused us to develop the coordination and collaboration skills necessary to cope with that new environment."[8] If one agrees with Admiral Loy that 9/11 will be talked about centuries from now, we have to wonder whether the response to 9/11 and the multiple measures taken to defend the United States will be talked about as well and, if so, will they be considered successes? Just because complex actions were taken quickly does not mean that they were wrong.

BEFORE DHS WE HAD THE OHS: HOMELAND SECURITY ON SEPTEMBER 12, 2001

On September 12, 2001, President Bush called his cabinet together and famously told his attorney general, John Ashcroft, never to let this happen again.[9] An investigative and prosecutorial Department of Justice (DOJ) was told to get into the business of preventing terrorist acts. The Departments of Defense, State, Energy, and others assumed new responsibilities as well. The president also appointed Tom Ridge, then governor of Pennsylvania, to be the director of the newly created White House OHS in October 2001.[10] This office was tasked to "develop and coordinate the implementation of a comprehensive national strategy to secure the United States from *terrorist threats or attacks*" (emphasis added).[11] It would assume responsibility for coordinating executive branch efforts to prevent, protect against, respond to, and recover from terrorist attacks within the United States.

However far-reaching these executive authorities granted to Governor Ridge and the OHS may have appeared, they were deemed insufficient by some members of Congress. Under the leadership of Senator Joseph Lieberman of Connecticut, Congress negotiated the creation of the DHS, a cabinet-level department with more expansive authorities, some new but most realigned from existing entities. Instead of a unilateral executive action creating a White House office, members of Congress wanted a greater role, making this the first of many battles between the administration and Congress over the form and function of homeland security. As a result of this interbranch negotiating and the broad consensus that developed, the American people were given a department with a sprawling mission. The institution to keep all Americans safe was finally in place, at least on paper.

During negotiations over the department, the still-functioning OHS in the White House created the first *National Strategy to Protect the Homeland*, clearly defining the broader homeland security mission set in relation to terrorism: "This document is the first *National Strategy for Homeland Security*. The purpose of the *Strategy* is to mobilize and organize our Nation to secure the U.S. homeland from terrorist attacks. This is an exceedingly complex mission that requires coordinated and focused effort from our entire society—the federal government, state and local governments, the private sector, and the American people."[12] Note the emphasis on coordination. The document identifies these strategic objectives of homeland security, listed in order of priority:

- Prevent terrorist attacks within the United States;
- Reduce America's vulnerability to terrorism; and
- Minimize the damage and recover from attacks that do occur.

These three objectives quickly became the *prevent, protect, respond, and recover* framework that permeates the homeland security lexicon today.

As of July 2002 the first presidential definition of homeland security was set. The authors of this document at the OHS were clearly aware of the work that occurred before 9/11; however, new questions and complications arose.[13] For example, who had responsibility for which mission sets? Although the president tasked the attorney general with ensuring a 9/11 attack will "never again" occur, and although the Federal Bureau of Investigation (FBI) is the lead domestic investigative agency of the federal government, Congress pinned the rose of terrorism prevention and protection on the DHS. Section 101 of the Homeland Security Act of 2002 unequivocally establishes DHS with the following mission:

1. In General. - The primary mission of the Department is to
   a. prevent terrorist attacks within the United States;
   b. reduce the vulnerability of the United States to terrorism; and
   c. minimize the damage, and assist in the recovery, from terrorist attacks that do occur within the United States.[14]

With an initial strategy and a congressional directive—and a corresponding budget—in place, the creation of the department was well under way.

THE DEPARTMENT, MARCH 2003

As the first secretary of the DHS, Tom Ridge led a massively complex start-up organization made up of pieces from all over the federal government, initially comprising 180,000 federal employees (increasing to over 210,000 after 5 years), seven operating components,

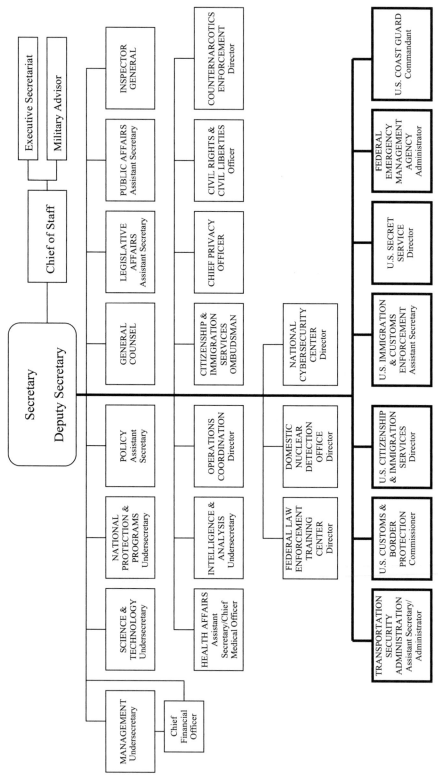

Figure 10.1   The Department of Homeland Security, 2009.

and many support offices. His first deputy secretary was Gordon England, soon followed by Admiral Jim Loy, who had been commandant of the Coast Guard on 9/11.[15]

The organization consisted of a cabinet secretary at the top, with seven operating components (see figure 10.1). The boxes between the top and bottom row represent the support functions of the department. Sometimes known as the gang of seven, these operating components are Transportation Security Administration (TSA), Customs and Border Protection (CBP), Citizenship and Immigration Services (CIS), Immigration and Customs Enforcement (ICE), U.S. Secret Service (USSS), Federal Emergency Management Agency (FEMA), and the U.S. Coast Guard (USCG).

The CBP embodies the unification of border enforcement authorities and associated work forces from four legacy agencies: (1) U.S. Customs (taken from the Treasury Department); (2) the U.S. Border Patrol (taken from the DOJ); (3) inspectors from the Immigration and Naturalization Service (INS; taken from the DOJ); and (4) inspectors from the Department of Agriculture. CIS provides all the services of the old INS, including citizenship and temporary worker status processing and adjudication. ICE agents and officers, formerly with U.S. Customs or the INS, investigate violations of immigration and customs laws and deport individuals through the detention and removal office. Just as a large police department has frontline officers and detectives, so too CBP acts as the frontline of border enforcement agency, combining the significant authorities of the legacy agencies behind one unified badge. Meanwhile ICE agents are the investigators—the detectives. The former INS was both a law enforcement and services agency. Now with the abolition of the INS and the movement of immigration authorities to the new DHS, immigration services were separated from enforcement and put under CIS.

TSA federalized the airport inspection work force and added the mission of securing all modes of transportation. The USSS and USCG remained largely unchanged, simply reporting to a new department. FEMA also became a part of the new department based on two beliefs: (1) that response and recovery must be an all-hazards mission; and (2) that the United States should avoid creating another FEMA by having one disaster agency for terrorist events and another for natural disasters. This location for FEMA continues to be hotly debated six years after the creation of DHS.

Support agencies include the office of management (which houses the CFO and CIO); national protection and programs directorate (including critical infrastructure and communications protection offices); and the department policy, legislative, and public affairs offices. An operations coordination office was created with no operational authority over the gang of seven. Instead it had the power to coordinate and de-conflict situations while keeping the secretary informed when the department responds to any incidents of national significance. The office of intelligence and analysis represents DHS as a member of the U.S. government's intelligence community (IC), coordinating information flows to and from the department's components.[16] There are also directorates for science and technology, and health affairs, privacy, and civil liberties, among others. The initial budget in FY 2004 for all of these DHS personnel and capabilities was $36.2 billion. Over the last six years this has grown to a $40.1 billion appropriation, plus $3.2 billion in discretionary fees and $9.3 billion in mandatory fees, for a total annual budget of $52.5 billion. Included in this budget is $4.2 billion in grants for state and local communities. Over the past six years, $32.1 billion in grant dollars has been allocated to state and local grant programs.

Many considered this department too large and yet, ironically in significant ways, it did not come close to the breadth and depth needed to accomplish its stated mission. However, the size of the organization and the scope of its mission far exceeded the new authorities provided to the executive and so authority accruing to DHS had to come from other departments and agencies, meaning that, by definition, DHS encroached on the historic responsibilities and authorities of other federal departments. Perhaps more significantly with respect to the initial lack of needed authority, when the federal government operates inside the borders of the United States for the purposes of preventing terrorist attacks or responding to any man-made or natural incident, in most instances it does so in support of local officials, not in control of those authorities.

The sheer complexity of sharing information among officials in intelligence, law enforcement, and federal and local entities makes addressing homeland security threats even more daunting. The private sector owns and operates most of the critical infrastructure on which the U.S. economy depends, therefore giving it a valuable and historically unique role in DHS collaboration.[17] Although the department has evolved since its creation on March 1, 2003, and although (thanks to committed leadership and public engagement) it has cleared up many of these historic ambiguities, much remains to be resolved.

2003–4: DHS LEADERSHIP IN THE GLOBAL WAR ON TERRORISM

Early on the morning of Wednesday, May 26, 2004, competing Washington press events caused enormous confusion when two political leaders clashed. They inadvertently but publicly confirmed the ambiguity of roles and missions to the public, Congress, and, perhaps most significantly, to hundreds of thousands of workers engaged in missions to protect the homeland. First, DHS Secretary Tom Ridge appeared on several nationally televised morning shows and, with great authority, asserted the primacy of DHS: "Homeland Security is responsible for coordinating a national effort to make us smarter and more secure using people and technology. We pulled together a variety of agencies within the federal government to say, what are we going to do now, how (sic) can we accelerate, and what additional things can we do over the next several months to just improve our security and make us safer? And that's precisely what we've been doing every single day."[18] Secretary Ridge did not discuss the specific role of any other department or agency, just DHS. A few hours later, Attorney General John Ashcroft, backed by FBI director Robert Mueller, asserted DOJ leadership in addressing terrorist threats by announcing "credible intelligence from multiple sources indicates that al-Qaeda plans to attempt an attack on the United States in the next few months." Ashcroft asked the public to support the DOJ and the FBI in finding terrorists. He mentioned DHS and Secretary Ridge only in response to a question from a reporter.[19]

The Global War on Terror (GWOT) legitimized the homeland security enterprise, but the creation of the DHS did not end these debates over roles and missions. Instead, as evidenced by the events of May 26, 2004, various national security institutions saw a jump ball and began competing for relevant homeland security responsibilities and funding.

DHS initially struggled in the interagency, as one might expect of a sprawling and immature department with a broad mission set. Its interagency problems can be traced back to two primary factors. First, DHS was a new entity with very little unified identity and many individual cultures and infrastructures. Simply put, it needed to get its own house in order before exerting unified strength across various agencies of the federal government. Second, DHS's mission was expansive in scope, wresting many authorities from other departments. In a zero-sum environment, some lost power while DHS gained power. So although DHS was a welcome player in the abstract, when it came to protecting turf, there were hostilities toward this new department that continue to this day.

The lack of a unified culture required a great deal of initial attention from Secretary Ridge. Some legacy components, such as the USSS and the USCG, were subsumed whole and transferred their historic mission sets intact. By contrast, TSA was created after 9/11 with no existing culture or history. Previous and deeply entrenched cultures at U.S. Customs—formerly under the Department of the Treasury—or INS, under the DOJ, had to be reset when those agencies were dissected to make way for the new department. All of this upheaval meant that the newest department of the U.S. government had to work harder than its peer departments across the interagency of the executive branch just to be cohesive and effective.

Even all of this focus on fragmentation and revamping of entrenched corporate cultures understates the DHS challenge. Secretary Ridge and his team may have had responsibility, codified into law, to protect the American people from another terrorist attack, but the authority and responsibility given to him by Congress and the president were not directly congruous. In order to accomplish his mission, he required the entire federal government to work together in ways never before accomplished, certainly not during the Cold War or the first Gulf War of 1990–91.

The threat from nonstate actors attacking us on our homeland required this new entity to organize itself in a masterful new way. As Jim Loy put it: "In the 1990s, we talked about the asymmetric array of threats, including terrorism, but 9/11 forced us to think and act very differently. We began to walk away from the traditional siloed processes of the Cold War and began to create the structures that would demand collaboration competencies from our leaders. DHS is one of those structures."[20] While DHS worked to organize itself for the new threat, others, including Congress, labored to make similar changes.

Congress has struggled to mature on the issue of national security in the post-9/11 world and this actually impeded DHS leadership's ability to accomplish its mission. Currently, DHS shoulders the burden of eighty-six congressional oversight committees, more than any other department of the U.S. government.[21] Despite the 9/11 Commission report's recommendation to consolidate congressional oversight, Congress failed to act, leaving this as the sole remaining commission recommendation not yet implemented.[22]

This lack of consolidated oversight is not just a matter of annoyance for DHS officials tasked with responding to multiple congressional requests on the same topics; it is a direct impediment to strategic planning department-wide. Many DHS components are accountable to different congressional committees, each with competing priorities and personalities. For example, CBP must answer to the Senate Finance Committee on issues of border security because of its trade and customs collections mission, while also engaging the Senate Commerce, Judiciary, and Homeland Security Committees. ICE must answer to the Judiciary Committee on intellectual property investigations as well as the Homeland Security Committee. This fragmentation gives competing congressional committees and members altered views of DHS's various roles, as each attributes to DHS different prioritized missions. By comparison, when the Department of Defense (DOD) was created in 1947, both the House and Senate consolidated their military oversight panels into two committees in each chamber (one authorizing and one appropriating), thus providing knowledgeable and strategic oversight of the new department. DHS has had to overcome far greater challenges than all the other departments in its relationships with the legislative branch just to assert its cohesive, united policy voice. In what some perceived as an irresponsible move, Congress refused to confer undersecretary status on the DHS head of policy—similar to the status in other major departments—to prevent the headquarters policy office from asserting greater authority over individual components.

Additionally, DHS's expansive and direct ties to citizens in many of its core missions present it with another challenge in how it approaches the interagency policy process. Unlike the Director of National Intelligence (DNI) and the Departments of State or Defense, for example, DHS interacts directly with over 3.3 million people on an individual basis each day.[23] Whether via TSA screeners at airports, USCG officers at sea, or CBP officers at the 314 ports of entry, DHS is the face of homeland security to the nation and the world.

Also, more than any other department or agency of the federal government, DHS must share information and coordinate actions with nonfederal institutions such as states, cities, counties, the commercial sector, private citizens, and the international community. These stresses on the number of stakeholders that DHS must incorporate into its policy decision-making process can inhibit that process's timeline and clarity, especially when compared to the constraints facing other departments of the federal government.

The 9/11 Commission alerted the public that the U.S. government knew a lot about the nineteen hijackers, but the government's failure to connect the dots impeded its ability to identify the threat posed by these people inside the United States.[24] In fact, Chet Lunner, DHS deputy undersecretary for intelligence and analysis, states that intelligence and information mean different things to different people and the first step to information and intelligence sharing across DHS is creating a facilitating network.[25] As long as different institutions claim exclusive ownership of the information they collect or maintain, the American people will have challenges managing the dots. Identity management and other aspects of cyber security appear critical to making progress on the information-sharing challenges.

Earlier we saw the DHS mission as having a threefold focus: "Prevent terrorist attacks within the United States; reduce the vulnerability of the United States to terrorism; and minimize the damage and assist in the recovery from terrorist attacks that do occur within the United States."[26] However, other agencies were already working on the *prevent, reduce,* and *minimize* missions and DHS's coordination role required a delicate balancing of authorities: domestic and international, military and law enforcement, federal and state, federal and local, and criminal and civil. A complex organization was created quickly. Now analysts and policymakers must evaluate: Was it the right action?

MARCH 2005: BORDER SECURITY AND IMMIGRATION REFORM WILL DEFINE DHS

Shortly after President Bush began his second term, he nominated Michael Chertoff to be the second secretary of DHS. This was a dramatic change from the previous political leadership, reflecting the shift in focus from quickly creating a department with a culture and mission of its own, to fine-tuning that department. Michael Chertoff, an expert on the U.S. Constitution who was a federal appellate judge at the time of his nomination, is a lifelong law enforcement advocate. He was a career prosecutor, first as a federal prosecutor in New York City and then as the U.S. attorney for New Jersey. Of great significance, he served as the head of the DOJ's Criminal Division on 9/11. In addition to Chertoff, the president selected Michael Jackson—a former deputy secretary of Department of Transportation under White House Chief of Staff Andrew Card who was a well-connected defense industry insider with expertise in acquisition and management—as the deputy secretary.

Secretary Chertoff was quickly confirmed and he ordered DHS to embark on what he called the second stage review (2SR) to determine what should be the "stable orbit" of DHS.[27] The 2SR was a systematic study of the department's operations, policies, and structures with the goal of creating a more responsive DHS better able to address homeland security priorities based on risk. The results of the 2SR included the following priority missions for DHS:

1. Increase preparedness, with particular focus on catastrophic events;
2. Strengthen border security and interior enforcement and reform immigration processes;
3. Harden transportation security without sacrificing mobility;
4. Enhance information sharing with our partners, particularly with state, local, and tribal governments and the private sector;
5. Improve DHS stewardship, particularly with stronger financial, human resource, procurement, and information technology management;
6. Realign the DHS organization to maximize mission performance.[28]

The goal to strengthen border security and interior enforcement and reform immigration processes soon became among the most prominent policy initiatives of President Bush's second term.

Secretary Chertoff identified border security as part of the comprehensive immigration reform initiative, and as a top priority for DHS. Finding terrorists among the thousands of people illegally entering the United States for work, whether for seasonal agriculture jobs or permanent jobs throughout the interior of the country, becomes a search for needles in a haystack and such efforts highlight a similarity of purpose between the goals of immigration reform and national security. Comprehensive immigration reform helps secure U.S. borders by decreasing the total number of people illegally crossing the border through funneling persons looking for economic access into legal avenues for immigration, leaving the universe of criminal actors who attempt illegal crossings to be pursued and apprehended by CBP and ICE. If we decrease the size of the haystack, DHS's argument goes, we can better find the most dangerous needles.

As the department finished the 2SR, the White House quickly engaged DHS in developing a comprehensive immigration reform plan. The initial DHS enforcement effort was called the border enforcement security initiative (BESI) and it quickly morphed into the secure border initiative (SBI). For the most part, both of these approaches looked internally within DHS to see what policies and processes the secretary could change using DHS authorities in an effort to step up border security and immigration enforcement.

Immigration reform became the issue over which DHS struggled to exert its planned pan-executive branch coordination role, ironically losing authority to the White House. If the earlier OHS had been the only institution that the federal government created, then having the White House run policies related to immigration reform would be logical. However, because the new cabinet-level department possessed not only the immigration authorities of the United States but also the coordination mandate, immigration reform became DHS's opportunity to shine; a failure to coordinate could call into question the very legitimacy of the department.

The immigration reform issue was so highly political that it transcended any cabinet, especially DHS with its law enforcement focus. An alternate viewpoint eliminated the DHS role, saying that the broader immigration reform issue should rightly have been run from the White House and not by any one cabinet department, and this is indeed what happened. Eventually other entities such as the DOJ; DOS; DOD; the Social Security Administration (SSA); and the Departments of Commerce, Treasury, and Interior (DOI) all reached in to tweak pieces of the proposals, but working through the White House, not DHS. Within the interagency process, the NSC and HSC did not end up as the leads in shaping comprehensive immigration reform (CIR) legislation. Instead, the White House domestic policy council prevailed, leading the process with subject matter expertise support.

While the domestic policy council at the White House resolved internal administration debates over immigration reform, DHS played an important yet supporting role. Congressional involvement in the drafting of the legislation produced an additional level of complexity. This meant Congress led the drafting of the legislation, thus forcing the administration, DHS, and other policy advocates to negotiate from Congress's many rewrites. The legislation failed in Congress because it attempted to accomplish too much with too little trust from the public.[29] However, out of this process came the August 10, 2007, White House initiatives highlighting twenty-six administration action items for improving border security and immigration within existing laws, without any congressional action aside from proposed budgeting.[30] Secretary Chertoff exerted leadership by having the legal authority and expertise to define what could be achieved without new legislation.

Secretary Chertoff led the creation of SBI while marshalling new reform policies through the interagency, displaying DHS leadership and assertiveness in the national security interagency process. Although broader comprehensive immigration reform legislation never passed into law, DHS successfully developed and implemented an impressive array of new policies and procedures. Although not granted all the powers necessary solely to accomplish the mission, DHS leadership had successfully acted and coordinated a series of policy successes. However, midway through the launch of the SBI, DHS leadership faced a new threat requiring even more authority and coordination.

AUGUST 2005: KATRINA BROUGHT ALL HAZARDS AND ALL THREATS

Hurricane Katrina occurred as the 2SR wrapped up and the BESI had become the SBI working group, but before Secretary Chertoff's significant border victories such as the end of catch and release.[31] DHS was on its way to exerting leadership and defining itself in the interagency, yet, in spite of impressive accomplishments, Katrina managed to define the department in ways damaging to DHS and, therefore, the U.S. government's ability to have an effective coordination department for national security.

The images from New Orleans in August 2005 are historic: people stranded on rooftops and highways; barges and boats on top of houses in destroyed neighborhoods; collapsed bridges; looting; children without food sweltering in the Louisiana heat—all while President Bush famously congratulated FEMA administrator Mike Brown on his strong performance. Most of the general public's perception of the DHS response to hurricanes Katrina and Rita is an equal mixture of information and misinformation, all wrapped together under the rubric of a failure of government. While many have chronicled various details, for our purposes, these failures can be seen as a result of the manner in which different institutions of government coordinated their efforts.

The inability of federal, state, and local partners to talk to each other, much less work together, was at the heart of the crisis. The state of Louisiana failed to plan with its city or federal partners for what was an obvious risk. The city quickly lost contact with those at the state level and within FEMA who could help the city most. And some federal government decision makers seemed disconnected from actual events on the ground.

Of particular concern for the federal government was the seeming disconnect between FEMA and DHS headquarters. At times it appeared to some that FEMA administrator Mike Brown was attempting to cut Secretary Chertoff out of decisions by withholding vital information. Because of the unusually large stature of such a small agency like FEMA in the federal bureaucracy, many believed that FEMA should report directly to the president, as during the Clinton administration. However, DHS did not exist during the Clinton years. Because Chertoff possessed significant authority to deploy thousands of USCG personnel, ICE and Border Patrol agents, and other DHS staff, this apparent FEMA failure to coordinate with headquarters had serious ramifications.[32]

Soon after Katrina devastated the Gulf Coast, in an address to the nation from New Orleans, President Bush ordered a comprehensive review of the federal response so he could make the necessary changes to be "better prepared for any challenge of nature or act of evil men that could threaten our people."[33] The president was directing the federal apparatus to be better prepared for all hazards. His orders resulted in conclusions that comprised *The Federal Response to Hurricane Katrina: Lessons Learned*, a report released on February 23, 2006.[34]

The report resulted in a fundamentally changed approach to how the federal government planned, prepared, and trained for all disasters. It also included new guidance on the importance of how the federal government should work with state and local partners in planning for disasters. Critical to the federal approach is the DHS directing other agencies in times of a disaster, regardless of the cause. The report set forth 125 recommendations: five of which apply to all departments and agencies and the other 120 of which are assigned to a specific department or agency responsible for implementing the recommendation. The report tasks DHS with most of the action items. As of January 20, 2009, the implementation of over seventy percent of the recommendations had been completed. The remaining thirty percent required legislation or other authorities not granted to the DHS secretary.

Over time, people appreciated what could have been obvious sooner—the complexity of the federal role in the homeland security enterprise. All incidents are local. Law enforcement occurs locally. The federal government may be expected to protect the domestic population, but it cannot act domestically in most instances without the invitation of state and local authorities. Across federal departments, individual authorities require coordination so that the federal government can deliver appropriate support to local prevention and response activities.

HHS devoted considerable personnel and resources to accomplishing its share of the recommendations and it has taken on a new, more proactive leadership role in overseeing the federal government's medical response to a crisis. With an expanded statutory mission given to it by Congress in December 2006, HHS has embraced its new role as the government's lead for medical emergencies and it is well positioned to contribute its assets and capabilities during future disasters. HHS works closely with the DHS chief medical officer in developing policies to respond to disasters. This was not as true in Katrina, but we have seen it most clearly post-Katrina as HHS and DHS have worked hand-in-hand to develop an interagency-approved plan to address the potential of a pandemic flu outbreak.

As a result of Katrina, DOD has also modified response efforts associated with domestic disasters. It has adopted a proactive response posture with predrafted mission orders that can be executed almost immediately in the aftermath of a major incident. DOD is better integrated with both FEMA and other DHS agencies and it has assigned a coordination element to FEMA in each of the regional headquarters. DOD has offered its logistics expertise and capacity to DHS as well, allowing FEMA to leverage DOD's mature procurement and distribution systems to provide needed commodities rapidly to emergency managers and disaster victims.

In 2008, during the run-up to the landfall of hurricanes Ike and Gustav, staff from DOD's northern command were full members of all FEMA conference calls and worked closely to ensure that plans were in place for contingencies they could support.[35] This was particularly useful for deploying military aircraft to move at-risk people and later in the use of military contracting vehicles to repatriate stranded evacuees. Additionally, FEMA's office of grants and training and the National Guard bureau are working with state staffs to provide planning personnel to help evaluate and address planning gaps.

DHS has made great strides to plan for pending disasters and terrorist attacks and it has produced interagency-cleared plans and frameworks to ensure coordination. The most important of these efforts is the National Response Framework of 2009, which replaced the National Response Plan on March 22, 2008. This document offers a framework for a uniform response system at all levels of government, each of which will focus on training and coordination, and it promotes interagency cooperation as vital to responding to a disaster.

Critical to the coordination of interagency operations, DHS created a national operations center (NOC) to serve as the coordination center for ensuring an integrated, interagency response to a disaster. Through the NOC and under the direction of the secretary of homeland security, DHS is able to closely monitor the contributions of interagency partners during a disaster to ensure that necessary services are provided.

Just as 9/11 forced the U.S. government to organize for the asymmetric threat and create DHS, Katrina complemented that wake-up call by forcing the reorganization of the federal government to address the coordination of response. Between 9/11 and Katrina's landfall, DHS and the national security community focused on law enforcement authorities and military authorities across all levels of government. However, Katrina highlighted the parallel need to focus on emergency management authorities and ambiguities across the offices of mayors, governors, federal civil authorities, and DOD support of civil authorities. The response to natural disasters, industrial accidents, and terrorist incidents requires largely the same capabilities; therefore, the DHS must effectively coordinate local, state, federal, and international efforts to prevent, prepare for, and respond to all hazards. DHS evolved from a post-9/11 GWOT mission to a broader enforcement and immigration reform mission and eventually to an all-hazards 24/7/365 mission.

In 2007, the *National Strategy for Homeland Security* received its first revision and, significantly, included the post-Katrina view of the coordination challenges of the homeland security enterprise:

> The purpose of our Strategy is to guide, organize, and unify our Nation's homeland security efforts. It provides a common framework by which our entire Nation should focus its efforts on the following four goals:
>
> • Prevent and disrupt terrorist attacks;
> • Protect the American people, our critical infrastructure, and key resources;
> • Respond to and recover from incidents that do occur; and
> • Continue to strengthen the foundation to ensure our long-term success.
>
> Today's Threat Environment: Our Nation faces complex and dynamic threats from terrorism. In addition, other threats from catastrophic events—including natural disasters, accidents, and other hazards—exist and must be addressed. We will continue to advance our understanding of these threats so we are better able to safeguard the American people.[36]

Five years of struggling to breathe life and legitimacy into DHS, combined with real-world events such as Hurricane Katrina, forced the evolution of the DHS mission well beyond terrorism. Its mission remained to prevent, protect, and respond and recover, but it grew to address threats from terrorism, natural disasters, infectious diseases, and industrial accidents.

Today the secretary of homeland security serves as the principal federal official (PFO) to the president of the United States in coordinating federal support to these mission areas, as well as reporting information to the president using the NOC and affiliated authorities and capabilities. Such coordination and information sharing must occur across all federal agencies of the U.S. government, across all states and local authorities, and internationally. The American people have invested significantly in building the institutional capacity across DHS to accomplish this mission. Some of these authorities rest solely within the DHS, such as border enforcement, customs, and immigration. Many authorities, however, rest primarily in other departments, or at the state level; however, the secretary of homeland security retains the coordination role for federal involvement (see figure 10.2).

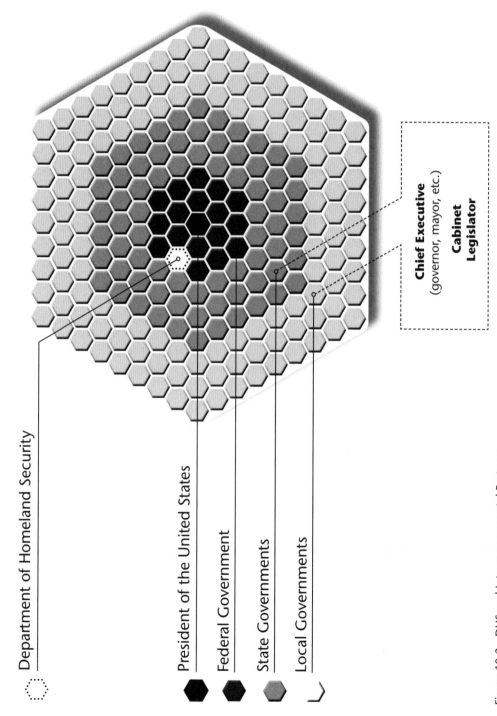

Figure 10.2   DHS and Intergovernmental Partners.

DHS EIGHT YEARS LATER AND BEYOND

DHS is the coordination department of the U.S. government. No other government department has built equally robust coordination channels across federal, state, local, tribal, territorial, commercial, individual, and international stakeholders. This will be DHS's strength over time.

Arguably, DHS touches more of the public on a daily basis than any other federal agency.[37] Because of this, DHS has demands placed on it that other interagency actors do not and DHS has benefited from the gained unique insight. The DHS work force of officers, agents, screeners, and sailors engages closely with local officials and law enforcement on a continuous basis. Additionally, thousands of DHS employees work outside the United States, attempting to identify threats long before they reach our shores. DHS employs more workers outside of the U.S. borders than the State Department—only the DOD has more federal employees overseas. This network of federal, state, local, tribal, territorial, commercial, international, and public contacts and partners will be crucial to DHS as it becomes more assertive in the interagency policy process.

DHS leads federal coordination in preparedness and response to incidents of national significance. DHS has worked through FEMA to strengthen FEMA regional structures, create regional planning, and fund regional training and exercise. DHS has also caused law enforcement fusion centers to be created across the states and territories of the United States and helps to staff these centers with federal liaisons. Although much work remains to be done, DHS has created a network of information-sharing nodes at the federal, state, and local levels. These act to prevent incidents better and to protect the American people and the critical infrastructure that our country relies on. In order for DHS to achieve its full potential in asserting the will of its stakeholders, the post-Bush DHS secretaries will have to involve themselves better in the policy process—from imagination to development to implementation.

DHS INTO THE FUTURE: FIRST LOOK

The United States needs a strong and respected coordinating element at the interagency table to address today's big security challenges: cyber security, domestic improvised explosive devices (IED), and smart borders.

Cyber security is chief among evolving threats that the federal government must train to confront through organization and planning. DHS has already been given some of the tools that are needed for this battle. The U.S. Computer Emergency Response Team (USCERT), housed within DHS's national protection and programs directorate (NPPD), addresses threats to the .gov and .com domains. The DOD's U.S. Cyber Command has been given responsibility for protecting the .mil domain. Although assignment of responsibilities for cyber security represents a significant step forward, the solution for exactly how to secure cyberspace remains undetermined. DHS will necessarily develop organic capabilities, as well as unique capabilities to coordinate with Cyber Command and the private sector. It is clear that the Obama administration will have to work to mesh the existing interagency efforts in cyber security together to form a useful, wide-reaching shield. In this discussion DHS should not only be a player but a leader, given the work it has already done and the power of its connections to the state, local, and business communities. But the role of the federal government must be held in check. Again, we have a story of responsibilities and authorities not aligned and the solution to be found in coordination.

In a more physically violent context, we must concern ourselves with the emerging domestic threat of improvised explosive devices (IEDs). Open-source intelligence has shown that IEDs could be deployed cheaply and widely against an unhardened public and with deadly effects.[38] DHS will largely be responsible for the federal contribution to preparing various aspects of the public including local communities, local and state law enforcement, and first responders for potential exposure to the terrorist use of IEDs.

Although the threat is known, the best manner in which to address IEDs is still uncertain. The DOD clearly has great experience in dealing with IEDs in war zones and it has gathered information that can and must be shared more widely with the interagency to prepare for domestic threats. DOD has also invested significant money and time researching how best to defeat IEDs encountered on the battlefields of the Middle East. Additionally, the IC is developing products that prepare communities better to address the tactics and methods of potential terrorists who deploy IEDs.

When immigration reform failed in late 2007, the result was a greater focus on the federal government as it proved its ability to secure our borders and as it tried to convince the American people that the leaders would take seriously the border security missions. At the end of President Bush's administration, DHS successfully completed 600 miles of fencing, it doubled the size of the border patrol from 9,000 to more than 18,000 agents, and it witnessed a historic drop in the number of illegal immigrants.[39] These efforts to secure the border were manpower-intensive and could prove difficult to maintain over time without additional resources. In an effort to develop those resources and further stem the flow of illegal immigrants, smugglers, and potential terrorists, DHS is working toward creating a smarter secure border.

The concept of a smart border applies not only to the use of smart technologies such as sensors and cameras between the ports of entry (POEs), but also to the use of advanced information, targeting, and technologies at the POEs. Both efforts at and between POEs require significant coordination within the interagency. Between the POEs, DHS must work closely with DOI and DOD and the landowners and operators of significant tracts of borderland to ensure cooperation in border management efforts. At the POEs, it is easy to say that DHS's task is actually more difficult. The POEs are significant economic engines for the United States and our land border and sea trade partners. Any effort to require more documentation or stiffer entry standards at POEs could adversely affect trade or travel. These issues are of great concern to the Departments of Commerce and State and they are often voiced loudly.

The December 25, 2009, bombing attempt, for example, demonstrates the challenges. Within DHS, the CBP makes determinations of admissibility and had planned to screen the suspect on arrival in Detroit Metropolitan Wayne County Airport (DTW). The TSA has responsibility for safety of flight, but does not have a work force deployed around the world. And, of great significance, the DHS possesses no legal authorities overseas, in Amsterdam or Nigeria. The IC had information on the suspect. The FBI had information on the subject. And the Department of State had information on the subject. However, the collective efforts of the federal government could not put the puzzle pieces together to prevent the suspect from boarding the aircraft in Schiphol with explosives sewn into his underwear. This threat is addressable through better coordination and deployment of off-the-shelf screening technologies. Like 9/11 and Katrina, a series of lessons learned will come from the incident and the federal government will make more progress on interagency coordination for homeland security.

Similarly, the May 1, 2010, Times Square attempted bombing shows distinct challenges for DHS. Although the December 25, 2009, attempt was the work of an international actor known to multiple members of the IC, the suspect in the Times Square effort was an unknown entity despite his training and contacts with the Taliban in Pakistan. And, like the December 25 attempt, alert citizens foiled the plot. And, once the plot was detected, the full DHS apparatus moved into action and—because of improvements made in aviation watchlisting in the wake of a number of previous incidents—CBP was able to arrest the suspect on an international flight to Dubai as he awaited takeoff.[40] These most recent incidents provide further evidence of the evolving threat environment facing DHS. To better face these threats in the coming years, DHS must participate forcefully at the national security interagency table. To meet the challenges of cyber security, domestically deployed IEDs, and border-crossing terrorists, DHS will have to assert itself more fully at the interagency to shape policy in a way that ensures the use of resources at the state and local levels to protect Americans best.

CONCLUSION

The secretary of DHS today must protect the American people from terrorist attacks, both as a leader and a coordinator, while responding to man-made and natural incidents. The secretary must facilitate trade, collect duties, and enforce the nation's immigration laws. DHS's new roles must include cyber security, domestic IED threats, and smart borders, all in budget requests to Congress. Sometimes the secretary is analogous to a commander, but the entire point of the post-9/11 action was to create better coordination. The secretary's job is to be the chief coordinator for the federal government's role in all hazards and all threats for the homeland.

How will we know if DHS has accomplished its goals? There have been no successful domestic terrorist attacks on the homeland as of the writing of this chapter, which means that DHS has met President Bush's initial directive not to allow another 9/11. Beyond that, it is hard to prove a negative, as anyone who works in the safety field knows. For example, how many people did not attempt to enter the United States illegally today and how many would have attempted if certain prevention measures were not in place? There is no way to know for sure. Are we spending the right amount on homeland security? The DHS's budget is about one-tenth of the DOD's. Is that the correct ratio? The December 25 Detroit attempt and the successful attacks in London, Glasgow, Madrid, and Mumbai demonstrate that extremist terrorists still plan and operate against allied countries. Only if DHS succeeds in becoming a fully legitimate leader in the interagency will we have appropriately used our opportunities to learn the lessons of 9/11.

NOTES

1. Gary Langer, "Support for Bush 2-1 Backing for War on Terrorism; Inaction Seen as the Greater Peril," *ABCNEWS.com*, September 21, 2001. http://abcnews.go.com/sections/politics/DailyNews/wtc_poll010921.html (accessed August 10, 2009).

2. Senator Joseph Lieberman, interview with the author, August 4, 2009.

3. Department of Homeland Security Public Affairs. "History: Who Became Part of the Department?" Department of Homeland Security. www.dhs.gov/xabout/history/editorial_0133.shtm (accessed August 10, 2009).

4. National Commission of Terrorist Attacks upon the United States, *The 9/11 Commission Report* (New York: W.W. Norton & Company, 2004), 400.

5. The United States Commission on National Security/21st Century. *Road Map for National Security: Imperative for Change* (Washington, DC: The Commission, 2001), vi.

6. USA Secure, "Management," USASecure.org., www.usasecure.org/about-who-management.php (accessed August 19, 2009).

7. Ashton B. Carter, John Deutch, and Philip Zelikow, "Catastrophic Terrorism: Tackling the New Danger," *Foreign Affairs*, November/December 1998.

8. James Loy, interview with the author, July 31, 2009.

9. John Ashcroft, interview, *Frontline*, PBS.org. March 12, 2007. www.pbs.org/wgbh/pages/frontline/homefront/interviews/ashcroft.html (accessed September 2, 2009).

10. "Governor Ridge Sworn-In to Lead Homeland Security." White House press release. October 8, 2001. http://georgewbush-whitehouse.archives.gov/news/releases/2001/10/20011008-3.html (accessed August 10, 2009).

11. "Executive Order Establishing the Office of Homeland Security." Executive Order 13328. October 8, 2001. http://georgewbush-whitehouse.archives.gov/news/releases/2001/10/20011008-2.html (accessed August 10, 2009).

12. Office of Homeland Security, *National Strategy for Homeland Security* (Washington, DC: Office of Homeland Security, 2002), vii.

13. Richard A. Falkenrath, "Homeland Security: The White House Plan Explained and Examined" (paper presented at the Brookings Forum, The Brookings Institution, September 4, 2002).

14. Homeland Security Act of 2002, Pub L no. 107–296, 116 Stat. 2135 (2002).

15. Loy led the creation of the TSA as the first deputy undersecretary at the Department of Transportation, and he became the second deputy secretary of the department in late 2003.

16. The Coast Guard, however, remains a separate member of the IC.

17. For example, the national infrastructure protection plan (NIPP) identifies eighteen critical sectors such as Energy, Healthcare and Public Health, Banking and Finance, and Information Technology. See the NIPP at www.dhs.gov/nipp.

18. "Interviews with Tom Ridge, Janis Karpinski" CNN.com. Aired May 26, 2004. http://edition.cnn.com/TRANSCRIPTS/0405/26/ltm.03.html (accessed May 29, 2009).

19. "Transcript: Ashcroft, Mueller Press Conference" CNN.com. Posted Wednesday, May 26, 2004. www.cnn.com/2004/US/05/26/terror.threat.transcript/ (accessed May 29, 2009).

20. James Loy, interview with the author, August 4, 2009.

21. Jenna Baker McNeil, "Congressional Oversight of Homeland Security in Dire Need of an Overhaul." The Heritage Foundation, Backgrounder #2161 (July 14, 2008). www.heritage.org/research/homelanddefense/bg2161.cfm (accessed August 10, 2009).

22. National Commission of Terrorist Attacks upon the United States, *The 9/11 Commission Report* (New York: W.W. Norton & Company, 2004), executive summary.

23. Department of Homeland Security, "DHS Fact Sheet: A Day in the Life of Homeland Security." Department of Homeland Security. Created May 28, 2008. www.dhs.gov/xabout/gc_1212011814375.shtm (accessed August 18, 2009). This includes 1.1 million people at our borders, 2 million air travelers screened by TSA, and a quarter of a million people contacting CIS about immigration benefits, but does not include the thousands of people receiving FEMA or USCG assistance every day.

24. National Commission of Terrorist Attacks upon the United States, *The 9/11 Commission Report* (New York: W.W. Norton & Company, 2004), 408.

25. Chet Lunner, "Whose Dot's Are They, Anyway?" unpublished speech given at Georgetown University, 2008.

26. Homeland Security Act of 2002, Pub L no. 107–296, 116 Stat. 2135 (2002).

27. Department of Homeland Security, "Secretary Michael Chertoff, U.S. Department of Homeland Security Second Stage Review Remarks," www.dhs.gov/xnews/speeches/speech_0255.shtm

28. Ibid.

29. Jonathan Weisman, "Immigration Bill Dies in the Senate," *Washington Post*, June 29, 2007, A1.

30. "Fact Sheet: Improving Border Security and Immigration within Existing Law," The White House. August 10, 2007. http://georgewbush-whitehouse.archives.gov/news/releases/2001/10/20011008-2.html (accessed August 10, 2009).

31. Michael Chertoff, "Remarks by Secretary Michael Chertoff at a Press Conference Announcing the DHS Fiscal Year 2008 Budget Request," Department of Homeland Security. February 5, 2007. www.dhs.gov/xnews/releases/pr_1170774601996.shtm (accessed August 10, 2009).

32. The USCG rescued most of the 40,000 people from roofs and buildings in flooded New Orleans.

33. President George W. Bush, address to the nation, Jackson Square, New Orleans, September 15, 2005, quoted in Homeland Security Council, *The Federal Response to Katrina: Lessons Learned* (Washington, DC: The Homeland Security Council, 2006), vii.

34. Homeland Security Council, *The Federal Response to Katrina: Lessons Learned* (Washington, DC: The Homeland Security Council, 2006), vii.

35. The DOD's U.S. Northern Command (NORTHCOM) was created in 2002 as the combatant command for North America and the Caribbean. NORTHCOM took over control of previous civil support and homeland security/homeland defense missions within the United States. Of interest here, it is responsible for DOD's response to domestic disasters regardless of origin.

36. Homeland Security Council, *National Strategy for Homeland Security* (Washington, DC: Homeland Security Council, 2007).

37. For example, CBP processes close to 1.1 million people crossing our borders every day, TSA screens 2 million air travelers, and a quarter of a million people contact CIS about immigration benefits. See note 26.

38. "Terrorism at home: domestic counter-IED office poised for expansion," *Security Beat: Homeland Defense Briefs, National Defense* (August 1, 2008), www.thefreelibrary.com/Terrorism+at+home:+domestic+counter-IED+office+poised+for+expansion.-a0183042574 (accessed August 10, 2009).

39. Thomas Frank, "Illegal Immigration Population Declines," *USAToday*, February 23, 2009.

40. "Times Square suspect had explosives training, documents say," *USAToday*, May 4, 2010.

Part II   The President's Partners and Rivals

Chapter 11   Congress: Checking Presidential Power

GERALD FELIX WARBURG

> I do not hesitate to say that it is especially in the conduct of their foreign relations that democracies appear to me decidedly inferior to other governments.
>
> *Alexis de Tocqueville, Democracy in America*

> There is no rational system whereby the Executive Branch and Congress reach coherent and enduring agreement on national military strategy, the forces to carry it out, and the funding that should be provided.
>
> *The President's Blue Ribbon Commission on Defense Management was informally named for its chairman, David M. Packard. Its final report was submitted to the White House on June 30, 1986*

Formulating and implementing national security policy in a democracy is a messy process. This is no surprise: the fight over who would have the power to make war and to fund its prosecution was at the heart of the American Revolution. The weak federal powers provided under the Articles of the Confederation were soon challenged by a Constitutional Convention tasked with devising a more effective balance. The system that emerged, and which endures today, ensures dynamic tension. The ensuing policymaking process permits the relative powers of the Congress and the president to expand and contract "like an accordion," as scholar Joseph Ellis has observed, "making the music required in different historical contexts."[1] That the enduring struggle between the legislative and executive branches is turbulent and partisan is to be expected. The competing interests clash by design: it is the American way.

This chapter examines the role of Congress in the national security enterprise, evaluating the tools legislators use to check presidential power. The central argument advanced rejects one of the most persistent myths in American political science, the notion that, by tradition, politics in the United States "stops at the water's edge."

In reality, politics have shaped most significant U.S. national security debates. Since supporters of Thomas Jefferson and John Adams fought in Congress over whether the U.S. should favor the British or the French, U.S. national security policy has been subject to bitter dispute among legislators. Similar dynamics were at work in 1939–41 when isolationists in Congress blocked many Roosevelt administration efforts to help nations under German and Japanese attack. Other examples include the "who lost China" recriminations in Congress after communists seized Beijing in 1949 and the congressional assaults on U.S.–Soviet détente in the 1970s. Study of such controversies makes clear that the American tradition is one of sharp partisan disputes over questions of war and peace. To appreciate the implications of this struggle, we must evaluate the congressional policymaking process established in the U.S. Constitution, the legislative culture on Capitol Hill, and precedents that shape national security debates.

PROCESS: HOW CONGRESSIONAL POWERS LIMIT PRESIDENTIAL OPTIONS

Congress has numerous tools to use in efforts to curtail presidential authority in national security. The U.S. Constitution enumerates the powers of Congress first. Congress funds, ratifies, amends, and restricts presidential foreign and defense policy initiatives. Article 1, Section 8 of the Constitution lists the primary foreign policy powers of Congress. The most significant of these include the power to appropriate funds, to declare war, and, in the Senate, to approve treaties and the appointment of ambassadors as well as many senior national security aides. From these powers are derived the key tools for congressional engagement in the national security enterprise. To impact policy, the best options include:

- the budget process (both authorizing and appropriating expenditure of funds);
- hearings and committee reports;
- ratification of treaties and confirmation of senior staff/ambassadors; and
- media statements and individual/group letters to executive branch officials.

The Constitution is silent on intelligence matters, thereby inviting repeated interbranch struggle. Yet where the Constitution is most explicit—granting exclusively to Congress the power to declare war—the law of the land has been followed only sporadically. In fact, Congress has not formally declared war on any nation since Pearl Harbor. Congress has instead given its tacit approval to, while aggressively funding, scores of foreign military actions since World War II.

Executive authority is more ambiguous. Where it is spelled out in the Constitution, there is a constructive tension that provides, as historian Edwin Corwin has observed, an "invitation to struggle."[2] The American system of self-government began with a Continental Congress and then a Confederation, neither of which provided any substantial executive authority. Constitutional power has since evolved to embrace a strong executive who directs all international diplomatic initiatives and commands U.S. military forces.[3] Only by building a domestic political consensus, however cumbersome, can the president advance a sustainable policy.

Abuses occur when Congress accepts a greatly reduced role in overseeing the president's national security policies. When legislators are intimidated or the majority in Congress defers to a president of its own party, oversight is lax. Legislative blank checks let mistakes go uncorrected and ensure that policy implementation will subsequently be subject to sweeping reversal in a cycle of reaction and counterreaction as party control changes. The role Congress plays in shaping national security policy is reactive, personality-driven, and greatly affected by the temper of the times. Participants' views on the appropriate level of presidential authority change as individual policymakers move from one branch to another, as party control shifts, and as circumstances and the national interest demand.[4]

Over the last decade, policymaking has proceeded in an atmosphere of near-constant crisis, which began with the 9/11 attacks and continued through wars in Afghanistan, Pakistan, and Iraq, then grew once more through a series of international economic shocks. This environment has provided fertile ground for sustained efforts to strengthen the powers of the White House and diminish those of Congress. Throughout the Bush-Cheney administration, proponents of a powerful executive sought new authorities. An important element in the argument they made was selective quotation of the *Federalist Papers*. Alexander Hamilton's arguments were used to defend presidential prerogatives for the conduct of military operations, intelligence gathering at home and abroad, and diplomacy.[5] Advocates asserted that presidents possess inherent powers to act in the national interest. They argued that the White House is obliged to counter restraining forces in Congress and the inherited executive branch bureaucracy.[6]

The process of shaping national security policies has always been dependent on countervailing forces to find balance. "Ambition counteracts ambition," as President James Madison once explained.[7] Authority goes to entrepreneurs who can seize and hold it. Commentators describe this competition as a "vigorous, deliberative and often combative process that involves both the executive and legislative branches. The country's Founding Fathers gave each branch both exclusive and overlapping powers in the realm of foreign policy, according to each one's comparative advantage."[8] It is through the competition to exercise these powers that U.S. national security policy is forged.

Throughout this process, Congress plays an arbiter's role. Legislators react to presidential initiative and wield their power to condition appropriation of funds for implementation of White House proposals. An essential tool is the power to scrutinize policy implementation in both public and closed hearings. Those who are suspicious of executive powers insist that congressional oversight "is meant to keep mistakes from happening and spiraling out of control; it helps draw out lessons from catastrophes in order to prevent them, or others like them, from recurring. Good oversight cuts waste, punishes fraud or scandal, and keeps policymakers on their toes."[9] Conversely, lessons derived from an era of congressional dominance and a weakened executive are often applied by champions of the executive branch who insist a strong presidency is required to meet international security challenges. Because the lessons learned differ, the contemporary policymaking process is guided by interpretations of precedents that are discordant.

The conclusions policymakers draw from past experiences evolve over time. For example, as a presidential candidate in 2000, then Texas Governor George W. Bush opposed the type of nation-building to which his predecessor President Clinton committed U.S. forces in the Balkans. Early in his first term, however, President Bush felt it necessary to commit substantial resources to far broader nation-building missions in Iraq, Afghanistan, and Pakistan. Similarly, Secretary of Defense Robert Gates publicly regretted the weakening of U.S. diplomatic options. He lamented in 2009 that "the gutting of America's ability to engage, assist and communicate with other parts of the world—the 'soft power' which had been so important throughout the cold war. . . . It is almost like we forgot everything we learned in Vietnam."[10] Although Gates helped lead the fight for more war funding as a member of the Bush-Cheney cabinet in 2007–8, his role as a Republican holdover under the Obama-Biden team placed greater emphasis on a draw down of Iraq forces and multilateral diplomacy.

In times of heightened international danger, the fractious nature of partisan legislative debate and the requirements for swift military action invariably empower the presidency. As historian Doris Kearns Goodwin has noted: "The presidential apparatus grew with the growth of military needs; the great steps forward in the expansion of presidential power were linked—whether as the effect or cause—with the great wars: the Civil War, World War I,

World War II, and the Korean War. Time and again, the law of national self-preservation was seen to justify placing extravagant powers in the hands of the President."[11]

Goodwin's observation was made at the height of the Cold War. Yet it has been borne out again a generation later by the American experience after the 9/11 terrorist attacks. The subsequent U.S. moves against al-Qaeda, as well as the prolonged U.S. military engagements in Iraq and Afghanistan, have brought the domestic political conflict over the appropriate balance of foreign policymaking powers into sharp relief. Congress has yielded extraordinary authority to the president, powers the legislative branch has recently struggled to reclaim. The recent international financial challenges have made legislators' task more difficult; the global economic recession of 2009 continued the post-9/11 trend whereby crises empower the presidency.

CULTURE: THE NATIONAL SECURITY POLICYMAKING ENVIRONMENT IN CONGRESS

There are stark contrasts in the workplace culture where legislative and executive branch policymakers operate. The former tends toward highly public combat. The latter relies on confidential internal deliberations to establish a uniform approach. Legislators and their sizable staffs have a different perspective on international challenges than those who inhabit executive agencies. Members of Congress and Capitol Hill staffers also have remarkable latitude to choose which issues they investigate. Staff jobs are secured through a mix of political contacts and substantive expertise, yet they remain influenced by home-state considerations. Horizontal alliances are formed between personal offices and committee staff, between House and Senate staff, between Republican and Democratic staff.

The five hundred and thirty-five members of Congress and their aides tend to have more sensitive political antennae than most executive branch bureaucrats. With the exception of the president and vice president, none of the thousands who staff a presidential administration is subject to popular election. A small percentage of the federal bureaucracy is made up of political appointees—including several hundred in the national security sphere. These political appointees often hold office for a short period of time and focus on a specific agenda. The vast majority of their colleagues remain career bureaucrats, who are more risk-averse and take pride in outlasting both presidents and congresspersons. National security issues are often carefully selected by members to highlight a broader agenda, one that calculates costs and benefits for reelection, along with national interests. The way these differences are manifest in the respective policymaking environments can be charted as shown in table 11.1.[12]

Congressional Culture Rewards Confrontation

Issues placed in stark relief generate headlines. Controversies energize voters and activate the electoral base on which politicians rely. By contrast, leaders of the executive branch abhor public dissent. Resignations on principle by senior executive branch policymakers are rare. Cabinet officers strive to speak with one voice; they are often frustrated in seeking similar unity from congressional leaders. Partisan legislators have ample opportunity to score political points attacking presidential leadership. Twenty-twenty hindsight suggests that many presidential initiatives opposed in their time by bitter factions in Congress

Table 11.1   Cultural Differences in Policymaking Environments

Congress	Executive
Follows public opinion	Leads public education
Encourages public dissent	Favors unitary action
Welcomes debate/shares information	Suppresses leaks and internal dissent
Focuses on thematic goals	Manages specific relationships
Promotes entrepreneurs	Protects team players
Subject to voter approval	Subject to presidential removal
Seeks sharp ideological contrast	Strives for bipartisan consensus
Initiates most spending	Commands military forces
Selective expertise on security matters	Highly specialized knowledge base
Uses procedure to shape policy	Alters policy to weather process
Multiple decision points	Unitary decision tree
Power contested horizontally	Power flows vertically

actually did advance U.S. security interests. Examples include recognition of the People's Republic of China (PRC), the Mexico "bail-out" loans of the 1990s, and détente with the Soviet Union. Indeed, the first major post-Vietnam foreign policy struggle, over treaties designed to return the U.S.-occupied Canal Zone to Panamanian sovereignty, was fueled in part by the presidential candidacy of a leading critic, former California Governor Ronald Reagan. Treaty opponents failed to block Senate approval of the Panama accords. Nevertheless, this legislative confrontation, and its appeal to a resurgent nationalism, played a significant role in Reagan's ascent to the presidency. Within just three years of ratification of the Panama Canal Treaties, twenty senators who voted for adoption of the accords were defeated.[13]

Congress Manipulates Media Coverage

Many legislative careers are built on public challenges to the White House. Congressional staffers are promoted, in part, on the basis of their ability to raise their boss's profiles and secure media coverage. Getting them quoted is a key part of the job for many Capitol Hill staffers. Elected officials gain colleagues' support for advancement based on their ability to assert the independence of Congress by confronting executive branch power. For example, Senator Harry Truman led early World War II efforts to ferret out waste, fraud, and abuse in defense procurement. The resulting favorable press was instrumental in Truman's being thrust onto Franklin D. Roosevelt's 1944 presidential ticket when the incumbent ran for an unprecedented fourth term.

Congress Uses Information Aggressively

Congress benefits from dissenting views that often originate with executive branch sources. Members of Congress tend to be confrontational in their use of such sensitive information, which they share in extensive offline networks. Because executive branch perspectives are far from monolithic, fault lines persist between political appointees and career bureaucrats. It is often these divides that produce leaks to the Congress and the media as one means for executive branch staffers to advance their dissents.[14] Administration officials enjoy an enormous structural advantage in the policymaking competition with Congress because virtually all diplomatic, military, and intelligence information flows first to the executive branch. An adversarial relationship ensues. National security information is shared with the Congress by the White House in a manner that is often inefficient and untimely. Administration officials abhor leaks to the media from the consultation process. For example, during President Nixon's first term national security advisor Henry Kissinger ordered wiretaps on his staff in an effort to discover the source of revelations regarding sensitive negotiations with North Vietnam. A special "plumbers" unit, driven by President Nixon and Attorney General John Mitchell's anger over leaks, ultimately led to the Watergate break-in and cover-up. The ensuing scandal and legislative response sharply reduced White House powers.

Congress Pursues Broad Function Objectives

Human rights and nuclear nonproliferation are examples of broad themes pressed by Congress, often without regard to their impact on U.S. bilateral relationships. This frustrates specialists at the Departments of State and Defense who are responsible each day for managing U.S. relations and military deployments abroad. For instance, congressional critics of China's one-party rule frequently complicate White House efforts to enlist PRC support for other challenges, from genocide in Darfur to balancing the exchange rate for Chinese currency. "China suffers from a caricature of what it really is," explained Assistant Secretary of State Christopher Hill in 2008. "It's a really complex society. I don't think it should be defined by one dimension, its economics, or security, or human rights . . . China has emerged as a country with whom we have to work globally on security challenges."[15] When newly confirmed Secretary of State Hillary Clinton espoused a similar version of *realpolitik* on her first trip abroad as a cabinet member early in 2009, she received withering criticism from human rights activists in Washington. The desire of members to pursue broad ideological goals generally pleases congressional campaign managers. Politicians seek contrast. Diplomats managing international challenges must often compromise general principles to achieve specific national security objectives.

Congress Exacts a Procedural Price

Executive branch policy initiatives are usually affirmed, but often only after they are amended, with conditions attached, as in the recent case of renewed U.S.-India nuclear energy trade. On occasion, Congress also links support for international policies to adoption of unrelated domestic policy changes. For example, Congress in the fall of 2008 tied approval of trade agreements with Colombia and South Korea to support for more domestic spending.[16] Senate confirmation of presidential appointees or ambassadors can similarly be made contingent upon assurances regarding future policies. Overhauls of U.S. policy initiated by Congress are often procedural in nature. Major reforms pressed in recent decades by Congress—including the Arms Export Control Act (1976); the Nuclear Nonproliferation Act (1978); and the Goldwater-Nichols Department of Defense Reorganization Act (1986)—changed the policymaking process more than they altered the substance of specific policies. Yet these procedural changes empowered Congress to insert itself more vigorously in subsequent policy disputes. These reforms also had a substantial deterrent effect on potential international engagements, curbing commercial nuclear trade and military weapons exports by limiting executive branch freedom of action.[17]

Congress Changes the Rules of the Game

Changes in legislative procedures create new avenues to challenge executive branch dominance. Post-Watergate reforms that decentralized congressional oversight powers and dispersed committee jurisdiction also produced sweeping inquiries into the intelligence community and Pentagon spending practices. Congress has created new panels on intelligence oversight and homeland security, funded military operations through both annual and supplemental spending, and created special procedures for closing military facilities. Legislative requirements have facilitated the doubling of congressional staff rolls over the last thirty-five years.[18] Added staff and requirements for numerous administration follow-up reports have given Congress more means for questioning executive branch policy implementation.

Congressional Expertise Often Grows from "Safe" Seats

Members often look to a small group of committee chairs, ranking members, and party leadership for direction. Expertise on national security issues resides with a handful of members—often those who have the luxury of defending seats where their safe reelection is a presumption. This establishes an informal succession of leaders whose ability to sway less expert and more junior members becomes central to any administration strategy to secure support in Congress. For example, veteran Senate incumbents such as Indiana's Richard Lugar, Michigan's Carl Levin, or California's Dianne Feinstein, who are secure against most electoral pressures, have accumulated seniority on committees focused on foreign policy, defense, and intelligence. Securing their public support, often after accepting some proposed amendments, is critical for White House lobbyists.

Elected officials in safe seats have the luxury of spending more time on international matters. Because their political base is so strong, they possess more freedom to negotiate with executive branch officials or stand up to their own partisans by taking unpopular positions. (The converse is true on domestic spending issues, where a handful of politically vulnerable centrists from swing states have enormous leverage to broker compromises in interbranch negotiations.)

There is, however, a danger that some legislators' political immunity can sacrifice closeness to the popular will. For example, during the Vietnam War era, entrenched incumbents on the defense appropriations committees strongly supported war funding long after a majority of the country had turned against the war. Similarly, from 2002–6, a thoroughly gerrymandered Congress, where relatively few members faced competitive races, continued to appropriate large sums for the Iraq occupation. When voter opposition to Iraq war spending achieved a critical mass in 2007–8, several congressional supporters of the Iraq war were unexpectedly defeated in reelection bids.

Congress Challenges Executive Branch Powers in Predictable Cycles

Executive branch champions expand presidential power in wartime. Subsequently, the Congress reasserts its authority and reforms the policymaking process. An illustration: the post-Watergate reforms empowered Congress and checked the imperial tendencies of the Johnson and Nixon presidencies. These reforms hampered the relatively weak presidency of Jimmy Carter, who clashed with congressional powers in his own party. His presidency was bedeviled by international challenges. U.S. diplomats were held hostage in Iran for more than a year, the strategic arms limitation talks with Moscow faltered, and the Soviet invasion of Afghanistan proceeded without effective U.S. challenge. One consequence was popular support for the vigorous reassertion of executive branch powers under Carter's successor, Ronald Reagan. Late in the second Reagan-Bush term, the Iran-Contra scandal empowered Congress. Legislators subsequently played a strong hand in shaping U.S. post-Cold War policies toward nations emerging from the shadow of Soviet power. The Clinton presidency challenged congressional powers in the 1990s; Clinton deployed troops to Kosovo without complying with terms of the War Powers Act and reinterpreted the ABM treaty without any effective congressional counter.[19] After 9/11, the Bush-Cheney administration systematically expanded the challenges to Congress. Then change came early in the Obama-Biden administration, when White House officials adopted a less extreme reading of presidential prerogatives on a host of issues, including signing statements, exclusion of war-fighting costs from annual budgets, and interpretation of U.S. obligations under the Geneva Convention.

PRECEDENTS: THE CYCLICAL BATTLE TO DOMINATE POLICYMAKING

A series of precedents are invariably cited by policymakers as they contest national security initiatives. Practitioners draw on these case studies to inform their actions. For example, an entire generation of international studies majors was schooled on the cautions suggested by Graham Allison's *Essence of Decision*, the landmark study of organizational behavior and nimble presidential maneuver during the 1962 Cuban missile crisis.[20] For a successor generation, divergent lessons from the failed U.S. military engagement in Vietnam produced starkly different conclusions, as for example in the respective presidential candidacies of war veterans John Kerry (2004) and John McCain (2008). The former drew the conclusion that the United States must not linger too long in an unpopular foreign war; the latter believed the United States abandoned a commitment to an ally too soon. These beliefs had a profound impact on the positions the senators pressed the Congress to take on U.S. engagement in Iraq in 2002–10.

Policymakers are driven invariably by a desire to refight the last battle, applying their own versions of lessons learned from the most recent major foreign policy confrontations. These threads of collective memory have shaped U.S. national security policy from the Cold War and Vietnam to Bosnia and Afghanistan. Those engaged in the national security enterprise struggle to avoid what they perceive as mistakes in recent national strategy and execution.

This phenomenon is both episodic and cyclical, as each generation reacts to the perceived excesses and failures of its predecessors. The danger of over-correction in this process is considerable. As historian Arthur Schlesinger Jr. noted, a politician such as John Kennedy—who came of age in the 1930s abhorring the isolationism of that era—predictably became an internationalist, supporting U.S. military interventions from Korea to Cuba to Vietnam.[21] Similarly, policymakers who came of age believing the United States abandoned Vietnam prematurely, invariably embraced a prolonged occupation of Baghdad to ensure the United

States held hard-won gains with an enduring military commitment. As one Iraq war critic put it, the Bush-Cheney policies risked "under the guise of exorcising the trauma of Vietnam, replicat(ing) the trauma of Vietnam."[22] Those who believe the United States left Vietnam too soon were committed to a long stay in Iraq and Afghanistan.

To facilitate military actions in the Middle East and Southwest Asia, the Bush-Cheney administration pressed a sweeping expansion of executive branch authority. "The assertion and expansion of presidential power," as one critical review of this era posits, "is arguably the defining feature of the Bush years."[23] It was no coincidence that this effort to strengthen the presidency was led in part by a veteran executive branch policymaker, Vice President Cheney, who had experienced firsthand the weakening of executive authority in the White House during the post-Watergate administration of President Gerald Ford.

From 2001–6, the Republican Party controlled one or both houses of Congress; legislators held less than fifty percent as many hearings on executive branch policies as had their counterparts in a comparable era of Democratic Party dominance, from 1961–68.[24] The effect of one-party rule was striking during this recent period, which featured strong support for new executive branch powers, limited congressional oversight, and not a single presidential veto. The expansion of executive branch authority was credited by supporters with helping to overthrow Iraqi dictator Saddam Hussein and to deter another al-Qaeda attack on U.S. soil. New cabinet agencies were created in Washington. New resources to increase the intelligence and defense budgets were found. Intelligence was very closely held. The political will and the ability of Congress to alter Bush administration policy were limited. "Decades from now," former Senate Judiciary Committee Chairman Arlen Specter of Pennsylvania reflected in 2008, "historians will look back at the period from 9/11 to the present as an era of unbridled executive power and congressional ineffectiveness."[25]

The 2008 election brought a predictable counterreaction. Congressional efforts to engage in national security policymaking began a new chapter with the advent of the Obama-Biden administration in 2009. Champions of a strong executive branch feared that a reform agenda might weaken presidential power when terrorist threats and an international financial crisis required strong executive action. Conversely, congressional Democrats who complained about lax Republican oversight of the White House during the Bush-Cheney years were challenged to show some intellectual consistency. They were now confronted with an executive branch team, led by many—from the secretary of state to the White House chief of staff—who were former legislative branch colleagues.

The ensuing struggle unfolded in a manner consistent with precedents established by several recent waves of reform. The first occurred in the wake of the Watergate scandal and the resignation of President Nixon, from 1974–76. A second set of reforms ensued after the collapse of the Soviet bloc and the end of the Cold War, from 1990–95. A third wave was launched early in the Obama-Biden administration as changes were made in the executive-legislative balance established by the Bush-Cheney team. Typically these reform movements featured efforts by legislators to reassert powers that had been eclipsed by presidential authority in wartime.

A common feature of these cycles is overreaction. Finding the most appropriate balance consistent with the national interest is ever harder because of globalization. Many issues formerly treated as domestic concerns now have complex multinational implications, from climate change to stimulus spending to stock market regulation.

It is instructive to note how such cycles have impacted one well-known legislative panel—the Senate Foreign Relations Committee (SFRC). Under Chairman William Fulbright in the 1960s, the committee was assertive. Democrats took the lead, commanding the national stage to challenge President Johnson's Vietnam policies from within his own party. The committee was relatively quiescent during the Nixon administration, before reasserting its powers under Democratic leaders John Sparkman and Frank Church. From 1975–80, the committee moved controversial reforms of war powers and export policies, then pressed ratification of the Panama Canal treaties. Under GOP Chairman Richard Lugar in the early 1980s, a changing SFRC majority again pressed a president of the same party, adopting sanctions against South Africa's apartheid government over President Reagan's veto and championing democratic reforms as conditions on U.S. aid to military-led governments in El Salvador and the Philippines.[26] The tide peaked before congressional efforts to exact the last word on presidential actions via a legislative veto were declared unconstitutional in 1983; the Supreme Court's decision was consistent with the counterreformation of such post-Watergate excesses.[27] The committee declined during the tenures of Presidents George H. W. Bush and Bill Clinton, as Chairman Claiborne Pell frequently deferred to the State Department. Even under hard-line GOP chairman Jesse Helms (R-NC), President Clinton, a former committee intern, had a relatively free hand in the Senate for policy initiatives from the Balkans to NAFTA to reinterpretation of the ABM treaty, although the Senate rejected the Comprehensive Test Ban Treaty in the months after impeachment efforts.

The SFRC again tried to reassert its authority late in the second term of President George W. Bush. Ironically, the committee was unable to realize its potential as champion of legislative branch powers, in part because several of its members were consumed by their own presidential bids. The SFRC actually provided *both* candidates on the winning Democratic presidential ticket for 2008, junior committee member Barack Obama of Illinois and his Senate mentor and chairman, Joe Biden of Delaware, who served alongside former presidential aspirants Kerry, Dodd, Lugar, and Brownback.

Throughout this period, the SFRC was undercut by the steadily growing power of the appropriations committees. The SFRC repeatedly failed to move major bills through committee and Senate floor debate to enactment. The appropriations committee route became the vehicle of choice for champions of many major policy provisions, including the House-originated Boland amendment that banned aid to the contras fighting Nicaragua's leftist regime. (Note that there are striking differences in culture among congressional committees. For example, the SFRC and its House counterpart tend toward more partisan ideological polarization in their staffs, a majority of whom have political and academic backgrounds. By contrast, Armed Services Committee staffers tend to come from military careers and focus on management and budget considerations.)

The pursuit of vigorous oversight by would-be reformers in Congress usually prompts executive branch resistance. Too much public prying into sensitive international issues can hamstring initiatives, as when the Church and Pike committees hampered the CIA's ability to conduct covert operations in the mid-1970s. So does too little inquisitiveness, as when recent congressional sessions gave a blank check for the costly U.S. invasion and occupation of Iraq, as well as the establishment of secret overseas prisons and suspension of *habeas corpus*. Striking a balance between such extremes is one of the great challenges in advancing U.S. national security interests.

One need not be a partisan of either branch to note the dangers when one partner in the system of checks and balances fails to play a steady role. The failures of both parties in Congress to provide vigorous oversight from 1998–2008 exacerbated federal government failures both domestic and foreign—see Hurricane Katrina, the housing bubble, financial derivatives speculation, and intelligence failures from pre-9/11 to Iraq's weapons of mass destruction (WMD). The inability to establish an equitable balance cut across major political parties and both policymaking branches of national government. As a leading Democratic critic noted early in 2008, "Republicans in the Congress did a disservice to the Bush administration by allowing it to be more secretive and by not using the institutional powers under the Constitution for oversight."[28]

Conversely, excessive meddling by Congress has often frustrated efforts of even the most determined presidents to pursue essential diplomatic opportunities abroad. For example, Congress consistently raised the bar on expansion of free trade with Colombia, insisting first on human rights reforms, then labor law changes, before finally in the waning days of the George W. Bush presidency, holding ratification of the U.S.-Colombia free trade agreement hostage to unrelated domestic political considerations. Similarly, hardline anti-communists in Congress for decades limited presidents' ability to alter ineffective Cuba trade embargo policies.

AUTHORIZING MILITARY ACTIONS AND FUNDING DEFENSE PROCUREMENT

Congress rarely launches major international relations initiatives. Despite decades of military engagements from Korea and Vietnam to Bosnia and the Persian Gulf, Congress has not adopted a declaration of war since 1941. The handling of the Iraq war authorization in 2002 was typical. For months preceding the key vote, legislators received classified briefings from Bush administration officials who already favored commitment to a military option. Cherry-picked intelligence on Iraq WMD efforts was offered to Congress by administration spokespersons, while dissenting analysis from the State Department and others in the IC was systematically quashed by Vice President Cheney and his staff. As with the Gulf of Tonkin resolution in 1964—which President Johnson used as an authorization for subsequent years of military operations in Vietnam—the key Iraq vote occurred not on a declaration of war, but rather on a conditional authorization for the commander in chief to take "all necessary measures" in the event diplomacy failed to induce Saddam Hussein's compliance with UN resolutions. Few congressional hearings were held. Those who questioned rosy scenarios regarding the costs of occupation were subject to rebuke. Potential critics within Congress muted their concerns in an excess of political caution. Key votes were held in the weeks immediately preceding congressional elections, when skeptics feared being portrayed as soft on terrorism and proponents of military action encouraged members to run for reelection on the basis of support for the war.

The timidity of Congress during the run-up to both the Vietnam and Iraq Wars was by no means unique. In practice, Congress rarely rejects presidential foreign policy initiatives outright, preferring to condition Hill approval before enacting enabling legislation. Even the prolonged fight over ratification of the Panama Canal treaties occurred over amendments, rather than on an up-or-down vote authorizing ratification of the treaties by President Carter.

When Congress does use its powers to take initiatives on national security issues, it is often to promote purchase of a military system. For example, the committees on armed services have traditionally been populated by legislators pressing home state interests in the production of one type of aircraft, naval vessel, or army weapon. Efforts to secure local jobs usually impact procurement debates, as with the 2009 congressional resistance to Pentagon efforts to terminate the F-22 production line, which yielded the first veto threat of the Obama presidency. Yet political interests are also manifest in executive branch defense budget decisions, especially in election years. Such phenomena have made it difficult for any administration—whether liberal or conservative, Democratic or Republican—to cut overall defense spending or cancel any weapons systems.

It was a war hero, Republican Dwight Eisenhower, who warned in the closing days of his presidency against the military-industrial complex of defense manufacturers and their champions in both the Pentagon and the Congress. Nearly half a century later, as defense analyst Richard Betts notes, "Washington now spends almost as much on military power as the rest of the world combined, and five times more than that of all of its potential enemies together."[29] The sheer size of U.S. defense and international spending—nearly $650 billion in 2008, not including nearly another $80 billion budgeted that year for homeland security and selected intelligence functions—guarantees that disputes in Congress over spending priorities will be advanced by parochial considerations and industry lobbyists. Ironically, while successful congressional challenges to major spending items are rare, controversy arises regularly over relatively miniscule amounts of funding that legislators attempt to commit or "earmark" for favored local initiatives, sometimes directives as small as $100,000 in a $500 billion measure. These are projects not requested in the president's budget, but instead funded by the appropriations committees at the urging of individual members, who insist on their constitutional prerogative to initiate appropriations.[30]

The confirmation process for presidential appointments, the ratification of treaties, and intelligence community (IC) oversight also afford Congress opportunities to curb national security options. When Congress does expressly prohibit the president from continuing an unpopular policy, as for example with the 1984 Boland amendment barring aid to the Nicaraguan contras, an aggressive executive branch can try to execute an end run. The conclusions of the congressional panel that investigated the ensuing scandal, however, offer an instructive caution. Congressional hearings on the Iran-Contra funding plan revealed an elaborate scheme developed by President Reagan's National Security Council (NSC) to, in effect, privatize certain foreign policy functions. The NSC program was designed to evade an explicit ban on U.S. support for the contras. This White House effort succeeded by pressuring other governments friendly to the U.S. to fund the Nicaraguan rebels, in part through proceeds of secret sales to Iran of surplus U.S.-origin military equipment. The ensuing congressional report was blistering. A bipartisan majority denounced those within the Reagan-Bush administration who advanced the scheme of a "cabal of zealots" who had broken "the letter and the spirit of the Boland amendment" with "pervasive dishonesty and inordinate secrecy," and thereby "undermined a cardinal principle of the Constitution . . . (the) most significant check on Executive power: the president can spend funds on a program only if he can convince Congress to appropriate the money."[31]

An equally strident minority report, signed by just eight of the twenty-six members of the Iran-Contra investigating committee, was drafted by staff to then Representative

Dick Cheney. Its broad defense of the contra assistance scheme became the oft-cited source for advocates for stronger executive branch powers. The Cheney-led minority concluded that the Congress had usurped presidential powers by passing a statute that interfered with "core presidential foreign policy functions." The view articulated here was that the president possesses inherent powers under the Constitution that Congress cannot challenge. This position was echoed a generation later when the Bush-Cheney administration was challenged by Congress over such programs as the 2005 warrantless wiretapping of American citizens.[32]

A more successful presidential effort to evade explicit prohibitions voted by Congress was the determined maneuver by President Franklin Roosevelt after the 1939 Battle of Britain. When isolationists in Congress continued to block White House efforts to aid Hitler's opponents, Roosevelt developed new means to circumvent them. Where consensus is possible, a wise president makes sustained efforts to include Congress via consultation before policy launches, both for political cover and international deterrence, including Congress, as Senator Arthur Vandenberg famously counseled in 1947, on both the "take-offs" as well as "the crash landings."[33]

JURISDICTIONAL BATTLES IMPACT THE POLICYMAKING PROCESS

Overlapping committee jurisdiction gives members more than one forum from which to challenge presidential power. This proliferation of legislative authority has greatly complicated recent national security policy disputes. Jurisdiction in Congress sometimes seems limitless. Foreign policy is by no means the exclusive domain of the international affairs committees. The relatively obscure House Committee on Government Reform, which has very little power to advance legislation, was used as a forum for critics of Iraq policy. The Senate Judiciary Committee did the same with counterterrorism policy through its hearings on the conduct of interrogations and domestic eavesdropping authorized by the Bush administration. The House Agriculture Committee took the lead in the 2010 efforts to lift curbs on U.S. travel to and on some trade with Cuba.

Co-optation sometimes limits congressional initiative. For example, on the Armed Services and Intelligence Committees, some members appear reflexive in their support for Pentagon or intelligence-gathering programs. One strong Bush administration backer and leading McCain presidential campaign ally, Senator Lindsey Graham (R-SC), described the problem as follows: "The Congress was intimidated after 9/11. People were afraid to get in the way of a strong executive who was talking about suppressing a vicious enemy, and we were AWOL for awhile . . . we should have been more aggressive after 9/11 in working with the executive to find collaboration . . . the fact that we weren't probably hurt the country."[34] Conversely, overreaction to international concerns by legislators can produce ill-conceived proposals with negative consequences. Congress is subject to popular passions and many members have limited international experience. Some greet crisis with demagoguery. Examples abound, from the notorious Smoot-Hawley tariffs that exacerbated the depression in the 1930s to contemporary China-bashing. In recent years, Congress has acted to block foreign ownership of port management contracts and to assail purchases of needed military hardware from foreign-owned producers, policies that appease domestic constituencies but do not necessarily advance U.S. national security interests.

Those who challenge executive primacy in a policy arena must frequently create new avenues for pressing policy-related issues. For example, efforts to curb promiscuous U.S. nuclear export policies in the 1970s were blocked until a bold move was made to eviscerate, then abolish, the powerful, industry-dominated Joint Committee on Atomic Energy (JCAE).[35] This was also true of House efforts to curb Vietnam War funding. Antiwar forces did not succeed until they bypassed defense appropriators, who supported more military spending in Vietnam until the bitter end.

Efforts to reduce jurisdictional conflicts often result in concentrations of power, while increasing the danger of "client-itis." For example, while reform efforts in the 1970s killed the JCAE, the only combined House-Senate committee with exclusive legislative jurisdiction, post-9/11 efforts to improve intelligence oversight led, ironically, to calls for establishment of an exclusive Joint Committee on Intelligence. The 9/11 Commission and scholars at the Congressional Research Service pressed for consolidating congressional jurisdiction on intelligence. Their solution: create a single committee to oversee authorization and appropriation of funds for all of the intelligence community.[36] Such concentrations of power have not produced beneficial results in the past (see table 11.2).

National security policymakers seeking congressional support today face numerous committees with jurisdiction, including defense appropriations, intelligence, and homeland security. Gone are the days when emissaries from the executive branch, or private sector lobbyists, could visit only a handful of powerful legislators in Congress to secure decisive support. The president's military, trade, intelligence, and international financial initiatives all face multiple points of contact and review in Congress. The bicameral legislature also requires executive branch officials to face the legislative gauntlet thrice: from the House, to the Senate, and then to conference committee.

Congressional relations officials at executive branch agencies often constitute an institutional barrier to better understanding of their work by those who oversee their agency budget in Congress. Most cabinet departments limit communications with Congress to those conducted through approved channels. Informal networks are deemed highly suspect by assistant secretaries who control department contacts with legislators' staff. This effort to control information flow may encourage end runs, leaks, and furtive communications. Overt collaboration and the routine sharing of perspectives might better serve the national interest.

There are frequent efforts to subvert these jurisdictional divisions. In recent years, there has been an inexorable growth in the power concentrated in the hands of so-called cardinals who chair the appropriations subcommittees, where specific dollar amounts are approved for every federal program. Authorizing committees such as foreign relations and armed services—which are responsible for establishing policy parameters and reviewing implementation of U.S. diplomatic and military initiatives—have been eclipsed. Their power has waned as fewer national security policy bills have been signed into law and more policy language has found its way into riders accompanying massive catchall appropriations measures.

Partisan gridlock has made the passage of comprehensive policy authorization bills exceedingly rare. Must-pass bills, including omnibus appropriations funding the entire federal budget, have become the vehicle of choice for unrelated foreign and defense policy matters. Extraneous issues—for example, in early 2009, proposed liberalization of policies

Table 11.2   Illustrative Chart of Recent Congressional Committee Jurisdiction

Issue	House and Senate Committees
Defense Spending	Defense Appropriations Subcommittees
Defense Programs/Policy	Armed Services
Foreign Aid Spending	Foreign Operations Subcommittees
Foreign Programs/Policy	Foreign Relations/International Affairs
Trade	Ways and Means (House)/Finance (Senate)
Intelligence	Select Committees on Intelligence
International Finance	Banking, Ways & Means, Finance
Agricultural Assistance	Agriculture, Appropriations Subcommittees
Homeland Security	Government Operations
Global Climate Change	Environment, Energy, Finance, etc.

on family travel to Cuba—have delayed passage of massive government funding measures on deadline. Such maneuvers further weaken the defense and foreign policy committees and add to the workload of already overburdened appropriations committee members.

SELECTED CASE STUDIES IN THE EXECUTIVE-LEGISLATIVE BRANCH STRUGGLE

From the scores of recent challenges to executive branch primacy in international policymaking, several are most often noted for the lessons protagonists take away from the battle. Each is a worthy topic of further study. They are charted in table 11.3 briefly, with the caveat that any selective summary is subjective.

A common feature is evident in most of the cases shown in table 11.3: while Congress debates the proper means of advancing U.S. policy, legislators amend but rarely terminate White House foreign policy initiatives. Even when Congress is most adamant, delay is often the best option available to legislators, as with the 2008 debate over ratification of free-trade agreements with Colombia and South Korea.

From these interbranch challenges there are derived a number of myths that persist. For example, some revisionist historians maintain that the United States would have won the Vietnam War if only Congress had not precipitously cut off funding. They argue that civilian politicians "would not let the uniformed services win" in Vietnam. Such assertions are highly dubious, given the actual timeline of the congressional funding ban, which occurred in 1975, years after most American combat troops had already been withdrawn under the Nixon administration's Vietnamization program.

Similarly, many progressives in Congress place exclusive blame on President George W. Bush for disappointments that followed the U.S. occupation of Iraq. Yet the Bush administration had majority support in Congress to proceed—including the votes, initially, of many Democratic presidential candidates, Senators Joe Biden, John Edwards, and Hillary Clinton among them. Congressional majorities continued to approve funding for the Iraq occupation for years. Indeed, the Obama-Biden administration found it necessary

Table 11.3   Key Cases in Struggle for Policymaking Primacy

Issue	Principal Congressional Action
Turkish Arms Embargo (1974)	Legislators blocked military cooperation with one key NATO ally to promote solidarity with another (Greece).
Arms Export Control Act (1974)	Congress amended AECA, legislating new requirements for pre-notification of major arms sales; specific means were provided for legislators to block execution of such agreements.
Panama Canal Treaties (1978)	Regional interests oblige U.S. government resistance to nationalist appeals.
Nuclear Nonproliferation Act (1978)	In response to Indian nuclear explosion, Congress conditioned nuclear power exports on acceptance of international inspection of all recipients' nuclear facilities.
Aid to El Salvador (1980s)	Critics of aid to the Salvadoran government legislated requirements for human rights and land reform as a condition of U.S. aid.
NAFTA (1993)	After insisting on inclusion of modest labor and environmental standards, legislators approved trade accords intended to promote regional stability, curb immigration pressures, and reduce consumer costs.
Iraq War Funding (2002–present)	Congress funded an increasingly unpopular military engagement both through annual Pentagon appropriations and through "emergency" supplemental funding measures—absent a declaration of war.
India Nuclear Trade Agreement (2006)	Bilateral ties can trump long-standing U.S. (nuclear nonproliferation) goals.
Armenian Genocide Resolution (2007–present)	House committee reported a commemorative resolution deploring the WWI-era genocide. Party leadership first pledged full House action, then retreated under pressures from White House and embassy of Turkey lobbying.
U.S.–Colombia Free Trade (2008–present)	Congress provided broad authority for White House to conduct "fast track" negotiation for trade accords; Colombia agreement was deemed valuable for anti-narcotics, pro-democracy efforts in region. Then, congressional leaders balked at approval, arguing assurances on labor standards and civil liberties were insufficient.

to maintain a costly military presence in Iraq while actually *expanding* U.S. military commitments in Afghanistan and Pakistan. These decisions bitterly disappointed antiwar voters on the left.

Recent cases such as the ones shown in table 11.3 serve to underscore the fact that tension between branches as they shape national security policy is intentional. It grows from the framers' design and evolves based on the temper of the times and the initiative of competing policymakers.

CONCLUSION: MANAGING INTERBRANCH COMPETITION IS ESSENTIAL TO SUCCESS

The conventional wisdom in much contemporary analysis holds that Congress is a meddlesome nuisance when it comes to national security policymaking. Foreign diplomats especially find legislators' roles vexing and harmful to consistent U.S. leadership. Similarly, U.S. war colleges and schools of foreign service often deplore the partisanship fueled by Congress; scholars lament how congressional engagement in the national security policy enterprise infinitely complicates matters.[37]

Congress makes unitary action difficult; this reality is undeniable. Congressional investigations prompt embarrassing revelations. Indiscreet legislators can undermine ongoing U.S. diplomatic efforts by striking discordant notes on visits overseas. At their worst, the two chambers put their most infuriating characteristics on display: the House, hyperpartisan, and the Senate, dysfunctional and beset by dilatory minority tactics. Legislative actions, and inaction, can make the United States a less reliable partner. Congress necessarily defines "national security" much more broadly than line officers or cabinet officials, who are responsible for a limited field of operations. For example, when then Democratic presidential nominee Barack Obama met with General David Petraeus in Iraq in July 2008, Petraeus pleaded for "maximum flexibility" in basing troops. Noting the costs of the occupation on a U.S. budget stretched thin, then candidate Obama conceded "if I were in your shoes, I would be making the exact same argument. Your job is to succeed in Iraq . . . my job as a potential Commander-in-Chief is to view your counsel and interests through the prism of our overall national security."[38]

Where you stand in the enduring debate over the appropriate role of Congress in the national security enterprise often depends on where you—or your champions—sit. Changing perspectives can often temper the rhetoric of critics, once they are forced to make hard choices. For example, as a junior legislator in 1849, Representative Abraham Lincoln decried the exercise of raw presidential power by James Polk in prosecuting war against Mexico. Little more than a decade later, it was President Lincoln who resorted to extra-Constitutional means, including suspension of *habeas corpus*, to defend the United States against Confederate secessionists.

Democracy is disorderly. Oversight and investigation of sensitive security policies can be unpleasant. Yet, like preventive medicine, their application can avert more grave dangers. If a policy initiative cannot weather public scrutiny by popularly elected legislators, it is unlikely the policy can be maintained. Secretary of State Colin Powell frequently noted that without public explanation and continued voter support, no U.S. military engagement can succeed over the long term.

Effective congressional engagement in national security initiatives, as well as vigorous legislative oversight of policy implementation, has the effect of inoculation. Transparency in many policymaking elements helps strengthen the resulting consensus. Five hundred and thirty-five would-be secretaries of state may include in their ranks more than a few amateurs, political hacks, and demagogues. Taken together, however, members of Congress are remarkably representative of how power is distributed in America. Certainly the elected members are far more representative than the thousands of unelected career bureaucrats and selected political appointees who populate the vast executive branch bureaucracy.

Senators and representatives mirror the hopes, fears, and passions of the electorate to an extraordinary degree. Once briefed and enlisted in support, members of Congress can play a crucial role in the public education essential to sustain any successful policy initiative. When power sharing works, U.S. national security policies are stronger. At its best, the policymaking process forges consensus while overcoming vulnerabilities. When this process fails, there are protracted partisan divisions and a legacy of unsupportable international commitments. Given these choices, efforts to provide interbranch cooperation are clearly an essential element of success in the national security enterprise. Congressional engagement, on an ongoing basis, is the *sine qua non* of sustainable international initiative in a democracy.

NOTES

1. Joseph J. Ellis, *American Creation: Triumphs and Tragedies at the Founding of the Republic* (New York: Knopf, 2007), 225. As Professor Ellis notes, even lifelong champions of limited federal and executive powers, such as Thomas Jefferson, can be opportunistic. To realize the opportunity of the Louisiana Purchase, Jefferson acted swiftly. His assertion of federal authority was, he privately conceded, "an act beyond the Constitution."

2. As quoted in Cecil V. Crabb and Pat M. Holt, *Invitation to Struggle: Congress, the President and Foreign Policy* (Washington, DC: Congressional Quarterly, 1984).

3. Andrew Jackson is considered to be the first to claim that the president was essentially the embodiment of the popular will, and thus asserted strong presidential authorities. See Ellis, *American Creation*.

4. Note, for example, how as senior executive branch staffers in the George W. Bush administration, UN Ambassador John Bolton and Justice Department counsel John Yoo, promoted executive branch primacy and the notion of "inherent" presidential powers. Both appeared to reverse position after November 2008 with their sudden championship of a strong congressional role. John R. Bolton and John Yoo, "Restore the Senate's Treaty Power," *New York Times*, January 4, 2009.

5. Proponents found justification for a dominant presidential role in international security matters in their analysis of *Federalist #70*; yet a careful reading makes clear that the "unitary" voice for the executive of which Hamilton writes here is explicitly limited to the conduct of wartime military operations. In the wake of the weak Articles of Confederation, Hamilton was calling for a unitary executive as opposed to a collective, committee-driven executive. Hamilton, champion of a strong president, insists in *Federalist #69* that, even in wartime, presidential powers are limited by congressional prerogatives. See discussion in Charlie Savage, *Takeover: The Return of the Imperial Presidency and the Subversion of American Democracy* (New York: Little, Brown, 2007), 125–27.

6. Veteran national security advisors to both Democrats and Republicans often agree that the permanent executive branch bureaucracy must be challenged. Nixon/Kissinger advisor Peter Rodman lauded his principals for outfoxing their own bureaucratic colleagues with secret diplomacy. McGeorge Bundy made similar warnings in a draft chapter about Vietnam lessons learned titled "Never Trust the Bureaucracy to Get It Right." See Peter W. Rodman, *Presidential Command: Power, Leadership, and the Making of Foreign Policy from Richard Nixon to George W. Bush* (New York: Knopf, 2009) and Gordon M. Goldstein, Benjamin Rochkin, and Benjamin Levine, *Lessons in Disaster: McGeorge Bundy and the Path to War in Vietnam* (New York: Holt, 2008).

7. Crabb and Holt, *Invitation to Struggle*.

8. Norman J. Ornstein and Thomas E. Mann, "When Congress Checks Out," *Foreign Affairs*, 85, no. 6 (November/December 2006): 67–82.

9. Ornstein and Mann, "When Congress Checks Out."

10. David E. Sanger, "A Handpicked Team for a Sweeping Shift in Foreign Policy," *New York Times*, December 1, 2008. Defense Secretary Gates noted that the United States had more members of military marching bands than foreign service officers.

11. Doris Kearns Goodwin, *Lyndon Johnson and the American Dream* (New York: Harper, 1976), 291.

12. After Stanley J. Heginbotham, "Dateline Washington: The Rules of the Game," *Foreign Policy* 53 (Winter 1983–84): 157. See also Gerald Felix Warburg, *Conflict and Consensus: The Struggle between Congress and the President over Foreign Policymaking* (New York: Harper, 1989), chapter 4.

13. See Abraham F. Lowenthal, "Ronald Reagan and Latin America: Coping with Hegemony in Decline," in *Eagle Defiant: United States Foreign Policy in the 1980s*, ed. Robert J. Lieber (Boston: Little, Brown, 1983). See also Crabb and Holt, *Invitation to Struggle*, 84. Note that there were actually two treaties involved in the Panama debate. While the Senate approves treaty ratification by a two-thirds vote on an authorizing resolution, technically it is the president who executes instruments of ratification.

14. See Rodman, *Presidential Command*. A vigorous proponent of presidential powers, Rodman overreaches in his startling revisionist notion that perhaps the "demise of Nixon was due to no less than the revolt of the bureaucracy whose power he had striven so assiduously to break in every sphere."

15. Helene Cooper and Scott L. Malcomson, "Welcome to My World, Barack," *New York Times Magazine*, November 16, 2008.

16. Congressional opponents of trade agreements, such as that President Bush negotiated with Colombia in 2008, also sought to withhold approval until foreign trading partners enacted reforms to their labor and environmental protection laws. See, for example, Reps. Linda T. Sanchez and Phil Hare, "U.S. Cannot Afford Free Trade Agreement," *Politico*, November 19, 2008.

17. See Gerald Felix Warburg, "Nonproliferation Policy Crossroads: The Strange Case of U.S.-India Nuclear Cooperation," Presentation for Stanford University Center for International Security and Cooperation, 2010.

18. Total congressional staff grew from some 10,700 in 1970 to 18,400 in 1980, to more than 23,000 today. See Crabb and Holt, *Invitation to Struggle*, 220.

19. President Clinton ignored the explicit provisos of the war powers resolution holding that appropriation of funds for military engagement in conflicts like Kosovo was not sufficient to authorize war. Note that in advancing such theories, the Clinton administration was on the same trajectory as his immediate predecessor and successor in asserting strong executive branch prerogatives versus those of Congress. See Savage, *Takeover*, 66–74.

20. See Graham T. Allison, *Essence of Decision: Explaining the Cuban Missile Crisis* (Boston: Little, Brown, 1971). Allison captures a strong-willed executive who ably resists pressures for a military strike. The deliberations bought time for an unexpected diplomatic opening few of the politicians or national security bureaucrats could discern. Nimble presidential maneuvers succeeded despite congressional pressures, on the eve of midterm elections, and on the brink of military strikes against nuclear-armed powers.

21. Schlesinger pays tribute to his father as an originator of this insightful theory of cyclical intellectual history. See Arthur Schlesinger Jr., *The Cycles of American History* (Boston: Houghton Mifflin, 1986).

22. Maureen Dowd, "Daffy Does Doom," *New York Times*, January 27, 2007.

23. Jonathan Mahler, "After the Imperial Presidency," *New York Times Magazine*, November 9, 2008.

24. Ornstein and Mann, "When Congress Checks Out."

25. Mahler, "After the Imperial Presidency," 45.

26. For contemporary reviews of the outset of the post-Watergate cycle of this ongoing battle, see, for example, Daniel Yankelovich, "Farewell to 'President Knows Best,'" *Foreign Affairs* 57, no. 3 (1978) or Douglas J. Bennett, Jr., "Congress in Foreign Policy: Who Needs It?" *Foreign Affairs* 57, no. 1 (1978).

27. Savage, *Takeover*, 41. The court ruling struck down scores of legislative veto provisos Congress had attached to statutes, especially from the prior decade.

28. Rep. Henry Waxman (D-CA) quoted in editorial, "Oversight Test for Dems," *The Hill*, November 24, 2008.

29. Richard K. Betts, "A Disciplined Defense: How to Regain Strategic Solvency," *Foreign Affairs* 86, no. 6 (November/December 2007). Even one of the most left-leaning think tanks, the Institute for Policy Studies, in its most radical proposals called for but a ten percent reduction in defense spending for FY 2008, a measure, Betts argues, of the enduring bipartisan support for robust defense spending.

30. Defenders of the congressional practice note that some earmarks are later hailed for their public policy benefits and are subsequently embraced by the executive branch. Two recent examples include congressional initiatives to fund development of unpiloted Predator drones capable of launching targeted missile strikes, as well as the legislative push to create a bipartisan Iraq Study Group to suggest a compromise policy strategy.

31. Savage, *Takeover*, 55.

32. See *Report of the Congressional Committees Investigating the Iran-Contra Affair*, November 1987, House Report 100–433.

33. See Crabb and Holt, *Invitation to Struggle*, 69.

34. Quoted in Mahler, "After the Imperial Presidency."

35. See Edward Cowan, "Joint Atomic Panel Stripped of Power," *New York Times*, January 5, 1977.

36. See Frederick M. Kaiser, "Congressional Oversight of Intelligence: Current Structure and Alternatives," Report RL32525 (Washington, DC: Congressional Research Service, September 16, 2008).

37. See, for example, James Q. Wilson, *Bureaucracy: What Government Agencies Do and Why They Do It* (New York: Basic Books, 1989), or Amy B. Zegart, *Flawed by Design: The Evolution of the CIA, JCS, and NSC* (Stanford, CA: University Press, 1999).

38. As quoted by Joe Klein, "Why Barack Obama Is Winning," *Time*, October 22, 2008.

Chapter 12 The United States Supreme Court: The Cult of the Robe in the National Security Enterprise

HARVEY RISHIKOF

> There is hardly a political question in the United States that does not sooner or later turn into a judicial one.
>
> *Alexis de Tocqueville*

> The absolute worst violation of the judge's oath is to decide a case based on a partisan political or philosophical basis rather than what the law requires.
>
> *Associate Justice Antonin Scalia*

> Some constitutional development comes about because judges evaluate significant facts differently from the way their predecessors viewed similar facts. The later judges discover some relevance to a constitutional rule where earlier judges saw none. Or they find an importance in some fact that once was thought trivial. In all sorts of ways the later judges see things that earlier judges did not see. Or they deal with facts that were not faced in earlier adjudication.
>
> *Associate Justice David Souter*

INTRODUCTION

It is now virtually impossible to discuss the national security enterprise (NSE) without discussing the role of the U.S. Supreme Court and the federal courts. Historically the federal courts had shown deference to executive power and Congress in the carrying out of foreign policy, national security, and war. Over the last few years, however, federal courts have increasingly injected themselves into issues concerning detention of prisoners, interrogations, state secret protections, domestic surveillance, and the applicability of the Geneva Conventions. These legal incursions have not been without controversy and have often revealed deep jurisprudential divisions among the sitting justices. Regardless of one's view on these issues, what has become clear is that the federal judiciary is helping to shape the policy environment of the NSE.

The constitutional framework, though, invites legal interpretations as a matter of text.[1] Articles I and II assign overlapping functions; many clauses are general, as in the case of presidential authority; and the language fails to prescribe or allocate power in the area of national security such as exactly when the writ of habeas corpus and may be suspended.[2] Because of these overlapping and shared authorities and the formulation of the foreign policy powers of both the president and Congress, a leading constitutional scholar noted the Constitution is "an invitation to struggle for the privilege of directing American foreign policy."[3] The modern national security arena has proven to be another invitation for struggle but this time including the federal courts as an active participant.

From the Supreme Court perspective, the two major precedents that previously established the power of the president and the Congress in the NSE are *Curtiss-Wright* and the *Steel Seizure* cases. In *Curtiss-Wright* the Supreme Court announced that in foreign policy the president was "the plenary and exclusive power" and "the sole organ of the federal government in the field of international relations."[4] The *Steel Seizure* case is famous for the concurring opinion of Associate Justice Robert H. Jackson that established the continuum of the three categories of presidential authority: (1) when the president acts pursuant to expressed or implied authorizations of Congress, his authority is at its *maximum*; (2) when the president acts in absence of either a congressional grant or a denial of authority, he relies only on independent powers but is in a *zone of twilight* in which he and Congress may have concurrent authority, or which the distribution of authority is uncertain; and finally (3) when the president takes actions incompatible with the expressed or implied will of the Congress, his power is at the *lowest ebb*, and he can rely only on his own constitutional powers.

In the recent war on terrorism, the Bush administration first asserted "sole organ" *Curtiss-Wright* authority in its view on legal interpretations of the Geneva Conventions and the law of armed conflict. When the Supreme Court rejected this view, the president then reasoned that according to the *Steel Seizure* doctrine, he enjoyed maximum power after the Congress passed the Military Commission Act. Again the Court rejected this view under its interpretation of habeas corpus and allowed for the detainees to have access to the federal system. The extent of the power of the Court on habeas corpus remains unclear and will be determined by further litigation.

What explains this culture of judicial independence? This was not the role envisioned by the founding fathers. To appreciate this phenomenon of judicial independence, the chapter will trace the creation of the culture of independence that marks the U.S. judiciary—its origins, budget, support organizations, rule making, remuneration, theories of representation, discipline/removal, and transparency. While to some these may seem to be merely bureaucratic or administrative issues, each critically reinforces an attitude of ideological independence. Part of the explanation of the ideological and constitutional independence of the federal judges rests on this unique historical organizational bureaucracy. To understand judicial independence, one must first appreciate the federal judicial bureaucratic culture. This analysis of the court culture will be followed by discussion of how a majority of the Supreme Court assessed their role in the NSE and required President Bush and the Congress to moderate their assertions and interpretations of the law in the war on terrorism by finding the right of habeas corpus in the detention process.

A GENERAL CULTURAL ANALYSIS

To understand the culture of the Supreme Court and the federal judiciary, one needs to appreciate the evolution and mix of constitutional vagueness, political power, and the internal administrative rules and traditions governing independence and autonomy. Skirmishes over budgets, support organizations, and the process of rule making have produced legal precedents that make the judiciary unique in its prestige and influence. An old joke about the popularity of the American judiciary abroad is that, despite the criticism of U.S. foreign policy, the three most popular U.S. exports remain Coca-Cola, jeans, and U.S.

judges. Many foreign judges under civil code systems continue to envy the power, salaries, and status of our federal judges.

The Inner Workings of the Court

The culture that the Supreme Court presents to the world is analytical—based on the written word—independent, apolitical, and detached. The method of interpreting the law is a case-by-case approach through the use of logical syllogisms both broad and narrow. Court debates and communications are formal and via memo. Each justice and his or her chambers approach a case independently. Cases are placed on the calendar when four justices vote to hear the case. The term runs from the first Monday in October to the last day in June.

A justice's chambers are composed of two secretaries, a court aide, and four law clerks, though the Chief Justice (CJ) is allowed five. The permanent staffs are lean, fiercely loyal, competent, and long serving. These public servants are loath to write kiss-and-tell memoirs. Though occasionally books such as *The Brethren, Closed Chambers,* or *The Nine* have been written to pierce the black veil, these are the exceptions and not the rule.[5]

To most observers the inner workings of the Court in the magnificent building built by Cass Gilbert in 1928 have remained opaque. As Walter Bagehot once noted in describing the British Crown, "a little mystery is a good thing." But in another sense the Court is transparent; its decisions are published for all to read and comment on.

The law clerks, considered the best and the brightest, have already clerked for a district or appellate court. They typically serve at the Supreme Court for only one term, after which many go on to significant government employment with the Department of Justice (DOJ) or the Congress, teach, or more recently, join the most prestigious law firms in the nation.[6] The clerks from each justice's chambers form a judicial family that usually meets annually or biannually; the justices remain tied by keeping up with the marriages and births of their extended families. The former-clerk culture is one of the key bases that have protected the independence of the judiciary. These clerks understand and promote the importance of an independent judiciary and can be counted on to support the institution whenever the concept of judicial independence is attacked.

The monastic-like imposed detachment of each justice is punctuated periodically by oral argument on a joined issue for usually one hour. The justices hold no press conferences, there are no lobbyists hanging around the chambers. Postargument the nine justices meet together to discuss the cases. Court protocol dictates that the CJ begins the discussion and, by tradition, the justices then discuss the case in turn by seniority. At the conclusion of the discussion, if the CJ is in the majority he chooses who shall be assigned to write the opinion. If the CJ is not in the majority, the most senior justice in the majority has the right to assign the opinion. In the most recent history, the Court has decided approximately eighty to ninety cases per term.

The opinions must be issued in the term in which the case was argued. If the opinion cannot be issued due to lack of a majority, then the case will be slated for reargument for the next term. Rarely, the Court will determine that the decision to hear a case was improvidently granted and dismiss the case. In such circumstances the decision of the lower court will stand. In this culture there are no ties; someone must win and someone must lose.

There is a way to duck the case per constitutional design, namely, when the court accepts the case but declines to decide it on the grounds that the issues present a political question. These cases have been brought at times to enjoin the president's military orders, or to contest war taxing and spending, asserting the unconstitutionality of a particular military action, such as the Vietnam War. Explaining the political question doctrine, Associate Justice William J. Brennan in *Baker v. Carr* advised against the court resolving cases that present "a textually demonstrable constitutional commitment of the issue to a coordinate political department; or a lack of judicially discoverable and manageable standards for resolving" the issue.[7] The jurisprudential debate among the justices focuses on which cases fall into this category.

Historic Origins

The place of the Court in our constitutional design begins with the U.S. Constitution. As is well documented, the U.S. Constitution does not specify the size of the Supreme Court. The only justice mentioned is the CJ, and the position is mentioned in the context of impeachment proceedings in Article I. Article III of the Constitution gives Congress the power to fix the number of justices. Over the years the number has fluctuated. The first Judiciary Act of 1789 set the number at six justices. The Court was expanded to seven members in 1807, nine in 1837, and ten in 1863. Then the Judicial Circuits Act of 1866 set the number at seven to be reached by retirement and the eventual removal of seats. As a result, one seat was removed in 1866 and a second in 1867. Before the goal of seven was reached, however, the Judiciary Act of 1869 was passed and the number of justices was set at nine, where it has remained until this day. Under Article III, the justices are the only actors that have life tenure and constitutionally protected salaries.

Although Article II contemplates removal by impeachment, no Supreme Court justice has ever been successfully impeached, though it was tried with Samuel Chase in 1804–5. This failure helped establish the principle that justices would not be removed for unpopular views or opinions. To understand this independence of mind, earlier in 1803 the paradigm-setting case of *Marbury v. Madison* established the Court's authority to rule a law passed by Congress unconstitutional, declaring "[It] is empathically the province and duty of the judicial department to say what the law is." President Franklin Roosevelt's failure to pack the Supreme Court in the late 1930s cemented the concept of an independent court.[8] These three historic events—*Marbury*, the failed impeachment, and the discredited court packing—enshrined American commitment to an independent judiciary as a counter-majoritarian institution to pure democratic or political rule.[9]

As reflected by these three events, any discussion of the American judicial culture requires a deep appreciation of American political and legal history. Many of the cherished values and rights now enjoyed by the citizens of the United States were borne of intellectual and political struggles. The results of these debates became enshrined as part of our constitutional framework and have been passed down from generation to generation. This is not to say, however, that once an issue has been settled in the constitutional sense, it is no longer open to debate. In fact, the opposite may be more the order of the day, whereby a dissent of yesteryear resurrects itself to forge a majority for the next generation. The best example of this phenomenon are the early dissents by Associate Justices Oliver Wendell Holmes Jr. and Louis D. Brandeis in the 1920s, concerning the right of privacy, which eventually became the law of the land forty years later under Chief Justice Earl Warren.[10]

Running the Courts

In the arena of judicial administration, similarly there have been decisions that have structured our legal system in a specific manner. In a sense *all* legal systems must confront general bureaucratic questions and ultimately resolve them. But the answers are not fabricated in a vacuum and must reflect cultural experience. Nevertheless, all judicial systems must resolve questions of judicial independence, budgetary allocation, selection of the judiciary, and the administration of justice. The resolution of these functions will create a structure that posseses its own interlinking logic. For comparative purposes such a framework of analysis allows for a discussion of terms, but the answers will be informed by the cultural legacy of each country.

For the purposes of the general historic cultural discussion, the analysis will begin by looking at two essential functions that all systems must address: budget formulation and support organizations in civil society.[11] Budgets matter because courts can be neutralized by financial cuts; support organizations also are essential so that an independent judiciary can weather unpopular decisions. Often critical choices must be made to create an independent administrative judiciary: the size of the judiciary, the method for legal rule making, compensation for judges, theories of judicial representation, discipline and removal, ethical codes, and transparency when dealing with the media. This is not meant to be an exhaustive list but rather an analytical rendering of the choices that have helped shape the American judicial culture of independence.

Budget Submission

How a judiciary submits its budget for appropriations is a critical administrative decision. Prior to the 1930s, the federal judicial budget, similar to many civil code jurisdictions, was submitted as part of the budget of the DOJ. In his biography, the Chief Judge of the Second Circuit in New York City, Judge Learned Hand, expresses his sense of humiliation and dependence of the judiciary as he made requests for basic necessities. In fact he becomes so dissatisfied with the thought of an administrative clique and judges involved in administrative matters that, when a central organization was created in Washington and inquiries were made as to what the Second Circuit position was to be, he replied, "We have no organization, no offices and no standing committees."[12]

On a political level the effect is more subtle. Representatives of the judiciary do not deal directly with the legislative branch but mediate the relationship through an executive agency, a department, or a ministry of justice. This allows the executive agency to comment on the submission and place the submission within the context of its own priorities, which may or may not be the priorities of the judiciary. The potential for mischief and petty penalization is great in such a system.

Although insulating the judiciary from the legislative process does have some benefits, there are potential costs if the executive branch then substitutes its own judgments for the judiciary's. In the 1930s the judiciary won the right to submit its budget to the appropriations committee with the executive playing only a minimal administrative role of including it in its general submission. However, could it be challenged? Under the Clinton administration, for example, the Office of Management and Budget (OMB), the executive agency charged with formulating the national budget, attempted to comment and reduce some judicial categories. This continued for some months until the president himself intervened to end the ill-conceived attempt of bureaucratic back-dooring and ordered the OMB to submit the judicial budget without comment.

Support Organizations: Internal and External

This complex machine of judicial administration could not work without the support of a number of critical internal support organizations all controlled by the judiciary. The Administrative Office of the United States (AO), the Federal Judicial Center (FJC), and the Office of the Chief Justice of the United States are composed of approximately 27,000 employees in both Washington and the thirteen circuits who handle the day-to-day administrative and clerical tasks.[13] What makes this administrative system distinctive is that ultimately all are reporting to and responsible to judges at all levels. At the end of the day, the Judicial Conference, a body composed only of federal judges, has the final word.

As a matter of constitutional law the Judicial Conference has no authority over the administration of the Supreme Court of the United States.[14] The Court and its nine members are governed by their own rules, regulations, and traditions, and the CJ is understood to be first among equals. As a matter of policy, most significant questions are decided by the Court in the weekly conference meetings. The Court's own budget of approximately $30 million is formulated by the Office of the Chief Justice and is presented separately by two justices selected by the CJ, to the appropriations committees of Congress. This presentation occurs before the chair of the Judicial Conference budget committee presents the total federal judicial budget.[15]

This process of independent submission and judge-controlled budget has now become an accepted part of the constitutional framework. It is viewed as an important instrument by which the American federal judiciary asserts and maintains its reputation for independence. The courthouses and facilities of the federal judiciary are not only the envy of foreign judges, but also of many American state judiciaries who look with awe at the resources controlled by the federal bench. Federal courthouses cost more per square foot than state courthouses, and federal judges and personnel are paid more than the average corresponding state judge or personnel. Although when these public sector salaries are compared to the private sector, the disparity is stark and the financial sacrifice of judicial service is clear.

The concept of having judges administratively *maitre chez nous* (masters of their own house) is strongly endorsed by the relevant civil legal organizations that help form public opinion. The American Bar Association, the largest voluntary association in the United States with a membership of over 350,000 attorneys and an influential political lobbying group, has stood by the federal judiciary in moments of crisis to protect this independence. In addition, the Center for State Courts, the American Judicature Society, the American Law Institute, and the American Association of Law Schools have helped develop an institutional network of public support for the judiciary. This support of civil society is a necessary condition for the American federal judiciary; its significance cannot be overestimated.

Selection and Number: Size Matters

There are a number of decisions over time that have contributed to the creation of the independence of the American federal judiciary both as a matter of jurisprudence and administration. The selection process of an Article III federal judge is a combination of local and national politics with both the president and the Congress playing a vital role. The requirement of the advice and consent of the Senate bestows a national legitimacy not shared by state and local jurists. Moreover, the decision to keep the number of life-tenured

Article III judges limited to approximately 1,000, of which 179 are appellate judges, has preserved the bench as a small elite with a high degree of esprit de corps.[16]

Needless to say, having life tenure insulates the judiciary from everyday politics. However despite the limit on federal judges, there has been a growth of parajudicial personnel over the last thirty years who have helped shoulder the increasing burden of legal work. The increased jurisdiction and growth of such functionaries as magistrate judges, bankruptcy judges rather than referees, permanent law clerks, and *pro se* clerks reflect a new cadre of judicial officials. These officials are chosen by councils or individual Article III judges and are supervised by, or report to, Article III judges.[17]

Rule Making: Internal or External

The process of rule making has a critical impact on the courts in the areas of the allocation of burdens of proof and the introduction of evidence into the courtroom, and the manner by which appellate review takes place. Although the legislature retains ultimate authority for the approval of procedural rules, the judiciary controls the process. The Rules Enabling Act provides that the Supreme Court and all the courts established by an act of Congress may from time to time prescribe rules for the conduct of their business.[18] Through a series of specialized committees that report to a general rules committee, the federal system has constructed an intricate process that includes private practitioners, academics, government attorneys, and judges. The process requires an extensive public comment period including the holding of public hearings to solicit comments from the lay public. This is important because the internal criminal, civil, and bankruptcy rules are controlled by the group charged with enforcing them. Although this may appear to be a rather technical point, and most of the points are technical in the rules area, it is significant. This is important because how burdens of proof, for example, are set affect the outcomes of cases over time. Rules tend to reward certain interests and a process overseen by neutral parties adds to the legitimacy of the court process.

Remuneration: Money Always Counts

A sensitive subject for most jurists is remuneration. Although as a matter of constitutional law an Article III judge's salary cannot be diminished, the founding fathers' failure to account for inflation has proven to be a point of aggravation for American jurists. Attempts have been made to create an automatic cost of living adjustment (COLA) that would be self-actuating. Due to political reasons, salaries of legislators and judges are linked together for budgetary purposes, and all efforts to separate the salaries of federal judges from those of the legislators have failed. Under the current statutory regime, if the salaries of judges are to have a yearly COLA, or if the base salary is to be increased, the legislature must vote each time, and any increase must also be awarded to the legislature itself.[19] For political reasons, legislators are reluctant to be seen as advocating for their own salary increases and, therefore, the salaries of both legislators and jurists have not kept pace with inflation.

In recent years many believe that due to the salary issue, an increased number of jurists have left the bench. Judicial compensation has not matched the increase earnings afforded to those in the private sector. Given their background and experience, federal judges could easily earn four to five times the government wage. Clearly a sense of dedication to public service and the esteem afforded a federal judge help explain why many are willing to make the financial sacrifice, but for many this decision is becoming increasingly difficult.

Theories of Judicial Representation: A Mixture of Systems to Avoid Oligarchy

Because all federal judges have life tenure and each judge is independent following his nomination by the president and confirmation by the Senate, each is a tall oak that can stand alone. Administratively, the governing structure has combined leadership by statute with fixed terms of service. For example, the chief judge of a circuit or a trial court can serve for a maximum of seven years. The CJ of the United States, on the other hand, chairs for life the Judicial Conference, the AO, and the FJC. The CJ's administrative appointment is also for life and is concurrent with his judicial duties, unlike, for instance, the Lord Chancellor of England, who tenders his resignation with the change of power in Parliament, thereby aligning the head of the judiciary with the new administration. In addition, the Judicial Conference also has elected trial judges by the circuit and representation by proxy for magistrate and bankruptcy judges, who by theory are represented by the appellate and trial Article III judges who have selected them to serve.

By statute though, magistrate and bankruptcy judges serve directly on the board of the FJC for a nonrenewable term of four years without any additional compensation.[20] In the continuing philosophy of not allowing for a permanent judicial administrative oligarchy, the director of the FJC must retire at the age of seventy.[21]

Discipline and Removal: Independence Is Not Absolute

As conditions of service and tenure, judges are required to be accountable in a variety of ways: publicly, personally, and intellectually.[22] In order to enforce the common-law rule of serving during good behavior, different countries have created specific judicial councils, tribunals, or panels allowing for the dismissal of a judge by the CJ. In the United States, along with Japan, Germany, and Brazil, an impeachment process that involves the political branch in a vote for removal has been incorporated into the constitutional framework for further protection.

Under Article III, federal judges "hold their offices during good behavior" and "receive for their services, a compensation, which shall not be diminished during their continuance in office." Removal from office is a drastic remedy and until 1986 the last judge removed from office in the United States was in 1936, at which point in American history only four judges had ever been impeached. Unfortunately, in the three years between 1986 and 1989 three district court trial judges, Harry E. Claiborne (Nevada), Alice L. Hastings (Florida), and Walter L. Nixon (Mississippi), were removed from office by the Senate. Prior to 1986, twenty-two of the thirty-five federal judges charged with serious misbehavior had resigned from office rather than endure the strain of an impeachment trial. For lesser transgressions, the power to discipline judges falls within the jurisdiction of the circuit judicial councils, but how far a council can go short of impeachment proceedings, due to the independence of each individual judge, is still a question that contains legal gray areas.[23]

Removal for unpopular decisions is why most legal systems have put into place screening mechanisms to separate legitimate claims from those that are frivolous. Because in every case one side must lose, in every case there is a potential disgruntled litigant ready to complain about the judge and the process. Criminal misbehavior such as bribes, payoffs, and personal criminal violations constitute acts warranting removal. Needless to say, there is a range of moral turpitude that does not honor the office but does not demand removal; this behavior in the American system is handled by our ethical codes.

Ethics and Codes: Maintaining Integrity with Self-regulation

The origins of judicial ethics in the United States stem from a variety of sources: the code of conduct for U.S. judges, the requirement for disqualification for bias or prejudice, the obligation of financial disclosure, the restrictions on outside earnings including gifts and honoraria, and the judicial oath of office.[24] The code of conduct is composed of seven canons focusing on: (1) the integrity and independence of the judiciary; (2) impropriety and the appearance of impropriety; (3) impartiality and diligence; (4) extra-judicial activities to improve the law, the legal system, and the administration of justice; (5) extra-judicial activities creating the risk of conflict with judicial duties; (6) reports of compensation for law-related and extra-judicial activities; and (7) political activity. As one can readily appreciate, the code concentrates on both the appearance and the reality of conflict of interest, and the subordination of impartiality for financial or political gain.[25] The American model combines both regimes of prohibiting certain activities and disqualifying for purposes of personal integrity.[26]

Transparency: Media, Efficiency, and Public Opinion

A recurring complaint of most jurists is the failure of the press and media to appreciate the judicial functions. Periodically in an open and free society, a judge, court, or opinion will be the subject of severe criticism in the press. How should the judiciary as a whole and the judge as an individual respond to the attacks?

Because federal judges have not created a specific press relations office to speak on behalf of the judiciary, there is no single organ to speak on behalf of the judiciary. Although the AO has a press office and a legislative office, the AO does not issue press releases dealing with the explanation of specific cases. The Canadian Supreme Court, for example, has an administrative assistant to the CJ who works with the media and helps explain opinions when they are released. In the United States, although the Supreme Court does have a press officer, he or she does not comment on any cases, as the dominant dictum is the opinion speaks for itself. From time to time proposals have been made to have regional press officers in each circuit or large district court, but each time the plan has been defeated.

First and foremost, a judge can point to his or her opinion to explain the reasons for the decision. The well-reasoned, albeit controversial, decision is on the public record and can be read by all parties. Given the prevalence of electronic forms of communication in the United States, most opinions are easily accessible to the general public within minutes of publication. On this question the external support organizations, the American Bar Association, American Association of Law Schools, and American Law Institute, are able to play an independent role in defending the judiciary or jurist unfairly criticized. By having a third party not directly involved in the dispute, the defense is more credible and should carry more weight with the general public.

As part of the accountability and transparency goal, however, the Civil Justice Reform Act of 1990 (Biden Bill) was passed to have more open and explicit reporting of court workings.[27] By the terms of the act, each trial court is required to implement *a civil justice expense and delay reduction plan* that would "facilitate deliberative adjudication of civil cases on the merits, monitor discovery, improve litigation management, and ensure just, speedy, and inexpensive resolution of civil disputes."[28] Each court has to evaluate both the civil and criminal dockets, the trends in filing, the causes for cost and delay, suggestions for new legislation, and in addition to this case-specific reporting, the amount of time taken by individual judges to resolve specific motions.

This form of reporting makes it possible to evaluate the efficiency of individual courts, in particular in comparison to other courts in the nation. To some this has deprived judges of a degree of autonomy, but with it has come a more open analysis of the internal operations of the courts and judicial docket management.

THE COURT: THE SHAPING OF A NATIONAL SECURITY LEGAL CULTURE

There are moments in the life of judiciaries that are founding moments. Critical decisions are made that affect the nature of the judicial function for long periods of time as a legal culture is created, recast, and nurtured by these outcomes. Paradoxically, although courts by and large are nonmajoritarian institutions, they are essential for the smooth functioning of majoritarian or democratic systems.[29] A court's legitimacy turns on its perceived impartiality. Impartiality is achieved differently in continental regimes than in common-law countries. Although there may be no life tenure, continental judges often directly control investigative teams and can conduct wide-ranging probes of governmental corruption. For Americans, judicial and administrative independence has been the chosen path. In fact administrative autonomy has helped support judicial independence. But what makes the American judicial system unique is that, while other common-law countries have created a constitutional structure permitting a simple majority of the legislature to overturn judicial decrees, in America a supermajority of two-thirds of the states is required to overturn a Supreme Court determination on constitutional matters under Article V.

When so much power is vested in one organ of government in order to adjudicate the constitutionality of the other branches, at times suspicion of motives becomes endemic to the process. Therefore, whatever institutional innovations can be made to ensure and foster impartiality can only strengthen the court system.

The court's independence though rests on its legitimacy as ultimately, the government must enforce the courts' judgments. Students of the judiciary often point out that in *Federalist Paper No. 78* Alexander Hamilton underscored the fact that the judiciary would control neither *the purse nor the sword,* in order to reassure opponents to the creation of a national court system. Enforcement of judgments has been the essential criterion of an effective legal system. Both the state and the citizenry must have confidence in the process and the content of the order both to enforce and to obey the order. When this fragile social contract is breached, the system no longer enjoys voluntary compliance and moves away from democratic impulses.[30] The recent detainee and interrogation cases in the global war against terrorism during the George W. Bush administration demonstrate how the court has asserted its place in the NSE and reformed the legal culture in the area of the laws of armed conflict.

After the 9/11 attack, Congress passed the Authorization for the Use of Military Force (AUMF), which authorized the president "to use all necessary and appropriate force against those nations, organizations, or persons he determines planned, authorized, committed, or aided" the attacks and recognized the president's "authority under the Constitution to take action to deter and prevent acts of international terrorism against the United States."[31] The president declared a national emergency, and as commander in chief, dispatched armed forces to Afghanistan to seek out and destroy the al-Qaeda terrorist network and the Taliban regime that had supported and protected it.[32]

The administration began by asserting a robust view of executive power, under a theory of the unitary executive in a time of war. Relying on the AUMF, the president asserted that he had the power to detain combatants captured anywhere in the world; determine whether and how the Geneva Conventions applied to these detainees for treatment and interrogation; establish military tribunals for adjudication; not follow the Foreign Intelligence Surveillance Act (FISA); and finally determine that the detention at Guantanamo base in Cuba was beyond judicial review.[33] Over a period of eight years the Supreme Court has rejected, modified, or reframed each of these claims of executive authority. The Court also became embroiled in debates with the executive branch and Congress over the definition of war, the due process owed to detainees, interpretations of the Geneva Conventions, and finally, the constitutional values that would shape the NSE as it battles extremism both at home and abroad.

In early January 2002, the first group of detainees arrived at Camp X-Ray in Guantanamo Bay and was housed in open-air cages.[34] The president determined the detainees were unlawful combatants and would not be afforded prisoner-of-war status under the Geneva Conventions, despite the objections of military JAG officers.[35] The choice of Guantanamo for detention was designed to avoid domestic U.S. law under the legal theory that the base in Cuba was not within U.S. territory and therefore, the federal courts would have no jurisdiction. This legal theory was based on an earlier court decision, in the context of immigration law, where the Supreme Court had ruled that Haitian boat people held at Guantanamo had no right to habeas corpus appeal to federal courts because the base was not U.S. territory.

Shortly thereafter, offensive pictures of the detainees were released and a habeas corpus lawsuit was filed, *Rasul v. Bush*.[36] Allegations concerning the harsh treatment of detainees in interrogations began to surface. The district trial court rejected the initial lawsuit so the detainees responded with a hunger strike. Over the next six months, a new facility was constructed (Camp Delta), and another habeas suit was filed, *Hamdi v. Bush*, involving an American citizen. By December 2002, the detainees were transferred to this new facility.

In early March 2003 on appeal to federal appeals court, the *Rasul* habeas petition (which had been consolidated with other appeals, Habib and Al Odah Khaid) was rejected but appealed to the Supreme Court, as was the *Hamdi* case. But as a result of the appellate court denial, a number of detainees were scheduled for trial by military tribunals; one foreigner, an Australian named David Hicks, was the first detainee assigned an attorney, and the defense counsel argued that a number of the rules for the tribunals were unconstitutional.

In June 2004, the Supreme Court decided the two cases *Rasul* and *Hamdi* on appeal. In *Rasul* the court rejected 6-3 the precedents of World War II prisoner-of-war cases, and the majority held that the federal courts have jurisdiction to determine the legality of the executive's potentially indefinite detention of individuals who claim to be wholly innocent of wrongdoing. This decision reversed the judgment of the court of appeals and remanded the cases to the district court to consider in the first instance the merits of petitioners' claims.

In *Hamdi*, again the Court rejected the administration's position and eight of the nine justices of the Court agreed that the executive branch did not have the power to hold indefinitely a U.S. citizen without basic due process protections enforceable through judicial review. In a plurality opinion, Justice O'Connor (joined by Chief Justice Rehnquist and Justices Breyer and Kennedy) argued that although Congress had expressly authorized the detention of unlawful combatants in its AUMF, due process required that Hamdi have a meaningful opportunity to challenge his detention. For Justice O'Connor, due process required notice of the charges and an opportunity to be heard. However, due to the ongoing military conflict, traditional procedural protections such as placing the burden of proof on the government or the ban on hearsay need not apply. In the opinion, O'Connor suggested that the Department of Defense create fact-finding tribunals similar to the Army rules for Article 5 hearings under the Geneva Conventions to determine a detainee's status, and she concluded that Hamdi should have a right to counsel. The plurality held that judges need not be involved in reviewing these cases for status, rather only an impartial decision maker would be required.

Justice Souter, joined by Justice Ginsburg, concurred with the plurality's judgment that due process protections must be available for Hamdi to challenge his status and detention, but disagreed that AUMF established congressional authorization for the detention of unlawful combatants. In an ironic twist, Justice Scalia, joined by Justice Stevens, dissented and based on Hamdi's U.S. citizenship reasoned that the government had only two options: either Congress must suspend the right to habeas corpus (a power provided under the Constitution only in times of invasion or rebellion, which had not happened), or Hamdi must be tried under criminal law. For Justices Scalia and Stevens, the executive did not have the power to detain U.S. citizens, and it was not the business of the Court to instruct the government on how to establish detention regimes. For these dissenting justices, Hamdi's status as a U.S. citizen afforded him special status. In the end, only Justice Thomas would have affirmed the lower court's ruling based on the AUMF and the president's war-making powers. The splits among the justices reflected the unsettled aspects of the law.

Immediately in July 2004 in response to the Supreme Court decisions, the administration established the Combatant Status Review Tribunals, consisting of three officers, to determine each detainee's enemy combatant status. Yet within five months, a district court judge again challenged the administration. The judge, James Robertson, ruled in the case of Salim Ahmed Hamdan, Osama bin Laden's alleged driver, that his military commission trial was unconstitutional due to the fact, among other things, that the accused could not be denied access to evidence; instead, the government should have held special hearings for detainees to determine whether they qualified as prisoners of war under the Geneva Conventions. Judge Robertson ordered that until the government provided the appropriate hearing, it could prosecute the detainees only in courts-martial as established by military law. On appeal in July 2005, the U.S. Court of Appeals for the District of Columbia Circuit Court (included on the panel was Judge John G. Roberts who would later be appointed CJ) unanimously affirmed the right of the president to create military commissions and overturned the Judge Robertson order.

Hamdan appealed the decision to the Supreme Court, asserting that the Geneva Conventions entitled him to an impartial hearing to determine whether he qualified as a prisoner of war and therefore to a traditional court martial unless he was found to be an unlawful combatant. There was much speculation that the Court would refrain from imposing itself in this war powers and foreign policy arena, but the Court to the surprise of many accepted the case. Its decision to accept the case reflected the Court's view that it had a role to play as fundamental rights were involved.

In the meantime, Congress, which had been largely silent on these issues, in December 2005 passed the Detainee Treatment Act (DTA), which restricted the interrogation techniques for the military and stripped detainees such as Hamdan of the right to file habeas corpus petitions, apparently making the Hamdan appeal to the Supreme Court null and moot. The Congress in the DTA made it clear that in its constitutional interpretation, this matter of national security is for the executive and the legislature; the Supreme Court should have no say in the matter, in other words, no jurisdiction for habeas petitions.

In a clear rejection of the views of both the executive and legislative branches, the Supreme Court in June 2006, in *Hamdan v. Rumsfeld* (a 5-3 decision), not only agreed to hear the Hamdan case rejecting the stripping of its jurisdiction but further held that the military commissions at Guantanamo violated U.S. and international law and that Common Article 3 (CA 3) of the Geneva Conventions applies to the detainees. CA 3 of the Geneva Conventions is a provision that guarantees minimum protections for detainees.[37] Justice Stevens, writing for the majority, concluded that CA 3 applied to the war against al-Qaeda, and is thus a part of the law of war as a matter of law. Military commissions, as constituted, did not meet the standard of CA 3 because they deprive defendants of protections that are basic to the courts-martial. Though the Bush administration had cited special dangers involved in fighting terrorism, Justice Stevens rejected the reasoning of the executive and concluded, "Nothing in the record before us demonstrates that it would be impracticable to apply court-martial rules in this case." For the majority, terrorism suspects fell under CA 3's prohibition against trials by anything other than "a regularly constituted court affording all the judicial guarantees which are recognized as indispensable by civilized peoples." Because the commissions were not properly authorized by Congress and did not match court-martial rules, the military commissions did not meet the requirements of CA 3.

In a scathing dissent, Justice Scalia, joined by Justices Thomas and Alito, violently disagreed with the majority's decision to hear the case and asserted their views on the exercise of executive power and legislative jurisdictional authority:

> On December 30, 2005, Congress enacted the Detainee Treatment Act (DTA). It unambiguously provides that, as of that date, "no court, justice, or judge" shall have jurisdiction to consider the habeas application of a Guantanamo Bay detainee. Notwithstanding this plain directive, the Court today concludes that, on what it calls the statute's most natural reading, every "court, justice, or judge" before whom such a habeas application was pending on December 30 has jurisdiction to hear, consider, and render judgment on it. This conclusion is patently erroneous. And even if it were not, the jurisdiction supposedly retained should, in an exercise of sound equitable discretion, not be exercised.

As a cultural matter inside the NSE, the Court's role could not have been clearer and more controversial. A majority of the Court had concluded that the Court had a role to play in the war on terrorism and was asserting its views under one of the great writs: the writ of habeas corpus and under its authority to be the ultimate organ on the interpretation of domestic and international law. For the minority of the Court, however, the extra-jurisdictional exercise of judicial power in the war and foreign policy arena was a violation of the constitutional balance and an exercise of judicial imperialism.

In the wake of the *Hamdan* decision, which had clearly stated that Congress had to be involved as a constitutional matter in the establishment of the military commission system and the interrogation process, the Congress finally responded. Within four months of the decision in *Hamdan,* Congress passed the Military Commission Act (MCA) in September 2006. The new MCA is designed to legalize military commissions and to clarify interrogation techniques that Central Intelligence Agency (CIA) officers may use on hundreds of terrorism suspects considered unlawful enemy combatants being held at Guantanamo Bay and other locations. The new act, however, grants the executive branch authority in deciding how to comply with treaty obligations regulating actions that fall short of "grave breaches" of the conventions and again restricts the writ of habeas corpus.[38] The MCA bars military commissions from considering testimony obtained through interrogation techniques that involve "cruel, unusual or inhumane treatment or punishment," which the Constitution's Fifth, Eighth, and Fourteenth Amendments prohibit.[39]

But the Court's role in this unfolding drama of constitutional authority and the NSE was not over. Again an appeal following the MCA made its way to the Court from a group of detainees in Guantanamo who asserted a writ of habeas corpus.

In June 2008 the Court yet again asserted itself in the detention process in the cases of *Boumediene v. Bush* and *Al Odah v. United States.* Lakhdar Boumediene was an Algerian living in Bosnia at the time he was captured.[40] He was arrested on suspicion that he was involved in a plot to bomb the United States embassy in Sarajevo. The Supreme Court of the Federation of Bosnia and Herzegovina—a court that the United States helped establish—released him because they could not find any evidence to justify his arrest. Despite the fact that the Bosnian court released him, the United States seized him and brought him to Guantanamo. This case is interesting because of the status of Lakhdar Boumediene. Boumediene is a non-U.S. citizen, seized in a nonbattlefield environment, who was then placed under U.S. authority.

As noted by the Court in *Boumediene*, this set of facts raises significant due process questions that must involve the Court. In yet another controversial 5-4 ruling, the Court held unconstitutional Section 7(a) of the MCA and reasoned that both citizens and non-citizens in Guantanamo Bay should have a right to challenge their detention in U.S. federal courts through habeas corpus petitions. Justice Kennedy, in his majority opinion, noted the unique nature of this war and its effects: "It is true that before today the Court has never held that noncitizens detained by our Government in territory over which another country maintains *de jure* sovereignty have any rights under our Constitution. But the cases before us lack any precise historical parallel. They involve individuals detained by executive order for the duration of a conflict that, if measured from September 11, 2001, to the present, is already among the largest wars in American history."

He then cites the *Oxford Companion to American Military History 849* (1999): "The detainees, moreover, are held in a territory that, while technically not part of the United

States, is under the complete and total control of our government. Under these circumstances the lack of a precedent on point is no barrier to our holding." The majority was creating new law for the NSE and was setting the values and norms for the executive and Congress when the U.S. would project force.

The dissenting Justices bristled with attacks on the overreach of the majority. Justice Scalia is scathing in his response: "Today, for the first time in our Nation's history, the Court confers a constitutional right to *habeas corpus* on alien enemies detained abroad by our military forces in the course of ongoing war. The *writ of habeas corpus* does not, and never has, run in favor of aliens abroad; the Suspension Clause thus has no application, and the Court's intervention in this military matter is entirely *ultra vires*."[41]

For Justice Scalia this expansion of judicial reach through the use of the writ was an unconstitutional expansion of power at the expense of the executive. Chief Justice Roberts, joining Justice Scalia's dissent, nevertheless was compelled to write on his own to note the unprecedented intrusion of the Court in national security areas: "Today the Court strikes down as inadequate the most generous set of procedural protections ever afforded aliens detained by this country as enemy combatants. The Court rejects them today out of hand, [this is Congress's actions] without bothering to say what due process rights the detainees possess, without explaining how the statute fails to vindicate those rights, and before a single petitioner has even attempted to avail himself of the law's operation." For the dissenters, the majority has generated shapeless procedures.

In the view of the dissenters in *Boumediene*, the DTA has met the standards of Hamdi as set by Justice O'Connor. Then why does the majority disagree with this interpretation? The disagreement harkens back to an understanding of due process and rights retained by those under U.S. jurisdiction detained against their will. In erasing the distinction between citizen and noncitizen, the majority is forging a concept of justice with an international character. This power, in turn, then shapes the environment for both the executive and Congress when it acts in its national security capacity. By doing so, the Court by *de jure* and *de facto* becomes a critical institution in the NSE by asserting its view as a matter of law. This was a prime example of the legal culture interacting with the NSE and shaping the parameter of power and force.

As is the nature of legal disputes, post-*Boumediene*, the district courts of the District of Columbia have been holding habeas hearings for scores of detainees from Guantanamo and slowly shaping the rules of evidence and judicial tests to determine, for example, what membership or "substantial material support" for al-Qaeda means. In essence, the legal skirmishing will continue both as a matter of law on the evidentiary level and as a matter of jurisdiction, as those being held under U.S. custody in Afghanistan will surely sue for similar habeas corpus rights as those in Guantanamo. Moreover the nature of the attack on the military commission process has called into question the legitimacy of military commissions and as of the fall 2009, the military commission process appears stalled.

CONCLUSION: THE INTERNAL BATTLE OF OUR JUDICIAL CULTURE IN THE NSE ARENA

This chapter has explored the independent culture of the Court and how it is institutionally maintained, and how in the last eight years it has participated in a constitutional dialogue with the executive branch and the Congress in the national security arena. To illustrate the Court's independence, the dialogue concerning the critical cases involving detention and detainee rights were explored. The Court's independence has been on display as it continually rejected both executive and legislative exercises of power. Other contentious issues such as wiretapping or leak investigations could have been chosen to illustrate the role of federal courts. The advantage of the detainee cases are that they strike at the heart of executive power while at war, demonstrate Congress's diffidence on the issue, and reveal the internal battle raging inside the Court on its appropriate role and on the judicial doctrine the majority argue should govern the detention process.

One legal commentator, Noah Feldman, characterizes the legal debate as reflecting the emergence of two schools.[42] In Feldman's view, one school begins with the observation that in the age of modern liberal democracy, law derives its legitimacy from being enacted by elected representatives of the people. From this standpoint, the Constitution is seen as facing *inward*, toward the Americans who made it, toward their rights and their security. For the most part, that is, the rights the Constitution provides are for citizens and provided only within the borders of the country. By these principles, any interpretation of the Constitution that restricts the nation's security or sovereignty—for example, by extending constitutional rights to noncitizens encountered on battlefields overseas—is misguided and even dangerous.

The opposing school defines the rule of law differently: law is conceived not as a quintessentially national phenomenon but rather as a global ideal. This position readily concedes that the Constitution specifies the law for the United States but stresses that a fuller, more complete conception of law demands that American law be pictured alongside international law and other (legitimate) national constitutions. The U.S. Constitution, in this cosmopolitan view, faces *outward*. It is a paradigm of the rule of law: rights similar to those it confers on Americans should protect all people everywhere so that no one falls outside the reach of some legitimate legal order. What is most important about our Constitution is not that it provides rights for us but that its vision of freedom ought to apply universally.

This is the legal cultural struggle reflected in the pluralities, dissents, and majorities of the decisions as the Court struggles with its role and as a judicial beacon both domestically and internationally. But this debate is unfolding while the branches of government are engaged in funding and directing lethal force and capturing detainees. The continuing cultural space of legal uncertainty undermines a coherent, logical, unified system of appropriate lethality, capture, interrogation, and detainment. Because the NSE is engaged in a struggle that is part criminal law, law of armed conflict, and immigration law both domestically and internationally, some intrusion of uncertainty is to be expected.

But for those charged with safeguarding national security it is deeply troubling, and yet it is our legal culture. The Court—because it determines appropriate due process, the distinction between citizens and noncitizens, the interpretation and applicability of the Geneva Conventions, and the war powers of the presidency and the Congress—has become a major force in the NSE. This independence to participate in the NSE dialogue stems not only from legal doctrine but a certainty of its bureaucratic base. The Court fears no bureaucratic attack on its budget or resources. Although it may not have the power of the sword or purse, the power of the judicial pen has proven to be in our democratic republic, at times, equally as powerful.

NOTES

I particularly would like to thank Trudi Rishikof and Roger George for their invaluable suggestions and assistance in writing this chapter.

1. For a discussion of the framework see the discussion in Dycus, Berney, Banks, Raven-Hansen, *National Security Law,* 4th ed. (Netherlands: Wolters Kluwer Law & Business, 2007), chapter 2.

2. Habeas corpus is Latin for "you have the body." Prisoners often seek release by filing a petition for a writ of habeas corpus. A writ of habeas corpus is a judicial mandate to a prison official ordering that an inmate be brought to the court so it can be determined whether that person is imprisoned lawfully and whether he or she should be released from custody. A habeas corpus petition is a petition filed with a court by a person who objects to his own or another's detention or imprisonment. The petition must show that the court ordering the detention or imprisonment made a legal or factual error. Habeas corpus petitions are usually filed by persons serving prison sentences. See www.lectlaw.com/def/h001.htm.

3. See Edward S. Corwin, *The President, Office and Powers, 1787–1984,* 5th ed. (New York: New York University Press, 1984), 171.

4. *U.S. v. Curtiss-Wright Export Corp.,* 299 U.S. 304 (1936); *Youngstown Sheet & Tube Co. v. Sawyer,* 343 U.S. 579 (1952); see *U.S. v. Curtiss-Wright Export Corp.,* 299 U.S. 304 (1936).

5. Bob Woodward and Scott Armstrong, *The Brethren* (New York: Simon & Schuster, 1979); Edward Lazarus, *Closed Chambers: The Rise, Fall, and Future of the Modern Supreme Court* (New York: Penguin Books, 1999); Jeffrey Toobin, *The Nine: Inside the Secret World of the Supreme Court* (New York: Random House, 2007).

6. *The Liberal Tradition of the Supreme Court Clerkship: Its Rise, Fall and Reincarnation;* with Bill Nelson, I. Scott Messinger, and Michael Jo, *Vanderbilt Law Review,* Vol. 62, No. 6 (Nov. 2009).

7. See *Baker v. Carr,* 369 U.S. 186, 217 (1962).

8. When the court appeared to be rejecting his New Deal legislation, Roosevelt introduced legislation to add an additional justice, up to a maximum of six, for every justice then serving who was seventy years and six months old.

9. William H. Rehnquist, *The Supreme Court—How It Was, How It Is* (New York: William Morrow, 1987); and *Grand Inquests,* (New York: William Morrow, 1992).

10. See dissent in *Olmstead v. United States,* 277 U.S. 438 (1928).

11. James G. Apple and Robert P. Deyling, *A Primer on the Civil-Law System* (Washington, DC: Federal Judicial Center, 1995).

12. Gerald Gunther, *Learned Hand* (New York: Knopf, 1994), 515.

13. Generally, § 601 et seq; generally, § 620 et seq.

14. Generally, § 671–677 et seq.

15. Harvey Rishikof and Barbara A. Perry, *Separateness but Interdependence, Autonomy but Reciprocity: A First Look at Federal Judges' Appearances before Legislative Committees,* 46 Mercer Law Review 667 (1995).

16. Bermant, Schwarzer, Sussman, Wheeler, *Imposing a Moratorium on the Number of Federal Judges* (Washington, DC: Federal Judicial Center, 1993).

17. Article III of the Constitution states that the judge enjoys life tenure, cannot have her salary diminished, and is confirmed by the Senate, as opposed to Article I judges, or legislatively created judges who do not have the same constitutional protections.

18. 28 U.S.C. §2071.

19. See §140 of Public Law No. 97–92, 95 Stat. 1183, 1200.

20. See 28 U.S.C. § 621.

21. See 28 U.S.C. § 627.

22. The discussion for this section draws on the work of Kersi B. Shroff, *Judicial Tenure: The Removal and Discipline of Judges in Selected Countries* from the Research Papers of the National Commission on Judicial Discipline & Removal Vol. II (1993).

23. See *Chandler v. Judicial Council of the Tenth Circuit*, 398 U.S. 74 (1970) as the leading Supreme Court case in the area of judicial discipline.

24. 28 U.S.C. § 144, 28 U.S.C. § 455 and Code of Conduct; 5 U.S.C. app. 6; Code of Conduct, Canon 5C; 18 U.S.C. §§ 203, 205, 216; 5 U.S.C. app. 7; 5 U.S.C. §§ 7351, 7353; 28 U.S.C.A. § 453.

25. This discussion draws on the work of Beth Nolan, *The Role of Judicial Ethics and the Discipline and Removal of Federal Judges,* from the Research Papers of the National Commission on Judicial Discipline & Removal Vol. I (1993).

26. The level of scrutiny of the code is reflected in the interpretation of canon 3C(1)(d)'s definition of "relative." A relative has been defined by the commentary that accompanies the code to include "a person related to either (the judge or judge's spouse) within the third degree of relationship, or the spouse of such a person. The degree of relationship is calculated according to the civil system and thus includes parents, grandparents, aunts, uncles, brothers, sisters, nieces, and nephews of the judge or the judge's spouse, or the spouses of any of those listed.

27. See 28 U.S.C. § 471 et. seq.; Pub. L. No. 101–650 (1990); due to Senator Biden's (D-DE) sponsorship as chair of the Judiciary Committee in the Senate, the bill became known as the Biden Bill.

28. See 28 U.S.C. § 471.

29. Ackerman has developed a theory of founding moments and counter-majoritarian courts in Bruce Ackerman, *We the People* (Boston: Harvard University Press, 1993).

30. *Federalist 78* (Rossiter ed. 1961), 465.

31. Authorization for Use of Military Force, Pub. L. No. 107–40, 115 Stat. 224, 224 (2001).

32. Proclamation No. 7453, Declaration of a National Emergency by Reason of Certain Terrorist Attacks, 66 Fed. Reg. 48,199 (September 14, 2001).

33. See Public Law No. 95–511, 92 Stat. 1783. The FISA issue or the use of domestic surveillance for intelligence purposes is an area of the law not well researched or explored. How to balance security, emerging technologies, and individual liberty with the Fourth Amendment has been an ongoing struggle since the passage of the legislation in 1978. The discussion will focus on the detention issue because the Supreme Court has been so active in this area of the law but the legal issues involved in domestic electronic collection of foreign intelligence and its role in the national security enterprise is worth a chapter unto itself. Some of the FISA issues are discussed in chapter 9 on the FBI.

34. The timeline and cases are drawn from the Guantanamo Bay Timeline found at http://projects.washingtonpost.com/guantanamo/timeline/.

35. See Lisa A. Turner, *The Detainee Interrogation Debate and the Legal-Policy Process,* 54 Joint Force Quarterly 2009.

36. See note 1.

37. Article 3 has been called a "convention in miniature." It is an article of the Geneva Conventions that applies in noninternational conflicts. It describes the protections that must be adhered to by all individuals within a signatory's territory during an armed conflict not of an international character (regardless of citizenship or lack thereof): noncombatants, combatants who have laid down their arms, and combatants who are hors de combat (out of the fight) due to wounds, detention, or any other cause shall in all circumstances be treated humanely, including prohibition of outrages upon personal dignity, in particular humiliating and degrading treatment. The passing of sentences must also be pronounced by a regularly constituted court, affording all the judicial guarantees which are recognized as indispensable by civilized peoples. Article 3's protections exist even if one is not classified as a prisoner of war. Article 3 also states that parties to the internal conflict should endeavor to bring into force, by means of special agreements, all or part of the other provisions of Geneva Convention III.

38. See Charles Babington and Jonathan Weisman, "Senate Approves Detainee Bill Backed by Bush Constitutional Challenges Predicted," *Washington Post*, September 29, 2006, available at www.washingtonpost.com/wp-dyn/content/article/2006/09/28/AR2006092800824.html.

39. The bar though is retroactive only to December 30, 2005, when Congress adopted the DTA to protect CIA operatives from possible prosecution over interrogation tactics used before that date; ibid.

40. Case descriptions and commentary drawn from Harvey Rishikof, *Powers, Distinctions, and the State in the Twenty-First Century: The New Paradigm of Force in Due Process* (Virginia Beach, VA: Regent Law Review, 2009).

41. *Ultra vires* is a Latin term meaning "beyond powers." The term is usually used to refer to acts taken by a corporation or officers of a corporation that are taken outside of the powers or authority granted to them by law or under the corporate charter; at http://definitions.uslegal.com/u/ultra-vires/.

42. See Noah Feldman, "When Judges Make Foreign Policy," *New York Times Magazine*, September 25, 2008. The following paragraphs are drawn and edited from the article.

Part III   The Outside Players

Chapter 13 Lobbyists: U.S. National Security and Special Interests

GERALD FELIX WARBURG

> The activities of lobbies representing foreign interests have contributed to the gradual erosion of the
> United States' credibility and influence in the world . . . the control of policy, once lost,
> may not be restored to capable, disinterested hands.
>
> *John Newhouse, "Diplomacy, Inc.: The Influence of Lobbies on
> U.S. Foreign Policy"*

> Americans are a collection of special interests, and one person's special interest is another's job or moral crusade.
> If people can't organize to influence government, then democracy is dead . . . the idea that the making of choices
> should occur in a vacuum—delegated to an all-knowing political elite—is profoundly undemocratic.
>
> *Robert J. Samuelson, "An Obama Gift for K Street"*

Success in the national security enterprise (NSE) requires policymakers to anticipate and engage competing interests. Foreign policy and defense initiatives cannot be advanced and sustained without recruiting domestic political allies and blunting the potential impact of critics. Developing tactics to promote a policy option often leads to deployment of experienced advocates to lobby in Washington to support proposals and to counter opposition.

This chapter explores the role lobbyists play in the NSE, both lobbyists employed full time on behalf of specific issues groups, as well as contract lobbyists engaged by a broad array of commercial interest groups. I examine who these lobbyists are, what they do, and how they produce results through interaction with policymakers. The focus is on how lobbying shapes national security policy options: what strategies, tactics, and precedents are most effective? The goal is to shed light on the impact of lobbying on the outcomes of defense and foreign policy initiatives.

NATIONAL SECURITY LOBBYISTS: WHAT THEY DO AND HOW THEY WORK

The ranks of registered lobbyists in contemporary Washington include representatives of business, labor, and environmental interests. Lobbyists working national security issues represent organizations as diverse as Amnesty International, the National Association of Manufacturers, and Boeing Corporation. They represent nongovernmental organizations (NGOs) as well as the broad array of ethnic American associations pushing for strengthened U.S. bilateral ties with nations from Ireland to India. Some organizations, such the U.S. Chamber of Commerce or the American-Israel Public Affairs Committee (AIPAC), seek to maximize influence by steering political contributions toward favored federal candidates, who are scored on votes of greatest interest to organization members. Others, like the National Rifle Association (NRA) or MoveOn.org rely heavily on members' strength at the polls to influence policies.

Although some of these organizations might not seem at the forefront on international security debates, their lobbyists have significant impact on international issues as diverse as birth control assistance, immigration reform, and climate change. For example, the NRA has thwarted efforts by the Mexican government to curb U.S. assault weapons sales that officials believe fuel narcoterrorism. Moveon.org—an organization that grew from domestic supporters of President Bill Clinton during his impeachment trial in 1998—subsequently evolved into a group that led U.S. opposition to Iraq war funding. Such lobbying organizations help shape U.S. national security policies in a contest of ideas, money, and voter organizing power.

National security lobbyists in the nation's capital typically spend their days developing information through an informal network of contacts, personal visits, and targeted research. Armed with insights into the positions views of possible allies and adversaries, they press talking points while trying to build a coalition to support clients' positions. They use each new bit of information to circle back and refresh existing contacts while cementing alliances with champions in each political party, Congress, and the executive branch. Favorable press commentary and public testimony are marshaled; third-party validation can affect possible outcomes. Lobbyists solicit emails and phone calls from grass-roots supporters. Lobbyists project votes, draft amendments and floor statements, and explore fall-back options. They try to organize informal caucuses of like-minded legislators and coordinate with allies in the executive branch agencies. Lobbying teams produce issue briefs and circulate sympathetic studies from respected academic organizations. Lobbyists seek alliances with representatives of related interests as they refine tactics to achieve success.

This type of lobbyist involvement to advance an issue with U.S. national security implications has become routine in the American system of government. Post-Watergate reforms and the increasingly transnational nature of many heretofore domestic issues have led to a substantial increase in the number of lobbyists in Washington. As of 2010, Washington had more than thirteen thousand lobbyists registered by the Congress, a figure that excludes legions of lawyers, consultants, and support staff who engage in the process without registering. Lobbyists who seek to change federal policies must file quarterly reports with the Congress under the Lobbying Disclosure Act (LDA). If they are paid by a foreign entity, they must file a Foreign Agent Registration Act (FARA) form. Thousands of national security-related LDA filings and hundreds of FARA registrations are produced annually, although those in noncompliance have, to date, rarely been punished.

Table 13.1 is an illustrative list of some recent lobbying expenditures that affect national security issues.[1]

National security lobbyists are most often employed on one of four types of engagements. First, many work in support of a specific commercial venture that needs federal licensing or guarantees, such as a major air force plane purchase or a multinational energy pipeline development. Second, they might work to deter a proposed U.S. policy action, such as sanctions against Iran or termination of the Cuba trade embargo. Third, they might work to develop broader sympathy for a particular bilateral relationship and its impact on other U.S. national interests, such as U.S. relations with Israel, Turkey, or

Table 13.1   Annual Lobbying Expenditures on Select Domestic and International Issues

Organization	Principal National Security Issue	Expenditures*
U.S. Chamber of Commerce	International Trade	$144,000,000
Boeing	Defense Procurement	$20,680,000
AFL-CIO	Labor Rights	$1,707,500
Johnson & Johnson	International Trade	$8,970,500
Amnesty International	Human Rights	$400,000
Chevron	International Trade	$15,087,800
Sierra Club	Global Climate Change	$730,000
AIPAC	U.S.-Israel Relations	$2,488,091
MoveOn.org	Iraq War	$39,860,865
Lockheed-Martin	Defense Procurement	$22,000,000

*Figures cited include lobbying costs for *both domestic and international issues*. Lobbying expenditures means the total amount each organization claimed in lobbying disclosure forms filed with Congress in 2009, when the U.S. Senate Office of Public Records reported total expenditures on registered lobbyists of $3.47 billion. Reported expenditures do not account for associated public relations and advertising campaigns designed to influence the policymaking environment, nor the salaries and overhead for full-time support staff at lobbying organizations.

China. Fourth, lobbyists also work in-house with NGOs championing such broad policy objectives as arms control, immigration reform, or human rights.

Some national security specialists are available for hire on domestic issues as well, particularly partners in the larger lawyer/lobbying firms such as Akin, Gump, Patton, or Boggs. Many lobbyists have special regional expertise based on prior U.S. government service. Most offer clients insights into the bureaucratic politics of specific U.S. government agencies, including the departments of State, Energy, or Defense, as well as "insider" information.

A further distinction can be made between lobbyists at not-for-profit organizations, who are wedded ideologically to a specific NGO agenda, and contract lobbyists, whose specialty skills and prior government service can attract large fees when they are hired, often by a diverse array of unrelated interests. The former group tends to rely more on grass-roots activists to mobilize support and sway policymakers. The latter group often engages heavily in campaign fund-raising to influence and reinforce existing contacts with legislative supporters. Some see a distinction without too much difference because both types of lobbyists are experienced professionals, paid advocates who use many similar tactics. Both seek to use their knowledge of procedure and bureaucratic politics to impact policy. Both are required to register, and under stringent Obama-Biden-era requirements, neither can move directly from lobbying to executive branch service without a waiver from White House counsel. Clearly, corporate lobbyists with prior government service and substantial fund-raising capabilities have built-in advantages over most NGO advocates.

Successful national security lobbying strategists must navigate an environment in which competing interests press their case. Public support is essential to sustain a program such as the U.S. military campaign in Afghanistan. Similarly, public backing proves vital to implement a specific proposal, such as increasing the procurement of F-22 fighter planes. For the preferred policy to prevail, proponents inside and outside of government must develop support by equipping allies and anticipating challenges from opponents.

NATIONAL SECURITY LOBBYING IN HISTORICAL CONTEXT

History offers ample precedents for factional lobbying of international policies. President Washington was beset by Francophiles and Anglophiles; his farewell address condemned those who agitated for intervention overseas. The presidencies of John Adams and Thomas Jefferson were bedeviled by bitter press attacks and street demonstrations regarding trade and foreign policy. In the 1840s, Representative Abraham Lincoln's loss of his congressional seat was attributed, in part, to his unpopular opposition to President Polk's war on Mexico. In 1914, Woodrow Wilson narrowly avoided defeat in his reelection bid because of grass-roots lobbying against U.S. intervention in Europe. The creation of FARA was prompted, in the mid-1930s, by congressional concerns that German American groups promoting the nationalist policies of new Chancellor Adolf Hitler might unduly influence U.S. policy. Heavy-handed lobbying by anticommunist backers of the Republic of China on Taiwan in the 1950s colored a generation of U.S. efforts to come to terms with Mao Zedong's People's Republic of China (PRC).

The influence of international activists on U.S. national interests remains a major concern for analysts of contemporary U.S. politics. Many scholars lament the influence of special interest lobbying on national security policies, pointing to the outsized voice of particular groups, including those who have supported Israel and those who opposed Iraq's Saddam Hussein. John Newhouse summarizes these arguments in his 2009 *Foreign Affairs* article, "Diplomacy, Inc.," complaining that pervasive lobbying influences in Washington erode American credibility and shift control of policy away from the "capable, disinterested hands" of executive branch experts.[2]

The historical record suggests that when there exists a modicum of transparency, a vigilant press, and an informed electorate, such dangers can be countered. The authors of the Declaration of Independence and the Constitution were driven by the express conviction that national security policy was too important to be left to an all-powerful executive. They sought to open government up, allowing competing interests to shape Americans' role in the world. Like Newhouse, the authors of the *Federalist Papers* deplored the trouble that factions can cause. Yet they assumed and invited their organization, rejecting the idea that issues of war, peace, trade, defense, and foreign alliance should be insulated from the popular will.[3]

COMMON ELEMENTS OF SUCCESSFUL LOBBYING CAMPAIGNS

At the center of Washington policymaking debates rests the assumption that the national security interests of the United States will remain paramount. Examples of first-rate lobbyists effectively pressing a foreign interest that stands in direct conflict with a U.S. national security priority are rare. Lobbying efforts usually push one alternative over another, or seek sympathy for the plight of foreign partners. Most lobbying campaigns express a common theme: it is in the *American* interest to adopt the preferred policy.

The creation of alliances proves crucial in many cases. For example, China's lobbyists in Washington argue that Beijing should not be assailed for policies that harm U.S. interests, including China's devalued currency or the PRC's suppression of democracy, because China is working with the U.S. on *other* national security concerns. These include crucial financing of U.S. debt, helping contain North Korea's nuclear program, and sanctions against Iran. To mute U.S. criticism, China's lobbyists seek help from stakeholders in such multilateral efforts. Similarly, foreign lobbyists search for American allies to validate the notion that their international client interests—be they British, Israeli, Pakistani, or Chinese—are altogether consistent with U.S. policy objectives. Much commentary on this process assumes that national security lobbying is a zero-sum game, that either U.S. interests or those of a pernicious foreign entity must prevail. Effective lobbyists try to offer a clear win-win option in which the national interest and their client's objectives are not in conflict.

In many cases, it is the president's team of lobbyists—who work on the public payroll—that seeks engagement with third-party allies to build support. Their tactics have much in common with those deployed by contract lobbyists and NGO representatives. For example, the White House staff in 2006 enlisted domestic proponents of closer U.S.-India ties before asking Congress to ratify a controversial nuclear trade accord; Bush administration allies included the American Nuclear Energy Council and Indian American groups. President George W. Bush publicly thanked Indian American community leaders when he signed the bilateral agreement lifting thirty-year-old U.S. sanctions on nuclear commerce with India.[4] Similarly, President Clinton's White House team extensively engaged such ethnic groups as Polish Americans to lobby in support of his proposals to enlarge NATO.

Executive branch-led lobbying campaigns can take more subtle forms. When the Bush-Cheney administration sought to make the case for action against Iraq's weapons of mass destruction (WMD) and Iran's nuclear program, executive branch staffers repeatedly armed pro-Israel lobbyists with sensitive information. These alarms were then shared with wavering members of Congress and sympathetic reporters who helped build the case for tough U.S. action. Similarly, pro-Taiwan lobbyists regularly benefit from executive branch sources concerned about China's growing military capabilities. Taiwan's advocates use information that casts the policies of the Beijing regime in a negative light. Supportive members of Congress responded by requiring an annual public report on PRC military budgets and capabilities. This document has become an effective tool for highlighting threats the PRC might pose to U.S. interests, including that of preserving Taiwan's nascent democracy. Its annual release ensures a regular cycle of news stories and hearings about the alleged Chinese threat to democracy in Asia. It is also used, not coincidentally, to justify defense spending requests from both the Pentagon and certain Asian defense ministries.[5]

Present, too, in many effective lobbying campaigns is money. The extraordinary amounts of money spent on lobbying in recent years (listed in table 13.1) have a substantial impact on outcomes. Money can act as a megaphone, skewing perceptions of the popular will. Lavish funding enables certain lobbying campaigns to spin the notion that they have broad voter support. Funds fuel advertising campaigns, placement of opinion pieces, grass-roots activities, and campaign contributions. Clues to the likely outcome of some policy initiatives can be discerned from analysis of how much money each side is spending on competing lobbying campaigns. Financial resources, however, are not necessarily decisive. Analysis of why certain policy outcomes occur needs also to factor in one's definition of the national interest, a question that remains entirely subjective. Should China have been permitted to buy CONOCO and its sensitive energy assets? Did the Pentagon need to buy more F-22s? Should the U.S. military have intervened against genocide in Sudan? Determining which lobbying campaigns *should* have prevailed in such policy disputes is not an empirical exercise. Virtue does not always rest with the under-funded. Maybe the winning side had reason, logic, and precedent on their side, along with financial advantages in the lobbying contest.

SECURING ACCESS TO DECISION MAKERS AND ENERGIZING VOTERS

Congress and the executive branch staff are relatively accessible. Members and aides alike usually remain open to new information and well-organized entreaties. These both come from professional contract lobbyists and grass-roots activists. Washington is regularly besieged by email campaigns, calls that inundate Capitol Hill receptionists, and door-knocking efforts of supporters bused and flown into the city by competing lobbies. Here, again, money matters. Contract lobbyists active in campaign fund-raising are more likely to meet directly with elected officials, whereas an NGO representative may meet first with staff—unless representing a constituency important to the member of Congress. Past donations and the prospect of more campaign funding colors debate on many national security issues, especially those involving defense procurement and sensitive bilateral relationships. However, the notion that money-equals-access and produces special-interest backed policies can be overstated. More important than the size of lobbying fees or campaign contributions is usually the potential impact of policy options on *voters*. Representatives who ignore the will of voters to appease campaign contributors risk exposure and rejection on election day.

Where organized interests have the most sustained success—for example, in the pro-Israel lobby—is when they make the case that voters will support champions of preferred policies and reject those who are unsympathetic. Politicians have strong survival instincts. Elected officials are remarkably sensitive to voter sentiment.

Effective lobbyists rely heavily on talking points, simply framed messages that become shorthand for policy. To prevail, lobbyists marshal information and build coalitions with like-minded groups to target pressure on executive branch and congressional decision makers. Campaign financing, issue advertising, and encouraging electoral support are important lobbying components; but good information and sound argument still make a difference. As Jeffrey H. Birnbaum, until recently the *Washington Post*'s resident lobbying critic, notes, "Lobbying is much more substantive and out in the open than its ugly carica-ture. Lobbyists primarily woo lawmakers with facts."[6] It is through effective use of these facts and their combination with a sound political strategy that many lobbying battles are won. Lobbyists who understand political imperatives confronting policymakers are more likely to advance winning strategies.

THE NATIONAL SECURITY LOBBYING ENVIRONMENT: EXPLOITING DIVISIONS

To understand how lobbying works on national security issues one needs to appreciate how organizational behavior shapes decision making in contemporary Washington. What is the organizational culture? What is the decision-making process? What are the key prec-edents lobbyists and policymakers employ in the NSE?

Executive branch officials rarely launch international initiatives such as the North American Free Trade Agreement (NAFTA) or Iran sanctions without engaging lobbying allies. To prevail, they need to compete and enlist organized support. If the argument is weak and the facts suspect, the merits of the position risk exposure by competing advocates in the decision-making process.

The executive branch is far from monolithic on national security questions. The president can shape the initial terms of defense and foreign policy debates by driving the interagency process, coordinating cabinet members' messages, and using the bully pulpit of the Oval Office. The team from the White House Congressional Relations Office then puts the best face on the executive branch position while papering over internal dissent. Yet in many national security lobbying efforts, dissenters from within the executive bureaucracy are the original source of key arguments employed by challengers in Congress to contest policy proposals. These critics within the executive branch deliberately leak their minority views or are sought out and exploited by lobbyists representing competing interests. These internal disagreements are often present between the departments of State and Defense as well as the various agencies that comprise the intelligence community where analysis of the implications of raw information is regularly the subject of dispute. As basic a decision as whether the United States should wage war in Iraq was heavily influenced by disputes among intelligence analysts about single assertions. Was an Iraqi government official present at a Prague meeting with an al-Qaeda recruiter? Did an Iraqi agent ask about buying uranium in Niger?[7] In these and scores of other cases, U.S. intelligence analysts disagree in interpreting specific events. Policymakers at other departments, driven in part by interagency rivalry and divided by different missions, often support competing policies.

Lobbyists thrive in this environment. Lobbyists seek out and use dissenters within the executive branch process as the point of departure in making their case with Congress, the media, and the voting public. New facts and interpretations often emerge and are used to challenge the original basis for policy proposals. An executive branch consensus (e.g., the allegation that Russia acted virtually without provocation when it massed forces on the international border and invaded the Republic of Georgia in the summer 2008) can later become the subject of dispute as more accurate intelligence leaks out—in this case intelligence indicating Georgia had provoked Russia by shelling civilian areas for hours before Moscow responded.[8]

CONGRESS AS A COURT OF APPEALS FOR LOBBYISTS

Congress becomes, in effect, a court of appeals where elected officials review and critique White House execution of national security policies. The most successful national security lobbyists are experts in this process by which the president formulates policy and the Congress revises it before ratifying or enabling its implementation. Lobbyists' best tool is often their substantial institutional memory. They have allies and former colleagues from previous policy fights. Veteran lobbyists often know the precedents, the legislative history, and the political sensitivities of individual legislators better than many of the executive branch's foreign policy and defense specialists. The latter are often technical experts operating at a distance from voters and the electoral process.

Lobbyists know which messages and messengers will have the greatest impact on undecided members. They carefully track the key go-to defense and foreign policy experts from among the respective congressional party caucuses. Lobbyists find out which commentators and news sources members look to first. They try to learn which home state VIPs might have the greatest influence on undecided members. They try to appeal to—or develop on their own—an informal caucus of members sensitive to a particular trade or bilateral relationship.

Such political insights are routinely exploited by interest groups and contract lobbyists. The best congressional relations team members in the White House do the same thing using the same types of information as they lobby to get support for the president's proposals. Similar pressure points are used by legislators themselves as they lobby colleagues to try to secure a majority vote.

Lobbyists collect and disseminate information from numerous sources, often seeking compromise through congressional amendment of the original executive branch proposals. A good illustration can be found in the work of labor unions and environmental activists, who often push to alter the terms of free-trade accords, including requirements for labor standards and environmental protection, before acquiescing to the pact's ratification. Similarly, lobbyists for defense manufacturers facing Pentagon termination of a program may plead with Congress to extend procurement for one more year in order to live to fight another day.

Lobbyists use the power of an assertive executive branch or the wounded pride of members of Congress to help shape outcomes to their clients' benefit. This is particularly true when pressing issues involving U.S. defense contracts, an area where the survival instincts of Congress and the power of defense lobbyists often frustrate efforts to curb defense spending. "Keep the production line open" or "maintain the American defense-industrial base" are phrases that ably capture the essence of lobbying messages used to challenge Pentagon procurement decisions. There are few more powerful arguments to an elected official than the creation or protection of jobs in their districts or states. Legislators on record favoring sharp reductions in defense spending usually make exceptions when weapons systems made in their home constituencies are imperiled.[9]

LOBBYING BY FOREIGN EMBASSIES IN WASHINGTON

The least effective lobbyists on international security issues are, ironically, often the professionally trained diplomats posted to Washington's Embassy Row. Constrained by the internal bureaucratic politics of their own governments, careerists from foreign ministries often become so concerned about protocol and hierarchy that they fail to demonstrate sufficient entrepreneurship. The risk-taking exceptions can be very successful diplomat/lobbyists. The British embassy has been particularly effective in gaining insights, famously knowing before many in the U.S. executive branch that a White House decision to invade Iraq had been made early in 2002. In terms of individuals, both Israeli Prime Minister Benjamin "Bibi" Netanyahu, as a deputy chief of mission at the embassy of Israel in the 1980s, and Prince Bandar, the long-time Saudi ambassador to the United States, developed extraordinary access to U.S. politicians and decision makers during their Washington tenure, as did the late Soviet Ambassador Anatoly Dobrynin. Such diplomats prove extremely effective by cultivating extensive back-channel relationships while operating in an unorthodox, freelance manner to advance their nations' security interests.

Foreign embassies in the United States sometimes hire advocates to press a position that appears in direct conflict with elements of U.S. policy. Such appeals face steep odds, unless they can be presented as consonant with U.S. national interests. An unusual example of a foreign government successfully blocking an initiative in Congress occurred in 2007, when the embassy of Turkey hired several prominent former members to help block adoption of a congressional resolution condemning the genocide against Armenians early in the twentieth century. Proponents of the resolution, long sought by Armenian Americans, believed that the U.S. government had a clear interest in demonstrating solidarity against an historical act of genocide. House Democratic leaders at first committed to a vote. Then opponents argued successfully that the risk of alienating an important NATO ally with a restive young Muslim population outweighed the benefits of a resolution restating troublesome historical facts. Their case was bolstered by feverish lobbying by the Bush administration and the embassy of Turkey's team of contract lobbyists, who coordinated efforts to get all living former U.S. secretaries of state on record opposing adoption of the proposed congressional resolution.[10]

Similarly, pro-Taiwan interests paid for a comprehensive lobbying campaign in 1995 to overcome State Department restrictions preventing U.S. travel by their elected head of state, Lee Teng-hui. In this well-chronicled episode, the traditional U.S. interest in free speech and democracy promotion clashed with the desire of policy pragmatists not to endanger efforts to get the one-party PRC government in Beijing to support other critical U.S. initiatives. Proponents of President Lee's visit framed the issue as one harming U.S. citizens. Lobbyists argued that communist authorities in China should not be permitted to limit Americans' rights to hear a democratically elected leader. They pressed their argument over outspoken State Department objections by highlighting recent U.S. visits of such controversial visitors as IRA leader Gerry Adams and PLO head Yasser Arafat.[11]

The most effective Washington lobbyists engaged by foreign interests are often former U.S. government policymakers or staffers who are retained with the unspoken understanding they will not challenge basic U.S. national interests. Veteran lobbyists take advantage of insights into executive branch divisions, the natural cleavages that separate political appointees from career bureaucrats, and divide one cabinet department from another. Some press their case without registering; they pose as legal counsel or strategic consultants. They maintain they are simply working to educate policymakers and develop sympathy for their clients' perspectives. They insist that they do not lobby per se, because they are not technically pressing for a specific legislative outcome and arguably not subject to registration with Congress or the Justice Department.

There is often a fiction that should be viewed with skepticism, because these paid advocates are often sharing information and opinions in an effort to influence policy. Such consultants often maintain robust communications with senior American policymakers, shaping the diplomatic tactics of foreign clients—and often encouraging them to accommodate U.S. concerns—while pressing senior U.S. government officials for support. Lucrative businesses developed by such former government officials and respected national figures as Henry Kissinger and Bob Dole have benefited from substantial consulting contracts for these types of engagements.

ETHICS REQUIREMENTS AND CORRUPT PRACTICES

Some lobbyists on international security issues, frustrated in their efforts to penetrate decision-making circles with legitimate merit-based presentations, become insensitive to evolving ethics requirements. Washington has a long history of overzealous foreign businesspersons and defense contractors trying to corrupt U.S. officials. In the 1950s and 1960s, supporters of Chiang Kai-shek and his anticommunist colleagues on Taiwan funneled money to those most outspoken against Mao's China. The Korea-gate influence peddling schemes of the 1970s and the ABSCAM scandal in the early 1980s produced reforms that curbed some abuses. More recent contracting scandals involving Boeing and air force officials appear also to have had a chilling effect on some corrupt practices.

The most ethically challenged national security lobbyists in the intensely competitive environment become lazy. Lacking confidence in the merits of their case, they rely excessively on efforts to curry favor by supporting endless campaign fund-raising events, donations to members' favorite charities, or lavish foreign fact-finding junkets. Among the recent cases of practices that allegedly crossed legal boundaries, the most notorious involved Paul Magliochetti Associates (PMA), an established lobbying firm of primarily defense appropriations specialists. The firm imploded in spring 2009 over reports that its principals recruited straw donors to make contributions to legislators who supported PMA clients' requests for earmarked appropriations.

National security lobbying is a highly regulated profession, with LDA, FARA, and Foreign Corrupt Practices Act (FCPA) requirements lending transparency and marking ethical boundaries. However, enforcement of regulatory requirements is lax and clumsy prosecutorial efforts, as in the 2008 trial of then Senator Ted Stevens of Alaska, make compliance problematic. Abuses have also undermined some legitimate efforts to expose members of Congress to diverse international views. For example, much foreign travel by working congressional delegations ("Codels" appointed by congressional leadership and parliamentary exchanges) involves members in serious fact-finding missions that inform key policy decisions. Official travel to war zones and allied capitals can increase understanding and build long-term support. Others, such as lobbyist-funded junkets to play golf in Scotland, are decidedly illegitimate, and risk discrediting all involved.

Members are warned by congressional ethics panels to avoid even the appearance of impropriety, yet many rely heavily on lobbyists for funds. Scrupulously following evolving congressional ethics rules is essential for Washington lobbyists. They can retain their effectiveness only by avoiding the many gray areas of ever-changing ethics requirements designed to lend further transparency to the policymaking process. Pressures from members of Congress for campaign funds from lobbyists create appearances that are awkward at best and will persist absent meaningful election finance reforms.

In the wake of the Watergate scandal of the 1970s, congressional reforms were put in place that dispersed concentrated power. Ironically, the creation of multiple legislative power centers and overlapping committee jurisdiction increased points of access for lobbyists, as have the growth of the cabinet and the appointment of numerous policy czars. This spread of jurisdiction has increased the degree of difficulty for execution of new policy initiatives; there are now far more decision makers to convince.

The dispersion of power has also opened up the possibility of panel shopping, much as attorneys maneuver for the best judge or venue before which to present their client's case. For example, there are more than eighty separate committees or subcommittees of Congress with jurisdiction over aspects of intelligence or homeland security. Lobbyists have also become more aggressive about using presidential transitions, the confirmation process, and fund-raising as opportunities to press their case. At the same time, ethics reforms have made efforts by registered lobbyists to impact the policymaking process more transparent, with timely reported information on some lobbying activities more accessible.

With the proliferation of think tanks and new media outlets, including blogs and web-sites, savvy lobbyists have refined techniques for making their case. Consider how effectively MoveOn.org was able to build voter opposition to the Iraq occupation.[12] Similarly, note the impact the U.S. Chamber of Commerce and agribusiness lobbyists have had on efforts to pass climate change/energy policy legislation. Each effectively uses grass-roots contact with business stakeholders and consumers, various internet platforms, as well as both earned and paid media. In recent years, even the most old-fashioned members have taken to such new communications platforms as YouTube and Twitter to reach voters and potential allies.

MILITARY PROCUREMENT, BASE CLOSURE, AND ENVIRONMENTAL ISSUES

Polices proposed by executive branch officials are often challenged by NGO lobbyists who coordinate grass-roots campaigns. Opponents of a proposed U.S. policy press their case via membership organizations, as MoveOn.org did on the Iraq war funding issue, or the Natural Resources Defense Council (NRDC) and the Sierra Club do on global warming/climate change issues. For example, as the fight to legislate caps on carbon emissions escalated in 2009, more than 770 companies and interest groups engaging more than 2,300 lobbyists worked to influence federal policy on climate change. Expenditures totaled more than $90 million in reported annual lobbying fees.[13]

Interests as diverse as coal manufacturers and birding groups hired advocates that included such prominent figures as former Democratic House Majority Leader Richard Gephardt and former Appropriations Committee Chairman Robert Livingston, a Republican. The marshaling of such disparate forces makes compromise inevitable and increases the likelihood of delay, worrying proponents of sweeping action. "The danger is that special interests will dilute and torque government policies," NASA's chief climate scientist James Hansen lamented in early 2009, "causing the climate to pass tipping points, with grave consequences for all life on the planet."[14]

Much of the lobbying conducted on national security matters is highly specialized. For example, if they seek to block a project in an environmentally sensitive area of Belize, the leadership of a Washington-based advocacy group such as NRDC must field a team that includes experts in development policy (to deal with the World Bank); Belizean contract law (to work locally); as well as lobbyists effective in dealing with members on key congressional committees (to press for enactment of restrictions via foreign aid or trade-related legislation.)

Lobbyists for defense manufacturers must know such diverse issues as contracting law and the voting records of potential congressional supporters. Defense lobbyists routinely encourage corporations to spread contracts widely to help secure local support from more legislators: the Stealth bomber and Seawolf submarine subcontracts were in as many of the four-hundred thirty-five congressional districts and fifty states as possible.

Reforms designed to insulate policymaking from politics usually lag behind successful lobbying efforts. Consider how a process explicitly designed to take the politics out of tough decisions to close military bases has itself become the focus of elaborate lobbying campaigns. The BRAC process, named for the Base Realignment and Closure Commission, has evolved into a sophisticated and highly competitive lobbying specialty.

What does a community do if it fears a major loss of local jobs and infrastructure investment because the Pentagon bureaucracy proposes closure of a long-standing military facility? It is not sufficient to rely on a single congressional champion to stand at the ramparts, though many members have found that the most important issue in their reelection campaign is their effort to save a local military facility from the threat of BRAC closure. Members from the region will make the public case against a Pentagon closure recommendation. City leaders in such vulnerable communities as Portsmouth, New Hampshire, or San Diego, California, will usually demand more and elect to work with local business and labor leaders in a coordinated campaign to save local jobs. Communities heavily dependent on defense-related jobs now often hire BRAC lobbyists with specialized Washington practices.

How does BRAC lobbying work? A good example can be found in the case of Los Angeles Air Force Base (LAAFB), an obscure California facility that plays a valuable role in procurement of communication and intelligence satellites used by scores of defense-related agencies of the U.S. government, from the Weather Service to those tracking al-Qaeda. It was tough for southern Californians to press the case for retaining LAAFB; it remains a Cold War anomaly, an urban facility on highly valuable land, but an air force base without a runway. It was originally proposed by Pentagon staff as candidate for inclusion on the 2003 BRAC closure list. However, a bipartisan community coalition funded a targeted lobbying campaign. Their team of lobbyists pored over Pentagon data used to justify closure and developed a series of counterarguments, noting that the facility needed to remain close to California's high-tech and defense industrial base. They also enlisted the backing of then House Appropriations Committee Chairman Jerry Lewis (R-CA) and veteran Senate Appropriations Committee member Senator Dianne Feinstein (D-CA).

The ensuing process of public debate and private persuasion did not remove politics from the final decision. Indeed, powerful legislators from New Mexico eagerly sought to transfer the LAAFB functions to their home state. Other California political leaders held a series of rallies at the Los Angeles base entrance and requested Chairman Lewis's intervention. Proponents of the base retention effort believe Rep. Lewis, who then played the lead House role in approving all Pentagon appropriations, argued the merits of their facility in direct conversation with Defense Secretary Donald Rumsfeld.[15] Although on the Pentagon's draft list of candidates for closure, the LAAFB was not on the final list of cuts approved by Congress in an up-or-down vote. Other survivors of BRAC rounds have employed similar lobbying strategies: politics most decidedly has remained a part of the base closure process.

BRAC cases expose the difficulty of putting national interests ahead of local concerns. Defense issues have proved especially vulnerable to coordinated lobbying and pressure campaigns. For the post-Vietnam generation, especially in the left-leaning parts of the Democratic Party, elected politicians have feared being labeled weak on defense. Post-9/11 events added the fear of being attacked as soft on terrorism. This has made members of both parties timid about reining in spending on defense, intelligence, or homeland security.

When the Obama-Biden administration and its GOP Secretary of Defense Robert Gates moved in 2009 to shut down the production line for a few weapons systems, some defense lobbyists assailed them for allegedly slashing Pentagon spending. They enlisted allies in lobbyists for local unions, who cited the sharp economic recession as a reason for continuing military programs the Pentagon said were not cost effective: "It doesn't make sense that our government is looking to save or create jobs at the same time it's talking about cutting something like this (the F-22 fighter jet program)," the head of the Georgia machinists union, Jeff Goen, complained.[16] Yet, the Obama-Biden administration's proposed Pentagon budget continued to grow at a rate of 4% in fiscal year 2010—and proposed procurement grew at 5.6%—even after liberal Democrats replaced conservative Republicans in the White House.[17] The threat of terrorists and nuclear proliferation warranted much of the spending, to be sure, as did instability in Russia, China, and the Middle East. Yet targeted lobbying once increased the challenge of controlling defense spending. Indeed, it took the threat of a veto for the Obama administration's first annual defense appropriations measure and an all-out coordinated lobbying campaign run by the White House congressional affairs—aided by arms control and taxpayer groups—for the administration to finally end F-22 funding in a close Senate vote in July 2009.

PRECEDENTS: LESSONS LEARNED IN RECENT POLICYMAKING FIGHTS

Lobbying on foreign policy and security matters helps shape and define the national interest. It is illustrative to chart some of the basic characteristics of recent lobbying battles, with the caveat that such an exercise is highly subjective. Table 13.2 is thus designed to be illustrative, not comprehensive, to provoke debate, and spur critical thinking among readers on the impact of recent lobbying campaigns.

Informed discussion of the case studies referenced in table 13.2 underscores the point that where you stand on the merits or desirability of the proposed policy course is often directly related to where you sit. Many could argue that some of the benefits of such lobbying battles also create national policy weaknesses and unwelcome outcomes, and vice versa. For example, those responsible for enlisting Chinese support for U.S. policy initiatives vis-à-vis North Korea and Iran doubtless find congressional resolutions pressed by pro-Tibet activists nettlesome. Such anti-China resolutions certainly put at risk important U.S. bilateral and multilateral policy objectives. Conversely, citizens championing human rights find it upsetting that pro-Turkey lobbyists succeed in discouraging U.S. House members from adopting a resolution acknowledging the fact that genocide was perpetrated by some Ankara officials against Armenians early in the twentieth century.

The openness of the American policymaking system affords the executive branch team several options if it is willing to engage in nimble maneuver. An example: the White House

Table 13.2   Impact of Lobbying on Selected National Security Issues

Putative "Benefits" to Policymaking Process	Illustrative Issue/Campaign
Manifests the interests of major employers	U.S. Chamber—NAFTA
Opens process to faith-based organizations	SaveDarfur.org's Sudan efforts
Increases Pentagon transparency	Boeing challenges Air Force tanker procurement decision
Renews key bilateral relationship/opens valuable energy market	Nuclear industry/Indian-American push for nuclear deal
Pushes for bipartisan consensus	Earmark funding an Iraq Study Group to devise exit strategy
Manifests popular U.S. concerns	Amnesty International campaign on Guantanamo Bay/detainee torture
Brings selected public concerns to bear	Environmentalists on climate change
Possible "Burdens" to Policy	Example
Can impose costly purchase requirements	Challenges to Air Force tanker deal
Can exacerbate diplomatic efforts	Pushing U.S. Embassy in Jerusalem or anti-Castro Cuba trade sanctions
Inflames sensitive bilateral relations	Anti-China resolutions
Imposes new requirements after the fact	Labor/environmental conditions on free trade agreements
Undermines global nuclear nonproliferation standards	U.S. India nuclear agreement

can use critics in Congress and the lobbying community to try to make the administration appear to negotiating partners as relatively moderate as, for example, in the recent U.S.-India nuclear agreement. If the administration wants the PRC to move on revaluing its currency, why not encourage members on Codels to China to vent constituents' anger that the PRC government's currency manipulation overprices U.S. exports and leads to dumping of subsidized Chinese products on the American market? Or, if the administration wants Russia to curb its harsh crackdown on domestic critics, why not quietly help Amnesty International and other NGOs to highlight abuse of civil liberties by the current Moscow regime?

In each case, using this kind of good cop/bad cop paradigm allows the White House to maintain bilateral relationships while encouraging organized lobby campaigns to press American concerns. This has proven an effective tactic; U.S. diplomats can impress on foreign leaders the desirability of working with the administration to address the concerns of NGOs, special interest lobbyists, and the U.S. Congress *before* implementing legislation is enacted. Diplomats can use the threat of congressional opposition to achieve many U.S. objectives in bilateral discussions.

In many cases lobbyists work with congressional leaders to avoid up-or-down votes, proposing amendments that deal with parts of the national security policy initiative, or conditioning its approval. Some of the most passionate critics of the congressional role in national security policymaking decry how lobbying pressures feed this institutional tendency to blink in a confrontation, an alleged political timidity that ducks or splits recorded votes.[18] This temptation to find political cover by voting on both sides of an issue has harmed a number of leading American political figures in recent years. For example, conservative critics assailed Democratic presidential candidates John Kerry and Hillary Clinton for flip-flopping because both first voted to give authority for military operations against Iraq, then later sought to curb war funding and ultimately oppose how the Bush-Cheney administration prosecuted the war and occupation. John McCain was similarly attacked by interest groups for first declaring it "immoral" to cut taxes in time of war, then reversing himself during the 2008 presidential campaign to embrace making the Bush tax cuts permanent. The crosscutting pressures of lobbying by national organizations can make such flip-flops tempting, if politically unwise.

The relative wisdom of alternative approaches to securing the national interest often requires passage of a generation before the merits become clear. How many of those conservative lobbyists who clamored in the 1970s to reject the Panama Canal treaties would argue seriously that U.S. interests would be more secure today had Washington insisted on occupying the Canal Zone in perpetuity? Similarly, how many of the liberal activists who assailed President Reagan's defense build-up would still insist that the threat of expanded U.S. military deployments played no role in intimidating Soviet leaders, bankrupting Moscow, and hastening the decline of Soviet-style communism?

The passage of time has not reduced debate over the merits of many national security lobbying campaigns, including efforts to secure U.S. government support for Israel. Dating back to the 1940s, American backers of Israel have been a major political force in Washington. Prompt U.S. recognition of Israel in 1948, when President Truman overrode nearly unanimous State Department opposition, became just the first success for this lobbying effort. Through the last decades of the twentieth century, the pro-Israel community in the United States, supported most visibly by AIPAC, argued that America had strong national security reasons for backing Israel against the threat of attack from hostile neighbors. American interests cited by lobbyists included the promotion of an anticommunist democracy, the need to back a moderate government in the unstable Middle East region, and the building of a bulwark against dangers from radical Islam. AIPAC lobbyists have worked with supporters in Congress and the executive branch to resist arms sales to Israel's foes. Pro-Israel lobbying campaigns have been countered by many U.S. diplomats, defense manufacturers, and oil company lobbyists, as well as some human rights organizations. These critics maintain that U.S. support for Israel alienates Arab nations and Muslim leaders while conflicting with U.S. principles and perpetuating the Palestinian diaspora. General David Petraeus, among others, has suggested that the U.S. failure to press Israel and Arab leaders for a resolution of the Palestinian issue has put American soldiers and American interests at risk. In recent years, breakaway groups within the pro-Israel community have alleged that AIPAC's unblinking support for positions taken by the most hard-line Israeli factions have harmed the interests of both the United States and Israel.

The success of AIPAC's lobbying efforts has attracted much highly charged commentary. The publication in 2007 of a study critical of AIPAC, authored by Professors Mearsheimer and Walt, sparked a series of bitter exchanges in the press over both the strengths and the dangers of the so-called Israel lobby.[19] The study's conclusions were controversial, alleging that the power of money (campaign donations) and lobbyists' threats (to withhold same) has distorted U.S. policy, abandoned Palestinians, and encouraged anti-American violence.

The existence of the formidable pro-Israel lobbying effort also produces clumsy scape-goating. For example, as recently as March 2009, an imperiled nominee for a senior intelligence post in the Obama-Biden administration, former U.S. Ambassador Charles Freeman, assailed AIPAC, alleging that "the Israel lobby" had blocked his nomination. Freeman's charge, detailed in a *Washington Post* opinion piece, ignored the fact that numerous political leaders, including House Speaker Nancy Pelosi, were on record in opposition to the famously abrasive Freeman for controversial positions he had taken on other international matters unrelated to Israel, such as human rights in China. Freeman's views on U.S.-Israel relations may have had little to do with the failure of his nomination. Yet Freeman's increasingly bellicose attacks on pro-Israel lobbyists were repeated as fact by many professional journalists, as well as amateurs in the blogosphere. Freeman's abrupt withdrawal from consideration for the intelligence post was cited by many as further evidence of pro-Israel lobbyists' power.

Here, as on other emotionally charged national security issues, the key question for intelligent analysis might better be "does the lobbying effort support or detract from the advancement of U.S. national security interests?" Critics of AIPAC's tactics are united in their view that U.S. policy is so pro-Israel as to endanger other U.S. security interests. Their conclusion, that nefarious lobbyists are to blame, is reflexive. The reality is that U.S. policy has, but for a few incidents since the Truman presidency, been firmly supportive of Israel no matter which party controlled the White House and Congress or who was lobbying the issue.

These examples serve to illustrate an essential characteristic of the national security policymaking process: by affording multiple points of access, the U.S. system creates numerous opportunities for effective lobbyists to exploit. From career agency bureaucrats to Senate-confirmed administration appointees to White House staff and the National Security Council, almost every decision-making layer of the executive branch bureaucracy is open to outside influence. In some cases, political appointees are more malleable than career bureaucrats. Nevertheless, the porous, complex system creates numerous pressure points. Similarly, with the diffusion of power in the post-Watergate Congress, lobbyists are provided a multitude of targets to attempt to persuade on the merits. The national security decision-making system in the United States is not, and never has been, a uniform process controlled by a single actor. It remains relatively open, subject to sustained lobbying throughout.

CONCLUSION: POLITICS AND THE NATIONAL SECURITY ENTERPRISE

Politics can no more be taken out of the NSE than can lobbyists be removed from the system designed by America's founders to shape U.S. laws. Indeed, some reform efforts designed to reduce concentrations of power often have an opposite effect. An illustration: in the 1990s, voters in the state of California imposed strict term limits on state legislators. The design was to use the populist legislation-by-voter-referendum to limit the power of entrenched incumbents, many of whom appeared to be in the sway of corporate or union lobbyists. The principal consequence of the California state term limits, however, is that when state assemblypersons and senators retire from office after only a few terms, the institutional memory in Sacramento resides to a much larger degree with lobbyists. Many of them are former elected officials. They know the precedents much better than their successors in the state legislature, where first-termers now routinely hold leadership posts. As with certain post-Watergate reforms in Washington, changes in California designed to curb special interest influence have actually increased the role lobbyists play in shaping policy.

Experience shows that hyperbolic appeals to take politics out of national security policy by curbing lobbying are unrealistic. The bitter divisions over U.S. policy toward Iraq illustrate the point. After September 11, 2001, President George W. Bush enjoyed extraordinarily high poll ratings, reaching ninety-two percent approval later that month. This patriotic support appeared to give his administration a free hand as his team sought to prevent more attacks on the United States. Criticism from Democrats in Congress was muted. Critics of proposed U.S. military responses were hard to find in the NGO community. Lobbying by the Bush-Cheney administration secured broad support for military action to counter the ongoing national security threats posed by al-Qaeda terrorists and their sympathizers. Administration cabinet members dominated the U.S. airwaves with ominous warnings. The administration's private briefings of swing votes in Congress reduced the threat of opposition.

Then the White House moved in 2002 to expand its lobbying campaign substantially. The administration chose to broaden its engagements against al-Qaeda and their Taliban allies headquartered in Afghanistan, making an emotional case for a new military campaign against Iraqi dictator Saddam Hussein. Internal executive branch dissent against this new tactic was systematically quashed. Months passed before lobbying by antiwar skeptics could effectively question the new priorities and challenge the credibility of intelligence regarding the nature of Iraqi threats to U.S. national security interests. Years passed before lobbying by human rights and civil liberties groups pushed to the forefront of public debate questions about Geneva Convention requirements, the alleged torture of prisoners by the United States, and the pressured involvement of U.S. allies in secret renditions of suspected terrorists. The wisdom of choosing to prosecute multiple wars at once instead of focusing first on al-Qaeda bases in Afghanistan went unchallenged.

The White House team leading the lobbying effort, headed by director for political affairs Karl Rove, exploited their temporary political advantage. The White House team portrayed critics of their tactics as soft on terrorism and unsupportive of U.S. policy in time of war. The short-term success of White House lobbying campaign was substantial. In the November 2002 midterm elections, for the first time since World War II, the incumbent president's party *gained* seats in both the House and Senate. Most successful GOP candidates heeded Mr. Rove's explicit advice to "run on the war."

Over time, however, lobbying by a broad array of constituencies eroded the domestic consensus forged in the wake of 9/11. The subsequent political disputes were pressed by grass-roots activists over such issues as Guantanamo Bay and Abu Ghraib interrogation methods, warrantless government eavesdropping on U.S. citizens, and the helpfulness of the U.S. invasion of Iraq to the Bush administration's declaration of global war on terror. Opposition legislators joined the effort belatedly, focusing their criticism on the conduct of the Iraq occupation. They argued that Iraq should be a lower priority for U.S. national security interests than rooting out al-Qaeda backers in Afghanistan.

Scholars have differing views on the wisdom of these competing lobbying efforts. Consensus should be attainable, however, on one central point: these are inherently *political* disputes about national priorities. The notion that only an elite group of military and diplomatic professionals should define the national interest on such key war and peace issues is without merit. Sustained lobbying on war and peace issues—by both national security professionals and grass-roots citizens—is the norm, not the exception. Throughout U.S. history, from "who lost China?" debates, to divisions over Soviet relations, to the bitter national divisions over Vietnam War policy, similar lobbying has occurred. Only in rare moments of national crisis, as in the immediate wake of Pearl Harbor and 9/11, have all but the most partisan voices been silent and an all-encompassing consensus briefly achieved. Politics, in fact, almost never stops at the water's edge.

The role lobbyists play in this competition to guide the NSE is increasingly transparent. In a regulated system, registered lobbyists are not unlike lawyers in the judicial branch: they serve as both messengers and advocates. Frustration about national security lobbying often appears as a desire to shoot the messenger. Understanding the tools available and mastering the policymaking process may prove more effective than deploring lobbyists' influence. The power of money to distort policy, spin facts, and intimidate opposition can be countered. Democracy is decidedly imperfect, but open competition, voter mobilization, and timely presentation of facts can help level the playing field. A vigilant press, an engaged voting public, and a modicum of transparency can ameliorate much potential harm caused by lobbying campaigns that would compromise national objectives to advance those of special interests.

The founding fathers believed competition among factions was distasteful, but necessary, to ensure freedom in a democratic system. The pressure from competing lobbying interests that influence the contemporary U.S. national security debate is consistent with what the architects of the American system anticipated. Opening the decision-making process in order to safeguard national interests—*especially* on issues of war and peace—was deemed the most efficient alternative.

No one branch of government is the font of all wisdom, nor is any singular elite group empowered by the Constitution to define U.S. national security interests. Washington today is a far cry from Plato's Republic; there are few of Newhouse's "disinterested hands" resident in the capital. Most parties to the NSE advance their particular interests, even as they invariably argue that their commercial or ideological priorities are consistent with the national interest. Constitutional checks and balances enable lobbyists to compete with other factions to shape policy outcomes. Well-funded interests are similar to mobilized electoral blocs; they mirror how power is actually distributed in contemporary American society, if not how partisans might wish power to be allocated in a more perfect democracy.

Lobbying to impact the national security policymaking process, like sausage making, is not pretty to observe. Nevertheless, it is the American way: inclusive, inelegant, and decidedly Darwinist. Participants in the NSE must compete vigorously and let the strongest campaigns, advancing the best arguments, prevail.

NOTES

1. Congressional Quarterly, CQ MoneyLine Lobby Database. United States Senate, Lobby Disclosure Act Database. Federal Election Commission, Campaign Finance Disclosure Database, available at www.fec.gov/disclosure.shtml. See also, Carrie Dann, "K Street Thrives Amid Economic Downturn," *Congress Daily*, January 30, 2009.

2. John Newhouse, "Diplomacy, Inc.: The Influence of Lobbies on U.S. Foreign Policy," *Foreign Affairs*, May/June 2009.

3. In *Federalist No. 10*, James Madison (writing as "Publius") defined factions as "a number of citizens, whether amounting to a majority or minority of the whole, who are united and actuated by some common impulse of passion, or of interest, adverse to the rights of other citizens, or to the permanent and aggregate interests of the community." Madison observed that liberty fuels factions as surely as air fuels fire, concluding that regulation and competition can ameliorate their negative effects. Clinton Rossiter, ed., *The Federalist Papers* (New York: New American Library, 1961), 78.

4. Note there were two key congressional votes—one in 2006 to get conditions for the negotiations, a second in 2008 to approve the pact. Gerald Warburg, "Effective Foreign Lobbying in Washington: Ten Steps to Success," Brookings Institution, Washington, DC, October 30, 2008, or "Nonproliferation Policy Crossroads: The Strange Case of U.S.-India Nuclear Cooperation," Stanford Center for International Security and Cooperation, Palo Alto, California, October 21, 2010.

5. Jay Chen and Sofia Wu, "Pentagon Required to Report on Taiwan Strait Security Annually," *CNA News*, May 28, 1999. Offered by the GOP leadership as an amendment to the annual Department of Defense spending bill, the provision is sometimes referred to as "the (Sen. Frank) Murkowski amendment" or the "Chinese power" report.

6. As quoted in Samuelson, "An Obama Gift for K Street" *Washington Post*, December 15, 2008.

7. For competing views on interagency disputes over Iraq war intelligence, see Tim Weiner, *Legacy of Ashes* (New York: Doubleday, 2007) or George Tenet, *At the Center of the Storm* (New York: Harper, 2007).

8. Nicholas D. Kristof, "Obama, Misha and the Bear," *New York Times*, November 20, 2008. The issue flared during the 2008 U.S. presidential campaign, in part because senior advisors to Senator John McCain's campaign had recently served as lobbyists for the Republic of Georgia.

9. See *Congress Daily*, November 20, 2008. Note that in the 2009 F-22 funding debate, many liberal legislators who often oppose defense budget increase—such as John Kerry of Massachusetts—opposed Obama administration efforts to limit more production.

10. See account in Newhouse, "Diplomacy, Inc."

11. Jim Mann, "How Taipei Outwitted U.S. Policy," *Los Angeles Times*, June 8, 1995. (Full disclosure: this author was involved, as Mann notes.)

12. Efforts to rally a lobbying group's donors can backfire. For example, the left-leaning MoveOn.org provoked backlash with its 2007 *New York Times* ad impugning the integrity of General Petraeus, who directed U.S. troops in Iraq. Juvenile wordplay questioning the respected General's patriotism (Petraeus rendered as "Betray-us") brought ridicule on the antiwar lobbyists and distracted from their efforts to curb U.S. funding.

13. Marianne Lavelle, "Lobbyists Warm to Climate Change Debate," *Politico*, February 25, 2009.

14. Ibid.

15. Jason Bates, "California Group Works to Shield Los Angeles Air Force Base," *Space News*, February 2, 2004. (Full disclosure: this author aided the California-based coalition.)

16. Dan Eggen, "Plan to Cut Weapons Programs Disputed," *Washington Post*, April 28, 2009.

17. Megan Scully, "Obama Seeks 5.6 Percent Boost for Weapons Procurement," *Congress Daily*, May 8, 2009.

18. Barry M. Blechman, with W. Philip Ellis, *The Politics of National Security: Congress and U.S. Defense Policy* (New York: Oxford University Press, 1992), 194.

19. John J. Mearsheimer and Stephen M. Walt, *The Israel Lobby and U.S. Foreign Policy* (New York: Farrar, Strauss and Giroux, 2007).

Chapter 14 Think Tanks: Supporting Cast Players in the National Security Enterprise

Ellen Laipson

> Bureaucracies do not invent new ideas. They elaborate old ones. . . . But where do politicians get new ideas? Many sources, obviously, but certainly think tanks. Think tanks become important incubators of policy innovation.
>
> *John Hamre, former deputy secretary of defense, now president and CEO, Center for Strategic and International Studies*

Think tanks are an important but unofficial part of the national security enterprise (NSE). Their contributions are indirect and informal. Think tanks do not make critical foreign policy decisions, face no public accountability, nor do they perform any inherently governmental functions. But they are increasingly integrated into the way the U.S. government conceptualizes its national security interests and devises responses to the diverse challenges and opportunities of national and international security. They can be seen as an organic part of the way in which policy ideas are incubated, tested, promoted, and evaluated. Government officials vary in the degree to which they seek input from think tanks, but the frequency with which very senior officials launch new policy initiatives at think tanks, or working-level officers seek critical input and feedback from think tank experts, suggests that think tanks are accepted as a normal and integral part of policy formulation and outreach.

Think tanks enjoy a different organizational culture from governmental agencies. They favor their independent status, cultivate individual expression, highlight personal achievement, and foster a work environment that supports intellectual productivity rather than programmatic teamwork and institutional process. The workforce of most U.S. think tanks includes substantive experts with years of government experience, alongside experts whose careers have been primarily in academia and think tanks, and these two groups can represent distinct subcultures within the think-tank environment. Some try to bring government-style methods into think tanks: note the memos to the president as think-tank advice to the new administration, for example, while others value scholarly articles and full-length books as the product that establishes value in the marketplace of ideas.

For the most part, American think tanks reside in an independent, nongovernment space; unlike their counterparts in Europe and Asia, they are less likely to be tied to political parties or funded by ministries of defense, intelligence, or foreign affairs. It is their independence that is the defining characteristic, which provides them an ability to speak honestly about governance gaps, failures, or successes without being seen as political actors with a stake in the outcome.

The degree to which a think tank is associated with a worldview or political preference also defines them, although many think tanks get labeled as liberal or conservative by observers when their internal self-concept is more neutral or bipartisan. Some think tanks advocate a political philosophy that is in fact outside of the U.S. mainstream, and those organizations never find a politician who fully satisfies their ideal. CATO, for example, which advocates libertarian policies, can be seen as being to the right of the Republican Party and the Institute for Policy Studies can be seen as being to the left of the Democratic Party.

The robustness of the think-tank world in the United States, larger by orders of magnitude than in other advanced democracies, is attributed to the relative weakness of American political parties, the developed philanthropic culture, and the public distrust of government.[1]

EVOLUTION OF THINK TANKS IN THE UNITED STATES

The history of think tanks in the United States goes back more than a century, when newly wealthy industrialists created a modern form of philanthropy, investing not in traditional charitable institutions but in the building of independent civil society. These Americans, including Henry Ford to Andrew Carnegie and the Rockefeller family across generations, created the network of public libraries, research institutes on scientific topics, and the first think tanks: the Carnegie Endowment for International Peace (1910), the Brookings Institution (1916), the Hoover Institute at Stanford University (1919), and the Council on Foreign Relations (1921).[2] These important institutions were initially funded by foundations that branded their family names and did so much to build American society as we know it.

By mid-century, think tanks competed with, or complemented, prestigious universities by providing intellectual talent for new presidential administrations. Experts with professional ties to the Brookings Institution, Hoover Institution, and the Carnegie Endowment can be easily found in the rosters of political appointees to Presidents Kennedy, Nixon, and Carter.

A next milestone in the evolution of American think tanks was the emergence of ideologically driven think tanks created to promote a coherent worldview and its associated policy ideas, and to work politically to support candidates with similar views. The most prominent example is the Heritage Foundation, created in 1973, which was closely associated with the Reagan revolution regarding the role of government, the uses of American power, and conservative social values.

The success of ideological think tanks on the right created pressures on the liberal or centrist-oriented policy world, in part because of the business model: conservative think tanks were funded lavishly often by individual donors who did not require the same formal review processes of the established foundations. This allowed the new think tanks to produce, and quickly, large volumes of polished and professional-looking publications targeted for a political audience. The older think tanks tended to follow a more academic model, with long gestation periods for the creation and publication of new policy ideas.

The end of the Cold War spawned a new generation of national security think tanks, pledging to take fresh approaches to public policy analysis based on a profoundly changed national security environment. This group would include the Henry L. Stimson Center (1989) and the Nixon Center (1994).

By the late 1990s, several new think tanks with a liberal or progressive orientation, or a single thematic focus, entered the scene, often funded by wealthy individuals. Donors, rather than large foundations, underwrote the establishment of the Washington Institute for Near East Policy (1987); the Center for Global Development (2001); and more recently, the Center for American Progress (CAP), founded in 2003 to provide the progressive movement with long-term leadership. Many observers think CAP represents yet another model for a think tank, the purpose of which is to provide a planning capacity for the Democratic Party when out of office.[3] CAP proved to be an indispensable part of the transition to the Obama administration; its president, former Clinton chief of staff John Podesta, served as the head of the Obama transition team and has had considerable influence on political appointments in the new administration. It remains to be seen how CAP will see its role now that its party is in power; will it provide direct support to the administration along the model of European party-affiliated think tanks or play a more independent role?

These examples are representative; there are an estimated three hundred and fifty think tanks in Washington, DC, alone and over one thousand in the country as a whole. Chicago has the Chicago Council on Global Affairs, Atlanta has the Carter Center, Los Angeles has the Pacific Council on International Policy, Boston has countless think tanks affiliated with its university community, and New York is home to the Council on Foreign Relations and other university-based think tanks.

It is hard to know where to draw the line between think tanks and other kinds of public policy organizations. Some of these newer organizations may call themselves think tanks but are in fact advocacy groups. Others cross the line to lobbying, and law firms and corporations call their directed research units think tanks. There are two additional categories of think tanks that are less central to the discussion of this chapter: in-government think tanks and federally funded think tanks that enjoy degrees of autonomy from official policy and procedure. The Congressional Research Service (CRS) of the Library of Congress is a government think tank created to support analysis for the legislative branch. Formed in 1914 as the Legislative Reference Service, it was expanded and renamed in 1970 and currently employs seven hundred people with a budget of $100 million. CRS covers all issues of interest to Congress; only a subset of its staff works full-time on national security issues. In the executive branch, the think tank most focused on the security agenda is the National Intelligence Council, which provides both classified and unclassified analysis, drawing on all the resources and agencies of the intelligence community (IC). The Office of Net Assessments in the Department of Defense can also be considered an inside think tank, although much of its work is directed by government planning requirements rather than initiated by the office's research staff.

The federal government also underwrites the core operating costs of several prestigious think tanks, including the Woodrow Wilson Center for Scholars and the U.S. Institute of Peace, both of which have independent governance structures and have strong reputations for quality scholarly work. The defense community has also created a series of federally funded research and development centers (FFRDCs) such as RAND, the Institute of Defense Analyses, the Center for Naval Analysis, and ANSER.

THE BUSINESS MODEL

Think tanks represent a range of business models. The large institutions formed in the early years of the twentieth century enjoy infrastructure and operating expense support from endowments, which they supplement through foundation grants for specific programmatic work, corporate donations, and individual contributions. The financial crisis that began in 2008 may force all think tanks to take appropriate cost-saving measures, but in particular, large think tanks that own buildings and run complex enterprises, full-time events staff, and communications teams may need to recalibrate how they use their founding fathers' endowments versus new forms of revenue.

Think tanks vary on the sensitive issue of government funding. Some eschew it entirely, while others accept U.S. or other government funding when programmatic interests are well aligned, and when they perceive no compromise to their reputation for independence. In the early years of the twenty-first century, many American think tanks branched out to collaborative relationships with prosperous countries in Europe and Asia, often through foreign ministry or development assistance channels.

In general, think tanks have diversified their funding, finding that grants from the large foundations (Carnegie Corporation, Ford Foundation, MacArthur Foundation, Hewlett Foundation, etc.) are no longer sufficient to cover the operating costs of organizations that have evolved from modest nonprofit organizations to more established parts of the mainstream urban economy, with long-term leases in business districts, competitive professional salaries, and modern infrastructure to provide services that are comparable to the business world.

THE PRODUCT

Think tanks play an important role in the policy process, but that does not mean interacting primarily with government. Think tanks have critical audiences in the scholarly community, with the media, the private sector, and the general public. The products of think tanks, therefore, need to be appropriate to these different consumers.

Think tanks make their contributions at many points along the life cycle of policymaking:

- Identify needs, gaps
- Generate new ideas
- Build support, constituents
- Formal approval through legislation or executive authority
- Educate, inform, persuade
- Monitor implementation
- Determine when change is needed to refine, retool, rethink

Some think tanks see their primary role as generators of big new ideas and they aim to directly influence the strategic course of government policy. Think tanks that work on health care reform, for example, may work for years on complex policy initiatives that would have significant implications for government programs and would likely require legislative or executive action.

Others focus their energies on current policies, offering feedback, criticism, and suggestions for new directions. The role of think tanks during the presidential transition in 2008–9 provides a flavor for this kind of policy input from the think tank world. Many think tanks offered policy advice on Iraq, Afghanistan, China, trade policy, etc., that constituted course corrections on the roster of existing problems rather than radical new directions.[4]

From the national security world, the work done in the aftermath of the Cold War that came to be known as Cooperative Threat Reduction is a compelling example of think-tank work at the beginning of a policy cycle. The end of the Soviet Union presented a dramatic challenge with respect to the Soviet nuclear arsenal; scholars at the Brookings Institution, working with colleagues at Harvard and Stanford Universities, were engaged in projects about the transition to the post-Cold War world that were embraced first by visionary members of Congress (Senators Nunn and Lugar, Congressmen Aspin and Murtha) and later became executive branch policy. Their ideas can be credited with a number of policy initiatives, from programs to employ former weapons scientists in times of great economic stress in Russia to new systems to manage and reduce fissile and other dangerous weapons-related materials.[5]

Sometimes the greatest contribution of a think tank is in information gathering and analysis rather than policy recommendations. Think tanks can sometimes do field research that would be difficult for government analysts or action officers. Research on the activities of Islamic organizations in countries where the official U.S. presence may be small or constrained by security conditions, for example, is a topic that could play to the strengths of a nongovernment research organization with Arabic- or Dari-speaking staff, eager to embark on research trips on policy-relevant topics.

In some respects, this information-gathering stage of the policy life cycle is comparable to intelligence work and think tanks have learned to collaborate with analysts in agencies of the IC. The tasks of collecting and interpreting data and analytic work in general are core to think-tank work, as they are to intelligence. The exchange of information and assessments of key national security topics can be rewarding to both parties. Government analysts are often constrained by large bureaucratic structures and by the press of producing daily reporting from collaborating across regional and functional areas; think tanks, by virtue of their smaller size, have a natural advantage in synthesizing across domains and producing more strategic outlooks. Think-tank experts may feel rewarded by knowing that their research and analysis is valued by government analysts, and may contribute in some way to the NSE.

But think tanks tread carefully in these relationships, to protect their reputations and images as independent organizations, and to avoid any associations that could present risk to the research staff themselves, particularly those who do field research in places that may be hostile to official Americans. It is also inappropriate for intelligence agencies to engage nongovernment experts to collect data for intelligence purposes; these protocols are well established and serve all parties' interests.

As part of the post-9/11 reforms of the IC, most intelligence agencies are eager to show that they have learned to engage in productive relationships with nongovernment experts.[6] The State Department's Bureau of Intelligence and Research (INR) and the National Intelligence Council (NIC), a senior body that produces national intelligence estimates and unclassified strategic analysis, and which reports to the director of national intelligence, are two components that have resources for regularized collaboration with think tanks. In the case of the NIC, the quadrennial Global Trends report, which provides each new presidential term with its assessment of major transnational developments that could affect U.S. interests, is now heavily based on inputs from think tanks around the world.

Later in the life cycle of a policy, think tanks play a useful role in monitoring the implementation of policies and offering ideas about improving the effectiveness of policies. The U.S. campaign to respond to the HIV-AIDS crisis, not purely as a humanitarian or health policy issue but as one with security implications for U.S. allies or for other U.S. interests such as in Africa, led to some creative work monitoring existing programs and providing useful input from target countries so that an ongoing and high-profile policy could be improved and increase its ability to save lives and reach the targeted populations.[7]

American think tanks provide new ideas and critical feedback to government actors other than the United States. The United Nations (UN) Department of Peacekeeping Operations (DPKO), and the newer Peacebuilding Support Office (PBSO), for example, have formed close research partnerships with American think tanks in New York and Washington, with goals of increasing awareness of UN activities in American constituencies, and working hard on the problems faced by UN experts on challenges related to deployments in postconflict or conflict-ridden countries.[8]

IRAQ CASE

The U.S. decision to go to war to oust Saddam Hussein, made by the Bush administration in 2002 and executed in 2003, is a disturbing case with respect to the role of think tanks, and serves as a warning that think tanks can be marginal or irrelevant players when an administration has strongly held views or solicits input only from like-minded thinkers. This case could weaken the argument of this chapter, that think tanks are often an integral part of national security policymaking, or it can be seen as an outlier or exception.

The Bush administration took power in 2001 with a clearly articulated worldview, and confident beliefs in American power as a force for transformation in the world. Bush had a national security agenda prepared by prominent defense intellectuals who advised his campaign, and Iraq was high on the list of problems that needed attention. It is the opinion of many Washington observers that President Bush was animated in part by a perceived failure on the part of his father's administration to solve the Iraq problem for once and for all. (The war aims of the conflict to oust Iraq from its occupation of Kuwait in 1990–91 were limited and did not include regime change. Prominent in the circles that defined that policy was then Chairman of the Joint Chiefs of Staff Colin Powell, who then faced the awkward situation of serving as secretary of state during a war that he did not fully support.) The team of ideologically driven officials believed that Saddam Hussein's continued defiance of international norms, his probable continued work on nonconventional weapons, and his dismal domestic record constituted a threat to U.S. credibility and authority. Removing Saddam Hussein's regime would benefit the Iraqi people, create prospects for a new regional political culture, and accrue important advantages to U.S. prestige worldwide.

Mainstream and conservative think tanks helped validate this thinking and provided additional documentation on conditions in Iraq, the dangers of an Iraq with weapons of mass destruction (WMD), and the potential benefits to the Middle East region once Saddam Hussein was removed. Titles from the Brookings website in early 2003, for example, are "The Dangers of Delaying an Attack on Iraq," "Why Iraq Can't Be Deterred," and "A Last Chance to Stop Iraq." From the American Enterprise Institute, "The False Allure of Stability."

Think tanks also helped staff the U.S. occupation of Iraq; dozens of young enthusiasts for the policy made their way to Baghdad for positions that were often intended for experienced civil servants.[9]

More avowedly liberal-leaning think tanks raised a number of issues about Iraq, including doubts about its weapons status and the downsides of a policy to remove Saddam Hussein by force. Of special note was the Carnegie Endowment for International Peace. With deep expertise on WMD, the Carnegie team developed alternative approaches for ridding Iraq of any possible WMD. Its main proposal was for coercive inspections, building on UN capabilities established in 1991 to detect, monitor, and eliminate Iraqi weapons programs. But their message was strategic: there are alternatives to war, and war will accrue terrible costs to the United States in human and reputational terms. No other well-established Washington think tank took as clear an antiwar position as Carnegie did.

Others addressed the larger, indirect costs of war and questioned how Iraqi society would respond to an abrupt change of fortune. But many of these analytic pieces accepted the inevitability of the Bush administration's decision to go to war, reluctantly or with satisfaction, and their purpose was to add value to that decision on the margins, not to assess the fundamental soundness of the decision.

Some think tanks are deeply interested in questions of governance, and the Iraq case seems a missed opportunity to examine more closely questions of decision making, authorities, and process. In general, journalists showed more interest in these important issues than think tanks.

Once the war began, think tanks displayed their impressive capacity for data collection and analysis, often presenting the picture on the ground in Iraq in more articulate and compelling forms than government bureaucrats did, at least in the public domain. Some new and creative partnerships were formed: the *New York Times* commissioned Brookings' Michael O'Hanlon to offer periodic graphic assessments of the costs of the war, measuring discrete categories of the war effort as well as casualties, both American and Iraqi.

A large set of secondary effects of the Iraq war were studied: Brookings contributed important work on Iraqi internally displaced and refugee populations, as well as analysis of the potential UN role in a postoccupation Iraq; CSIS offered deep analysis of the impact of the war on U.S. military readiness; AEI, the Washington Institute, and the U.S. Institute of Peace (USIP) became venues for the new Iraqi political class to engage with Washington pundits and researchers.

USIP, in a special category of think tank as a federally funded but independently governed research institute, provided perhaps the most significant platform for bipartisan, cross-disciplinary work on Iraq after the fall of Saddam. At the request of Congress, and with the reluctant acquiescence of the Bush White House, USIP convened, with three other think tanks as cohosts, what came to be known as the Iraq Study Group (ISG). Cochaired by former Congressman Lee Hamilton and Republican Party statesman James Baker, the ISG spent much of 2006 grappling with how to improve the effectiveness of the U.S. intervention in the face of spiraling violence in Iraq and political anguish at home. Its mission was to identify some new directions for U.S. policy without labeling the entire Iraq effort a devastating failure. The Bush administration, in the fall 2006 election period, seemed to dismiss the study's findings but later quietly

Table 14.1 Think-Tank Work on Iraq, 2002–7

	2002–3	2004–5	2006–7
AEI	Strong support; war as justified act of preemption and liberation of oppressed population	Analysis of events on the ground, worsening of violence, few policy recommendations	Policy recommendations supporting the idea of the surge, emphasis on giving new strategy a chance to succeed
Brookings	Mixed support; some scholars supported invasion and regime change; others criticized lack of debate in Congress	Developing pragmatic solutions for increasing security in Iraq, some analysis of mistakes made by the United States in planning for war/reconstruction	Analysis of current events on the ground and the effects of the surge and new Bush administration strategy, cautious optimism tempered with a wait-and-see approach
Carnegie Endowment	Generally opposed to military action, focus on WMD, not regime change; idea of a region-wide wave of democratic reform a dangerous fantasy: invasion is "reckless"	Analysis of the decision to go to war in Iraq looking back after one to two years, realist and pragmatic policy solutions for deterioration of situation in Iraq	Realist approach: policy recommendations leading up to the surge, focus on what to do next, not how we got here
CATO Institute	No support; Iraq not proven to be an imminent threat to the United States, costs of invasion too great	Analysis of the Bush administration's policy and its failures, recommendations for exit strategies	Realist approach: analysis of current events related to the American side of the political debate surrounding the surge
CSIS	No opinion; focus on capabilities of Iraqi army, repercussions of invasion on international relations and oil markets	Ways to improve security issues, analysis of the many elements affecting the progress and setbacks of U.S. and coalition forces, broad strategic development of the war effort	Ways to improve security issues, analysis of the many elements affecting the progress and setbacks of U.S. and coalition forces, broad strategic development of the war effort
Council on Foreign Relations	Mixed support; main point of dispute centered on whether Saddam's regime could be contained or disarmed without military action	Wide range of issues, general consensus on the need to develop a new strategy to end insurgency, to promote the Iraqi democratic process, and for the United States to finish what it has started	Wide range of issues, particular attention to analysis of current events/reports, general consensus that the United States has been largely unsuccessful, mixed support for troop surge
Heritage Foundation	Strong support; threats from Saddam in larger context or war on terror, act of self-defense, criticized lack of teeth in UN sanctions	Political focus: analysis of current events on the ground and reports such as the Iraq Study Group, policy recommendations for the short term	Analysis of current events on the ground, policy recommendations for short term, greater focus on U.S. politics
Hoover Institute	Strong support; war with Iraq inevitable, regime change as part of grander strategy to spread democracy, focus on future challenges of the reconstruction effort	Iraq war as part of larger war on terror, consensus that despite the rise in violence the United States must stay and finish the job	Reasons why victory in Iraq is necessary, strong support for troop surge, ambivalence regarding ISG report
International Institute for Security Studies	No support; directly refuted CIA analysis of Iraq's WMD program/procurement criticized lack of evidence	Focus shifts to other issues: Iran and Syria	Focus shifts to other issues: Iran and Syria
Institute for Science and International Security	No opinion; IISS' Strategic Dossier extremely influential in the creation of Tony Blair's Iraq Dossier and the United Kingdom's decision to back the war effort	Analysis of the Iraqi political system, progress and elections, analysis of U.S. mistakes in planning for war/reconstruction	Iraqi government and issue of state building, limited work on Iraq

began implementing some of the ideas, including its recommendations related to engaging with Iraq's neighbors.[10] The experts groups that advised the Study Group continued to meet informally and address Iraq's political and security developments through occasional publications and in a politically inclusive way.

USIP's special relationship to government, including its obligation to spend its Iraq program funds according to State Department guidelines, was both a virtue and a handicap. USIP has enjoyed the unique status of being both a think tank and a do tank; many think tanks claim to have a field mission that is action oriented, but USIP's peacebuilding work in Iraq is the most credible and comprehensive do-tank work of any Washington think tank. Yet its closeness to government, in an institutional rather than political way, was also a constraint. They on occasion chose silence over truth telling when it would seem to expose too raw a nerve, or when they were unable to forge an all-parties position at moments when the debate over Iraq policy was highly polarized and emotional. Their funding sources (congressional appropriations for operating expenses and State Department grants for Iraq program work) enabled them to work at a higher economy of scale than most think tanks, and with more security protection inside Iraq, but it also diminished their independence, as complying with State Department regulations often made them seem as much an adjunct of U.S. embassy programming as an NGO.

Some U.S. think tanks, irrespective of their position on the decision to go to war, have tried to help the new Iraq build its own think-tank culture. USIP, Brookings, AEI, WINEP, and Stimson among others have hosted new civil society leaders in Iraq, traveling on U.S. embassy and State Department programs. In some cases, U.S. think tanks conducted capacity-building workshops as a way to strengthen democratic practice and culture in Iraq. In these different fashions, think tanks accommodated themselves to Iraq as a government priority during the Bush years and found diverse ways to contribute to stability in Iraq as an American interest, irrespective of their views on the decisions of 2002 and 2003. It could be argued that, with very few exceptions, think tanks demonstrated that they are only supporting cast players in a national security play whose heroes or villains are government officials. Think tanks can bring some color and texture to the performance, but are unlikely to drive the plot.

IDENTITY ISSUES

For the twenty-first century think tank, a new set of issues arises: Are American think tanks only American? Many think tanks approach the foreign policy landscape from the globalization paradigm, and increasingly see themselves as part of a global community.[11] The U.S. Carnegie Endowment launched a new initiative of rebranding when it opened offices in Beijing, Brussels, and Beirut and pronounced that Carnegie was the "first global think tank."[12] Other think tanks are increasingly part of a global network, through collaborative relationships with non-U.S. think tanks, through funding relationships, and through the reach of their publications and ideas, in the information age. Think tanks are beginning to formalize their relationships, through consortia that cross-publish and promote each other's work, work jointly to seek funding for collaborative work, and host international meetings where individual and joint work can be featured.

Identity issues are not limited to the global versus national issue. Political labeling is also a challenging identity issue. Think tanks' internal culture, which often values individual positions more than institutional ones, and which often perceives itself as nonpartisan or bipartisan, can be injured by a facile press reference to the presumed political preferences of the entire organization. Think tanks are often labeled by outsiders as liberal or Democratic, even when a quick study of their boards or their governing principles would suggest a more neutral identity.

Think tanks may also bristle at the ease with which universities, law firms, lobbyists, corporations, and governments refer to their own activities as think tanks. These entities often served a more directed purpose: to analyze a political situation from the perspective of a client, or a weapons system from the perspective of a market player, for example. They are often not intended to promulgate knowledge for knowledge's sake, or for a public policy purpose.

One scholar sees harm to think tanks from this pressure to market their products and see their work as a commodity, or from the need to mimic the tactics and methods of interest groups. In this view, the "research" done in think tanks has come to resemble "polemical commentary" rather than empirical truths or objective analysis.[13] But a quick review of think tanks' websites would dispute this critique; think tanks are generally competent at providing accessible data and information, as well as interpretation and policy recommendations.

THINK TANKS FROM THE POLICYMAKERS' POINT OF VIEW

There is no single view on the part of policymakers about the utility or value of think tanks; just as government officials vary in their use of information and their strategies to master the issues for which they are responsible, so too do they differ in how they value the contribution of nongovernment expertise in their work. What is clear is that increasingly, government officials consider it a normal and constructive way to perform their official duties by following carefully what think tank experts are writing and saying, and by engaging directly with think tanks to solicit their input on key policy issues. It has long been common for government officials to engage informally with experts they know, from graduate school or through social networks. It is particularly true of political appointees, who often bring their information-gathering practices established in other professional settings to their work in government. But it appears increasingly common for government officials to make overtures to think tanks, either as they familiarize themselves with a new account, or begin a new policy initiative, or consider ways to change an existing policy.

Some in government may harbor the view that think tank work is superficial, or is not informed by deep inside truths. Think tanks for the most part have no access to intelligence or other insider information, and their analysis and recommendations may suffer from this factor. But the challenge is for actors in the NSE to use appropriately and effectively knowledge and judgment of think tank experts in the interest of wiser policymaking and policy implementation. Think tanks are not intended to substitute for the insider policy deliberations, or to compete with work done in government teams and interagency meetings. Yet think tanks can provide unique data in some cases and deep wisdom and judgment in others that cannot be acquired inside the bureaucracy.

NOTES

1. James McGann, *Think Tanks and Policy Advice in the United States: Academics, Advisors and Advocates* (New York: Routledge, 2007), 8.

2. The Council on Foreign Relations is also a membership organization, funded by dues of members. It has functioned as both an elite club and as a think tank. The Pacific Council on International Policy is also a membership organization.

3. CAP describes itself as nonpartisan. The planning function is also identified by the Center for Strategic and International Studies as a core mission: President John Hamre wrote, "CSIS is committed to undertake strategic planning for the US government." In McGann, *Think Tanks and Policy Advice in the United States*, 90.

4. Think tank advice to the Obama transition includes: "A better deal: Twelve Suggestions for the new US President" (RAND); "Advice to President Obama" (MIT Center for International Studies); "Foreign Policy for the Next President" (Carnegie Endowment for International Peace); "Presidential Inbox 2009" (The Stimson Center).

5. I am grateful to Laura Holgate of the Nuclear Threat Initiative for her recollections of the early intellectual churning that led to the cooperative threat reduction programs.

6. See in particular *The Commission on the Intelligence Capabilities of the United States Regarding Weapons of Mass Destruction*, March 31, 2005 (Washington, DC: US Government Printing Office), 387–429.

7. In January 2003, a delegation of health leaders formed by the Center for Strategic and International Studies (CSIS), under the umbrella of its Task Force on HIV/AIDS, visited China "to examine [its] approach to HIV/AIDS and to explore the possibility of expanded U.S.-Chinese collaboration." Drawing explicitly for the findings of this delegation, the Presidential Advisory Council on HIV AIDS (PACHA) passed a resolution on August 8, 2003, calling for "the President, the Secretary of Health and Human Services, and the U.S. Congress to provide strong international leadership and technical assistance to China, India, Russia and other nations to fight the HIV/AIDS pandemic."

8. The DC-based Better World Fund, for example, hosts high-ranking UN officials in meetings with the Washington community and makes a case for the UN on Capitol Hill. The Stimson Center has worked both directly and through government grants to supply lessons learned research to DPKO's Security Sector Reform Team, analysis and doctrine development support to its Police Division, and field research for its Best Practices Section. Stimson has reviewed drafts of major UN policy statements on peacekeeping doctrine, security sector reform strategy, and how best to benchmark peace-building activities, the latter for PBSO. The New York-based International Peace Institute has seconded personnel to help draft the Secretary-General's 2009 report on peace building, and the Center on International Cooperation at New York University publishes an annual compendium of peacekeeping activities, in collaboration with DPKO.

9. Rajiv Chandrasekaran, "Ties to GOP Trumped Know-How among Staff Sent to Rebuild Iraq," *Washington Post*, September 17, 2006. Adapted from Rajiv Chandrasekaran, *Imperial Life in the Emerald City* (New York: Knopf, 2006).

10. James A. Baker III and Lee H. Hamilton, cochairs, *The Iraq Study Group Report: The Way Forward—A New Approach* (New York: Vintage Books, 2006).

11. James G. McGann and R. Kent Weaver, *Think Tanks and Civil Societies: Catalysts for Ideas and Action* (New Brunswick, NJ: Transaction Publishers, 2002). This book and other online surveys by Mr. McGann are useful catalogues of the global network of think tanks.

12. One could easily call the International Crisis Group, created with an international board and offices in sixty countries, the first global think tank. It was initially conceived with an activist mission as its primary function, pressing foreign ministries to engage to prevent or resolve conflicts, but it is its research and analysis work for which it has become best known.

13. Andrew Rich, *Think Tanks, Public Policy and the Politics of Expertise* (Cambridge, UK: Cambridge University Press, 2004).

Chapter 15 The Media: Witness to the National Security Enterprise

John Diamond

> I hate newspapermen. They come into camp and pick up their camp rumors and print them as facts. I regard them as spies, which in truth, they are. If I killed them all there would be news from Hell before breakfast.
>
> *Gen. William Tecumseh Sherman*

> I am partial to the Infantry; always have been. . . . There, in the mud, is where war is most visible and easiest understood. There no one will lie to you; no one will try to put a spin on the truth. Those for whom death waits around the next bend or across the next rice paddy have no time and little taste for the games that are played with such relish in the rear. No one ever lied to me within the sound of the guns.
>
> *Joe Galloway, "The Military and the Media: One Man's Experience," remarks prepared for delivery at the Commandant's Lecture Series, Air War College, Maxwell Air Force Base*

INTRODUCTION

In today's information age, asserting that the media has an impact on national security decision making is almost akin to saying that geography has an impact on national security decision making. The ways in which the dynamics of mass communication influence the military and national security leadership are countless and as complex as the influences of geography, politics, logistics, or any number of other factors beyond the balance of forces at the scene of conflict. As with any of these other influences, each situation in which media dynamics play a role in the development, execution, and outcome of military strategies must be regarded as unique, making broad, academic generalizations or principles difficult to propound with any confidence.

The broad point is so obvious in today's information-saturated age, that proving it through academic discipline is no longer really necessary. What is useful, however, is examining how the media-national security dynamic works by looking at situations where media influence is pronounced, and other situations where it is less so and trying to discern the reasons behind the differences.

The aim of this chapter is to draw on the author's twenty-five years of experience as a journalist, most of it covering national security affairs, in identifying and describing important themes in the media and national security dynamic. Overriding principles may be elusive in a field in which the contributing factors are so numerous and, at times, random. Instead it examines a number of themes or dynamics that can inform national security decision making under media scrutiny.

There can be little doubt that the media can influence events in international relations and national security, sometimes by design, sometimes by accident. New studies on the end of the Cold War have brought out vivid examples of how even when the media gets the story wrong it can change the course of history. In November 1989, for example, a widely viewed West German news broadcaster reported that the Berlin Wall had been opened. The report was erroneous, or, as it turned out, premature, for the report itself helped spark the flood of East Berliners who had flocked to the wall after seeing the news broadcast.[1]

The years since the 9/11 attacks have been years of extremes in national security journalism. In the aftermath of the terrorist attacks, multiple official investigations as well as saturation media coverage examined the events leading up to the attacks in forensic detail, always focusing on the tantalizing and ultimately unanswerable question: Were the attacks avoidable? At the very time when these inquiries were at their most intense, the run-up to the U.S.-led invasion of Iraq wound up putting U.S. media under intense public scrutiny for having been too ready to buy the Bush administration's allegations about Iraq's supposed arsenal of weapons of mass destruction (WMD). Under assault for missing the story, elite U.S. media rebounded in the ensuing years with exposés on torture, secret Central Intelligence Agency (CIA) prisons, decrepit housing for wounded veterans of the Iraq War, and a secret program to conduct warrantless domestic wiretapping. As of this writing, with two wars ongoing, the American newspaper industry is coping with a financial crisis of unprecedented severity, struggling simply to keep reporters in the field, let alone influence world-changing events.[2] This weakness is creating openings for new media, or nontraditional media. A public furor in the summer of 2010 over disparaging remarks by Army Gen. Stanley McChrystal, the commander of U.S. forces in Afghanistan, and by his staff—remarks directed at President Obama, Vice President Biden, and other senior civilian officials—stemmed not from a major media outlet's reporting but from an article in *Rolling Stone* magazine.[3] Weeks later, major media outlets in the United States, Britain, and Germany published accounts of some 92,000 pages of classified documents unearthed not through their own sleuthing but by a website called WikiLeaks.[4]

This chapter examines aspects of these and other media episodes. First, though, it is important to discuss national security media in more general terms to give readers unfamiliar with this arena a sense of the landscape. It is important to keep in mind that some of the dynamics between the media and U.S. national security could just as easily apply in civilian contexts. Among the aspects of the media-military relationship that stand out are the importance to the information flow of relationships of trust between reporter and source, the highly sensitive nature of some of the information and the reasons for sharing it, and the often compressed timeframe of crisis, decision making, and result.

THE TRIBES OF NATIONAL SECURITY MEDIA

U.S. media coverage of national security breaks down into four broad types: correspondents based in Washington and focused on diplomatic and military policymaking; foreign correspondents based in foreign capitals and focused on world news, but with an emphasis on news of interest to U.S. audiences; war correspondents assigned to a combat area who may at times be embedded with U.S. forces; and U.S.-based regional journalists who work near major military installations in places such as San Diego; Norfolk, Virginia; and Tampa.

The first group, the Washington-based correspondents, includes journalists with extensive experience and a deep base of sources. Reporters such as David Martin of CBS News,

Eric Schmidt of the *New York Times*, Tom Ricks of the *Washington Post*, Barbara Starr of CNN, and Tony Capaccio of Bloomberg News have been covering their beats for years, in some cases, decades. It is not uncommon for journalists such as these to develop sources of midlevel civilian or military rank and then stick with those sources for years, through promotion to increasingly senior positions.

These reporters have been on the job so long that, at times, they may know the political and policy landscape better than the colonels and one-stars and assistant secretaries they cover. At times this can make things easier for official Washington because such reporters do not need an elementary-level education in the issues, policies, and operations they cover. They start with a broad and deep base of knowledge so the national security officials dealing with them need not fear some gross distortion of reality based on ignorance of the way things work, nor do they have to spend precious time walking these reporters through the basics. On the other hand, these reporters can pose a significant challenge to officials because they know the right questions to ask. It is a basic reality of official Washington that bureaucracies are fairly willing to share information, but quite often will do so *only if asked*. It therefore takes a reporter of some experience to know the right questions and drill past the surface to gain a deeper understanding of what is going on. This class of national security journalist has access to trusted sources that will provide unofficial and sometimes contrasting perspectives on the storyline that an administration or cabinet office is trying to disseminate. They report in a milieu filled with contrasting opinions and perspectives, whether it is the ranking minority-party member of the Senate Armed Services Committee, a former cabinet secretary now out of government at a think tank, a retired intelligence officer, or an executive at a defense contractor embroiled in heated competition for a new weapons program. Finally, these reporters work in an environment where official self-examination and criticism is standard procedure. The military and intelligence community (IC), more than most other government institutions, engage in lessons-learned exercises. These combined with congressional oversight reports, blue-ribbon commission studies, and after-action reviews form a steady stream of critical (if not uniformly negative) information available to the national security beat reporter.

The environment in which these reporters work may vary from assignment to assignment. Pentagon correspondents go through a clearance process to get a building pass. The clearance does not provide them access to classified information, but it does give them freedom to roam all but the most secure corridors of the vast building, a great asset for bumping into senior officials at coffee stands or in cafeteria lines, and for dropping in on various offices where a face-to-face conversation (whether authorized or not) may elicit information more quickly than a phone call or email. Because the State Department press corps includes a large contingent of foreign reporters, a State Department press pass limits reporters' access to the first two floors, far below the senior executive suites where the key decision makers work. The casual drop-by is not an option at State; reporters must hustle from photo opportunities to briefings to the occasional public ceremony to get access to principals. Select members of the Pentagon and State Department press corps travel with the secretaries of State and Defense on official trips. This is an expensive proposition and not all news organizations can afford to pay the hotel bills and air fare (equivalent to a first-class ticket) on weeklong trips making multiple stops in world capitals. But the payoff is considerable, for unlike the restricted access typical in Washington, an international trip can afford journalists extensive access to senior officials including the cabinet secretary, whether in in-flight briefings, casual conversations en route, or over hotel meals during the trip. Being in the bubble does not always mean being first to get the news. During U.S.-brokered Arab-Israeli peace negotiations in 2000, for example, Israel Army Radio often broke stories before any of the journalists traveling with Secretary of State Madeleine Albright. This had little to do with the traveling arrangements and much to do with the desire of the State Department, acting as intermediary in the talks, to avoid leaking information sensitive to either negotiating party at the wrong time.[5]

Unlike the Pentagon, State Department, and White House, the CIA provides no filing center for reporters, though journalists who cover the agency can make the occasional appointment to come to CIA headquarters for a carefully monitored deep-background interview. The CIA, like the White House, is often best covered from the outside in. Rather than trying to get a reticent organization to yield closely held information, better to go to those who are the CIA's overseers—the House and Senate Intelligence Committees—or its customers, the many people across the U.S. government with regular access to intelligence reports. Reporters with long experience covering U.S. intelligence, such as the *Washington Post*'s Walter Pincus, have learned the value of developing sources among the large community of CIA retirees, many of whom continue to do sensitive work for the government long after they have handed in their agency badges.

Foreign correspondents are sometimes quite senior in rank but not always, particularly in recent years. For much of the twentieth century, foreign postings were the capstone on a career. In his account of the *New York Times*, Gay Talese tells the story of A. M. Rosenthal's long-delayed quest to become a foreign correspondent. Rosenthal, who would go on to become the paper's executive editor, slogged through years of domestic assignments before finally getting a foreign posting.[6] Today, a young reporter with ability in a difficult foreign language or a willingness to go to dangerous places can jump ahead in line. Thomas Friedman's early career experience in Lebanon for UPI and then the *New York Times* in the late 1970s and 1980s, and Richard Engel's reporting on the Iraq War for ABC News and then NBC News are examples of this phenomenon.[7]

In the nineteenth and twentieth centuries, a typical foreign correspondent did well to locate near a major foreign capital. These days it is, perhaps, more important for a foreign correspondent to locate near a major international airport. As the ranks of foreign correspondents have dwindled, the job of the foreign correspondent has had less to do with covering the goings-on of the government of the country in which the correspondent is based than it does with using the overseas posting as a base of operations for covering stories within a much larger geographic base than any one country.

Generalizations on the output of U.S. correspondents reporting from overseas are much harder to make than for Washington-based national security correspondents because the type of story and circumstances of assignment vary so widely. It is safe to say that a foreign correspondent will have ample opportunity to find officials and prominent citizens willing to criticize the policies of the United States. A foreign correspondent will often be well positioned to produce stories that suggest that the reality on the ground or the impact of a policy forged in Washington differs greatly from the view of events at the White House or State Department. There is generally no shortage of opportunities to report on the views of foreign officials who believe Washington's aims or demands to be unreasonable. Foreign correspondents may, at times, be able to draw attention to crises or developments—famine, ethnic cleansing, corruption in a foreign government—that have been ignored or overlooked by official Washington. In a breaking news context, the reality is that a single foreign correspondent, even one who happens to be close to the scene of the crisis, often has to rely heavily on local or regional media coverage to put together a complete story.

News organizations are under economic pressure from multiple directions: newspapers facing the flight of classified advertising to the internet, networks facing increasing loss of viewership to cable, or cable stations confronting the rising cost of maintaining round-the-clock operations; and they have responded by cutting back on foreign correspondents. The added costs of providing security, drivers, translators, and guarded living and office space in Iraq and Afghanistan have only accelerated the trend.[8] Wire services and local hires have filled the void only up to a point. The ability of a foreign editor at a major U.S. metropolitan daily to spot an interesting trend overlooked by other news organizations and to deploy reporting resources to get the story is waning.[9]

Creative ideas are emerging for finding new ways to finance foreign coverage. And in the information age, torrents of information unavailable from any source even a decade ago have altered the dynamic of the way information is collected around the globe.[10] The wide circulation of mobile phone images of police brutality in Iran following national elections is only the most recent example.[11] But new business models at mainstream media organizations have not fully emerged. Hiring foreign nationals to provide coverage has the advantage of providing a U.S. news organization with deep local knowledge and language skills, but with the corresponding absence of familiarity with the U.S. readership or viewership, or of U.S. sensibilities and priorities. An election in Pakistan, for example, might present innumerable interesting local angles as factions and well-known personalities vie for advantage. But to the U.S. audience the only thing likely to matter much is which candidate or slate is deemed most desirable for U.S. interests, and which most threatening.[12]

War correspondents may come from the ranks of Washington national security reporters, foreign correspondents, regional writers focused on the military, from nonmilitary beat assignments, or, in a few cases, straight out of school. For news organizations big enough to maintain foreign bureaus, war correspondents are often drawn from the ranks of foreign correspondents. Typically a Mideast correspondent based in Cairo or Jerusalem would be deployed to conflict in the Mideast. Correspondents based in Berlin, Rome, or Paris were often called on to cover the Balkan wars of the 1990s. Correspondents based in Nairobi or Johannesburg might be called on to cover any one of the seemingly endless African wars virtually anywhere on the continent. Under this model the image of the foreign correspondent as an urbane figure hobnobbing with diplomats in elegant foreign capitals gives way to the reality of dangerous assignments, months away from family and home, and few creature comforts. World geography and time zones mean that in most cases, foreign reporting entails extremely long hours, as a full work day of reporting typically would end in Europe, Africa, or much of Asia at about the time editors are arriving at work at U.S. news organizations. This then requires long evenings and nights of interaction with headquarters before stories (and reporters) are put to bed.

The issue of embedded journalists has been chronicled extensively and a detailed treatment is beyond the scope of this chapter. The concept of attaching reporters to military units, placing them under their care and protection, and, to varying degrees, limiting or

Box 15.1   The State of the News Media

Journalism is under stress. Numerous studies document the decline in media coverage of international issues. For example, the number of foreign correspondents has declined steadily in this decade. Writing in the *Washington Post* in 2007, a former foreign correspondent noted that the ranks declined from 188 in 2002 to 141 by 2006. Major news dailies like the *Baltimore Sun* and the *Philadelphia Inquirer* now have no foreign bureaus.[1] While CNN, NPR, the *New York Times,* and the *Washington Post* continue to send reporters out to cover the world, other major news outlets are cutting back on foreign bureaus and resorting to parachute reporters—that is, nationally based reporters who are dropped into foreign countries as breaking news happens. Although more cost effective, some experienced journalists believe this trend sets up news stories that lack the historical context, miss comparisons with other events, and encourage clichés and stereotypes.

The decline in foreign reporters, not surprisingly, has tracked with a decline in foreign reporting. According to the Project for Excellence in Journalism, by almost all measures foreign news is losing out, with foreign coverage "rapidly losing ground at rates greater than any other topic area." Two-thirds of newsroom executives acknowledge that foreign coverage continues to decline, nearly half say they have cut resources to international topics, and only one in ten thinks foreign coverage is "very essential."[2] This seems to apply across the board, whether the newspaper is large or small. Other studies of American newspapers conclude that "coverage of international events is declining more than any other subject."[3] Some attribute this trend to the clash among news, profits, and technologies that transformed news outlets into

"profit centers" that had to make money or face reductions and staff cuts. As papers get literally smaller, even major news dailies like the *Los Angeles Times* experience staff cuts and a recurring battle between editorial staffs and corporate management over whether newspapers should become local or try to remain national news providers. Citizen reporting—via blogs and the internet—also challenged traditional media outlets in providing trusted as well as easily accessible and cheap forms of current news. As of 2010, advertising losses reached nearly twenty percent for the second year in a row, causing so much shrinkage in news coverage that the Pew Project for Excellence in Journalism now warns that there is so little "throw-weight" to American dailies that they cannot reach the front porch.[4]

Ironically, while the nation is engaged in two wars as well as a global economic crisis, coverage in 2010 fluctuated widely. Afghanistan, which got scant attention in 2007 and 2008, was a big story in 2009 as the administration deliberated on its strategy, but it still marshaled only one-third the attention President George Bush's surge in Iraq had generated only two years earlier.[5]

1. Pamela Constable, "Demise of the Foreign Correspondent," *Washington Post,* February 18, 2007.
2. Pew Research Center, Project for Excellence in Journalism report, *The Changing Newsroom,* see, "Changing Content" chapter, July 21, 2008, www.journalism.org.
3. Tricia Sartor and Dana Page, "Foreign Coverage Shrinking, Not Gone," Pew Project for Excellence in Journalism, posted July 23, 2008, www.journalism.org/node/12042.
4. Pew Project for Excellence in Journalism, *State of the News Media, Annual Report on American Journalism,* 2010, www.stateofthemedia.org/2010/newspapers_summary_essay.php.
5. Ibid.

controlling what they can report goes back generations. The term "embedded" took on a sort of official status, however, in connection with the U.S.-led invasion of Iraq in March 2003. Some eight hundred reporters from scores of U.S. news organizations signed contracts with the military giving those reporters the ability to travel with advancing troops but also limiting what and when certain information could be reported. The Pentagon was particularly concerned about reports that would pinpoint the location of U.S. troops. As a result, there were a number of "Somewhere in Southern Iraq" datelines on stories during the invasion phase of the conflict. This concern was not necessarily the result of a new, antipress freedom attitude at the Department of Defense as it was recognition of the instantaneous nature of today's journalism. Not only wire services and broadcast and cable outlets but daily papers and even weekly news magazines now have online outlets that can disseminate information about troops' dispositions in real time.

What turned out to be far more restrictive and controlled was the choice available to news organizations as to which units they could cover.[13] During the Vietnam War, correspondents made their own decisions, hopping choppers out of Saigon to frontline operations in any one of a number of locations. In Iraq the Pentagon decided which reporters went with which units, the result being that news outlets spending exorbitant sums of money to cover the conflict sometimes found their correspondent in the field assigned to a unit far removed from the most important action.[14] The Pentagon also proved understandably sensitive on reporting about the details of enemy attacks, particularly attacks that succeeded in destroying or damaging their targets, so as not to give Iraqi forces or insurgents valuable information. And there was a consciousness at the Pentagon of the impact of reporting on public opinion that drove some restrictions, such as photographs of damaged or destroyed U.S. military vehicles or of coffins of U.S. war dead returning to the United States.[15]

Although the embed policy began as a Department of Defense initiative, there were inconsistencies in the way information was distributed in the field. The Marines, for example, gave out no information about the details of Marine Corps killed in action. A casualty notice would simply name the fallen Marine and the date and general location of the event. Army casualty notices, by contrast, included at least some information as to the circumstances, for example, explaining whether a soldier was killed by an improvised explosive device while riding in a Humvee or in a firefight during a raid on a suspected insurgent hideout.[16]

Generally, the power of policy restrictions on media as against the power of information flow turned out to be a highly one-sided contest in favor of information flow. The Army could try to control or limit the release of a photo of a damaged tank, for example, to prevent the enemy from learning the points of vulnerability on a tank's armor. But there was no way to stop the avalanche of video and photographic information flowing from Iraq, whether from media cameras, civilian cell phone images, insurgent reports posted online, or video clips exchanged via email between U.S. soldiers.

The fourth group of U.S. national security correspondents—those based at regional news organizations in areas with heavy military representation—can be a vitally important source of news and quite often beat Washington journalists to important developing stories. Gregory Vistica, reporting for the *San Diego Union-Tribune,* uncovered the U.S. Navy "Tailhook" scandal in the 1990s; the *Birmingham News* broke many of the important Gulf War Syndrome stories in the 1990s, to name just two examples.

An important scoop in AP history—the report that the Nixon administration had elevated the U.S. military to "Def Con III" readiness status in the midst of the Arab-Israeli crisis of 1973—broke out of the AP Washington bureau. However, it depended on reporting from regional reporters filing from bureaus near some of the U.S. military bases where alert status manifested itself in convoys, flights of aircraft, and other activities visible to outsiders.[17] Veteran AP Pentagon correspondent Fred Hoffman got the story by walking the Pentagon hallways in the wee hours of the morning. The Soviet Union had delivered what amounted to an ultimatum on the United States, threatening to insert Soviet troops unilaterally into the Arab-Israeli conflict if the United States did not agree to send in troops as well. Hoffman was called into the Pentagon in the middle of the night after reports filtered in to AP's Washington bureau from bureaus around the country where reporters near military bases were picking up evidence of sudden and urgent mobilization of forces. Hoffman not only broke the story of the alert, he was also the only reporter to learn the reason behind it: the Soviet ultimatum. As one commentator observed: "Implicit in Hoffman's experience was a mutual recognition between reporter and source that normal military operational security did not apply to a political and military confrontation of this magnitude between the superpowers, and that the public had a right and need to know the reason for the sudden military alert."[18]

Typically a major scoop, once out the door, can be rapidly matched by competing news organizations which, as a result of the scoop, now know the right questions to ask and can get their sources to divulge the same information, or at least confirm the accuracy of the initial report. In this instance, the Nixon administration took the highly unusual step of adamantly refusing to confirm the story in any way. Initially, this was a frightening prospect for the AP, because it raised the specter that the story might be wrong, but ultimately it was a boon to the wire service, and to Hoffman's reputation, because for nearly a week competing news organizations could do nothing but credit the AP repeatedly for its reporting coup.[19]

THE MEDIA–NATIONAL SECURITY ENVIRONMENT

Reporting on the national security enterprise occurs within a particular media environment. For example, President Obama's decision in December 2009 to send thirty thousand more troops to Afghanistan to halt a deteriorating situation there followed a sequence typical for major developing national security stories. On its face, it would appear the sequence began with a scoop, a report by *Washington Post* reporter and editor Bob Woodward that the U.S. commander in Afghanistan, Gen. McChrystal, was warning of mission failure if he did not receive reinforcements.[20] It is important to remember that the Woodward story was not the beginning of the chain of events; it only seemed that way because of the prominence of the story and the clarity of McChrystal's confidential memo. The turn for the worse in the Afghan conflict was well known publicly and was already subject of intense discussion inside the Obama administration, which had had McChrystal's assessment for three weeks by the time the *Post* published Woodward's story. But by giving readers an insider's view of the debate—almost a seat-at-the-table view of the discussion among the U.S. high command—Woodward gave public prominence and focus to a debate that had been, up to that point, muddling along.

The White House may have been caught by surprise by the leak, but it should not have been. Woodward had been allowed by the Pentagon to travel to Afghanistan with the president's national security advisor, retired Marine Corps Gen. James Jones, shortly before publication of the story, a trip that undoubtedly gave him extensive information on the problems outlined in the report. There has been much critical commentary on the propriety of the leak, but the document itself, while confidential—and one would hope that a war strategy memo from a field commander to a president would be at least that—was clearly stamped "unclassified."[21] That was an invitation for someone on the report's broad distribution list to share it with the press. The story neither identified the source of the document nor his or her motivation. (In recent years some organizations such as the *New York Times* have adopted the practice of explaining the motivation of an anonymous source, particularly in cases where it is partisan.) As commentator Peter Feaver pointed out, the Woodward story made matters harder for Obama by making it clear to the public that a decision against sending more troops would run directly against the advice of his military commander. But it simultaneously aided the no-reinforcements camp by laying out so clearly the many ways in which the situation in Afghanistan was deteriorating. That deterioration, particularly the weakening of the central government and increasing corruption, added legitimacy to claims that we were helping an unworthy ally and should consider cutting our losses.[22]

The administration deliberated quite publicly for more than two months, during which time stories ran indicating near unanimity within the president's inner circle to sending more troops but disagreements over the accompanying strategy. Former Vice President Dick Cheney publicly chastised the president for "dithering" while the situation in Afghanistan worsened, an attack that lacked some zip because it was, of course, the previous administration's policy that had left things in Afghanistan in such sorry shape.[23]

The policy announcement then followed a well-established Washington pattern. Major newspapers carried stories in the days leading up to a major address by the president on Tuesday, December 1, 2009, outlining the basic elements of the White House posture, including support for sending more troops. The precise details were withheld to allow for at least a small bit of news the day of the actual speech. For example, the president wound up deciding to send an additional thirty thousand troops, though the number had been reported (from anonymous administration sources) as thirty-four thousand only a day earlier. The difference may have reflected an actual last-minute policy shift, a technical adjustment in deployment schedules, a reporting error in adding new foreign troops to the total, or perhaps an attempt to set the president up to appear at least somewhat measured in the military steps he was approving.[24] One element briefed to select reporters was that Obama had decided to accelerate the troop deployment. This reflected a civilian president's impatience with plodding Army deployment schedules and also enabled Obama to appear even more hawkish than his own commanders. It also provided a hawkish front end to the speech to offset its dovish back end—the announcement of a date certain (July 2011)—for the beginning of withdrawal of U.S. troops from Afghanistan.

The president spoke in prime time from the United States Military Academy at West Point in a speech aired on the major network and cable news stations. Earlier in the day senior national security officials briefed White House correspondents on background, withholding their names not because the information they were conveying at that point was particularly sensitive but so that the focus of named commentary out of the White House that day could be limited to the president himself. Days after the speech, continuing in a well-established pattern for managing such announcements, White House officials briefed select reporters on background, providing a behind-the-scenes look at the president's decision-making process. This led to largely flattering stories, known in the trade as "tick tocks" because they attempt to follow the president and his top advisors almost minute by minute through the key days of decision. The coverage depicted Obama as fully engaged in the details of policymaking, supportive of the commitment to success in Afghanistan, but not merely a rubber stamp for recommendations sent up from below.[25]

Through these critical few months there was something of a media reversal of order that went on: Coverage of the conflict in Afghanistan served as a kind of backdrop to the seemingly more important drama in Washington. It was more important in the sense that the situation in Afghanistan was static, holding steady at the bad level, to put it crudely. The situation in Washington was dynamic, as the president deliberated on a fateful decision to escalate the conflict. As is true of every major policy development, there were some elements that could be controlled by the president (his own policy deliberations; the timing of his announcement; the news media management surrounding that announcement; and his ultimate policy choice) and some he could not (the decision by someone down the chain of command to leak a document; a prominent reporter's scoop; the timing of that story; the actions of Afghan insurgents; the reactions of lawmakers and other key stakeholders; and the comments of prominent critics such as Cheney).

Months later, another media-military drama tied to the Afghan conflict—one that ended McChrystal's career—played out in similar fashion. The key difference was that the media outlet involved was not one of the mainstream players in national security coverage such as the *Washington Post*, but rather *Rolling Stone* magazine, a publication that focuses on popular music and culture and only occasionally delves into high policy. In a colossal exercise in bad judgment, McChrystal granted insider access to a freelance reporter writing for *Rolling Stone*. The access became extended when a volcanic eruption in Iceland grounded aircraft all across Western Europe. It was good news for McChrystal in that he and his staff were marooned at the Paris Ritz Carlton Hotel, but bad news in that *Rolling Stone*'s freelance reporter, Michael Hastings, was with them. Gradually, the general and his staff relaxed while the reporter kept taking notes. McChrystal may have said enough to get himself fired just in the way he disparaged diplomatic meetings in general and meetings with French diplomats in particular—the original reason for his stop in Paris—as wasted time. But he and his staff did not stop there, venting comments about the general's disappointment on his first meeting with Obama by saying the president seemed "uncomfortable and intimidated" in the encounter; about Gen. Jones, the national security advisor, referred to by a McChrystal aide as a "clown"; about Vice President Biden, or "Bite Me," as one of McChrystal's aides called him; and about special envoy Richard Holbrooke, whose emails the general openly dismissed as not worth opening.

The published comments were shocking in their disrespect for the civilian chain of command. "Honestly, when I first read it, I was nearly sick . . . literally, physically . . . I couldn't believe it," Admiral Mike Mullen, chairman of the Joint Chiefs of Staff, told reporters at a Defense Department news briefing.[26] Within 24 hours McChrystal was being summoned to the White House for a very brief and undoubtedly frosty meeting with Obama in which the general was relieved of command.[27]

Several things were notable about this media flameout. First, the complaints were directed at an administration that had given McChrystal just about everything he had requested. These were not the gripes of a frustrated commander whose entreaties to Washington were being ignored. The request for more troops—aired in the earlier *Washington Post* story—had been granted by the president. From the point of view of the White House, McChrystal was guilty not only of poor judgment but of ingratitude. Second, the removal of McChrystal brought with it no change in the overall war strategy. Obama named as his replacement McChrystal's erstwhile boss, Army General David Petraeus, then-head of the U.S. Central Command, the military headquarters in charge of operations in the Middle East. Petraeus had not only groomed McChrystal for the Afghan command, he had authored the counterinsurgency strategy being undertaken in Afghanistan, a strategy that Obama made clear was not going to change. Third, it was not the existence of tension within the U.S. civilian-military team in charge of the war; such tensions, especially in wars not going particularly well, are common enough to be the rule rather than the exception. Rather it was the public airing of that tension, particularly in the insubordinate form of disrespectful comments aimed at the civilian—which is to say, upper—chain of command that evinced outrage.

It should be noted that although it is not unheard of for senior officials to grant extended access to a reporter for purposes of a lengthy feature article, it is usually done under strictly negotiated and controlled circumstances. Presidential candidates, for example, have in recent years taken to allowing one or two reporters—usually from one of the newsweekly magazines—special access, but on condition that the material be used for publication *after* the election. Presidents have granted similar access to historians under similar ground rules. McChrystal reportedly agreed to talk to *Rolling Stone* because the military recruits from a young audience and possibly because he believed the questions might be less barbed. After the extended exchanges with the reporter, McChrystal and his staff belatedly realized their mistake and tried, to no avail, to get the reporter to cut out some of the more incendiary remarks as having been made "off the record." The reporter, Hastings, was having none of it, having been quite clear on the ground rules, which allowed him to use the comments either on background or verbatim if he was quoting McChrystal. On the eve of publication the general telephoned Biden to apologize for and to alert him to what was coming. The call was the administration's first inkling of the public relations storm that was about to burst. *Rolling Stone*, meanwhile, managed to lose its own scoop when the editors decided not to post the article online until the print edition was ready for distribution. In the meantime, the magazine had emailed copies to various administration officials for comment, copies that soon made their way to other media outlets, including the new media publication *Politico*. Without hesitation, these news organizations quoted extensively from the piece; in some cases blogs and websites posted the article in its entirety before *Rolling Stone* had the piece on the streets.[28] Still, "The Runaway General" was a triumph for the magazine and a black eye not only for McChrystal but for the Washington media expected to have the lead on such scoops. The columnist Frank Rich said the episode once again showed that insider Washington media were too cozy with the subjects they covered, to the point of protecting senior officials from their own gaffes so as not to "burn" a source. Rich called Hastings "a Washington outsider who seemed to know more about what was going on in Washington than most insiders did."[29]

THE CULTURE AND MYTHS OF ANONYMITY

The nonjournalist is sometimes overly impressed by the aura of anonymity that often surrounds media stories. The concept of an unnamed source brings to mind Woodward and

Bernstein and their Deep Throat source meeting via potted geranium signal in a downtown Washington parking garage. Without question, important stories burst on the scene on occasion as a result of courageous risk-taking by a source or, as some would undoubtedly view it, reckless disregard for national security. Far more often, however, the reasons for anonymity are prosaic rather than profound. Perhaps the most common explanation stems from a combination of haste and a preference for the somewhat more frank information that can be conveyed on background as compared to the polished, not to say canned rhetoric that would flow from an on-the-record statement. A reporter speaking to a midlevel officer or civilian in a military or intelligence public affairs office might call wanting to know the agency's view on a congressional report, a think-tank study, a piece of pending legislation, or a remark made that day on the Senate floor. Given enough time, an on-the-record answer could be obtainable. In that case, the staffer taking the call would have to take the question up the chain of command, probably propose an answer, and get the most readily available principal figure to sign off on having his or her name attached to the statement. Depending on the subject matter, such a process could take anywhere from a few hours to days. Far better, then, journalists usually conclude, to get the information on background and get it out on the wire, or into the paper, or on the air, and spare a lot of waiting around. The source agency might well prefer it that way as well, the better to get a more pointed response in circulation without having to stand by it in case it provoked a harsh reaction. Of course this method has two major faults: It enables the bureaucracy to disavow the content of the on-background response if, for some reason, changing circumstances or political miscalculation make it no longer the appropriate answer. This method forfeits the opportunity to hold the agency accountable later on for its position. The other, far more important fault, is that readers, viewers, or listeners are deprived of the elemental ability of being able to, as the saying goes, consider the source.[30]

Reporters often prefer keeping sources anonymous to prevent other reporters from knowing who is talking. Perhaps journalists like to think they build sources by dogged hard work, painstaking development of relationships of trust—and perhaps sometimes they do. But quite often journalists build sources by paying attention to who is being quoted by competing media outlets and calling up the same people. This is one of the main reasons why it often seems that the same names keep cropping up as talking heads on cable television or in daily coverage of a long-running story such as a presidential campaign. To prevent this kind of source creep, journalists will try to horde their sources by keeping them anonymous for as long as possible.

In recent years media organizations, in the wake of newsroom scandals involving journalistic fabricators, and in response to increasingly strident reader objections, have instituted policies strictly limiting the use of anonymous sources.[31] Because the national security arena remains the place in American journalism where anonymity continues—of necessity—in frequent use, journalists and sources have developed new methods for getting on-the-record material into circulation. One method is for a reporter to conduct an interview on background, pull together the story, select those quotes from the interview that seem most useful, and then run the quotes by the source for permission to use those selected remarks on the record.

As an alternative to veiled sourcing, this method may be preferable. But it has problems as well. One problem with this approach relates to the issue of special treatment for people of high rank. When reporters run to cover a fire or a flood, or to interview the neighbors of a person who has suddenly become notorious, the people the reporter questions do not get the benefit of a later call-back or email from the reporter seeking permission to use selected quotes. The reporter gets a name and runs to file. The kind of special treatment involved in allowing a source to review quotes before they go to press is a privilege offered only to those of high rank who are able to negotiate this special treatment by holding out the threat of providing the reporter with nothing. This, it seems to the author, is a serious concession by the journalist.

When Is Information Really Sensitive?

In August 2006, a longstanding source—a person with whom the author had developed a relationship of trust—provided information about a development in the war going on that summer between Israel and Hezbollah forces in Lebanon. U.S. intelligence had captured spy satellite imagery of Iran's military loading powerful antiship missiles onto cargo planes at a base near Tehran for shipment to Syria and, from there, on to Lebanon. The shipment, a direct threat to Israel's navy, had been halted with the aid of the intelligence. U.S. officials worked with air traffic controllers in Turkey and Iraq to either deny Iran overflight privileges or demand that the planes land for inspection. The fact that Iran's activities had been captured by U.S. spy satellites was sensitive information. Perhaps even more sensitive was the assistance provided by two predominantly Muslim countries to the United States in furtherance of Israel's security. The source's motivation was twofold: help to undergird the U.S. government's assertions that Iran was a major arms supplier to Hezbollah, and document a U.S. intelligence success story. A number of sources provided confirmation and backup, but the main narrative was based on this single source.[32]

None of the several IC and administration sources contacted about the shipment—including official spokespersons for key agencies—had requested that the story or certain details be withheld. So, it was surprising when one source expressed concern about the coverage after publication. The issue was not the main story—the account of the detection and tracking of the missile shipment—as one might expect. Rather, the concern arose over a sidebar that had been included with the main story to help readers understand how the shipment had been detected.[33] Editors had asked a very reasonable question before publication: If the missiles were crated up in boxes at the time the Iranian cargo plane was being loaded, how did U.S. intelligence know what was in the boxes? The answer was one of those esoteric words out of the IC: crate-ology. It referred to a sort of science developed in the secret world of intelligence imagery analysis by which weapons, components, ammunition, and other military hardware could be identified by the size, shape, and characteristics of the crates that contained them. Some in the IC were deeply disturbed that this detail of an intelligence operation had made its way into the newspaper. What made this reaction surprising was that this sidebar story was based on open sources, including a book published many years earlier.[34] While reporters often believe they have a good understanding of the reasons for the sensitivity of their stories, this episode nevertheless illustrates that even professional journalists may not fully understand the reasons why some information is considered sensitive.

The difference between news and sensitive information came into sharp relief in July 2010 with the online posting of some 92,000 classified U.S. government documents relating to the war in Afghanistan. The website WikiLeaks obtained and posted the documents, but allowed three media organizations—the *New York Times*, the British newspaper *The Guardian*, and the German magazine *Der Spiegel*—advance access to the material so they could analyze and put into context, not to mention confirm as legitimate, the material. A consensus emerged quickly that the documents, despite their volume, did not convey much about the war that was not already generally known. Although commentators drew many a comparison to the leak of the Pentagon Papers in 1971, there was a key difference in that the WikiLeaks material tended to confirm that the Obama administration had been telling the truth about the war, or at least not hiding it, while the Pentagon Papers pointed up the false optimism that attended the U.S. effort in Vietnam and especially of the Johnson administration's systematic concealment of the war's aims, strategy, and cost.

Despite the absence of startling news content in so large a cache of material, the Obama administration was at pains to point out that their public release represented a serious breach of national security. Claims by WikiLeaks founder Julian Assange to the contrary, the Pentagon maintained that the material posted online had not been fully scrubbed of references to sensitive sources inside Afghanistan who were risking their lives by cooperating with U.S. and allied forces. Again, it was Admiral Mullen in a Pentagon briefing who had the most vivid comment: "Mr. Assange can say whatever he likes about the greater good he and his source are doing, but the truth is they might already have on their hands the blood of some young soldier or that of an Afghan family. Disagree with the war all you want, take issue with the policy, challenge me or our ground commanders on the decisions we make to accomplish the mission we've been given, but don't put those who willingly go into harm's way even further in harm's way just to satisfy your need to make a point."[35]

The message was clear: The reading public in the United States might not be poring over the memos, cables, and field reports, bereft as they were of new perspectives on America's longest war, but the enemy was, and in great detail. Publication of such details as the home village and occupation of an otherwise unnamed source was as good as putting the source's name up in lights, the Pentagon maintained. Not only did it jeopardize the life of a source, as if that were not enough, it also made it much more difficult for the Pentagon and other U.S. intelligence branches to recruit sources.

Although some regarded the WikiLeaks case as an example of the future of media, with new, online sources working in coordination with mainstream media, *New York Times* executive editor Bill Keller told NPR that he regarded WikiLeaks not as a collaborating news organization but as a source, the only difference being that while in the past sources leaked to the press and the press had exclusive control over what was made public, today's online culture enabled individuals to self-publish.[36] WikiLeaks had no control over how the *Times* handled the material, nor did the *Times* have any say over what WikiLeaks decided to post. The *Times* went to lengths to contrast its handling of the classified documents with WikiLeaks, noting that it consulted at length with multiple U.S. government agencies, including the Pentagon, over what could be safely published. WikiLeaks withheld some 15,000 documents but did not directly engage with the Pentagon over publication.[37]

The episode points up an emerging problem that goes along with the new media forms available in the online world. More and more information can now be related without any filter to readers and viewers. While this sometimes, perhaps most times, brings with it benefits of getting more material out to a wider audience, it can short-circuit the journalist's role of assessing, weighing, reviewing, and contextualizing material before publishing or broadcasting it. However one may want to praise full, rather than filtered, availability of information, the practical reality is that very few Americans are going to sit down and plow through 92,000 documents, but many will hear about the story through the filter of brief—sometimes extremely brief—media reports. To be sure, critics in the national security community are hardly satisfied with the job the mainstream media does at filtering. At about the same time as the WikiLeaks controversy, the *Washington Post* published an extensive series on the vast expansion of the U.S. intelligence community since the September 11, 2001, terror attacks. Both in print and, in greater detail, online, the *Post* showed how, largely outside of public view, an immense network of public and private contractor organizations had sprung up around Washington and across the country doing intelligence work wholly outside of public scrutiny. As did the *Times* in the WikiLeaks case, the *Post* consulted extensively with the U.S. government over what to publish and what to withhold. Still, there were complaints that some of the material amounted to a road map to potential terrorists who might wish to attack or attempt to penetrate U.S. intelligence installations.[38]

The problem the Pentagon encountered in the WikiLeaks episode was not entirely the result of an online organization with no compunction about publishing classified material, nor of a source (suspected of being a 22-year-old private already facing charges in an earlier leak investigation).[39] Indeed, the WikiLeaks story and the *Post* series on the intelligence community had a connection beyond the publication of sensitive information. Because, as Defense Secretary Robert Gates acknowledged, the extensive detail in the 92,000 documents on the war in Afghanistan and their wide distribution (and with it the increased risk of a leak) stemmed from a lesson learned in the Persian Gulf War and reinforced in the wake of the 9/11 attacks. The lesson was that intelligence needed to be shared and, in the case of military intelligence, needed to be pushed forward to the warfighter and given the widest distribution possible.

"The interesting thing is," said Gates, "and it really was one of the lessons learned from the first Gulf War in 1991, was how little useful intelligence information was being received by battalion and company commanders in the field. And so there has been an effort over the last 15 or so years in the military, and I would say really accelerated during the wars in Iraq and Afghanistan, to push as much information as far forward as possible, which means putting it in a secret channel that almost everybody has access to in uniform." The publication of the war documents not only exposed past communications, some of them containing sensitive information, it also carried the risk of denying war-fighters future communications. Because, as a result of the leak, Gates said, the high command was "going to have to look at . . . should we change the way we approach that, or do we continue to take the risk?"[40]

9/11: MEDIA AS POLICY CHANGE AGENTS

The simplest process by which media coverage can play a role in shaping governmental decision making is one in which coverage draws attention to a hitherto overlooked issue; the outrage or shock or interest generated by the coverage then spawns political action. This impulse to appear responsive to a problem raised by media attention can stem from a sincere desire to address the problem or from a cynical play on the part of elected officials to draw media attention to themselves. A familiar sequence of events ensues: enterprising journalism draws public attention to an issue; public attention spurs political action to address that issue; resulting reform efforts help generate a journalism award. A journalist who can say his or her reporting led to a special commission investigation or the passage of a new reform law is a journalist with bragging rights.

This process is not the only route by which the media can shape events. At times the mere anticipation of major media attention can have an impact. A case in point is the 9/11 Commission inquiry into the September 11, 2001, terrorist attacks. From the beginning of their inquiry, Commission investigators were aware that President Bush had received a briefing one month before the attacks that warned that al-Qaeda was planning to strike the U.S. homeland.[41] This was no ordinary briefing but a CIA-drafted *President's Daily Brief* (PDB), without doubt the most highly classified recurring intelligence document produced by the U.S. government.

Created as a result of intense public pressure led by family members of 9/11 victims, the Commission had pledged not only to investigate the facts but, to the greatest degree possible, present them to the public, even though much of the material would necessarily come from the world of intelligence. The existence of a pre-9/11 presidential briefing that touched on the potential terrorist threat against the U.S. homeland had been reported by CBS News in May 2002, well before the 9/11 Commission had even been formed.[42] This initial disclosure was an important story but by itself not enough to create a media furor because the precise content of the intelligence report had not yet been revealed. It took the Commission, with its power to demand access to even highly classified documents, and with its power to advocate, if not compel, declassification of as much information as possible, to elevate the story into a major public controversy.

With its title, "Bin Ladin Determined to Strike in U.S.," it was easy enough for the Bush administration to anticipate what would follow disclosure of even part of the actual briefing paper with its August 6, 2001, date just over a month before the 9/11 attacks. A story line already gaining currency would gain the backing and credibility of a document known to have been shown to the president: The White House had been warned and it did nothing.

At first the Bush administration tried to withhold release of the PDB to the Commission altogether, then to prevent its contents from being made public.[43] Eventually a compromise was worked out: The relevant portions of the PDB could be disclosed, but only if a similar PDB entry dating to the Clinton administration was also released. Dated December 4, 1998, the article in the PDB was titled "Bin Ladin Preparing to Hijack U.S. Aircraft and Other Attacks."[44] Days before the 9/11 Commission report itself was made public, Bush administration officials helpfully briefed reporters on the warning the CIA had given the previous administration.[45] That ensured that the warning the Clinton administration received got separate press attention and would not be lost in the blanket coverage of the release of the entire Commission report. The operative issue for the Bush administration was not press coverage, but *anticipated* press coverage, and the goal was to create a sort of media counterpunch, the point being, "Yes, we were warned, but so were they—*nobody* really saw this coming." Thus, anticipatory media pressure drove a series of events: the Commission's determination, in response to pressure from 9/11 families, to make as much as possible public regardless of who might be embarrassed by the information disclosed; the realization by the Bush administration that certain documents, particularly this clear warning a month before the attack, would draw intense media scrutiny; and the demand that a similar document from the preceding administration be made public as well.

The public uproar the August 2001 PDB generated more than justified the concern in the White House that preceded its release. A couple of points should be noted, however. The overall theme of the story concerning the level of vigilance (or lack thereof) on the part of the Bush administration concerning the terrorist threat before 9/11 had already been amply established by other facts long since made public. Notable among these was the repeated warning by counterterrorism advisor Richard Clarke, a holdover from the Clinton administration, that the threat was real and that the Bush White House needed to focus its attention on that threat, and the failure of the Bush administration to heed that warning. What the PDB did was dramatize the story. As with the Bob Woodward story about the leaked McChrystal report on the state of the war in Afghanistan in 2009, the post-9/11 reporting on the Bush PDB put it in stark terms that the public could easily understand. In newsrooms reporters and editors talk about the phenomenon of being able to tell an entire story in a single sentence. With the release of the PDB that sentence was, "The CIA warned the president, and the president did nothing."

Release of the Clinton-era PDB did not have the intended effect of deflecting criticism away from the Bush administration. The problem was that there was ample evidence that President Clinton, unlike Bush before 9/11, had focused on the al-Qaeda threat, particularly in the wake of the 1998 bombings of the U.S. embassies in Kenya and Tanzania. The Clinton administration counterattacks on al-Qaeda did not stop the terror group, but it was difficult to say that the Clinton White House had failed to heed warnings about the al-Qaeda threat.

Lost in this boiled-down version of reality were the nuances that made it harder to reach the conclusion that the president had failed to heed a clear warning. The August 2001 PDB did indeed raise the specter of an al-Qaeda attack on the U.S. homeland, and it did mention unconfirmed rumors that hijackings might be one form of al-Qaeda attack. But the document provided no information that suggested the IC was on to a specific plot or had made any specific recommendation for presidential action. The possibility of al-Qaeda hijackings was raised by way of saying that the IC could find no information to *confirm* rumors that this type of attack was in the offing. In the view of 9/11 Commission chairman Thomas Kean, the problem was not failure to heed clear warning but the absence of any specificity to the warning in the PDB. When first given access to not just one but all of the potentially relevant PDBs from the pre-9/11 period, Kean came away with the distinct impression that they were "garbage" and that relative to specific, clear warnings, "There really was nothing there—nothing."[46]

Also lost in the simplified storyline was a point raised by a few national security experts. The furor over the PDB seemed founded on a concept of the president as action figure. The furor focused on presidential inaction. Thus the implied correct course of action envisioned the president setting the national security apparatus in motion as a result of the warning contained in the PDB. The sequence of events under this supposedly ideal scenario would be as follows: intelligence bureaucracy gets wind of an attack, collects the relevant intelligence, moves that information up the chain of command all the way to the president, and *waits for instructions*. This, of course, is an absurdity. If the IC had information on an impending attack on the U.S. homeland, the president will be informed without delay, of course. But one hopes that the intelligence, military, and law enforcement bureaucracies will be capable of taking preventive steps without waiting for a go-ahead from the Oval Office following a morning intelligence briefing.

Media as Amplifier

The 9/11 Commission investigation was an enormous media event for obvious reasons, but a controversy surrounding the appointment of the Commission chairman provided an example of a case in which a story developed in spite of the media, not because of it. The circumstance concerned the initial appointment of former Secretary of State Henry Kissinger to chair the panel. It turned out to be a serious false start. Family members of 9/11 victims were the driving force behind the establishment of the Commission and the panel's commitment to transparency. Upon Kissinger's appointment they raised questions about the former secretary of state's postgovernment career as a consultant to foreign governments. Concerned that Kissinger's client list might well include Saudi Arabia, home of the powerful and wealthy bin Laden family and locus of at least some of the radicalism that led to 9/11, family members pressed for the client list to be made public. When Kissinger refused, the ensuing furor ended with his resignation from the panel and his replacement by Kean, the former New Jersey governor who was much better able to communicate with and relate to the family members—many from his home state—who had lost loved ones in the attack.[47]

None of this was all that surprising. Kissinger had long been a controversial figure, distrusted by both the political left and right—the left for his hawkish policymaking role during the latter years of the Vietnam War, the right for his development of the détente policy with the Soviet Union. What was surprising was that it was the 9/11 families—private citizens not schooled in the subtleties of Washington machinations—who drove the story, not the media. To the contrary, the objections to Kissinger's appointment by 9/11 family members stood as an embarrassment to the media. For years Kissinger had been a columnist, opining on the pages of the *Washington Post* and other major newspapers on foreign affairs; he had been a regular guest as expert pundit on network news and cable television. And through all those postgovernment years as a sought-after expert, the media was all too happy to bask in the glow of Kissinger's considered opinions, without ever demanding to know whether those views might be influenced by the clients who had retained him at his consulting firm. Once the 9/11 families were on to the problem, the media, with its enormous power as a megaphone, elevated the story and drew public attention, but the media did not initiate the story and, indeed, seemed keen on avoiding it altogether until the issue was forced upon it by a group that could not be ignored.[48]

IRAQ WMD: MISSING THE REAL STORY

The preceding example demonstrates that it is not enough for the press to report a well-known story. It must do so in a compelling and prominent fashion. An example of a far different sort would be media reporting on WMD prior to the Iraq war. The conventional wisdom is that the media missed the WMD story—it uncritically accepted the Bush administration's fear mongering and served as a credulous tool in the administration's public relations campaign to lead the country into war.[49] The political left finds this story-line particularly compelling, for it absolves the left of responsibility for acquiescing in a radical and tragically ill-thought-out war policy. In fact there was media reporting that raised questions about the WMD story, and despite what many have claimed, Knight Ridder News Service was not the only news organization that raised questions about the WMD charges.[50] The problem was that the coverage raising questions about the veracity of the WMD charges did not get prominent play from any news organization nor was it picked up and amplified by critics of the Bush war policy. The underlying assumption of the criticism aimed at the media was that if only the coverage had been persistent enough to gain a prominent place in the prewar debate, that coverage might have slowed or stopped the march to war. There is no way to answer that hypothetical question. The point is that a vocal group of critics of the war policy believed this to be so.

There is no doubt that the media was far too credulous of the WMD allegations emanating from the White House. Stories skeptical of that case were relatively rare and tended to run inside newspapers rather than on the front page, while uncritical news reporting of the administration's charges about Iraq dominated the front pages, to say nothing of the hyped coverage on cable television, replete with titles and slogans for the pre-war coverage.[51] The problem was not that the media, collectively, had made a decision to back a war policy by refraining from fact checking the Bush administration about its WMD claims. The problem was that the contrary story—that Iraq might *not* have WMD—ran so counter to the assumed and accepted truth that Iraq had WMD capability that there was neither a significant editorial push behind that storyline nor any great number of sources pointing up that possibility. Furthermore, the stories that did raise questions about the WMD charges drew little if any notice. Given the intensity of the Bush administration's warnings of Iraqi capability, what is surprising is not how few stories raised questions about the Iraqi threat, but rather how many were ignored. The author of a University of Maryland study of media coverage of the Iraq-WMD story noted that amid a general tendency to uncritically report the Bush administration's charges, several news organizations did run skeptical stories. "Despite the apparent failures in reportage, not all journalists covered the WMD arc of stories poorly. Reporters Barton Gellman, Walter Pincus and Dana Milbank of the *Washington Post*, Bob Drogin of the *Los Angeles Times*, David Sanger and William Broad of the *New York Times*, Warren Strobel, Jonathan Landay and John Walcott of Knight Ridder, and Dafna Linzer of the Associated Press were prominent exceptions to the general pattern of WMD reportage."[52]

That is quite a large number of exceptions, especially as it does not include the reporting of *USA Today*, the nation's largest circulation daily. Entirely overlooked by those who have criticized the prewar coverage, *USA Today*, at the time the nation's largest-circulation newspaper, began raising serious questions about the case for invading Iraq in July 2002, three months before Congress voted to authorize the use of force and eight months before the actual invasion. It ran a story indicating that the Bush administration was seeking to find a legally defensible cause for the attack.[53] A July 29, 2002, story reported that "Bush administration lawyers have concluded that establishing a link between al-Qaeda terrorists and Iraq would provide all the legal justification the administration needs to launch military action against Saddam Hussein's regime, U.S. officials say."[54]

When, despite strenuous administration efforts, the al-Qaeda-Iraq link did not initially gain a great deal of public or official credibility, the Bush administration shifted the case for war to the WMD threat. As already noted, these charges fell on receptive ears because of a general assumption that Iraq had retained its banned weapons. But to those who followed intelligence issues day to day, the administration's case for war went beyond what the U.S. IC had been saying about Iraq for several years, which was that there was suspicion—but no proof—that Iraq had kept weapons programs going, and that there was no clear evidence of actual WMD stockpiles. At risk of their careers, dedicated intelligence professionals expressed their dismay that nuanced reporting on the Iraqi threat was, in the Bush administration's hands, being transformed into unqualified and dire warnings of danger. For example, on September 17, 2002, *USA Today* reported: "The Bush administration is expanding on and in some cases contradicting U.S. intelligence reports in making the case for an invasion of Iraq, interviews with administration and intelligence officials indicate. In some cases, top administration officials disagree outright with what the CIA and other intelligence agencies report. For example, they repeat accounts of al-Qaeda members seeking refuge in Iraq and of terrorist operatives meeting with Iraqi intelligence officials, even though U.S. intelligence reports raise doubts about such links. On Iraqi weapons programs, administration officials draw the most pessimistic conclusions from ambiguous evidence."[55]

Still, the attempt to link al-Qaeda with Iraq persisted, despite reporting that raised serious doubts. For example, on September 27, 2002, two weeks before the vote to authorize force in Iraq, *USA Today* reported, under the headline, "Experts Skeptical of Al-Qaeda-Iraq Tie": "The Bush administration has intensified efforts to link al-Qaeda terrorists with Iraq, charging that senior al-Qaeda members were in Baghdad recently and received training in chemical and biological warfare. But several intelligence experts, including some within the U.S. government, expressed skepticism about the reports. A Pentagon official, speaking on condition of anonymity, called the new assertions an 'exaggeration.' Other intelligence experts said some of the charges appeared to be based on old information and that there was still no 'smoking gun' connecting Iraq with the Sept. 11 attacks on the United States."[56]

What is most notable about all of this coverage is not how prescient it was but rather how little impact it had on the debate. None of the stories the author has cited here played on page one, unsurprising because they raised questions and reported doubts within the government but did not absolutely disprove the administration's assertions. But the problem was more than one of page placement.

A key element of the media dynamic, whether the subject is military issues or other concerns, is the need for a two-way flow between report and audience, with the media serving as a megaphone for a particular line of inquiry *combined* with an audience *receptive* to that line of argument and positioned to echo and further amplify it. In the Iraq-WMD case, the latter half of that dynamic was missing. Given that the Bush war policy was controversial, one would have expected stories such as these to be read aloud on the House and Senate floor, entered into the *Congressional Record*, posted up on the screen by Tim Russert, then the host of NBC's *Meet the Press* program. It did not happen. A handful of Democratic senators drew attention to a CIA warning that the one U.S. policy most likely to provoke Iraq's Saddam Hussein into using WMD would be an invasion. In that case, even among Democrats opposed to the war policy, the concern was not that the Bush administration's allegations about Iraqi weapons might prove false, but that the Bush administration war policy might provoke Iraq into using the (alleged) weapons.

The media could have and should have made at least an attempt at a speculative style of reporting in the run-up to the Iraq invasion. Either scenario—that Iraq had WMD or did not—was speculative. The difference was that the speculation in favor of Iraq possessing WMD was coming from the White House and was linked to a controversial invasion policy. The speculative case against Iraqi WMD had no constituency, other than Iraq, and was disconnected with any specific policy option other than the status quo. The specter of an Iraq able to destroy American cities certainly carried more news punch than the possibility of an Iraq less heavily armed than the White House alleged. But the latter scenario raised a critically important, and totally overlooked question: What if we invade and there are no WMD? What will happen to U.S. credibility? What will happen to the war effort itself? This line of speculation was not quite as sensational as, What if Saddam attacks New York with biological weapons? But the questions were serious, as were the consequences once the absence of a WMD arsenal became clear. The media, often scolded for speculative reporting, would have done a service by doing more.

Among the many reasons why the media, and even elected officials not supportive of the Bush administration, tended to believe the WMD allegations is that disbelieving them required a fairly significant assumption. For Iraq to have no WMD would have meant that a combined policy of economic sanctions, aerial overflights, occasional air strikes, and international weapons inspections had succeeded in forcing Saddam to abandon his weapons and that, to some degree, Saddam had cooperated. This, in fact, is precisely what happened. But it was also an entirely unprecedented development, one that not even the participants—the inspectors, the intelligence analysts, the policymakers from the first Bush administration and the Clinton years—could allow themselves to contemplate.

IRAQ WAR: BEING THERE TO GET THE STORY

As a reporter covering the first two years of the Iraq war, the author covered developments from a desk in Washington, DC. From there the story existed at the macro level, dealing with questions of whether troop strength was adequate, how soon more body armor and stronger vehicular armor could be fielded, the futile search for WMD, the discovery of vast stocks of conventional weapons, and why the Bush administration seemed to have been caught so off guard by the strength of the insurgency. The administration may not have had tight control of the war, but it maintained tight control over information about the war. Off-message stories out of Washington came aplenty from critics of the war policy, but seldom from inside. This tight hold made it difficult to penetrate what was actually happening on the ground.

The circumstances for reporters in Iraq were markedly different—provided they had the time and freedom to get out of Baghdad and visit forward-operating bases. In early 2005, when the war was transitioning from a relative lull to its most violent phase, the author had the opportunity to do this kind of reporting and was amazed at how much more freely information flowed at combat outposts. Here the exchange of sensitive information did not depend on carefully cultivated sources and longstanding relationships of trust but from proximity to the action. Troops going through the day-to-day business of fighting an insurgent war are too busy coping with the threats coming at them every day to bother thinking up phony stories or spin to tell reporters. They were not particularly enamored of the media. In fact, some were openly hostile to a press they believed was, at times, working against them. Partly to set straight reporters they suspected of bias, frontline troops openly shared their frank assessments of what was going on, without checking to see if their version matched up with the line coming out of Baghdad's Green Zone or Washington.

In the case of the Iraq War, the term front line was used loosely, as this was an insurgency where the enemy wore no uniforms and could turn up almost anywhere in any fashion, from an ambush in the desert to a roadside bomb to a mortar attack on a forward-operating base. Still, there were clear differences between the Pentagon filled with colonels and one-star officers, or a forward command center still heavily populated by senior officers, and a forward-operating base, where a lieutenant colonel is God.

By this point in the conflict, the policy of embedding journalists had changed along with the circumstances of war. The operations no longer consisted of an active military advance but rather had become a more static occupation along with a targeted counterinsurgency. After a fairly elaborate accreditation process, this reporter could board a military helicopter and be taken to a forward-operating base. But there was no active censorship of any stories, nor any papers to sign promising government prepublication review of filed reports.

At forward-operating bases, then, American reporters were often invited—without much pressing—to sit in on tactical briefings, intelligence read-outs, discussions of upcoming operations, and frank assessments of regional political leaders. At a forward-operating base outside of Baghdad, a morning briefing with officers and senior enlistees stands out. Among the topics: an upcoming raid at a mosque suspected of being used as an insurgent supply depot. The briefing occurred on an off-the-record basis, to give this reporter a feel for day-to-day activity without exposing time-sensitive information to the public, or more particularly, to the enemy. The lieutenant colonel in command at the base requested withholding any reporting about the mosque, at least until the unit had been able to carry out its raid. Later an intelligence officer attached to the unit took me through a PowerPoint presentation showing charts, graphs, and the occasional photograph. One showed a crippled M1A1 Abrams main battle tank. It had been struck from above and behind by a rocket-propelled grenade. Somewhat sheepishly, the officer skipped past the photo, saying, "You're not supposed to see that." Seeing that the reporter did not understand at first what was so sensitive about a crippled Abrams tank, the officer explained that the Iraqi insurgency was gradually discovering vulnerabilities in the 60-ton Abrams. It was heavily armored to withstand attack from the front; in keeping with its intended use in conventional war against the Soviet Union, but not particularly well suited to urban environments, where the enemy could get above and behind the tank and aim at less heavily armored points. There was no point in helping the enemy to kill Americans even though stories were already filtering out that the Abrams tank had vulnerabilities, and the reporter readily acceded to the officer's request not to disclose the information. But the willingness, indeed eagerness, of frontline soldiers to share their direct experience with reporters writing to a domestic audience, and the actual information shared, helped immensely in filling out a more accurate overall picture of the challenges U.S. troops faced.

ETHICS, WAR, AND THE REPORTING PROFESSION

During the North Africa campaign in World War II, U.S. commanders struggled with operational security issues created by American correspondents trying to outdo one another in getting a bead about where the next offensive or battle was likely to occur. Eventually, General Eisenhower hit upon an approach that worked better than he could have hoped. It served as a model for at least some press dealings in the European theater for the rest of the war. With the war correspondents speculating—increasingly accurately—that the next Allied move would be toward Sicily, Eisenhower decided to neutralize the security threat by bringing the journalists into the fold. One month before the invasion, American correspondents assigned to cover the U.S. forces campaigning in North Africa were briefed on the broad outlines of the planned assault on Sicily. The correspondents got the briefing on the promise they would not publish anything about it until given the go-ahead by Army press handlers. The idea was that reporters made privy to what was going on would cooperate in holding the information, while reporters kept on the outside would struggle constantly to break stories, and would inevitably succeed. The results of this approach exceeded expectations. Not only did the speculative reporting about an assault on Sicily halt, the reporters actually policed one another, imposing an effective form of peer pressure on any correspondent in the inner circle who violated the bond of trust with the Allied high command.[57]

The episode adds some perspective to the later deterioration of relations between the military and the media, particularly during and after the Vietnam War. One offshoot of the deterioration is a hypothetical question journalists who cover the Pentagon are asked frequently by military officers, particularly junior and midlevel officers. The question goes like this: You, the correspondent, have managed to insert yourself into the confidence of an enemy insurgent force and are traveling with them as they go about planning attacks on U.S. forces. You become aware that the insurgents, tomorrow, will mount what is sure to be a lethal attack on a U.S. convoy moving through the area. You know where, when, and how the attack will unfold. Do you keep quiet and let the attack unfold or do you somehow try to get word back to U.S. forces so they can evade or repel the attack?[58]

To this reporter's knowledge, no scenario of this type involving an American journalist accompanying guerilla fighters has ever occurred. This is an urban myth, a tale that has taken on real form through multiple retellings. Military worries along these lines trace their origins to an article in *The Atlantic Monthly* that described a conference involving former military officers and prominent journalists in which a hypothetical scenario of this sort was proposed. In the panel discussion, CBS News correspondent Mike Wallace defended the proposition that the hypothetical reporter's response should be to report the ambush on the U.S. forces "simply as another story."

In this case, the hypothetical question was not well thought through. A reporter running with the insurgents, once having been told about plans to mount an ambush on U.S. forces, would not likely be allowed by internet-savvy insurgents to file a story about this impending attack. If the insurgents were remarkably clumsy, a reporter could, at great risk, try to sneak away and convey the information back to his domestic bureau to be broadcast or put on the wire or online. Such a reporter might well convey the information directly to a U.S. military official hoping not only to save lives but to build good will that would help the reporter on future stories. Journalistic excursions with insurgents—in those rare instances in which they occur—usually take place under extremely tightly controlled circumstances. In the unlikely event that an attack set for the next day on soldiers of the same nationality as the journalist were disclosed to that journalist, the disclosure would almost certainly take place under strict controls—the reporter's communications equipment confiscated; the information kept sufficiently vague as to conceal the key details; and so forth.

The scenario depicts a reporter suddenly finding himself in a deeply uncomfortable situation upon realizing an attack on U.S. forces is about to occur. Well, if you are covering the enemy, isn't that to be expected? The CNN reporters who found themselves in the middle of a U.S. air attack on Baghdad at the outset of the Persian Gulf War never faced criticism for failing to notify the Pentagon that Iraqi anti-aircraft guns were about to open fire on U.S. warplanes; the Pentagon was perfectly aware of that fact and did not need CNN's warning; it could simply watch the action unfold on television like everyone else.

The reality is that in the wars in Iraq and Afghanistan, such access to frontline enemy insurgents has been virtually nonexistent. What little reporting has surfaced usually originates from foreign reporters—perhaps some grainy footage of insurgents making and planting a bomb, footage that might turn up on an insurgent website. Reporting by U.S. correspondents from within the enemy camp has tended to be confined to those much-celebrated instances like CNN reporting from Baghdad or cable news coverage of the first attacks on Baghdad in 2003.

The scenario laid out in this frequently asked question is thus highly unlikely, bordering on unheard of. Moreover, there was another element missing from the equation, namely, any recognition that if an American correspondent was able to spend a few weeks traveling with insurgents, the reporting would be of keen interest to U.S. intelligence as a rare inside look at the operating methods of the enemy.

WHEN "NEGATIVE" NEWS DOES GOOD

Over the past several years, national security reporting has detailed delivery delays of armored vehicles to the combat theater in Iraq, squalid conditions at Walter Reed Army Medical Center for injured veterans, Army investigations into prisoner abuses at Abu Ghraib, CIA's extreme interrogation techniques at secret detention centers, and the secret and warrantless domestic surveillance program begun after the 9/11 attacks. These kinds of stories are often seen within national security organizations as negative in media terms. But like the old saying about it being an ill wind that blows no good, it is the rare story that has no upside, at least for someone. To the extent that critical stories about the Army's sluggish response to the urgent need for body armor and more heavily armored vehicles accelerated the efforts by the Pentagon and industry to get better protective equipment into the field, then those stories benefited the troops in need. If a few generals and acquisition officers were embarrassed, so what? Within days, if not hours, of the *Washington Post*'s publication of the problems at Walter Reed, living conditions started to improve. What, precisely, is negative about that? The debate rages on about whether coverage of the Abu Ghraib abuses and the CIA's interrogation program harmed national security by serving as a recruiting tool for Islamic extremists. To Americans who actually care about what is being done around the world and at home in their name, the Abu Ghraib and secret CIA prison stories cleared the way to halting deeply objectionable policies.[59] In the case of the surveillance story, the disclosure opened the way to reining in what many viewed was an imperial executive branch—not to mention galvanizing the legislative branch into performing its oversight responsibilities—that had stepped far beyond legal and constitutional boundaries in the name of domestic security and the international war on terrorism.[60]

For purposes of better understanding what can drive or elevate a story, it would be well to examine briefly some of the characteristics of these stories. The Water Reed housing story was a classic media exposé. An enterprising reporter found the problem and reported on it at a time when, in official circles, the decrepit housing in which recuperating soldiers were living had been entirely overlooked. The Abu Ghraib story brought to light an ongoing internal investigation. That is to say, the government had already discovered the scandal and was investigating—but in secret—and the news media brought before the public what was going on, most especially the photographs of abusive treatment. The other major contribution of the Abu Ghraib coverage was in taking the story beyond the initial investigation and up the chain of command, bringing to light links as high as the White House to official backing for some harsh interrogation methods. The existence of secret detention centers exposed secret policy, as did the disclosure of warrantless domestic wiretapping as part of the larger war on terrorism.[61] Both raised questions of legality, inviting greater court and congressional involvement to ensure that the American constitutional system was not being undermined on grounds of national security.

In addition to the simple power to expose and to draw public attention and sometimes condemnation of officials and policies, these stories illustrated the media's power to accelerate events. At Walter Reed, top officials were fired and repair work began with stunning speed as a result of the news coverage, while the problem had languished, entirely ignored, before the media became involved. Abu Ghraib and the complex issues surrounding secret detention and overseas prison and harsh interrogation techniques showed the media's ability to spark immediate and intense public debate, whereas the actual machinery of government—investigation, legislation, court action, and elections—moved on a much slower time scale. The surveillance story is an interesting exception because the *New York Times* chose to hold the story for a year at the request of the Bush administration. In that case, the *Times* moved with a deliberateness that mirrored that of government. Publication in the newspaper may ultimately have been driven not by a change in the fact set but by a simple matter of competitive advantage: James Risen, the reporter who broke the story, was also writing a soon-to-be-released book which, as a result of the *Times* hold on its story, risked scooping the newspaper.

CONCLUSION: REPORTERS ARE ACTORS, NOT JUST OBSERVERS

The foregoing discussion of the national security journalist's environment, culture, and dynamics suggests that more than anything else, a reporter is not just an observer but an action player in the national security enterprise. If one needed any proof of this, consider the experience this reporter had in the 1990s when covering the CIA and being asked to lecture to a National Defense University class of midcareer military officers and civilians involved in national security and intelligence matters. A CIA careerist from the D.O., or Directorate of Operations—the clandestine service—taught this course. Imagine addressing a group that included many who regarded journalists with a mixture of horror and disdain; horror that the media sometimes published classified information and disdain that journalists had any notion of the damage they might be causing. The talk tried to methodically walk the class through a journalist's day-to-day working life. As a beat reporter assigned to cover national security and intelligence matters, source building was a key job requirement, and the key to source building lay in developing relationships of trust with people who could responsibly and accurately share sensitive, though not necessarily classified, information. These sources were placing their careers into the reporter's hands. If the story came out wrong or information was mishandled, or made too obvious who had provided it, the consequences could be dire—at the very least for them, and potentially for the country. Journalists needed to know that their sources possessed access to the information; they, in turn, needed to know that the journalist had the depth of background needed to understand and handle the information appropriately.

Every word in the phrase "developing relationships of trust" is operative. "Developing," because valuable reporter-source relationships take time to build. They might get off to a decent start by a reporter demonstrating that he or she was not just assigned to cover a defense or intelligence story on a random Tuesday but was devoting all his working hours to the national security beat. The source might become familiar with the reporter's work by reading or hearing his reports, and might, in some cases, be able to test the reporter's handling of a complex story with his own understanding of what had happened. "Relationship," because the best sources work with a given reporter for months, even years at a time. Officials in sensitive positions do not share closely held information with reporters they do not know or will not be seeing again. They do not leak to reporters who are parachuting in to cover a single crisis. In a constructive reporter-source relationship, the reporter might get to know a source on an official trip or on a battle front—where there is enough time to establish a rapport and discover common interests. "Trust," because neither the reporter nor the source has a great deal of leverage over the other, and because the consequences of a miscommunication or betrayal are so severe.

At the end of the presentation, the professor, a career intelligence officer with years of experience overseas in sensitive CIA assignments, said to the class, "Well, as you can see, what Mr. Diamond does in his day-to-day work is remarkably similar to what we do in the Directorate of Operations." And in a sense, the journalist is every much a part of the national security enterprise as is the case officer, the diplomat, or the warrior, although his culture and world are very different.

As often as not, the issue of the media's influence on national security could just as well be described in terms of national security's influence on the media. Even in this era of bloggers and online media, national security journalism is a source-intensive business where the desire for the scoop or exposé is at least somewhat tempered by the journalist's realization that there will be other stories to write tomorrow, stories that may well require the same sources.

At certain times and in certain places there is no small amount of hostility between the media and military and national security decision makers. But we would probably do well to assume that, given the generally longstanding tenure of reporters who cover the military, well-established relationships of trust are developed between source and reporter that are the driving force behind the new information the media is able to bring to light.

Public criticism of the media in the WMD case underscores the point that whether or not the media can be said to influence military and national security affairs, there is a widespread belief that this is so. That belief, then, becomes the dynamic that drives the cycle of reporting, leaking, reacting, and re-reporting that makes this system go. But as there is a fog of war, so there is a fog of journalism; stories emerge not fully formed, sometimes based on wrong assumptions, occasionally warped by bias or politics, and in an environment of decision making that is far from unified within the government. Stories can and do take on a life of their own and get out of the control of their original sources, reporters, or subjects. That, more than anything, may be what can make them at times so powerful.

NOTES

1. Timothy Garton Ash, "1989," *The New York Review of Books*, Vol. 16, No. 17, November 5, 2009, 4.

2. See, for example, Marisa Guthrie, "Cover Story: Networks Face Grim Cost of War: Budgets are trimmed, coverage is more perilous—and ratings are falling," *Broadcasting & Cable*, August 13, 2007, available at www.broadcastingcable.com/article/109953-COVER_STORY_Networks_Face_Grim_Cost_of_War.php; and Stephen Hess, "Covering a 'War Without End': Terrorism, Homeland Security, U.S. Politics, Media & Journalism, Governance," The Brookings Institution, November 3, 2009, available at www.brookings.edu/articles/2003/11terrorism_hess.aspx. For more on the newspaper industry crisis see David J. Collins, Peter W. Olson, and Mary Furey, "The Newspaper Industry in Crisis," *Harvard Business Publishing*, March 11, 2009.

3. Michael Hastings, "The Runaway General: Stanley McChrystal, Obama's top commander in Afghanistan, has seized control of the war by never taking his eye off the real enemy: The wimps in the White House," *Rolling Stone*, June 22, 2010.

4. C. J. Chivers, Carlotta Gall, Andrew W. Lehren, Mark Mazzetti, Jane Perlez, and Eric Schmitt, "The War Logs. Inside the Fog of War: Reports from the Ground in Afghanistan," *New York Times*, July 26, 2010.

5. Author's notes. The author covered the peace talks as State Department correspondent for the *Chicago Tribune*.

6. Gay Talese, *The Kingdom and the Power: The Story of the Men Who Influence the Institution that Influences the World, New York Times* (New York: NAL, 1969), 280–81.

7. See Thomas L. Friedman, *From Beirut to Jerusalem* (New York: Farrar, Straus, Giroux, 1989), 3–18; and Richard Engel, *A Fist in the Hornet's Nest: On the Ground in Baghdad Before, During and After the War* (New York: Hyperion, 2004).

8. In a specific case, the *Washington Post* recently explained that its Baghdad bureau was costing roughly $1.5 million a year, as it had sent nearly eighty reporters to cover the war. According to the *Post*, a foreign bureau might run from $5 to $10 million annually to cover salaries, travel, war zone insurance, relocation expenses, cost-of-living adjustments, security personnel, and local support staff. Andrew Alexander, "A Changing Future for Foreign Coverage," *Washington Post*, December 13, 2009, A26.

9. For an overview, see John Maxwell Hamilton, *Journalism's Roving Eye: A History of American Foreign Reporting* (Baton Rouge, LA: Louisiana State University Press, 2009).

10. John Maxwell Hamilton and Eric Jenner, "The New Foreign Correspondence," *Foreign Affairs*, September/October 2003.

11. Patrick W. Quirk, "Iran's Twitter Revolution," *Foreign Policy in Focus*, June 17, 2009, at www.fpif.org/fpiftxt/6199.

12. Mark Glaser, "GlobalPost Aims to Resuscitate Foreign Correspondents Online," PBS, *Media Shift* website, January 8, 2009, at www.pbs.org/mediashift/2009/01/globalpost-aims-to-resuscitate-foreign-correspondents-online008.html.

13. For an example of the media criticism of the embed policy, see Ameen Izzadeen, "Embedded: Prostituting Journalism and Producing Bastardized News," *Daily Mirror*, March 28, 2003. For a different perspective, see Albert Eisele, "Embed Cavallaro sees war from the inside," *The Hill*, March 31, 2005.

14. U.S. Department of Defense transcript, meeting of Assistant Secretary of Defense—Public Affairs Victoria Clarke with news bureau chiefs, January 14, 2003, at www.defense.gov/transcripts/transcript.aspx?transcriptid=1259.

15. See, for example, Joe Strupp, "MRE Criticizes Expelling of Embeds Over Pix of Shot-up Humvee," *Editor & Publisher*, December 15, 2005.

16. The website icasualties.org has compiled detailed casualty information and battlefield reports where the differences between Army and Marine Corps reporting can be examined.

17. Author's notes. See also Henry Kissinger, *Years of Upheaval* (Boston: Little Brown, 1982), 588–90. For an account of the AP scoop, see Robert B. Sims, *The Pentagon Reporters* (Washington, DC: National Defense University Press, 1984).

18. Ed Offley, "When to Keep Secrets," published on Committee of Concerned Journalists website, November 19, 2001, at www.concernedjournalists.org/when-keep-secrets.

19. Offley, "When to Keep Secrets," and see also Ed Offley, *Pen & Sword: A Journalists Guide to Covering the Military* (Portland, OR: Marion Street Press, 2001).

20. Bob Woodward, "McChrystal: More Forces or 'Mission Failure.' Top U.S. Commander for Afghan War Calls Next 12 Months Decisive," *Washington Post*, September 21, 2009, A1.

21. Headquarters International Security Assistance Force, Kabul, Afghanistan, Stanley A. McChrystal, General, U.S. Army, Commander, United States Forces—Afghanistan, "Commander's Initial Assessment," August 30, 2009. The *Washington Post* made the document public at http://media.washingtonpost.com/wp-srv/politics/documents/Assessment_Redacted_092109.pdf?hpid=topnews).

22. Peter Feaver, "Bob Woodward Strikes Again! (McChrystal Assessment Edition)," *Foreign Policy*, September 21, 2009, at http://shadow.foreignpolicy.com/posts/2009/09/21/bob_woodward_strikes_again_mcchrystal_assessment_edition.

23. Michael D. Shear, "White House and Cheney in a war of words over Afghanistan," *Washington Post*, October 23, 2009.

24. Karen DeYoung and Scott Wilson, "34,000 troops will be sent to Afghanistan: President details plan for allies, other nations to be asked for more forces," *Washington Post*, December 1, 2009, A1.

25. Peter Baker, "Inside the Situation Room: How a War Plan Evolved: Advisers Detail Obama's Decisive Moment in a Tense Decision on Afghanistan," *New York Times*, December 6, 2009, 1A. (This was the lead story on the heavily read *Times* Sunday edition.) See also Anne E. Kornblut, Scott Wilson, and Karen DeYoung, "Obama pressed for faster surge: Afghan review a marathon, 'What was interesting was the metamorphosis,'" *Washington Post*, December 6, 2009, A1.

26. U.S. Department of Defense briefing, Secretary of Defense Robert Gates and Adm. Mike Mullen, chairman of the Joint Chiefs of Staff, June 24, 2010, transcript available on Defenselink.mil at http://www.defense.gov/transcripts/transcript.aspx?transcriptid=4647.

27. Helene Cooper, Thom Shanker, and Dexter Filkins, "McChrystal's Fate in Limbo as He Prepares to Meet Obama," *New York Times*, June 23, 2010, 1A.

28. David Carr, "Heedlessly Hijacking Content," *New York Times*, June 27, 2010.

29. Frank Rich, op-ed column, "The 36 Hours that Shook Washington," *New York Times*, June 25, 2010.

30. For references on the well-chronicled subject of anonymous sourcing in journalism, see the Poynter Institute's *Poynter Online* web page, "Anonymous Sources," at www.poynter.org/column.asp?id=49&aid=64013.

31. For an account of *USA Today's* tough policy on anonymous sourcing, see David Folkenflik, "USA Today Cuts Use of Anonymous Sources," National Public Radio, August 29, 2005, at www .npr.org/templates/story/story.php?storyId=4815420.

32. John Diamond, "Officials: U.S. blocked missiles to Hezbollah," *USA Today*, August 18, 2006, at www.usatoday.com/news/world/2006-08-17-iran-missiles_x.htm.

33. John Diamond, "Trained Eye Can See Right Through Box of Weapons," *USA Today*, August 18, 2006, at www.usatoday.com/news/world/2006-08-17-missiles-iran_x.htm.

34. For more on crate-ology, see Dino A. Brugioni, *Eyeball to Eyeball: The Inside Story of the Cuban Missile Crisis* (New York: Random House, 1993, updated edition); and Roger Hilsman, *To Move a Nation: The Politics of Foreign Policy in the Administration of John F. Kennedy* (New York: Doubleday, 1967).

35. U.S. Department of Defense briefing, Defense Secretary Robert Gates and Adm. Mike Mullen, chairman of the Joint Chiefs of Staff, July 29, 2010, transcript available at www.defense.gov/tran-scripts/transcript.aspx?transcriptid=4666.

36. David Folkenflik, "WikiLeaks: An Editor-in-Chief Or Prolific Source?" *NPR Weekend Edition*, interview with *New York Times* executive editor Bill Keller, July 31, 2010, available at www.npr.org/templates/transcript/transcript.php?storyId=128870288.

37. See Eric Schmitt, "In Disclosing Secret Documents, WikiLeaks Seeks 'Transparency,'" *New York Times*, July 26, 2010, 11; and by *New York Times* staff, "Piecing Together the Reports, and Deciding What to Publish," *New York Times*, July 26, 2010, 8.

38. Dana Priest and William Arkin, "Top Secret America: A Hidden World, Growing beyond Control," *Washington Post*, July 19, 2010, A1 and online at www.washingtonpost.com/top-secret-america/.

39. Voice of America News, "Army Private in WikiLeaks Case Transferred to U.S. Military Jail," July 20, 2010, available at www.globalsecurity.org/military/library/news/2010/07/mil-100730-voa07.htm.

40. DOD Briefing, Gates and Mullen, op. cit. July 29, 2010.

41. President's Daily Brief, "Bin Ladin Determined to Strike in U.S.," August 6, 2001, declassified April 10, 2004. Available on National Security Archive website at www.gwu.edu/~nsarchiv/NSAEBB/NSAEBB116/index.htm. Note: U.S. government documents transliterated the terrorist leader's name "Usama bin Ladin." I quote spellings in official documents as they appear but use in my own text the spelling "Osama bin Laden" that became more widely used in the media.

42. Thomas S. Blanton, "The President's Daily Brief," online article, the National Security Archive, updated April 12, 2004, available at www.gwu.edu/~nsarchiv/NSAEBB/NSAEBB116/index.htm.

43. *CBS Evening News*, on May 15, 2002, broke the story of the pre-9/11 intelligence briefing for President Bush that warned of al-Qaeda's intention to attack the United States. For White House reaction to the story and initial resistance to release of the full briefing, see White House press briefing, May 16, 2002, White House spokesman Ari Fleischer.

44. The PDB is reprinted in the *Final Report of the National Commission on Terrorist Attacks upon the United States*, *The 9/11 Commission Report* (New York: Norton, 2004), 128.

45. Susan Schmidt, "1998 Memo Cited Suspected Hijack Plot by Bin Laden," *Washington Post*, July 18, 2004, A17.

46. Quoted in Evan Thomas, "Book of the Times: Tragicomic Tale of the 9/11 Report," *New York Times*, February 4, 2008, a review of Philip Shenon, *The Commission: The Uncensored History of the 9/11 Commission* (New York: Twelve, 2008).

47. See "Kissinger resigns as head of 9/11 Commission," *CNN.com*, December 13, 2002. Former Senate Majority Leader George Mitchell had previously resigned as vice chair of the commission, citing demands that he sever ties with his Washington law firm.

48. An exception in the media's general failure to initiate questions about the Kissinger appointment appears in Christopher Hitchens, "The Latest Kissinger Outrage: Why is a proven liar and wanted man in charge of the 9/11 investigation?" *Slate*, November 27, 2002. Hitchens's reputation as an extreme critic of Kissinger may have dampened the article's impact.

49. See, for example, Frank Rich, "All the President's Flacks," *New York Times*, December 4, 2005, at http://select.nytimes.com/2005/12/04/opinion/04rich.html?_r=1.

50. For one of many examples in which reporters and editors claimed that theirs was the only reporting that was skeptical of the WMD case prior to the point in 2002 when Congress authorized the use of force in Iraq, see Max Follmer, "The Reporting Team that Got Iraq Right," interview with John Walcott and Jonathan Landay, *The Huffington Post*, March 17, 2008, at www.huffingtonpost.com/2008/03/17/the-reporting-team-that-g_n_91981.html.

51. For a detailed study of media coverage prior to the U.S.-led invasion of Iraq, see Susan D. Moeller, "Media Coverage of Weapons of Mass Destruction," Center for International Security Studies at Maryland, University of Maryland, March 9, 2004.

52. Susan Moeller, "Weapons of Mass Destruction and the Media: Anatomy of a Failure," *YaleGlobal Online*, April 14, 2004, at http://yaleglobal.yale.edu/content/weapons-mass-destruction-and-media anatomy-failure. For the detailed media study Moeller authored, see Moeller, "Media Coverage of Weapons of Mass Destruction," ibid.

53. Recently, amid the severe downturn in the news business, the *Wall Street Journal* has passed *USA Today* as the circulation leader.

54. John Diamond, "Attack on Iraq requires clear al-Qaeda link; Administration's view: Direct ties provide legal justification," *USA Today*, July 29, 2009, 7A.

55. John Diamond, "U.S. Assertions Go beyond Its Intelligence: Questions Raised on Iraq Evidence," *USA Today*, September 17, 2002, 4A.

56. Barbara Slavin and John Diamond, "Experts Skeptical of Al-Qaeda-Iraq Tie: Link Could Help the Case for War, But Some Say It's Weak," *USA Today*, Sept. 27, 2002, 4A.

57. Dwight D. Eisenhower, *Crusade in Europe, A Personal Account of World War II* (New York: Doubleday, 1948), 169–70.

58. James Fallows, "Why Americans Hate the Media," *The Atlantic Monthly*, Vol. 277, No. 2, February 1996, 45–64.

59. Dana Priest, "CIA Holds Terror Suspects in Secret Prisons: Debate Is Growing within Agency about Legality and Morality of Overseas System Set Up after 9/11," *Washington Post*, November 2, 2005, A1.

60. See, for example, Blake Morrison and John Diamond, "Pressure at Iraqi Prison Detailed," *USA Today*, June 17, 2004, 1.

61. James Risen and Eric Lichtblau, "Bush Lets U.S. Spy on Callers without Courts," *New York Times*, December 16, 2005, A1.

Chapter 16 Conclusion: Navigating the Labyrinth of the National Security Enterprise

HARVEY RISHIKOF AND ROGER Z. GEORGE

> It's hard to convey how difficult it is for bureaucracies to adapt to radical change. But generally, government
> work is like any other line of work; most people will tend to approach tomorrow's problems with the
> solutions that worked today. . . . In the private sector, there's almost always a bottom line—profit—
> that causes organizations to change their approach. But in political and policy work, there's seldom
> a clear bottom line, and each faction behind a given policy can almost always rationalize why its
> plan works best or would work best "if only" this, that or the other were altered.
>
> *James Baker, The Politics of Diplomacy*

CRITIQUING THE SYSTEM

The chapters in this volume examine some of the key organizations and institutions that make up the national security enterprise (NSE). As the book's title suggests, navigating the labyrinth of this enterprise is a daunting challenge. Even our collective effort to describe and analyze the process is incomplete and subject to some oversimplification. For example, this book uses an inside-the-beltway perspective to elucidate a bureaucratic cultural viewpoint of how U.S. national security policy works. One could write another volume on many organizations' field activities and operations—be they embassies, commands, or news bureaus—that provide even more insight into the workings of these national security players. Moreover, there are other agencies that must be considered part of the NSE deserving their own treatment such as the U.S. Agency for International Development (USAID), Department of Energy (DOE), and Treasury, among others. Space considerations and availability of authors unfortunately dictated hard choices for this book but perhaps in future editions we will revisit these decisions and approaches.

The NSE has proven to be a very resilient and evolving set of organizations, institutions, cultures, and processes. For the past sixty years, the American system has functioned well enough to successfully avert a major nuclear war with the Soviet Union and contain its influence to bring an end to the Cold War. As Michael Warner and Jon Rosenwasser note in their historical treatment of the system, that is a monumental achievement. On one level the national security system has adapted, weathered the legislative and court battles against executive power, and endured and perhaps benefited from the intervention of outside lobbyists, pressure groups, and think tanks. That is the American system of checks and balances. A conventional view suggests that whatever changes need to be made to confront new issues facing the United States can be managed through the traditional pulling and hauling of those interagency and political processes.

We, however, respectfully dissent. For more than a decade, major commissions and outside studies have been arguing that a more fundamental set of changes is required. First, the world is far different than anything that the creators of the 1947 National

Security Act could have imagined. The range of issues, their complexity, and their global dimension simply are far more diverse than what the Trumans or Achesons imagined. As the National Intelligence Council's Global Trends 2025 notes, the international system is being transformed and will be unrecognizable by 2025. Such changes are being driven by economic, climate, demographic, energy, and social shifts that were hard to imagine only a few years ago. Moreover, the multiplicity of actors, the rise of Asia as well as non-government players, and the shift of economic power suggest the United States will be a much less influential player, although not without considerable leverage.[1]

Second, the growth of the NSE itself has now reached a point where complex inter-actions among agencies and organizations are particularly bewildering. As many of the chapters in this book illustrate, the day is past when a single government agency or organization—even one as large as the Department of Defense (DOD)—can manage a key foreign policy issue. This was true to some extent even in the late 1940s but today there are no clear agency lanes in the road for twenty-first-century problems. When the Clinton administration talked about complex contingency operations in the 1990s, it was only beginning to appreciate what that would entail. The failure of the Bush administration to handle postconflict reconstruction and stability operations, as authors Grossman, Smith, and Miller note, was a perfect storm of unanticipated prob-lems, poor planning, and the obsolete notion that a single-agency approach could han-dle all the issues. To cite another example, one can point to the complexity of today's proliferation problems and how many elements of the U.S. government are struggling to map out what is needed to counter the spread of dangerous weapons and technolo-gies. As figure 16.1 highlights, the pieces of government involved—only the executive branch in this case—can barely be put on a single chart or be comprehended without a magnifying glass.

Third, the once clear line between domestic and foreign security threats has now almost completely dissolved in regard to counterterrorism as well as other transnational issues like climate, immigration, and health. As the book's discussion of homeland security illus-trates, coordinating aspects of global terrorism, emergency responses to natural disasters, and border control involve agencies and authorities that range from the federal to the state to the local levels. Separating out these responsibilities is nearly impossible. A key role for the NSE is ensuring that these levels of government can exchange information, share responsibilities, and collaborate to avert or at least minimize damage to U.S. foreign and domestic interests.

This complex picture has been laid out in numerous studies. As far back as the 2001 Hart-Rudman Commission, there was an appreciation of the new twenty-first-century challenges facing the national security enterprise. The report, presented to the George W. Bush administration only a few weeks after it began its term, warned that the new century would require agencies to adjust their portfolios and achieve a level of interagency coop-eration and partnering with nongovernment organizations as well as allies to a degree not anticipated during the Cold War. A decade later, many of the same recommendations are to be found in the Project on National Security Reform (PNSR). Like the seven-volume 2001 Hart-Rudman report that preceded it, the PNSR displayed in copious detail and in multiple volumes the tasks ahead in redesigning the NSE. Similarly to Hart-Rudman, the PNSR saw the necessity of whole of government approaches that integrated the operations

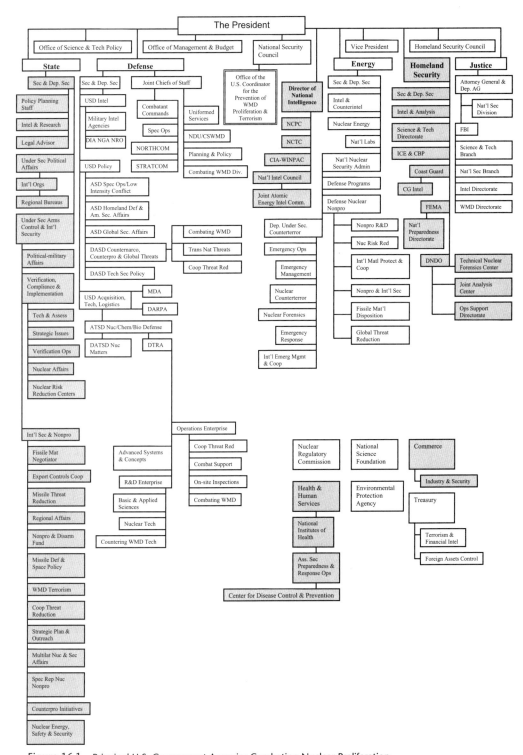

Figure 16.1   Principal U.S. Government Agencies Combating Nuclear Proliferation.

Source: Leonard S. Spector, director, James Martin Center for Nonproliferation Studies, and Anya Loukianova for the illustration.

of very different organizations and developed mechanisms for overcoming many of the organizational and bureaucratic obstacles that stood in the way of effective interagency national security planning and implementation. The PNSR noted: "U.S. national security missions are shifting, broadening, and becoming increasingly interdisciplinary. In light of today's multidimensional national security challenges, the system's inflexible stovepipes demand reform. . . . The [PNSR] vision is for a collaborative, agile, and innovative national security system that horizontally and vertically integrates all elements of national power to successfully meet 21st-Century challenges and opportunities based on timely, informed decisions, and decisive action."[2]

This book focuses on a critical underlying assumption embedded in all the major studies conducted on improving the NSE. That is, the various organizations, agencies, and institutions of government will be able to adapt their own unique cultures to work better with other parts of the U.S. government in the pursuit of effective national security policies. These same studies routinely complain that more agile and innovative policies typically run afoul of narrow and parochial organizational interests. Often, organizations and institutions prefer to operate using their well-developed processes and traditional missions, rather than adapt to new conditions or surrender control to other agencies. How can such diverse organizations and their cultures effectively adapt and yet maintain this uniqueness? To a large extent this is the conundrum on which the book is focused.

There are a number of propositions that flow from chapters focused on the different institutions and their cultures. The first proposition is that in the NSE, no one entity is capable of designing grand strategy. And American grand strategy confronts a complicated myriad of organizations, institutions, and cultures that attempt to reshape or bend the strategy in their own images. Describing these "organizational" or "professional" cultures for the practitioners and students of national security is a first step to understanding the expanding NSE. These cultures are not all bad nor all good. Appropriate evaluation of a culture turns on the context: what new goal or new mission is the organization challenged to meet as its critical priority? Even the National Security Council staff (NSCS), which is charged with orchestrating national security strategy, is incapable by itself of achieving this goal. For one thing, it is far too small a staff with far too limited an institutional memory to be saddled with the function of drafting grand strategy; for another, it lacks any real strategic planning element, which has been a constant complaint of numerous studies of national security reform. Moreover, there is strong institutional prejudice that the NSCS not be operational, in the sense of running day-to-day operations, and coordinate as best it can.

Indeed, as more and more interagency functions are added to the NSCS set of tasks, it will tend to become more of a traffic cop, scheduler of meetings, and mediator rather than a grand strategic planner. Yet, it is instinctive to recommend more directorates for the NSCS to coordinate, as the latest Council on Foreign Relations report does for Prevention/Stabilization/Reconstruction and Development/Governance.[3] These added duties will only be successful if one envisions a very much more expanded NSCS of twenty-five hundred or so, a combat command so to speak. As has been noted by analysts though, the size of the NSC has grown over the years and then cut back; however, this growth has been, even at its zenith, modest in comparison to other agencies or combat commands.[4] Both the Congress and other department secretaries have always resisted a large NSCS. One think tank report has suggested that the executive and legislative branches jointly establish a standing *independent strategic review panel* of experienced and senior experts to review the strategic environment over the next twenty years and provide prioritized goal and risk-assessment recommendations for use by the U.S. government for each new administration.[5] This report would become the basis for the NSCS to implement. Such suggestions point to the urgent need to define a clear set of national interests and establish an organization with the authorities to implement the necessary strategy to achieve them.

A second proposition is that so-called organizational fixes—that is, adding new units on top of existing ones or realigning agencies or their elements—are not sufficient to address the new boundary-crossing issues. If one needs proof of this, the chapter on the Department of Homeland Security (DHS) makes it clear that placing twenty-two different agencies under a single secretary for homeland security did not ensure common purpose or clear missions; rather, it multiplied the challenges of creating a common culture as well as multiplied the number of missions for which it was responsible. Similarly, the director of national intelligence (DNI)'s creation has not ended the interagency disputes within the intelligence community (IC) or integrated its functions smoothly. Rather, new turf battles seem to have cropped up between the DNI and the Central Intelligence Agency (CIA) over who serves the president and who represents the IC overseas. So, organizational changes are only part of the solution and may be part of the problem if cultures do not adapt and shift along with the line charts and reporting responsibilities (see box 16.1).

A third proposition is that organizational cultures can change but they will do so only if the incentives for change are stronger than the incentives to remain the same. At the same time, care should be taken to preserve what is best in the cultures so that the proposed changes do not undermine what needs to be preserved. The 9/11 shock produced substantial reforms in priorities within the FBI, CIA, and other national security agencies. The promotions and recognition coming from those who worked counterterrorism were suddenly much more obvious to those working inside these agencies, and the need to share became the dominant mantra over the need to know. But those incentives might weaken over time as new demands on those agencies arise and agencies' priorities shift again. As described in chapter 10, DHS has been buffeted by emerging crises, causing it to zigzag from a focus on counterterrorism to emergency management (Hurricane Katrina) and then to border controls (immigration). Likewise, the tendency of most agencies is to allow their organizations to return to business as usual, be that arresting criminals, recruiting agents, or preparing for traditional war operations. The failed Detroit Christmas bombing plot of December 2009 will only reinvigorate the debate of core DHS counterterrorism functions but not resolve its responsibility for its other missions. Hence, there will be a tendency to regress or drift back to traditional core missions over time, unless new incentive structures are put in place that outlast the current set of presidential advisors and agency leaders.

A fourth proposition is that various models of orchestrating the national security enterprise—be they NSC-centric, single-agency-led, or special-envoy-driven—all require that those issue leaders understand the organizations and the cultures they represent. As Marc Grossman notes, when Henry Kissinger came into the State Department he had little idea what the foreign service ethos was. Kissinger came to admire many career diplomats but he also realized that the best diplomats did not necessarily make the best strategists. The vision thing was not what State Department did, and generally speaking, he was not

Box 16.1   Crafting an Intelligence Community Culture

The 2004 intelligence reforms that created the Director of National Intelligence (DNI) were based on the presumption that the sixteen federal agencies performing intelligence functions are in fact a community. As many practitioners and critics will acknowledge, the concept of community is a work in progress. Instead, a loose confederation of agencies operates with different missions and organizational cultures, competing for attention, personnel, and dollars. Agencies only superficially like the idea of a DNI who is charged with integrating and directing them. These agencies, the Central Intelligence Agency (CIA) especially, guard their special relationships with other foreign intelligence services with territorial vigilance.

The recent DNI-CIA disagreement over selection of the senior officer in overseas missions to represent the intelligence community (IC)'s interests illustrates the challenge. These days, those interests touch on the missions of agencies far beyond CIA to include the National Security Agency (NSA), Defense Intelligence Agency (DIA), Federal Bureau of Investigation, Drug Enforcement Agency, and Department of Homeland Security, suggesting the DNI should select the representative. On the other side, the CIA insists it is the agency with the deepest ties and most critical missions overseas, namely clandestine collection and covert action. Hence a CIA officer must be the senior-most officer in-country, commonly called the chief of station. Anything less would undermine the CIA's ability to conduct its clandestine mission and undermine the long-established bilateral relations between the United States and host country intelligence services.

The National Security Advisor's decision in favor of the CIA does not settle the question of whether the CIA can truly represent the entire IC, because the IC lacks officers trained in and knowledgeable about the IC. Agencies continue to train, direct, and promote career professionals entirely separately from each other. Creating a "jointness"

equivalent to the military is a necessary step if an IC culture is to emerge.

All intelligence officers must have more opportunities to train together and get to know each other's cultures. To do this, the purported National Intelligence University—at the moment a virtual, on-paper institution—needs to become a bricks-and-mortar facility where officers from across the community are educated about each other and their professions.

Intelligence professionals must serve together. There are limited opportunities for officers now, largely in the centers focused on counterproliferation and counterterrorism. To many, the best example of "jointness" may occur overseas where different intelligence agencies are collocated under the direction of the ambassador as chief of mission. The DNI has made a start at this by instituting a joint–duty-assignments list that places aspiring officers in each other's agencies for broadening experiences. This must become a serious professional requirement for senior responsibilities—with no waivers—if the IC is to create a multi-agency perspective among the few leaders of the IC. This "jointness," which the military has been working on for decades, is only a baby step at this point in the IC.

Finally, when officers within the community are about to be promoted into the senior ranks—"flag equivalents" or the civilian senior executive service—a joint promotion board of the sixteen agencies should be convened to pass on candidates. Individuals who have demonstrated an unwillingness to be community players should not be promoted. In addition, there should be a required course that throws these future executives from CIA, NSA, DIA, etc., into a month-long training experience to develop their sensitivity to other parts of the IC, build personal networks, and give them a broader sense of community than currently is inculcated in the agency-specific training they have received throughout their careers.

going to be able to rely on careerists to produce new approaches to foreign policy problems. By the same token, the NSC-centric model seldom produces comprehensive policies, unless of course the national security advisor is a Henry Kissinger who carries strategy inside his head and has a special relationship with the president. More than most national security advisors, he disdained the interagency process and sought to develop overarching policies on his own with presidential support and approval.

Launching a strategy development process inside NSCS is one objective of the Obama administration. Its first national security strategy appeared in May 2010 and received little attention and polite applause. Many called it an unremarkable document, while others credited it with projecting a more realistic view of America's limited resources.[6] At this point, the NSCS that produced this document will have to do more to sell it as a truly ground-breaking statement that reflects America's grand strategy. Whether a planning cell can keep the "crisis-du-jour" NSCS focused on longer-term horizons will be a challenge. Historically, such strategy development efforts have lapsed, with those NSCS confining their efforts to outreach and public diplomacy more than actual strategy development. As is inevitable in such circumstances, NSC-driven initiatives cause potential tensions with cabinet secretaries who may feel marginalized, depending on how the policy is created and implemented. Likewise, single-agency leads or special envoys still invite only partial understanding of the complex interactions of different elements of the U.S. government bureaucracy. Unless the agency lead or special envoy for an issue understands where each bureaucracy is coming from, he is unlikely to know how to mold those activities into a coordinated whole. Moreover, the special envoy approach by its nature is an end-run approach around the bureaucracy and little organizational legacy is institutionalized.

ORGANIZATIONS ARE "US"

As mentioned in the introduction to this book, national security studies devote little attention to the specific dynamics or underlying organizational cultures that often drive the bureaucratic politics of American foreign policy. Scholars who do are more the exception than the rule. Recently, for example, Peter Hall and Michele Lamont have focused on how institutional and cultural structures affect societies that are successful in providing health care for their citizens.[7] Drawing on the literature of organizations, Hall and Lamont conceptualize institutions as sets of regularized practices with a rule-like quality that vary according to how expectations are established, whether by formalized sanctions or by informal mechanisms that create perceptions to serve mutual interests and shape appropriate behavior.[8] A similar analytical approach was pioneered in the 1970s for national security issues. For example, Morton Halperin's work on bureaucratic politics touched on the organizational essence that drove defense decision making. Likewise, Graham Allison's early work and later collaboration with Philip Zelikow reexamined the bureaucratic and organizational behavior evident in the Cuban missile crisis. Both efforts remain the basis for serious thinking about the organizational dimension of security.[9] These works tend to focus on explaining policy outcomes that are the result of the pulling and hauling of organizations and of effective bureaucratic entrepreneurs. They do not pretend to be in-depth studies of the individual organizations, although they do rely on key organizational behaviors that social scientists have discovered in examining many other government and private sector organizations. More recently though, Amy Zegart has focused on the organizational behaviors of the CIA and FBI, noting how dysfunctional these organizations became when asked to take on new tasks or work with other organizations in new ways.[10] She too, however, focuses on generalities in laying out how these organizations operate given her questions and does not explore the subcultures of the structures. Finally, Richard Haass has written about the "bureaucratic entrepreneur" and how an ambitious bureaucrat must assess his or her own organization's operational style and that of others if he or she is to flourish in the national security organization.[11] While laying out important traits of the successful organizational man or woman, this useful contribution makes no attempt to analyze the radically different organizational perspectives found inside the executive branch, which are laid out here.

This book argues that a more systematic and detailed understanding of the various organizations and cultures will help scholars and practitioners to navigate the NSE. It has focused on three key aspects to this enterprise. First, the key executive branch agencies—including the NSC, the State and Defense Departments, the CIA, the Office of Management and Budget, and broader IC and the domestic/law enforcement agencies (chiefly, FBI and DHS) that make up the formal interagency process that leads policy development and implementation. Second, we have discussed the operation of the two other branches of government. The Congress, with its unique cultures and operating styles, has the ability to frustrate or redirect policy in ways not intended or desired by the executive branch; but also the Supreme Court, with its seemingly remote and detached view of policy, has lately become a more prominent feature of the national security enterprise. And third, the book examined the important role of outside actors and their agendas. In particular, the media, the think-tank world, and lobbyists can influence and inform but also can amplify or distort the development of foreign policies. Our concluding thoughts will address each of these three levels in turn.

THE INTERAGENCY PROCESS

The interagency process today is far more than the NSC, the State and Defense Departments, the military, and the CIA as envisaged by the 1947 National Security Act. New players like FBI and DHS are increasingly being drawn into high politics, as lines blur between purely foreign and domestic policies. The combining of NSC with the Homeland Security Council staff by the Obama administration reflects the desire to integrate these spheres. This interagency process has become the target of much of the criticism for ineffective policy formation and implementation. But more attention needs to be placed on the clash of cultures that often lies underneath the lack of cooperation or information exchange.

The Special Relationship: State–Defense

The challenge of managing the vital State–Defense relationship is a central part of the book's chapters on these two organizations. The authors of the State–Defense chapters seem to agree that some rebalancing is required in terms of raising priorities on nondefense resources for national security. However, as Marc Grossman notes, simply giving the State Department more people and funding will not solve the problem. Ultimately, the solution lies in changing the mission and necessarily the culture of the State Department, whereby foreign service officers (FSOs) see their role as problem-solvers as much as negotiators; likewise, DOD civilians and military officers alike will also need to accept that military operations other than war are now part of their skill set until such time as the rebalancing of defense and nondefense resources is accomplished. But this new relationship will also require the Congress to fully fund a civilian foreign office with a budgetary training mandate that has been hitherto avoided. Historically, the approach has been to use local talent and not FSOs to maintain a small diplomatic footprint for very practical foreign policy reasons.

One recurring theme found in many of the chapters focused on single agencies is that they are all inhabited by subcultures. One internal coordination mechanism for the military, for example, are the tribes of the Army built around weapons systems: armor versus artillery versus special forces. Comparable tribes exist in the U.S. Air Force and Navy. Added to this set of subcultures is the grooming of senior officers that takes place.[12]

While the diplomat is the poster child for the State Department, there are many varieties depending on the bureau or region in which an FSO serves. Its subcultures, driven by political, economic, public, or consular affairs career tracks, make a difference in their outlook and loyalties. Sometimes these loyalties can produce internal governmental interests that act as single-issue nongovernment organizations. One bureau committed to human rights will veto agreements being negotiated by other bureaus and sabotage programs if those programs do not comport with views of the prevailing approach on human rights. This can result in a battle between different careerist factions. Or the State Department, like DOD and some other institutions, can be divided between the careerist and political appointee cultures. Getting the career subcultures as well as the political appointees to agree on a policy is often difficult. NSC frustrations, as related in the chapter focused on that institution, often stem from its impatience with the State Department's inability to formulate its own internal policy, much less coordinate with other agencies.

A recent trend toward appointing special envoys that can carry both a department and White House imprimatur seems aimed at giving State more clout and an ability to overcome internal State Department wrangling. The Obama administration is now full of special envoys from Afghanistan-Pakistan to Arab-Israeli to Sudan.[13] Is this reliance on envoys an admission of failure on the part of career ambassadors and assistant secretaries to implement policies? Does this solution only serve to accentuate the careerist-political appointee tensions, or can it help make the careerists more effective and galvanize them? To be sure, the appointment of envoys avoids a congressional confirmation process. Much will depend on whether this strategy of bringing in powerful outsiders is seen as intended to discipline a bureaucracy or to advocate for it.

The Pentagon, however, suffers from exactly the opposite problem. Well resourced compared to other agencies, with plenty of personnel and hardware, it has become the interagency's 911 for doing anything hard or rapidly. More than many other organizations, the DOD has acknowledged the existence of its separate military and civilian cultures, as civilian–military relations have long been recognized as a major flashpoint historically. Similarly, though, it has internalized "jointness" in a way other agencies can only envy: it has not solved all the problems of unique service cultures scrambling for resources and mission relevance. Likewise, the DOD's battles to hammer out a joint policy between the military services—represented by the Joint Staff—and the civilian leadership found in the Office of the State Department (OSD) can be time consuming; moreover, after the Goldwater-Nichols reforms, the Pentagon now is allowed to come to the table with separate Joint Staff and OSD positions, which further complicates the integration of separate agency perspectives. In fact, authors Michael Meese and Isaiah Wilson also point out that the effectiveness of the Pentagon is still undercut by its sheer size and power; the multiple competing organizational structures and internal bureaucratic cultures make change within DOD exceptionally problematic; and finally, extraordinary management structures needed to ensure that its tremendous budgets and personnel lists do not encourage waste and inefficiency also limit its agility and innovation.

Redefining the Lanes

The twenty-first century has forever blurred the distinctions formerly recognized as the domestic-foreign policy divide and the law enforcement-security divide. As the chapters on FBI, DHS, CIA, and the DNI highlight, there are no clear lanes anymore in the realms of terrorism, proliferation, and other global threats to American citizens. The 9/11 case illustrates how both CIA and FBI were tracking parts of this threat. The importance of interdependence among agencies is reflected in the Detroit Christmas bombing plot of 2009. Today, agencies must acknowledge this interconnection if they are to fulfill their own missions. Moreover, they must examine where their own cultural norms prevent, or hinder them from playing well with others. So the FBI faces the challenge of adapting its special-agent-in-charge culture of prosecutions and arrests into something closer to the CIA's analytical-operator culture, but in a domestic context. Similarly, the CIA needs to remake its current self-image of the detached analytic provider of information to the policy process or the clandestine solo operator conducting covert action into more of a team player who straddles the line between intelligence and policy. As the chapter on the CIA notes, there is a gray area where the CIA must be both an intelligence agency but also a policy implementer. This gray zone is precisely where the CIA runs the risk of being accused of politicizing its intelligence, or at least allowing itself and its analysis to become politicized by the decision makers pushing a certain agenda. Or in the case of unmanned armed vehicles operated by CIA employees where questions arise as to whether their actions are covered by the protections of the Geneva Conventions.

In the field of counterterrorism, however, the model of the National Counterterrorism Center (NCTC) has been offered as the best practice so far in terms of melding together the diverse cultures and organizations fighting global terrorism to create a fusion center. The NCTC, although it was at first a creation of a presidential order as a follow-on to the previously executively created Terrorist Threat Integration Center, became congressionally mandated and lodged in the Office of the Director of the National Intelligence under the 2004 Intelligence Reform Act.[14] The NCTC was unique in how it blended both its intelligence and policy functions, but also in how it joined the law enforcement and intelligence organizations together. Not only was NCTC tasked to develop intelligence on terrorism threats both foreign and domestic, but it also had the responsibility to develop counterterrorism strategies and operations. Moreover, the position of the NCTC director, a Senate-confirmed office, was unique in government. For analyzing and integrating information pertaining to terrorism (except domestic terrorism), budget, and programs, the NCTC director reports to the DNI. However, for planning and progress of joint counterterrorism operation (other than intelligence operations), the director reports directly to the president. Operationally, the director works through the NSC and White House staff.[15]

The goal was to bring together law enforcement, military, and intelligence organizations in one place. The assignment of more than thirty intelligence, military, law enforcement, and homeland security networks including FBI, DHS, DOD, and IC officers to this center was envisioned to create more "jointness" among the diverse organizational cultures. However, the failure of the NCTC to coordinate and analyze critical information in two cases in late 2009 called into question the effectiveness of the center in forging information sharing. First, the November shootings at Fort Hood Army base in Texas by Major Nidal M. Hassan and the failed December Detroit bomb attempt by Umar Farouk Abdulmutallab caused President Obama to characterize the bombing attempt as a systematic failure. The immediate response, as one would expect, was a call for better technology to help analysts connect information; better technology at airports; wider and faster distribution of intelligence data; smarter guidelines for watch lists; and a clearer responsibility for the chain of command to investigate leads of plots to harm the United States. But even with such reforms, organizational cultural questions remain for Congress to consider, in addition to the perennial distinction between analysts versus operators. What were the consequences of the dual-reporting scheme for the director to both the president and DNI; how did the NCTC interact with the CIA's Counterterrorism Center and State Department's Immigration bureaus; and, finally, how did the NCTC interact with the NSCS over policy proposals? In addition, how can counterterrorism officials overcome the resistance of the military to share personnel files with law enforcement, as in the Fort Hood incident, and the rights of U.S. citizens to protect sensitive medical information?[16]

The 2009 Detroit Christmas airplane bomber incident, however, reflects a deeper cross-cultural challenge on two levels. First, a February 2010 study by the Project on National Security Reform found that the counterterrorism arena was still a spiderweb of overlapping missions and ambiguous lines of authority and that the different departments and agencies also continued to interpret their responsibilities based on their own statutes, histories, and bureaucratic cultures. In short, these entities were not accountable to NCTC's directorate of strategic operations (DSOP), and there were insufficient bureaucratic incentives to fully support the interagency integration process of the DSOP.

Second, even within the field of law enforcement national and cultural differences could complicate cooperation. When U.S. and European Union authorities attempted to exchange law enforcement information for travel while ensuring the protection of personal data and privacy, they discovered their different interpretations of the definition of law enforcement purposes. The United States defines law enforcement purposes as the use "for the prevention, detection, suppression, investigation, or prosecution of any criminal offense or violation of law related to border enforcement, public security, and national security, as well as for non-criminal judicial or administrative proceedings related directly to such offenses or violations." In contrast, the European Union defines it more narrowly as the use "for the prevention, detection, investigation, or prosecution of any criminal offense."[17] Such different definitions of "law enforcement" are significant as they implicate different actors, agencies, processes, and types of information that need to be coordinated and involved in the different countries.[18] While fusion centers such as the NCTC may be the way to attack the domestic and international coordination of transnational travel issues, successfully bridging these different organizational and national cultures requires a full understanding of them. Securing movement of people for travel, migration, and the management of borders will require a new mindset that reorganizes the bureaucracies and approaches information with a twenty-first century understanding of data.[19]

Needed: Coordinators and Integrators

The chapters on the formation of the DHS and DNI highlight the problems of responding to new transnational threats by creating organizations intended to break down traditional jurisdictional boundaries and integrate disparate parts of the government. In both cases, the creation of new structures has met with confusion if not conflict.

In the case of the DHS, this step toward horizontal coordination of federal, state, and municipal authorities to deal with homeland security issues has been a step forward. Yet, as Gary Shiffman's chapter highlights, an American legal and constitutional framework that separates domestic and international arenas hampers the coordination of authorities at all these levels. Unity of command is fractured by congressional oversight involving eighty-six subcommittees of the Congress. The recommendation of the Hart-Rudman Commission to consolidate these committees remains unheeded. Although the chapter details the courageous effort by the DHS secretaries to create a unity of effort, the narrative illustrates how difficult the separate and overlapping authorities among all the moving parts of government make for coordination. The examples of the department's secure border initiative, cyber coordination, and the eventual failure of comprehensive immigration reform are prime examples of problems facing the new department on the block.

The creation of the DNI in 2005, like the chapter in this book, is only the introductory chapter in this new organization's evolving role in the NSE. Barely five years old, already having had five directors, it promises to be a work in progress. Reforms introduced in the midst of wars in Afghanistan and Iraq also have to be measured carefully. But the DNI, along with the creation of the NCTC and the National Counterproliferation Center have now added to the menagerie of organizational cultures that populate the IC. In the longer term, however, the DNI's role is unclear both within the executive branch but also within the DNI itself. With more than a dozen intelligence agencies, there are nearly as many views of what the DNI should or should not become. And as the DNI is largely staffed by those agencies, views even within the DNI diverge on nearly every issue. The intent for having a DNI appears pretty clear. On the one hand, the job was designed to turn a collection of sixteen specialized agencies into a more integrated, single enterprise; on the other hand, the legislation also aimed at correcting the specific problems that contributed to the September 2001 strategic surprise and the 2003 flawed Iraq weapons of mass destruction estimate. Arguably, the DNI has done less well on the former than on the latter set of metrics, but even its proponents admit there is more room for improvement.

As noted by Thomas Fingar in chapter 7, there can be no single DNI organizational culture until the sixteen separate agencies' cultures adapt and accept the role of the DNI and until the DNI is less dependent on those agencies for its own staffing needs. Amending the relevant executive orders to reflect the need to give the DNI more authority than previous DCIs would be a step forward. But moving the DNI beyond being just a coordinator of the community to being truly its integrator—comparable to how the secretary of defense integrates the military services and unified commands—will require both time and superb leadership. There have been four DNIs in its five years of existence; if there is to be a true head of the intelligence community who analyzes and plugs the gaps, this function will have to be supported by the president.

THE INSTITUTIONAL PROCESS—CONGRESS AND THE COURTS

Neither the constitution nor existing statutes dictate any precise internal structure to the legislative-executive management of the NSE, and so it has remained an invitation to struggle as a number of the authors have noted. But the playing field is a crowded space with an often divided executive confronting the Congress (itself divided between the House and Senate), the medley of media outlets, think tanks ranging from conservative to liberal, and assorted lobbyists working both ends of Pennsylvania Avenue for contending interest groups. One of our claims for the book is that to fully grasp the NSE, one needs to understand that more than just the government is a player. As detailed in a number of the chapters, the actions of the media, lobbyists, and think tanks affect power relations as different institutional players jockey for advantage in the policy process. Moreover, the professionalism of the agencies shapes the cultures of the organizations. When approaching issues, a culture of professionalism becomes the behavior pattern in which the individual and organization approach the interagency process. Talented professionals roam the corridors of power using all the elements of the playing field to influence and shape policy.

The constitution lays out the battlefield of overlapping national security powers. In chapter 11 on the Congress, Gerald Warburg makes it clear that this was more by design than most people wish to acknowledge. The constitution grants shared power between the Congress and the executive, and different contexts favor power concentration in one or the other. War, for example, tends to concentrate power into the hand of the executive and reinforce its tendency for secrecy, while Congress's ability to shape national security tends to be reactive, personality driven, and most assertive on large, ideological issues in times when external threats seem to be diminished.

Due to the different structural and cultural settings of the House and the Senate, the Congress tends to pursue broad ideological objectives such as human rights or nonproliferation and not view national interests with the nuanced lens required by the executive branch. The Senate will extract concessions by withholding confirmation of appointments to the executive branch and both the House and Senate will attach amendments to legislation reflecting specific interests, such as the Boland amendments during the Iran-Contra affair. Whether war financing, genocide resolutions, or free trade agreements, the Congress will find ways to assert their ideological views that can be at loggerheads with the administration. The House is marked by hyperpartisan top-down leadership, while the overlapping committee jurisdiction structure of the Senate can be arenas for struggle against the administration that bestow powerful influence on individual senators. Further complicating the executive-legislative management of lawmaking is the fact that the House, the Senate, and the president each have weapons to stall the process: the Rules Committee, the filibuster, and the veto, respectively. In other words, the president and thirty-four senators can stop sixty-six senators and four hundred and thirty-five House members.[20] The tendency is toward deliberative deadlock and incremental change until a crisis supports more sweeping change.

While oversight of the NSE is a fundamental function of the Congress through jurisdictional and appropriations committees, the Congress has been sporadic in its effectiveness. In the intelligence arena, it has tended to act after the fact and legislated reform, but then returns to a passive role especially during times when the same party controls Congress and the executive branch. While in the military appropriations arena, the military-industrial-congressional complex has rarely lost battles and has usually been able to override the proposed termination of weapons systems. Nonetheless, when the stars are aligned, some weapons systems can be terminated, or at least cut back, such as the example of the F-22 aircraft.[21]

On the issue of self-reform, for example, to create a more coherent oversight system for new departments like DHS, the Congress has been an abysmal failure. In short, the congressional cultures and structure favor the status quo, leaving coalitions in the House and powerful senators in the Senate to extract concessions on particular NSE issues, depending on the nature of the issue involved and the will of the executive to respond.

As underscored in chapter 12, it is now virtually impossible to discuss the NSE without discussing the role of the U.S. Supreme Court and the federal courts. Historically, the federal courts had shown deference to executive power and Congress in the carrying out of foreign policy, national security, and war. Over the last few years, however, federal courts have increasingly injected themselves into issues of executive power concerning detention of prisoners, interrogations, state secret protections, domestic surveillance, and the applicability of the Geneva Conventions. Using the doctrine of habeas corpus, the courts have demonstrated to both the president and the Congress that when it comes to the protection of rights and the applicability of international conventions, the Court will have the last word.

The *Boumediene* case, which eroded the legal distinction between citizens and noncitizens held in custody outside of the United States, is a watershed precedent whose effects await further adjudication. The D.C. district courts will now be setting the policy on who can be detained as a member of al-Qaeda based on the legal tests the courts establish. In addition, many have lamented the legalization of armed conflict and the new role "juridical warfare" or "lawfare" plays in the projections of force.[22] As the distinctions between domestic and international spheres continue to erode due to the nature of transnational threats, more and more the issues of privacy and state needs will come into conflict over appropriate surveillance technologies. The federal courts, given their capacity for independent action, will continue to shape the NSE in potentially unexpected ways. It is hard to imagine the courts now retreating from this expanded role in the NSE process. The court culture of doctrinal independence, grounded in administrative autonomy, has been supported by the domestic political culture regardless of the nature of the decisions. To paraphrase Tocqueville, "all national security enterprise issues will sooner or later turn into legal ones."

OUTSIDE PLAYERS: SETTING THE AGENDA

Think tanks, lobbyists, and the media all influence and shape the political environment for the national security debates. Some individuals rotate among these professions at different times in their careers. Although one cannot quantify their influence, the cultures of outside players are pervasive and significant in the policy process.

As described by Ellen Laipson in chapter 14, the think-tank culture has become increasingly integrated into the way the U.S. government understands its national security interests and formulates policies and solutions. These organizations have become accepted as a normal and integral part of the policy formulation process. The different institutes have become convenient locations for government officials to launch new policy initiatives and attract the media. Think tanks not only have critical audiences in the scholarly community but very specific connections with the press, the private sector, and the general public. Policy ideas are "incubated, tested, promoted, and evaluated" in these organizations. Often populated by recently retired, aspiring to be, or seasoned veterans of the government, all these individuals have extensive indexes of contacts and influence.

Think tanks can make their contributions at many points along the cycle of policymaking: identifying needs and gaps in policy; generating new ideas and approaches; building support for announced policies among constituents; assisting in gaining formal approval of ideas through legislation or executive authority; and monitoring implementation and issuing reports. In short, think tanks educate, inform, and persuade and are a transmission belt of ideas and information between government and the governed.

As noted by Laipson, in the national security world the work done in the aftermath of the Cold War that became known as Cooperative Threat Reduction was a perfect example of how think tanks can influence policy. The collapse of the Soviet Union presented a dramatic challenge with respect to the Soviet nuclear arsenal. Scholars at the Brookings Institution, working with colleagues at Harvard and Stanford, were engaged in projects about the transition to the post-Cold War world that were embraced first by concerned members of Congress and that later became executive branch policy. The ideas from this working group helped launch a number of policy initiatives, from programs to employ former weapons scientists in times of great economic stress in Russia, to new systems to manage and reduce fissile and other dangerous weapons-related materials.

This role of influencing current policy took an unprecedented leap in January 2010 when Major General Michael T. Flynn, then deputy chief of staff for intelligence for the International Security Assistance Force in Afghanistan, chose the think tank Center for a New American Security to publish a scathing critique of the U.S. IC's performance in counterinsurgency in Afghanistan.[23] To many, it was curious that a think tank and not the Pentagon was the vehicle for such a report by an active duty officer. Only time will tell if this approach of administration–think-tank collaboration will become an accepted way to provide policy analysis.

What explains the robustness of the think-tank world in the United States? As Laipson notes, some attribute it to the relative weakness of American political parties, the developed philanthropic culture, and the public distrust of government.[24] Whatever the explanation, they are here to stay and will continue to be a force with which to be reckoned.

If think tanks approach the NSE as a battle of ideas, lobbyists are the critical implementers of the warring ideas and play a very significant role advocating interests in the struggle over the political agenda. As insightfully stated by Gerald Warburg, politics can no more be taken out of the policymaking process than can lobbyists be removed from the system designed by America's founders to shape U.S. laws.

To be successful, lobbying campaigns create an alliance of interests securing access to decision makers and energizing voters. The role lobbyists play in this competition to guide the NSE is readily apparent. Lobbyists are expert in navigating the national security labyrinth because they understand the access points, the interests of the major players, and how to cobble together the necessary coalitions of interest groups. In a regulated system, registered lobbyists are not unlike lawyers in the judicial branch: they are both messengers and advocates. Frustration about lobbying designed to impact U.S. international policy often appears as a desire to shoot the messenger. Lobbyists, money, and access are all part of the executive and congressional branches. To some this use of money and access can distort the process and undermine what is best for the national interest. For Warburg, however, understanding the tools available and mastering the policymaking process is more effective than railing against the allegedly excessive influence of lobbyists. Many come to the NSE with the view to solve the lobbyist problem; the so-called problem, though, is embedded in the enterprise itself. There have been recent efforts to change the process around the edges, such as the calls to eliminate all earmarking involving for-profit entities.

In many senses, the media is like the culture of lobbying. Students of the NSE may rail against its influence but, like the tides and the moon, for practitioners the media is a force of nature. There is little doubt that the media can influence events in international relations and national security, and set the agenda, sometimes by design and sometimes by accident. As explored in chapter 15, anonymity plays a crucial role for both the media and government officials. The critical issue is when is information sensitive, and when can the strategic leak be used to affect policy? For the profession of the media, debate centers on when the story trumps national interests. Will a reporter compromise an exclusive story and disclose the potential whereabouts of Osama bin Laden to assist the U.S. military, or for professional reasons not pass on the information until after the interview? Regardless of the answer to this question, as John Diamond explains, even negative stories can have positive results as when incompetence or dereliction is exposed, and legitimate grievances are heard and remedied. Due to its nature, the media is a controversial player in the NSE but due to our values, it is a critical and necessary one for our culture of governmental accountability.

John Diamond catalogues how historically the different correspondent cultures—whether Washington-based, foreign, war, or regional—place a premium on being on site and interpreting the story or getting the scoop. Increasingly, though, given the competition from the other new technologies, reporters add value by being able to provide in-depth analysis that places events in context. It is clear that the media is undergoing a revolution as traditional papers and television networks struggle to adapt to the information revolution and the new emerging technologies. From a business perspective with two wars ongoing, the American newspaper industry is coping with a financial crisis of unprecedented severity and laboring simply to keep reporters in the field. Television networks are in a desperate effort to transform themselves from a static medium to one linked to home pages, the internet, and 24/7 live coverage. This internal business struggle within the media will affect how the NSE will be covered in the future. Media concentration combined with a democratization of forums paradoxically restricts and expands points of views at the same time. Increasingly, it is becoming harder to keep secrets as individuals with cell phone cameras, global tracking technology, and access to massive databases become private investigative reporters with blog pages.

The 2010 series in the *Washington Post* on "Top Secret America"—based on open-source documents—was an extensive exposé of the intelligence community's growth since

9/11.[25] The three-part reporting series asserted that the government had built a national security and intelligence system so big, so complex, and so hard to manage that it is questionable whether anyone knows if it is fulfilling its primary purpose of keeping us safe. In the process, the series revealed facts previously not generally known to the pubic concerning the size of the community, locations of facilities, and a number of programs. At about the same time, the news organization WikiLeaks released on its dedicated web page 92,000 classified reports covering the war in Afghanistan from 2004 to 2010, titled the *Afghan War Diary*. This was an extraordinary set of reports written by soldiers and intelligence officers describing lethal military actions involving the U.S. military; however, it also is alleged to include intelligence information, reports of meetings with political figures, and other details. As of this writing, the release of some 15,000 additional reports, that were to be redacted to protect certain information, are expected to be released. Senior officials, including Joint Chiefs of Staff Chairman Admiral Michael Mullen, have warned that such releases might endanger lives. Even the original set of released reports are alleged to contain the names of Afghans who had assisted the United States and its allies, which might put them at risk.[26]

The *Washington Post* story became possible in part due to the ability of technology and data banks to be cross-referenced from public sources and public electronic reports—the electronic risk of public data storage. There was no leaker, per se; it was an investigation of public electronic databases. WikiLeaks was a bit different. A few observers have compared the WikiLeaks disclosure to the *Pentagon Paper* leaks during the Vietnam War. Yet, what made this latest disclosure different was that all the original material could be stored electronically on a public website that then could be instantly accessed, searched, and downloaded by friend and foe for information on U.S. approaches to the war in Afghanistan. This reflects the new age of computer technology. The future national security media environment will become ever more transparent, confusingly diverse, and potentially unreliable as a source of solid facts.

THE FUTURE FOR THE NATIONAL SECURITY ENTERPRISE

We have detailed in the book why it is hard to navigate and reform the current institutions and cultures of the NSE. Why coordination and reform is so difficult stems in part from one of the central tenets of the Washington bureaucracy—the mandarin algorithm of power:

$$J = FTEs + \$.$$

(Translated as: Legal jurisdiction over function or task [J] = Full-time equivalents or employees [FTEs] plus Money [$].)

Bureaucratic entrepreneurs know that if they can acquire statutory jurisdiction for a problem or issue, they will eventually acquire FTEs or hiring authority and funding from Congress. This is one reason why turf battles are so pitched inside the beltway: what appear to be parochial concerns of statutory jurisdiction are really about people and money—the lifeblood of power. So how does the NSE overcome this combined problem of the culture of organizations and the algorithm of the culture of power, given the challenges of the future?

To create more of a unity of effort among the senior career managers, much more must be done to coordinate interagency career paths, provide pay incentive programs, and combine training and joint educational opportunities. To some, these suggestions may appear to support an antidemocratic proposal for the creation of an elite set of career managers. To be accurate, we already have a managerial elite, the senior executive service, and over the last few years some have become the gorillas in the cylinders of excellence that have undermined collective efforts. This reform though, even if successful, may not eliminate the deep cultural and organizational rivalries. Goldwater-Nichols, the model of reform for "jointness," has not been the panacea for the military as highlighted in a number of our chapters.

Unfortunately, we believe that if all the innovations fail, or are not even tried, significant change will come only with different scenarios of institutional failure. A massive attack on the continental United States will be understood as a critical domestic crisis. The ripple effects would be felt through the entire structure. The U.S. Northern Command (NORTHCOM) and the National Security Agency (NSA) would be scrutinized to reevaluate their effectiveness and missions. It is predictable that the domestic departments and agencies charged with protecting the homeland—DHS, NSA, FBI, CIA, NORTHCOM, and DOD—would come under severe political attack, and once again there would be pressure to create a domestic intelligence agency. Potentially, a new domestic agency would be proposed to house all of the component parts for domestic intelligence currently scattered in the different departments. At the very least, a major effort will be launched to review and assess the allocation of authorities.

Whether such a failure would also spur internal congressional reform of our present fractured oversight structure remains unclear. Presidential power would be strengthened in the short term as cries for action and executive response would be made. The environment would be supportive for massive institutional change; for us, effective change would require a full understanding of the cultures of the NSE. One reason we have written this book is to precipitate change before such a domestic crisis occurs.

Internationally, failure in Iraq and/or Afghanistan would similarly cause soul searching on whether the current balance of resources between the military and all the other agencies charged with political, economic, and social development is the proper mix. Yet again, debates would occur over the definition of our vital interests and when we should venture abroad with the projection of force. Much ink will be spilled on how to deploy smart power with new and improved national security structures, empowered and well-resourced state departments, and effective modern development plans for fragile states and ungoverned spaces. To be sure, there would be support from some for a return to neoisolationist policies and a withdrawal or cutback of overseas commitments without allied support. Reform of the NSE process would again be part of the debate, particularly if there was a consensus that the United States needed to be more involved in an international duty to protect vulnerable minority populations in failing states. Again, we contend reforms will not be effective unless the cultures of the agencies are understood.

Historically, the United States has always proven to be resilient. The Cold War NSE served us well. We now confront global climate change, a weakening U.S. dollar, failing or fragile states, rising economic powers, an information revolution, the potential spread of nuclear and biological weapons, increasing transnational terrorism, and an evolving hybrid for warfare. Creating new institutions and navigating a new labyrinth of power is fraught with risk and is not for the fainthearted or for those with wobbly integrity. We are hopeful that our generation, like the generations before us, will craft policies that will appeal to our better angels and overcome the tendency of the triumph of parochialism and turf. It is our goal that this book will assist in the conversation needed to foster reform of the NSE.

NOTES

1. See National Intelligence Council, *Global Trends 2025: A Transformed World*, November 2008, Executive Summary, vii–xi. Or the The United States Institute of Peace, *The QDR in Perspective: Meeting America's National Security Needs in the 21st Century; The Final Report of the Quadrennial Defense Review Independent Panel* (July 2010) at www.usip.org/files/qdr/qdrreport.pdf. (Five key global trends: radical Islamist extremism and the threat of terrorism; the rise of new global great powers in Asia; continued struggle for power in the Persian Gulf and the greater Middle East; an accelerating global competition for resources; and persistent problems from failed and failing states.)

2. Project on National Security Reform, *Turning Ideas into Action*, executive summary, September 2009, iii. This latest report is part of a multiphase study, funded by Congress and led by James M. Locher, but which included notable members of the new Obama administration, including General James Jones (ret.); Admiral Dennis Blair (ret.); James Steinberg; and Michelle Flournoy, to name a few of those who have taken senior positions within the executive branch.

3. Paul B. Stares and Micah Zenko, *Enhancing U.S. Preventive Action* (Council on Foreign Relations Special Report No. 48, October 2009).

4. David Rothkopf, *Running the World* (New York: Public Affairs, 2004).

5. The United States Institute of Peace, *The QDR in Perspective: Meeting America's National Security Needs in the 21st Century; The Final Report of the Quadrennial Defense Review Independent Panel* (July 2010) at www.usip.org/files/qdr/qdrreport.pdf.

6. For contrasting views see Stephen Walt, "Snoozing through the National Security Strategy," *Foreign Policy* (May 28, 2010) at www.walt.foreignpolicy.com/posts/2010/05/28/snoozing_through_the_national_security_strategy; and Leslie Gelb, "Obama's Forgettable New Strategy," The Daily Beast, at www.thedailybeast.com/blogs-and-stories/2010-05-27/obama-presents-a-new-national-security-strategy/.

7. Peter A. Hall and Michele Lamont eds., *Successful Societies: How Institutions and Culture Affect Health* (New York: Cambridge University Press, 2009).

8. Ibid., 14.

9. See Graham T. Allison and Philip Zelikow, *Essence of Decision: Explaining the Cuban Missile Crisis*, 2d ed. (New York: Longman, 1999); and Morton Halperin, Priscilla Clapp, and Arnold Kanter, *Bureaucratic Politics and Foreign Policy* (Washington, DC: Brookings Institution Press, 2007).

10. See Amy B. Zegart, *Spying Blind: The CIA, the FBI and the Origins of 9/11* (Princeton, NJ: Princeton University Press, 2007); and *Flawed by Design: The Evolution of the CIA, JCS, and NSC* (Palo Alto, CA: Stanford University Press, 1999).

11. Richard Haass, *The Bureaucratic Entrepreneur: How to Be Effective in any Unruly Organization* (Washington, DC: Brookings Institution, 1999). Haass argues that an individual must develop his/her compass to navigate among the North, South, East, and West poles that shape the national security field.

12. This phenomenon found in the Army is recently detailed in *The Fourth Star*, a book about the Department of Social Sciences (Sosh) at West Point. The department attracts both generals-in-waiting and dissidents, from Generals Peter Chiarelli to David Petraeus. At Sosh, intellectual ties and relations are forged that can follow and assist rising general officers until they are finally awarded the fourth star of command. See David Cloud and Greg Jaffe, *The Fourth Star* (New York: Crown Publishers, 2009), 54–60.

13. As of the time this book was completed, the Obama administration has already established special envoys for Afghanistan-Pakistan (Richard Holbrooke), Arab-Israeli (George Mitchell), Sudan (Gen. Scott Gration), and climate change (Todd Stern).

14. See Richard A. Best Jr., "The National Counterterrorism Center (NCTC)—Responsibilities and Potential Congressional Concerns," CRS, R41022, January 15, 2010.

15. Ibid.

16. Ibid.

17. Hiroyuki Tanaka, Rocco Bellanova, Susan Ginsburg, and Paul De Hert, "Transatlantic Information Sharing: At a Crossroads," Migration Policy Institute, January 2010, 3–4, at www.migrationpolicy.org/pubs/infosharing-Jan2010.pdf.

18. Ibid.

19. See Susan Ginsburg, *Securing Human Mobility in the Age of Risk – New Challenges for Travel, Migration, and Borders* (Washington, DC: Migration Policy Institute, 2010).

20. See W. Lee Rawls, *In Praise of Deadlock—How Partisan Struggle Makes Better Laws*, (Washington, DC: Woodrow Wilson Center, 2009), 25.

21. See "Gates Announces Major Pentagon Priority Shifts," at www.cnn.com/2009/POLITICS/04/06/gates.budget.cuts/index.html.

22. See Major General Charles J. Dunlap Jr., "Lawfare amid Warfare," *Washington Times*, August 3, 2007; and Harvey Rishikof, "Juridical Warfare: The Neglected Legal Instrument," *Joint Force Quarterly*, Issue 48 (1st Quarter 2008).

23. Major General Michael T. Flynn, USA, Captain Matt Pottinger, USMC, and Paul D. Batchelor, "Fixing Intel: A Blueprint for Making Intelligence Relevant in Afghanistan," Center for New American Security, January 2010. The report opined that the "vast intelligence apparatus is unable to answer fundamental questions about the environment in which the U.S. and allied forces operate and the people they seek to persuade. Ignorant of local economies and landowners, hazy about who the powerbrokers are and how they might be influenced, incurious about the correlations between various development projects and levels of cooperation among villagers, and disengaged from people in the best position to find answers. . . ."

24. James McGann, *Think Tanks and Policy Advice in the United States: Academics Advisors and Advocates* (New York: Routledge, 2007), 8.

25. See Dana Priest and William M. Arkin, "Top Secret America," *Washington Post*, July 19–21, 2010, at projects.washingtonpost.com/top-secret-america.

26. Greg Jaffe and Joshua Partlow, "Joint Chiefs Chairman Mullen: WikiLeaks Release Endangers Troops, Afghans," *Washington Post*, July 30, 2010, at www.washingtonpost.com/wp-dyn/content/article/2010/07/29/AR2010072904900.html.

Contributors

Gordon Adams is professor of international relations at the School of International Service at American University and Distinguished Fellow at the Stimson Center. From 1993 to 1997 he was the senior White House official on national security budgets as associate director for national security and international affairs at the Office of Management and Budget. He has written widely on defense and foreign policy budgeting. His book on national security and foreign policy planning and budgeting, *Buying National Security* (coauthored with Cindy Williams), was published in 2009.

David Auerswald is associate dean of academic affairs and professor of strategy and policy at the National War College. Before joining the National War College he previously served on the faculty of the George Washington University and was a staff member for the U.S. Senate Foreign Relations Committee. He has also served as a member of the 2008 Central Command Assessment Team tasked to review the command's regional operations.

John Diamond spent 25 years as a daily journalist and covered defense, foreign policy, and intelligence issues from 1989 to 2006 for the Associated Press, *Chicago Tribune,* and *USA Today.* He is the author of *The CIA and the Culture of Failure: U.S. Intelligence from the End of the Cold War to the Invasion of Iraq,* published in 2008 by Stanford University Press. He currently works as a communications director in the U.S. Senate.

Thomas Fingar is the Oksenberg-Rohlen Distinguished Fellow and a senior scholar at Stanford's Freeman Spogli Institute for International Studies. He served as the first deputy director of national intelligence for analysis and chairman of the National Intelligence Council from 2005 to 2008 after nearly two decades at the State Department's Bureau of Intelligence and Research.

Roger Z. George is adjunct professor at Georgetown University in the security studies program and is associate professor of security studies at the National War College. He was a career CIA intelligence analyst who served at the State and Defense departments and was the national intelligence officer for Europe. He is coeditor with James B. Bruce of *Analyzing Intelligence: Origins, Obstacles, and Innovations* published by Georgetown University Press in 2008.

Marc Grossman is a vice chairman of the Cohen Group and teaches at the Georgetown University Edmund Walsh School of Foreign Service. He was a career foreign service officer from 1976 to 2005, having held many senior positions, including undersecretary of state for political affairs, director general of the Foreign Service, assistant secretary of state for European affairs, and U.S. ambassador to Turkey. He is a future of diplomacy fellow in the Future of Diplomacy Project at Harvard University's John F. Kennedy School of Public Policy, and was a public policy scholar at the Woodrow Wilson International Center for Scholars.

Jonathan Hoffman is a principal with an Arlington, VA-based homeland security consulting firm. He previously served four years in senior roles at the Department of Homeland Security, most recently as a deputy assistant secretary of homeland security and on the White House Homeland Security Council staff under President George W. Bush as the director of international programs and border security policy. He earned a Juris Doctorate from the University of Virginia School of Law and is a judge advocate general with the U.S. Air Force Reserves.

Ellen Laipson is president and CEO of the Stimson Center, a post she has held since she retired from government service in 2002. She has worked on Middle East issues as an analyst at the Congressional Research Service, as well as at the State Department's policy planning staff. She has also served as the director of Near East and South Asian affairs at the NSC and as national intelligence officer for Near East and South Asia. Before assuming her responsibilities at the Stimson Center, she was the vice chairman of the National Intelligence Council.

Michael J. Meese is the professor and head of the Department of Social Sciences at West Point, having previously taught at the National War College. He has served as an advisor for senior military and civilian leaders in Afghanistan, Iraq, Bosnia, on the army staff, and on the Defense Science Board and Defense Policy Board. He is the author of numerous books and articles on national security including, most recently, *American National Security*.

Franklin C. Miller is a principal at the Scowcroft Group. He served as a career defense policy analyst in the Department of Defense from 1979 to 2005, having risen through the ranks from an action officer to office director, deputy assistant secretary, principal deputy assistant secretary, and acting assistant secretary. Before retiring from government service he was a senior director at the National Security Council and special assistant for defense policies to President George W. Bush.

Harvey Rishikof is professor of law and national security at the National War College. He is the chair of the American Bar Association standing committee on national security law and is a senior consultant for intelligence issues. He is a member of the Council on Foreign Relations and the American Law Institute. He also served as administrative assistant to the chief justice of the U.S. Supreme Court, a federal law clerk, a tutor in social studies at Harvard University, and legal counsel for the FBI.

Jon J. Rosenwasser was a professional staff member for national security affairs on the U.S. Senate Budget Committee, a fellow at the Council on Foreign Relations and the Brookings Institution, and a consultant to the Defense Department. He has also served as an adjunct professor at the Graduate School of Public Policy at George Mason University. He has been a senior strategist in the Office of the Director of National Intelligence since 2006.

Gary M. Shiffman is professor and director of Homeland Security Studies at the Center for Peace and Security Studies, Georgetown University, and he is managing director of the Chertoff Group. He is an economist focusing on national and homeland security issues both in and out of government. He has been an industry executive in emergency management and infrastructure protection as well as chief of staff at U.S. Customs and Border Protection. He is the author of *Economic Instruments of Security Policy: Influencing the Choices of Leaders.*

Frederick C. Smith is vice president for the Institute for 21st Century Energy at the U.S. Chamber of Commerce. He joined the Department of Defense in 1978 and served there until 2004. He held various positions including director for Near East South Asia, deputy assistant secretary of defense for Asia-Pacific, and principal deputy assistant secretary of defense for international security affairs.

Gerald Felix Warburg is professor of practice of public policy at the Batten School, University of Virginia, and executive vice president of Cassidy & Associates. He previously served as a legislative assistant on international issues for members of the U.S. House and Senate leadership, where he helped draft the Nuclear Nonproliferation Act and the Anti-Apartheid Sanctions Act. He is author of *Conflict and Consensus: The Struggle between Congress and the President over Foreign Policymaking,* as well as *The Mandarin Club.*

Michael Warner is a historian for the Department of Defense and was previously a historian with the Office of the Director of National Intelligence. He is also adjunct professor at the American University School of International Service and has written widely on intelligence history, theory, and reform. Most recently he contributed to the volume edited by Jennifer Sims and Burton Gerber, *Vaults, Mirrors, and Masks,* published by Georgetown University Press in 2008.

Isaiah Wilson III is professor and director of the American politics, policy, and strategy program at West Point. He has taught previously at the National War College. He was the chief of plans of the 101st Air Assault Division in Mosul, Iraq, contributed to the army's first assessment of Operation Iraqi Freedom, served as an advisor and planner in Kabul, Afghanistan, on civil-military integration, and is the author of numerous articles and books, including *Thinking beyond War.*

Index